HIGHLIGHTS *of*
THE BOYER LECTURES
1959–2000

The **Boyer** Collection

SELECTED *and* INTRODUCED *by*
Donald McDonald

ABC
BOOKS

Donald McDonald was appointed chairman of the Australian Broadcasting Corporation in July 1996.

A commerce graduate from the University of New South Wales, he has been involved in the administration of arts enterprises for over 30 years. From 1968 to 1972 he was with the Australian Elizabethan Theatre Trust and The Australian Opera, of which he was the first general manager. He was chief executive of Musica Viva from 1972 to 1978, a period of significant growth during which he co-sponsored the formation of the Australian Chamber Orchestra. With his wife he co-directed an arts management firm that administered the ACO, the Australian National Playwrights' Conference and the Confederation of Professional Performing Arts Organisations.

From 1980 to 1986 he was general manager of the Sydney Theatre Company, a period that saw the company's first international touring, the establishment of The Wharf, and such outstanding successes as *Nicholas Nickleby*.

Returning to The Australian Opera in 1986, Donald McDonald was the company's chief executive for a ten-year period that has been described as a golden age of opera production and presentation in this country.

In 1993 he was a visiting fellow to the University of Edinburgh, and in 1997 completed a four-year term as a fellow of the Senate of the University of Sydney. In 1997 he succeeded Sir Ninian Stephen as chairman of the Constitutional Centenary Foundation. From 1998 he was a member of the documents reference group of the Council for Aboriginal Reconciliation. He was a director of the Australian Tourist Commission from 1993 to 1996, and chairman of the State Opera Ring Corporation in South Australia.

Chairman of The Really Useful Company (Aust) Pty Limited, he is also a director of Focus Publishing Pty Ltd, and a member of the board of the University of New South Wales Foundation.

He is married to Janet McDonald AO and has two adult children.

He was made an Officer of the Order of Australia in 1991.

Acknowledgments

I am indebted to a number of people for their kind and generous help and for their patience in the preparation of this anthology. They include Helen Wallace, my Executive Assistant; Matthew Kelly, the then Publisher of ABC Books; Susan Morris-Yates, my Commissioning Editor; Marjorie Wearne the ABC Librarian; Natasha Marfutenko and Guy Tranter of ABC Archives; Mae Gannon of Radio National.

Special acknowledgement must be made of *Chronicle of the 20th Century*, published by JL International Publications, and *What Happened When: A chronology of Australia*, compiled by Anthony Barker, from which much valuable information was gleaned for the timelines in this book.

My gratitude also to my fellow Board members and the senior management for their support and encouragement. And to Janet for everything, as ever.

Published by ABC Books for the
AUSTRALIAN BROADCASTING CORPORATION
GPO Box 9994 Sydney NSW 2001

First published June 2001

National Library of Australia
Cataloguing-in-Publication entry
The Boyer collection: highlights of the Boyer lectures
    1959–2000.

    ISBN 0 7333 1003 6.

    1. Speeches, addresses, etc., Australian. 2. Radio addresses, debates, etc.
    I. McDonald, Donald, 1938– . II. Australian Broadcasting Corporation
A825.3

Text designed by Helen Semmler
Jacket designed by Graham Rendoth/Reno Design
Set in 11.5/13 pt Joanna MT by Midland Typesetters Maryborough, Victoria
Colour separations by Pageset, Victoria
Printed in Australia by
Australian Print Group, Maryborough, Victoria

5 4 3 2 1

Contents

Sir Richard Boyer and Mr Jawaharlal Nehru, New Delhi, 1956

Introduction

I had just turned twenty-one when the ABC launched the Boyer Lectures in 1959. Although I was brought up on a radio diet almost exclusively based on the ABC, it has to be admitted that I wasn't immediately aware of the advent of the lectures, perhaps because I wasn't at home very much listening to the radio in that year. But the lectures did engage more mature minds, and they soon became an important element in public discourse in Australia. Initially called the ABC Lectures, they were the idea of my distinguished predecessor, Sir Richard Boyer, and renamed in his honour after his death in 1961. The lectures were modelled on the Reith Lectures, which the BBC had started in 1947. They grew out of ABC Radio's already well-established traditions of discussion and debate and the practice of providing a platform for a respected public figure to present views of interest to the audience unmoderated by an interviewer.

One of the earlier talks programs of this sort was 'Guest of Honour' on Sunday evenings, which had begun during the war and continued into the 1970s. The Boyer Lectures were different because they involved—initially—four weekly half-hour lectures that later grew to six lectures. While it was a demanding commitment for the lecturer, it was an invitation to be regarded as an honour; and the scale of the commitment did provide the guest who had something to say with a significant opportunity for doing so, enhanced by the subsequent publication of the lectures.

Now, over forty years on, the Boyer Lectures are as highly regarded as at any time in their history. The choice of lecturers has, in the main, been the prerogative of the Board of the ABC. Consistent with that prerogative, the Board decided that, in celebration of the Centenary of Federation and as part of our end of the century stocktaking, an anthology of this remarkable body of Australian thinking should be published for the interest and enjoyment of readers who would be unlikely to have collected all or indeed many of the lectures over those 40, indeed now 42, years.

In choosing the lectures to be included in this anthology, I have sought to convey the breadth of subject matter dealt with, but also provide examples of the thinking of those lively, intelligent and justly celebrated Australians who have been the lecturers. At the time of delivering their lectures, most were already famous in their own fields; many went on to significantly greater success and celebrity. In at least one case—RJL Hawke's lectures in 1979—the lectures can be seen as an important building block in that later success. In all cases, the choice of subject matter reflected one of the lecturer's major preoccupations of the time, and the lectures should be read in the light of those times. The thoughts expressed are not necessarily the lecturers' last thoughts on the subject matter, but in making my choices I have selected from each series the lecture which has best stood the test of time and which provides something of a revelation of the thinking of the authors.

In only three years out of 42 has there been a departure from the format of one person presenting all the lectures in a series: in 1988, as part of the Bicentenary celebrations, six previous lecturers were each invited to deliver a single 'Postscript' lecture; in 1991 there were two lecturers; while in 1993, in acknowledgement of the International Year for the World's Indigenous Peoples, seven Australian indigenous people each delivered a lecture. None of the 1988 'Postscript' lectures has been reproduced here, while two of the seven lectures delivered in 1993 have been included.

I have presented the chosen lectures chronologically. Some might have preferred that they be grouped by subject matter, which would have provided the opportunity for readers to compare at closer range the thoughts of distinguished Australians on a similar subject separated by as much as 40 years. Indeed that is the basis on which I began, but the subject matter grouping seemed to me to be increasingly arbitrary and potentially misrepresentative of the intentions of those lecturers who ranged widely in their expressed interests and who deserved to be read in their historical perspective. So for each ten-year period I have provided some sketch notes to remind the reader of some of the major events surrounding the presentaton of each lecture series.

The world of my twenty-first birthday, into which Sir Richard Boyer introduced his idea for a lecture series, was one that now seems at once familiar and remote. It was a time of hope and apprehension; a time of very great change. Many commentators in this country now seek to characterise the 1950s and, by inference, those who lived through them as being unchanging, unresponsive, inward-looking. The events of 1959 alone don't support such a description. For one thing it was a year of significant political activity in Australia: in Western Australia the Brand Coalition government was elected; the Playford government was re-elected in South Australia in time to celebrate its twentieth anniversary; in New South Wales the Cahill Labor government was re-elected although Mr Cahill died in the October to be succeeded by RJ Heffron; and in Tasmania the Reece Labor government was re-elected. The Menzies government had been re-elected in November of the previous year with a substantial majority helped by DLP preferences; it was the tenth year of Menzies' government. In Queensland, the Nicklin Coalition government had gained power in August 1957, ending 25 years of Labor rule, and Henry Bolte had begun his Liberal rule of Victoria four years earlier, in 1955.

There were significant technological milestones in 1959: the first Snowy Mountains Scheme power station opened at Tumut; commercial computers arrived in Australia; Qantas took delivery of its first Boeing 707; the first Australian high-speed freeway was built from Perth to Kwinana; the ferry *Princess of Tasmania* began running between Melbourne and Launceston; and work began on the Sydney Opera House. The country was moving faster and the rest of the world was coming closer. Australia restored diplomatic relations with the USSR and Egypt, and opened an embassy in Saigon.

Beyond our shores De Gaulle had become the first President of the Fifth Republic; Castro took power in Cuba; Khrushchev claimed the USSR was leading the space race and he toured the USA where his host was President Dwight D Eisenhower in a year that saw the end of an era with the death of John Foster Dulles. Indira Gandhi was elected leader of the Congress Party. In the first weeks of the next year Harold Macmillan would deliver his famous *Winds of Change* speech in Africa.

Religious life was at a turning point: Pope John XXIII had been elected in October of the previous year, while evangelist Billy Graham led his first crusade to Australia in 1959.

Cultural life was also not as dull as some current commentators would have it. Morris West published *A Devil's Advocate* and Mary Durack published *Kings in Grass Castles*; Peter Kenna's play *The Slaughter of St Teresa's Day* was produced in Sydney and *My Fair Lady* opened in Melbourne just two and a half years after its Broadway debut. The Czech Philharmonic Orchestra was the first overseas orchestra to tour Australia and was jointly managed by the ABC and Musica Viva, NIDA was established, the ABC started 'Six O'Clock Rock', the Myer

Music Bowl opened in Melbourne, and there was the vicarious pleasure in Joan Sutherland's London success in *Lucia di Lammermoor*. The six ABC Symphony Orchestras presented a wide range of concerts in their annual seasons with an amazing roster of soloists. Albert Namatjira died, while in Melbourne the self-styled Antipodean Group formed to oppose the growing use of abstract expressionism and included Arthur Boyd, John Perceval, Clifton Pugh, John Brack and Charles Blackman; in Sydney, William Dobell's portrait of Dr E.G. MacMahon won the Archibald Prize. In Melbourne, Ava Gardner, Gregory Peck and Fred Astaire were filming the end of the world in Neville Shute's *On the Beach*.

Our national love affair with sport continued: Jack Brabham won the world motor-racing championship and was the first ABC Sportsman of the Year, Australia regained the Davis Cup with Neale Fraser, Roy Emerson and Rod Laver, and we won the Ashes Series in Australia 4–0.

Daily life was changing in many ways. Australia's population reached 10 million, having received 1,500,000 immigrants since 1945; hire purchase was booming; the Uniform Code of Divorce Law was introduced into Federal Parliament; and the Reserve Bank was formed to take over the central function from the Commonwealth Bank.

It is one of my regrets that Sir Richard Boyer himself did not deliver a series of lectures. It may not have been to his taste to do so but one can be reasonably sure that he would have had stimulating insights to convey to an audience.

He was a remarkable man who embodied many of the characteristics of the great leaders of his generation. Born in 1891, he graduated with an MA Honours from Sydney University in 1915 and entered the Methodist ministry. Having hoped for an appointment, which did not eventuate, as a chaplain in the AIF, he enlisted in 1915. He fought at Gallipoli and on the Western Front where he was gassed near Passchendale. Feeling unable to return to the ministry, he went jackerooing near Morven in Queensland. He took up a large holding in 1920 and married Elenor Underwood, who had nursed him during the war. Despite initial difficulties as graziers, the Boyers succeeded as sheep producers. He became increasingly involved in the affairs of the wool industry to the extent that he became President of the Graziers Federal Council of Australia (1942) and sat on the Australlian Meat Industry Commission. Having placed their property in the hands of a manager, the Boyers took up residence in Sydney in 1940. His interest in foreign affairs had been stimulated by attendance at the 1938 British Commonwealth Relations Conference, but he avoided direct involvement in domestic politics.

In 1940 Richard Boyer accepted appointment to the Australian Broadcasting Commission and became chairman in April 1945. His truly remarkable period of service as ABC chairman did not end until his death on 5 June 1961; he had planned to retire on June 30 of that year. He made other notable contributions to Australian public life, but none eclipses his service to the ABC to which he brought a disarming idealism, legendary tact, and liberalism together with a steely determination to maintain the ABC's independence; his judgment was trusted, he was a shrewd and patient tactician. The ABC was especially blessed in Sir Richard Boyer; it was a particularly felicitous decision that, in renaming the lectures in his honour, the ABC ensured that his contribution would not be forgotten.

The early Boyer lecturers responded to the very big issues of their time. The first, by Dr David Forbes Martyn, *Society in the Space Age*, addressed the relatively new space exploration which had begun as a search for knowledge, but soon became the space race. The Russian Sputnik had first traced across our southern skies in 1957. By 1959 Kruschev's claim that Russia was leading the race was based on the successful launch of Lunik, the first spacecraft to escape gravity, although the USA had safely brought a monkey back from space.

Reflecting the nature of the Cold War which threatened to boil up on a number of occasions, lecturers in the following years chose subjects related to international security and the fear of nuclear war—Professor Julius Stone in 1960, Professor JDB Miller in 1963, and George Ivan Smith in 1964. Lecturers have not returned to that subject since, perhaps reflecting a more sanguine view of prospects of survival.

The first lecture by a woman did not occur until 1975 when Dame Roma Mitchell, the first in so many other areas, addressed *The Web of Criminal Law*. There was no immediate female successor; Shirley Hazzard was the next in 1984 with *Coming of Age in Australia*.

If lecturers in the main turned away from international affairs after 1964, they became vividly interested in defining Australia and Australian-ness from 1984 onwards, with at least five lecturers addressing that general area.

The history, interests and voices of Australian indigenous peoples have been the subject of several lectures, most notably in 1968 and

1993. *After the Dreaming* was the umbrella title of Professor William Stanner's historic lecture series, which became a basic reference text and was reprinted at least seven times. In 1993, to mark the International Year of the World's Indigenous Peoples, seven Australian indigenous lecturers were invited to make their singular contributions under the umbrella title of *Voices from the Land*. I have included two of the most significant in this anthology—'Towards a Koori Healing Practice' by Dr Ian Anderson and 'Mabo: Towards Respecting Equality and Difference' by Noel Pearson.

The law, medicine and biology, population trends and the shape of the future, government, art and aesthetics, history: all have been subjects on which Boyer lecturers have shed the light of their knowledge and insight.

Reading all of the lectures to choose this anthology has been a source of immense pleasure to me and of pride in the ABC. The Boyer Lectures represent for me what is unique about the ABC, and what is best.

DONALD MCDONALD AO
Sydney, 2001

THE SIXTIES

EVENTS 1959 – 1969

1959

JANUARY	Charles de Gaulle inaugurated as first President of Fifth Republic
FEBRUARY	Fidel Castro became Cuban President, aged 30
APRIL	Australia's population passed 10 million mark
MAY	The World Bank warned that the 'poverty gap' threatened the world more than Cold War
	US Secretary of State John Foster Dulles died
	ALP voted to retain the White Australia Policy
NOVEMBER	David Ben-Gurion's Labor party won Israel general election

1960

JANUARY	Harold Macmillan made 'Winds of Change' speech
MARCH	The first Adelaide Festival opened
JULY	Neale Fraser beat Rod Laver in an all-Australian final at Wimbledon
AUGUST	Malaya state of emergency lifted
	Jack Brabham became Formula One World champion
	Beyond the Fringe opened at Edinburgh Theatre
	Rome Olympics opened (concern that stimulant drugs were being taken)
	East Germany closed border with West Berlin
SEPTEMBER	Julius Nyerere became first Prime Minister of Tanganyika
DECEMBER	Pope John XXIII met with the Archbishop of Canterbury (Dr Fisher)
	Sir Macfarlane Burnet won Nobel Prize for Medicine
	Australia and West Indies played first tied Test match

1961

JANUARY	John F Kennedy sworn in as 35th President of USA
	Oral contraceptives went on sale in Australia
APRIL	Adolf Eichmann put on trial
	Soviet Union put first man in space—Yuri Gagarin
MAY	South Africa became a republic and left British Commonwealth because of apartheid policies
JUNE	Carl Jung died

JULY	Ernest Hemingway died (suicide)
AUGUST	Berlin Wall built
	First screening of 'Four Corners'
SEPTEMBER	UN Secretary-General Dag Hammarskjold died in air crash—
	North Rhodesia
	Bob Dylan's New York debut
	U Thant elected Secretary-General of UN
NOVEMBER	US military advisers sent to South Vietnam
	Catch 22 by Joseph Heller published
	West Side Story film opened

1962

JANUARY	EEC nations reached agreement on common agricultural policy
FEBRUARY	First American—John Glenn—orbited the earth
MAY	Adolf Eichmann hanged
JUNE	Writer Victoria Sackville West and conductor Eugene
	Goossens died
JULY	US TV program delivered live by satellite for first time to
	Europe
	Independent Algeria proclaimed by France
	Rod Laver won all-Australian Wimbledon final—goes on to
	win Grand Slam
AUGUST	West New Guinea ceded by Dutch to Indonesia despite
	protests by Australian Prime Minister Menzies
	Marilyn Monroe died
OCTOBER	Cuban missile crisis ended with Soviet withdrawal
	First James Bond film—*Dr No*—released
NOVEMBER	Nelson Mandela jailed for five years
DECEMBER	Dame Mary Gilmore died

1963

JANUARY	British entry to EEC closed off by French President de Gaulle
	The Beatles record first LP *Please Please Me*
APRIL	First issue of *Oz* magazine
JUNE	David Ben-Gurion resigned as Israeli Premier
	Pope John XXIII died
	Pope Paul VI elected (Cardinal Giovanni Montini)

	Profumo sex scandal in Britain
	John F Kennedy visited Berlin
AUGUST	Great Train Robbery
	Civil Rights movement rally in Washington heard Martin Luther King 'I have a dream' speech
SEPTEMBER	Federation of Malaysia created
OCTOBER	Nigerian Republic proclaimed
	Harold Macmillan resigns—succeeded by Alec Douglas-Home
	First West German Chancellor Konrad Adenauer resigned—succeeded by Ludwig Erhard
	Jean Cocteau died
	Edith Piaf died
	'Beatlemania' was born
NOVEMBER	John F Kennedy assassinated
DECEMBER	Sir John Eccles won Nobel Prize for Medicine

1964

FEBRUARY	HMAS *Voyager* sunk
	George Papandreou won Greek general election
MARCH	UN peacekeeping force sent to Cyprus
APRIL	General Douglas MacArthur died (aged 84)
	Sir Owen Dixon retired as Chief Justice, succeeded by Sir Garfield Barwick
	Ian Smith elected Prime Minister of Southern Rhodesia
MAY	Jawaharlal Nehru died—India's Prime Minister since Independence in 1947—aged 74
JUNE	Creation of Palestine Liberation Organisation
JULY	Roy Emerson beat Fred Stolle in yet another all-Australian Wimbledon final
	Malcolm X founded Afro-American Unity to seek independence for Black Americans
AUGUST	Turkey and Greece accepted UN cease-fire in Cyprus
	Kenneth Kaunda elected first President of Zambia—formerly Northern Rhodesia
SEPTEMBER	Indonesian paratroopers landed in Malaysia
	Harpo Marx died

OCTOBER	Opening of Tokyo Olympic Games
	Labour won British general election—Harold Wilson became Prime Minister
NOVEMBER	Lyndon Baines Johnson won US Presidential election, defeating Barry Goldwater
	Viet Cong launched a major attack on US base at Bien Hoa
DECEMBER	Canada adopted maple leaf as national flag

1965

JANUARY	Sir Winston Churchill died
	TS Eliot died
FEBRUARY	Malcolm X shot dead
	Ron Clarke broke 5000-metre world record at 13 minutes 33.6 seconds, concurrently held world records for 3 miles, 6 miles and 10,000 metres
MARCH	Vietnam conflict escalated, with US sending 3500 marines to Da Nang
	Sir Thomas Playford defeated in South Australian elections after 26 years as Premier
JUNE	Joan Sutherland returned to Australia for a triumphant season of operas after 14 years abroad
JULY	Roy Emerson again beat Fred Stolle in another all-Australian Wimbledon final
	United Kingdom's House of Lords unexpectedly approved Bill to abolish hanging
AUGUST	First West German Ambassador sent to Israel
	Singapore seceded from Malaysia
	Le Corbusier died
SEPTEMBER	India and Pakistan at war over Kashmir
	Australian Ballet arrived in London for first overseas tour and Sydney Symphony Orchestra on tour in Japan
	Dr Albert Schweitzer died
NOVEMBER	Rhodesia issued Unilateral Declaration of Independence
	Jean Shrimpton wore miniskirt at Melbourne Cup
DECEMBER	Ferdinand Marcos sworn in as President of Philippines

1966

JANUARY	Sir Robert Menzies resigned after 16 years as Prime Minister, succeeded by Harold Holt
SEPTEMBER	Prime Minister of South Africa, Dr Hendrik Verwoerd 'father' of apartheid assassinated
OCTOBER	President LB Johnson visited Australia
DECEMBER	Rhodesia left British Commonwealth
	Walt Disney died
	'Swinging London' claimed to be fashion capital of the world

1967

MAY	British Prime Minister Harold Wilson announced Britain will apply for membership of the EEC, but rebuffed by President de Gaulle
	Majority of 90 per cent voted for referendum to count Aborigines in the census and to allow Federal Government to make special laws for them, previously the preserve of the States
JUNE	Archbishop of Krakow, Karol Wojtyla named a Cardinal
	Israel won six-day war against Arab states of Egypt, Jordan and Syria
SEPTEMBER	Prime Minister Harold Holt established Office of Aboriginal Affairs
OCTOBER	Che Guevara shot dead by Bolivian Army
DECEMBER	Harold Holt drowned in surf
	In Cape Town Dr Christiaan Barnard performed world's first heart transplant operation

1968

JANUARY	John Gorton sworn in as Prime Minister
	Poet Dorothea Mackellar died
	Alexander Dubcek became leader of Czechoslovakia
FEBRUARY	Sir Howard Florey (1945 Nobel Prize winner) died
MARCH	President Johnson announced he will not contest the presidential election
APRIL	Dr Martin Luther King assassinated
	John Farnham had first hit song—'Sadie'
MAY	Students rioted in France

JUNE	Robert F Kennedy assassinated
	Charles de Gaulle won landslide re-election to French presidency
JULY	Pope Paul VI refused any concession on birth control
AUGUST	Russian invasion brought an end to Dubcek's 'Prague Spring'
OCTOBER	Mexico Olympics opened
	Australia's first heart transplant operation performed
NOVEMBER	Richard Nixon elected US President

1 9 6 9

JANUARY	Rupert Murdoch purchased British newspaper *News of the World*
MARCH	Concorde made maiden flight
APRIL	Bass Strait gas piped to Victoria for first time
	President Charles de Gaulle resigned
JUNE	Georges Pompidou elected French President
JULY	Neil Armstrong and Edwin Aldrin landed on the moon
SEPTEMBER	Bob Hawke became President of the ACTU
OCTOBER	Willy Brandt elected Chancellor of West Germany
	Gorton coalition Government re-elected
NOVEMBER	Standard-gauge rail link from Sydney to Perth completed
	Norman Lindsay died

David Forbes Martyn

David Forbes Martyn was chief officer of the uppert atmosphere section of the CSIRO. Born in Scotland in 1906, he was educated at Plymouth College, the Royal College of Science, and the universities of Glasgow and London, from which he was awarded a PhD.

He emigrated to Australia in 1929 as a researcher for the Radio Research Board of the Australian Council for Scientific and Industrial Research. Early work on ultra-high frequency communication led to his selection to a group invited by the British government to study radar in 1939.

On his return to Australia he headed the CSIRO's new radiophysics laboratory at the University of Sydney. In 1944 he moved to the Commonwealth Observatory at Mount Stromlo in Canberra and ultimately to the independent Upper Atmosphere Section of the CSIRO.

The importance of his theoretical work was widely recognised: he was elected a fellow of the Royal Society in 1950 and became president of the Australian Academy of Science.

Dr Martyn was vice-president of the International Radio Science Union from 1950 to 1954. He was a convenor of the Australian National Committee of the International Geophysical Year (1957–58) and, in 1959, he was chairman of the Australian National Committee for Space Research and chairman of the Australian National Committee for Antarctic Research. From 1962 until his death in 1970, he chaired the United Nations committee on the peaceful uses of outer space.

It was that interest in particular which informed his lectures, entitled *Society in the Space Age*. I chose for inclusion here Dr Martyn's first lecture, 'World Inherited', partly because his opening paragraph provides a thrilling reminder to my generation of our first glimpse of a space craft, but also because in 1959 he could boldly and accurately proclaim a new age—the Space Age—which had begun only two years previously. Happily he lived to see man land on the moon. His three other lectures were entitled 'World in Transformation', 'Other Worlds' and 'World of Tomorrow'. At the end of that fourth lecture he uses a beautiful quote from Masefield to inspire all seekers after knowledge:

> *Adventure on, for from this littlest clue*
> *Has come whatever worth man ever knew;*
> *The next to lighten all men may be you.*

WORLD INHERITED

Society in the Space Age

David Forbes Martyn

• 1959 •

Historians will probably decide that on 4 October 1957, man entered a new era—the Space Age. As the first Sputnik soared round the earth, high above the atmosphere, it was already widely recognised that we were witnessing man's first big step into outer space. The feelings aroused were like those that greeted Columbus' discovery of the New World.

Mixed with reactions of astonishment and awe there seemed to be almost a feeling of relief; we had heard repeated warnings that the world would soon be overcrowded; those who did not appreciate such warnings were at least fully aware that nuclear bombs had made the earth no longer a secure habitage. Could it be that here was a way out? Was a path being blazed to guide future generations to new and safer worlds? Consciously or subconsciously these thoughts went through our minds as satellite after satellite went into orbit, as probes reached out to the moon and beyond.

In these talks I am going to try to answer this question. We shall look first at the world we have inherited, see what we are making of our inheritance, look at other worlds, and venture on predictions of what the future may hold.

It is always difficult to see ourselves in perspective against both the past and the future; we have a built-in tendency to regard the present as extending fore and aft with only minor changes. This is particularly unfortunate when we live, as we do today, in a world which is changing infinitely faster than ever before, and not only is it changing rapidly—the tempo of change accelerates as never before.

In 1950 the famous Kinkakuji—the Temple of the Golden Pavilion—was burned to the ground in Kyoto, medieval capital of Japan, deliberately set alight by a young man in a crime that shocked all Japan. The psychology of the incendiarist is examined in a novel by Mishima, who considers it an act of rebellion against the strain of living with feudal traditions in the rapidly changing modern world. It is ironically fitting that the Japanese have reconstructed the Golden Pavilion, beam for beam, so that it now stands glittering in the sun exactly as in 1397.

Writing of Mishima's novel, Anthony West says:

> He touched on one of the major discomforts of his generation in every country—the feeling that the modern world is so different from the old that the greater part of its cultural legacy has become merely an irrelevant burden, inhibiting and stifling the creativity of those who wish to deal with life as it is, and not as it was, or is supposed to have been.

I would go further than Anthony West. I would say that this modern dilemma is more than a major discomfort; it is the crucial problem facing the human race; its resolution may decide whether we can survive upon this planet. The pages of natural history are strewn with examples of species of animals that vanished from the earth because they failed to adapt themselves to changing environment—to climatic changes, to the arrival of new predatory species, or to competition with other animals whose mode of life was better suited to their surroundings. For one or other of these reasons the dinosaur and the dodo have disappeared.

Man is tougher. With superior intelligence he has managed to adapt himself to living on almost any part of the earth's surface. He has survived for months in the blizzards of the South Pole; for moments at least on the top of Everest. He can even live and travel for weeks hundreds of feet under the surface of the seas.

It can truly be said that we have conquered our immediate environment. Not only are we finding how to live in difficult parts of the world; we are making such areas more hospitable. By conserving water we are making deserts fruitful, bringing electric power to areas remote from other sources of energy. From a material point of view it is truly a Golden Age.

Nor is this all. Besides securing ourselves the basic necessities— food and warmth—we have made enormous strides in subduing our natural enemies. It is probably thousands of years since any other predatory animal was a real threat to the human race; the animals that survive do so by our grace. In recent times our most dangerous enemies have been parasites—insects and bacteria that thrive in and upon our bodies and blood, preying on us in microscopic forms too small for the eye to see.

It is a last-ditch kind of struggle, and one which at best could only result in a Pyrrhic victory; for if the parasite kills its host it too must die. Even this battle is now substantially won; the great killers of past centuries—plague, cholera, smallpox, yellow fever, typhus, malaria—have been either eliminated or at least confined to ever-shrinking areas.

We have overcome the big animals; we have made microscopes to study and help us destroy those too small to be seen. Now our main enemies are the viruses—too small to be visible by ordinary light in conventional microscopes. It is reasonable to think that new tools such as the electron microscope will soon let us control even those tiny enemies. Man's outlook seems promising indeed. He now substantially controls his physical and biological surroundings; they are safe to live in.

With survival seemingly secure, we have turned to broader fields. We are no longer content to dwell on one small patch of earth. We have become civilised, which means in essence that a substantial proportion of us live in cities. We need transportation, for food, for the necessities of city life and industry, and to coordinate activities between cities and countries. This we now have—by land, by sea, and by air.

Some may grumble and point out that trains were faster 50 years ago; others may complain how tiring and uncomfortable are long journeys by air. But, although we may have to hang by a strap or sit up all night with bent knees, we do get there; if we have the money we can move anywhere about the earth.

And if we don't choose to move ourselves, we can communicate. Couriers will take our written messages speedily across the world at small cost. At somewhat greater expense we can talk directly with friends or associates anywhere around the globe. The voice we hear may be distorted and liable to abrupt crescendos and diminuendos; there may even be an accompaniment of crashes and bangs from elemental storms.

Nevertheless the fact that we can understand and communicate almost instantaneously right around the earth is not only a great technical feat; it binds the human race together as never before. It ensures that events happening in one part of the globe can be realised and rapidly assessed everywhere; if necessary, world reaction can take effect in hours or days. In their present development, speedy, modern transport and communications have welded the human race into one organism of interconnecting reactions.

> Let observation with extensive view,
> Survey mankind, from China to Peru;
> Remark each anxious toil, each eager strife,
> And watch the busy scenes of crowded life.

These eighteenth-century words of Samuel Johnson, written from the standpoint of an armchair philosopher, are now applied by men of action. Disasters or aggressions in remote islands or jungles can result in the speedy arrival of a team of international observers, and sometimes in international succour.

We have reached out and surveyed almost every part of the earth's surface. Today there remain to be mapped only a few rocky outcrops on the continent of Antarctica. It is certain that these, too, will be fully known within the next few years.

The years 1957–58 saw the greatest cooperative study of man's environment in history. In this International Geophysical Year more than 50 nations planned and made extensive observations of earth, sea, and air, and of the particles and radiations reaching us from the sun and outer space. With delicate seismographs we studied the travel of both natural and man-made vibrations through the earth's crust. Plans are afoot even to drill a hole right through this crust— to the mantle some ten miles down.

A great effort was made to study the circulation of the atmosphere at all heights. Irregularities in this circulation are the cause of what we call weather—alternations of fine clear skies with heavy winds, cloud, and rain. It is only when the general circulation over the globe is fully understood that we can hope to predict the birth, death and movement of storms for days or weeks ahead. Of special interest to Australia was the unprecedented concentration of meterological observations in the Antarctic, a zone which controls our weather, at least in the southern and most populous states.

Very important for men, too, is the carbon dioxide (CO_2) in the atmosphere. It is little—in volume less than a thirtieth of one per cent—but it acts like the glass in a conservatory; it keeps in the heat of the earth by preventing infra-red radiation from escaping into space. Some scientists even suspect that man is increasing CO_2 in the atmosphere by as much as 70 per cent in 40 years, by burning fossil fuels like coal and oil at a great rate and by denuding the surface.

If true, this means that temperatures will steadily rise all over the earth, glaciers will retreat, the polar ice-caps will melt, and the great seaports of the world will find themselves below sea-level. Very sensitive methods of measuring CO_2 were developed during IGY to keep track of the amounts of this gas in the atmosphere. We should know soon whether man is prejudicing his environment in this way.

But perhaps the most exciting fruits of the IGY came from rockets and satellites. It is difficult to realise just how important our atmosphere is. We can't see it and we don't feel it unless it is stirred up by cyclones to blow against us as wind. Yet it is vital to our very existence. Besides providing oxygen for our lungs, it cushions us against the deadly bombardment of particles and radiation from outer space. These range from meteorites, tiny particles travelling with 20 times the speed of a rifle bullet, to atomic particles travelling with speeds approaching that of light—186,000 miles a second; from ultra-violet rays capable of burning our skin to a crisp, to X-rays capable of immediate profound damage to our blood cells, and of future genetic damage to our children. To all such dangers the atmosphere is our shield. It provides us, too, with convenient means of locomotion; it can propel ships round the globe; it supports airships and aircraft in their travels.

On the debit side the atmosphere makes it difficult to study what is going on in outer space. From that point of view the protective cushion of air becomes an undesirable blanket that screens many phenomena from our earth-bound instruments, distorting our vision of the phenomena that do penetrate to ground level. Stars twinkle and give unsteady images; we sometimes think we see canals on Mars, but can't be sure; long radio waves, that we think must exist in outer space, we can't detect at all.

To the scientist who seeks to know more of other worlds the atmosphere is a serious nuisance. To get an adequate view he must rise above it, and since he wishes to rise above its support, he must use rocket propulsion, which can operate in empty space.

The rocket makes use of Newton's third law; that is, to every action there is an equal and opposite reaction; if material is ejected from its tail the rocket will be propelled forward. We can calculate that a rocket using any known or likely chemical fuel can penetrate the atmosphere but will remain only for a few minutes in outer space before falling back to earth. If we wish to send it far into space, or to make it orbit the earth, then we must use a multi-stage vehicle—a large rocket carrying a smaller rocket in its nose, the latter carrying a still smaller one. By firing these stages successively we can project an object into space in such a way that it will remain there for any desired time. During IGY some hundreds of rockets were fired through the atmosphere, and a small number of satellites were put into orbits around the earth.

From the scientific viewpoint a satellite carrying recording instruments which relay their findings back to earth is much more valuable than a brief rocket ascent; one month of such observations from a satellite is equivalent to 3000 rocket ascents. The satellites and rockets launched during IGY have already established that there are two unsuspected zones of deadly high-velocity particles, outside the atmosphere, but tied to the earth at heights of about 6000 miles and 14,000 miles. Space travellers of the future must brave these zones.

I have given only the briefest outline of the great cooperative enterprise which is IGY, and have touched on only a few of its highlights. Years must elapse before the full fruits are known. Perhaps history will record as the greatest achievement that here for the first time all the major nations, and nearly all the smaller ones, combined harmoniously and effectively to study and record the physical phenomena of our earthly environment. There have been no political barriers and no secrets; the results obtained by all are freely available to all.

But man is concerned now with more than his tangible physical surroundings. He is increasingly aware of the importance of his intangible environment, of the molecules and atoms and particles of which he and all else is made up. When I went through university it was thought that all matter was made up of two kinds of particles—protons and electrons. This great simplification, due in large measure to a New Zealand physicist—Rutherford—had great intellectual appeal.

I well remember pondering on Bertrand Russell's philosophical deduction that if only there were a great computing brain, and it were given the position and speed of every proton and electron in the universe, then it could calculate all that would happen to everything in all future time. A magnificent concept, if depressing; one which we now know to be untrue in at least two aspects. For if we specify the position of a particle accurately we cannot so specify its speed. And now it is known that there are at least 32 instead of only two fundamental particles; in addition to the proton and electron we have the positron, the neutron, the mesons and many others.

The horizons of the physicist are expanding rapidly—almost embarrassingly so; the seeming atomic order of the 1920s dissolves and proliferates into a challenging new chaos.

Recently Heisenberg, the author of the 'uncertainty principle' which I've mentioned, and another physicist, Pauli, believed that they had made an important step forward in explaining elementary particles. Pauli explained the theory in New York before an audience which included Neils Bohr, Rutherford's famous theoretical collaborator. When he had finished, Bohr summed up the general opinion: 'We are all agreed,' he said, 'that your theory is crazy. We can't agree whether it is crazy enough to be likely to be true. I myself feel it is not crazy enough.' This incident illustrates the current ferment in fundamental theoretical physics.

What is needed is the grand and apparently crazy simplification of which only genius is capable.

The parallel with the current state of art is striking. In many countries, in Europe, Asia and America, art is reaching out into new forms. To the uninitiated there is something crazy about the apparent distortions and abstractions of Picasso, Braque, Chagall, Klee and Mondriaan, the sculptures 'with holes' of Henry Moore, the harmonic dissonances of Schoenberg and Stravinsky; art, too, is in a ferment. Aristotle said, 'It is the mark of a poet to see a connection between apparently incongruous things.'

It is also the mark of the scientist, the artist, the sculptor, and the musician. The great innovations and simplications are never easy, before the event. When first made they incite incredulity, hostility, ridicule; later they come to be regarded as beautiful, if obvious.

It is remarkable indeed how close is the parallel between progress in the arts and sciences; the 'golden mean' of Greek art has mathematical significance; the rectangular abstractions of some modern artists are almost perfect solutions of certain problems in the theory of electrical networks. Moore's sculptural innovations have parallels in the geometer's studies of connected spaces. The love of music widely shown by mathematicians seems to manifest an underlying unity of purpose.

The processes at work in these fundamental developments may always baffle the non-expert; they may not be understood even by the expert. The innovators are often asked: 'What does it mean? What use will it be?' These seemingly sensible questions are usually distracting when put, and are often unanswerable for years. It was the question put to Michael Faraday after he had shown a lady his primitive magnets and coils of wire. 'Mr Faraday,' she said, 'what is the use of all this?' 'Madam,' said the father of modern electric technology, 'what is the use of a new-born baby?' That answer is as valid today as it was more than a century ago.

We welcome and encourage the arrival of the human baby unquestioningly. Should we not do the same with potentially fruitful ideas or discoveries? This is a question which the community has now to face with mounting urgency. As recently as 30 years ago it posed no serious problem. The scientist in his ivory tower could get along without much outside assistance. All he asked was a roof and some 'glass, string, and sealing-wax'.

Nowadays fundamental advances in science increasingly require elaborate and expensive equipment, giant cyclotrons, giant radio or optical telescopes, giant rockets or satellites, things that cost millions of pounds. The expenditure of such large sums now begins to have an appreciable effect on a country's economy, and increasingly involve decisions at government levels. This raises difficulties, as it is still rare to find politicians or top civil servants possessing the scientific background necessary to make the informed decisions which become increasingly important.

Until now our top-level administrators have been drawn almost exclusively from the ranks of those with professional training in such matters as law, accountancy, or the humanities. This has worked well in the past; the lawyer, for example, is experienced in assessing the reliability of evidence, and the relative soundness of proponents in conflict. In this space age, when complex scientific issues are ever more widely and deeply involved in political decisions, it becomes increasingly difficult for men of such relatively narrow training to grasp the full implications of the matters they have to decide.

There appears to be urgent need in our leaders of the broader outlook that a sound knowledge of science can provide. But there is one important difference between the study of the humanities and of the sciences. The arduous disciplines of science cannot be picked up by part-time study, either in undergraduate years, or later; it is much easier for the scientist to gain knowledge and understanding of the humanities at any stage of his career.

Here is a fundamental difference between the Western democracies and the Soviet bloc. To guide us, we rely upon humanists with a smattering of science. On the other side of the Curtain the pre-eminent role of the scientist becomes increasingly obvious. The relative effectiveness of these methods—so far as material progress goes—may become apparent within the next decade.

Economically the world has never been healthier. The general prosperity reaches into all segments and age-groups of society in all save a few under-developed countries. It seems unlikely that we shall ever again see a catastrophic depression like that of the early 1930s; it is recognised now that the effects on the community of slumps in private business can be substantially cushioned by increasing public spending—by doing, in other words, just the opposite of what we did in the Great Depression.

The condition of the unskilled and semi-skilled worker has never been better; it is now so good that there is barely adequate incentive for boys and girls to embark on long courses of study leading to professional or semi-professional careers with very little extra material reward. This is one sign that the social pendulum may have swung too far. Another is the careful preservation of the so-called 'right to strike', a meaningful phrase when applied to a group of underprivileged workers at the mercy of a wealthy private boss; a mere shibboleth when demanded by a powerful group of key workers holding the whole community to ransom.

Perhaps the most obvious index of current prosperity is the motor car. In the United States there is now almost one automotive for every two persons; the entire population of the US could take to the roads in cars tomorrow and still leave as many empty in the garage.

In world politics we have reached a power stalemate. Each of the two main groups engaged in the Cold War now has power to destroy the other. I am not an optimist, but I do not think this power will ever be used; the fruits, or rather lack of fruits, are clearly realised on both sides. It seems likely that reason will gradually—perhaps only very gradually—prevail.

The dangers facing the world from nuclear warfare, though real, seem less serious than those I will discuss in my next talk.

Truly we are living in a Golden Age. Will it continue for centuries, or at least for generations? Or is the worm of decay already in the apple?

Julius Stone

Julius Stone was a distinguished international lawyer.

A Yorkshireman born in
1907, Julius Stone graduated
with a first in law from Oxford.
He worked for three years as a
solicitor in Leeds and then
became a Rockefeller fellow in
Social Sciences at Harvard.

From 1933 to 1936 Professor
Stone was Assistant Professor of
Law at Harvard University, Pro-
fessor of International Law and
Diplomacy at Fletcher School and
then, in 1938, Professor and Dean
of the Faculty of Law at Auckland
University, New Zealand.

Appointed Challis Professor
of International Law and Juris-

prudence at the University of Sydney in 1942, he remained there until
1972, twice serving as acting dean of the faculty. In 1973 he became
Professor of Law at University of New South Wales.

In 1961 Professor Stone was an official observer for the international
commission of jurists at the Eichmann trial in Israel. He published books
on law, the philosophy of law and international law, as well as being a
regular guest and commentator on ABC Radio. Honoured by the American
Society of International Law in 1956, he also received an award from the
Royal Academy of Arts and Sciences in 1964. Professor Stone was awarded
the OBE in 1973 and the AO in 1981. He was made an honorary QC in
1982. Professor Stone died in 1985.

The title of his six lectures—*Law and Policy in the Quest for Survival*—reflects the
anxiety of that Cold War period with its potential for the destruction of
the human race. His concern was that aggression should be contained and
world order maintained through the development of legal sanctions, but
he was not optimistic; how could he be in the light of the events of the
twentieth century to that date? The titles of the other lectures in the series
give some indication of his concerns: 'Is There a Rule of Law Between
Nations?', 'Judgement and Survival', 'Law Force and Survival', 'Outlawry
and Revolution in the Relations of States' and 'What Can We Do To
Survive'. We reproduce here Professor Stone's fifth lecture.

INTERNATIONAL LAW AND THE PRICE OF SURVIVAL

Law and Policy in the Quest for Survival

Julius Stone

• 1960 •

It should have become obvious from what I have said in these lectures that I am not sanguine about the power of international lawyers to produce any early or quick relief to the fear of war which confronts all thoughtful people. The responsibility of making the world safe for the human race rests on all of us, and on all our governments, throughout the nations. If we meet this responsibility, the results of our success will, no doubt, come to be recorded in a very much revised and strengthened international law; but the decisions necessary for this revision must be taken by ordinary men, and by governments on their behalf.

It is by no means possible even to be sure what these decisions should be. It is easy enough of course to formulate common objectives which all people share. But you will usually find when you look closely at these so-called common objectives that, somehow, the conflicts between nations manage to go on behind them. Behind the common objective, peace, lie the gravest conflicts as to what each side requires in order to assure it of peace. Almost everybody wants peace; the problems arise because people also want other things which they may not be able to get without war. Behind the objective of justice for all, lie conflicting national versions of what justice means. Behind the objectives of human welfare lurk the conflicts arising from the uneven economic development of peoples, and the tensions deriving from demands for a more or less equitable redistribution of the goods of the world. Behind the common objectives of disarmament lie conflicts as to the means for bringing it about. Behind the objective of a free united Germany are the intractable questions: What kind of a Germany and on what terms? The hard problems indeed, of international politics, are not so much problems of ultimate objectives, as problems of what should be the next steps towards the objectives, and what sacrifices each nation should be willing to make to render them achievable.

The decisions which must be made before international law can be remodelled into the workable code of a peaceful world have never, indeed, been more numerous and more difficult than they are today. This is because the dynamics of our age have added to the numerous unsolved problems of traditional international law, vast new problems, including some for which it is difficult at the moment to see any answer.

I must at the outset, tonight, give you some impression of the range and difficulties of these vast new problems. And while my purpose is not to lead you to alarm and despondency, it emphatically is to dispel any impression that we might awake one bright morning to find that the world is a safe and orderly place.

First of all, we have by our technology and energy transformed and expanded the physical world which the law must regulate. We have given land surfaces different values, penetrated downwards under the land and under the sea, and outwards into space. By shrinking distances we have made most peoples into neighbours; making all states problems to each other, whether as rivals or enemies or allies or helpmates. World-wide political organisation is made physically possible, and so is world-wide destruction; but as long as the powers of destruction cannot be placed solely in such an organisation, it cannot be an assured guarantee of the peace.

At present rates, world population will approximately double between 1955 and 1985, much of it among the new states of Asia and Africa. As from 1960, the existing 3000 million people, at the present rate of 50-millions per year, will increase to 4250 millions by 1985. In the still undeveloped states, as Gunnar Myrdal has pointed out, the cultivation of nationalism rather than internationalism is almost a political and economic necessity, as a source of morale and energy for facing the grave tasks of economic survival and growth. Yet, as Toynbee stressed in his recent Azad lectures, unless some of these countries can control their explosive birthrate, their national goals of economic development as well as the international goals of peace will all be defeated.

There are a number of reasons why the drastic effects on peace of such changes are only now fully emerging. German, Italian and Japanese population growth underlay the military bids of these countries; but all three were defeated. While Asia had her teeming millions in the nineteenth century, these peoples were weak and without military friends; and voluntary humanitarian drives—for instance, for relief of Chinese flood victims—diverted pressure of human needs away from the state system as such. This nineteenth century free enterprise world still regards the standards of life of different peoples as a private matter and not a State concern. The universal franchise and the votes of depressed classes forced the advent of the Welfare State in the West. Not only the votes in the United Nations of the 40-odd African and Asian states but the instability of a world of contrasting living standards, are now forcing the issue of a kind of 'welfare world'. For, in a world in which each starving people looks daily over the fence onto the more prosperous life of its neighbours, through the growth of world-wide communications, violent contrasts of standards become a new kind of provocation.

International economic aid through such measures as the Marshall, Colombo and US Technical Assistance Plans and the projected International Development Fund, represent a major new field in which international law must be worked out. Clearly such aid, as well as bilateral aid (of which the United States is this year providing four billion dollars), cannot be handled quite like nineteenth century philanthropy as selfless generosity. We can scarcely expect the United States happily to pour generous aid into a Cuba which is campaigning against her, and inviting Soviet entry into the American continent; it was natural therefore for the Senate to bar this aid to any states which would pass it on to Cuba. Yet on the other hand, it will also not improve the human situation very much if aid is distributed merely as an act of foreign policy, to consolidate client and ally relations. The emotional problems of colonialism are too near us for that. The effort to collectivise aid through the abortive SUNFED (Special United Nations Fund for Economic Development), and the still promising International Development Fund, is thus one of the touchstones of our future.

Critical both to living standards and to military power are the problems arising from the increasing demand for industrial raw materials. This old problem again is vastly intensified today by the more advanced stage of industrialisation in the West, by the industrial ambitions of the new nations, and by the related disappearance of the old colonial empires. States well endowed with raw materials, technology, and population, such as the United States and the Soviet Union, become super-powers. Where industrial States lack raw materials there is a tendency for the weaker States to use their endowment for hard bargaining and even blackmail. And the same applies to the channels of supply, as the Suez crisis of 1956 well showed. Despite the massive growth since World War II of all sorts of organs, treaties, and codes for regional and general economic cooperation and planning, this is still an area in which the design for a peaceful world has not yet even reached the drawing board.

But it is of course the revolution in weapons which is most central to the crisis in international life. It is related that the second Lateral Council of the Church denounced the newly invented cross-bow as 'odious to God' in 1139. Destructiveness of weapons has grown ever since; but it is only with atomic weapons that mankind has had to contemplate limitless destructive capacity from which neither side can expect to escape, and against which no real defence can be expected to emerge. It is easy to say that the limitation, control and even prohibition of these new weapons, are absolute essentials for human survival, and must therefore be a common human objective. But the question still remains: What are the feasible next steps in this direction? And when we come to this, the most self-evident truths turn out to be deathtraps. You might suppose, for example, that the lower level of retaliatory (that is, offensive) weapons on both sides, the better. But, in fact, if this level is below the point at which each side would continue to have a substantial power of retaliation, after it has suffered a surprise attack, the effect of the drastic reduction of the level of armaments would be vastly to increase the risk of them being used. For the check on surprise attack now existing from the virtual certainty of effective retaliation would then disappear.

So again, it seems a self-evident truth that agreed reduction of armaments will be safer and surer in proportion as the mutual inspection system is full and comprehensive. But the truth seems rather to be that, beyond a certain point, full and frequent information by each side of the location and strength of the potential enemy's retaliatory bases will rather promote war. It would allow each side to calculate, almost from day to day, not only how vulnerable the enemy is, but also what measure of retaliatory damage to itself it need expect if it decided to make a surprise attack on its enemy.

This particular problem illustrates a most important truth for modern man. What we most complain of is the awful uncertainty of our situation—for instance, as to what one side of the Iron Curtain is preparing for the other. Yet in some situations, and the case of atomic armaments is one of them, that very uncertainty of each side about the state of preparedness of the other may be the best assurance available against the greatest disaster of all. And one of the most important lessons, that all of us have to learn, is the need to accept the uncertainty and tension as an unavoidable background for living and planning. Our greatest dangers are likely to come when we yield to the temptation to think that 'Anything would be better than this'; and it is not true, anyhow, as a general proposition.

I am not here saying that we should give up looking for feasible next steps in atomic disarmament. Some steps may be feasible. For instance one great danger, looming over both sides, is that the other may achieve a technological breakthrough, either defensive or offensive, which would so disturb the balance as to tempt that side to make a surprise attack on the other. If somehow both sides could become aware immediately of any such development, this particular element of uncertainty might come under control. Unlike the other proposals mentioned, this one would usually only discourage warlike initiative; the negotiations for controlling testing of new weapons are thus particularly important. And it is true, even if paradoxical, that the testing of new means of defence should fall within corresponding principles.

But even if all sides showed the maximum intellectual ingenuity, and reasonableness and good faith in agreeing, no early step could free us of the danger that a leader might arise in some nation, who values some particular goal, sane or insane, sordid or sublime, more than he values the survival of mankind. It is, I fear, almost inconceivable that mankind will ever again be free of fear of general destruction by instruments of its own creation.

We must learn, as I said some years ago, the wisdom of the maxim: 'It is not for thee to complete the task, but neither art thou free to desist from it'. Or, as Niebuhr has recently said, the terrifying facts of modern history prove that 'historic responsibilities must be borne without the certainty that meeting them will lead to any ultimate solution . . . but with only the certainty that there are immediate dangers which may be avoided and immediate injustices which may be eliminated' (p. 298).

All this highlights the central modern issue concerning the nature of man himself. Despite the hopes based on the great humanitarian pacifist movements of the last century, and the opening of the present one, technology and totalitarianism have again confronted us with the deep roots of human cruelty and savagery, with homo homini lupus. With many peoples what appeared to be deep moral tendencies built up over millennia of civilisation, have turned out to be pathetically fragile in crisis, or at the hands of the psychopath manipulator. At moments, indeed, it seems as if modern techniques of mass manipulation, combined with the depersonalised methods of mass destruction, can harness to State policy a savagery compared with which the tramp of Hannibal's elephants over the bodies of the wounded seems like good clean fun.

Never has it been so difficult, in any case, to trace back the crimes of States to the moral responsibility of individual men. Before modern democracy, when the monarch could declare L'Etat c'est moi it made sense for Grotius and the early writers of international law to address the heads of state in terms of conscience and morality and to threaten them at any rate with the wages of sin and of divine displeasure. By the same token, State policy was not so subject to the ignorance, prejudice and hysteria of mass opinion, and to the malice or caprice of the manipulators of opinion. The modern democratic State, of which the United States affords a good example, splits and disperses moral responsibility for State action. Modern dictatorships, where dominating individuals still control decision making, tend to be headed by men rather free of moral inhibitions, and able to manipulate mass opinion through propaganda, in any way they choose.

In either case, State action tends to become detached from human responsibility, and to be fastened onto abstract entities, like public opinion, self-defence, vital interests, retaliatory or pre-emptive military necessity, which cannot be brought to the bar of justice, morals or compassion. From the abstraction the command moves forward, dispersing, as it goes, into the hierarchy of command, often to be almost lost in the complex apparatus of decision-making before it emerges as dramatic action. Modern atomic warfare as it looms before us carries this tendency to great extremes. The most massive destruction can proceed from acts whose authors feel little personal association, let alone moral responsibility, for the results. Scientists and technologists invent the weapons, technicians and industrialists produce them, the armed forces release them from land, sea or air, at a distance in space which may be thousands of miles from the designed point of impact, and in time, years remote from the genetic and other radiation effects. Any remaining moral sensibility in the men who act is insulated by space and time from the terrible consequences of action. Very correctly has it been said that technology, considered apart from what use is made of it, is 'a paralysing triumph of the means over the end'.

The depersonalising of opinion and conviction is not perhaps as extreme as the depersonalising of weapons. But the tendency is clear enough for our convictions as individuals to be merged (or submerged) under floods of matter which pass through the media of mass communication, into the entity known as 'public opinion'.

If an assertion is made or agreed to by enough people, it is thought to sustain and determine State organs and policies, regardless of what basis there was for making it, and even if it originates merely from indoctrination by manipulators who themselves do not believe it. Indeed, with great perverseness, the weight of so-called 'public opinion' seems to increase as its basis becomes inscrutable.

Nor, in the present state of human knowledge, is it easy to check this moral chaos by appeal to scientific knowledge. Even in the natural sciences the field of human knowledge has ceased to be within the sweep of any existing human mind. Even the masters in a field command increasingly small corners of it. But the sciences which become increasingly vital for us to master, those concerning men's life together in society, are affected also by other difficulties. Politics, as the physicist Einstein once observed, is much harder than physics. And the social sciences continue to sprawl their chaotic way, suffering from ill-distribution of tasks, from capriciousness of frontiers, and bad communication across frontiers. These very difficulties have provoked among social scientists a kind of idolatory of natural science, leading them to expect far more from the idol than it can possibly give, and to forget that natural science creates more problems for the peace and security of mankind than it is ever likely to solve.

However intimidating they may be, these are some of the movements of growth, change and disruption, which frame the present international struggle, and any attempt to control it by law. The mastery that man has won over natural forces requires him to assume responsibility for controlling them on a global and even transglobal scale. Formerly he could rely on natural processes to repair the physical and biological harm produced by his folly or ineptitude; he can no longer do so. Moreover, as population takes its explosive course and higher living standards are demanded, there is a danger that each generation will begin living on the capital which rightly should provide for the generations to come.

Quite apart therefore from the more sensational perils of sudden destruction, our generation should rightly bear a vastly increased moral responsibility, demanding a sensible adjustment between the interests of the living and of those yet to be born.

Our moral responsibilities have undergone a vast expansion both in space and time corresponding to the expanding range of man's dominion. We must learn to bear these responsibilities, even as we learn to acknowledge the finite limits of our capacity to meet them.

The unavoidable frustrations of history must not weaken the search for feasible next steps to be taken, nor self-righteousness our will to understand and accommodate, nor dreams and yearnings our patience and will to wait.

W D Borrie

Wilfred David Borrie could be described as the father of population studies in Australia. He was born in New Zealand in 1913 and educated at the University of Otago and at Cambridge.

He held research and teaching positions at Sydney University from 1942 to 1948 including senior lecturer in Society History.

Associated with the Australian National University from 1948, first as a Social Science research fellow, he was appointed Professor of Demography in 1957, the first chair of demography in the world, and remained there until his retirement in 1978.

Professor Borrie was the Australian delegate to the UN World Population Conference in Rome in 1954; chairman of International UNESCO Conference on Migration in Havana in 1957; and a vice-president of the International Union for the Scientific Study of Population. He served on the Australian government's immigration planning councils from 1965 to 1981 and assisted in formulating immigration policy. From 1970 to 1978 he directed a national population inquiry, known as The Borrie Report, into the history and future of Australia's population. He chaired the government's ethnicity committee in the early 1980s.

He wrote and contributed to a number of books, publishing his last in 1993.

Professor Borrie was awarded an OBE in 1969 and a CBE in 1979. He died in 2000.

The strength of the science of population studies in Australia owes a great deal to the work of Professor Borrie. It is a science that can provide the rational basis for this currently important debate in Australia. Indeed, it has been a recurrently important debate since European settlement, now needing a resolution of not necessarily conflicting issues of net migration benefits, environmental sustainability, encouragement of natural increase, and population ageing. We reproduce here the third of the four lectures in his Boyer series titled *The Crowding World*. The individual lecture titles were to the point: 'The Vital Revolution', 'Western Man's Victory Over Death', 'Births, Deaths and Poverty', which is reproduced here, and 'The Future'. As he put it so succinctly at the outset of his first lecture, he was writing 'about life and death, or more precisely, about the consequences of the changing relation between these two factors for human societies.'

BIRTHS, DEATHS AND POVERTY

The Crowding World

WD Borrie

• 1961 •

In my last talk, I discussed the nature of the vital revolution that occurred amongst many European countries in the nineteenth century, and described the pattern of the life cycle that now prevails throughout a great part of the European world. The dominant features of that pattern are controlled fertility, extremely high expectations of life and therefore very low mortality, and, compared with any previous period of man's history, extremely high average incomes. I emphasised that this life cycle pattern is unique in man's history.

In my first talk, I also indicated some of the broad features of the current situation in countries in which per capita income is still low, in which processes of industrialisation are for the most part still rudimentary, and in which the forces of life and death are comparable rather with Europe before the nineteenth century than with Europe today. Yet the parallel cannot be drawn too closely because there are several features of these 'low-income', or so-called 'underdeveloped' areas of today's world which had no parallel in European societies.

One striking difference is that, whereas many parts of Europe were thinly populated when their period of demographic expansion began, and whereas there were still many new lands to be discovered and populated, most of today's 'underdeveloped' areas are relatively thickly populated. But density figures by themselves do not mean very much. What is the significance of stating that, in terms of persons per square kilometre, Australia carries two people, Burma 29, Europe 84, India 118, Ceylon 136, Taiwan 257 and Japan 243.7? Clearly there is little correlation here between density and levels of living, for Japan, one of the most densely populated areas of Asia, has a relatively high income and Burma, a relatively thinly populated area, has a low income. Nor is Australia's high income primarily a function of low density, but rather of its overseas trading system. Density, in other words, is less important than the endowment of the land with physical resources, methods and techniques available to use those resources, international trading systems for the interchange of goods and resources, and so on. Yet there can be little doubt that Asian countries, which today are attempting to achieve a 'take off' process in economic growth, start initially at a considerable disadvantage in relation to a population-resources ratio than European people did in the nineteenth century. Nor have they the same reserves of capital for investing to improve efficiency in the use of those resources. For example, the Swedish economist Dr Gunnar Myrdal has pointed out that income per head in India is perhaps only a third or a fifth of what it was when today's high-income, developed countries started out on the process of economic growth a hundred and more years ago. As he observed: 'They could rise as small islands in a large ocean of under-developed peoples . . . Now it is, instead, this whole "outside world" which is rising and craving for economic development . . .'

Thus, whether examined in terms of resources or capital, today's low income areas present a considerable contrast to the situation of the western European countries at the time when they were launched upon their economic and demographic transition.

Another contrast in the two situations is that there are no longer any new lands to be colonised. Undoubtedly the present population of Europe, plus the population living beyond Europe but of European origin, form a considerably larger total than would have been the case had there never been any emigration in the nineteenth century. Since the beginning of the nineteenth century about 60 million people emigrated from Europe and the populations derived from these immigrants now number at least 300 millions. Many of the lands to which these emigrants went are still amongst the world's most thinly populated areas—for example, Australia and New Zealand with a combined average of only two persons per square kilometre, North America with only nine, and Latin America with a similar figure. Furthermore the low density of many of these particular areas is not evidence of a lack of natural resources but rather of a lack of sufficient time to acquire larger populations or to achieve complete economic maturity, as well as of restraints imposed upon immigration in order to protect the ethnic homogeneity, economic standards and social and political structures of the present inhabitants.

Yet it cannot be assumed that the opening of these relatively empty lands to the free flow of the surplus population growth of today's high fertility areas would itself make any substantial contribution to the problem of over-population. The resettlement of 60 million Europeans overseas in the last 150 years is by far the greatest inter-continental migratory movement of history; yet it represents only two years of the current natural increase of the Asian part of the world! Population growth has now reached quantities far beyond the point where migration alone can provide any substantial relief from the pressures it is imposing upon the resources of 'underdeveloped' countries.

This conclusion should not, however, be used to support arguments in favour of further restrictions upon international migration: the right to move, from one country to another, including to Australia, has to be examined in terms of basic human rights rather than in terms of its demographic consequences; and countries with space for new settlers and with resources surplus to their own needs have a moral obligation in this crowding world to press on with plans that will ensure the most efficient use of those resources. These plans must include positive immigration programmes where these will help to meet this criterion of efficient use, and restrictions to international movement based primarily on race and colour are likely to be increasingly open to attack in the councils of the nations.

A third set of factors distinguishing the problems of today's economically 'underdeveloped' countries from those of Europe a century and more ago is concerned with patterns of marriage and fertility. The last talk emphasised the comparative restraint of Westerners in regard to marriage and fertility. It was stated, for example, that as many as a quarter of women often remained unmarried at the age of 35. Nor did fertility usually attain the high average figures of, say, the Hutterites or the Cocos Islanders today. Instead of an average of about eight or nine births in a reproductive lifetime, averages of five or six were more common. There are undoubtedly areas of Asia in which considerable restraints upon fertility do apply. For example, there is some evidence that among the Chinese middle-classes at least, very high proportions of men and women remained unmarried in the seventeenth and eighteenth centuries. But in contrast to this we have the situation in India where the betrothal of women in their early childhood is common practice. In many parts of India the average at which females are formally married seems to be as low as 13 years, with the age at which cohabitation begins as low as 15 years. Furthermore, marriage is practically universal. In most south-east Asian countries, while the age at first marriage is much higher than in India and may indeed be almost as high as the United States today, the proportions which ultimately marry nevertheless remain at very high figures, and considerably less than 10 per cent of women can be expected to remain single by age 30.

Likewise, in regard to births, the average number of children born during the female reproductive cycle appears to have been higher in most Asian countries during this century than it was amongst most areas of Europe, although this does not mean that there have not been many customs, such as restraint upon re-marriage, frequency of divorce, or prolonged suckling of infants, which have imposed some restraint upon fertility. But these customs have on the whole been less restrictive than those applying earlier in pre-industrial Europe.

Consequently, in contemporary 'low income' areas, found throughout most of Asia, or in Latin America or the Caribbean, birth rates frequently exceed 40 per 1000 of population, and sometimes rise as high as 50 per 1000. As death rates have tended to come down from 20 and over per 1000 to 12 and under per 1000, these birth rates have produced growth rates of up to 3 per cent and more a year. So far as Asia is concerned, rates approaching 3 per cent are typical of the relatively small countries in which there is less dire poverty, and less pressure of human numbers against natural resources than in the great central landmasses of Asia. Examples of the former are Taiwan, Malaya, Ceylon and Thailand. In India also however, despite the continual warnings that India's economic plans to increase food supplies and other basic resources are lagging far behind their targets, the rate of population growth appears to be still expanding steadily, for whereas growth was placed at an average of about 1.9 per cent a year by 1951, the latest census of 1961 appears to suggest that growth rates may now be in excess of 2 per cent a year. Yet this has been achieved in the face of mortality which is still appalling by almost any contemporary standard and with life expectations which probably do not yet exceed 40 years. Yet appalling as that average of 40 years may sound, anyone with an historical perspective of demographic development, will realise that an expectation of life of even 40 years is relatively high compared with any earlier time. But India is still far behind many of the smaller Asian countries, where, as previously emphasized, expecta-tions of life of up to 60 years are now not uncommon.

For the student of population history, one blessing of British control over India is a series of censuses which, although by no means completely accurate, can at least provide some indication of the pattern of Indian growth over the past 90 years, during which time population has increased from 255 millions to 435 millions.

The striking feature of this pattern has been short bursts of growth over some periods followed by periods of stagnation and even loss over others. Between 1881 and 1891 population growth averaged almost 1 per cent a year. In the next decade growth was negligible, to be followed by another burst of growth at 0.6 per cent a year between 1901 and 1911, after which there was another set-back culminating in the loss of 12 or 13 million people in the influenza epidemic after 1919. In short, Indian demographic history up to this point appears to have been one of a great people struggling to get above subsistence levels only to be driven back by disease and frequently famine.

This is the pattern which all today's low income, underdeveloped areas are striving to destroy. They are striving to achieve that break-through whereby early death can permanently be placed under human control and whereby the majority of babies born may be expected to grow through to adult life generation after generation; and despite all the dire warnings based upon statistics of food production, demographic evidence may suggest that India is so far succeeding. Since 1921 growth rates in India have not fallen below 1 per cent, and, as already emphasised, are now probably above 2 per cent. An expectation of life of even 40 years would also put India into the European demographic time scale of the early nine-teenth rather than the eighteenth century, and from the early nine-teenth century no European country reverted to the Malthusian demographic controls. Admittedly the problems ahead of India, whether expressed in terms of land resources, capital literacy or the re-location and full employment of labour, seem gigantic compared with those faced by England, Germany or France about 1830 or 1840. But if the slow but inexorable expansion of the rate of popu-lation growth of the last 40 years in India means what census statis-tics suggest, then conclusions based upon other statistics that food production has been continually lagging behind population growth are probably not showing the true position. For, as food production began in the 1920s from a base barely above subsistence, as is suggested by earlier failures of population to sustain growth, there should by this argument have been recurring and increasingly severe death control through famine since the 1920s. Admittedly while the census statistics of population upon which this conclu-sion is based also contain errors, they are almost certainly more trustworthy than the statistics of food production.

If India's success in the battle against death is full of hope but yet by no means complete, not even this much is known about Mainland China. There is very substantial evidence that Chinese population was expanding steadily from about 1700 until 1850 at higher rates than the population of the Western world. The estimated population of 430 millions by 1850 may have been three times the population in 1700. Major factors contributing to this growth were probably the introduction of the new and improved food crops, and more land which could still be brought into cultivation, together with long periods of relatively stable government and freedom from external invasion. But as in India, the later nineteenth century also seems to have brought a recurrence of checks to growth of a Malthusian character. For example the great wars of the mid-nineteenth century appear to have had a most devastating effect upon the Chinese population and there were recurrent outbreaks of disease and famine.

The last population count made in China in 1953 provided a figure of 583 million people. If correct, this figure would imply an average growth rate over the previous hundred years of only 0.3 per cent compared with 0.7 per cent between about 1750 and 1850. Contemporary students of Chinese population tend to consider the official 1953 figure an undercount, but even if it was correct, growth rates of 2 per cent a year since then will have produced the rather staggering total of 700 millions today. This would mean that communist China now comprises close on a quarter of the world's people. The figure also implies that during this century China may have again been undergoing a period of steady population growth. As there is no adequate system in China of registering births and deaths it is impossible to establish with any precision the vital rates which are applying over this vast population, but on the evidence of other countries estimated to have similar age and health patterns and from a study of some information supplied from within China itself, an estimated birth rate of over 35 per 1000 of population would not seem unreasonable. It may in fact be a good deal higher. Of the death rate little is known, but there is at least no evidence to suggest that it should be higher than about 15 per 1000. This means that growth rates in China may be at least between approximately 1.8 and 2 per cent a year, and if this is the case and if these growth rates persist, the result will be 1300 or 1400 million Chinese before the end of the century. Yet this does not necessarily mean that China has broken from the traditional population controls of poverty and disease, and the widespread evidence of current famine in China is a reminder of this fact.

Now the basic features of the current demographic situation of all these non-European areas to which we have referred are falling death rates without any substantial control so far in birth rates.

It is now quite apparent from the comparisons of today's 'under-developed' areas with those of Europe of an earlier time mentioned in our previous talk that, in terms of death control, much of Asia is already far ahead of the situation which obtained in most of north-eastern Europe until well into the nineteenth century. In fact, assuming that improvements in life expectations began from a common base of about 35 years, with technical assistance and the application of the long experience of the West, many of these Asian countries have developed as far along the road of mortality control in about 30 years of this century as most Western countries did before them in about a century. The pessimists looking at the Asian situation tend to conclude that improvements in mortality cannot continue at rates which have recently applied: the improvement in life expectations from say 35 years to 50 years is easy, but can the pace be sustained? In this regard the point made earlier needs re-emphasising, namely that since 1900 western European countries have added as much, and often more than Asian countries to the expectation of life, even though the Europeans began the century with levels of expectation around 50 years, whereas many Asian countries started from much lower figures ranging approximately between 35 and 40 years. The point is that modern medical science can continue to bring great improvements in mortality even after expectations of life exceed 50 or even 60 years, provided that the basic requirements of food and shelter can be supplied by the economic systems. The longevities enjoyed by the Western world certainly require the application of every known device of medical science, but not necessarily of Western calorific and protein intakes or of Western levels of investment in motor cars and refrigerators.

Yet obviously, very complex problems of economic growth remain to be solved in all the world's high fertility and low income areas. Man cannot live for ever on medical science. Population analysis has shown that growth rates of 3 per cent and over are quite possible for periods stretching over many generations, but such growth rates produce population structures in which there are very heavy burdens of young dependants compared with those who must provide for their subsistence. In Australia approximately 27 per cent of our population is under the age of 15. In some Asian countries this ratio rises above 40 per cent. The economic disad-vantages of this burden of dependency are offset to some extent in these Asian countries by their small proportions of old people, but even so their total burden of dependent groups remains con-siderably higher than in high-income countries like Australia. The contrasts might perhaps best be illustrated in terms of the proportion of populations between the ages of 15 and 59 years. For Asia as a whole this proportion is about 55 per cent compared with over 60 per cent in the case of Europe. On the other hand the ages at which people begin and end their working lives are much less easily determined in low income, peasant type societies than in the high income industrial societies, and no doubt in many of the former considerably more than 55 per cent of the populations are engaged in productive employment.

The major point to be emphasised is, however, that a large part of the burgeoning juvenile populations of Asian countries in which death rates have been falling so rapidly cannot possibly be employed much longer in traditional agricultural pursuits. In some countries of south-east Asia in which growth rates are amongst the highest in the world, there is still some scope for more intensive use of land already occupied and some new land that can be brought under cultivation. Probably the same applies to Mainland China. In India the prospect is much more gloomy. But clearly, with the growth rates now prevailing the limit of agricultural settlement must be reached in all these countries in a comparatively short time.

What has to happen, if the growth rates now applying from the partial victory that has been achieved over death control are to be consolidated, is that the volume of production of basic foodstuffs must go on increasing at levels of 2 and 3 per cent a year. It is generally agreed that these targets must be achieved less through a commensurate increase in areas under cultivation than through higher production and more efficient farming methods in areas already cultivated. Hence in all current plans of Asian economic development the essential first clause must relate to measures to sustain and increase food production.

This, however, is only the first step. Increased food production does not necessarily mean increased employment. The basic avenues for employing the expanding numbers of young people must come from growth of non-agricultural sectors of Asian economies. With ample manpower, these economies can probably achieve short-term goals with a much lower level of capital investment per worker or per unit of output than is found in the United States or Australia; but even if the ratio of capital to output ratio remains as low as 3:1, compared with the more generally accepted ratio of 4:1 in our type of 'developed' society, population growth rates of 3 per cent will require capital investment each year at the level of 9 per cent of national income if the economic system is to function at levels sufficient to sustain existing living standards. To improve living standards would of course require even higher annual rates of capital formation—rates which would be commensurate with those in many of the relatively affluent 'developed' societies. Attaining the necessary levels of capital formation is one thing: the efficient use of that capital is another. Where land resources are known to be capable of further development some labour will have to be employed in avenues which will increase agricultural productivity, for example in the construction of dams, irrigation works and the production of fertilisers. Where land resources are short, the burgeoning labour force will have to be employed in the production of goods that can be sold in international markets in return for essential foodstuffs and raw materials. The whole process of economic growth also needs a literate population, so that heavy investments must be made from the outset in the extension of basic education services.

The necessity for virtually simultaneous attacks upon so many fronts at once arises from the fact that population growth rates have increased as a result of the application at one level only (mortality control) of a technique (Western medical science) which was extraneous to and far more sophisticated than other features of the economic and social systems of underdeveloped countries. When medical science and public health began to learn how to reduce death in European societies they were already lagging behind developments in the industrial and agricultural fronts. In today's underdeveloped world the reverse is the case, and the consequence is a set of problems infinitely more complex than those with which European man had to grapple.

Clearly these problems could be greatly simplified if the low income countries in today's world could follow another example of Western man and bring about reductions in their levels of fertility. In this regard, the controls so far exercised in most Asian and other low-income countries have few of the unique characteristics of the West. The essential determinant of population growth rates is still the level of death rates, whereas the essential determinant of growth in Western societies is the level of fertility. Fertility is not likely to rise much higher in these low income countries, but very probably mortality will continue on its downward course. This assumes that there will be moderate success in achieving the levels of economic growth to which I have just referred. Some observers consider that this economic battle is already being lost, but as already emphasised in relation to India the evidence of continually rising rates of population growth do strongly suggest that some of the statistics upon which such extremely pessimistic views are based may not be telling the whole story. On the other hand, it does seem quite clear that economic reorganisation and the re-direction of millions and millions of workers into non-agricultural employment must proceed from now on at an increasing pace unless the gains of recent years are to be lost; and the chances of success of such re-organisation will be immeasurably enhanced if the rate of popula-tion can be slowed down.

So I turn finally to the whole issue of population control, and there the pessimist tends to be far more in evidence than the opti-mist. There are some of course who hopefully argue that the population prospect ahead of the world, assuming the contin-uation of present trends of birth and death rates, is not a subject to be concerned about, because the ingenuity of man, which has already achieved so much will find new outlets for the teeming millions of the next few generations, if not on other planets, then at least on manned satellites orbiting the earth, an environment in which illiterate peasants surplus to the require-ments of 'terra firma' are not likely to have a very high expectation of life, even if they can be persuaded to try the experiment. Being less imaginative than this I am going to assume that there are only two alternatives within the next century—either the extension of the system of rational control of family size, now so widespread amongst Europeans, to the rest of mankind, or a return of the rudi-mentary controls of rising death rates which for centuries upon centuries held mankind in thrall.

The next and last talk will endeavour to assess the prospects for such population control.

W G K D u n c a n

Walter Duncan was born in Sydney and was a graduate of the universities of Sydney and London. He was a Commonwealth Fund Fellow at the Universities of Chicago, North Carolina and Berkeley. From 1934 to 1950, he was director of tutorial classes at the University of Sydney and was a director of studies for the Australian Institute of Political Science. In 1951, Duncan became Professor of History and Political Science at the University of Adelaide. He was also a president of the Library Association of Australia.

Professor Duncan gave his five Boyer lectures under the title In Defence of the Common Man. His title could be taken as a cri de coeur against 'caffe latte-drinking urban elites'. His great theme was enunciated towards the end of his first lecture: 'The real problem of democracy is how to make the voice of the people at once audible, well-informed and discriminating.' Talk-back radio surely cannot be the complete answer. The questions he addressed included: 'Should Government Be Left in the Hands of Experts', 'What Type of Leadership is Needed in a Democracy' and 'How Should We Encourage Such Leadership?' We reproduce here his fifth lecture.

Writing in 1962, Duncan's interest in the needs of democracy and the sources of its strength was not surprising. Totalitarian governments in their most brutal forms were to be seen behind the Iron Curtain, in China, in South Africa and elsewhere, yet the winds of change in Macmillan's evocative phase were blowing through Africa; democracy had survived the establishment of the Fifth Republic in France in 1959, was surviving chaotically in Italy but was not yet in prospect in Spain. Democracy's well-springs and sustenance were of vital importance in 1962. At the conclusion of his second last lecture he posed the question: 'Is the public to be thought of (as Hamilton, one of the American Founding Fathers, regarded it) as "the great Beast", to be feared and kept in its place, or as "the great Audience" (Lord Reith's conception of it—Reith who succeeded in establishing the BBC as a public corporation, with public responsibilities). Beast, or Audience, then? Fear or respect? This is of the essence of democracy and the education system that it implies.'

THE GREAT BEAST OR
THE GREAT AUDIENCE?

In Defence of the Common Man

WGK Duncan

· 1 9 6 2 ·

In this final talk I must try to pull together the various threads of my argument, and show how they all derive from a certain view of democracy. I started out by saying that government was not a matter that could, or should, be left to the 'experts'. It is for the common man, or the lay public, to determine the general shape and direction of policy, even though experts are increasingly needed as advisers and administrators. But common sense, or native shrewdness, is not enough, these days, to cope with a rapidly changing world, and no real effort has yet been made to keep the public well-informed, or balanced and discerning in its judgments. Education in a democracy needs to be both universal and lifelong, to provide conditions, that is to say, in which all people—not just the gifted few—can go on growing, in understanding, width of interests and emotional maturity, as long as they live, not just while they're at school.

Even within our schooling system, I argued, the provision of scholarships for the brainy few (those with high IQs) doesn't amount to anything like effective equality in educational opportunity, and in any case the purpose of education should be to enable people to 'live a life', not merely to 'get on', and 'succeed', in a worldly sense. In particular, a democratic system would not set out to educate a chosen few—an 'elite'—for 'leadership'. It would allow scope for it, of course, in its public affairs—bold, imaginative leadership, if necessary—but it would not presume that such leaders are to be recruited from the well-to-do families nor that they can be produced by specialised training in select schools. The greater the power vested in its leaders, the more wary a democracy needs to be, lest they become corrupted by its exercise. The long-range purpose of a genuinely democratic leader, I argued, was similar to that of a good parent, namely, to make himself unnecessary—or at the most to convert himself into a desirable (but by no means indispensable) colleague.

This sense of shared purposes and mutual respect should be felt and encouraged not only between leaders and led, but between different sections and groups within the community. Just because a democracy believes in liberty and diversity—in allowing people to grow up and live their lives in their own way, as far as possible—it is especially considerate of the rights of minorities. But if it is to hold together, as a community, lines of communication must be kept open between the various groups. Isolation breeds misunderstanding, and eventual hostility. The way to get the necessary social cohesion is to mix people up, and encourage criss-crossing loyalties, so that people divided on some issues will be united on others, and as a result less inclined to push their differences to extremes. It is especially important that children, while impressionable, should learn to respect differences in outlook and belief, and this is far more likely in a common schooling system than in schools segregated according to the race, religious belief or income level of the parents.

To appreciate and respect differences is clearly not the same as trying to eliminate them, and yet the stock criticism of a common schooling system is that it would result in uniformity and standardisation—the products being as alike as a string of sausages coming out of a machine. This is far less likely, I suggest, in schools which set out to foster critical, independent thinking than in those whose avowed purpose is to implant dogmatic religious beliefs. And if, as is often alleged, there is, in fact, a good deal of indoctrination in state schools (resulting among other things in a narrow and dangerous nationalism) then the thing to do is to show it up, and to insist on genuine education in those schools—not try to counter one betrayal of it by fostering another, in a separate set of schools.

But schools, whether common or otherwise, and however honest and skilful the teaching provided within them, will never be able to provide the educational service and stimulus needed within a democracy. People in their adult years have needs and interests and powers quite different from those of youngsters, and no comprehensive or properly integrated scheme has yet been devised to meet such needs. It would clearly require not only immense resources, but a great effort of the imagination to think out appropriate ways of catering for people of widely different ages, interests and levels of ability. But some interesting lines of approach have already been suggested. Here are a couple of examples.

The first is by way of documentary films. The word 'documentary' is now quite fashionable, and has come to mean many different things. But the kind I'm referring to is the sort of film produced by people like John Grierson. His chief interest was not in films as such—as an 'art form' say—but in the possibility of arousing men's minds by the use of this new medium. Let me quote his own words:

> The documentary idea was not basically a film idea at all . . . This medium happened to be the most convenient and the most exciting available to us. The idea itself was a new idea for public education; its underlying concept that the world was in a phase of drastic change . . . and the public comprehension of the nature of that change vital. There it is, in the films themselves, from the dramatisation of the workman and his daily drag . . . to the dramatisation of social problems: each a step in the attempt to understand the stubborn raw material of our modern citizenship, and to make the heart and the will to their mastery.
>
> Where we stopped short was that, with equal deliberation, we refused to specify what political agency should carry out that will; or associate ourselves with any one of them. Our job was to make the heart and the will: it was for the political parties to make to the people their own case for leadership.[1]

There, I think, we have the heart of the matter. A documentary film is an authentic (or well-documented) portrayal of something; it is a 'human document', full of human interest, for it depicts the life of real people; it is a dramatic interpretation of our everyday life and problems, designed to appeal to our hearts and our imagination, as well as to our intellects, to stir our wills to action, to civic action, to the readjustments needed in a changing world. But it does not prescribe the answers to our problems. That is for us to work out for ourselves. That is a political decision, which the film-maker as artistic expert has no right, or authority, to make for us. Here, at least, we have one expert—John Grierson, a world authority in his field—who yet knows his place, and doesn't presume to run our lives for us.

Grierson had great hopes that documentary films would help to close the 'gaps' which he felt were developing in modern, large-scale communities—gaps not only in understanding between the well-informed 'insiders' and the man in the street, but gaps in sympathy between different sections of the community, leading very different sorts of lives. He tried to make us realise the effort and elaborate organisation that lie behind services we take for granted—such as the supply of fresh food to large cities, the delivery of letters to our homes, and the availability of pure water, whenever we turn the tap on. He tried to bring home to us the problems of handicapped children, of old people, the problems of slum clearance and town planning, and so on. This imaginative appreciation of the way other people live, and this awareness of the extent to which we are all dependent on the services of other people, are basic ingredients in any genuine sense of community.

This sense of community is not, of course, peculiar to democracies. It may well be stronger in authoritarian regimes, where it is often explicitly cultivated, by large-scale propaganda campaigns. What is needed to give this sentiment a distinctively democratic flavour is a widespread feeling of having an effective say in community affairs. And this means much more than turning up to vote on election day. It means active participation in affairs and a willingness to accept personal responsibility. How is this to be fostered? This brings me to my second example.

I take it from Mr Alec King, of Perth, who published a little booklet some years ago called 'Everyone's Business'. Education, in his opinion, was 'everyone's business', but to have any great width of appeal it would have to consist, not of lectures or formal classes, but of *activities*, with an educational content, appropriate to the needs and existing interests of people. This is the way he put it:

> We confuse the whole problem of adult education in the ordinary man's mind by presenting it as a special service for 'students', more or less closely connected with other formal educational services . . . Ordinary adults do not want to be 'students'; they want to live more successfully. They will not take to adult education unless it is felt to be a way of dealing with, or enriching, their own already active interests . . . The whole secret of adult education, I suggest, is to see it as any person with cultivated interests sees it, as part of the normal environment.

One of the best ways of making education part of the normal environment was, he suggested, to establish in each neighbourhood a Community Centre—a place in which people could try, in association, to discover and fulfil their leisure-time needs and interests. Notice that it should be a neighbourhood affair: the area to be served by such a centre must not be so large that there is little sense of a community of interests; that it is meant to foster a common effort by groups of neighbours, to discover something (as well as to fulfil existing interests); an effort to discover their own leisure-time needs, as well as interests.

Leisure is now within the reach of us all, and it looks as though it may become something of a 'problem', for the common man has no traditions of leisure, and has to acquire the skills needed to gain genuine refreshment from it This refreshment is at once more needed, and more difficult to attain, in our machine age: more needed because mass-production tends to destroy the interest craftsmen once took in their work and the satisfaction they derived from it, and more difficult because the glamorous amusements of today tend to seduce us into a passive acceptance of the ready-made. Amusements are all right in their place, but they don't bring refreshment to the spirit of men bored by routine jobs.

Men *need* (even if they don't realise it) an outlet for their own personalities: some kind of activity in which they can express themselves, and win the respect and esteem of their fellows. We all want to feel significant, in some way or other, but of what significance can the average man feel when employed in a huge industrial undertaking? How can he make his voice heard when confronted with the huge political machine of party politics? He feels overwhelmed and impotent. This, I'm sure, contributes to the apathy and cynicism I spoke about, in my first talk.

The very fact, then, that this is an age of large-scale organisation and impersonal planning, makes it the more important that we preserve some field of activity in which the ordinary man and woman can take a personal interest, and for the management of which they will accept some personal responsibility. This is why Community Centres would be so valuable. They would not only provide facilities for the kind of leisure-time activities which commercial interests tend to neglect because unprofitable, but they would provide also opportunities for small groups of people to manage their own affairs. There would be among them a sense of active *participation*, which, to my way of thinking, is essential in a democracy.

It is generally admitted that democracy is at its best when it is rooted in the daily lives of small groups of people. For it is then local, personal and intelligible. The people themselves help to shape its programme and feel responsible for its success. Here is a way, then, through Community Centres, of establishing practical training schools for democratic citizenship, or, as the Americans put it, of fostering democracy 'at the grass roots'.

Community Centres are, as yet, few and far between, and may long remain a mere aspiration. Even where established they are not, and never will be, patronised by everybody. They are merely one of the many possible ways of supplementing existing institutions—

such as the home, the school and voluntary associations—all of which could and should also be 'practical training schools for democratic citizenship'. Now is this really feasible? Can homes, or schools, be run on democratic lines? Well, why not? There are, of course, limits to what can be expected of immature children. But democracy doesn't mean simply taking a vote on everything—so that children would be asked to say what time they'd like to go to bed, or what lessons (if any) they'd like today at school. (There are, I believe, one or two schools in England that allow even this, but I'm afraid you'd need specially gifted teachers to cope with the resulting problems.) But it should be possible to provide a democratic 'atmosphere' in both the home and school, and to show, in practice, respect and consideration for others—for all members, not just for those in a position of authority.

You may remember what I said a few weeks ago about the difficulty of recruiting officials in post-war Germany with the right habits of mind, because so many of them came from authoritarian homes. Well, let me add to that now a word about voluntary associations in general, and trade unions in particular, for many of these organisations seem to be breeding the wrong outlook and habits of mind for a democracy. In these organisations, as within the state's own machinery, a good deal of the trouble springs from the sheer scale of activities. Any large organisation tends to develop into a bureaucracy, with a hierarchy of full-time officials, wielding considerable power, possessing 'inside' knowledge, and increasingly impatient with any attempt at rank-and-file control. Branch meetings of trade unions are generally poorly attended, control gets into the hands of an inner group, and the ordinary member is expected to do little more than endorse (or otherwise) the cut-and-dried proposals put to him by his leaders. Many rank-and-file members are, of course, quite content with this. A good leader, for them, is one who 'gets results', in the form of improved wages and conditions, no matter how irregular or high-handed his methods. And many trade union leaders have enjoyed years and years of this unquestioning loyalty, and when, as many of them now do, they move over into the political arena, they expect the same kind of support from party members and the public at large.

Many trade unionists—both leaders and rank-and-file—imagine that democracy is simply a matter of 'government by majority vote'. If over 50 per cent say Yes to any proposal, then that settles the matter. Does it really? If so, Hitler's regime was one of the most democratic on record, for well over 90 per cent of the voters said Yes in several plebiscites he put to the people. Likewise the Communist regime in Russia always wins elections by almost unanimous votes. Does that make it democratic—in our sense of the word? Surely we need to look behind the voting figures and ask: Was the counting honest? What pressure was put on people to vote in a certain way? Were they given any real alternative? An effective alternative implies freedom to criticise, opportunities for discussion, means of publicity. Were these available under Hitler? Are they enjoyed today in Russia?

Do trade unions provide them for their members? I know of one trade union in America which does; which allows an organised 'opposition' to exist within the union, just as we have an official Opposition within Parliament. But this is a conspicuous exception to the general rule, and the conditions which account for it are peculiar to this union—of type-setters. All too frequently in trade union circles independent thinking is treated as equivalent to disloyalty. Unity and solidarity are, of course, essential to trade unions as fighting organisations, but even in times of war the genuine democrat refuses to identify criticism with treason.

The worship of majority opinion is, of course, not confined to trade unionists. The standing excuse offered by those who control the daily newspapers and the TV chains, when attacked for glamourising the trivial or exploiting the sensational, is that they are giving the people what they want, and that this, surely, is the democratic thing to do. What right, they ask, has any minority of self-appointed improvers of society—to tell the majority what it should see and read?

Quite a lot would need to be said to answer such a question at all fully, but all I shall attempt to do, in the minute or so at my disposal, is to challenge the assumption that a democrat, who claims to respect other people, should confine himself to offering the public what it wants, and that it is in some way arrogant or presumptuous on his part to offer other things, however good he thinks them. To start with, what does the public want? That's not the same as to ask what will it most readily and passively accept, because it has been conditioned into a limited range of expectations by the powerful interests whose chief concern is to sell it something. The public is carefully protected from unfamiliar ideas and disturbing experiences by those who think of it, not as people, but as potential customers. This may be legitimate enough for salesmen, but is it good enough for everybody?

Let me quote you an entirely different approach, from a recently published book:

The surest way of giving the public what it really wants is not by trying to reach the lowest common denominator of effortless acceptance but by encouraging those who have specialised in the various departments of human activity to give of their best . . . Those who are more literate and more experienced and more discriminating than their fellows have an obligation so to convey news or entertainment as to help those who receive it to become themselves more mature, independent in judgment and capable of worthwhile enjoyment. If they exploit the undeveloped palates of those they serve by offering them only spicy tit-bits and meretricious sweets, it is not surprising that those who are not sickened by these offerings should begin to lose their taste for solid food . . .

Human equality demands that those who can exercise influence over their neighbours, whether through large-scale media of communication or in any other way, should show respect for those whom they address. It is their task, whether they are trying to instruct, inform or entertain, to help others come to share what they have honestly found to be good. It is here that they find true equality. To exploit the weakness, ignorance and prejudices of their neighbours for their own gain, and to use their gifts and education to do so, is the reverse of what most people mean when they speak of the 'democratic ideal'. It amounts, in fact, to 'the treason of the educated'.

That passage is taken from a book by Mr D Jenkins called *Equality and Excellence*, and it is to this relationship between equality and excellence that I propose to devote my final remarks. The issue can be summed up very briefly: Is equality the enemy of quality, of all kinds? Wouldn't a genuinely egalitarian society mean the end of outstanding achievement, and even of aspiration to attain it? Wouldn't it tend to glorify the mediocre and to level everybody down to a drab uniformity? Wouldn't it prove itself the enemy of liberty and variety? And, in any case, isn't the whole effort wrong-headed, flying as it does in the face of facts—the facts of heredity, which show that people are very differently, and unequally, endowed at birth, and the facts of history—which is a record of the achievements of a creative minority? These are the sort of questions, or rather unquestioned assumptions that you'll find throughout the literature on politics for the past hundred years or more. And these assumptions seem immune to criticism, which suggests that they are the product of what has been called 'wishful thinking', rather than of logical or clear thinking. Wishful thinking by those who think in terms of an 'elite', entitled to special privileges.

To start with, as I've already said more than once, the democratic claim to equality has nothing whatever to do with biological fact. It is a statement of moral value, and a suggested principle of social organisation. It is a claim that all people, however much they differ in talent and ability, are equally entitled, as human beings, to consideration and respect. To say that men are equal, in rights, is not to say that they are identical in personal qualities. GK Chesterton put this point in a characteristically vivid way when he suggested that all men are equal in the sense that all pennies are equal. Some men are bright, some dull, just as some pennies are bright and others dull. But all have, in the end, an equal value, for all pennies are stamped with the image of the king, just as all men bear the image of the King of Kings. This is the Christian claim that all men are equal, as sons of God, but the same claim can be made in secular terms—and was in fact made in such terms by the Stoics, centuries before the Christian era.

Likewise, equality in rights does not imply uniformity of treatment. To say that everyone is entitled to a good education does not mean that everyone should be given the same type of education. Some differences, such as differences in wealth, are irrelevant in a genuinely democratic educational system; but differences in the interests and capacities of the people to be educated are (or should be) the basis from which the educators start. The very equality—in rights—that is claimed springs from a recognition of such differences. The reason why equal 'consideration' should be given to people is that every single person is in some respect 'unique' and different from his fellows. It is from respect for such differences that the democrat derives his belief in equality; because of it he tries to provide the individual with as much freedom to develop, in his own way, as is possible within an organised society; and from such mutual respect, that he hopes society will come to be informed by a spirit of fraternity, or fellowship.

Perfect equality—or perfect anything—is not likely to be achieved, in any society. The important thing is to know in which direction to move, and what goals to set ourselves in public policy. Take an analogy: if we were lost in the bush it might be literally a matter of life or death to know in which direction to move. If we were lucky enough to have a compass with us, or could tell from the stars where North lay—and because of this succeeded in getting out of the bush—we could then decide how much farther North we wanted to go. Few of us want to get to the North Pole. So with a social policy, aiming at equality, say. As we attain an increasing measure of it, we can decide, step by step, how much more we want. For myself, I think we need far more of it than we have at present. I accept Matthew Arnold's advice to his generation: 'Choose equality', he said, 'and flee greed'.

[1] Documentary News Letters, June 1942.

JDB Miller

John Miller was born in Sydney in 1922, and enrolled in the Faculty of Economics at the University of Sydney as an evening student while working during the day, first at a bank and then, in 1939, with the ABC as an announcer and talks officer. He graduated in 1944, and two years later joined the staff of the University of Sydney as a tutor in adult education.

In 1952 he went to study at the London School of Economics, joining the staff in the following year. In 1955 he was appointed lecturer in politics at the University College of Leicester and was made professor in 1957.

In 1962 he returned to Australia as the Professor of International Relations at the Research School of Pacific Studies at the Australian National University. Since 1987 he has been Emeritus Professor.

Professor Miller has also held visiting professorships at the Indian School of International Studies, New Delhi, in Government at Columbia University, at Yale University, at Princeton, and was Smuts Visiting Fellow at St John's College, Cambridge.

He was a member of the Australian Population and Immigration Council and the Australian Research Grants committee and the Australian National Commission for UNESCO. From 1989 to 1991 he was the executive director of the Academy of the Social Sciences in Australia.

Professor Miller has published a number of books. He was also the editor of *The Australian Outlook*, the journal of the Australian Institute of International Affairs, and chairman of the editorial advisory board for Australian documents on foreign relations. He was Canberra correspondent for *The Economist* between 1962 and 1987.

The titles of Professor Miller's five Boyer Lectures about Australia and foreign policy, were 'The Limitations of Foreign Policy'; 'The Problem of National Interest'; 'Ideology, Trade, Defence', which is reproduced here; 'Party Traditions' and 'Diplomacy and the Public'. He delivered his lectures in the wake of the assassination of John F Kennedy, but had prepared them prior to the President's death. Sad and significant though that event was, it in no way altered the contentions advanced by Professor Miller. Rightly deploring the notion that foreign policy is 'a series of dramatic flourishes', Professor Miller nevertheless delivered a series of dashing lectures which still make important reading. In his foreward he says: 'Our foreign policy as I see it is essentially a problem for us. It is for us to examine, to assess and finally to understand the meshing of the great forces about us, so that we may better take our place in the world and ensure our survival.'

IDEOLOGY, TRADE, DEFENCE

Australia and Foreign Policy

JDB Miller

• 1 9 6 3 •

The last lecture was about the difficulty of deciding what we mean by the national interest, and the folly of assuming that any particular policy can be sustained permanently on the ground that it represents a national interest. This time I want to consider three things which are sometimes referred to as determinants of foreign policy. They are ideology, trade and defence. I shall be suggesting that none of these is as clearcut as it may seem at first glance. Let us look at them in some detail.

Ideology is the most difficult of the three to describe accurately. It is a term used to describe dominant ways of thinking, the ideas which seem to be most widely accepted and to underlie the actions of the people in question. Sometimes we refer to an ideology as a 'system of ideas', but this is probably too neat; most countries do not display a systematic structure of ideas, in which each part is clearly related to each other, but a medley of ideas and assumptions, held in different measure by various sections, and often in conflict with one another. If I were asked to describe the Australian ideology I should be hard put to it to give a short, satisfactory answer. It would be necessary to include the notions that lie behind our system of parliamentary democracy; the various views of society and social status which contend within our community; the distinctive notes struck by our poets and novelists; something about the way our education is carried on; some estimate of the effects of religion on our thinking; some assessment of the influence of our press and our political parties, some distillation of the things that are said by our leaders on solemn and ceremonial occasions. Out of all this, no doubt, would come some impression of an ideology. It would be rather confused and ambiguous, but there would be a shape to it; and people who knew Australia well would either recognise the shape at sight or would have some idea of what was wrong with it.

The point about one's national ideology in regard to foreign policy, and the world at large, is that it would be greatly affected by conquest. If some other country imposed its rule on us, the standards we had been accustomed to would be changed. Not everything would change; it would depend on who the conqueror was, and how harshly he pressed conditions on us. Much would depend, too, on how long conquest lasted. But it is clear, I think, that if Australia, which has a very long experience of independent development, were conquered and then subjected to occupation and to a deliberate attempt to re-make our society, there would be a conflict of ideology. Efforts would be made to establish new rules of thought and new beliefs. I am not suggesting that our ways of thinking would automatically become those of the conqueror. The experience of such countries as Japan under American occupation and France under German occupation certainly suggests otherwise. On the other hand, if occupation is prolonged and there is no opportunity for indigenous forces to make their presence felt, a new ideology will certainly appear, as in parts of eastern Europe. At any rate, the whole ideological structure will be changed. And not only ideas, of course, ideas are important, but they are very hard to separate from the rest of our life. It is in actions and institutions that ideas find their expression. It is these which would be changed— the courts, the parliament, the civil service, entertainment, art, the practice of religion, the nature of education. The tone and quality of our common life are the ultimate expression of ideology; changes in the things I have just mentioned would be the most accurate measure of what differences in ideology were being imposed. People who say 'better dead than Red' are presumably referring to their fear of changes which might be brought about in our institutions by Chinese or Russian conquest of Australia, and by the kind of government which the conquerors might be expected to set up. What was affected would be our own way of doing things and thinking about them; much would remain, but what did remain would operate in a different setting.

Yet it is not this identification of ideology with our own specific way of doing things that people usually have in mind, I think, when they raise the ideological issue in foreign politics. At those times we are usually described, not as ourselves in our own terms, but as 'Christian' or 'democratic' or as part of 'the free world'. The implication is that we share an ideology with a number of other countries, and that it is not just something of our own. How are we to view this? The difficulty, I think, arises from the absolute nature of the ideological terms used in such circumstances. For example, there is the description of Australia as a 'Christian' country. Plainly, much of our thinking derives from Christian experience, and we are officially Christian in an undenominational way when it comes to public occasions. But only a minority of our people go to church, and one does not have to be a Christian to occupy positions of high eminence. We are Christian up to a point. Our governments are not animated by the specific teachings of any church, yet many of our actions are explicable only against a Christian background. Is this the same as being Christian in the sense in which the term would be understood in Spain or Italy? Clearly it is not. Yet we do share some part of our Christian heritage with these countries: it is only that we do not share the whole, or operate on the same immediate assumptions.

Again, to call us 'democratic' raises difficulties. I am sure that, if there is such a thing as democracy, we have it in Australia; but I know from long experience how hard it is to get agreement on what constitutes democracy, and how puzzling it is to distinguish the countries which are just inside or just outside democratic limits. All too often, 'democratic' is nothing more than a term of approbation: we call countries democratic when we like them, and undemocratic when we don't. Of the three ideological labels I have listed, this, I think, is the least useful.

'The free world' is a bit more descriptive, but it has its failings too. Its fault lies in the ambiguity of 'free' in this connection. 'The free world' can mean either those countries with free institutions, or those with independence from external control, usually, in this context, control by the Soviet Union or Communist China. The two lots of countries are not the same. Countries with free institutions are a small minority of the hundred or so sovereign states. Countries which have practical independence are much more numerous; but many of them are essentially authoritarian in their government, and possess very little of that ideology which the countries with free institutions—in Europe, Asia and the Americas—can be said to share in some measure. Too easily we equate the first group with the second in discussion, and then have to find excuses for calling 'free' certain countries which are blatant dictatorships. If we said 'the non-Communist world', this would be more to the point. But it would still demand that we distinguish between the different sorts of states, and different ideologies, within that variegated array.

My point is that we ought to be sure what we mean when we claim to share an ideology with other countries, and ought to be cautious in equating their institutions and assumptions with ours. Basically, the national ideology is the strongest there is; it is what animates countries' policies most often. And, when it operates, it does so not simply in terms of ideas, but as an expression of the complex of institutions and practices common to the people in question. Sometimes these will have much in common with what goes on in other countries. A shared ideology will then exist to a certain extent. But we must not confuse this with the temporary identity of policy that exists when states of disparate character unite to face a common enemy, as in the coalition against Germany in World War II. That is a different thing. When we go to war, it may be in alliance with other countries with whom we have sympathy and much in common. The ideological bond will then help to strengthen the alliance. But, given the nature of world politics, we may fight alongside countries whose ideas and practices are alien to ours, but with whom circumstances have flung us together. We cannot pick and choose too delicately in this regard. What we are defending, in the last resort, when we go to war, is not the parliamentary system or the independent courts or the ideas that lie behind them, but the distinctive life we lead in this country, of which these institutions and ideas are essentials but only part. Foreign policy is basically a national thing, not the pursuit of a philosopher's abstraction.

Now I turn to trade. Many tough-minded people pooh-pooh the notion of ideology as a basis for foreign policy, and fasten on economic aims as the only ones which can be clearly formulated and have real driving force. One does not need to be a Marxist to hold this view. The phrase, 'just an ordinary trade war', applied to World War I, has some importance in Australian history, and the author was not a Marxist. When one looks at the statements being made about Australian foreign policy by intellectuals just before World War II—for example, at the 1938 Summer School of the Australian Institute of Political Science—it is notable how many of them assumed without argument that Britain would have to support Australia in a war, and Australia Britain, because they traded heavily with one another. This sort of statement is less often heard now, though I think it is not just a case of economic conditions having changed; the discoveries being made about imperial expansion and war in the 1880s and 90s, the crucial period for historical evidence on this point, suggest that facile generalisations about economic imperialism, based on the works of Lenin and JA Hobson, had less substance than we used to think. At any rate, times have changed; we in Australia trade much more widely than we did 25 years ago, and so do the British; and our dependence on trade as such for our prosperity is not what it was. However much men deliberately shaped their foreign policy in the past to achieve greater trade, I find it difficult to believe that they do so now. I mean that I find it difficult to believe they would take trade so seriously as to make the preparations and approaches which imply a readiness to make war—for this is the ultimate kind of policy which shows you are really in earnest. Certainly we should expect trading nations to go out of their way to make friends with countries which might increase trade with them, but not, I think, to the extent of determining their major alignments in this way. The Japanese, for example, are anxious to extend their trade, especially in South East Asia, but they are very wary of getting caught in the shifting political attachments of the area. Whatever its place may previously have been, trade takes a back seat now as a determinant of a country's alignment. To take an extreme example, it is not because he wants to buy wheat in North America, or sell oil in Europe, that Mr Khrushchev has relaxed some of the tensions of the Cold War. Nor is it a desire for trade that has caused President Kennedy to respond to these overtures.

I think it unwise, then, to assume that trade is a major factor in deciding the direction of foreign policy. What it can do, however, is complicate the broader issues of our associations with other countries. Take the issue of trading with Communist countries, as that applies to the United States, Britain and ourselves. The basic American posture in the 1950s was that it was wrong, or at any rate imprudent, for America and her allies to trade with Communist countries. This attitude has now been largely relaxed in regard to the Soviet Union and the satellite countries in eastern Europe, but it remains in regard to China and Cuba. The British have stuck to the letter of the law, but have made no secret of their view that greater trade will do no harm to world peace. Australia, understandably, has been somewhere in between these two positions. We have not hesitated to sell wheat and wool to China, and, although we do not recognise the Chinese Communist government, we have not gone to the same lengths as the Americans in preventing our people from entering China and buying things from there. In part, the attitudes of the three countries reflect the differing extent of their need for trade. Yet genuine questions are involved on which allies can legitimately differ. There is the major question whether selling necessities like food and machinery to a Communist regime simply helps it to consolidate its power, or enables the grip of authoritarianism to be somewhat relaxed. I have found myself taking both sides of this argument at different times. Again, there is the difficult matter of the effect of trade with Communist countries upon the non-Communist countries concerned. May it make their economies dependent upon Communist orders for ships or wheat or whatever the products are? May it force them to provide opportunities in their own markets which ought to go to their allies? Does it create distrust between them? It is easy to put the answers in extreme terms and make a moral issue out of these questions; in fact, I think the answers are very difficult to arrive at. One cannot easily isolate the effects of Communist trade as such upon the non-Communist countries; nor can one say, with much assurance, what political and economic effects trade has upon the Communist states. Certainly, however, the issue does complicate what might otherwise seem a more clearcut division. That is my main point, that trade is a complicating factor in the general sphere of foreign policy.

It becomes even more so when one takes into account the matter of economic aid, which is now part and parcel of diplomacy. Each developed country's strategy of foreign policy now includes a place for foreign aid. Yet the recipient countries complain that, while the developed ones are prepared to give them certain kinds of aid, especially technical assistance, their aid and trade policies are contradictory: commodity prices, the world prices of the raw materials which under-developed countries produce, do not rise as fast as the prices of manufactures, and aid is not sufficient to fill the gap or to increase incomes in the under-developed countries. In this field, as in some others, there is constant danger that our right hand will not know, or not care, what our left hand is doing.

It is important, if we can manage it, to get some genuine connection between trade policy and foreign policy, and not to have them working against one another. One of the great virtues of the Cobdenite free trade policy in nineteenth century Britain was that it combined economic and political advantage, as more than one writer on foreign policy has pointed out. It gave Britain cheap goods and gave other countries opportunities to sell in a rich British market; it operated at a time when British foreign policy was not to cultivate alliances but to practise general goodwill. Please do not think I regard this as a pattern which can be universally applied, by Britain or anyone else. But a similar consonance between foreign and trade policies, including economic aid, is something greatly to be desired. It is not easy to attain, since trade and foreign policies are usually the responsibility of different departments, responding to different domestic pressures. In Britain there is often tension between the views of the Foreign Office, concerned with general political considerations and especially relations with the United States, and those of the Board of Trade, very much affected by the demands of British exporters. Perhaps similar tensions occur here. It would be surprising if they did not. But, even if the departments agree, it is important that the Cabinet should not regard itself as solely an assembly of departmental spokesmen, but should look for co-ordination at a level above that of agreement about one another's budget.

Defence is a similar case in many ways. It is often represented as an absolute, something which must prevail whatever else goes to the wall. 'The defence of Australia' is sometimes put forward by former military men as an entity in itself. But defence is no absolute; it is a case of who does it, with what, and to whom. Defence policy has to decide which of the services ought to have the most resources and why; what weapons, aircraft, ships and so on ought to be provided, and in what quantity; and to be used with what allies in what situation against what sort of enemy. This is a formidable range of variables. No policy will meet all possible eventualities. There have to be decisions about allies and enemies, and these are essentially decisions of foreign policy. Our own position is fairly clear in one particular: cooperation with the United States seems to be enjoined by our experience in the last war, and to be agreed on by all but a handful of people. Yet the matter is not settled by agreement about cooperation. The United States is committed to us, but not solely to us, she has numerous other allies, in other parts of the world, and various projects in which necessarily we do not share. So we cannot hope for undivided American attention, or for an assurance that we shall find agreement when we have something to suggest. Also, American policies, like those of any other country, are determined in part by domestic considerations. It would be foolish for us to assume that we were pledged in advance to all of them, whether they came from President Kennedy or a possible President Goldwater. Along with these cautionary considerations goes the fact that no country has discovered how to control American policy in its own interests; it cannot be done. A year after the Cuba crisis, the *Manchester Guardian Weekly* made the point in this way: 'In the last resort, in a fast-moving situation, one man has to decide; and nobody now is likely to challenge the skill and sanity of Mr Kennedy in his action. But the fact remains that senators from California and Arizona were flown back to Washington for urgent and secret consultations; London and Paris were no farther away, but senior Ministers were not invited to take part in the White House discussions.'[1] The *Guardian* writer was thinking specifically in terms of the Atlantic Alliance, but the point applies to the Pacific allies of the United States too.

Thus, our defence situation is complicated by the fact that we cannot order about our chief ally as we might wish. Moreover, any help we might get does not absolve us from full responsibility for defence to the limit of resources we can manage here in Australia. Just as, in pre-war times, the assumption was that the Royal Navy would protect us in global terms, but that we would be responsible for dealing with attacks on our own territory, so now it can be assumed that the United States will help us in major matters but cannot be expected to help us out of any local difficulty we might encounter. Moreover, we have commitments in regard to Malaysia which do not involve the United States, but are jointly undertaken between Britain, New Zealand and ourselves.

This situation indicates how much defence is connected with considerations of foreign policy at the planning stage; but it is also connected with domestic considerations at the implementation stage, like trade. We cannot fully decide in advance the degree of our participation in what quarrel and with what weapons and what assistance. We *can* decide in advance the extent of our resources in weapons and trained men. A country's decisions here are usually made in terms of two things, money and whether men will be compelled to serve; both are essentially domestic in their ramifications, as more countries than Australia have found.

Defence and foreign policy do not follow one another in any logical order; they interlock and have mutual effects. Defence may sometimes get the lead, as when we deploy forces in an ally's territory and are thus committed to it; even here, however, broader considerations may prevail later, and forces be withdrawn to serve some greater end, as with the British withdrawal from France in 1940. Defence is not certain. As James Thurber puts it in one of his Fables for our Time, 'there is no safety in numbers or in anything else'. But foreign policy is of little consequence in major matters unless military force is there to back it in extreme situations. Certain possibilities, however remote, have always to be kept in mind; in our case, these would presumably include involvement in a world war, or in a war with Communist China, or in one with Indonesia. Defence policy has to think of all these. Foreign policy has to try to prevent them. The two sorts of policy must not trip each other up.

The upshot of considering ideology, trade and defence is, I think, that we must not use these words as incantations: we must not simply say that our policy abroad should maximise each of them, and leave it at that. Each is clearly affected by the others. There is no federal Department of Ideology, but that does not make consideration of ideology, as I have defined it, less important than consideration of trade and defence, even though there are federal departments to look after those. Each of these three affects the others. Our view of the world, and of countries' responsibilities towards one another, has necessarily been coloured by our experiences of the effect of trade on our prosperity, and our previous participation in wars. In particular, Britain and the United States are not abstract entities to us; they are countries with which we have been allied in two great conflicts, apart from our other connections with them. But the practical point about the interlocking character of ideology, trade and defence is that, as far as possible, we ought to be assured that the people who advise our Cabinets on these are constantly in touch with one another, and can tender either agreed advice or an honest choice of alternatives, when external dilemmas arise. The ultimate choice of policy, of course, lies in our system with the politicians. Next week I shall examine the traditions in foreign policy of our political parties.

[1] *Manchester Guardian Weekly*, 31 October 1963, p. 1.

George Ivan Smith

George Ivan Smith was a man of the world. He was born in Sydney in 1915. After education at Bathurst, Goulburn and Sydney, he trained as a reporter, and later became a literary critic and feature writer for Australian newspapers.

In 1937, he was appointed Talks Editor for the ABC. Later, in 1939, soon after the outbreak of World War II, he established and became the first director of the ABC's overseas broadcasting service, now known as Radio Australia. In 1941 he was invited to London by the BBC, there to become director of the Pacific service of the BBC Overseas Service. He also served on the BBC Advisory Panel on literary output. In 1945 he jointed J Arthur Rank as adviser and producer of documentary films on international affairs for world theatrical distribution.

George Ivan Smith joined the United National Secretariat in 1947 and held various positions there, including that of director of the UN Information Centre in London.

In 1958, Smith was made director of the external relations division, based in New York, then in 1962 became director of the UN's press division. During much of this time he was also personal assistant to the Secretary-General. This was a period of particular distress for the UN with the death of Dag Hammarskjold in an air crash in Northern Rhodesia; Hammarskjold was succeeded by U Thant.

From 1962 George Ivan Smith was appointed personal representative of the Secretary-General for East and Central Africa and East Africa regional representative for the United Nations Technical Assistance Board and Director of United Special Fund Programs.

Subsequent to delivering his Boyer Lectures, entitled *Along the Edge of Peace* he took leave from the United Nations in 1966 and 1967 to take up visiting professorships in political sciences at Princeton University and at Fletcher School of Law and Diplomacy in Boston, but returned to the United Nations as director of the London office in 1968. He remained in this post until 1974 when he became senior consultant for the International Institute for Environment and Development until his retirement.

George Ivan Smith was also the author of several books. He died in 1995.

The titles of his five Boyer Lectures have a journalist's dash about them. They were 'The House with the Golden Key'; 'The Human Factor at Work in the World'; 'The Golden Eggs'; 'The International Civil Servant', which is reproduced here, and 'Australia and the World'. George Ivan Smith's engagement with international diplomacy at the highest levels did not diminish his belief in the unique style of international contribution to be made by Australia.

THE INTERNATIONAL CIVIL SERVANT

Along the Edge of Peace

George Ivan Smith

• 1964 •

During the course of this talk, world population will increase by about two-and-a-half thousand—a nett increase. Every day there are 60,000 additional human beings to feed, to educate and later to work if jobs can then be found.

It took a century for world population to double by 1900. It will double again in 35 years. Man moves to the stars in spaceships and leaves behind on earth human society, fretful, confronted by danger, depleted by anxiety. The most remote spot on earth is within military range, nuclear explosions can poison the atmosphere. One more paranoic with access to power, like Hitler, could extinguish life on earth. There have been many like him, how do we bar them in the future?

Yet for every peril on earth, and they do seem to flock like vultures around the kills of change, there are balancing weights of purpose. The new tools of science could help to fill the granaries of the world, to conquer epidemics, to build highways along which new trade and life could be made to flow if only—yes, the ancient voice from the well—if only we can achieve a matching development of human understanding and determination, while there's still a chance to move towards world order.

The two world wars caused tides of change to flood the earth. New discoveries, techniques, jet aircraft, weapons, mass media, they all fling us together into one small world; and interdependence has been changed from a phrase of purpose to a brooding political fact.

The swords have been turned into ploughshares that cut deeply into human society, ploughing furrows through old systems— colonialism, even paternalism—that have been broken up. New shapes are being formed, often in bloodshed, often with failures and a slowness that is agonising to watch against the need of the hour.

It's this urgency, the swinging of the pendulum between peril and purpose, that has brought the United Nations into being, with technical agencies of every conceivable type, because everybody is suddenly in everybody else's backyard; and with the new agencies come the International Civil Servants. They're not agents for change, they're servants of change. The very phrase 'International Civil Servant' in itself reflects a change of concept and a concept of change. In the UN alone there are some 5000 of us working at headquarters or in the field, as I do. We work in every continent, in over a hundred countries, we come from some 80 different nations and on appointment we take an oath of office swearing or affirming that we shall neither seek nor accept instructions from any government. So professionally our loyalty is to the world community.

But we're not expected to become cultural eunuchs, we're actively encouraged to maintain loyalty and links to our own peoples and homelands because an International Secretariat, to function effectively, must be renewed and enriched constantly by ideas, qualities and expressions of peoples from all parts of the world; and in our kind of a world, nations impinge upon one another, not only in political and economic fields but in scientific, social and cultural fields, too. Consequently our service includes technicians and scientists in a rich variety, civil aviation experts, economists, meteorologists, statisticians, and so on, all working in a world perspective.

In remote villages in every continent, there are doctors, nurses, teachers, farmers, on international service. They work through various agencies and they assist governments to battle against hunger and poverty and the deadly waves of disease.

There can be no peace for people who are living in the dark corners of desperation, nor for us who observe it. Whether we work in the field to raise the standard of life or in the political field, and I've been lucky enough to be involved in both, in either case it is work of reconciliation. Our thousands of technical aid experts, many Australians among them, are engaged there because governments realise that the gap between the high standards of living for about one third of the world's peoples and the appallingly low standards for some two thirds, quite apart from the humanitarian aspect, is a definite and a constant threat to peace.

You have only to see the dusty legs of Africa to know that or to go into villages of Latin America where families are obliged to live in conditions that no Australian would accept for an animal, and it's in such places that the germs of war begin to breed. Throughout history many have attempted reconciliation. It's a struggle that must go on, for generation after generation, until success is achieved.

A group of Chinese philosophers, 350 years before Christ, went from State to State, helping people to settle differences, arguing against wanton attack and pleading for the suppression of arms.

They wanted their age to be saved from its state of continual war. I suppose in those days, and even at the Congress of Vienna, the stakes seemed high—relatively, they were. However, there was nothing like the pressure that must govern action towards international cooperation in this age. Change has delivered an ultimatum.

I've been an International Civil Servant for some 18 years, and I'd like to share with you something of the feeling of the world that comes from having the world as your boss, 115 Member States at this stage. It wouldn't be appropriate for me to describe or assess the failures, successes or difficulties of the Secretariat to which I belong—that's a job for an historian and probably in another medium, but on a more personal basis may I recall a few stories about just one operation in which I was involved. The points illustrated could as easily have been taken from experiences my colleagues or I had in other missions when at different times and places the alarm bells began ringing and we were rushed out to our posts along the edge of peace.

It was a cold grey dawn just outside Naples in November 1956, at an airfield called Capodichino. We stamped about in the waiting room trying to keep warm. The room was filled with uniformed soldiers from more than half a dozen countries— Scandinavians, Latin Americans, Indians.

Some of us were about to board an aircraft to fly to a military airfield on the bank of the Suez Canal. It was a piece of history but we were too cold to notice it. This was the height of the Suez crisis, and I was going down with the advance guard of the first fully international police force in history.

For days, huge troop transports had been flying practically around the world bringing troops from every continent for this extraordinary and rapid operation. At times of crisis one learnt many times that speed and communication could determine success or failure. One day lost might be the very day on which the positions of the parties became too fixed to negotiate further, or the day on which extraneous elements became attached to complicate the controversy—perhaps beyond repair.

Consequently the staff work for sending out UN Missions starts as soon as the authorising resolution has been passed. I saw it for the Lebanon in 1958—the first observers were in Beirut within 24 hours; it was fast for the Congo and for Suez. The climax to the crisis—the attack on Egypt—had occurred only two weeks earlier, and then began the cycle of action and reaction that one has learned to expect. Emergency sessions, Security Council or General Assembly, hundreds of private meetings, ambassadors from several countries or between regional groups and then between different groupings, Commonwealth Members, Afro-Asians, Scandinavians. At times of such crisis it's essential to have a place like the United Nations where communication can take place, views exchanged, new ideas tested, the valuable release of anger in private.

This whole process of communication is as important to the sound health of international life as to individuals. Our sanity depends on it and so does international sanity.

Dag Hammarskjold and a small staff, of which at times I happened to be one, worked all through the day following up the assignments and the actions flowing from the resolutions and neg-otiations or offers of aid, and we worked until four or five o'clock in the morning; then home for a warm bath, two or three hours' sleep, and back by ten o'clock the same morning for another long day.

Sometimes Hammarskjold would drop in at a 'hamburger joint' on Manhattan's East Side for some breakfast about four o'clock in the morning, and I shall never forget the astonishment of taxi-drivers and night shift workers when they saw the Secretary-General and his aides joining him for coffee at that hour. In fact Richard Miller, writing about this and similar experiences, said 'The United Nations has some critics in New York City to be sure, but at least the few of them who observe these strange scenes must have formed a new idea of what's involved in peace-making'.

Hammarskjold did have greater energy and power of concentra-tion than I've ever seen in another man. Forced to be without sleep several nights running because of some hideous situation in the Congo, he could at three o'clock in the morning write a legal docu-ment, that was critically important to the operation, that would take its place in political and diplomatic history, and it stood up—it had to stand up—to the meticulous scrutiny that it was going to be given for varying and sometimes opposing reasons in foreign offices in all parts of the world.

Aides like myself had very modest responsibilities and much more sleep, but I tell you frankly that many times during about five crises I personally found it hard to keep going—and now, after weeks of the tensions in London and New York, I found myself on this Italian airfield ready to fly south to Suez as dawn broke.

We took off. I looked around the aircraft and there I saw about

50 riflemen. There were another 50 in the second aircraft. There were a few rifles and kitbags, and for some altogether inexplicable reason, about half a dozen bicycles.

At that stage I can't say that the view filled me with an overwhelming sense of confidence in the mission. The rifles seemed ancient and the idea of patrolling the Sinai Desert on bicycles—well, I tried just not to dwell on that.

Instead, I closed my eyes and recalled the almost unbelievable speed at which the majority of Member Nations had responded. When the danger's great enough, international action generates itself. Scores of States from every continent had offered troops, money, transport, services of all kinds to try to unsnarl the tangle in the Mediterranean. In such situations, delegations and the Secretary-General worked to provide the correct legal and legislative framework in which efforts could combine to reduce tension. It could too easily be increased and the problem made more complicated, if timing or action is miscalculated.

Speed is important, but never at the risk of tipping more political balances; and consequently every single step forward has to be repared diplomatically—not always publicly at every stage—urgently and thoroughly, to test the ground in every known direction; and that interlacing of the diplomatic preparation and of speed in action characterised the international effort over Suez.

Naturally it involved risks. For example, within hours after the UN had approved its plan, many countries announced they had troops standing by to be lifted into Egypt. There was pressure to get moving. But on the other hand Egyptian national sovereignty had to be respected, and Hammarskjold was still negotiating for that consent before a force could operate on Egyptian soil. Before those negotiations were completed he had to try to gain a few days by starting to move troops across the world to some staging point near Egypt, and to do it so that it couldn't be an influence upon the negotiation for entry.

Italy seemed to be about the right spot, and the Italian ambassador was invited to see the Secretary-General that night at ten o'clock. By the very next day the ambassador announced that Naples Airport was ready for our use, and immediately a fleet of transports flew out across different oceans. One flight from Germany had a flash 'Proceed to Norway, take off, we'll let you know in flight which airfield can accept you'.

There were scores of such examples, actions that normally took months to negotiate were made possible in an hour or so because the danger was so great; and new historical patterns were being established. For example, we were flying to Suez in an aircraft made available by the government of Switzerland. Now the Swiss, proudly defiant about their neutrality, had probably never before transported armed and uniformed soldiers of other nations; and not for centuries had Swedes, Norwegians, Danes and Finns been partners on a joint military operation.

For the next month, shuttling back and forth between Cairo, the Desert of Sinai, London, New York, you caught the different atmosphere and texture at each of these places, like sections fitting into one pattern of crisis. In Egypt our build-up of troops went ahead very rapidly, 1000 in the first week, building up to 6000 and gaining stronger international flavour all the time.

One remembers minor sketches, how Scandinavians down from their northern winter began in their first week to look like uniformed lobsters from the Egyptian sun; and I went out with patrols into the desert to an oasis where our Yugoslav soldiers had swept and packed the sand around the palm trees, making it the tidiest oasis on earth; and an unforgettable visit to remote Sharm el-Sheikh on the tip of the Gulf of Aquaba—the ancient gateway for Alexander the Great.

There, where the Red Sea is indigo blue; where the sky is white with heat; and where rose-red basalt cliffs leap up from the shore like fluted columns of an ancient empire: In that silence and in that place where beauty had been resolved into an essence, we posted a contingent from Finland. There they built their own Finnish Sanna bath—the first, I imagine, in that ancient part of the Mediterranean.

On Christmas Eve, on the beach at Gaza—close to where Samson sported with Delilah—I watched Swedish soldiers trying to do traditional long dances in the heavy sand, and just before midnight we went up on a fairly high hill overlooking Israel where the Colombian contingent had erected a huge army tent in which to hold a midnight church service. All sides of the tent were raised, and from where I sat I could see a field of stars burning with unusual clarity and the faces of hundreds of soldiers who'd come from all corners of the earth to the Holy Land on a mission of peace. And it *was* Christmas Eve.

I talked with many of the soldiers later—Brazilians, Colombians, Swedes, Danes, Canadians, Norwegians—and I found them all fascinated by this new role in which they were expected to use the many excellent qualities of military training—organisation, discipline, precision—for positive and peaceful purposes. The individual soldier, wherever he came from, seemed to sense an increased dignity and purpose in endowing him as an individual, because he was expected to help people by example instead of snuffing them out with rapid bursts of fire.

And every week, flying in from such outposts to London, I attended many of the Suez debates in the House of Commons. There were sometimes very angry scenes from both sides of the House, and I used to sit there privately wishing—like Danny Kaye's Walter Mitty—that I could go down for a moment to take part.

I wanted to tell them about the men in the desert wearing different national uniforms, but the same blue helmet and blue armband to show that they were part of a world peace force.

From the gallery you felt like a witness to the cavalcade of Darwinian evolution—one cell acting in this way, other cells having to compensate in other ways.

The way that the Suez operation worked out is a matter of record and not really part of this story—the canal was cleared, the shareholders were paid and, contrary to many stories circulating at the time, the Egyptian personnel were able to operate the canal not only with great efficiency, but they continued to handle much greater volumes of traffic than ever before.

But in crisis after crisis one has been made aware—as in a drama—of the great difference in atmosphere between the first act and the last. In the first act there is a tempest of emotions in the heat of crisis—it's a dangerous time; in the last act, if the right steps have been taken diplomatically from all of the wings, a discreet and sometimes even a furtive tying together of the loose ends. Peter Quince described it well: 'Gentles, perchance you wonder at this show, but wonder on till truth makes all things plain.'

The role of an International Civil Servant in trying to make all things plain was described by Hammarskjold in 1953 on the day that he arrived to take up his new job as Secretary-General, described by his predecessor, Trygvye Lie, as the most impossible job on earth. The press was there in full to greet the new victim, and they questioned him on the great international issues.

He said: 'My personal views on those questions didn't interest the world last week before appointment and should not today. Now the private man should disappear and the International Servant take his place. The International Servant helps those who take decisions that make history. We have to listen, to analyse and to try to understand fully the forces at work and the interests at stake, to be able to give the right advice when the situation calls for it.'

All Civil Servants, whether National or otherwise, are trained to be objective, but writing a report for the United Nations is like sitting for an examination under the glare of 115 spotlights and with scrutineers from every part of the world. Hammarskjold discussed the neutrality of the International Civil Servant once at a News Conference, and a correspondent had suggested that the human mind was incapable of freeing itself. 'Impossible,' he said, 'for any human being to be objective or neutral.'

Hammarskjold agreed that in a deep human sense there is no neutral individual, because if he's worth anything, he must have ideas and ideals that are not only dear to him but which he must be prepared to defend.

'But,' said Hammarskjold, 'even a man who is in that sense not neutral can very well undertake and carry through neutral actions, because that's an act of integrity.'

Such acts of integrity are carried out daily in many countries by judges—indeed, all connected with the legal profession—and by National Civil Servants. The only difference so far as we're concerned is that we try to apply the same principle of impartiality and the respect for law into an international field where such operations are not made easier by the ideological conflict or the other conflicts, and by the fact that at this stage of development, standards and backgrounds vary so much that communication becomes difficult. The same symbols and images may communicate entirely different ideas to different groups of peoples.

But whatever the difficulties, the strength and the effectiveness of an International Secretariat will depend upon trust in its impartiality, experience and maturity of judgment, as Hammarskjold once told us in a staff meeting.

'Those qualities,' he said, 'are your weapons, and they're as hard to forge as guns or bombs.'

I was privileged to work with him at many times of crisis. He gave his life in a diplomacy of reconciliation. I doubt if I ever saw him or heard him waste time on subjective judgments or trying to allocate blame. He was always trying to fit pieces together to make possible another beginning or, as he said so often, 'to get them back on to the tracks'.

I shall never forget Cairo, 1956, when he was engaged in an extremely complicated attempt to reduce tension in the Middle East. I was Duty Officer, and at two o'clock in the morning a telegram came in indicating a stand by one of the parties which would wreck the whole operation and probably spark off a war, and at the very least it eliminated all that Hammarskjold had tried to do in the preceding weeks. Well, as a man he was entitled to explode with anger. So with some trepidation I woke him up.

He read the signal, he paused for a few seconds, and then he said:

'We need a fresh approach. Wake up the secretaries.'

It would be superficial and misleading to imply that such affairs can be settled because a man has a calm outlook—that's only a starting point. The force of action, the cutting edge, is what follows. Send for the secretaries by all means, but when they arrive the new approach will be constructed precisely within the legal and the political limits. To succeed it must mesh into the gears of Foreign Offices and their diplomats all over the world and to all other elements that are capable of lending a positive drive towards reconciliation.

But since this series of talks has concentrated on the individual role, one may note that the coolness of peace cannot be achieved without the coolness of approach in men who are working for it.

Hammarskjold, just before he set out for the Congo mission which killed him, spoke to the whole staff in New York and said: 'It would be too dramatic to talk about our task as one of waging a war for peace, but it is realistic to see it as an essential and, within its limits, effective work for building dams against the floods of disintegration and violence.'

The floods of disintegration, the tides of change. In a sense they inject evolutionary processes that may result in a new species—International Man. His capacity is being sketched in daily; jet aircraft and rockets increase his speed and his reach; with electronics his sight stretches even to the far side of the moon; muscle and sinew have been given explosive nuclear strength, but with an ingredient of restraint, because that power is so great that one man's State cannot destroy another's without destroying his own in the process.

The new tools to increase production may give man some incentive to work for a system of world order, but the balance of terror commands him to do so. He's confronted by the knowledge that human survival may well depend upon establishing a system of world order and by the knowledge that it can no longer be achieved by force. But do we therefore cease to work for the establishment of law; do we cease to be engaged at problem after problem, impatient and often frustrating negotiations in the direction of more effective world order; engagement with open roads we've not yet dreamt of; concepts as yet unborn? The theme of these talks has been that the spirit of man has the power to do the unexpected—the unimaginable—when he has the inspiration, the faith and the sense of purpose.

If at the end of this new evolutionary cycle International Man does not appear, it may well be because National Man sold the past and Man became extinct in the process.

Sir John Eccles

John Carew Eccles was a Nobel Laureate with a world reputation as a research worker and teacher in physiology. Born in 1903, he graduated from Melbourne University with first class honours in medicine and science, and went on to Oxford as a Rhodes Scholar where he gained an MA and PhD. From 1934 to 1937 he was a fellow and tutor of Magdalene College, as well as a demonstrator in physiology. He returned to Sydney in 1937 to become director of Kanematsu Memorial Institute of Pathology. He remained there until 1944 when he was appointed Professor of Physiology at the University of Otago, an appointment he held until 1951 when he went to the John Curtin School of Medical Research at the Australian National University.

At the time of his delivery of the Boyer Lectures under the title of The Brain and the Person he was a world authority on the physiology of the brain. In the following year he went to the Institute of Biomedical Sciences in Chicago and was Professor (later Emeritus) of Physiology and Biophysics and head of the research unit at the State University of New York until his retirement in 1975.

In 1941 he was elected a Fellow of the Royal Society and in 1962 he was the Royal Medallist. From 1957 to 1961, he was president of the Australian Academy of Science. He was knighted in June 1958 for his distinguished contribution to physiological research.

In 1963 Sir John Eccles was awarded the Nobel Prize in Physiology or Medicine. He shared his prize with Professor AL Hodgkin and Professor AF Huxley of Britain. His international reputation was based on his contributions to the fundamental knowledge of the nervous system.

A few days before the Nobel Prize announcement, he was awarded the Cothenius Gold Medal of the Deutsche Akademie der Natuforscher Leopoldina, the first overseas scholar to win this award. That year he was also named Australian of the Year.

John Eccles died in Switzerland in 1997.

The titles of Sir John's five Boyer Lectures were 'Conscious Experience', which is produced here, 'Knowing Our World and Acting In It'; 'The Brain in Consciousness and Learning'; 'The Evolution of the Brain and the Possibility of Intelligent Life Elsewhere in the Universe' (unlikely, he concluded); and 'The Unity of Conscious Experience'. He draws us into his fascination with the interaction of the brain and conscious mind and willed actions, while maintaining a clear focus on our 'primary reality', which is our consciousness. His lectures called for a 'renewal of faith in the great mystery and dignity of human existence'.

CONSCIOUS EXPERIENCE

The Brain and the Person

Sir John Eccles

• 1965 •

First of all, I am going to talk to you generally about the title for this lecture. And while I do this, I want each one of you to participate with me in an effort to grasp the meaning of what I am trying to say and to apply it to yourself. If you do this with me, we shall have a kind of dialogue in thought, so that my thoughts communicated in language will give you thoughts that parallel mine. You become then not my audience, but my collaborators in this conjoint effort to reach an understanding of what is central to our being.

The series of talks that I am giving will be an attempt to see how far we can answer the question: What am I? This is a question which each of us can ask ourselves and which is quite unashamedly a looking within ourselves—an attitude which is called subjective and introspective.

I am not alone in posing this question and attempting to answer it. For example, Schrodinger, the physicist who was awarded the Nobel Prize for his wave mechanics, wrote in his book *Science and Humanism*: 'Who are we? The answer to this question is not only one of the tasks, but the task of science.' This assessment would have been supported by Sherrington, the founder of modern neurophysiology, and many other scientists would be in agreement. I can mention Eugene Wigner, Hinshelwood and Michael Polanyi.

I have chosen to talk to you in the field of the philosophy of the person, because I wish to do all I can to restore to mankind the sense of wonder and mystery that arises from the attempt to face up to the reality of our very existence as conscious beings. Too often we have statements that a man is but a clever animal and entirely explicable materially. And again, we are often told that man is nothing but an extremely complex machine and that computers will soon be rivalling him for supremacy as the most complex machine in existence, and that they will have performances outstripping him in all that matters.

I want to discredit such dogmatic statements and bring you to realise how tremendous is the mystery of the existence of each one of us. It is beyond my competence to go further and deal with the way in which religion is related to this mystery of existence.

First of all, let us consider what I mean by 'conscious experience'. This is strangely difficult to define, but fortunately I do not think a definition is necessary. I hope that, as my talk develops, you will come to appreciate just what I am talking about when I refer to 'conscious experience'. I could have used other words, such as 'consciousness' or 'mind' or 'mentality'; but I have chosen the expression 'conscious experience' in order to stress the experienced character of consciousness in all its aspects. It will comprise all of your experiences in waking life and also your dreams.

Some of you may have come under the influence of philosophers, such as Ryle and Ayer, who have attempted to discredit the usage of such a word as 'mind'. They assert that there is no significance or meaning in this word and that we should instead describe and study the behaviour of people and, in particular, their use of language, instead of introducing an assumption of mind as some spiritual existence underlying this behaviour or this use of language.

I hope that I shall be able to bring you to see how unjustified and illogical are the claims of such philosophers. In fact, their work has recently been very severely criticised by the psychologist John Beloff, in a book called The Existence of Mind, and also by the philosopher Kneale, who has re-established the philosophic status of mind in his book On Having a Mind. For example, Beloff begins his book by stating: 'The thesis of this book, if it can be stated in two words, is that Mind exists, or, to be more explicit, that minds, mental entities and mental phenomena, exist as ultimate constituents of the world in which we live'; and also: 'Those who take seriously the existence of Mind are often taunted with being worried by a "ghost in the machine"; I suggest it is high time we refused to let our critical faculties be paralysed any longer by this pert gibe.'

This counter-attack is very encouraging to neurophysiologists and neurologists, for many of us, despite the philosophic criticisms, have continued to wrestle with the problem of brain and mind, and have come to regard it as the most difficult and fundamental problem concerning man. However, as far as possible, I am not going to employ such words as 'mind', 'mental' and 'mentality', because they have been used in a most confusing manner; for example, it has been frequently stated that even inorganic matter has some primitive quality of mind or mentality. To me such statements are quite meaningless, and to avoid confusion, I am going to use instead the term 'conscious experience'.

My approach to conscious experience is, in the first instance, based on my direct experience of my own self-consciousness. I believe this to be the only valid way in which I can begin to talk to you about this problem that lies central to our being. I want you to understand that this initial position of myself in regard to my own consciousness must also be adopted by each of you in regard to your own self-consciousness. I am aware that a philosophical position of this kind is often criticised, because it is alleged that it gives rise to the exclusive attention of each one of us to our own conscious experiences—an attitude which is called solipsism. However, for a start, I want each of you to face up to the problem discussed in this lecture in this way, and it will soon become apparent that we move from this restricted initial position into the wider field of vision, where we recognise the existence of other conscious selves or persons. That recognition provides, of course, the basis of social life, and it is the denial of solipsism.

So let me now start with this experience that each of us has as a kind of inner illumination. I am going to state quite categorically that this conscious experience is all that is given to me in my task of trying to understand myself, and similarly, this is true for each one of you. Further, I am going to state that only because of and through my conscious experience do I come to know of a world of things and events and so to embark on the attempt to understand it; as, for example, I do in my work as a scientist. This again is true for each one of you, and in all that you do in your own individual lives.

In developing the significance of this conscious experience, I would like to quote from a recent lecture, 'Two Kinds of Reality', by Eugene Wigner, Nobel Laureate in Physics in 1963. These quotations illustrate how important and urgent is the problem of consciousness to one of the most eminent theoretical physicists in the world today. I quote: 'There are two kinds of reality or existence—the existence of my consciousness and the reality or existence of everything else. This latter reality is not absolute, but only relative. Excepting immediate sensations, the content of my consciousness, everything is a construct; but some constructs are closer, some further, from the direct sensations.' You will see from this quotation that the whole of what we call the material world, that is, the constructs, is regarded by Wigner as having a second order of reality in contrast to the absolute reality of our conscious experiences, and he develops this theme in the course of his lecture. Wigner continues: 'As I said, our inability to describe our consciousness adequately, to give a satisfactory picture of it, is the greatest obstacle to our acquiring a rounded picture of the world.'

I shall further reinforce this primacy of our conscious experiences by two quotations from recent lectures by eminent scientists. Sir Cyril Hinshelwood, in his lecture 'The Vision of Nature', says: 'To deny the reality of the inner world is a flat negation of all that is immediate in existence: to minimise its significance is to depreciate the very purpose of living, and to explain it away as a product of natural selection is a plain fallacy.'

Julian Huxley, in his lecture 'Higher and Lower Organisations in Evolution', states: 'To start with, let us recall that the only primary reality is the reality of our subjective experiences.'

Of course, reality, as used in these quotations, must not be confused with truth. Let me illustrate by such experiences as those reported of flying saucers. Recently, a lady wrote me a long documentary account about flying saucers and what they do. To her they were as real as ordinary saucers, but she did not convince me. They are real to her but not to me. You will appreciate that the question of their actual existence is not implied. I am merely stating my disbelief—not dogmatising on their non-existence!

You may think that, as a scientist, I have some privileged insight into truth. On the contrary, I am not able to claim to have made an absolutely true statement that has scientific value. The most I can say is that this scientific explanation or hypothesis is in accordance with all known facts as given in experiments, though probably it will not be reconcilable with further experimental investigations. The most that I can claim is that my scientific hypothesis is an approximation to truth. As St Paul says, 'We see as in a glass darkly.'

After this digression on reality and truth, let me return to the reality of conscious experiences.

I would now suggest to you that conscious experiences are of two kinds. One is what I call the inner experiences; and the other the perceptual experiences that are derived from the stimulation of some sense organ or other, with the consequence of an almost immediate sensory experience. Both of these experiences, of course, belong to our single unitary self that I will speak of in more detail later.

It is entirely from such perceptual experiences as vision, hearing and touch, for example, that I get to know the external world of things and events, which is a world other than my consciously-experiencing self. You may be surprised to hear me say that a special part of this external world is, in fact, my own body, which I actually only come to know because of such senses as vision and touch; and in this same way I come to know of innumerable other human bodies that appear to belong to selves like my own self.

This is, of course, so self-evident that it may appear to you to be a trite statement. Nevertheless it is of great significance, in that it leads me to believe in the existence of other persons or selves like myself with bodies and conscious experiences. It leads to the rejection of solipsism. For example, Julian Huxley states: 'We can only deduce that other human beings have subjective experiences like our own. This is not only scientifically legitimate and necessary; it is justified pragmatically and operationally: human existence would be impossible unless we did so.'

From our earliest childhood days, we have learnt to exchange communication with other selves by all kinds of movements or signals. For example, we do this in babyhood by gestures; and as we become progressively more educated, we use speech and writing; and of course, we learn to exploit still more sophisticated and subtle means of communication', as in the shared joy in aesthetic experience and imagination that even make words seem too crude.

This takes us into the world of communication by artistic creation and by shared appreciation. But no matter how intimate is our linkage with some dearly loved person, we still remain separated in a most heart-rending way. We are dependent on some movement that gives to the other a sensory experience. Never does there seem to be direct communication of one conscious self to the other. At least, I shall say that the direct thought transfer postulated in telepathy appears to be a very inefficient way of communicating between selves. I would not deny the possibility of telepathy, neither do I think it proved. We need further rigorous investigation in this most difficult scientific field.

Thus we come to believe that there is a world of selves, each with the experience of inhabiting a body that is in a material world comprising innumerable bodies of like nature and a tremendous variety of other living forms and an immensity of apparently non-living matter. I would agree with Wigner that this material or objective world has the status of a second-order or derivative reality.

Let me now talk about the other kind of conscious experience. Inner experiences, as I call them, are of a much more varied character than perceptual experiences. For example, experiences arising from a memory recall have the character of some past sensory experience and are recognised as such. Thus we can remember, in what we appropriately call our 'mind's eye', some striking scene or happening, or we can remember a musical tune, and even tastes and smells; but much more important are the extremely complex memories that we have of other people, particularly of those dear to us.

You will recognise that, because of memory, each of us links his life together into some kind of continuity of inner experience, which is what we mean when we talk of a self or person. This involves a recognition of unity and identity through all past vicissitudes. Of course, we do not have a continuity of conscious experience. You will appreciate that the continuity is broken every time we go to sleep or lose consciousness in some more unpleasant way. But we wake up after each period of unconsciousness, recognising, because of memory, our continuity with the self of the preceding day, and we continue with its trains of experiences.

Is it not a curious experience that, when we wake up in the morning, we slowly come around to recognise that we are in just the same room as when we lost consciousness the night before? Thus we bridge the periods of unconsciousness and identify ourself in the morning with the person who went to sleep the night before. It is the same self that awakes to another stream of consciousness for another waiting day.

Moreover, by my inner experience, I do not mean just the recall of my past experience in memory, but I also include in my inner experience the extraordinary texture of thoughts and ideas, the deliverances of imagination, emotional feelings, wishes, desires and volitions. In addition to all of these experiences of waking life, one also has such bizarre phenomena as dreams and hallucinations, about which I shall speak in a later lecture. All of this is part of our conscious experience, and the whole assemblage throughout our lives has contributed to the formation of ourselves, to each one of us as a person.

I want you to understand that there is a unity of the self through all these diverse conscious experiences, each of which is assimilated to the self; and this even occurs in dreams, as I think you will readily agree. For always in a dream we find ourselves as the agent central to the whole play of imagery; and this likewise occurs with hallucinations and the fantasies of waking life that we may call daydreams.

I want you to recognise that each of you can look back in memory through, as it were, the thread of the long years of accumulated experiences that make up your life, so that eventually you come to your earliest memories, where you have the amazing experience in retrospect of waking up in life in the very limited environment of a young child. Each of you has a personal identity from these earliest times, which is built up from remembered experiences.

I want further to suggest to you that in literature we have not just a description of the behaviours of people going through motions in some determined and stereotyped manner and observed always from the outside. But instead—central to literature—there are descriptions of inner experiences with thoughts and motives and the emotional feelings of the characters that the author, as it were, brings to life in this way.

You can yourself recollect all the range of emotional feelings of love and friendship and hate and antipathy, as well as your experiences of fear and terror and of delight in the beautiful. All of these contribute to the richness of your direct inner experiences.

This richness of our experiences is enormously developed, when we fuse, as it were, our immediate perceptual experiences with an imaginative range of inner experiences. This occurs particularly in aesthetic experiences. The artist attempts to express not some exact rendering of what he sees, but his vision, which has a creative enrichment given by his imagination. In great art this artistic creation has for the artist some compelling necessity. Unfortunately, much imitative work masquerades as art, though in itself it is only an artificial contrivance. Superficially, there is, of course, much resemblance between this imitative contrivance and true artistic creation. For this reason, in attempting aesthetic evaluation and understanding, we often need art critics and historians to guide and inform us—but not, let me add, to compel us.

I now return to perceptual influences by asking the question: How can my perceptual experiences in vision, hearing, touch and movement give me such an effective knowledge of the objective world that I can find my way round in it and even manipulate it with such success?

So effective is this practical operation that I am not conscious of this problem in my whole experience of practical living; my body and its environment appear to be directly known to me. This attitude towards perceptual experiences can be termed naive or direct realism; but this belief must be rejected, because it is based on a misunderstanding of the way in which we come to know of the external world by means of our sense organs and our brains.

In response to some sensory stimulation, I experience a private perceptual world which must be regarded, neurophysiologically, as an interpretation of specific events in my brain that we will be considering in more detail in a later talk. Hence I am confronted by the problem: How can these diverse cerebral patterns of activity give me valid pictures of the external world?

Usually this problem is discussed in relation to visual perception. There seems to be an extraordinary problem in explaining how information from my retinae, when relayed to, and activating, my cerebral cortex, gives me a picture of an external world with all its various objects in three-dimensional array and endowed with brightness and colour. This problem has led to much philosophical confusion when it has been discussed on the assumption that fully patterned visual perception is an inborn property of the nervous system. On the contrary, my visual perception is an interpretation of data provided by my eyes, that in a lifetime of experience I have learned to accomplish, particularly in association with sensory information provided by receptors in muscles, joints, skin and the special receptors for spatial orientation in my inner ear, and in addition, with the central experience of my willed effort.

Apart from trivial differences, such as colour blindness, we agree with one another about the external world, because we can point to things and talk about them, and others know what we are talking about. This is the world we call objective, because it can be tested, reported upon and agreed upon. And amongst sane people there is a tremendous measure of agreement.

As I shall suggest in a later talk, we have specific patterns of activity in our cerebral cortex for every detailed event we can remember and for every visual image that we can recollect. When we experience an object, we can see it and confirm its presence by touch. We can lift it, examine it, and by virtue of complex reactions in our brains, we can give it secondary properties like colour, texture and weight. This all comes about because diverse sense organs are busy signalling to the central nervous system and so transmitting information. The richness of our sensory experience derives from the great diversity and wealth of interaction of all the information pathways into the brain.

Many philosophers will not agree with this, saying, for example, that the taste is in the apple, or the colour in the flower. The taste is not in the apple; certainly it is the result of chemical substances that are in the apple, which act on the taste buds, stimulating specific pathways leading to the brain and evoking therein specific spatio-temporal patterns of activity; the result is a taste you can remember, report on, talk about and compare. But the taste itself is primarily the result of a specific cortical activity; and, of course, likewise with colour, where all that the observed object emits is a complex of spectral wave lengths that is transmitted in coded patterns to our cerebral cortex and there transmuted into the perception of colour.

In my next lecture, I shall be dealing particularly with the way in which we come to learn to interpret all the information that comes from our sense organs and to derive from it our experience of an external world in all its detailed variety and richness.

Sir Macfarlane Burnet

Frank Macfarlane Burnet was Australia's other great Nobel Laureate for medicine in the 1960s. He was born at Traralgon, Victoria, in 1899. He was educated at Geelong College and completed his medical degree at Melbourne University.

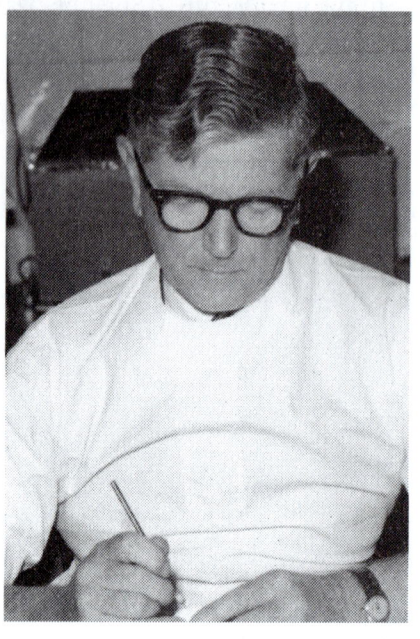

His first research work in virology was begun at the Walter and Eliza Hall Institute of the Royal Melbourne Hospital in 1923 and, except for periods overseas, his professional career was spent at the Hall Institute.

From 1926 to 1927, he worked at the Lister Institute of Preventative Medicine, London, and in 1932–33 at the National Institute for Medical Research, Hampstead. In 1931 he discovered with Jean Macnamara that there were at least two strains of poliomyelitis. He also undertook research into the influenza virus.

Macfarlane Burnet returned to the Hall Institute in 1934 and was appointed director in 1944. He was also Professor of Experimental Medicine at the University of Melbourne.

Sir Macfarlane's work covered several fields, but until 1957 was primarily concerned with virology. In that year he switched the focus of the Hall Institute to immunology.

In 1960, he shared the Nobel Prize for Physiology and Medicine with England's Sir Peter Medawar 'for the discovery of immunological tolerance.'

Sir Macfarlane retired as director of the Hall Institute in 1965 but continued his association with the University of Melbourne as Guest Professor of Microbiology until 1977. He was also president of the Australian Academy of Science from 1965 to 1969 and chairman of the Commonwealth Foundation (1966–69).

Among his many awards were the Royal Society's Royal Medal (1947), the Copley Medal (1958) and the Mueller Medal (1962). He delivered many noted lectures, publishing prolifically.

Sir Macfarlane Burnet died in 1985.

At the time of his 1966 Boyer Lectures, entitled *Biology and the Appreciation of Life*, Macfarlane Burnet was a towering figure in medical science who also had a keen interest in its wider implications as exemplified in the titles of his individual lectures: 'The Beginnings of Science'; 'The Pasteurian Revolution'; 'The Darwinian Approach'; 'The Ethics of a Biologist' reproduced here, and 'Education for Life'. His reverence for life informs all these lectures, as in his concluding words: 'Life is everywhere—to be wondered at or understood, as it presents itself in the culture tubes of the laboratories; as the living fascinating inhabitants of earth, air and sea, or in our own human form, behaviour and aspirations.'

THE ETHICS OF
A BIOLOGIST

Biology and the Appreciation
of Life

Sir Macfarlane Burnet

• 1 9 6 6 •

As far back as men have written down their thoughts, they have dreamt of a world in which people could live together in amity and banish war and cruelty, poverty, hunger and disease, and death itself. The great religions arose in response to those dreams, to keep hope alive in the midst of an almost unbearable reality and to strengthen those aspects of social behaviour that made the life of human communities more tolerable.

In the last hundred years, the situation has changed in a fashion that would be wholly inconceivable to the great moralists and philosophers of the eighteenth century and earlier. Poverty, hunger and disease have virtually vanished in the affluent societies like our own. That is the work of science and invention. For the great majority of people for most of their lives, war, serious crime and death can all be half-forgotten. Yet war and crime and violence are all with us in increasing intensity, and our achievement of general health and prosperity has brought new social and medical problems, such as over-population and the mounting incidence of coronary disease.

To a scientist, there can never be final answers—truth in science is that complex of recorded observations, generalisations and theories which in the opinion of competent scholars have not yet been proved to be wrong. Equally, there can be no final statement as to what is good, and only too clearly can we recognise the changing nature of what is said to be beautiful.

In this talk, I want to discuss only the question of whether in the modern world our increasing knowledge of human biology can provide us with a working picture of what is 'good'.

I think I can indicate the sort of approach I will adopt by quoting a few lines from an American professor of anthropology (SL Washburn). He said: 'Throughout most of human evolution, man was adapted to ways of life radically different from those of today, and there has been neither the time nor the control of breeding to change human biology from what was adaptive in the past to what is adaptive now.' Washburn was concerned mainly with aggression and violence, but his remarks are equally applicable to many other aspects of human life.

The evolution of man seems to have taken about two million years, and, as far as can be gathered from skull and brain size, men physically similar to ourselves were in Europe 20,000 years ago, before there were any agriculture, domestic animals or any of the other precursors of civilisation. What has happened since then has been the development of new cultures and an always increasing amount of learned and transmitted technical know-how. The physical background of brain structure and the basic patterns of instinctive or easily learnt behaviour were developed over at least a half-million years, and civilisation is no more than a few thousand years old. In the eyes of the modern anthropologist, the problem of today is how to use the intelligence of a relatively small number of men and women to devise ways in which patterns of behaviour, laid down in a million years, can be modified, tricked and twisted, if necessary, to allow a tolerable human existence in a crowded world. There are three imperatives: to reduce war to a minimum; to stabilise human population; and to prevent the progressive destruction of the earth's irreplaceable resources. At the present time, none of these seems possible, but it may be that, by thinking, writing, experimenting and observing, they will gradually become more nearly approachable.

I was trained as a physician, and though I have been a laboratory scientist for more than 40 years, my approach to ethics is deeply influenced by the doctor's point of view. There can be all sorts of answers to the question of what is good, but no sane man or woman will deny that vigorous health, appropriate to an individual's age, is good and desirable. This universally accepted principle has, however, some important implications for human behaviour. It means education in the fundamentals of healthy living; it means baby health centres; immunisation of children; good water supply and sanitation; and dozens of other things that we take for granted. It means good hospitals and good doctors; and it calls for things which we haven't yet been able to develop. Far too many people are killed by accidents on the roads. Men who eat too much, smoke too much and take too little exercise, are candidates for heart attacks. And although everyone nowadays knows that cigarette-smoking is wholly responsible for most lung cancer, deaths from that disease continue to move steadily upward each year. One of the best things

I know about doctors is that they are the only group of people who have mostly stopped smoking, and in England, they are the only group whose incidence of lung cancer is falling.

Can I now try to suggest and discuss four rules for a modern ethic? The first rule then would be this:

> To ensure for every individual the fullest measure of health that is allowed by his inheritance.

If physical health is desirable, so is mental health, and, like physical health it can be assessed objectively. The intelligent, socially-adaptable individual is recognisable as easily in Russia or China as in Australia or Japan, and in all countries it is now a clear objective that every child should be educated to the limit of his capacity and desire to learn. This again has immense implications for society. Once we begin to visualise and ponder on the distribution of ability amongst individuals, the nature of mental disease and the infinite gradations of mood, personality and behaviour that run from the normal to the insane, the problem seems infinite. Education can do much, but there are other possibilities. One day, we may know enough about the genetics of mind and brain to devise eugenic programmes that will reduce the numbers of children born with sub-standard brains. And in quite a different approach, already well under way, drugs which can modify mood and emotion may make people socially adaptable who would otherwise have to be kept under institutional care.

For the great majority of sane individuals, with their range of intelligence and manipulative skills from genius to dullness and from the born artist or mathematician to the inept, education must be made available to bring out in each individual his best value to the community and to himself.

Now let me suggest the second rule for this modern ethic:

> To provide for every individual the opportunity to develop intellectual and manipulative skills to the limit of his inherited capacity.

Health and a trained mind are good in themselves, but there is a third aspect of human life that is equally acceptable to people of all sorts as good. This is that achievement and success should be recognised. There are so many thousands of different fields in which a man or a woman may exceed that there should be few individuals without the possibility of feeling a sense of achievement. One person's success may temporarily hurt his direct competitors, but by and large, people like seeing another's success in any of the thousand activities in which they are not competitors.

So I come to the third rule, with just the faintest reservation that it may not always be accepted as valid. It would be:

> To ensure to all, the opportunity for achievement, and the recognition of success.

All three of these rules are concerned simply with the individual, but still staying within the limitation of the doctor's outlook we have to look at the future as well as the present. Darwin and Mendel, Galton, Malthus and Margaret Sanger have taught us to look at the implications of reproduction and inheritance, both in regard to quality and quantity. We have all suddenly become aware of the dangers of over-population and of the availability of the pill and of mechanical methods of birth control. There is no doubt about the desirability, for both affluent and under-developed countries, to attempt to stabilise their population by reducing the birth rate. Even if this were successful, it would still leave some very important long-term biological problems. As Darwin and his successors have so often pointed out, throughout the whole range of animals many more individuals are born or hatched than survive to reproduce themselves. Twentieth-century man is the only exception, and he may have to face the consequences. With medicine removing Nature's method of maintaining genetic quality by selecting against harmful mutants, it is conceivable that in a few thousand generations more than half the people will carry what we now regard as severe genetic disabilities like haemophilia or diabetes. In quite a different direction, it seems entirely possible that one or other of the industrial wastes or specific chemicals that are beginning to poison air, earth or water, may have severe and unexpected effects on the health of this or future generations.

This regard for the future calls for a fourth rule. It is this:

> To ensure that opportunity to attain bodily and mental health and to find satisfaction in achievement, will be available to all future generations in measure not inferior to what we now enjoy.

I believe that those four imperatives are sufficient to cover all those human objectives that can be regarded by all intelligent and knowledgeable men, irrespective of race and culture, as desirable, right and good. Taken together, they represent the humanist approach, by which human welfare is the sole measure of what is good.

There are, however, other matters quite closely related to the fourth point but expressible in non-human terms. They allow us to express what might be called the conservationist approach. This is, I think, self-evident enough for me to condense it into a few brief statements.

The resources of the Earth must be maintained for the use and enjoyment of future generations by ensuring four things:

First: That irreplaceable mineral resources shall not be exhausted before effective substitutes can be made from always-available materials.

Second: That energy from fossil fuels will be replaced in time by perpetually renewable sources of energy.

Third: That the environment shall not be poisoned by industrial and military wastes.

Fourth: That adequate areas shall be preserved, to allow the indefinite persistence of all significant forms of wild life and many areas of natural beauty or special interest.

In principle, few would disagree with any of these aspirations: in practice, no one seems to regard them as of any significance whatever.

To express these things as an ethical basis for action, in terms that come naturally to a scientist with a medical-biological background, may be helpful to some and can do no harm to anyone.

To be a biologist or a medical man is to be a realist. May I quote two more short passages from Washburn? The first:

> Throughout most of human history, society has depended on young adult males to hunt, to fight and to maintain the social order with violence . . . (using) aggressive action which was socially approved, learned in play and personally gratifying.

And the second:

> Evolution has equipped us with the ability to learn certain things easily: we learn to speak easily, we learn easily to use tools or to handle weapons . . . These things have been built into us by evolution. It does not mean that they are inevitable but it does mean that they are probable.

Men carry the marks of their evolution and we have to recognise that capacity to exert dominance over one's fellows, aggressive courage in the face of danger and identification of one's own group with oneself were all absolutely necessary for survival, except in times and places where a well-policed and stable civilisation could develop. Those characteristics have been bred into every race of men, and the whole art of civilisation is to find ways by which the instinctive drives towards dominance and violence can be directed into relatively harmless channels and the capacity for identification with one's group directed toward progressively larger groups.

So we come squarely against the central dilemma of our times: that, men being what they are, stability of social life is only possible by the constant availability of force to stamp out any anti-social violence with the more effective violence of an organised and disciplined police.

In a scientifically based civilisation, where the power of weapons has suddenly expanded to something which makes nonsense of biology, an effective police force at the world level is an obvious and urgent necessity. It is illuminating to see that the ostensible reason for military action nowadays is always to counter anti-social violence by the enemy. Perhaps a world police force may come into being in one way or another sooner than we think.

It is not the job of a biologist to solve major human problems, but it is his job to look at those problems from his own highly relevant point of view and to ask that men with the responsibilities of power should become aware of the lessons of human biology as well as those of human history.

In the last 15 or 16 years, I have been fortunate to have travelled widely to nearly all those countries where active medical and biological research is going on. My interests have been in one of the fields of human knowledge that has always had a rather specially privileged place in the public mind—the prevention of infectious disease. I have been to a dozen or more specialised conferences on ways of preventing polio, and influenza, and twice I have acted as chairman of a full-international committee. What has impressed me about these experiences has been the relative ease with which agreement can be reached on matters which are based on science— on accurate knowledge obtained by methods which are the same in every country. And it is the almost universal experience that, if the language barrier can be overcome, people doing this sort of work together find that they like each other. Perhaps it is only a desperate hope to find some way of escape from the threat of extermination that hangs over us all, but this ease of intercourse amongst technically trained and intelligent men seems to give promise that, if we can only widen the understanding of human affairs at the scientific level, the possibility of escape may gradually increase.

Perhaps the position can be summarised in two propositions. The first is concerned with what favours aggression and violence; the second with the equally important factors that can prevent or minimise violence.

First then, we look at those inborn qualities that are needed for survival, which developed during human evolution. We can, if we like, call them instincts, but psychologists tend rather to speak of attitudes or actions that are specially easy to learn. There are three such qualities, all more evident in men than in women:

First: All human beings appreciate a chance to dominate or feel superior to other people.

Second: On the background of the group and territorial instincts of primitive man, they readily develop loyalty to much larger groupings.

Third: Most men find it relatively easy and gratifying to use weapons effectively.

But the other side is equally important, equally natural. The second proposition is that with the development of stable human communities, means have been developed over the centuries which can virtually eliminate overt violence. The use of intelligence and commonsense to see the implications of violence, plus group feeling and to some degree a broadening of family affection, see to that.

To a human biologist, the hope is that the second set of factors which do allow people to live together in communities as large as the USA or the USSR, can gradually be applied even more widely.

Two things interest me particularly: the first I have already mentioned. It is the ease with which scientific and technical discussions can be fruitful, effective and happy across any set of frontiers. Art and music are by tradition equally international, but science comes much closer to the realities of power, and interchanges at the scientific level are likely to be more helpful.

The second is the small, but growing, proportion of international and inter-racial marriages amongst scientists and scholars. In the last analysis we are unlikely to see 'One World' in any stable sense, unless the strong social taboos in nearly every community against marriage outside the accepted groups can be broken down. There is no sound biological reason against inter-racial marriage, and there is some evidence that, where many human stocks are blended, vigour and capacity for achievement may be increased. England and southern Germany are the classical examples. Sooner or later, race prejudice will be broken down, and what the anthropologists call mating groups, and the geneticists gene pools, will be enlarged to include essentially the whole human species. I think we begin to see the first steps in that direction, even if we fully realise the strong feeling against racial inter-marriage which undoubtedly exists in most parts of the world.

All that I should like to leave with you is the feeling that the only way in which we can overcome the inborn instincts that have made war and conflict the pattern of history, is by the application of intelligence and commonsense—and the scientific approach is no more than systematised intelligence and commonsense. There are clear indications from human biology—from the scientific study of our own species—as to the aims that will allow the full achievement of human potentialities. I may be quite unduly optimistic, but I look to progressive education in human biology as the most likely agent to help us to move in the direction which we all desire; and in my last lecture, I shall touch on the problems and potentialities of education in human biology.

Robin Boyd

Robin Boyd was a distinguished architect and noted commentator. He was born in 1919 near Melbourne, son of the artist Penleigh Boyd. He studied at the Melbourne Technical College and the Melbourne University Architecture Atelier.

Following his war service in New Guinea, Robin Boyd wrote a weekly column with the *Age* newspaper in relation to the Small Homes Service set up by the Royal Victorian Institute of Architecture. Boyd remained the director of the Service until 1953. In 1953 he designed the Peninsula house, Australia's first project home.

In a wide-ranging career, Robin Boyd was the architect of many domestic, commercial and academic buildings, including Menzies College at La Trobe University, Melbourne, the zoology building at the Australian National University and Churchill House, Canberra. He was the exhibits architect for the Australian pavilion at Montreal's 1967 Expo and at Osaka's in 1970.

In 1950 he won the Robert and Ada Haddon Travelling Scholarship. He became a Fellow of the Royal Australian Institute of Architects, a Fellow of the Royal Society of Arts, a Fulbright Scholar and Visiting Professor of Architecture at the Massachusetts Institute of Technology in 1956–57, a trustee of the National Gallery of Victoria, and a member of the National Planning Authority.

He wrote for the *Australian* in 1964–65 and in that paper's Sunday edition from 1970, and regularly contributed architectural criticism to international journals. His books included several established classics: *Australia's Home*, *The Australian Ugliness*, which was particularly influential, *The Puzzle of Architecture* and *Great Australian Dream*.

He received an honorary Doctor of Letters from the University of New England in 1967, the Royal Australian Institute of Architect's gold medal in 1969, and the honorary fellowship in 1970.

His five Boyer Lectures, *Artificial Australia* were vintage Boyd. He was urgent in his hope that Australians would open their eyes and really look at the cities and suburbs around them. Their individual titles were 'Creative Man in a Frontier Society'; 'The Architecture of Ideas' reproduced here, 'Integrity in the Artificial Object'; 'The Environmental Arts in Australia' and 'The Australian Myth in the Modern World'. In that last lecture, he argued in support of the proposal to establish a national arts council similar to the Canada Council. He lived to see his wish fulfilled when the Gorton Government acted on Harold Holt's decision and established the Australian Council for the Arts in 1968, later to become the Australia Council.

THE ARCHITECTURE
OF IDEAS

Artificial Australia

Robin Boyd

• 1 9 6 7 •

In the first lecture in this series I spoke of Australia's great need to cultivate ideas, and promised to try to define this rather loose term 'ideas' in relation to my own fields of architecture and design. This I will do now, and I will concentrate on the timeless and international problem of the design of the biggest artificial, useful object: a building. In later lectures I will relate the question to other objects and more specifically to Australia. But I speak of architecture first, for she is the mother of all design, and if she can be satisfied most of her children will follow dutifully.

I use the word idea as meaning the conception of a principle, and in architecture the need for such ideas occurs at two levels.

First, for most men or women seriously engaged in the creation of buildings, there is a hunger for a theory, a need to define to himself in some satisfying way what is the ultimate object of all building, what is the aim of architecture.

Then, at the second level, the need for a motivating idea arises afresh with each new problem. The architect must seek a concrete idea, of structure and form, which satisfies all the problems as he sees them and which will be his guide vision through the long processes of preparation and construction.

But to take ideas at the first level first, I must explain at the start that it takes many different kinds of architect to make a world, and not all architects are convinced of the need for any overall theory. To some the object of architecture is so evident that any theorising is an irritation. The object is simply to erect a building that works and is beautiful. While few architects would contest that, to others of us such an easy explanation is not enough. It leaves undefined two vital qualities. What must a building be or do in order to 'work'? And what is 'beauty'?

Just as many good people of the highest intelligence find satisfaction in the concept of God as a substitute for further discussion in seeking answers to the ultimate questions of life, so many fine architects and sensitive patrons of architecture are satisfied by the word beauty as a substitute for theory and for principles in building. However, among those who are not so satisfied, the father figure is a famous old man of Roman architecture, Vitruvius, who wrote ten volumes of theory just before the birth of Christ. Horrified by the contemporary architecture being run up around him in Rome, Vitruvius looked back wistfully to Greece and asked himself what was it that made Athens a dream to set the spirit soaring, and what was it that made Rome, which was stolidly copying all the outward shapes and symbols of Athens, a clumsy, lumpish city. He saw that architects need to be directed by more than their eyes. They require a little heart and intellect as well: in short, an idea. 'Theory,' he wrote, 'is that which is able to explain and analyze material constructions by the exercise of . . . reason.' Vitruvius then gave his definition of what architecture is, or should be. He specified three essentials to good building: strength, utility, and beauty. And this has remained the classical definition, although the words have been pulled around a lot. For instance, Sir Henry Wotton in 1624 paraphrased the three virtues as 'commodity, firmness and delight', and last century John Ruskin, after much evident mental torment, arrived back at virtually the same conclusion when he said that a building should 'act well, speak well, and look well'.

The Vitruvian theory served well enough, with few dissenters and few diversions, through nearly 1900 years, through classical, Renaissance, Gothic and other Revivalist styles, until about 115 years ago. But then a change in the technique of manufacturing the artificial products of the world forced a reconsideration. The change was the Industrial Revolution, and the re-examination which it forced upon architects and all designers of artificial objects of use was centred on the mystery which was cloaked by that facile word, beauty.

Industry raised a fascinating new problem. Before this there had never been such a thing as vulgar design. The aristocrats had had their fine things artfully enriched, and the peasants had had serviceable things artlessly crafted. Now industry made it possible for reproductions, or caricatures, of the rich man's artifacts to be interminably repeated, and for cheap products to be elaborately dressed in ornaments, and it opened the door for everyman to previously barred delights of colour and texture. As we all know, people without any advantage of education or experience of art responded greedily to every curlicue of ornamentation that could be applied, and the period of decadence in design known to us as the Victorian era came into being. However, as well as vulgar ornament, the Industrial Revolution brought iron frames and steel suspension bridges and the mass production of glass and other portents of revolutionary building techniques.

Our present-day ideas of architecture and of the design of all useful things began to take form at that time—in the middle of last century. Some prophets, excited by the mighty, imaginative, inspiring bridges and horrified by the excesses of petty ornament, began to seek a new theory of design, a new artistic concept, to fit the new conditions.

Looking at those magnificent bridges and towers like the Eiffel, they had a revolutionary idea. It was that everything made by man for his own use should be shaped according to its function—to the job it had to do—with no concessions to tradition, no false over-coating to give a 'better' appearance, no extra frills or ornamentation of any sort. Everything was to be cruelly honest, completely naked and unashamed; and have no fear, the prophets said, the results will not be ugly but as beautiful as nature. 'In nakedness I behold the majesty of the essential instead of the trappings of pretension', wrote Horatio Greenough of America in 1853.

This new concept, this artistic bombshell, was of course called Functionalism, and its supporters could gather corroborative evidence from many quarters. Without question, complete visual satisfaction—assuredly, beauty, if of a hitherto unrecognised kind—could be found in many objects traditionally shaped for use only, without any pretensions or visual aspirations. The revolutionaries pointed to many humble tools and utensils (think of the superb sculptural shape of a scythe). As for architecture, a functional tradition was strongly rooted in charming unadorned farmhouses, wharves and numerous other utilitarian buildings.

As the nineteenth turned into the twentieth century, the Functionalist ethic gained a lot of ground. Architecture sometimes deliberately followed the lead of primitive buildings and finished up as a little knot of whitewashed boxes. Simplicity was prized highly in the progressive quarters of most of the visual arts. And every now and then some spectacular proof of the concept appeared, some vindication of the most extreme theories of Func-tionalism. Imagine, for example, the joy of the early Functionalists when they beheld an aeroplane. Here was an instance of an unques-tionably twentieth century product that had to be made scientifically and honestly, that had to ban ornamentation and false nostalgic effects or it would never get off the ground; and yet it was beaut-iful. If ever the time came when all things were made as honestly

and as plainly as an aeroplane, then—thought the Functionalists—
we would have the visual millennium. For many years they fought
against the majority of people who had no theoretical, moralistic
desire for design to be honest and who much preferred to cling to
the visual effects handed down to them by past generations, to
costly familiar styles like the Gothic and the Georgian.

Nevertheless, a new way of building—which is still known, for
want of a better term, as Modern Architecture—slowly conquered
the world. If I may be permitted to simplify history to a gross
extent, I can say that it began in Europe and built up strength gradually, standing on the shoulders of the English honest craft movement of William Morris, and the Art Nouveau movement of Van de
Velde and Mackintosh, and the concrete constructional freedom of
Perret. It grew with the formal freedom suggested by Peter Behrens,
and the moral antiornament ethics of Adolf Loos. It reached a first
plateau of success and acknowledgement shortly after the First
World War with the appearance on the world stage of the stars of
the first act: Le Corbusier, Walter Gropius and, as yet playing the
butler, Mies van der Rohe. But, as I say, that is gross oversimplif-
ication. In fact, another great star was working in another theatre,
and the impulse of his work affected the Europeans I have
mentioned. This other star was Frank Lloyd Wright, the American,
whose intensely individual development of what he called Organic
Architecture preposterously complicates the telling of modern
architectural history. Nevertheless, considering the central stream of
the movement only we can gain a reasonably accurate picture. This
central, European stream produced by 1925 or so a vision that was
as sharp and memorable as that produced by any major style of the
ancients. In its classic form it was a stark white flush box, flat-
roofed, and slit by a few random windows. When the function
served was complex, as in a multi-purpose school or a civic centre,
the box broke up into several parts, each shaped more or less in
accordance with some special internal requirement.

Thus, in a rather stolid architectural way, the complex sometimes
looked like a machine, in which the many parts were related by the
purity of the geometry and the sense of common purpose. As a
matter of fact, the architects of the time were disproportionately
moved by the beauty of machinery. Although they still had to work
most of the time with conventional materials, they dreamt of a time
when all buildings could be stamped out by giant machines like
Chevrolets were. (Do you happen to remember an exciting film
made by Alexander Korda to HG Wells' scenario *Things to Come*? It was
made at the height of the Functionalist movement about 1936 . . .

In it Wells pictured buildings of a Utopia to come being made by huge robot machines fitting into place steaming, enormous slabs of white plastic.) In the meantime, the real-life architects of the 1920s and '30s had to make do with humble old materials like brickwork, but they plastered it, hoping that no one would catch them in the act, to look like something plastic. For a decade or two more this style was the vision of progressive building, the symbol of Functionalism. It had its problems—banning by Hitler and by Stalin included—but, as it crept slowly round the world, to Scandinavia in the early 1930s, to England, America, Australia, it became known more and more as the International Style. And after the Second World War was over, it gained official international recognition. It was accepted by the United Nations as the style for its headquarters in New York. The 40-storey slab of the UN Secretariat was the biggest, bravest box in the world. It was also the climax and the curtain of the first act. The glass and concrete boxes which followed, magnificent as were many of them, were anti-climaxes.

Now the second act of modern architecture opened, and it took a surprising turn. It was romantic, even sentimental. It began when architects had had time to digest the success of the rectilinear boxes. By this time boxes were in use for almost all functions—offices, theatres, churches. It suddenly dawned on some architects that, if a cube could be made successfully to house a number of different functions, then why not move on to any of a number of other more exciting shapes, more particularly the shapes ruled by a circle—the pure and perfect shape which had fascinated designers since Stonehenge.

Thus an era of great shapes began. There were buildings made in the shapes of cylinders and domes, and alphabet houses in O, C and S shapes. At first there was no conscious revision of the Functionalist ethics. Many of these exciting shapes were derived from function. What could be more logical, for instance, than a building shaped like the letter O, if the outlook was good all round and a fine old tree was left standing in the hole or court in the middle? Thus a reasonable and Functionalist attitude could marry, in some circum-stances, with a romantic form. (Indeed, this may be the ultimate goal of architecture.)

But then some of the braver architects went further. Eero Saarinen, who was the bravest of them all, the brightest star of the 1950s, made the TWA terminal building at Kennedy Airport in New York in a symmetrical but free shape, with great wings symbolic of flight. It became known as the giant bird. While he was working on this project, Saarinen was called to Sydney to join the judging panel on an international architectural competition for a building beside the harbour, and he selected another great shape from the entries: a concrete dream of great white sails.

By this time the cause of Functionalism had retreated out of sight. The aim of the star architects now was to discover for each job in hand something which they called 'significant form'. The shapes were imposed on the functions of the building. Nevertheless, they were not entirely arbitrary. The shapes were meant to signify visually some essence of the function of the building and its part in society. Often they were assisted to their exciting visual consummation by brilliant new feats of engineering involving shell concrete or tensile steel.

With remarkable speed this movement sank into decadence. Soon the 'significant' forms were shaped with no real motivation except to be different, and thus an enviable monument to their architect. Practically all reference to the natural shape of the activities being housed was subjugated to impressive external imagery. And now that the stern ethic of Functionalism appeared to be abandoned by the leaders, the other ranks of architecture, with obvious relief, felt free to break all disciplines. Often they reverted backwards out of the twentieth century, to ornament and false arches. At the height of this movement, in the late 1950s, it was commonplace to hear the statement from architects that honesty in building was a shibboleth best forgotten and that Functionalism was a dreary maxim now as dead as any fashion that has run its course.

Was Functionalism just a fashion? The plastered white box was; there can be no doubt about that. But the principles behind it were much bigger than the box and inevitably they began to surface again. A reaction against overexciting shapes began to set in some time before 1960.

You may have noticed that the latest architecture, as illustrated in photographs of completed buildings from abroad—or projected buildings here—no longer has that bland, one-piece look. The two most apparent reactions to those sophisticated great shapes of the 1950s have been a return to rugged, rustic textures and to fragmentation. In place of the flush plaster of the earliest modern, and the classic marble and polished metal loved by many of the men of the romantic second act, we often find ourselves nowadays back with coarse bricks, undressed timber and bare concrete. But, more importantly, there is a reaction against that one-piece look, that monumental, monolithic form which can be taken in at a glance and is retained in the eye without effort. Buildings are showing again their separate parts. Indeed, they often seem to break themselves up for no apparent reason, so that their walls and roofs are fractured into many vaguely related sections. This is sometimes done just to be fashionable, as is the swing from feminine to masculine textures, and should not be taken any more seriously than Carnaby Street clothes. However, behind the frivolous fragmentation and tough texture there is often today a much more significant revision of architectural principle.

There is often again these days a proud exposition of the separate functional elements of the building, so that you can often guess from the outside what happens inside—in general terms. You say to yourself: there's the office wing; there's the service block (look at that flue); there, obviously, is the council chamber. It is reasonable and right that these things should be apparent, and unreasonable when all such diverse elements are packed against their will into an exercise in pure geometry. By that I don't mean that all geometrical, monumental ideas in architecture are necessarily unreasonable, any more than all fragmented complexes are necessarily reasonable and right. My point is only that ideas in architecture are not necessarily the obvious sort of brainwaves detectable in simple, monolithic shapes. A simple, exciting shape may be reasonable for the problem in hand, and therefore right. But it may be unreasonable, and therefore, in terms of architectural integrity, wrong.

The rumours of Functionalism's death appear to have been exaggerated. It has made a remarkable recovery, and these days, in its new sporty clothes, it is as young in heart as ever. I don't mean that the argument about Functionalism is over. It will continue as long as men build, while other motivations from time to time will undoubtedly divert the main stream of architecture. I don't mean by this that form should follow function so slavishly that it has no will of its own. I mean that function is the major factor distinguishing architecture from all the other arts, and to serve function means only to serve people, and that is what architecture is here for. I don't mean that the old Vitruvian three-part definition is cast aside. Good buildings still seek strength, utility and beauty. But the emphasis is different. The motivation is the central factor: utility or function. The starting point is people—not strength, not beauty. Those two follow as a matter of course. Finally, among these things I don't mean, I don't mean that people should be served by a building at the expense of art. I mean that the art of architecture is serving people.

After a decade or so of beautiful delinquency, I think that architecture is back on the rails and recognises its first responsibility, to function. The worship of irrelevant beauty, the falsifying of structure and the twisting or cramping of function for the sake of a striking monument, are becoming abhorrent again in the little world of the architects' drawing offices. Abhorrent is not, I assure you, too strong a word. You would probably find it hard to believe, if I were to tell you how passionately many architects feel about the integrity of building. What we know as 'dishonesty' in architecture; that is, presenting an effect that is not true to the structure behind it, like a false column added just for visual symmetry or a domed ceiling hung inside a perfectly sufficient flat ceiling and pretending to be the real structure—these pretty tricks are repugnant.

Why do such things grate so badly on some of us? Often the falsity is well disguised and only the experienced observer can detect the subterfuge. Often the visual effect is satisfying, orderly, familiar, even imaginative. Then why should it move some of us to immoderate opposition? The rather embarrassing answer is this: numbers of architects anthropomorphise buildings outrageously, virtually applying a human morality to the bricks, steel and concrete. In more sentimental days a century ago, they spoke of buildings as an extension of God's work, a continuation of the life force flowing out through the mason's hand into the building stone. In this more rationalising age, the argument tries to cut away excessive sentiment. The principal claim now is that building is too important as a social activity, and too conspicuous and influential on the whole culture of society, to allow room for tricks disguising the truth. Nevertheless, the passion remains under the reasoning. Falsity seems in almost every respect as distasteful as dishonesty in a person. Architects are perfectly aware that such an attitude appears ludicrous to many better and saner people, who are satisfied if a building looks all right, and have no desire or intention to crane around corners to see if it is theoretically 'dishonest'.

Nevertheless, many of us can't help feeling this way. Some architects are inclined to be even more emotional and unreasonable in such matters than any artists in other fields when they are faced with bad work in their own medium. Architects are not so easily prepared as some others to be philosophical and to laugh off the bad. They seem, to many observers, to take themselves or their work too seriously. I suppose this is the result of the insistence on principles that I have mentioned, the hunger for ideas at the first level.

Ideas at the second level, relative to each building problem, are inclined to be more sympathetically received by non-architects. These ideas cannot be abstract, and are usually evident to all in the finished building. At least one of the ideas of the building on Benelong Point, for instance, is clear at first sight: the idea of covering whatever it is inside, not with walls and a roof but with a series of great sail shapes inter-related in form. The motivating idea or concept behind Sydney's Australia Square tower also is clear immediately: it is a shaft thrust up into the sky, and feeling itself thus in command of the city, it looks out all round: hence a circular shaft or needle, braced against the stresses of the four winds by regular tapered sinews all round.

The idea behind some houses is clear to all. The classic vision of a luxurious residence in Egypt, at Pompeii, and still today in many parts of the world, including Australia, is something like a square in plan shape with all main rooms looking on to a courtyard in the middle.

Ideas as obvious as those were more common in the second act of modern architecture to which I have referred. Nowadays, the idea in each building tends to be more subtle, but it is present still in some form in every building worthy of any close attention or admiration; by which, I regret to say, I refer to only about one building in every hundred.

This idea at the second level, the concept for a building, may at the start have nothing to do with shapes or a concise external image. The oldest architectural idea in the world, as in every Egyptian or classical building, is symmetry. A new idea, like Moshe Safdie's idea in that already famous stack of concrete flats known as Habitat built at Montreal's Expo '67, may have no symmetry, nor even any discernible visual pattern. Yet its idea and the ancient architects' ideas have one thing in common. That is, they have order—a sense of order apparent immediately to every observer, a sense which grows with investigation. Such order is not achieved by luck after a bit of sketching on the drawing board. It is intellectual. It is achieved only by an architectural idea, old or new. At the very beginning, before he has designed anything, probably before he has put pencil to paper, the architect has devised some orderly shape, structure, system or theme which is suited to the nature of the building and will hold all its parts together. He has had an idea.

Now, how can this sort of specific, concrete idea—an idea at the second level—be consistent with the overall ethical idea which I have discussed at the first level? It is not difficult. There is no conflict with the Functionalist ethics when the idea for a building springs from the function.

This is not saying the same thing as if I were to quote the famous slogan of Louis Sullivan (Frank Lloyd Wright's great early master): 'Form Follows Function'. What I am saying is that an architect, when designing, when searching for the motivating concept or idea for the building, should be above all most conscious of how the building will serve the people who will use it, serve them in the fullest sense. He does not follow function best by letting every little functional requirement state its own terms for the shape required to house it. These shapes may well conflict unless he first studies the whole problem and all the functions and finds an order which char-acterises or averages out all these functions. He then imposes this order on the whole programme of requirements of the building. The idea, the order which he picks, is the essential creative act of architecture. The spirit, or poetry, or art of architecture enters at the point when this order is conceived. The architect has in this act determined what he perceives to be the overall functional character of the building. He has, if you like, perceived the function in an emotional light, and has conceived a formal order around this perception. He has taken the decisive step that can make the finest and most exciting art out of the ancient and pedestrian activity of building.

WEH Stanner

Anthropologist WEH Stanner was born in Sydney in 1905 and educated at the University of Sydney and the London School of Economics.

Between 1932 and 1935, he undertook fieldwork for the Australian National Research Council in the Northern Territory. In 1938, after taking his doctorate at London, he joined an Oxford University fieldwork trip to Kenya.

During his war service he rose to the rank of lieutenant colonel. He supervised post-war reconstruction in British North Borneo (Sabah).

Various field studies took him to Uganda, Tanganyika (now Tanzania), Kenya and the south-west Pacific. Appointed Reader in Comparative Social Institutions at Australian National University in 1949, he undertook further field research to northern Australia throughout the 1950s.

Professor Stanner took the chair of anthropology at the Australian National University in 1964 until his retirement in 1970. He then became visiting Fellow of the Research School of Pacific Studies from 1972 to 1974, and in the department of prehistory and anthropology at the ANU.

In 1961 he convened the Commonwealth Conference on Aboriginal Studies, which directly led to the establishment of the Australian Institute of Aboriginal Studies, of which he was the first executive officer in 1961–62. He served on the Council for Aboriginal Affairs from 1967 to 1977.

Winner of the 1971 Mueller Medal and the 1972 Cilento Medal, he was conferred with an honorary doctor of letters by the ANU in that year. His books include *The South Seas In Transition* and *On Aboriginal Religion*, *After the Dreaming* and *White Man's Got No Dreaming*.

Professor Stanner died in 1981.

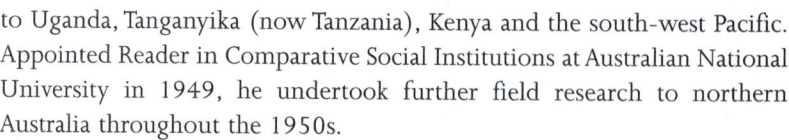

Stanner's Boyer Lectures were delivered in the wake of the 1967 referendum question which passed with a 90 per cent majority vote that the

Constitution be amended to permit Aborigines to be counted in the census and to allow the Commonwealth to make special law for aborigines, previously the preserve of the states. His lectures had a significant continuing impact, being reprinted at least seven times (up to 1974), and are still considered a major reference source.

Given under the title *After the Dreaming*, the lecture subjects are 'Looking Back'; 'The Great Australian Silence' reproduced here; 'The Appreciation of Difference'; 'Confrontation' and 'Composition'.

These are watershed lectures, amazing for their relevance, prescience and balance.

THE GREAT AUSTRALIAN SILENCE

After the Dreaming

WEH Stanner

• 1 9 6 8 •

In my first lecture I spoke about a structure of racial relations that had come about between us and the aborigines in the early days and had stayed more or less unchanged for 150 years. I tried to sketch something of the frame of mind and vision we had when we saw the skeleton beginning to walk in the early 1930s.

Why it began to walk then, and not earlier, or later, is a question to which I cannot give a very satisfactory answer. There was scarcely any interest in the aborigines of the settled areas of the east and south. Concern over them is a very recent development indeed. What had aroused public feeling in 1926 and afterward were reports of atrocities in the outback and the subsequent disclosure of many bad practices. But I do not think that pastoralists, miners and other employers had suddenly become harder on their aborigines than in the past. I doubt if authority had suddenly become more observant or active; indeed, one of the great difficulties of the time was to get the executive, administrative and legal arms of authority to notice what was afoot, let alone to move. The people whom WK Hancock acknowledged in his book *Australia* (1930) as ever-present—'the enthusiastic friends' of the aborigines—were active but I doubt if their ranks were any stronger. Perhaps there had been a true rise of public sensibility but I find it hard to pin down any changes of conditions that may have brought it about. The explanation may simply be that just as in earlier times the view from Exeter Hall had been clearer than the view from Sydney, so now it was clearer from Sydney than from a town like Alice: and there was now much more to see. The road, the motor car, the aeroplane and the radio had put an end to the old isolation of the bush. It was a humdrum affair to drive from Sydney and Melbourne to Cape York and the Kimberleys. There was a piling up of evidence or near-evidence into a presumption that intolerable things were happening in the lonely places, and a certain taint of hugger-mugger about some of the official disclaimers did nothing to allay suspicion. What I am suggesting then is simply that people heard more, and heard more quickly, about a pattern of outback life that probably had not changed greatly for the worse.

Some people consider that 1934 was the main 'turning point' of aboriginal policy. I cannot say that I recall anything about that year that suggests a sudden access of public virtue or a new vision at all widely shared. It seems to have been just another year on the old plateau of complacence.

In 1931 the Prime Minister of the day, Mr Scullin, still showed little inclination to credit that much could be amiss in Common-wealth territory and seemed not ill-content to plead the constitu-tional limit on his responsibility for events in the States. In 1932 the Federal Minister for Home Affairs, Mr Parkhill, went very close to giving the Northern Territory a coat of whitewash. Even after the Arnhem Land affair of 1933 and 1934 the Prime Minister of that time Mr Lyons, thought it appropriate to continue substantially with the existing policy. There was, perhaps, a certain softening of official attitudes and if so I do not think we can altogether dissoci-ate the fact from inquiries which had been made by the Dominions Office through the High Commissioner in London. But we are hardly justified in placing the 'turning point' before 1938 when Mr McEwen, the then Minister for the Interior, placed before the Commonwealth Parliament the proposals which later became known as 'the New Deal for the Aborigines in the Northern Territory'. It was then that the new concept of 'assimilation' came into use although another ten years had to pass before its effects became at all noticeable.

It is an interesting question whether we should connect the change with another 'turning point' which is supposed to have taken place at that time. I refer to RM Crawford's theory that a 'New Australia'—the phrase is Peter Coleman's, not Crawford's—came into being in the second half of the 1930s, and that from then on the whole stream of Australian life and thought, in public policy, social and economic attitudes, culture and letters, took a new course. The new and the stretched ideas and activities that have been cited in evidence do make an impressive list. The writers who have discussed the matter would include the great expansion of CSIRO, the recruitment of graduates to the Commonwealth Public Service, the generous patronage of culture, art and letters by the ABC and the Commonwealth Literary Fund, the formation of the Literature Censorship Board and the Contemporary Arts Society, the welcom-ing of Jewish refugees from Europe and the new liberalism towards immigration in general, the new confidence in industry and trade, and even such developments as the penetration of key unions by the Communist Party and the establishment of the National Secretariat of Catholic Action. These are perhaps the leading items from a catalogue which could of course grow to almost any size by the same principle of selection, that is, to take a handful of roughly contemporary things and regard them as a connected bundle.

As far as I am aware, no one yet has put the new aboriginal policy into the bundle. The omission is surely significant. But of what? Part at least of the answer, I suggest, can be given by extending the examination into the war years. So far as domestic affairs were concerned the main power-house of progressive social thought was the Department of Post-War Reconstruction. I have good authority for saying that the idea of taking the aboriginal situation as a challenge simply never occurred to the collective mind of that exciting and vital department. That more than anything else confirms me in my view that for all the quickening and deepening of the national stream only a trickle of new thought ran towards the aboriginal field, and it ran around the edges, not through the middle. The only natives we were prepared to think about at all seriously at this time were those of New Guinea. The aborigines came a bad second. This is not to say that the war years were a blank. There was some progressive thinking in the Northern Territory, where some excellent men found themselves too far ahead of government to make their ideas felt, and the new Commonwealth Department of Social Services also made some useful advances in association with federal and state aboriginal agencies and with missionary bodies. But aboriginal Australia simply could not compete with New Guinea either for public resources or for public interest. What with one thing and another the new policy of assimilation hung fire for more than a decade. I know that even in 1952, when I returned to the Northern Territory after a long absence, I could start to work very much where I had left off without any acute sense of change in the aboriginal life around me or in their relations with white Australia. There were some changes but they were more the effect of war and the new price-inflation than of policy.

I am therefore inclined to argue that the two 'turning points' had precious little to do with each other. I suspect that the achievement of the new policy of assimilation was the product of a compartment of Australian thought and experience quite separate from and much weaker than that which led to the great energising of the rest of Australian society and culture. The 'feedback' from the greater into the lesser movement—the 'trickle' I spoke of—was entirely minimal. There is small doubt in my mind that that continues to be the case, and that it is one of the main reasons for the slowness with which we are mastering our aboriginal problems. It is absurd that so small a part of the talent and ingenuity that exist in our departments of state, our great private industries, our universities and our research organisations should be turned toward these problems.

I will not pursue that theme further for the moment, although I will come back to it. I want instead to pick up a dropped thread. It seems clear to me now that the change of attitude and policy towards the aborigines which we trace back to the 1930s was confined very largely to a rather small group of people who had special associations with their care, administration or study. Outside that group the changes made very little impact for a long time and, within the group, it was a case of the faithful preaching to the converted about a 'revolution' which in fact had arrived only for them. The situation has altered very considerably in the last five or six years—witness, for example, the Referendum of 1967—but has a very long way to go before we are justified in using words which, like 'revolution', suggest a total change of heart and mind.

Turning this thought over in my mind the other day I asked myself whether it could be tested for truth-value even if only in part. If, for example, the two 'turning points' were not as I suggested distinct and separate, but were connected in some vital way; that is to say, if more than a very few people had been aware of a struggle waged and won in the aboriginal field, surely (or so I argued) there should have been a marked response from the 'New Australia' that was coming into being after the late 1930s; surely the serious literature from that time on should show some evidence of a consciousness that here was another old, cluttered field to renovate by the new progressive thought. I put to one side the large array of technical papers and books expressly concerned with the aborigines, such as Paul Hasluck's *Our Southern Half Castes* (1938) and *Black Australians* (1941) and EJB Foxcroft's *Australian Native Policy* (1941), and looked instead at a mixed lot of histories and commentaries dealing with Australian affairs in a more general way. They seemed to me the sort of books that probably expressed well enough, and may even have helped to form, the outlook of socially conscious people between say, 1939 and 1955, by which time some objections of a serious kind were beginning to be made to the idea of assimilation.

The first book I looked at was M Barnard Eldershaw's *My Australia* (1939). The aborigines figure quite prominently in it; their affairs, indeed, make up nearly one tenth of the book; but it is only too clear that they are marginal, and in a deeper sense, irrelevant to the author's story. Hardly a word on the other 280 pages would have to be changed if they were dropped from the prologue ('A mask of Australia for inaudible voices') and if one chapter ('The Dispossessed') were snipped out.

The writers take over from WK Hancock his thesis that 'in truth, a hunting and pastoral economy cannot co-exist within the same bounds', but they do not like his plain language, and they prefer to say that 'the twentieth century and the Stone Age cannot live together'. They also have it that the white man did the black man 'very little wilful harm' and that the rest was 'inevitable'. The revolution of attitudes had certainly not arrived for these writers. In the next book, Hartley Grattan's Introducing Australia (1942), we are given a good thumbnail sketch of old, familiar facts. I could not deny that Grattan has a sense of change: he mentions it in one sentence on one of his 300 pages. But Brian Fitzpatrick's The Australian People (1946) does not show even this degree of awareness. Only one or two of his 260 pages makes any mention of the aborigines and, although it says well what it has to say, it is all backward-turned.

Much the same is the case with HL Harris's Australia in the Making: A History (1948). There are some fragments about Dampier, Banks, Cook and Sturt, but there it ends. The next book, Geoffrey Rawson's Australia (1948), has a chapter entitled 'Aborigines', which also deals with wild life, so the title could as well have been 'Aborigines and Other Fauna', after the style of John Henderson, who in 1832 wrote some 'Observations on Zoology, from the order Insecta to that of Mammalia; the latter including the Natives of New Holland'. I then turned to the 1950s, hoping for rather better things. My hand fell first on RM Crawford's splendid little book Australia (1952). There is a chapter on the aborigines; not the shortest chapter, and not a tail-piece, but one full of good information and well-moulded general statements, and—a great novelty, this—a lively awareness of questions which historians ought to have but apparently had not, asked; for example, what were the relations between the squatters and the aborigines? But there is little that bears on either of the 'turning points'. The next was George Caiger's The Australian Way of Life (1953), in which the word 'aboriginal' is not to be found; no, I am wrong; it does occur—once, in a caption under a photograph which displays two of Australia's scenic attractions, the aborigines and Coogee Beach. To the next book, WV Aughterson's Taking Stock: Aspects of Mid-Century Life in Australia (1953), there were ten contributors. Only one of them, Alan McCulloch, the art critic, has anything to say about the aborigines, some passing but perceptive observations on their art. Incidentally, the book opens with a chapter entitled 'The Australian Way of Life', written by WEH Stanner, who can safely be presumed never to have heard of the aborigines, because he does not refer to them and even maintains that Australia has 'no racial divisions like America'. (At this point in my reading I could hardly resist feeling that all the authors so far mentioned should surely have used M Barnard Eldershaw's title 'My Australia'; that, clearly, was what they were writing about.) The intense concentration on ourselves and our affairs continues in Gordon Greenwood's *Australia: A Social and Political History* (1955). The other books by comparison are in the light or middleweight divisions; this one is nearly a heavyweight. It sets out to give a broad but comparatively detailed study of our history; to discover significant elements and the organic relations between them; to reveal the essential spirit and the dominant characteristics of each stage; and, more, to show 'what gathering forces transmuted the existing society into another, different in outlook and constitution'. It is written by six eminent scholars and has been reprinted half a dozen times, so it seems to have been influential. How does it deal with the aborigines? It mentions them five times—twice, quite briefly, for the period 1788–1821; twice again, as briefly, for the period 1820–1850; once, in sidelong fashion, for the period 1851–1892; and thereafter not at all.

Here I was, then, 17 years after the 'turning point' in aboriginal policy, only to find that some of our most perceptive thinkers seemed to be unaware of it or if they were had nothing to say about it. Perhaps they were right; perhaps in 1955 there were still no 'gathering forces' seeking to 'transmute' aboriginal-European relations; perhaps my theory of two unrelated compartments of Australian life and thought could have something in it. By picking and choosing a little I went on to persuade myself that for a number of writers the lack of interest ran on even into the 1960s. For example, Peter Coleman's *Australian Civilization* (1962) leaves little of our life and thought unexamined but by its total silence on all matters aboriginal seems to argue that the racial structure which is part of our anatomy of life has no connection with our civilisation past, present, or future.

I need not extend the list. A partial survey is enough to let me make the point that inattention on such a scale cannot possibly be explained by absent-mindedness. It is a structural matter, a view from a window which has been carefully placed to exclude a whole quadrant of the landscape. What may well have begun as a simple forgetting of other possible views turned under habit and over time into something like a cult of forgetfulness practised on a national scale. We have been able for so long to disremember the aborigines that we are now hard put to keep them in mind even when we most want to do so. It might help to break the cult of disremembering if someone made a searching study of the moral, intellectual and social transitions noticeable in aboriginal affairs from the 1930s to the 1960s. It seems to me to beg to be written.

I am no historian and I should stick to my last but the history I would like to see written would bring into the main flow of its narrative the life and times of men like David Unaiipon, Albert Namatjira, Robert Tudawali, Durmugam, Douglas Nicholls, Dexter Daniels and many others. Not to scrape up significance for them but because they typify so vividly the other side of a story over which the great Australian silence reigns; the story of the things we were unconsciously resolved not to discuss with them or treat with them about; the story, in short, of the unacknowledged relations between two racial groups within a single field of life supposedly unified by the principle of assimilation, which has been the marker of the transition. The telling of it would have to be a world—perhaps I should say an underworld—away from the conventional histories of the coming and development of British civilisation. I hardly see that it could afford two assumptions. One is that it satisfies the canons of human relevance and social influence to allow men of the kind I have mentioned to flit across the pages as if they were the Benelongs and Colbys of the day. The other is that the several hundred thousand aborigines who lived and died between 1788 and 1938 were but negative facts of history and, having been negative, were in no way consequential for the modern period. In aboriginal Australia there is an oral history which is providing these people with a coherent principle of explanation of which I will speak later. It has a directness and a candour which cut like a knife through most of what we say and write. We would have to bring this material—let me be fashionable and call it 'ethno-history'—into the sweep of our story.

One consequence of having given the aborigines no place in our past except that of 'a melancholy footnote' is both comical and serious. Comical, because one of the larger facts of the day is the aboriginal emergence into contemporary affairs but about all we can say, on the received version of our history, is the rising twin of that immortal observation, 'from this time on the native question sank into unimportance'. Serious, because the surfacing of problems which are in places six or seven generations deep confront us with problems of decision, but we are badly under-equipped to judge whether policies towards the problems are slogans, panaceas or sovereign remedies, or none of them.

In one sense, of course, the historians have been right. It is incontestable that few of the great affairs of the past took any sort of account of the continued aboriginal presence. It is also the case that some great affairs of the present—the plans for the development of sub-tropical Australia—take all too little account of the continued aboriginal presence there. But it is precisely this situation which calls for a less shallow, less ethnocentric social history. Fish swim in water, and what we do with our fins, gills and tails is not un-related to the permissive-resistant medium in which we move. For example, it occurred a long time ago to WG Spence, that father-figure of trade unionism, that the weakness of our system of local government was connected with the rapid decimation of local native populations. As he saw it we did not devolve protective and other powers locally because there was no need to do so. The medium was in that respect permissive. But a poorly working parish pump is at one end of a scale. Let me go to the other end. All land in Australia is held in consequence of an assumption so large, grand and remote from actuality that it had best be called royal, which is exactly what it was. The continent at occupation was held to be disposable because it was assumed to be 'waste and desert'. The truth was that identifiable aboriginal groups held identifiable parcels of land by unbroken occupancy from a time beyond which, quite literally, 'the memory of man runneth not to the contrary'. The titles which they claimed were conceded by all their fellows. There are still some parts of Australia, including some of the regions within which development is planned or actually taking place, in which living aborigines occupy and use lands that have never been 'waste and desert' and to which their titles could be demonstrated, in my opinion beyond cavil, to a court of fact if there were such a court. In such areas if the Crown title were paraded by, and if the aborigines understood what was happening, every child would say, like the child in the fairy-tale, 'but the Emperor is naked'. The medium, in this matter once permissive, is now turning resistant, and the fact is one of the barely acknowledged elements of the real structure of Australia which is working its way towards a more overt expression. Like many another fact overlooked, or forgotten, or reduced to an anachronism, and thus consigned to the supposedly inconsequential past, it requires only a suitable set of conditions to come to the surface, and be very consequential indeed.

I hardly think that what I have called 'the great Australian silence' will survive the research that is now in course. Our universities and research institutes are full of young people who are working actively to end it. The Australian Institute of Aboriginal Studies and the Social Science Research Council of Australia have both promoted studies which will bring the historical and the contemporary dimensions together and will assuredly persuade scholars to renovate their categories of understanding. If we could have done this in the 1920s and 1930s, perhaps we would not have had to wait until the middle 1950s to see any real product of the new 'positive' policy. For example, the effort to preserve the aborigines within inviolable reserves was the last ditch of an older policy, and we were then beyond the last ditch. I do not recall that we asked ourselves at all clearly: what comes *after* a policy which *by definition* is one of *last resort*? The inability to ask the question in that way left us, not rebels without cause, but doctors without a diagnosis, and it is interesting to recall how few people then thought in terms of some of the notable advances that have in fact come about—the grant of equal political status, the suffrage, the extension of civil liberties, the ending of legal discrimination, the right to social services, and other things of the kind. One wonders what equivalent astigmatisms may affect our contemporary vision. I will suggest later that one of them is a certain inability to grasp that on the evidence the aborigines have always been looking for two things: a decent union of their lives with ours but on terms that let them preserve their own identity, not their inclusion willy-nilly in our scheme of things and a fake identity, but development within a new way of life that has the imprint of their own ideas. But that is a topic for another lecture, and I want now to round out what I have been saying.

The impulse to make radical changes in the aboriginal situation had little force or product until the last decade. Twenty years of the 'revolution' were thus years of the locust. The ideal of assimilation took shape when no one dreamed that galloping development would overrun all of aboriginal Australia, and no one devised a very convincing human strategy or technical method even for the older circumstances. We thus enter on a new time with a heavy backlog of unsolved older problems. A glance at the human map of Australia still shows one of the worst of them. The map is disfigured by hundreds of miserable camps which are the social costs of old-style development that would not let any consideration of aboriginal interest stand in its way. Development over the next 50 years will need to change its style and its philosophy if the outcome is to be very different. I have begun to allow myself to believe that there is now a credible prospect of that happening. A kind of beneficial multiplier could be starting to have effect. One notices the coming together of things from different starting points. The private industries which use and in some measure may depend on aboriginal labour do not all resist as they once did the idea that it is in their interest to habilitate this broken society. We may see a market take shape in private industry for workable proposals. The public instrumentalities concerned with aboriginal affairs have a head of steam towards their tasks which was not the common rule a few years ago. The flow of public funds specifically earmarked for aboriginal advancement is relatively generous. Some very worthwhile ideas are starting to come forward from some sectors of the aboriginal population. Perhaps the one thing now needed to increase the power of the multiplier is a projection of the costs, monetary and social, that will be a charge on the national pocket in default of a rapid advance of the aboriginal people to self-support. A native population which promises to double itself well within 20 years will otherwise become a fiscal problem of magnitude.

One cannot talk of everything, even in a generous series of lectures of this kind, and I must now narrow my span to one of the things that interfere with our judgment of a scene that is being transformed under our eyes. That is to say, our folklore about the aborigines. It had a lot to do with the making of our racial difficulties and it still has a lot to do with maintaining them.

Sir Zelman Cowen

Sir Zelman Cowen is a former Governor-General, lawyer and educator born in Melbourne in 1919 and educated at Scotch College and the universities of Melbourne and Oxford. He was the Victorian Rhodes Scholar for 1940 and won the Supreme Court Prize in 1941.

After war service in the RAN, he went to Oxford and became a Fellow and tutor of Oriel College. From 1951 to 1966, he was Professor of Public Law and Dean of the Faculty of Law in the University of Melbourne. He was appointed Emeritus Professor there in 1967 and in the same year became vice-chancellor of New England University, a position he held until 1970. Professor Cowen was the vice-chancellor of the University of Queensland until 1977. In that year he was appointed Governor-General, succeeding Sir John Kerr, serving until 1982.

Sir Zelman, who was knighted in 1977, was provost of Oriel College at Oxford from 1982 until 1990. During that period he was chairman of the British Press Council from 1983 to 1988.

Sir Zelman has held a number of visiting professorships, many to American universities, including twice to Harvard. His awards and honours are too many to mention here. He has served on numerous boards throughout his career, including the board of governors of Tel Aviv University, honorary Master of the Bench at Gray's Inn, London, chairman of the Australian National Academy of Music, president of the Order of Australia Association, the board of The Australian Opera, among many others. He was a non-executive director of John Fairfax Holdings 1994–97.

As well, he has written extensively on political and legal topics and was the biographer of Sir Isaac Isaacs, the first Australian Governor-General.

His Boyer Lectures, titled *The Private Man*, examine the manifold threats to the privacy of the individual and suggest how this problem might be addressed as a matter of social policy and law. There were no doubt issues which engaged Sir Zelman, in particular during his subsequent service to the British Press Council. 'The Right to be Let Alone' was his first lecture and is reproduced here; it was followed by 'The Goldfish Bowl'; 'The Clandestine Observer'; 'The Computer and the Dossier', which was a remarkable early warning message, and 'The Beleagured Private Man', the conclusion to which includes: 'The protection of privacy will be better assured by appropriate legal protections and procedures, but it also depends to a very great extent upon the attitudes of men and women in democratic society to the values which are enshrined in the claim to privacy'.

THE RIGHT TO BE
LET ALONE

The Private Man

Sir Zelman Cowen

• 1969 •

No man, wrote John Donne more than three hundred years ago, is an island entire of itself. Hell, says Jean-Paul Sartre in our times, is other people. Both men look at the human situation from very different points of view, and both have valid things to say about it. Few would deny the reality of human interdependence: we have responsibilities and obligations to one another, even though our performance is often inadequate, even woeful. But it is also the case that the apparatus of political and social organisation erodes our island quality, our personal autonomy. In some senses modern urban society affords more privacy than an older village society; the size and impersonality of our cities and suburbs, the character of our dwellings, our occupational and residential mobility allow of some escape from the watchful prying eyes and tattling voices of neighbours. But in other respects we live lives crowded in upon one another; our political masters demand of us an ever growing accounting of our lives and affairs. It is not only our political masters who call for this, for the recording of details and histories and performance and malperformance is carried on by corporations and enterprises for a variety of purposes. The sellers, the pollsters, the social scientists and investigators, the employers and their agents the management consultants, the peddlers in motivation research, call for a great mass of information about us. 'In our record-keeping civilisation,' we are told, 'the man whose name is not inscribed on the tab of someone's manilla folder simply does not exist. Each of us from the day he is born begins to deposit information about himself in various public and private files. By the time he emerges from school and the armed forces, the ordinary young adult cannot have escaped becoming the subject of at least a dozen personal information files. Our necessary social interdependence assures an acceleration at the rate at which personal data are accumulated and stored.' Until yesterday it has been manilla folders; it becomes increasingly a computer record, which stores and organises an even wider range of data about each of us.

Virginia Woolf has written with disdain about the peculiar repulsiveness of those who dabble their fingers in the stuff of others' souls. I have so far spoken about the mass, and the increasing accessibility of the mass of recorded information, there are other forms of surveillance, psychological and electronic. Some men earn their keep by prying into the lives of others, to inform their clients for fee whether those overseen or overheard are criminal, adulterous, employable: worse still, some peddle their machines and devices to titillate the dirty-minded. Then there are the claims of the media of mass communication to 'the right to know' and to make known. Edward Shils, the American sociologist, has written of the growth of the popular press which produced a 'new sector of the profession of journalism that regarded the penetration of the private spheres as its main occupational task. It justified this penetration by reference to the satisfaction of popular desires and the freedom of the press to enlighten the public.' The mass of people, so far from resisting these intrusions, welcome and encourage them. Candid cameras give pleasure, 'the intimacies of other persons are "interesting", and when they are degrading to the mighty and great, they are all the more acceptable.'

The objector to all of this is charged with being captious, with seeking to impose restraints on activities which lie at the heart of democratic processes, with impeding the legitimate and difficult operations of law enforcement. There are good points here, and one who argues for the imposition of restraints in the interests of the protection of privacy, cannot do so in absolute terms. The constant search, in democratic society, we are reminded, must be for the definition of a proper boundary line in each specific situation and for an overall equilibrium that serves to strengthen democratic institutions and processes.

I have called these lectures The Private Man because I am becoming increasingly troubled by the threats to the privacy of the individual citizen. In the face of all the pressures and threats, I believe that the claim to privacy is a matter of great and increasing importance in our crowded society with its unbelievable technological resources and inventiveness. A man without privacy is a man without dignity; the fear that Big Brother is watching and listening threatens the freedom of the individual no less than the prison bars. The reference to Big Brother, as most will know, is to the late George Orwell's 1984 and to the society which he foresaw less than 40 years on when an all enveloping political organisation would have totally destroyed the individuality of its people; when simply by flicking a switch, Big Brother could know at any time what anyone was doing. Twenty years of Orwell's time have already run out, and his cautionary tale remains vivid in many minds. An article in an American journal last year bore the chilling title '1984—minus 16 and counting'. A little earlier, the London Economist noted that 'there are only nineteen years left until 1984, but American electronic listening devices will meet the deadline easily'. In all of this, there is naught for our comfort.

Why *should* we have concern for the private man? There are many who say that he has no place at all in our world. In the totalitarian states of recent days and our own day, the claim to privacy is utterly rejected. The man whose time cannot be accounted for, who has a life concealed from others, is likely to be suspected of treasonable or at least non-conforming activities. The totalitarian master assails the claim of the private man as 'immoral', 'anti-social', as 'part of the cult of individualism'. Expressed in more general terms, it is said that the individual has meaning only in a social context, so that the claim to privacy is simply an exhibition of caprice, triviality and irresponsibility. The moral realisation of the individual depends entirely upon the degree to which he identifies his interests and duties with the value structure appropriate to the particular society in which he finds himself. Unlike democratic society, totalitarian organisation claims secrecy for the regime and full surveillance over the lives of groups and individuals. I reject this utterly; I believe very deeply that the political structure is a collectivity whose legitimacy derives from and depends on the private individual judgments of the persons who are comprised in it. I say with the American writer, Clinton Rossiter, that:

> Privacy is a special kind of independence which can be understood as an attempt to secure autonomy in at least a few personal and spiritual concerns, if necessary in defiance of all the pressures of modern society . . . (It) seeks to erect an unbreakable wall of dignity and reserve against the entire world. The free man is the private man, the man who still keeps some of his thoughts and judgments entirely to himself, who feels no overriding *compulsion* to share everything of value with others, not even with those he loves and trusts.

It seems to me that this is a modest but persuasive statement of the claim to privacy. It is a claim for individuals and for groups; it is based upon a psychological judgment that the growth and development of the individual person depends in part (and of course only in part), upon a conceded area of solitude and anonymity; it asserts that without privacy one cannot in a meaningful sense be an individual. Only those who can sustain an absolute commitment to the ideal of perfection can survive total surveillance, and I do not believe that they exist among ordinary men in ordinary society. A man must therefore have some place, some area of 'social space' into which he can withdraw in solitude and anonymity. Who among men can know what he thinks and feels if he never has the opportunity to be alone with his acts, thoughts and feelings? A crucial aspect of the autonomy of the individual, therefore, must be his claim to make his independent decision when to 'go public'. A man's privacy is his safety valve; he has in it his permissible area of deviation, his opportunity to give vent to what he would not express or do publicly; within these private limits he may share confidences and intimacies with those he trusts and he may set boundaries to those confidences. What is involved in the claim to privacy is well stated by Alan Westin when he says that:

> the basic point is that each individual must within the larger context of his culture, his status and his personal situation, make a continuous adjustment between his needs for solitude and for companionship; for intimacy and general social intercourse, for anonymity and responsible participation in society; for reserve and disclosure. A free society leaves this choice to the individual, for this is the eve of the 'right of individual privacy'—the right of the individual to decide for himself with only extraordinary exceptions in the interests of society when and on what terms his acts should be revealed to the general public.

It is worthwhile stressing the points which emerge from this: the claim to privacy protects an individual's *solitude*, his *intimacy* in various groups of his own choosing, his *anonymity*, his ability to be lost, without identification, in a crowd, his *reserve*, his shutting himself off from unwanted intrusion.

To me, this claim to privacy is clear beyond doubt; I see it as one of the truly profound values of a civilised society. I believe that it is important that it should be so recognised: important because the contemporary political and social organisation, aided by a formidable technology, has forced us to become aware that the privacy which until now we took for granted and even casually presumed as an ingredient of moral action, simply can no longer be presumed but must be specified. What also must be specified are the threats, actual and impending, to that privacy, and the action to be taken to meet those threats.

The problem is not without recognition. It has been recognised in various international declarations, instruments and statements. Article 12 of the Universal Declaration of Human Rights adopted by the General Assembly of the United Nations in 1948 stated that 'no one shall be subjected to arbitrary interference with his privacy, family, home or correspondence, or to attacks upon his honour and reputation'. The terms of the Declaration emphasised protection against the activities of secret police and the officers of public authority, and the abominable activities of the Gestapo were then fresh in memory. But the terms in which the right was expressed were broader than that. The same principle was written into the later United Nations Convention on Civil and Political Rights which further provided that 'everyone has the right to the protection of the law against such interference or attacks'. At a non-official level, an international Conference of the International Commission of Jurists at Stockholm in 1967 made a more comprehensive and specific examination of the right to privacy and of the steps necessary to protect it. In 1968 an international conference on Human Rights convened by the United Nations at Teheran called for an international study of problems with respect to human rights arising from developments in science and technology, particularly with regard to (1) respect for human life in view of recording techniques, (2) protection of the human personality and its physical and intellectual integrity in view of developments in biology, medicine and biochemistry, and (3) the uses of electronics which may affect the rights of the person and the limits which should be placed on their uses in a democratic society. In the 20 years which have elapsed between the adoption of the Universal Declaration of Human Rights and the Teheran Conference, it is significant to note the stress on the development of technology which has made it possible for a close surveillance to be maintained over the lives and activities of individuals and groups.

Historically, the most famous piece of writing on privacy—at least from a lawyer's standpoint—was an article published in the Harvard Law Review in 1890 by two lawyers, Samuel Warren and Louis Brandeis. The article was said to have been provoked by excesses of press publicity, of which Warren and his family were the irritated victims. In arguing for a legal remedy to protect individual privacy, the authors drew attention to 'recent inventions and business methods (which) call attention to the next steps which must be taken for the protection of the person, and for securing to the individual . . . the right "to be let alone".' There followed a disquisition on the iniquities of the press:

> The press is overstepping in every direction the obvious bounds of propriety and of decency. Gossip is no longer the resource of the idle and of the vicious, but has become a trade, which is pursued with industry as well as effrontery . . . To occupy the indolent, column upon column is filled with idle gossip which can only be procured by intrusion upon the domestic circle. The intensity and complexity of life, attendant upon advancing civilization, have rendered necessary some retreat from the world and man, under the refining influence of culture, has become more sensitive to publicity, so that solitude and privacy have become more essential to the individual, but modern enterprise and invention have, through invasion upon his privacy, subjected him to mental pain and distress, far greater than could be inflicted by mere bodily agony.

It was strongly stated, and what the authors sought was a remedy in the law to protect the privacy of individuals and groups against such excesses.

Almost 40 years later, and by this time a distinguished Justice of the Supreme Court of the United States, Brandeis returned to the matter. In a case in which the issue before the Supreme Court was whether evidence obtained by eavesdropping, by telephone tapping, was admissible against a man charged with crime, Brandeis, in dissent, declared that it was not. In a famous and prophetic passage he declared:

> Discovery and invention have made it possible for the Government by means far more effective than stretching upon the rack to obtain disclosure in court of what is whispered in the closet. . . . The progress of science in furnishing the Government with means of espionage is not likely to stop with wire-tapping. Ways may some day be developed by which the Government, without removing papers from secret drawers, can reproduce them in court, and by which it will be enabled to expose to a jury the most intimate occurrences of the home. Advances in the psychic and related sciences may bring means of exploring unexpressed beliefs, thoughts and emotions. The makers of the Constitution . . . sought to protect Americans in their beliefs, their thoughts, their emotions and their sensations. They conferred as against the Government the right to be let alone—the most comprehensive of rights and the right most valued by civilized man.

Brandeis' phrase 'the right to be let alone'—which indeed had been used by Cooley before him—has virtually passed into the language. It took 40 years for the doctrine he expressed in dissent to become, by reversal of the earlier decision, the law of the land. We shall see a little later how in the intervening years American courts came to grapple with more general questions relating to the privacy of the person. Apart from what has been done by the courts, there have been many notable voices of public men and of scholars in the United States raised against the perceived and serious threats to privacy. In his State of the Union Message to Congress in January 1967, President Johnson referred specifically to Brandeis' right most valued by civilised man in calling for the prohibition by law of wiretapping both public and private, with limited exceptions to safeguard the national security, and even then only under the strictest safeguards. The President called for a major effort to outlaw electronic eavesdropping and snooping generally. Senior officers of the administration, officers of state governments, and committees and individual members of both Houses of the Congress have addressed themselves to various aspects of the problem of protecting privacy: to such issues as wiretapping and eavesdropping, the existence and use of computer data banks, personality and polygraph tests, and to the protection of privacy generally.

In the United Kingdom, writers, judges and members of parliament have written, spoken and acted on problems arising out of threats to privacy. Some years ago, a distinguished Liberal leader, Lord Samuel, introduced a Liberties of the Subject Bill which dealt with some issues bearing on privacy. In 1961 Lord Mancroft introduced a Bill in the House of Lords 'to give every individual such further protection against the invasion of privacy as may be desirable for the maintenance of human dignity, while protecting the right of the public to be kept informed in all matters in which the public may be concerned'. In 1967 a member of the House of Commons introduced a Right of Privacy Bill 'to protect a person from any unreasonable and serious interference with his seclusion of himself, his family or his property, from the public'. Private members have proposed particular measures, all bearing on questions of privacy. In 1967 there was an Unauthorized Telephone Monitoring Bill, in 1968 an Industrial Espionage Bill, and this year a Data Surveillance Bill. These are not the voices of 'far out' men; a number of sponsors have been Conservative members. The present Lord Chancellor, Lord Gardiner, has written and spoken on the need to protect privacy, and groups of lawyers, practising and academic, have argued powerfully and persuasively in favour of general and particular action to this end. The British National Council for Civil Liberties has recently mounted a campaign to draw attention to the wide front on which the privacy of the individual has been threatened.

In Australia, there is a growing concern with the problem. Sir John Barry of the Supreme Court of Victoria has been an articulate and eloquent writer on the threat to privacy, and has drawn particular attention to the dangers posed by the use of electronic and eavesdropping devices. Mr Justice Selby of the Supreme Court of New South Wales has called firmly for legislation to regulate their use, pointing to the threats they pose to privacy and freedom of expression. Commonwealth legislation imposing substantial restrictions on the tapping of telephone conversations has been in operation for some years, and there has been recent discussion at conferences of Commonwealth and State Attorneys-General of the specific issue of bugging and eavesdropping, and legislation has been introduced in Victoria and New South Wales to deal with listening devices. I shall speak later of this particular problem and the Australian legislative responses to it. There has been some discussion of the protection of privacy on a wider front at the first Australian Convention of the Council of Civil Liberties in 1968 when some able and well informed papers were presented. The problems posed by computer data banks have also been discussed somewhat technically at computer conferences, but with an awareness of the privacy aspect, and some legal scholars have published papers dealing with various aspects of privacy. It is some-what surprising in face of this that in the recent and comprehensive study Freedom in Australia by two able and senior Australian academic lawyers, privacy is all but ignored as a matter of serious concern. Even in a selective examination of the state of liberties in Australia, I am puzzled by this. There is, moreover, little general public awareness of the problems. This, I fear, is symptomatic of attitudes to civil liberties generally; it seems to me that we are too often inert and unseeing in the face of what seem to me to be serious invasions of the liberties of free men. In the case of privacy, these threats are often subtle and not readily perceived, and the appropriate responses are not always very clear. But in face of a fast developing technology the threats are very real. It is encouraging, then, that a body of active younger Australian citizens, the St George Jaycees, should have undertaken as a major project a study and report on the problems of protecting privacy. Their strong and detailed report entitled The Invasion of Privacy presented to the National Convention of Jaycees in 1968 is a notable document.

Their general conclusion is uncompromising:

> ... The right to personal privacy is being severely challenged by the demands of modern society in its never ceasing quest for efficiency and conformity. ... The growing awareness of a few thoughtful people is not sufficient to safeguard the right to privacy. There is a need to place before our community and business leaders the challenge of maintaining the dignity of the individual in a changing environment. There is also a need for us to realize our obligations to our fellow men. Bureaucratic zeal and the pursuit of efficiency have blinded many men to the need to preserve the basic dignities and freedom of their fellows.
>
> To maintain the role of free men in a free society we must insist on the right to be let alone.

THE SEVENTIES

EVENTS 1970 – 1979

1970

JANUARY
Muammar al-Qaddafi became Premier of Libya

First jumbo jet, Boeing 747, launched

FEBRUARY
Three Melbourne TV stations agreed to pay the VFL a total of $225,000 a year for four years to screen replays of VFL matches

Bertrand Russell died

APRIL
Australian Prime Minister, John Gorton, began troop with-drawal from Vietnam

Bicentennial celebration of landing by Captain Cook at Botany Bay

Sir William Dobell died

JUNE
Edward Heath became UK Prime Minister when Conservatives won election

SEPTEMBER
President Nassar of Egypt died, succeeded by Anwar Sadat

OCTOBER
West Gate Bridge, Melbourne, collapsed, killing 35 men

NOVEMBER
Salvador Allende became President of Chile

Pope Paul VI made first papal visit to Australia

Charles de Gaulle died

DECEMBER
Germaine Greer published *The Female Eunuch*

1971

JANUARY
Aswan High Dam across the Nile River in Egypt opened

Coco Chanel died

FEBRUARY
Idi Amin seized power in Uganda

MARCH
Malcolm Fraser triggered a dispute within the Liberal Party leading to the fall of Prime Minister John Gorton, who was succeeded by William McMahon

APRIL
President Nixon vowed to withdraw US troops from Vietnam

MAY
Neville Bonner selected by the Liberal Party to be a Senator for Queensland; became first Aboriginal Member of Parliament

Chips Rafferty died

JUNE
ALP Conference abandoned White Australia Policy

Japan became Australia's largest export market

JULY
Josip Tito re-elected for another five-year term as President of Yugoslavia

	All-Australian women's singles final at Wimbledon when Evonne Goolagong beat reigning champion Margaret Court
AUGUST	David Williamson play *Don's Party* opened at Melbourne's Pram Factory
	Prime Minister McMahon announced most Australian troops would be home from Vietnam by Christmas
	Oz Magazine editors jailed in UK for obscenity
SEPTEMBER	Former Soviet leader Nikita Khrushchev died
NOVEMBER	Australian Vietnam veterans given a great welcome home after the end of Australia's combat role
DECEMBER	Pakistan launched full-scale war against India—India won two weeks later

1972

JANUARY	Evonne Goolagong named Australian of the Year
	Britain joined EEC
FEBRUARY	Bangladesh (formerly East Pakistan) became separate country
	President Nixon visited China
	US resumed intensive bombing of North Vietnam
MAY	President Nixon visited Moscow; signed pact with Soviet leader Brezhnev
	J Edgar Hoover died
	Duke of Windsor, ex-King Edward VIII, died
JUNE	Knighthood conferred on Aboriginal Pastor Douglas Nicholls
JULY	Ord River Dam opened by Prime Minister McMahon
	All US land troops withdrawn from Vietnam
AUGUST	Opening of Munich Olympic Games
SEPTEMBER	Nine Israeli Olympic hostages killed after being seized by Arab guerillas at Munich Olympics
OCTOBER	Snowy River Scheme officially completed
NOVEMBER	Richard Nixon re-elected President in a landslide win over George McGovern
DECEMBER	Labor party, led by Gough Whitlam, won election for first time in 23 years
	Harry Truman died
	President Nixon ordered halt to Hanoi bombing
	David Malouf published *Johnno*

1973

JANUARY	Lyndon B Johnson died
	Peace Treaty brought Vietnam war to end
MARCH	Noel Coward died
APRIL	Pablo Picasso died
	Four senior White House aides resigned in wake of Watergate scandal
JUNE	Soviet leader Leonid Brezhnev visited US
	West German chancellor Willy Brandt visited Israel
JULY	Arthur Calwell died
	Bob Hawke became ALP President
	Nancy Mitford died
SEPTEMBER	Chile's President Allende killed in coup
	WH Auden died
OCTOBER	Sydney Opera House opened
	Pablo Casals died
	Oil prices increased by 70 per cent
	Patrick White won Nobel Prize for Literature
NOVEMBER	Egypt and Israel signed peace pact
	Self-government for Papua New Guinea
	California Governor Ronald Reagan visited Australia
DECEMBER	Referendum on control of prices and incomes defeated in every state

1974

JANUARY	Tertiary education fees abolished as Commonwealth takes over states financial responsibilities
	Film studio owner Sam Goldwyn died
FEBRUARY	Alexander Solzhenitsyn exiled from USSR
	Sir John Kerr appointed Governor-General by Whitlam Government, to succeed Sir Paul Hasluck
MARCH	WA Liberal–Country Party swept Labor from office, making Sir Charles Court Premier
APRIL	'Gair Affair' brought about double dissolution of Federal Parliament
	Following a public opinion poll, Whitlam Government announced 'Advance Australia Fair' as new national anthem
	Golda Meir resigned as Israeli Prime Minister
	French President Georges Pompidou died

MAY	Australian Presbyterian Church split over union with Methodist and Congregational Churches
	Dr Donald Coggan became Archbishop of Canterbury
	Helmut Schmidt became Chancellor of West Germany
	Sir Frank Packer died
	Artist Ian Fairweather died
	Duke Ellington died
	Giscard d'Estaing became French President
	Whitlam Government returned in narrow win
JUNE	Yitzhak Rabin became Prime Minister of Israel
	Joan Sutherland created a Dame
	Mikhail Baryshnikov defected from Soviet Union
JULY	General Franco handed over power to Prince Juan Carlos
	President of Argentina, Juan Peron died
AUGUST	President Richard Nixon resigned in face of impeachment charges; Gerald Ford became US President
	Unemployment in Australia topped 100,000 for first time since Depression
	Portugal gave independence to Angola and Mozambique
SEPTEMBER	Australian radio and television licences abolished
	NZ Prime Minister Norman Kirk died in office, succeeded by Wallace Rowling
	Haile Selassie, Emperor of Ethiopia, overthrown in coup after 44-year reign
OCTOBER	Violinist David Oistrakh died
	Colour telecasts began in Australia
NOVEMBER	Frank Crean sacked as Treasurer by Whitlam
DECEMBER	Cyclone Tracey hit Darwin

1975

JANUARY	Tasman Bridge in Hobart collapsed after being rammed by bulk carrier *Lake Illawarra*
FEBRUARY	Governor-General John Kerr announced establishment of Order of Australia
	Margaret Thatcher elected Tory leader
MARCH	Malcolm Fraser elected as Opposition leader
	Charlie Chaplain knighted
APRIL	Fall of Saigon

MAY	Khemlani loans scandal broke
	Mother Teresa visited Melbourne
JUNE	Whitlam sacked Jim Cairns and Clyde Cameron
	Lance Barnard resigned
	Swaziland re-opened
JULY	Medibank heath scheme started
AUGUST	Dmitry Shostakovich died
	Haile Selassie died
	Indonesia intervened in East Timor civil war against Portugese control
SEPTEMBER	Papua New Guinea became independent
	Former NSW premier Jack Lang died
OCTOBER	Malcolm Fraser provoked constitutional crisis by blocking supply
	Rex O'Connor resigned from Cabinet
NOVEMBER	Whitlam Government sacked by Governor-General Kerr. Election called
	General Franco died; Spanish monarchy re-established
DECEMBER	Coalition won Federal election in a landslide
	Picnic at Hanging Rock film was a success

1976

JANUARY	Zhou Enlai, first premier of People's Republic of China, died
FEBRUARY	Pat O'Shane became first Aborigine admitted to the Bar
MARCH	Harold Wilson resigned as British Prime Minister
APRIL	James Callaghan became British Prime Minister
JULY	US celebrated Bicentenary of Independence
	Montreal Olympics opened
AUGUST	'Blue Hills' ended after 27 years on air
SEPTEMBER	Mao Zedong died
NOVEMBER	Jimmy Carter elected US President, defeating Gerald Ford
DECEMBER	Benjamin Britten died

1977

JANUARY	Granville train disaster
FEBRUARY	ABBA toured Australia
MARCH	Celebration of Queen's Silver Jubilee
	Don Chipp resigned from Federal government to establish new party: the Australian Democrats

MAY	'Advance Australia Fair' confirmed as national anthem after winning a poll with one million margin out of six million votes lodged
	Kerry Packer launched World Series Cricket
JUNE	Uniting Church of Australia formed
	Spaniards went to polls for first time in 41 years
JULY	Sir John Kerr resigned as Governor-General, succeeded by Sir Zelman Cowen
	Donald Mackay disappeared in Griffith
AUGUST	Groucho Marx died
	Elvis Presley died
SEPTEMBER	Maria Callas died
	South African anti-apartheid activist Steve Biko died in detention
OCTOBER	Bing Crosby died
NOVEMBER	Egyptian President Anwar Sadat visited Israel
DECEMBER	Fraser Government returned in general electon with clear majority
	Bill Hayden became Labor leader
	Refugees began fleeing Vietnam as 'boat people'

1978

JANUARY	Aboriginal Land Rights Act proclaimed in Canberra, restoring some Northern Territory land to Aborigines
FEBRUARY	Sydney Hilton Hotel bombing during CHOGM conference
MAY	Government approved intake of 9000 Indo-Chinese refugees
	Sir Robert Menzies died
	Italian statesman Aldo Moro murdered by Red Brigade
JULY	Northern Territory achieved self-government
	Solomon Islands became independent of Britain
	Gough Whitlam resigned from Parliament
AUGUST	Pope Paul VI died
	President of Kenya, Jomo Kenyatta, died
SEPTEMBER	Pope John Paul I (Cardinal Luciani) elected, crowned, and died 33 days later
	South African Prime Minister Vorster resigned, succeeded by PW Botha

OCTOBER	Polish Cardinal Wojtyla elected Pope John Paul II
	Menachem Begin and Anwar Sadat shared Nobel Peace Prize
	Spanish Parliament adopted democratic constitution
	Johnny O'Keefe died
	Jacques Brel died
NOVEMBER	Martial law declared in Rhodesia
	Margaret Mead died
	Norman Rockwell died
DECEMBER	Golda Meir died
	Fundamentalist uprising in Iran against Shah

1979

JANUARY	Shah of Iran driven into exile
	Rhodesian whites voted for black majority rule
FEBRUARY	Chinese troops invaded Vietnam as punitive measure for Vietnam's invasion of Cambodia
MARCH	Ayatollah Khomeini took control in Iran—said there is no place for democracy in Islamic republic
	Egypt and Israel signed peace treaty
APRIL	First black Prime Minister of Rhodesia elected, Bishop Abel Muzowera
	Idi Amin overthrown in Uganda
	Ex-Prime Minister Bhutto executed in Pakistan
MAY	Margaret Thatcher became British Prime Minister in Conservative election victory
JUNE	Rhodesia renamed Zimbabwe
	Pope John Paul II visited Poland
	President Jimmy Carter and Soviet leader Leonid Brezhnev met for first time and signed SALT Treaty
JULY	Australian intake of Indo-Chinese refugees rose to 14,000 annually
AUGUST	Lord Mountbatten and family members killed by IRA bomb

HC Coombs

Herbert Cole 'Nugget' Coombs was born in Kalamunda, Western Australia, in 1906. He was educated at the Perth Modern School, the University of Western Australia, and the London School of Economics.

With a brilliant academic record, Dr Coombs rose rapidly through the public sector; he was appointed assistant economist of the Commonwealth Bank in 1935, economist to the Commonwealth Treasury in 1939, and director of rationing in 1942. He performed the influential role of director of post-war reconstruction from 1943 to 1949 when, at only 42, he was appointed governor of the Commonwealth Bank at a time when it combined savings, trading and central bank functions. When Prime Minister Menzies created the Reserve Bank in 1959, Coombs became its first governor. He held this position until 1968, having influenced the Australian economy for almost 30 years, advising seven prime ministers.

Dr Coombs was associated with the Australian National University from its foundation, and was its chancellor from 1968 to 1976. He then became a visiting fellow in the University's Centre for Resource and Environmental Studies.

He was deeply committed to Aboriginal issues and concerns. He chaired the Australian Council for Aboriginal Affairs, which he had initiated, from 1968 to 1976. He published extensively on Aboriginal matters.

Dr Coombs also displayed a long commitment to the arts: he was founding chairman of the Australian Elizabethan Theatre Trust from 1954 to 1968, a period when it effectively created The Australian Ballet, The Australian Opera and the state theatre companies. He was founding chairman of the Australian Council for the Arts (now the Australia Council) from 1968 to 1974.

Dr Coombs was Australian of the Year in 1972.

He died in 1997.

Dr Coombs chose as the subject of his Boyer Lectures *The Fragile Pattern—Institutions and Man*. He was extraordinarily well qualified to write about institutions for he was a founder of institutions: institutions ranging from wartime rationing structures to post-war reconstructions, performing arts bodies to arts funding structures, the Australian National University to the Council for Aboriginal Affairs.

As implied by his individual lecture titles—'Institutions Maketh the Man'; 'Are Good Intentions Enough'; 'Is Man Another Crown of Thorns' reproduced here, 'Shall We Join the Dropouts' and 'The Measure is Man'—Dr Coombs was concerned 'that we assert our control over the institutions we have made and the influence they exert over us.'

IS MAN ANOTHER CROWN OF THORNS?

The Fragile Pattern: Institutions and Man

HC Coombs

• 1970 •

In my last talk I looked at some successes which had been achieved in adapting our economic system to the welfare of those who work within it but went on to note some unhappy side effects of these successes—side effects which led one to question the absoluteness of the objective of growth which underlies our present economic strategy.

Another factor contributing to the built-in growth of a modern industrial economy is the increasing provision for military activity and preparedness. Modern warfare having become so technically sophisticated, the influence of military institutions on other parts of society must cause profound disquiet. No one would consider the late President Eisenhower an alarmist. Having been himself a distinguished soldier before he faced the problems of political decision in affairs military, he was well equipped to assess the pressures of professional and economic interest which can be brought to bear on such decisions. In his farewell address he said:

> Our military organization today bears little relation to that known by any of my predecessors in peacetime or by the fighting men of World War II or Korea.
>
> Until the latest of our world conflicts, the United States had no armaments industry. American makers of ploughshares could, with time and as required, make swords as well. But we can no longer risk emergency improvisation of national defence: we have been compelled to create a permanent armaments industry of vast proportions. Added to this, three and a half million men and women are directly engaged in the defense establishment. We annually spend on military security more than the net income of all United States corporations.
>
> The conjunction of an immense military establishment and a large

arms industry is new in American experience. The total influence—economic, political, even spiritual—is felt in every city, every State House, every office of the Federal Government. We recognise the imperative need for this development. Yet we must not fail to comprehend its grave implications. Our toil, our resources, our livelihood are all involved: so is the very structure of our society.

In the councils of government we must guard against the acquisition of unwarranted influence, whether sought or unsought, by the military-industrial complex. The potential for the disastrous rise of misplaced power exists and will persist.

We must never let the weight of this combination endanger our liberties or democratic processes. We should take nothing for granted. Only an alert and knowledgeable citizenry can compel the proper meshing of the huge industrial and military machine of defense with our peaceful methods and goals so that security and liberty may prosper together.

These are wise words—meet to be heeded by us all—even in countries where the concentration of military and industrial power is not yet so overwhelming. There is, however, a third element in this concentration to which the late President gives no mention but which in some ways is even more disturbing—i.e. the degree to which science (the search for knowledge and understanding of the Universe) is itself geared to the military complex. We have in the past thought of scientists as men dedicated to the pursuit of truth—deriving their opportunities and their incomes from independent and disinterested sources and their status from the professional judgment of their fellows. Increasingly over the post-war decades the problems with which they have been concerned, and the financial material resources which they have employed in their study of them, have derived increasingly from the military establishment. It may already be that among some the independence and integrity of learning and of research are being corrupted by this dependence.

Furthermore, who could be sure that, threatened with economic disorder from serious contraction of military spending, and bewildered by ignorance and special pleading, the citizenry would, as the late President hoped, be sufficiently alert and knowledgeable to defend their peaceful methods and goals. We have in our own time seen in Germany a community lay down its resistance to domestic tyranny and acquiesce in aggression against its neighbours for the promise of employment and of profits for industry.

I would like to turn now to an aspect of the human condition which is another example of apparent success producing side-effects of potentially disastrous order. The combined efforts of the economic system and the medical profession equipped with modern science and technology have made man the dominant species in every environment he inhabits. This dominance is so absolute that his numbers are growing at a staggering rate while all other species, except those felt by him to contribute directly to his dominance, are threatened with extinction, if they have not already succumbed.

AD Hope, in a light-hearted rhyme, some years ago wrote:

No hunter of the age of fable
Had need to buckle in his belt;
More game than ever he was able
To take ran wild upon the veldt.
Each night with roasts he stocked his table
Then procreated on the pelt,
And that is how, of course, there came
At last to be more men than game.

A pleasant and amusing jingle but unhappily an inadequate explanation of the population explosion. In the age of fable it is more likely that hunters in their leisure time would be competing for territory or other conventional prizes and that access to game would go only or primarily to the winners—and that furthermore partners in the joys of procreation would go also to the winners, leaving the least successful not merely hungry but wife-less and without posterity. In this way balance between the numbers of hunters and of game was preserved through the ages. It was only when the hunter became a breeder of animals as well as of children, when he stocked his table with home-grown grain and other vegetables, as well as with roasts, that a dissonance crept into the harmony of this little idyll. These developments were the beginnings of the technology which has grown exponentially towards its modern explosion.

Particularly in this century, man has increased in numbers to an extent which now threatens to run beyond the capacity of the earth to feed, house, clothe and equip the bodies concerned—at least at the kind of level to which members of the more affluent societies have become accustomed. Advancing technology so far has successfully pushed this threat forward into the future but the march of numbers is inexorable and the reckoning is but delayed.

Ecologists have for years emphasised that man lives naturally in a symbiosis with other species and that the extent and character of our interrelationship with them is too complex for us fully to understand it with our present knowledge. In the circumstances the only safe thing is to avoid drastic and sudden change in the total environment, to study and measure the changes that are in fact taking place, and to seek by patient research to set conservative limits to what is acceptable.

It is not my intention to discuss at length the general themes of conservation, pollution and the ecological approach to man's affairs. After long years of indifference—indeed of the dismissal as cranks and rat-bags of those who have spoken of these issues—the community and its political leaders are suddenly aware of their urgency. Accordingly I propose to speak only of matters which I think still in Australia lack acceptance as part of this newly emerged consensus. First I want to emphasise that the current tendency to think that population pressure is not and cannot for many generations be a problem for Australia needs urgent reconsideration. Secondly I want to crave attention for that aspect of the population pressure which shows itself in the decay of overgrown cities, which is making them no longer a cradle of civilisation but rather the potential coffin of the illusions of progress with which technology has beguiled us.

We have for long thought of Australia as an isolated underpopulated country, threatened by alien forces—historically by the French, the Russians, the Japanese, and now vaguely by the underdeveloped hordes of Asia. The demands of defence and the need to justify the occupation of a continent by one people have led us to policies—fiscal and social—which are designed to encourage large families and to migration programmes adding massively to our numbers, giving us in post-war years a population growth of more than 2 per cent per annum—a very high and indeed burdensome rate for a European-type community. I believe that so far there have been definite gains from this policy. We are still benefiting from the economies of scale which come from a growing domestic market while so far avoiding the worst inflexibilities and bureaucratic ineptitudes. Furthermore, despite an almost obsessive concentration on preserving apparent racial homogeneity, migration policies have brought us welcome accessions of skills, interests and cultural diversity. We are thereby the richer.

But I believe the time has already come when we must dispute the validity of this image of the empty continent, question the importance of numbers to our national future, and shift our emphasis to our need for diversity and to the quality of life which we can offer our people.

On present trends there will be some 25 million people in Australia by the end of the century and, unless we plan boldly and successfully to the contrary, most of them will be crowded into the already overtaxed capital cities where deterioration in health and in the quality of living can be avoided, if at all, only at astronomically increasing cost.

In a world of international trade it is impossible to set limits to the numbers of people who might be supported in any given area if they can produce goods and services valued by the rest of the world. If these are services of a predominantly rare and expensive character it is possible to conceive very small communities living richly by providing specialised services at high cost while buying its daily requirements from others. Monaco, selling the services of its casinos and croupiers under the calculating patronage of the celluloid princess, is perhaps an example. It is possible to conceive a nobler one—an England serving the world with scientists, writers, artists; with knowledge, experience, and administrative capacity; with imagination and wisdom: a great research and development establishment for the culture of the Western world. This is a role which we too in our more modest way could play for the emerging countries of South East Asia—if we can use wisely and generously our greater technical advancement, the benefits of a high standard of education, and avoid casting to the winds the freedom from the taint of imperialism which in the first instance we so remarkably, if unjustifiably, possessed—a freedom which sadly we seem determined to jeopardise.

Apart from such romantic notions we are a wealthy and well endowed community. There is no reason to doubt that we can with energy earn the means to pay for the things we need to buy abroad—even for a much larger population. But domestically the ecological shoe will pinch much more rapidly. In terms of water Australia is the most poverty-stricken of all the continents—and this may well prove the limiting factor to our population growth. With this growth concentrated in our already overtaxed capital cities— which we are apparently expecting to see double their populations within the next 20 or 30 years—we are likely to be experiencing the agonies of water shortage and pollution of worse than the present United States intensity well before then.

It is time therefore to reconsider our population objectives. Without seeking to answer the unanswerable question of what the ultimate population for Australia might be with advantage to its people, we can be sure that our present rate of growth is bringing us face to face with ecological problems to which we as yet have no answer with a speed which is as unnecessary as it is unwise. We have before us the desperate plight of American cities, which in many ways have been our models, whose dreams we have shared in almost servile imitation. Let us look at New York, or at Los Angeles, that city chosen 50 years ago by the infant movie industry because it was the 'city of sunshine'. Let us look at the hundreds of millions of dollars their city tax payers spend year by year—not yet to make things better but to avoid them becoming impossible.

Returning the other day from overseas I was reading as the aeroplane approached Sydney an account of some studies of the smog problem of Los Angeles. This account referred to a puzzling quality of the Los Angeles pollution that, even when dust and the more obvious physical effluents of industrial and motor vehicle exhausts had been removed, there remained a characteristic brownish haze. This haze had markedly deleterious effect on the health of the residents, provoking painful irritation of eye, nose, throat and other membranes. The haze was in due course identified as being derived from nitrogen dioxide produced from the chemical processes flowing from the effects of *sunshine* on certain components of motor vehicle exhausts. As the plane dipped to land at Sydney airport I glanced out to see hanging over the city and the harbour the same characteristic brownish haze. I commend to those responsible for the planning of the future of Sydney and of Canberra the reports of these Los Angeles tests. In these two Australian cities, each in its own way so beautiful and so full of promise, as in many others potentially in Australia, those two elements—sunshine and motor vehicle exhausts—are brought together in densities rapidly approaching those of Los Angeles. Why should we hope that, without action by us, the results here will be different? I remember a few years ago an American friend and visitor saying to me: 'Sydney has the climate that California advertises'. Soon perhaps we Sydneysiders will be visiting Perth and Adelaide (until they too are engulfed) and saying sadly that they have the sunshine we once with justice boasted of.

Our city fathers and state political leaders should spend some time in Canberra—not just to bite the ear of the Treasurer, but to look at the rational family of cities which is coming into being there. In less than 20 years John Overall and his National Capital Development Commission, with the patient (if sometimes sceptical) support of government, of Parliament and the local community, have devised a rational Australian model for the urban-suburban city—flexible yet human in scale, a city designed for children to grow up in and for men and women to live in in civilised diversity.

Most of us who remember our own childhood remain confirmed suburbanites of smaller cities—if Barry Humphries will forgive us. We envisage for our children and for ourselves a home with the bush or the beach at the back door and a short and easy walk or ride from the front to the school, the playing fields, the university, the theatre, the restaurant or the home of friends. Within a decade or two when the more sophisticated urban delights are more fully developed Canberra will, I believe (subject only to the threat of the motor vehicle), be the nearest approximation to that image that we are likely to be able to create for city dwellers.

I believe it would be possible and profitable for states to create new cities. All that is needed is an economic nucleus around which a planned environment could grow and a firm determination to halt the growth of cities already too large. Canberra was established as a centre for government and administration. These functions were bolstered by education and research, but the city has now 'taken off' in independent growth. It has become simply a good place to live and an economic place to work. The present capital cities of the states themselves had basically the same origin—they were centres of government which attracted to the market of their populations a steadily increasing flow of industrial and commercial activities. Perhaps it is time to transfer our state capitals to new centres. We would then have half a dozen counter growing points of potential city scale to which new enterprises could be bribed or otherwise persuaded—even coerced a little—while we spent some time and money on the regeneration of our present capitals.

To be able to buy land now at rural valuations—to plan the design and development of a city—to create urban values where only grass grew before sounds like a land developer's dream. Who could not over 50 years make a handsome capital profit from such an enterprise? It is worth even a politician's thought. To dispose of the vast quantities of state-owned city real estate could contribute to the development cost of the new cities, help finance the regeneration of the old, or even simply provide space for parks and gardens to give new lungs to the smog-choked city dwellers.

Finally we must look at the influence which the dependence of the economic system on growth exerts upon man himself. The fact that a growing system most readily avoids the problems of depression and unemployment has led us to value growth as an end in itself—to see the condition of man as being absolutely measured by the increase in the Gross National Product and to believe that all else must be subordinated to greater output of the commodities to be sold in the market. Recently Professor Fritz Machlup solemnly took us to task for daring to set such ephemeral things as the pleasures of the bushland, the beach, the theatre and the concert hall, the joy of solitude and of conversation, of the contemplation of the universe in all its splendour, above the urgent need to expand our industrial output. He drew our shocked attention to the fact that the increase in our GNP per head of population was lagging behind that of the most advanced countries of the world. Obviously we must with more extravagant advertising budgets whip our indolent consumers into new and greater wants; we must sternly turn our backs on the sybaritic but unmanly delights of leisure and of idleness and return grimly to the lathe and the office desk. 'Life is real and life is earnest.'

Thank goodness most Australians had the wit and understanding to laugh at this solemn pundit but did he not express an attitude of mind which we are increasingly coming to share? Sometimes one feels that in our society culture has little to do with joy or with the arts. The characteristic structures of our age, which I hope will be puzzled over by historians and archaeologists of the future, are clover leafs and flyovers; hospitals and towering office blocks have taken the place of cathedrals and palaces and of the gracious terraces and squares of Georgian cities. Technology expands everywhere to save man from the consequences of its previous achievements. The new agriculture was made necessary by the flooding population stimulated by the old agriculture; atomic energy by the threatened depletion of fossil fuels. Every day makes us more dependent on greater and more rapid technological achievements and to drive ourselves to them we raise growth to the pedestal of the absolute good. To the extent that we come to believe this, then, we shall for the present at least achieve growth but we will do so at the expense of other values. Growth is indeed a jealous god. Galbraith says:

> If we continue to believe that the goals of the industrial system—the expansion of output, the companion increase in consumption, technological advance, the public images that sustain it—are coordinate with life, then all our lives will be in the service of these goals. What is consistent with these ends we shall have or be allowed; all else will be off limits.

It is well known that the Scandinavian lemming has a population explosion every few years, when vast herds of lemmings cross the country, swimming river after river, until they reach the sea and then they swim until they drown. This phenomenon has puzzled naturalists for generations and theories of a genetic 'death-wish' have been seriously advanced. The latest hypothesis is that the lemming is merely short-sighted. He has successfully crossed a number of stretches of water temporarily to solve his problem of survival and he is at the end unable to distinguish the sea from the streams he has successfully crossed so far.

Mankind would be unwise to assume that, because technology has enabled him to cross so many rivers of threatened scarcity to reach survival, he will be able to deal with the oceanic problem of numbers which bring him into absolute conflict with the total environment of which he is a part.

Indeed were it possible to take a God-like view of the human species in his environment—physical and social—one could readily conclude that the whole species had become itself a disease. Even if the God-like viewer were one with a special covenant with Mankind and did not view all his creatures with equal tenderness and concern, he could properly conclude that the human species was like a cancerous growth reproducing itself beyond control and living parasitically on, rather than symbiotically with, the rest of creation and threatening to destroy not merely the environment but itself also.

Basil S Hetzel

Basil Hetzel is a distinguished researcher and educator. Born in London in 1922, he was educated at King's College and St Peter's College, Adelaide, and graduated in medicine from the University of Adelaide in 1944. After initial postgraduate studies in clinical medicine and clinical research, he was a Fulbright Scholar in the United States at the Cornell Medical Centre, New York, from 1951 to 1954 and research fellow at St Thomas's Hospital in London from 1954 to 1955. He returned to the department of medicine at the University of Adelaide in 1956, where he subsequently became  Michell Professor of Social and Preventive Medicine at Monash University, Melbourne, in 1968. From 1968 to 1975 he was Foundation Professor of Preventative Medicine at Monash University, relinquishing that post to become chief of the CSIRO division of human nutrition, a position he held until 1985. From 1986 to 1995 Professor Hetzel was executive director of the International Council for Control of Iodine Deficiency Disorders. He became its chairman in 1995.

From its establishment in 1965 until 1972, Professor Hetzel was a member of the Council of the University of Papua and New Guinea. He was chancellor of the University of South Australia from 1992 to 1998.

He was chairman of the Centre for Research in Aboriginal Affairs at Monash University, and vice-chairman of Australian Frontier from 1968 to 1972. He has published extensively on health and nutrition.

Professor Hetzel was awarded the Companion to the Order of Australia in 1990 and was Lieutenant-Governor of South Australia from 1992 to 2000. He was awarded the RSL Anzac Peace Prize in 1997.

Professor Hetzel's Boyer Lectures were titled *Life and Health in Australia* and they present a difficulty of choice for the purposes of this anthology, not because his lecture subjects were unimportant, quite the contrary, but they were clearly meant to be useful in the debates current in 1971 and contain frequent references to then-current policy shifts which may confuse some readers now. This in itself is a reminder of the complexity of health policy making and the variety of attempts that have been made to achieve the best outcomes. In his fifth and concluding lecture, 'Health and Community Action', which is reproduced here, Professor Hetzel emphasised the need for health policy to be based on health education and planning for the delivery of care through proper coordination of community and hospital services.

HEALTH AND COMMUNITY ACTION

Life and Health in Australia

Basil S Hetzel

• 1971 •

In each of my previous four talks, I have pointed out the need for community action in relation to health problems in Australia. In this fifth and last talk, I want to consider community action itself. I have noted already the 'application gap' between knowledge and its use by the community. This delay is an interesting and important phenomenon.

I believe that this gap arises not only because of ignorance or lack of communication, but mainly because of the difficulty of implementing the change which the application of new knowledge usually requires. Implementing change is particularly difficult if it requires change in an existing institution such as a government department. Recently, I heard Dr Donald Schon, the 1970 BBC Reith Lecturer, describe government departments as 'a series of memorials to old problems'. He, as an American, pointed out that the titles on the doors of government offices have remained the same throughout the period of the great technological and social revolution of the last 30 years. This description is most apt. Let me hasten to say that the departmental officers are not necessarily primarily to blame for this, but it is true that many able and conscientious men and women are labouring within a framework to meet a situation which no longer exists or problems which have since been solved. We are, as Dr Schon says, 'very inept at public learning'.

This is particularly true of the health field, where we have not yet been able to catch up with the changed pattern of illness, injury and disability. Recent hospitals are memorials to past problems—acute illness rather than chronic illness, physical disease rather than psycho-social morbidity, and so on. However, I do believe that mass media, and particularly television, is significantly accelerating social change by increasing awareness of problems not only in the community at large but also within government departments, industry and educational institutions.

However, many of our government Health Departments are

caught in a web where change is extremely difficult, if not impossible. Many officers recognise the problem, but such a situation cannot be accepted. The use of advisory committees made up of suitable qualified people from the community is one way to assist change but such bodies are all too rare in Australia although I have been impressed with the possibilities from my own experience on two such committees.

The problem of traffic accidents does not fit neatly into any existing health institution—it is not an environmental health problem—it is not a mental health problem—it is not a hospital problem, though in a sense it overlaps into all these areas. The same applies to alcoholism. Traffic accidents and alcoholism are urgent present day problems for which there is no simple means of applying what knowledge is available. It is to the credit of the Royal Australian College of Surgeons that they have taken up the problem of traffic accidents, and by an aggressive approach made some headway in bringing about the new organisation necessary. By contrast with accidents, heart surgery has made rapid progress in Australia. It is purely a hospital problem that can be solved with hospital resources of highly trained staff and specialised facilities.

In general, the community can exert its will and take action on the results of research along three main lines: education, legislation, and provision of suitable health services.

Education in health matters is a much neglected area in this country. Some effort is being made at primary school level, but the academic pressures at the secondary school level have largely prevented the development of broader subjects in the health and social field. Education in the field of men/women relationships is urgently required in the light of the evidence of widespread ignorance, and the social harm resulting from hasty marriages and illegitimacy. However, beyond this is the need for an understanding of human growth and development, the various stages of the life of man and their significance for society and community life.

Of course, education does not depend only on school curricula. Understanding of personal relationships comes from the home and wider family, from membership of other community groups such as clubs and church congregations, but there is a need for community activity to supplement the existing defects in school and family life. Much is being done by organisations like the Marriage Guidance Council, and the Family Life Movement.

Why can't we use television to more creative purpose in this field? Certainly there is plenty of effort made by special groups on television to advertise their products which are inimical to health.

It is one of the disadvantages of a society believing in individual enterprise that the activities of certain groups go unchecked, in spite of the damage that is done to the health of the young, with future heavy personal and economic cost to the community. In the face of present television commercials, we can hardly be surprised at the results of the survey of the smoking habits in 26,000 children carried out in 1968 by the National Health and Medical Research Council. This revealed that by the age of 15, 26 per cent of boys and 16 per cent of girls were smoking three to five cigarettes per day. In its report to the government in 1969, the National Health and Medical Research Council has drawn up a comprehensive program for action, including education, yet no decisions have yet been made on this report and certainly little has been done to control television commercials. This inaction contrasts with recent initiatives of the Canadian government which has banned all cigarette advertisements on TV, radio and in the newspapers from January 1972.

Let us now look at *legislation*. We have already seen the way in which legislation brought about the sanitary revolution earlier this century. Legislation in the health field follows community awareness which has been stimulated by scientific advance. Legislation in the form of the Commonwealth State Tuberculosis Agreement of 1948, provided the basis for the successful control of this disease in Australia. We are now much more aware of the dangers to the physical environment than we were, and suitable legislation is essential to safeguard this. The prevention of water pollution by segregation of enough ground around reservoirs was recently enforced by legislation in South Australia; the preservation of adequate recreational areas in city and suburban municipalities is now an urgent matter as population density increases. The importance of motor car exhaust in air pollution calls for legislation to reduce the carbon monoxide content. Industry is now under much greater pressure because of the dangers of air and water pollution from industrial wastes.

In relation to traffic accidents, legislation has recently been introduced to permit breathalyser testing of a driver suspected of alcoholic intoxication, and penalties enforced if the level is above 0.05 per cent in Victoria, or above 0.08 per cent in other states. Recent legislation in Victoria permits 'spot checks' of drivers, a method of further discouraging the alcoholic driver. Compulsory blood alcohol tests are now being considered as a further step in Victoria, but legislation is also needed to ensure safety measures being incorporated in the design of motor cars. These are now mandatory in the USA; they should be made mandatory in Australia as soon as possible. The recent introduction of legislation to make seat belts compulsory in Victoria is an example of important legislative advance in which we have led the world.

Another matter which requires attention is cigarettes. Apart from the much needed control of advertising, there is the question of tar content. It is not possible to prohibit smoking in Australia today, but there is every reason to believe a safer cigarette could be produced. The tar content of the various brands of cigarette varies widely from 5 mg to 26 mg per cigarette. There has been a reduction in tar content of various brands in the last two years following the announcement of the result of the analyses being carried out by the Victorian AntiCancer Council. I believe suitable legislation favouring low tar content cigarettes, for example by taxation benefits, would quickly accelerate this tendency to the considerable benefit of the smoker, whose increased health hazard from cancer of the lung is in direct proportion to the tar content of cigarettes.

Today, in a society which regards man as free of the old paternalisms of church and state, legislative action tends to be unpopular, but the beneficial effects are apparent as, for example, in the use of breathalyser tests. Inaction seems scarcely credible when faced with indisputable evidence of personal tragedies and mounting costs for medical care for avoidable disease. The fall in lung cancer in British doctors following curtailment of smoking of cigarettes, and a similar fall in heart disease, provides conclusive evidence of a causal relationship.

There are other more difficult areas where legislative amendment is probably necessary, such as children at risk from maltreatment or neglect by their parents, the apprehension of sexual deviants, and those attempting suicide. The legal framework needs to take account of medical advance—the importance of social and psychological factors, the unsatisfactory effects of penalties, and the need for a therapeutic approach. New methods of therapy require properly organised research studies so that maximum benefit can be obtained. The question of compulsion to undergo therapy has to be considered in the case of some of the more serious situations, such as the young chronic alcoholic driver. The analogy with a sufferer from tuberculosis has already been pointed out, and I believe treatment should if necessary also be made compulsory for the young alcoholic.

It is clear that increases in knowledge are bringing about changes in the climate of opinion more rapidly than ever before—especially through mass media coverage. Legislative provision is a particularly powerful means for the promotion of health—both by increase in control, as with alcohol and cigarettes, or by decrease in punitive measures in the case of attempted suicide, sexual deviation or problem families.

The health services are the most obvious expression of the state of our knowledge, if not of health then of disease.

The critical issue facing the health services in Australia is the delivery of adequate medical and health care to the whole population. Health care is now regarded as a right and not a privilege, but the implications of this view are still not generally recognised.

The present system of voluntary hospital and medical insurance supported by the Commonwealth government was introduced between 1951 and 1953 in order to subsidise the delivery of private medical care. Last year, after 20 years, substantial increases in cover were introduced by the Commonwealth government through the voluntary insurance system. However, the mounting health care bill is a major problem for the state and Commonwealth governments, and the establishment of an agreed scale of fees between the profession and the government is essential for control.

One finding of the Nimmo Committee of Enquiry into Health Insurance concerned the evidence of hardship to the poorer groups in the community, resulting from a contributory system in which income levels are not taken into account. I believe an alternative system whereby health costs could be met by a compulsory contribution, with income tax deductions in proportion to tax paid, would be a much more equitable and preferable method of financing health care. Such a plan could be introduced without affecting the present system of private practice.

One serious disadvantage of the subsidy of private practice by health insurance in Australia has been its effect on medical education. The teaching hospitals provide the basic opportunity for both undergraduate training of medical students and postgraduate training of specialists such as physicians, surgeons, obstetricians, paediatricians and psychiatrists. However, the teaching hospitals can no longer attract as many patients because of the preference for private care. This has caused a dearth of patients in the public wards and outpatient clinics, which have in general much less attractive amenities. Unfortunately, most private patients in Australia receive treatment in separate private hospitals, even though the technological facilities available are much less developed than in public teaching hospitals. There is widespread concern in universities and medical schools about this problem, which is seriously hampering teaching at both undergraduate and postgraduate level. Many of the relatively few private patients in teaching hospitals have agreed to assist teaching when requested to do so—modified arrangements are going to be necessary so that many more private patients can have this opportunity, otherwise training of future medical students and specialists is going to be severely jeopardised.

Some more effective coordination of the various arms of the health services—public health, mental health, hospital and community services and medical education—has become an urgent need to enable a more adequate response to be made to the pattern of modern illness and morbidity. At present, the various arms of the health services function more or less independently. There are historical and sociological reasons for this, but the barriers must be overcome if a high quality of health care is to be provided, and if general practice is to take its rightful place in the health care system. It is clear that adequate delivery of health care to a rapidly increasing and culturally diverse Australian population will require much more effective organisation and a consensus between different arms of the health services as to what is to be done, together with the full involvement of the general practitioner.

The prominence of chronic illness and disability in older age groups following the control of so much infectious disease has changed the nature of the demand on the health services of the community. Chronic illness and disability require, above all, teamwork between doctors in the different specialties that have developed with the increase in our knowledge of the mechanisms of disease. These conditions also require teamwork between doctors and nurses, social workers, physiotherapists, occupational therapists, clerical staff and volunteers. Well trained administrators are also essential for the complex task of running the modern hospital and other health services. In many ways, the modern hospital is one of the most complex institutions—its organisation and optimum function needs much more study. The cost of hospital care is now a major source of embarrassment to Commonwealth and state governments.

There is a danger of the personal needs of the individual patient being overlooked in the complex machinery of modern medical treatment, especially in hospitals. This indicates the need for better organisation of the care of the personal needs of the patient. More time is now allowed for visiting by family and friends, but the provision of befrienders for those (and there are many) who do not have family and friends available is of considerable importance. The development of volunteer auxiliaries who look after the needs of patients' families while they are in hospital and continue with their support, if necessary, after discharge is also beginning in some hospitals and should be encouraged. The provision of chaplaincy services on a full time basis for chaplains who have undergone special training for ministry to the sick is being recognised in modern hospitals, and some governments have subsidised these services. The importance of the social worker with specialised knowledge of welfare provisions and of personal problems is obvious.

The difficulties all major Australian hospitals face today are partly a reflection of the inadequacy of community services— services designed to care for the sick and disabled in their homes or in some other less costly environment. The natural leader in this field is the general practitioner, the doctor of first contact who has a distinguished tradition of service in this country. The recent great increase in knowledge which has led to the many specialties in medicine has left the general practitioner somewhat uncertain of his role. There is a fall of recent graduates willing to enter general practice which bodes ill for the future. There is already evidence of a shortage of general practitioner services, particularly in rural areas, but also in inner urban areas of large cities. Patients and families are coming to hospital in increasing numbers seeking first contact care, a function for which hospitals have not been designed and which they are unable to fill adequately without considerable reorganisation.

These difficulties are leading to a reappraisal of general practice. There is an urgent need for a new form of organisation, recognising the principle of teamwork between doctor and nurse and other health professionals such as the social worker, physiotherapist, and the community with its governmental and voluntary services. This new organisation is beginning to occur overseas with the provision of what are called health centres.

In Australia, we can learn from these overseas experiments and should develop some pilot projects in suitable areas as soon as possible. Obvious examples that come to mind are inner urban areas and rural areas, where existing services are inadequate, and new suburban areas where they have yet to be developed—where their development can benefit from more recent advances in concepts of medical care. Such a centre would be a great advantage for both undergraduate arid postgraduate teaching more related to present day needs.

I believe that we could secure a much higher return for the investment of our health dollar than we do at present. By international standards, the expenditure on health services in Australia is above that of the United Kingdom and Sweden, but below that of Canada and the USA. We are not niggardly in our expenditure on health, but we are careless in the way we spend the money without any effective coordination and planning of the services which it finances.

I believe the most urgent need is for a better organisation of community services because of their ultimate preventive value. There is a need for the development of a metropolitan regional approach, with proper integration of hospital services with community needs and community services. Increasing organisation is inescapable for a more effective delivery of the rapid advances resulting from medical scientific endeavour in the last 20 years. With the help of improved communication made possible by advances in electronics and the rapid handling of large masses of information by computer technology, greatly increased efficiency of services becomes possible.

In keeping with our lag in 'public learning', however, this can only develop following acceptance of the principle of rational study of needs and how they can most efficiently be met. Proper recognition of this still has to be given by those ultimately responsible for decisions in the health field in Australia, namely both Commonwealth and state governmental authorities, as well as the organised medical profession.

As a Professor of Social Medicine, I am much concerned with the relation of health to society, and therefore I am very interested in whether health is being promoted or hindered by social factors. One important criterion by which we can judge our society is its concern for the health and welfare of its individual members. In looking at man in society, I am an optimist. I agree with the great American, Thomas Jefferson, when he said, following the American Revolution over 150 years ago, 'I am among those who think well of the human character generally. I consider man as formed for society, and endowed by nature with those dispositions which fit him for society. I believe also . . . that his mind is perfectable to a degree of which we cannot yet form any conception'.

With the advent of mass media, powerful new social forces have been introduced. In line with Jefferson's prediction, I believe man is, in fact, in process of becoming a new being, partly as a result of mass media. Man has created a new social environment for himself, and then by reacting to it produced a new intensity of living. I believe this new phase of living offers exciting possibilities for the health and life of man.

However, we must recognise the need for new organisations to respond to present day needs. We cannot get to the moon in a

T-model Ford—we cannot meet our current health problems with the equipment fashioned to meet earlier situations which no longer exist. However, we need a positive approach to health in our society—not just the absence of disease, and the treatment of disease, but recognition of prevention by action at individual, family and community level whereby the 'perfectability of man's mind may be increased', to use Jefferson's phrase. We have seen that many of our current health problems are largely preventable—all we need is the will to take the action indicated by scientific investigation, both individually and as a society. A national health policy incorporating these principles is urgently required. This policy should include recognition of the need for promotion of health by appropriate education and legislation. It should recognise the need for planning and organisation in the provision of health services. It should accept the principle of compulsory health insurance. A positive social approach to health policy will challenge the community to take responsibility—both individually and at various levels of organisation. The experience of giving must be facilitated so that we really are a concerned and vital society. This raises the ultimate question of the choice between our will to live a creative life meeting the challenge of our times, or our desire to die prematurely to escape our responsibilities. Health is a by-product of our way of life—do we, as individuals and as a nation, wish to live such a creative life that our health can be maintained in the face of the constant challenge of our environment?

Dexter Dunphy

Dexter Dunphy was born in 1934 and educated at the University of Sydney and at Harvard, where he received his PhD. Before going to the United States in 1961, he taught in the New South Wales Education Department and lectured in education at the Sydney Teachers College.

He spent further years at Harvard, first as a teaching fellow, then as lecturer in Social Relations, and later as Associate Professor of Social Relations and Business Administration.

He returned to Australia in 1967 to become senior lecturer in sociology at the University of New South Wales and then Professor of Business Administration and head of the department of organisation behaviour in the Faculty of Commerce at that university in 1970.

In 1983 Professor Dunphy took up the position of Professor of Management at the Australian Graduate School of Management at UNSW, heading the Centre for Corporate Change for a number of years. In 2000 he moved to the University of Technology in Sydney as Distinguished Professor in the School of Management in the Faculty of Business.

Professor Dunphy has published many books, particularly in the area of managing organisational change, human resource management and corporate sustainability.

The title of his Boyer Lectures was *The Challenge of Change* and has potency still, nearly 30 years later. For those who think that the rate of change is now too rapid, it is worth remembering that within the year prior to Professor Dunphy's lectures much was altering: Australian troops were withdrawn from Vietnam, David Williamson wrote *Don's Party*, Britain joined the EEC, Nixon visited China, the Munich Olympic hostages were killed, Nixon was re-elected in a landslide and, in the period when the lectures were being put to air, Gough Whitlam led the Labor Party to federal victory for the first time in 23 years. Change happens, and rapid change is no recent phenomenon.

His individual lectures are titled 'Riders in the Chariot'; 'The Searching Self' reproduced here; 'The World of Work'; 'Principalities and Power' and 'Designing Utopias'. 'The Searching Self' deals importantly with rapid change and the ways in which individuals must deal with it. As he put it in his concluding words: 'Ultimately, the only way to understand the future is to have the courage to begin to live with it'.

THE SEARCHING SELF

The Challenge of Change

Dexter Dunphy

• 1972 •

I spoke in my first lecture of the accelerating rate of technological and social change in modern society. Responsibility, I suggested, rests in attempting to plan, guide and control change, not in its technical aspects alone but also in its impact on the lives of men.

In later lectures I will be speaking about 'collective' responsibility but, in the last analysis, responsibility is exercised by individuals. We operate increasingly in a world where decisions are made by groups but, even in group decision making, individuals give or withhold consent, if only sometimes by opting out. Responsibility is ultimately an individual matter. If we are to have responsible collective decisions, we will only get them by having decision making groups made up of responsible individuals.

In this lecture therefore I want to concentrate on the individual—to discuss what responsibility is for people like you and me. Once again I want to link my discussion to the notion of change. If we live in a world of constant flux, what does this mean for us individually? Does this rate of change threaten our personal stability? What are the personal characteristics we need to cope effectively with rapid change? Can we plan, guide and control change in our personal lives and, if so, to what ends shall we direct it?

If change offers us new opportunities, we must use these opportunities to find genuine fulfilment in our personal lives. For if a changing society doesn't offer me that, it offers me nothing.

Accelerating change affects us individually in a variety of ways. At the level of technology, we are constantly bombarded by new products, new machines, new processes, new procedures, new ideas, new experiences.

Each of these demands a corresponding change on our part. Of course, the changes may be simple. A new can opener? I may learn the required skill of operating it in a few seconds. It may take longer to learn to cope with a new kind of gear shift in my car and I may have trouble discarding some of the old responses practised daily over a number of years. However, if I am a tradesman, a new kind of lathe may make obsolete years of training and experience. Or if I am a small shopkeeper, a new supermarket may shatter a lifetime's learning, effort and investment. New technologies not only bring problems of adjustment and learning; they often bring distinct and immediate benefits too. If I am a housewife, a new dishwasher may release me from hours of drudgery each week; if I am an invalid, a new drug may relieve me from years of pain.

For better or for worse, each innovation I encounter affects my life. But these examples have only dealt with simple and direct responses to novelty. A new approach to mining or to oil refining may completely escape my notice but it may initiate a series of changes such as strikes and price adjustments which affect many aspects of my life—from transport to work, to the cost of basic items of living. It may affect my life in ways I do not even understand.

But there is a deeper, more persuasive sense in which accelerating change affects our personal lives. Man is a symbolic animal and he seeks meaning in life. He does not live by bread alone. He searches actively for significance and finds it in symbols: in words, signs, places, flags, scents, sounds, and significant personal relationships. It is at the symbolic level that accelerating social change hits us hardest, because it so frequently tears apart symbols which have provided our lives with meaning and continuity.

Primitive man experienced less mobility and less dramatic changes than we do. The Australian Aborigine, for example, lived his whole life on his restricted tribal grounds. Each significant physical feature—rocks, pools, trees, hills—had meaning for him and his people. He walked a territory inhabited by mythical figures of the 'dreaming time'. His tribal ceremonies celebrated the events of the dreamtime in song, dance and ritual. He lived as his fathers had before him and their fathers before them. He hunted the same animals, observed the same rituals, lived out the same social customs, held the same values. Life was bounded and confined by tradition but at the same time it was infused with profound meaning. A meaning derived from community life with strong historical continuity.

Rapid social change destroys a symbolic meaning of this kind. Modern man lives in a world in which whole landscapes are swept away and remade in short intervals of time. Bulldozers tear down what was there, gigantic machines throw up high rise buildings from the ruins and roll out superhighways across the horizons.

What disappears is not just a landscape but a way of life and a set of meanings. Within our minds an inaudible bomb has been dropped on a set of reference points. In our naive delight in the power of technology, we have assumed that we can wipe out the symbolic landscapes of a man's mind, deprive him of the sights and sounds and familiar routines in which he was nurtured, and that this will not hurt him. Unfortunately it is not so.

We are discovering that symbols are not replaced as easily as tyres, rebuilt as readily as houses or manufactured as directly as detergent. A chainsaw takes minutes to rip down a tree which took centuries to grow. In the same manner technology seems to be much better at cutting the roots of our identity than re-establishing our identity.

For a long time we have assumed that we could make up this loss of meaning to people with the readily apparent benefits of progress—that plentiful wealth and goods could adequately substitute for the loss of psychological satisfactions deriving from persons, places and possessions dear to us—that roles could replace persons, a motel replace a home, a parking lot replace natural bush-land, syndicated glamour replace the warmth of human friendship.

In all this we forgot that identity needs roots, needs nourishment, needs meaning, continuity, reference points; that meaning is a deposit refined relatively slowly from experience and that therefore there is a limit to the speed with which symbols can be formed and invested with feeling. To uproot symbols indiscriminately is to destroy the stable sense of individuality and identity which is the basis of any meaningful personal and community life. The modern world of advertising and political propaganda has specialised in manufacturing substitute symbols—but plastic flowers are not real flowers and plastic people are not real people.

Oddly enough we are also discovering that the age of affluence and dynamism requires higher ethical qualities than the age of scarcity and stability. Necessity forced most people into the role of honest, hardworking citizens and the police took care of the rest. When parents told their children, 'if you don't be good and work at school, you may starve and will certainly amount to nothing in life', there was plenty of evidence about to make the threat credible. How many young people would regard the threat seriously now?

The certainty of change and the possibility of catastrophe combine to tear from us the traditional sources of meaning for living—these sources of meaning were continuity with the past and congruity with the values of the past.

The other side of the coin of course is that change also offers hope—hope springing from the exercise of choice, the possibility of escape from traditional patterns of meaning and significance which smother the human experience; hope springing from the loosening of relationships that limit, curb and destroy personal growth. Change offers a freedom to create new meanings and symbols, to seek new and more satisfying personal relationships, to experiment with patterns of behaviour we choose ourselves. In fact to stand at the helm of our own life and steer a course into unnavigated waters if we wish, rather than to accept uncritically a course chartered for us by forgotten generations. Change offers the hope of freedom.

There are some who would argue that to raise this hope is to foster an illusion. That our sense of freedom is only an unrealisable and forlorn wish and that we are bound to react automatically to an environment over which we have no control, an environment which controls us as surely as a puppeteer controls a puppet by pulling strings. One psychologist who argues this way is BF Skinner of Harvard University. In his most recent book, *Beyond Freedom and Dignity* he continues his lifelong argument that we are products of conditioning by our environment, we are shaped by the forces that impinge on us. Choice and freedom are illusions. This modern form of predestination is the latest salvo of an ancient argument about the extent to which man is free to shape himself and his environment.

Is it true that freedom is an illusion? I do not believe it is so. My answer must be a simple statement of belief as there is no logical way to derive an answer to this essentially metaphysical question. But I do share Skinner's pessimism somewhat for I believe that there are real limits to the extent that we can take responsibility for directing our lives and that, further, within these limits, the exercise of responsibility is a difficult thing to attempt and, for most of us, a scary thing.

On the other hand, the search for this limited freedom is the core of what a fully human life is about and ultimately it is the source of the joy and maturity which leads to a life lived in the fulness of hope rather than the darkness of despair. In a world that is increasingly dynamic, accepting responsibility for the direction of change in our lives offers the only source of meaning that can replace the given meaning of a stable tradition, and that is a source of meaning less and less available to us. Freedom lies in facing the future, fully conscious of our limitations but stubbornly prepared to use the leverage we have to force the future to yield us the fulfilment of our deepest needs.

I have said that man is a symbolic animal—that he is in search of an identity, of a notion of self that conveys significance to his actions. In confronting change and coping with it, we have a great deal going for us. The self is not essentially static—it is born in change, nurtured in change; the self is a growing thing.

Sigmund Freud drew up the first significant chart of the way in which the child develops a personality of his own. Theorists and researchers since Freud have built on and revised his original contribution and have constructed a clearer picture of the way in which we develop a sense of identity. We know now, for example, that our self, our personality, is a product of our relationships with others. Deprived of human relationships, particularly loving human relationships, small children die almost as surely as they die when deprived of food.

A French researcher, Renee Spitz was puzzled to discover the high death rate in larger, hygienic, well-run orphanages as compared to the smaller, rather squalid orphanages. Children in the former were provided with scientifically selected and prepared diets, were kept clean and received good medical care; unfortunately, however, there was a high death rate and their psychological health and mental ability declined as they grew older. In the smaller, more squalid, less professionally run orphanages, these problems were not in evidence. Why the difference? Careful research tracked it down to the lack of personal responsibility for children in the larger orphanages where the staff worked in shifts. The staff were not given responsibility for particular children, and so they did not become attached to them, did not pick them up, fondle them or talk to them. In the poorer orphanages, one nurse typically had care of eight or so babies whom she regarded as 'hers'. She became emotionally attached to them, fondled and talked to them and they lived and grew despite the dirt. Through studies such as this we have found that the growing self needs nutriment too. Its prime nutriment is a relationship with a responsible, caring human being.

The newborn infant, if hungry, will actively search for his mother's breast, the source of food he needs. For years, many philosophers and psychologists regarded the infant as the passive recipient of forces impinging on him and they saw his mind as an empty slate on which civilisation would write messages of its devising. But the infant is no more passive in his search for psychological nutriment than he is in his search for food for his body. The infant contributes actively to the emergence of relationships with others about him. He seeks stimulation from his environment, is attracted by movement and by varied patterns. He will choose some patterns from others and pay particular attention to them. But the patterns he seeks most are *people patterns*. Infants of even two to six days old will pay more attention to a disc with a human face painted on it than to any other object of equal shape or size. Even at that early age, the infant recognises intuitively the food he needs for psychological growth. And he becomes increasingly selective. At three months he can distinguish not only people from objects, but his mother from strangers. By six months his behaviour in relation to people is *highly* selective—he is responding with movement, gurgles and smiles to his mother and other familiar people.

Is it simply the satisfaction of his physical needs that leads to this attachment? No. The growing child responds most to those who respond to him—and who take an active interest in him, and not just to the hand that holds his bottle. Any fond grandparent knows this.

So, from infancy onwards, we are active partners in social encounters. We seek a response from others and search for significant social contact. These reciprocal human relationships are the basic building blocks we use in constructing a sense of self. We learn about ourselves by seeing how others respond to us. Our psychological health, our independence, autonomy and freedom to react confidently and spontaneously depend on secure personal relationships. The healthy person seeks these relationships—he has a searching self.

What is true of the infant is just as true for the child, the adolescent and the adult. Whatever deprives us of human response deprives us of life, hope and happiness. The danger is that we need human relationships so much that we cling to them and fear that they may change. But change in social relationships is essential to growth. The small child, faced with his mother's new demand to feed himself, rather than be fed, feels threatened. He reacts with alarm and at first becomes more dependent than less. But the child who had learned to trust his mother can cope with her new demands. As he finds that she does not withdraw her love, he learns to master change. He finds that change, rather than a threat, can be the basis of a new sense of competence and an enhanced experience of life.

When we are young, we depend on others to provide us with the basic conditions for life and personal fulfilment. If we find that they do so, we are increasingly able to sense and to seek the conditions necessary to satisfy our own needs by ourselves, to choose those relationships which will sustain our growth, to avoid those which threaten to destroy us.

But what if our early experiences of human relationships do not satisfy our basic needs? If we seek food and find a stone? We become confused and fearful, we lose our sense of trust and our confidence in life. We become frightened to reach out for living relationships. We feel hurt and we begin to build powerful defences against being hurt again. We are determined not to be vulnerable.

We experience the loneliness and emptiness of isolation from others. We cradle ourselves, cry on our own shoulder, build protective armour about ourselves and allow our life to become a sea of meaningless despair. We are now increasingly unable to do what the infant does naturally—to search for the responsive human relationship that is the life of the self. So we seek substitute symbols of satisfaction. We indulge in excessive eating that never satisfies us because we are satisfying the wrong hunger—we accumulate symbols of security—bigger bank balances, more lavish houses, longer cars. These provide no security at all, because the security that we want is the security of being loved and loving. We sink into hopeless passivity, or try to run from our hopelessness by engaging in a frenzy of busyness, or become actively destructive to those about us.

One thing is sure. The immature, unfulfilled person is too frightened to cope effectively with change. Another way to express this is to say that our ability to be responsible varies directly with our level of maturity. Eric Hoffer once wrote: 'We can never really be prepared for that which is wholly new. We have to adjust ourselves, and every radical adjustment is a crisis in self esteem. It needs inordinate self-confidence to face drastic change without inner trembling.'

It is the fulfilled person who is most free and who can exercise responsibility of a high order. The unfulfilled person who has been severely deprived in the satisfaction of his most basic emotional needs cannot cope with change. Like Linus, the character in the Peanuts cartoon, he is too concerned about losing his security blanket. He is also likely to become severely frustrated and hostile. I think of the Melbourne taxi driver who recently drove me to the airport from La Trobe University. He began by saying how he would like to line up all the radical, long-haired students and shoot them. Then he told me how he spent half the year slaughtering kangaroos and showed me coloured photographs of their bleeding carcases. He complained of the fact that he couldn't get anyone to take away the huge pile of empty beer bottles stacked alongside his house almost to roof level. He was a symbol of the unfulfilled and frustrated person, oscillating between anger and depressive drinking, frightened and frightening in his hostile loneliness.

There is a lot of evidence that my taxi driver is not an isolated case—that Australians have chosen to avoid responsibility on a grand scale. Australia is a land remarkably lacking in traditions—its culture consists of shallow symbolism and synthetic meanings. It is a kind of lotus land in the Pacific—a land of escapism with a suicide rate and an automobile death rate as high as any in the world. Australians also consume huge quantities of drink and drugs and spend record amounts on gambling. We might ask ourselves why these forms of escape—death and fantasy—are so popular in Australia. Surely it is not because we are leading personally fulfilling lives?

We are the most urbanised nation in the world but we have little tradition of community life. We pursue an ideal of conformist individualism which keeps us locked into isolated boxes in the ever-extending reaches of suburbia, usually with our eyes glued to the flickering tube. Recently, an Australian TV executive stated that the television industry's main role was to provide entertainment to the majority of people who were 'tired, bored and in the main disillusioned with life. Most of them don't like the job they have got, don't like their life style and a lot of them don't even like the person they are married to,' he said. 'Their horizons and the scope of their lives are limited. At the age of 21 a lot of them have faced the fact that they have reached, substantially, the level of income they are going to have until they die. Life has come almost to a full stop.'

When we do come together, it is generally a shallow, conventionalised groupiness where feelings can only be loosened through a haze of alcohol and cigarette smoke. Or we participate in the mass ceremonies of the football field where individual restraints are swept away in crowd hysteria.

Individually, we lavish more loving care and attention on our cars than each other, finding it easier to relate to something that responds automatically than to the unpredictable responses of real human beings. Our behaviour is standardised and conventionalised—to be unconventional and non-conforming is to excite bewilderment, embarrassment or anger. We still have headmasters who dismiss youths with long hair and girls wearing slacks.

In many of our schools, the main lesson taught is conformity with a capital C. The ideal seems to be to have every child dressing in the same way, behaving in the same way, writing in the same hand-writing, painting the same vase of flowers. Many Australian schools are paramilitary organisations—saluting flags and drilling in stiff parodies of military precision to compete for weekly marching honours. Relationships are stereotyped rather than responsive.

The vast changes of modern life seem to have passed by the bulk of our schools which are still geared to produce a majority of unquestioning workers fit to tend machines without asking why. All the predictions for the future point to the need for educating for a new man—one who is not a mindless conformist. An innovator, ready to experiment, to question, and to assume responsibility.

When our schools are not inculcating conformity, they are stuffing children with knowledge. Don't ask if the knowledge will still be relevant when the child comes to use it! (I am told that it takes five years for an engineer's training to be 50 per cent outdated—what of the usefulness of what the child learns for ten or 20 years later?) But knowledge as such will be less important in the future anyway. We can leave the storage of knowledge to computers which will also give us ready access to it. What will be important will be the ability to integrate knowledge and apply it with a well developed sensitivity to social values. The key man of the future will not be a specialist but a creative generalist who can implement change in human systems. Dennis Gabor has argued in fact that an EQ or ethical quotient will be as necessary as an IQ or intelligence quotient for those who occupy significant social positions in the future. Our schools are still trying to produce conformists, with knowledge stuffed brains; the result is children who are ethical morons in terms of the central issues of the modern world.

Out of school, our students will not learn to be innovators by participation in a rich community life. At home they will be under the care of mothers who make up the female serfdom of suburbia. Most housewives are excluded from the main stream of political and economic life. And when young people move away from the home, what then? Out of school and out of home, there is a dearth of provision for youth—our municipal councils don't provide for youth in the way they do in Great Britain for example. With a few exceptions, our local councils cannot see higher than their own curbs and gutters.

There remains the church. Religion in Australia has generally provided a ghetto refuge from the modern world; an emotional support for people frightened by the pace of change. Some churches have been oases of communal life in the suburban desert, but few have forged new and viable patterns of community life for the future to take up. The notion of responsibility taught in most churches has been a spiritless rectitude, a guilty over-conformity to outdated social rules.

Yes, ours has been a derivative culture, inculcating a blend of individualism with no individuality, conformity with no community, morality with no responsibility. Vast changes have rolled across our culture and the culture has reacted slowly, very slowly, revealing our fear of change, our frightened immaturity, our massive evasion of the issues.

The challenge is to create a society which fosters the human qualities needed to handle the revolutionary changes which lie ahead.

I believe that many people today are disillusioned with our traditional way of life, with its personal isolation, lack of communication and absence of significant meaning. For this reason many people, particularly young people, are experimenting with new patterns of group and communal living. In recent months I have been a guest in a number of so-called 'communes' where eight or ten people, some married, some not, are living together in a large house. These young people are involved in an experiment that may provide direction for social life in the future. Similarly many housewives are escaping boredom and neuroticism by forming social action groups in local communities. They are enlarging their intellectual understanding and directing their creative concern to horizons beyond their front fence. There is yet another quiet social revolution which is beginning to be noted in the newspapers. This is the increasing number of people involving themselves in sensitivity training or encounter groups; I have myself been involved in these groups for ten years. They are temporary communities where people come to deepen their understanding of themselves and further their own emotional growth. Encounter groups are a serious attempt to cope with change at the personal level and use it to forge a new and more satisfying identity.

Responsibility for change begins with an active awareness of our potential and a willingness to choose to change and grow. The easy alternative is to take refuge in the false security of routines and responses chosen for their familiarity rather than their relation to a changed reality. Social change offers increased alternatives for personal fulfilment. But too often we react in fear, either clutching the familiar or seizing the novel, without assessing the relative worth of either for our emerging maturity. We can only contribute effectively and responsibly to social change if we are ourselves confident and changing. Ultimately, the only way to understand the future is to have the courage to begin to live it.

Sir Keith Hancock

Keith Hancock was a distinguished historian and social scientist. He was educated at the University of Melbourne and, as a Rhodes Scholar, at Balliol College, Oxford. In 1923 he was the first Australian to be elected a Fellow of All Souls College, Oxford.

In 1926, he returned to Australia as Professor of Modern History at Adelaide, and then in 1933 he accepted the position of Professor of History at the University of Birmingham. From 1944 to 1949 he was Chichele Professor of Economic History at Oxford.

During World War II, he worked in the War Cabinet offices in London and subsequently edited 30 volumes of the 'Civil' series of British war history. From 1949 to 1956, he was director of the Institute of Commonwealth Studies at the University of London.

He returned to Australia in 1957 to become director of the Research School of Social Sciences at the Australian National University, and was Professor of History there from 1957 to 1965. He was made a university fellow in 1966 and Professor Emeritus in 1968.

Professor Hancock's achievements were widely recognised and he received honorary degrees from universities on three continents.

He wrote numerous publications. His book, *Discovering Monaro: A Study of Man's Impact on his Environment*, won the Foundation for Literary Studies Award as the best book published in Australia in 1972 dealing with an aspect of Australian life. His 1930 book, *Australia*, was considered to be a seminal work. Professor Hancock's last book was published in 1982.

He was knighted in 1965. He died in 1988.

Sir Keith's beautifully crafted Boyer Lectures were titled *Today, Yesterday and Tomorrow*. His graceful writing displays a deep concern for environmental problems and a love and respect for the English language. 'A Little Lower Than the Angels' was the fourth of his five lectures. The preceding lecture

'Pollution' ends as follows: 'Man sometimes makes deserts and sometimes makes the desert blossom like the rose. Man makes gardens; sometimes he neglects them; sometimes he tends them with loving care. Is man a naked ape? Or is he a living soul? "What is man, that Thou art mindful of him?" '

A LITTLE LOWER THAN THE ANGELS

Today, Yesterday and Tomorrow

Sir Keith Hancock

• 1973 •

I still retain the vivid memory of a picture that I saw half a century ago. It is the 'Scapegoat', by Holman Hunt. Among the red rocks and sands of a vast desert the goat wanders alone and in agony, bearing the burden of all the iniquities of the Children of Israel.[1]

What those people were doing with ritual care 3000 years ago we today do carelessly. When things go wrong for us any scapegoat will serve our turn. Consider for a moment the rich choice of scapegoats that is offered to us in the 'doomsday' books. We can put the burden of our iniquities upon the economist; he is the callous calculator of our ill-gotten gains. Or we can put it upon the scientist; he is the inventor of our destructive technologies. Or we can put it upon the Jew and the Christian; their teaching has polluted our minds. So, at any rate, we are told.

The chance is 50:50 that the next book you read about the environmental crisis will contain a censorious reference to 'The Judaeo-Christian tradition'. This contribution to the conventional wisdom of our time may be traced to a single article, *The Historical Origins of Our Ecologic Crisis*, by Professor Lynn White of the University of California.[2] Jews and Christians, he maintains, would have lived companionably with Nature, just as the pagan peoples do, had not the Bible put them on the wrong track. On the first five days of creation, the Bible says, God made the universe and the earth and all the creatures of the earth with the exception of man. On the sixth day God made Adam and—I quote:

> ... as an afterthought, Eve to keep man from being lonely. Man named all the animals, thus establishing his dominance over them. God planned all this explicitly for man's benefit and rule: no item in the physical creation had any purpose save to serve man's purposes. And, although man's body is made of clay, he is not simply part of nature: he is made in God's image.

Christianity, he continues, has inherited from Judaism man's arrogant conception of his powers and rights as the lord of creation.

It seemed to me, when I read this dissertation, that its author was building a tall tower of theory on a fragile foundation of fact. His reading of the Old Testament had come to a dead stop with the second chapter of the first Book. But the Old Testament contains 39 Books. Almost every Book is the work of different writers who lived at different times and put into literary shape traditions that had been handed down over long periods of time from one generation to the next. Taken together, the 39 Books constitute a miscellany— history books, law books, song books, prophecy books, wisdom books. They tell the story of a small nomadic tribe striving to conquer and hold a territory and to make itself a nation: this story is heroic, tragic and all too often murderous. Interwoven with it is another story of the same tribe or nation asking tremendous questions about the universe and its scheme of government, about the earth and its creatures, about man and his place in the scheme of government and his relationship with the creatures. The answers given to this last question are more various than is asserted by Professor Lynn White. If he were logically consistent, he would applaud the animistic symbolism which the prophets and the poets quite often employ. In the Book of Isaiah, for example, natural creatures are joyful and companionable with man; their songs mingle with his songs; the beasts of the field and the dragons and the owls praise the Lord; the heavens and the mountains and the lower parts of the earth sing for joy; the trees on the little hills sing and clap their hands. In the Psalms, contrasting moods find expression. Psalm 8 re-echoes the Genesis story of man's domination; but in Psalms 19, 96 and 148 man's voice mingles with many other voices. The heavens declare the glory of God and the firmament showeth his handiwork; the sea and its creatures praise him with a loud roar; the mountains skip like rams and the little hills like lambs; the fruitful valleys shout and sing for joy. All God's creatures join the exultant choir—the angels and hosts of the Lord, the sun and moon and stars, the waters above the heavens, the dragons and all deeps, fire and hail and snow, vapours and stormy winds, beasts and all people, young men and maidens, old men and children. In the Psalms, as in Genesis, man is the climax of creation; but he is not an irresponsible tyrant. He holds his power from God and is accountable to God for the use he makes of it. The thought of the poets and prophets, notwithstanding its exuberant imagery, is neither animistic nor anthropocentric, but austerely monotheistic.[3]

Lynn White makes no attempt to trace this thought to its

historical source. Early versions of the creation story had been incised in hieroglyphics on Mesopotamian stone a very long time before a Jewish literary genius composed that superb first chapter of the Book of Genesis. Moreover, people in the Euphrates valley had been domesticating animals and plants, digging irrigation channels, building cities and inventing the calendar for some thousands of years before the idea occurred to them that a story of their achievement ought to be told. *The fact* of man's mastery over nature existed before the story. Lynn White appears at times to regret the fact. He looks back nostalgically to pagan animism, when 'every tree, every spring, every stream, every hill had its own *genius loci*, its guardian spirit'. Pagan man, he asserts, 'respected the feelings of natural objects'. A logician or a grammarian might say that to have feelings is a capacity of subjects not objects; but let us ignore this quibble. The question has still to be asked whether or not pagan man respected 'the feelings' of natural objects when he set fire to forest and scrub. He was an inveterate incendiary.

'The historical origins of our ecologic crisis' are not so easily identified as has been suggested. Let us now return to the Old Testament with some different questions in mind. Abraham and the other pastoral infiltrators brought with them from Mesopotamia to Palestine a rich collection of stories—Creation, the Fall of Man, the Flood, the Covenant, the Tower of Babel. Of these, the Covenant has particular interest for historians, because its successive versions throw light on cultural change. Noah belongs to the cosmopolitan, urbanised culture of the Euphrates valley; in consequence, God's Covenant with Noah embraces the whole of mankind. But the cultural situation is different when the Covenant is re-enacted with the Bedouin invaders of the land of Canaan. In their imaginations, the Lord God of the universe becomes the Lord God of Israel. The commands of this Lord God to his chosen people are terrible—not only to destroy the enemy armies but also to destroy the populations—men, women, children and even the animals. If ever the Children of Israel practise even a little humanity, they become transgressors of the Covenant. The Lord God smites the transgressors. They repent and amend their ways. Carnage continues as before.[4]

Nevertheless the universalist vision does not completely fade. In a land ravaged by war and murder tender plants of human sympathy come once more into leaf. The serene story of Ruth, a daughter of Moab who finds blessing in the land of Israel, speaks to the heart of man. In the Psalms we sometimes hear the music of mankind.

What is man, that thou art mindful of him?
and the son of man, that thou visiteth him?
For thou has made him a little lower than the angels, and has
crowned him with glory and honour.[5]

Proverbs and Ecclesiastes, the wisdom books, are documents of an emergent humanistic culture. In the later prophetic books the signs are clear that Jewish exclusiveness is coming under challenge. By now the time is not far distant when Palestine will become a province within the cultural world of Greece and the political world of Rome. Zealots will fight to the death for the old ways; but other Jews will come to terms with the new ways. The idea will emerge that God's chosen people are not a tribal or racial community, but a community of the faithful within which no distinction is made between Jew and Gentile. The Church will be born.

I propose now to attempt a long leap from the world of the Old Testament and the early Christian Church into the modern world.[6] My leap takes off from a famous theological controversy of the fifth century AD. A sturdy British monk named Pelagius had the temerity to argue that man is not born under the curse of Adam's sin: on the contrary, he is born with the capacity to act not only sinfully but virtuously: by the exercise of his own free will he can make himself either good or bad: he may even make himself perfect. This sanguine view of human nature brought down on the head of Pelagius the wrath of Saint Augustine. The Fall of Man, he retorted, is a continuing calamity: because of Adam's sin 'the whole mass of mankind is cankered at the roots': some men are chosen for salvation by the grace of God, but no man ever has been saved or ever will be saved by his own will and effort. This sombre Augustinian theology prevailed. The Pelagian doctrine of free will was declared heretical. Pelagianism, however, was not so easily killed. It seeped into the Catholic Church. It provoked the Protestant revolt. To this very day, Augustinians and Pelagians, although they no longer know themselves and each other by these names, remain locked in combat.

The theological controversy has been secularised. Among the secularisers the Florentine Niccolo Machiavelli holds pride of place. In his political writings Necessity ousts God: 'men never do any good', he asserts, 'except by Necessity'. A statement such as this, with its emphasis on the sinfulness of man, may sound Augustinian; but the sound is deceptive. Machiavelli has inherited the Christian terminology of goodness and sin, but uses it cheek by jowl with a pagan terminology which he ascribes to the writers of republican

Rome. Consider the word 'goodness': there is Christian goodness, which is contemptible, and pagan goodness, which is admirable. If you want to be good in the Christian way, he says, you will have to go into a monastery; but if you want to live in the world as it is you will have to learn how and when not to be good in the Christian way—how and when to be predatory, miserly, deceitful, cruel. These Christian vices are pagan virtues. His word for them is virtù, by which he means courage and competence in political combat. He loved combat. He also loved shocking people. He could so easily have used mealy-mouthed words which would have offended nobody; he could have called the miser economical, the liar discreet, the cruel man severe or firm. All appearances to the contrary, he is not an Augustinian. Nor is he quite a Pelagian. Perhaps we may most fittingly remember this lively, intelligent Italian as the founding father of value-free political science.

Machiavelli died in AD 1527. Two centuries later, a Dutch physician who had settled in London, Bernard de Mandeville, became a founding father of value-free economic science. He is remembered today by his book, *The Fable of the Bees, or Private Vices, Public Virtues*. Struggle, he says, is the law of economic activity; the great commercial nations of Europe owe their wealth and power to the pride, greed and envy of thrusting individuals. De Mandeville's robust vocabulary lends itself as easily as Machiavelli's does to insipid translation. In modern textbooks his 'private vices' are called 'incentives'. Adam Smith called them 'natural propensities'.

Adam Smith was riding the crest of a great Pelagian wave. Historians call this wave the Enlightenment—a good name, because it was much in use among European philosophers of the eighteenth century. A conspicuous hero of the Enlightenment was the Marquis de Condorcet, who grew up with mathematics and physics, blossomed as a philosopher and plunged into the politics of revolutionary France. While the Jacobins were hunting him to his death he was writing a book to prove the perfectability of human society.[7] He died firm in the faith that a tyrant like Robespierre is like chaff before the wind in comparison with Bacon and Descartes, Galileo and Newton—men who had discovered a method of reasoning which made it certain that progress would continue by its own momentum through all the vicissitudes of politics:

> Nature and Nature's laws lay hid in night
> God said, 'Let Newton be!' and all was light.[8]

Condorcet looked forward to the day when the same light would reveal not only the laws of physics but the laws of human society. Immanuel Kant held the same faith: Nature, he declared, would in her own good time bring forth a second Newton to formulate the universal law of human development. These enlightened men pitched their hopes too high. Nevertheless the great optimistic wave rolled on with gathering force through the nineteenth century and into the twentieth. Then it crashed on the rock of world war.

There had always been a pessimistic undertow. To exemplify it, I shall choose Dean Swift's Gulliver. He is cast ashore in the land of the *Houynymhnms*, a race of noble horses who live comfortably with the rules of reason. The menial tasks of their society are performed by detestable creatures called *Yahoos*. When Gulliver reports to the Master Horse the achievements of European civilisation, that wise creature comments as follows:

> That he looked upon us as a Sort of Animal, to whose Share, by what Accident he could not conjecture, some small Pittance of *Reason* had fallen, whereof we made no other Use than by its Assistance to aggravate our *Natural* Corruptions, and to acquire new ones which Nature had not given us.

To his horror, Gulliver recognises himself as a Yahoo. He is denied the felicity of spending the rest of his years with the wise and magnanimous Honynymhnms. After many adventures he returns home.

> As soon as I entered the House, my Wife took me in her Arms, and kissed me; at which, not having been used to the Touch of that Odious Animal for so many years, I fell in a Swoon for almost an Hour.

As might have been expected, an expurgated version of Swift's satire has been many times re-published as a story for children.

In our own century, the returning tide of gloom was heralded by the poet WB Yeats during the chaotic years that followed the First World War.

> . . .
> Things fall apart; the centre cannot hold;
> Mere anarchy is loosed upon the world,
> The blood-dimmed tide is loosed, and everywhere
> The ceremony of innocence is drowned;
> The best lack all conviction, while the worst

Are full of passionate intensity
Surely some revelation is at hand;
Surely the Second Coming is at hand.

. . .

And what rough beast, its hour come round at last,
Slouches towards Bethlehem to be born?

I called those lines to mind at the end of the Second World War when I learnt the truth about Auschwitz.

Two world wars and the environmental crisis have made more urgent than ever the great debate which began so many thousands of years ago in the valley of the Euphrates. What is Man? Two distinguished biologists, Jacques Monod and René Dubos, have come to close grips with that question.

Monod is a Nobel Prize winner and the Director of the famous Pasteur Institute. In his book, *Chance and Necessity*, he reports the rapid progress that has been made since the Second World War in scientific knowledge of the large molecules that are contained within the cells of all living creatures. He gives clear and precise explanations of the mechanisms of cellular inheritance (the DNA story); of the purposive functioning of cells (the protein molecule story); of mutations and—moving now from the microscopic to the macroscopic level—of natural selection. Monod's specialist colleagues in Paris, Cambridge and elsewhere endorse his explanations. The lay student of the book admires Monod's forceful prose and his crusading fervour. In his first chapter, he declares war against superstition—in particular, against the erroneous belief that knowledge of the universe can be reached 'by interpreting phenomena in terms of final causes—that is to say, of "purpose"'. In the concluding chapters he claims total victory for science over superstition.

> Pure chance, absolutely free but blind, at the very root of the stupendous edifice of evolution: this central concept of modern biology is no longer one among other possible or even conceivable hypotheses. It is today the *sole* conceivable hypothesis, the only one compatible with observed and tested fact. And nothing warrants the supposition (or the hope) that conceptions about this should, or even could, be revised.[9]

That very typical statement is not completely immune from strictly scientific criticism. In a broadcast discussion last year with Jacques Monod, Sir Peter Medawar gently suggested that the scientist who uses phrases like 'the sole conceivable hypothesis' is running great risks.[10] But Monod is an ardent risk-taker. In the last ten pages of his book he invents a new epistemology, in which objective scientific knowledge is 'the only' source of truth. He invents a new ethic, 'the ethic of knowledge'. He invents a new transcendence within the soul of man,[11] to take the place of cosmic purpose. Finally, and for good measure, he invents a new Utopia, socialism without Karl Marx. To me it seems surprising that the pure seed of his scientific objectivity should produce so plentiful a harvest of subjective proclamations. However, I do not want to score a debating point. The crucial issue is Monod's epistemology—whether or not scientific objectivity is the only source of truth. I do not believe it. As an historian, I take pains never on any account to distort the evidence; but my approach to the evidence, whether it starts with sophisticated theory or with a hunch, invariably expresses my point of view.[12] If we can believe Einstein and Niels Böhr, points of view have some significance even for physicists. Do they have significance for biologists?

René Dubos, my second spokesman for biological science, suggests some answers to this question in his book *So Human An Animal*.[13] Formerly a member of the Pasteur Institute, Dubos has been for many years an American citizen and a professor of the Rockefeller University in New York. By training a microbiologist and experimental pathologist, he is today pre-eminently an ecologist. He holds different ideas from those of Monod about the scope and method of biological study. He pays eloquent tribute to the success of the molecular biologists in explaining the chemical machinery which is operative within the cells of all living creatures, from the simplest to the most complex; but he also insists that this is only part of the story of life. Living creatures have to be studied, he maintains, not only by analysis in laboratories, but also by observation in the field. They have to be studied as organisms in complicated interplay with other organisms, all responding to environmental challenges within the habitats which they share. This, surely, is scientific truth as the soil scientist sees it; the clod of earth on which he stands is the habitat of hundreds of thousands of interacting micro-organisms. It is scientific truth as the plant pathologist sees it; his diagnosis of disease in the root of a plant is unlikely to prove successful if he has paid no attention to the funguses and viruses of the surrounding soil. It is scientific truth as the student of animal behaviour sees it when he is observing, recording and measuring mother–infant relationships among rhesus monkeys. It is scientific truth not only for the biologist, but for the historian or the philosopher whose field of study is 'man umbilical to earth'. It is scientific truth for humanists.

In their different ways, both Monod and Dubos are humanists; but the humanism of Dubos seems to me both more spacious and more realistic than that of Monod. I can best illustrate the contrasting philosophies of the two men by quoting some methodological observations made by Dubos.

> The methods used by the investigator determine and limit the kind of observations he can mate. If scientists elect to study man only by physicochemical methods, they will naturally discover only the physicochemical determinants of his life and find that his body is a machinery of atoms. But they will overlook other human characteristics that are at least as interesting and important. One of them is that man hardly ever reacts passively to external forces. The most characteristic aspect of his behaviour is that he responds not only actively but often unexpectedly and creatively. He is the more human the more vigorously he converts passive reactions into creative responses. The mechanical definition of human life misses the point because what is human in man is precisely that which is not mechanical.[14]

Frankly and firmly, René Dubos puts man into the centre of his world-picture.

I have found it fascinating to see him making his way along successive knife-edges of thought and just managing to retain his balance: nature and nurture; man shaped by his genetic and cultural inheritance yet still a rebel; freedom inevitably constrained, yet none the less real. I have neither the time nor the competence to pursue those themes; but I must declare my solidarity with Dubos on an issue that is crucial for me as an historian. He rejects the theory of knowledge propounded by Jacques Monod: namely, that 'the principle of objectivity' is the only road to truth.[15] It is not the only road for poets; nor is it the only road for biologists. René Dubos finds truth of different kinds in science, poetry, parable and myth. If you were to ask him whether the Garden-of-Eden story is scientifically true he would tell you not to believe a word of it. Nevertheless he quotes more than once in his book a sentence from that story: 'And the Lord God took the man and put him into the garden to dress it.' Precisely that, he believes, remains man's responsibility.

If Dubos allows himself to find truth in Genesis, I may allow myself to find it in the Psalms. According to the psalmist, man is a little lower than the angels.[16] That poetic statement expresses realistically man's status in the order of the universe. Man is a good deal less than a god; but a good deal more than a naked ape. I recall the fighting declaration of a sorely afflicted Afrikaner humanist, Jan Christiaan Smuts: 'It is a great thing to be a man'.

1   Leviticus 16:21–22. Holman Hunt's picture was painted in 1854. Like Russell Drysdale a century later, Hunt studied the desert landscape before he painted it.
2   *Science*, vol. 55, no. 3767, pp1203–07.
3   Isaiah 43:20. Psalms 19:1; 60:13; 96:11; 148 *passim*.
4   The most gruesome stories of slaughter will be found in Joshua, Judges and Samuel.
5   Psalms 8:4–5.
6   My colleague John Passmore illuminates this highway of the history of ideas in his superb book, *The Perfectability of Man* (Duckworth, 1970).
7   Condorcet was found dead in his cell on the day which followed his capture by the Jacobins. His unfinished book is entitled *Sketch for a Historical Picture of the Progress of the Human Mind* (trans.).
8   Alexander Pope, 'Epitaph intended for Sir Isaac Newton'.
9   Jacques Monod, *Le hazard et la nécessité* (Paris, 1970); English translation by A. Wainhouse (Vintage, 1972), p110.
10   *The Listener*, 3 August 1972. Medawar recalled that JS Haldane (not, JBS) had asserted that the existence of a chemical substance akin to DNA was 'inconceivable'.
11   On pp. 148–9 Monod (op. cit.) refuses to surrender 'the soul'.
12   See the study entitled 'Bias' in WK Hancock, *Attempting History* (ANU Press, 1969).
13   I have used the London edition (Rupert Hart-Davis, 1970). (A new edition was published in 1998.)
14   Dubos, p132.
15   Cf. *The Listener*, 3 August 1972, Medawar to Monod—'You say that objective knowledge is the only source of truth. But that is not true, is it? Truth may come from all sources, however unlikely.' In *The Art of the Soluble* (London, 1966) Medawar acclaims imagination as the generator of creative science work.
16   Theologians have ascribed to angels a comparatively modest rank in the spiritual hierarchy. According to the fifth century writer known as Dionysius the Areopagite, they occupy the third place in the third 'choir'.

Hugh Stretton

Hugh Stretton was born in Melbourne in 1924, and was educated at the Scotch College and the universities of Melbourne, Oxford and Princeton. He became a Fellow of Balliol College, Oxford, in 1948, where he taught history and political science until he returned to Australia in 1954 as Professor of History at the University of Adelaide. He gave up his chair in 1968 but continued to lecture at the university as a Reader until 1989. He has been visiting fellow in economics at the university since 1990.

Among Stretton's most influential books was *Ideas for Australian Cities*. He was deputy chairman of the South Australian Housing Trust from 1973 to 1989, as well as being a member of the Australian Cities Commission (1974–75) and on the board of the Australian Housing Corporation (1975–76).

Professor Stretton was also a visiting lecturer or researcher at a number of Australian and overseas institutions including the Australian National University, the University of London, the Centre for Environmental Studies, London, and York University.

Hugh Stretton's role as both an advisor to governments and an implementer of public policy is summarised in his Boyer Lectures title *Housing and Government*. Given that statistics relating to housing approvals and expenditure are still a source of remarkable interest to economic commentators, Stretton's analyses and criticisms of many economic theories of housing make challenging reading. His individual lecture titles are 'The Conventional Wisdom'; 'Home Economics—How People Use Space and Time' reproduced here; 'How to be Free and Equal and Productive' and 'A National Housing Policy'. Throughout runs the thesis that citizens usually understand their own housing needs and economic priorities better than most economic and urban experts. These are subjects of abiding importance, especially in our larger cities. Stretton sets out his concerns at the outset of his first lecture: 'The hard problems of housing are not chiefly technical, they are problems of justice, social values, social and economic understanding; and they are riddled with conflicts of interest.'

HOW PEOPLE USE SPACE
AND TIME

Housing and Government

Hugh Stretton

• 1 9 7 4 •

How should we decide what to invest in home and neighbor-hood?

I have suggested that it helps to think of two economic systems, a commercial one and a domestic one. The commercial one includes all the paid labor and the goods exchanged for money, so it includes most of both of what are commonly called the public and private sectors of the economic system. The domestic economy is everything we make and do for ourselves and one another by free labor, mostly at home but also between relatives, friends, neighbors, and in unpaid community services and associations.

The two systems can't be compared too precisely but, applying some rough common sense, the commercial system probably uses more than half of all our capital and labor, and the domestic system uses more than a third. Orthodox economic theory counts the capital costs of both systems, but it counts the labor and output of only one of them. So it says that investment in housing produces no output, and keeps us poor by preventing economic growth.

You may not think a society like ours needs much more economic growth. For environmental or other reasons, some people doubt it. But suppose you are still interested in growth. Look at its history. Industrial societies all went through a phase of very fast growth when coal and steam, then other sources of power, trans-formed their methods of production. Through that phase it was the organized commercial use of paid labor that contributed most to the growth of productivity. But now that the factory and transport revolutions have transformed about as much of our work as they can, growth is much slower. Most of it now has to be in labor-inten-sive services—people paying each other for their skill and time. But in the meantime a lot of the factory output has gone to build and equip and service our houses. That equips us to do more for ourselves. The domestic economy can be as well equipped as most commercial services, and it can contribute as much as they can to growth. It can often contribute more. Once the commercial services have full employment and a limited working week their further growth is severely limited, and mostly depends on getting more housewives back to commercial employment. But domestic productivity responds just as well to investment, and on top of that it can draw on big reserves of under-used labor—especially because so much of it is not hard labor but quite welcome activity, often with the double value that the work and its product are both enjoyable and both deserve to count as goods. So it looks sensible to put a good deal of the capital where the spare labor is.

But if you're interested in growth you won't learn much about it from a science which ignores about half of it. And if you're less interested in economic growth and more interested in other qualities of life, or in environmental care, or in fairer social shares, you'll learn even less about those from the orthodox theories.

So what should we do instead? We could correct one bias by putting shadow prices or notional money values on what we make and do at home, and counting them into national income and product. That may be educational, but it still won't reflect the values most people put on a great many non-measurable pains and pleasures of home and social life: the personal frustrations and fulfilments and freedoms, and the easy or strained human relations, that are affected in so many ways by the space and resources that people can have at home. We really need to make broader judgments that take into account quantities and qualities, economic goods and a great many unmeasurable goods and evils too. There's nothing wrong with judgments of that kind. We live by them, and expect our politicians to take most of their decisions in the same broadminded way. But they can still be careful rather than careless, and based on the best information they can get.

In deciding how to allocate capital between the two economic systems we should really consider three kinds of questions. First, the systems may produce different goods. It's not efficient to smelt steel at home, or on the other hand to bring up children in institutions if you can help it. So we should decide what balance of goods we want and invest accordingly. But there's also a wide range of goods that can be produced by either system—most personal services, for example. With them the question is less what you want to consume, and more how you want it produced. The real costs may be much the same either way, but using paid instead of free labor is likely to affect distribution of income. So in making these choices the third thing to bear in mind is the effect they'll have on social shares.

To illustrate all three, think about flowers. As a consumer you may like your own best, or the ones that come from market gardens. As a producer you may enjoy growing them, or you may find it a chore. But even if you don't like growing them yourself that may be the only way you can afford them. If you think pensioners ought to be able to have flowers you can invest in private land for them, or in market gardens and flower shops. But if you choose the commercial method it won't work unless you also increase taxes and pensions, because unless you drive the pensioners back to wage labor, you've replaced a productive possibility by a distributive problem. By giving the land to commercial gardeners rather than pensioners you've switched capital out of the domestic system into the commercial system. That has ruled out some free labor, reduced overall productivity, and increased inequality—though as usual the national accounts will probably say the opposite. If the taxpayers want to give flowers to pensioners, they'll stay richer themselves if they give capital rather than consumer goods; and most of the pensioners will do better that way too.

That sort of choice affects bigger things than gardening. It affects a lot of maintenance of land, buildings, equipment, clothing and health; some care of children; a lot of culture and recreation; and plenty of other goods and services. It's the options between paid and free labor that many commercial interests and economists do their best to deceive us about. They'll defend themselves by saying that the customer spends his money how he likes, on equipment or consumer goods, and investment responds to demand. That may sometimes be true of the choice between buying a packet of seeds or a bunch of cut flowers—though even then it's only true if the customers have land so that they have real choices. In practice a great many of the customers' choices are predetermined for them by government or business decisions, and especially by the private space and opportunity the customers can or can't have to make their own labor productive and enjoyable.

Housing and its land are the most expensive of those domestic resources. In most affluent societies government does a great deal to influence the size, type, standard, financing and distribution of new housing, and in doing that it determines a good deal of the distribution of new capital between the commercial and domestic systems. If it can't get sensible advice from its economists, what other advice can it look for? It can ask housewives what they think; and it can ask some other social sciences what they know about those reserves of time and labor and freedom that go to work—or go to waste— outside the money economy and the 40 hour week. Off work, how do people use their time, their equipment, their mobility, their houses and gardens? What do they do with those resources and how do they value them?

I can't possibly summarize or even list the sources of knowledge about those subjects. I can only sample four of them (with apologies to scores of Australian researchers left off the list). First there was an international study of how people used their time in 1965 in the United States and nine countries of east and west Europe. Its results are collected in a book by A Szalai and others called *The Use of Time* published in Holland in 1972. There are similar reports of the use of time by people in the London region in 1970 in a book called *The Symmetrical Family* by the sociologists Michael Young and Peter Willmott, published in 1973; most of the book is about what's happening to family life. Then there are two Australian examples, neither finished yet. One is a survey of family use of time, and housewives' feelings about it, in parts of Melbourne and Albury/Wodonga. It was conceived by Norman Kirkan with help from Frank Lancaster Jones (both sociologists) and is being done for the Cities Commission by the market research firm of McNair Anderson and Associates. Finally there's a study of how urban Australians use their gardens, being done by Ian Halkett, a research student in geography at the Australian National University.

Only one of those studies was conceived by government. In passing, notice how most of the city-building branches of government allocate their research resources. Australians average at least ten times as many waking hours at home and around the neighborhood as they spend in cars on roads—and those home hours have many more variable possibilities of enjoyment, productivity or frustration. But the relevant authorities spend hundreds of times as much on road research and planning as they spend on studying the value and use of home resources. In three south-eastern cities alone in the last ten years several million dollars' worth of road research have recommended knocking down about 100,000 houses, without ever sparing a dime to investigate the personal effects or the social economy of doing that, or the citizens' opinions about it, or the fortunes of people who have been bulldozed in the past. Some are now doing better—though it tends to be the new, egg-headed agencies that are doing it. The South Australian government finished its asphalt research then suspended its urban motorway program a good many years ago, and it does now spend money on urban social research. So do the new urban department of the Australian government, and some of the development corporations, and some planning authorities and consultants. But the branches of government which traditionally build our cities still design most of their research to make sure it won't discover anything human. The experts who tell us we'll be better off without private houses and gardens never expose that opinion to research. The people who plan roads—and the Treasuries who insulate road finance but not housing finance from stop-and-go—never study the personal or social harm their policies may do. There is currently a lot of research into ways of producing houses from factories, but not much of it is asking how people experience the various kinds of industrialized housing, some good and some bad, that we and other countries have already. In these fields the distinctive contributions of expert-ise are one-eyed biases—more by products of theories which define housing as shelter and the work of the home economy as worthless.

To return to the sociologists who do investigate the use of home resources: there's not much disagreement between the studies I mentioned. They're all consistent—and so are scores of others—with conclusions which could be summed up like this: Most people put high value on private space, indoor and outdoor. They're aware of the private and social costs of their domestic resources but think them well worth paying. And the way to get people out to join in community and public life is generally to give them more home space and resources, not less; but city, local and home resources do need to match and complement each other. They're not so much alternatives as mutual multipliers.

Halkett's garden studies dispose of the idea that the Australian suburban block is useless. Remember that story that we only need back yards for the few years we have small children? Otherwise they're millstones round our necks, compulsory boredom and lawnmowing forced on us by stupid municipal rules, or social conformism? Europeans have more sense than to want them, and we'd be happier without them? The fact is that Europeans in Europe grab private land if they can get it. Europeans in Australia are keener on it than home-grown Australians are. In Halkett's sample more of them want it, they want more of it, and they use it more actively—more fruit and vegetables and chickens. Thirty per cent of native Australians say they'd like the smaller gardens that go with medium density housing; only half that proportion of immigrants would be content with so little. Are our blocks nevertheless bigger than they need to be? Well, the bigger they are the more intensive and varied use they tend to get. But we do seem to have the right number of big and little ones to meet demand, though they're not all meeting it—the number of people who want bigger blocks than they've got is neatly matched by the number who'd like smaller ones.

As you'd expect, households with children use their gardens most, most actively, through most months of the year. But adults as well as children use them; and adults without children still use them a good deal. More than 90 per cent of parents use their gardens for some sort of recreation, and more than 70 per cent of adults without children do the same. More than half of our back yards see at least 15 hours a week of social or recreational activity. (That's additional to the work done in them, though it may some-times count different activities going on at the same time.) And more than half of all our hours of outdoor recreation happen in our gardens. Halkett notices ruefully that a national seminar on leisure was held in Canberra earlier this year; it went on for three days, but the place where people spend more than half their outdoor leisure, and the recreations they pursue there, were scarcely mentioned. (More expertise, based on more theories of the same old one-eyed kind.) Most of these facts are not peculiar to Australia. We may spend more garden hours, because more of us have gardens, and warm weather. But majorities in all affluent societies, including the Europeans with the sociable cities we envy, spend most of their leisure at home; and just as we do, they spend four or five times as much of their purely social time with family and kin as they do with other friends and acquaintances or with strangers.

More from Halkett: If his Adelaide sample represents Australian cities fairly, two thirds of us keep pets or chickens. Nine out of ten grow some fruit or vegetables; one household in ten grows a quarter or more of its needs. Five out of six grow flowers. Very few households spend more than two man-hours a week cutting lawns; nearly half spend an hour or less. One in ten of those who do the gardening thinks gardening is nothing but a chore. A third think it's part work, part pleasure. More than half think it's a pleasure or a major hobby. Front fences? Most people like whatever they've got, with one exception: of the people with no front fences at all, more than half would like to have them, though more for reasons of appearance and conformity than privacy.

It's in front of the house that Halkett's findings don't directly contradict the critics of suburbia. People don't use their front gardens much, and they design them chiefly to be looked at. I'm not sure why the critics think that's such a worthless thing to be doing. Designing gardens to look good, and live well with their neighbors and streetscape, isn't necessarily slavish—or if it is, so are most of the visual arts. Halkett didn't ask people to compare front with back gardening, but they didn't volunteer any different feelings about them.

Nevertheless if you want to save land it's clear what you can take with least loss of active social or home life. First you can take half the street—more than half if you plan more cur-de-sacs—then half the front gardens, especially if you let householders fence the other half. For the land you save, there will then be choices between commercial and domestic uses. You can use the saved land to make the city denser—to shorten the walk to shops or transport stops. Or it can provide more local parks and pedestrian ways, if you don't mind higher taxes to pay for more commercial gardening and maintenance. Or you can leave the old map as it was, but narrow the streets and shift the houses forward to give people deeper back gardens; then you'll have reduced commercial capital and running costs, and increased private resources. The best thing to do will vary with circumstances and local opinions. Meanwhile planners and local councillors may like to hear that their traditional block sizes seem to have been about right, even if their street-plans and setbacks and fencing rules don't.

But if you take away too much of the private land you'll turn the clock back in more ways than one. To see how complicated and drastic the losses would be, it is necessary to stand back and look at home resources in a more general and historical way, as Michael Young and Peter Willmott do in *The Symmetrical Family*. For us this book has the disadvantage of being about English rather than Australian life; but plenty of it holds for life in most affluent democracies. Simplified, one of its historical themes is this:

Two hundred years ago most people lived off the land, in one way or another. They farmed, or if they worked at other trades they often worked near home much as farmers do. There were tasks for most members of the family, and they all helped to produce goods for market as well as goods for themselves. So however poor they were, families were often cooperative producers, with a good deal of control of their own tasks and timetables.

The first industrial revolution—the factory revolution—broke up that co-op. Work moved out of the family into the factory. Labor had to live in walking distance of the factory, so people moved into the crowded slum housing of the early industrial cities, where there was neither space nor spare time to do much more than eat and sleep. Members of the family went off singly to long hours of low-paid wage-labor, and at home they had to live on what they could afford to buy. They were slaves of the commercial economy right around the clock, and the statistics of economic growth looked wonderful. More and more housework was commercialised. To keep home up to any genteel standard took long hours of labor, with the primitive gear they had; so to look after the rising numbers in the expanding upper and middle classes, low-paid domestic service became the biggest single occupation in the commercial economy. But there wasn't much chance for genteel housekeeping in the laboring classes. Child-rearing was short. Children went to work young, and learned most of what they needed to learn on the job. Many of their mothers as well as their fathers worked long hours for wages. So the house was just shelter. The family wasn't together much, it didn't do much together or produce much. It was at its most degraded and unimportant as an institution.

But then came the second industrial revolution: mass-produced household goods, network water and gas and electricity, more versatile transport; and another great shift of productive resources. The first industrial revolution had moved production out of the family into the factory; the second industrial revolution moved a lot of it back again. The housewife got equipment which saved time and made her work a bit more enjoyable. It allowed her and her family to do more: between them they could produce better living standards and more enjoyable uses of their time together. As the factory economy got more efficient it used less labor for shorter hours; so it did the double service of giving people more private capital, and more free time to use it. Also more power—today's British housewife commands as much mechanical horsepower as the British factory worker did 60 years ago. We think of vacuum cleaners and washing machines and do-it-yourself tools and materials. But the thing people wanted most, and have been getting steadily all over the affluent world, was simply space: bigger and better houses, with a room each for more members of families, and versatile private garden space outside, and more public space in the schools and parks of the local neighborhood. To most people the richest gift of powered transport has not been mobility so much as private space. Since the first railway, London's population has multiplied by five. And that fivefold population have several times the private space per head they used to have, so the city has sprawled over 20 or 30 times its old area. But the average time it takes to get from home to work or city has scarcely varied through all those years—it's about the same now as it was in the London of Charles Dickens. The marvellous achievement of the commercial economy has been to give private households not just consumer goods, but space and time and freedom to produce for themselves—to produce goods, and to enrich their time and social experience in ways freely chosen by themselves.

With these new freedoms the nuclear family turns out to be more popular than ever, especially where it can get comfortable living space. A higher proportion of people than ever now live in family households. If they leave home young, or get divorced often, it's usually to form new nuclear households very soon. It's been said that the family has come full circle from being a producer co-op to being a consumer co-op. That's half true, but it makes the same old theoretical mistake of only counting the commercial goods. A great many of the things a family 'consumes' or enjoys these days it produces for itself, using commercial goods as raw materials or working capital. It's a cooperative producer again. In fact it's both. Plenty of both production and consumption (if you want to insist on the distinction) have moved back into homes and gardens and free public places.

I have talked about housework and humdrum games and hobbies, but the same is true of more formal culture. Many writers write at home. Most composers compose at home. Some painters paint at home. And a lot more than half of all the enjoyment of that sort of culture now happens at home. That's where most people now hear most music, read most books, see and hear most drama, read and see and hear most of the world's news and most of the analysis and commentary on it. This doesn't mean that public community and city life has stopped—that we do nothing but sit at home plugged in to our electronics. Since the kids got trannies, they spend more time at live pop gatherings. The people with most gramophone records are the people who go out to most live concerts. The people who have most books at home make most use of libraries and educational services. It's where the home resources and the television programs are poorest that low-income families stay home and watch most television. They do least of that where the home resources and the television quality are best—in English houses with gardens, for example. One thing that has moved back home is watching sport; at least in England, more people go out to play it than to watch it; and they play more, the better their home resources are.

What holds for city life can hold for country life too. Norway is a good example. Norwegian city life tends to be dull because the Norwegians seem to prefer country recreations. They love their summer countrysides and seasides, and they spend more winter hours than any other Europeans out on their snow. Does this mean that they need less housing and private land at home? No, they average the biggest houses in continental Europe, with the highest percentage of private gardens, and the highest percentage of households with two houses, one in town and another for holidays. Because of this a lot of their activities and pleasures can be uncommercial. So they show a little poorer and less equal than the Swedes do in the official figures of national income. But they have much fairer shares of more generous home resources than the Swedes do, so in fact they're probably richer—more productive and also more equal—in real goods and enjoyments that they really value. Once again good home resources go with more use of public resources away from home.

Young and Willmott are specially interested in the way the new home resources affect human relations within families. Women go out and earn; men do more of the work around the house; they do more things together; so their roles are growing more similar. Some still work harder than others. A few managers and professional men average the longest hours. Next come a third of married women, the ones who combine some housework with full-time jobs. Then come the next third of married women who combine part-time jobs with rather more housework. Next come most married men, with full-time jobs plus (in England) an average hour and twenty-five minutes a day of work around the house. Last come the remaining third of married women, mostly the ones with small children, who average six or seven hours of work at home and don't go out and earn at all.

So the relations between commercial and domestic work, and between husbands and wives, are still far from equal, but in England they are moving in that direction. And (except for the few hardest-working men at the top) the better-off people get, the further they move in the equal direction. As English husbands rise up the income scale, they do more both at work and at home. Unskilled laborers do the shortest hours at work and are the laziest husbands at home. But there are less and less of them, as more and more of the population get better off, and more cooperative at home.

This is a humane and valuable process of change, but it may not be happening in quite the same way in Australia. Some early figures from the Australian time study seem to differ from the international averages. Husbands in Melbourne and Albury/Wodonga appear to do less than a third of the housework that husbands in Bulgaria do; about a quarter as much as Czechs do; and scarcely a third of what English husbands do. The second-laziest husbands on record are the Americans, and we are more than twice as bad as them. Some of the differences may be due to different survey methods. Perhaps Australian fathers spend more time with their children in ways that don't count as work. But there seems to be no doubt of one sinister difference: Australian husbands don't improve much with affluence. From poorest to richest they average worse than the lowest-paid lumpenproletarians of the London region. These figures seem to confirm a number of popular beliefs. Perhaps the toffee-nosed English who think all Australians are vulgar working class have some evidence at last. And Australian women who believe they have the world's most unhelpful husbands are correct. Furthermore they'd better watch the male economists who want them back at more hours and years of wage-labor, on top of the housework they already monopolise. On Colin Clark's calculations of the value of housework we've only got to combine Australian husbands' habits with English wives' willingness to go out and earn, and Australian men can collect three-quarters of the national income while Australian women do more than two-thirds of the nation's work. I'm not sure that we're far short of that now.

But shifting more of the wages to the women might not make much real difference. Married women spend most of their earnings on the house and other members of their families. And not much of it goes where the critics of suburbia say it goes, to buy things merely to possess, or show. People may be greedy, but it's more to do things than to have things. After the shelter and necessaries, a high proportion of family income goes on the means of *doing* more enjoyable or productive things, at home or away from home. Whatever some married male motorists may waste on doubling the size or speed of their cars, I don't think the same goes for most expenditure on most houses. People don't want their houses chiefly to look at, or sit about in. They have them to use—and a high and steadily rising proportion of people seem to use them as well as the resources of house and neighborhood allow.

These are only a few patchy samples of the information there is, in women's heads and in the libraries of social science, about the values and uses of home resources. And information by itself doesn't tell us what to do. Next I'll discuss some relations between home and neighborhood resources and environmental values; then I'll try to draw these themes together and bring them to bear on the question of what we should do.

Dame Roma Mitchell

Dame Roma Mitchell was born in Adelaide in 1913, and was educated at St Aloysius College and the University of Adelaide.

She was admitted to the Bar of the Supreme Court of South Australia in 1934. She entered the practice of law in 1935 and was appointed Queen's Counsel in 1962—the first woman to hold the position in Australia. She was elevated to the Bench of the Supreme Court of South Australia in 1965—again, the first woman judge appointed in this country—where she sat until 1983.

Roma Mitchell lectured in family law at the University of Adelaide for ten years prior to appointment to the Bench, was chairman of the Parole Board of South Australia from 1979 to 1981, and in 1981 became the first chair of what she considered to be the most important body she served on—the Commonwealth Human Rights Commission. She held this position until 1986.

She became deputy chancellor of the University of Adelaide in 1972 (another first), and the first woman in Australia to be appointed governor—of South Australia—from 1991 to 1996. From 1996 she was the chair of the Ministerial Board on Ageing for South Australia.

Roma Mitchell was made a Dame in 1982, became a Companion of the Order of Australia in 1991, Commander de la Legion d'Honneur in 1997, and Commander of the Royal Victoria Order in 2000 just a few days before her death.

Dame Roma's Boyer Lectures entitled *The Web of the Criminal Law* are straightforward, scholarly, delivered in the best educational manner—statement, re-statement, elaboration, conclusion. Much of what she proposed in her five lectures has subsequently come to pass. Her subjects were 'Protection'; 'Apprehension'; 'Prosecution'; 'Reparation' reproduced here, and 'Rehabilitation'. The fourth lecture, 'Reparation' is of vivid current interest and importance. The imposition of penalty following conviction for a crime, together with the roles of retribution and deterrence in the aims of sentencing are of continuing significance given the general public, and sometimes strident media, interest in such matters.

REPARATION

The Web of Criminal Law

Dame Roma Mitchell

• 1975 •

The consequence of a conviction for crime is the imposition of a penalty. In earlier times the convicted person was likely to be hanged or mutilated, flogged or transported, and retribution was a substantial purpose of sentencing. So it was said: 'We should punish not simply to prevent crime, but to show our hatred of crime.'[1] While execution, corporal punishment or transportation was the lot of the convicted person, the prison was primarily a place in which he was detained until the penalty could be carried out. In the nineteenth century more humane ideas of treating prisoners began to prevail in British countries, and imprisonment itself was frequently the penalty imposed for an offence. Imprisonment is now the ulti-mate penalty imposed for serious crime and, while there may be an element of retribution in the sentence pronounced by the court, questions of deterrence of the prisoner himself and of others from committing the like crime, and of rehabilitation of the prisoner loom larger in the determination of the sentence.

I say that retribution and general and particular deterrence continue to be among the aims of sentencing. No one doubts today that the main aim should be the rehabilitation of the offender, not only for his sake but also for the sake of the community into which he must at some time return to live, and in which he must take his place. There are those, however, who say that this aim should be effected by treatment of the offender, and that the law should renounce all ideas of punishment as such. It has become fashionable to refer to the treatment rather than the punishment of offenders.[2] The use of the word 'treatment' may seem to suggest that the convicted person is suffering from a disorder which may be cured, and it may follow that the person should be required to submit to treatment until cured. There is no doubt that many offenders do suffer from personality disorders; some of course from actual mental defects. Some such persons may have defective intelligence or a structural defect of the brain, or may suffer from a neurosis or psychosis. Other persistent offenders, who do not have any recognisable mental disease but who appear not to learn from the experience of punishment, are sometimes called psychopaths. Some psychopaths are aggressive and commit violent crimes, other psychopaths are non-aggressive. Many other persistent criminals are said to have personality defects. One criticism of the concept of treatment in lieu of punishment for convicted persons is that the term required for treatment may be indefinite and extensive, and may lead to the offender being held in custody for a period far longer than the crime which he has committed would justify. The compulsory exclusion from the community of mentally deficient persons who are not dangerous is now discouraged by the medical profession. The psychiatrist will probably go further and say that the community should permit the mental defective to live without restraint even where there are some risks of violence by him. A person who has committed a crime should not suffer longer imprisonment than he would otherwise suffer merely because he has a mental disorder, but the mental disorder in itself may warrant detention for treatment. I do not think that the community should be in a position to force treatment, as such, upon a person who, knowing his own propensity to commit crime and knowing that if he does not undertake treatment he is liable to suffer extended terms of imprisonment, nevertheless is unwilling to undertake any particular treatment. Nor do I think that what is in fact a penalty for a crime should be confused by calling it treatment although the penalty may, in an appropriate case, include an order that specific treatment be afforded to the convicted person. Nor should it be assumed that all persons who commit crimes are in need of treatment. It may be and usually is desirable, in their own interests and in the interests of the community, that they change their behaviour, but they may be quite capable of electing not to change and to continue upon a life of crime. They should be free to make this election, but should know that, if they make it, the protection of society will require that they be incarcerated for longer and longer periods, and they should be encouraged to choose a different mode of life.

I recognise the paradox inherent in prescribing imprisonment as a corrective measure. Those who offend against the law are frequently ill-adjusted to the community in which they live, and removal from that community will be likely to render them even less capable of later filling a satisfactory role within the community. The persistent offender is likely to become institutionalised. He may be a model prisoner, but be quite incapable of living independently outside prison, and so he falls back upon his old ways and, probably without intending it, finds himself back in the security of prison life. It has been said that you cannot train men for freedom in a condition of captivity. Thus any prison sentence may be seen as self-defeating. This is one reason for the view held by many reformers that imprisonment should be abolished and our prisons razed to the ground. Nevertheless it seems to me impracticable in the foreseeable future to envisage the substitution of any sentence alternative to prison for persistent offenders or for those who deliberately commit heinous offences.

If we agree that a conviction against the criminal law leads to punishment and not necessarily to treatment the aims of punishment must still be defined. It is clearly to the advantage of the convicted person and of the community that the reformation or rehabilitation of the criminal should predominate. In speaking of the advantage to the convicted person I am not speaking of those who make their livelihood by committing crime for gain. Such persons may prefer to live in luxury unless and until their nefarious acts are discovered, than to engage in lawful employment and perhaps live in only modest comfort. They voluntarily choose the life of the outlaw, in that they are never secure from apprehension. They probably hope, and may even expect that they will evade the tentacles of the law, and if they are detected and convicted of any offence they regard a sojourn in prison as merely an interruption in a chosen way of life. As far as such persons are concerned only their removal from society for substantial periods will be of any benefit to the community. This does not mean that no attempt should be made to encourage a change of outlook in such persons. But it is only realistic to assume that many of them will be recidivists.

By far the greater number of persons however who perpetrate crimes do so only sporadically. Between the commission of crimes they follow lawful occupations. There are others who commit only one offence in their lifetime; and that may be a grave offence such as murder. A murderer may be no further danger to the community. There may be no likelihood that he will again succumb to the temptation to do violence to anyone. If we were concerned only with rehabilitation he could safely be freed without punishment. There is no need to impose a penalty in order to deter him from further crime. He may be mentally sound and may not need any psychiatric treatment. Nevertheless the community would be outraged if he were discharged without a penalty. In his case the law has to consider questions both of general deterrence and of retribution. If the idea were to get abroad that an obnoxious spouse could be disposed of by killing rather than divorce without condign punishment, there might be a spate of attempts to dispatch husbands or wives. If a substantial sentence did not follow conviction for murder, the family and friends of the murdered person might seek retribution outside the law. It seems to me therefore that there must be some place for the ideas of retribution and general deterrence in sentencing offenders.

Of course we do not know to what extent a sentence does deter others from committing the particular crime for which the sentence is imposed. I am tempted to believe that most criminals are persons whose philosophy includes the confidence that 'this cannot happen to me'. The fear of capital punishment did not appear to deter thieves when this was the penalty for anything other than petty larceny. It may be said, of course, that in those days life was cheap and bitter for the poor. But I do not believe that life has ever been so bitter for people in general that they have wished to depart from it at the end of a hangman's rope. Statistics do not speak with a sufficiently reliable voice to enable the courts to know whether the imposition of a particular sentence has acted as a deterrent. A diminution in the number of charges of breaking and entering and larceny after the imposition of increased sentences for this offence, may mean that the sentences have deterred other potential wrongdoers but it may be that those likely to commit the offence have reformed, or that they have moved on to greener pastures; or police methods in the district may have become less effective, or victims may have become discouraged by the low proportion of the clear-up rate of offences or, for other reasons, have ceased to report offences. All these possibilities make it difficult to say with confidence that an increase in sentences imposed for particular crimes has led to a diminution of such criminal conduct.

In any event there is always the problem as to whether the remarks of the judge in sentencing have reached that section of the community to which they are directed. The news media are not charged with the duty of full court reporting, and it is necessarily fortuitous as to whether remarks upon sentence are reported or not. Whatever the judge may say, his remarks may or may not reach that section of the community to which they are directed, depending upon whether those who publish reports of court proceedings regard the remarks as being worthy of reporting, and whether the criminally minded persons for whom they are intended read or listen to any report which may be made. It is useless to suggest that one of the purposes of a sentence is to deter others from committing a similar crime, if the knowledge of such sentence does not come to those who are likely to commit the crime. Frequent offenders probably associate with other frequent offenders, and I have no doubt that what is regarded as the appropriate tariff for conviction of a particular offence is passed by word of mouth in the circles in which they move; but the novice may not have the admission to such circles. Some judges and magistrates tend to clothe their remarks in florid language which is likely to appeal to reporters. This, in my view, is a practice to be deprecated. It may be desirable that persons who are likely to commit a particular offence shall be warned that in a particular court in a particular district the penalty for such offence is likely to be imprisonment. Nevertheless it is undesirable that the court shall be so zealous to deter that it uses intemperate language in sentencing merely to attract the attention of the reporter who may otherwise be taking a post-prandial doze. I believe that responsible journalists and reporters appreciate that fair reporting of criminal proceedings is a service to the community, and that the fact that such reporting is necessarily selective is a matter of some concern to them. There is no easy answer to the problem. The report of a sentence imposed upon a convicted person may bring additional suffering not only to him but also to innocent members of his family, and this is an extra penalty suffered by those whose sentences are reported in the press or over the air. If, however, no publicity at all is given to sentences it seems idle to refer to general deterrence as part of the function of a sentence. It has been suggested that there should be official reporting of criminal cases and particularly of sentencing, such reporting to be intended for perusal by members of the public. Whether reports of this nature would be read by those members of the public who need to be deterred from crime seems to me doubtful.

I return to the question of punishment or treatment. I have said that the rehabilitation of the convicted person should be the main aim of the law. Crime and the consequences of crime cost the community dearly in terms not only of money but of human suffering and inconvenience. The suffering includes that of the victim and his relatives and the wrongdoer and his kin. In the case of the wrongdoer himself there may be little sympathy for his suffering, but most people will feel sympathy for his spouse and children. If the punishment or treatment devised for him means that he will not re-offend, there is an obvious advantage to society. The community therefore is sometimes lacking in wisdom when it criticises what may appear at first sight to be too lenient a sentence. I refer particularly to the non-custodial sentences, such as probation or community service orders or to sentences which are suspended. If the person sentenced in this way satisfactorily completes the terms of probation, complies with a community service order, does not re-offend during the time that his sentence of imprisonment has been suspended, at the very least the state has been saved the considerable expense of keeping him in prison. At best he may have been dissuaded from further criminal activities for the rest of his life. During the term of his sentence he has been able to support his dependants who would otherwise have been a charge upon the community. The measure of success which he has achieved may have been attained only through his own efforts and self-control, or he may have been assisted by the supervision of a probation officer, or even by medical or psychiatric treatment which he may have been ordered to take as part of the condition for his release. So that to some extent there may have been treatment of the criminal. Some people with inadequate personalities respond to active support which encourages them not to re-offend. In this field of work the trained probation officer gives valuable service to the community. We should not grudge the cost of the probation services which, by and large, need extension. In most places the probation officer is carry-ing too burdensome a work load. We achieve substantial savings in respect of each offender who is dissuaded from further crime and remains a member of the work force, thus being a contributing member of the community rather than a charge upon it.

The courts are sometimes criticised for making the release of a prisoner conditional upon his undertaking treatment, particularly psychiatric treatment. The psychiatrist would prefer to treat a person who comes voluntarily for treatment because, in those circum-stances, the motivation will assist the treatment. The psychiatrist may feel that the court unreasonably expects him successfully to treat a patient who is under some form of duress in relation to the taking of treatment. The courts do not expect anything. They know that the success rate for any non-custodial sentence or, for that matter, for any sentence at all is likely to be low. Nevertheless a judge who hears evidence that a prisoner will be likely to benefit from psychiatric treatment may be willing to impose a non-custo-dial sentence rather than a sentence of imprisonment only upon condition that the prisoner does undertake treatment. He knows that the prisoner, while in the dock, may be filled with excellent intentions, and may believe, at that time, that he will undertake whatever treatment it is desirable for him to have, but that those intentions are likely to vanish when the prisoner is once more at liberty and joins a few friends in the bar for a drink. He thinks it preferable that the prisoner knows that he is to remain at liberty only if he does undertake treatment. It may not be the ideal situation in which to seek psychiatric treatment, but it may be better that he has it under those conditions than that he does not have it at all, or than that he serves a gaol sentence.

Where a custodial sentence is imposed the treatment of the prisoner ceases to be a matter for the court and passes to the prison administration. In my next lecture I shall discuss the rights of prisoners and their rehabilitation generally. Today I mention only a few of the questions relating to treatment of prisoners in prison. The United Nations Standard Minimum Rules for the Treatment of Prisoners say:

> Imprisonment and other measures which result in cutting off an offender from the outside world are afflictive by the very fact of taking from the person the right of self-determination by depriving him of his liberty. Therefore the prison system shall not, except as incidental or justifiable segregation for the maintenance of discipline, aggravate the suffering inherent in such situation.
>
> The purpose and justification of a sentence of imprisonment or a similar measure deprivative of liberty is ultimately to protect society against crime. This end can only be achieved if the period of imprisonment is used to ensure, so far as possible, that upon his return to society the offender is not only willing but able to lead a law-abiding and self-supporting life.
>
> To this end, the institution should utilise all the remedial, educational, moral, spiritual and other forces and forms of assistance which are appropriate and available, and should apply them according to the individual treatment needs of the prisoners.[3]

As a member of United Nations we should not merely pay lip service to the minimum rules which have been drawn up after much consideration and consultation. Primarily it is the duty of the Minister whose portfolio includes the department responsible for the maintenance of prisons and the care of prisoners, and of those who administer and work in that department to ensure compliance with the rules. But they should receive public encouragement in any efforts which they make in that respect.

Whenever a new prison is constructed, and has modern plumbing, murmurs of 'motel accommodation for prisoners' are heard. To this the prison authorities will reply that people are sent to prison as punishment and not for punishment. We who have not suffered incarceration can not fully appreciate the situation of those who are in prison. As the late Sir John Barry said:

No one who is not an inmate, or, possibly, a member of the prison staff, can really know the bleak realities and the warped values of prison life.'[4]

The deprivation of liberty alone is a grave punishment for most people. A former Superintendent of the Women's Rehabilitation Centre in Adelaide which is, in appearance, a pleasant building with motel-type bedrooms for the inmates told me once that her stock reply to criticisms that the prison was too comfortable was 'Well I should not enjoy spending months locked inside the best hotel in Australia'. Most people with any sensitivity would agree with her.

Probably no one would dispute that while a prisoner is in gaol he should be given any medical and psychiatric treatment which may assist him to re-establish himself in the community after his release, and which may tend to prevent recidivism. In some cases it has been found that cosmetic surgery to correct a disfigurement will be beneficial, in that it gives to the prisoner the confidence to face life as an ordinary citizen, and makes him realise that he is not confined to association with derelicts and misfits. Sometimes even the removal of tattoo marks which betoken past criminal associations may assist in rehabilitation. In New Zealand I was told that the tattoo mark of a star upon the forehead was likely to indicate that the owner of the mark had undergone Borstal training. In one prison which I visited I noticed a youth who had three such tattoo marks. Apparently one was for each period of Borstal training. I do not know whether it would ever occur to him that this was not the best recommendation of him to any future employer.

Apart from any question of medical or psychiatric attention in prison the treatment of the prisoner is important in so far as it relates to work and the training for work. At some time every prisoner will return to society, and it is desirable that he will be fitted to take employment in that society. Prison industry in Australia seems to me to be a very neglected sphere of prison reform. Traditionally there is opposition to prisoners, who personally receive very little payment for their work, competing in the general market with those who work outside the prison. There is a case for payment of prisoners for their work at the going rates. If this were done proper deductions should be made for their upkeep in prison. If the deductions included the cost of providing prison officers and of the general maintenance of the prison, there would probably be very little, if any, credit balance for the prisoner. In any event if prisoners were to be paid full wages then it would be proper that they should be called upon to support their dependants from their own earnings. This is a difficult subject and one in which, as far as I have been able to ascertain, there has as yet been no satisfactory solution. I do believe that the proper treatment of prisoners requires that they be given greater encouragement to work a 40 hour week; that the work be productive, and that, where necessary, it should include the training of the prisoner in up-to-date methods of production. All this would require considerable capital expenditure and would increase the costs of running prisons. The increased costs could be offset, at least to some extent, by revenue from work undertaken. Coldingley prison in Surrey, England, which I visited three years ago, was run on the lines of a modern factory. Contracts were obtained by tender in which prison labour was charged at the rates paid to workmen outside the prison. The amount paid to each prisoner was still low, but was graded according to the type and amount of work which he performed. The prisoners did receive a complete training in some form of factory work. This was of course a modern gaol, and I know that at the same time in other prisons in the United Kingdom prisoners were necessarily kept in their cells for 16 to 18 hours a day owing to the inability to care for them outside the cells.

I think that we should, without delay, move away from the practice of leaving a prisoner locked in his cell for any extended period beyond sleeping time. In some cases this may necessitate the erection of new buildings, in many the adaptation of old ones. The expenditure of large sums on prisons is doubtless not popular. Nevertheless whatever crime a person may have committed, the conscience of the community should revolt against putting him into a pen and forgetting him. Many prisoners will more readily move towards rehabilitation if they are fully occupied during their time in prison. At all events they will be better able to cope with the pressures of life outside the prison and more inclined to remain in employment, if they have been accustomed to working a full week while in prison.

Some prison activities can best be described as occupational therapy. Prisoners are encouraged to develop artistic, musical or literary skills, and in some cases their efforts go beyond occupational therapy and are capable of being judged by professional standards. Thus we have had plays written by prisoners produced on the professional stage; we sometimes see other literature written by prisoners published by outside publishers. Some paintings by prisoners are worthy of exhibition. Some disgruntled exponents of a particular art have been known to express the view that preference is given to works by prisoners.

I think that it is unfortunate if this happens. I believe that prisoners should be encouraged to develop their talents, but I do not believe that their work should be judged as though it were the work of a child or of a mentally defective person so that all proper criticism is stifled. Once again it is to be remembered that in due course the prisoner will face life as a member of the outside world. If his creative efforts in prison have received undue praise, he is liable to become severely depressed by the contrast with which they are greeted when he is an ordinary member of the community. If he is likely to remain always an amateur and not even a very gifted one, it is better for him to know this from the start, and better for him to realise that, although what he is doing may continue to be an interesting spare time activity for him, it is never likely to earn for him great approbation when it is judged on its merits and not as a curiosity because it is produced by a prisoner.

I believe that every person who embarks upon a sentence of imprisonment should expect that he will have to conform to the discipline of the prison. That discipline should be designed towards ensuring that all prisoners will so regulate their conduct as not to give any ground for the belief that they will be a danger to themselves or to others including the prison officers and fellow prisoners. Prisoners should be entitled to privacy for their rest periods and to attend to their own bodily functions. They should be entitled and required to work at some productive work for a full working week. They should be entitled to recreation and should be encouraged to take an interest in hobbies. They should not be encouraged to regard themselves as freaks, or to believe that what they have achieved in any creative field is remarkable merely because it has been achieved by a prisoner. They should at all times be assisted to prepare for the day when prison life will no longer be theirs.

1   Sir James Fitzjames Stephen, *A History of the Criminal Law of England* (London 1883), Vol. 2, p75.
2   cf. *The Sentence of the Court: A Handbook for Courts on the Treatment of Offenders* (HMSO, 1969).
3   Rules 57, 58 and 59; adopted at the First UN Congress on The Prevention of Crime and the Treatment of Offenders, 30 August 1955, and most recently confirmed at the fifth such Congress in September 1975.
4   *The Court and Criminal Punishments*, p40.

Manning Clark

Manning Clark was born in Sydney in 1915, but after his family moved to Victoria he was educated at Melbourne Grammar School, the University of Melbourne, at Oxford, and, briefly, at Bonn Am Rhein.

His teaching career began at Geelong Grammar in Victoria in 1940, but in 1944 he returned to the University of Melbourne to teach politics. In 1949 he became Professor of History at Canberra University College, later the Australian National University. He held the chair of history there from 1960 until 1975 when he became Professor Emeritus. Clark became the first visiting professor of Australian Studies at Harvard in 1978.

Manning Clark became Australia's best-known and most controversial historian with the publication of each volume of his six-volume work, *A History of Australia*. The first volume was published in 1962, and the last in 1987. Among the awards for his writing were the 1989 Christina Stead Award, the 1989 Herb Thomas Literary Award, the NSW Premier's Award for Non-fiction in 1979, the *Age* Book Prize in 1974, and the Australian Literary Society Gold Medal in 1970. He also won the Henry Lawson Arts Award in 1969. In addition to his *A History of Australia*, he wrote a volume of short stories, two autobiographical works, a book on Russia and one on Henry Lawson.

In 1974 he received the honorary degree of Doctor of Letters from the University of Melbourne, and in 1975 was made a Companion of the Order of Australia for his contribution to Australian literature and history. He was named Australian of the Year in 1981. Manning Clark died in 1991.

Manning Clark's work often provoked controversy but he played an undeniably important role in exciting public interest in the history of his country.

Titling his Boyer Lectures *A Discovery of Australia*, he explains at the outset that they are an account of how he discovered 'one way of writing the history of Australia given on the assumption that there are many ways of looking at the past.' His individual lectures were: 'Being an Historian'; 'Having Something to Say' parts 1 and 2; 'Collecting the Material' and 'Telling the Story' reproduced here.

He concluded his author's note thus: 'As Henry James pointed out in a sentence of unwonted brevity: "A man gives what he has: the rest belongs to the madness of art". Perhaps in our country so far we have been too timid to surrender to that madness.'

TELLING THE STORY

A Discovery of Australia

Manning Clark

• 1976 •

I am coming now to the part of a historian's work which is the most difficult of all, namely learning how to tell the story. As it is a subject on which it is difficult to speak of one's own experience without either claiming too much or claiming too little, I am going to begin with a reply by Ralph Vaughan Williams to a man who asked him how he wrote his music. Vaughan Williams said: 'It's a rum go.' I am also going to quote the reply by Bach to someone who asked him how he performed such a miracle. He said: 'Hard work.' Perhaps I feel so strongly about that because every volume of a history has to be written at least three and sometimes four times, and, as each volume contains nearly 200,000 words that means over three-quarters of a million words have to be written to get out a volume. A man has to be single-minded to keep going.

Well, now, how does anyone set about telling the story? I do not know the answer. I can only say the obvious things such as that just as there is no such thing as history, but many kinds of history, so there are many ways of writing a history. Telling the story, or writing narrative history, is only one way. There are also all sorts of ways of telling a story. If the story is about the past, the writer has to be careful about the facts. He cannot invent facts, or put into the mouths of characters words which they never used. If he does, he slides over into fiction or imaginative biography.

Also, in both fiction and narrative history the writer can only give what he has. His first task is to find out what he has to say. That happens in all sorts of ways. Some writers know before they put pen to paper what they want to say, and how they are going to say it. Happily, that is not true of all writers. Thomas Hardy seems to have added that sentence about 'the President of the Immortals' finishing his sport with Tess after he had made a fair copy of the whole work. Tolstoi was well into the first part of *War and Peace* when he heard great bells tolling in his head, and began to realise what he wanted to say.

I happened to be one of those people who stumbled on a method of telling the story, which would give me a chance to get down on paper something of what was in my head. There always was a gap between what one believed was in the head, and what one managed to get down on paper. The only thing a man can hope for in that perpetual source of torment for a writer is that after many, many efforts and the passage of a long period of time the gap becomes narrower. But, again to borrow the words of another man, between the conception and the creation falls the shadow. The vision is often vivid, the execution generally tame and halting. At the end of every major scene, every great confrontation, I find myself muttering in bitter disappointment, and dismay: 'No, that's dreadful: that does not do justice either to the characters or to the events'.

Just on 20 years ago I saw the first chink of light at the end of what was then a very dark tunnel. At that time I was trying to write a text-book history of Australia in two volumes—the first to end in 1861 with the news coming back to Melbourne of the death of Burke and Wills, and the second to end with another disaster—the fall of the Chifley Government, and the temporary ascendancy of what was for me the 'dead hand' out of our past. It was going to be very academic, very careful, very much a 'Yes' and 'No' performance, with genuflexions in the direction of Mr 'Dry-As-Dust', and anxious looking back over the shoulder at the people I liked, hoping they were not as bored or lost as I was. It was all hopeless, lifeless, meaningless and false. I was in England, writing about Australia, writing about a country I did not really know, and about a country with which I had a love–hate relationship. The truth was I had nothing to contribute to that most valuable human activity— academic history. I suddenly realised when I got to Quiros that there was a story I wanted to tell—a story about the coming of a great civilisation, a civilisation which had produced Bach's Mass in B Minor, to an ancient, barbaric continent, and what that continent did to that civilisation and its people, and what those people did to each other. I wanted to tell the story of how three quite different visions of the nature of God and man— Catholic Christendom, Protestant Christianity, and the Enlightenment—confronted each other in Australia.

The way in which a story is told depends on what the writer wants to say. All history is about conflict. The writer has to know what he wants to say about that conflict. He may want to say something about the environment. This is a conflict to which every narrative historian in Australia must address himself. From the remarks by those early Dutch seamen down to our present landscape painters every man of sensibility has had a shot at this subject. Even the language of seamen who are normally so content to fill their log books with readings of the latitude and longitude, and on the winds and the state of the sea, became informed with a simple majesty when they described their reactions on first seeing the coasts of Australia. The first prose poem about our country was possibly that sentence in which the Dutch summed up all their disenchantment and disappointment at what they had found: 'He who would know this country must first walk over it'. Those men, the first explorers by land, were either so cast down or so exalted by what they saw that they became the first writers to achieve literary distinction in Australia. Indeed it could be said that our literature begins with magnificent descriptions of the environment.

It took almost 100 years before poets like Adam Lindsay Gordon and Henry Kendall and prose writers like Marcus Clarke had anything to say about the human situation in Australia. It was going to take well over 150 years before the men of sensibility in the Old World and North America were to think of Australia as a place which produced men and women with something to say. Every narrative historian will try to evoke the spirit of the place, and its effect on human beings. He will do that by weaving into his narrative the remarks of the contemporaries of his subject, and at the same time, but very unobtrusively, almost without the reader's noticing it, he will get across whether he is a recoil in horror man, a nostalgia for England's green and pleasant land man, an exile at heart man, or a man who has the great good fortune to see the fragile beauty in our ancient continent, a man, that is, who has had at least one great love in his life. This is what the imaginative writers like D H Lawrence, Marcus Clarke and Patrick White have done so superbly, as, indeed, have the painters like Sidney Nolan, Arthur Boyd and Russell Drysdale, and what the historians have done so badly. No one would know after reading many of our history books that the spirit of place was the mother of creative literature in this country.

One other conflict is class conflict. From the beginning of squatterdom's domination until the present day, class conflict has played a major role in our history. In the early period there was the struggle between the squatters and the bourgeoisie for control of the colonial parliaments. At the end of the nineteenth century, that conflict was almost healed so that both classes might protect their class interests against the threat from the working classes. In the twentieth century when the influence of the environment on human behaviour declined because of the use of more and more machines with which men have asserted their mastery over the environment, and with the decline of the influence of religious doubts about the capacity of human beings to control their destiny, the class struggle has become more prominent. At the moment the capitalist class and the working class are like two bulls locked in combat in which neither will allow the other to take a step forward. One of the tasks of a historian is to prophesy the victor—to be that prophet who sees that the victor will come from another herd.

Because class conflict, or the polarisation of society, has taken up the central position on our stage of life there will probably be more and more history written by authors with Marxist values. This will throw light on the past; it may also mean that for a while our history books may read like the history of commodities rather than the history of human beings. As nearly all the history of mankind is written by the victors, or at their dictation, whichever Marxist group seizes power in Australia is not likely to be very merciful or generous in their judgment of those who stood in their way. There are only rare moments in the history of mankind when writers are not obliged to take sides. Gibbon was lucky enough to live in such a period. We have just lived through such a period, but it looks as though it is about to be replaced either by some variety of a people's democracy, or the spread of a new barbarism over our continent.

The other conflict is the conflict within the heart of a man. Some say the heart of a man is a battlefield between God and the Devil: some say it is a battlefield between good and evil: some say that the men who leave a mark on their generation are divided and tormented men: some say creative men are Merlins—part devil and part innocent child. Dostoievsky said one of the great mysteries about human beings was that the ideal of Sodom and the ideal of the Madonna lived side by side in the human heart. The difficult thing for a writer is to paint what goes on in the heart of a man. In the Book of Jeremiah there is a harsh remark about the human heart. 'The heart,' writes the Prophet, 'is deceitful above all things.' But Jeremiah then went on to put the question of questions: Who can know it?

The truth is there are often many persons within the one human being. The writer has to take care lest he confound one of these with the man himself. The contemporaries of Henry Parkes have left many contradictory descriptions of him. There is the ungenerous description of him by Alfred Deakin in which vanity and delusions of grandeur provide the key to the man. There is the salacious Parkes in the stories related in the journal of AG Stephens in which Parkes, when over 70, was claiming to perform feats in bed which would have dwarfed the fantasies of an adolescent. There is the account by the imaginative writer 'Price Warung' who described more in sorrow than in anger the man of principle being corroded by all those expediencies to which he was driven to earn a living for his family. There is the portrait of Parkes by Tom Roberts in the Sydney art gallery in which the ravaged face tells us something about the humiliations the man had endured, and also that Parkes was both the man who was petty enough to be concerned about where his name appeared in a list of public men, and yet of such magnanimity that he had dreamed a great dream about the future of Australia.

To do justice to such a man, a historian must create scenes in which he knew both glory and damnation, both honour and humiliation, both principle and expediency. It would take an Ibsen to create a Henry Parkes—to show, for example, the chapel-goer living on in such a fiery furnace of a man that no woman was said to be safe in his presence, to show the chartist and future-of-humanity man sinking so low as to ask his advisers to give him information on the number of Catholics in his electorate, and the man who had loved much fervently repeating the responses at a Christian service.

I am not sure that anyone can say anything very helpful about how that could be done. It is possible to say what not to do. I will do that comforted by the thought that civilisation for a few thousand years was kept together by some rather frightening 'Thou shalt nots'. Here is a narrative historian's list of don'ts. Don't use the verb to be; don't use the passive voice; don't use more than one adverb to modify a verb, for if you feel you must then your choice of verb has failed you; don't use jargon, such as 'however', or 'of course', 'in the light of', 'with a view to' etc etc etc; don't discuss the problems of writing with the reader; don't tell the reader what is happening, or comment on what is happening—that is, don't act the role of a coach captain on a tourist bus and comment on the scene, but let the scene speak for itself. All the great stories of mankind are told without any comment at all. Perhaps that is why they have outlived their generation, and said something to men at all times and in all places. If the writer intervenes then he puts the stamp of his own generation on his work.

As for the tone of the work, that too depends on what the writer wants to convey. A historian should probably not write in the comic vein, because the comic writer is looking down on his characters; belittlers are like the mockers: they besmirch people on whom it behoves every writer to confer a dignity. That presents a great difficulty for an Australian historian, because the comic imagination and mockery are by now part of the national consciousness. A historian should probably try to write his story as though it were an epic, because that gives him the chance to turn his creation into what all such works should be—a hymn of praise to life. It also gives him the chance to present the case for acceptance side by side with the passionate plea that men deserve something better, that men have the capacity for better things. That is to say the historian sees clearly those things which are from eternity and will never change, but paradoxically, those things which can and must be changed. It is his duty both to describe the world, and show how the world can be changed.

He has to learn how to prepare his readers for what he is going to say. I find it helpful to have a look at the writers who are masters of the art of reader preparation. At the beginning of *Anna Karenina*, Tolstoi prepares his reader to see under his microscope what he had seen about the relations between men and women, and about marriage and the family—that never healing wound in his life. Here is the beginning of that work:

> All happy families resemble one another, but each unhappy family is unhappy in its own way. Everything was upset in the Oblonskys' house. The wife had discovered an intrigue between her husband and their former French governess . . .

And away he goes to introduce the reader to the characters in one of his families—that great life lover Stiva, and that weeper, Dolly. By contrast the first sentence by Thomas Babington Macaulay in his *History of England* is both brash and full of confidence:

> I purpose *he declared* to write the history of England from the accession of James the Second down to a time which is within the memory of men still living.

He lived in an age of confidence. We who live at a time when a new savagery and barbarism threaten to destroy our ancient civilisation, are so much more aware of all the evil done under the sun that we would probably use the vocabulary, the rhythms and the sentiments which would prepare the reader for a melancholy tale, or give him the strength to survive the cleansing fire that is sweeping over the earth.

A writer also has to learn how to tell a story. How that is done I do not know. All that can be said is that some people can tell a story, and some cannot. Again, there is a point in having a look at the stories which have lived on—stories such as Noah and the Flood, Susannah and the Elders, the Prodigal Son, and the great folk tales which preserve the wisdom of a people. One of the things on the debit side for us is that we have no such tales of our own. We never created a Christ figure or the Holy Mother of God in our own image. We never created a distinctive music which one can listen to feeling that it conveys what it is like to be a human being in Australia. All stories which have lived on have four things in common: they are memorable; they have a high seriousness of tone; they create human beings; they make a point about life; or, to extend this a little, they make us explicitly aware of what we had vaguely noticed before, of what life is like, of what will happen to us if in our folly or in some mad passion we defy the wisdom of humanity. That after all was what the word historian meant. He was the wise man or the judge who told a story about the past so that his readers might know what life was like, or, as one sometimes dares to hope, so that all men might have life and have it more abundantly.

My purpose was to tell the story of what happened when a great civilisation was transplanted to our ancient continent. My purpose was to show that the more successful our ancestors were in planting that civilisation in the Australian wilderness, the more disastrous it was for the original tenants of the soil. My purpose was also to show how human beings responded to the decline of the faiths which had comforted human beings for thousands of years, and to portray the pilgrimage of man from the Kingdom of God to the Kingdom of Nothingness. My purpose was also to present the choice which confronts us at the moment: whether we shall drift into the role of defenders of an over-ripe society, or join those who in their zeal to wipe a society based on moral infamy off the face of the earth, lapsed into spiritual popery, conformism and greyness of spirit, or shall build a society in which men can be both happy and wise. I was very lucky: I had a great dream. My great regret was that I was never able to find the words which would enable me to portray the child of my heart.

Douglas Stewart

Poet, playwright, critic and biographer Douglas Stewart was born at Eltham, New Zealand, in 1913, and came to Australia in 1938 to join the staff of the *Bulletin*. From 1940 to 1960, he was the *Bulletin's* literary editor, or 'editor of the Red Page' as the post was called, and so came into contact with a wide range of poets, short story writers and novelists. His generous influence on a generation of Australian writers continued even after he left the *Bulletin* in 1961 to become literary adviser to Angus & Robertson Publishers.

Stewart published a number of volumes of poems beginning in 1936 with *Green Lions*, and including *The Dosser in Springtime, Sun Orchids, The Birdsville Track* and *Rutherford*. Stewart's *Collected Poems 1936–67* appeared in 1967, and *Selected Poems* in 1973, and he also published four verse plays, *The Fire on the Snow, Ned Kelly, The Golden Lover* and *Shipwreck*, all of which were broadcast on the ABC. In addition, Stewart wrote two books of biography and reminiscence: *Norman Lindsay: A Personal Memoir* and *A Man of Sydney: An Appreciation of Kenneth Slessor*, as well as a book of criticism and an autobiographical account of his early years.

In 1967 he received the Sidney Myer Award for the best volume of poetry that year and in 1968 the Britannica–Australia award for the humanities.

Douglas Stewart received an OBE in 1960 and an AO in 1979. He died in 1985.

Douglas Stewart called his Boyer Lecture *Writers of the Bulletin*. The titles of the individual lectures give some indication of their content. They are: 'JF Archibald's Paper' reproduced here; 'The Bulletin As I Knew It': 'Ronald McCuaig's Poetry' and 'Books of the Bulletin—Part 1—AG Stephens to SH Prior' and 'Part 2—The Endeavour Press and After'. The lectures have a rambling conversational charm with endless names, many of which would have been distant memories in 1977. But that is one of Douglas Stewart's objectives: to try to halt cultural forgetfulness.

JF ARCHIBALD'S PAPER

Writers of the Bulletin

Douglas Stewart

• 1977 •

I should like to say something about the *Bulletin* and the part it has played in the development of Australian literature; and perhaps I should start by saying what the Bulletin was, and how it came into being—for it is a long time since it has been seen about the streets in its full majesty, and its origins are far and dim.

The *Bulletin* of course still exists today, or a magazine by that name exists, and quite a good paper it is. It does in fact preserve, in a modernised, streamlined form, many of the elements of the earlier *Bulletin*, as a mirror of Australian society. Nevertheless it is a fact that when the paper was taken over by Consolidated Press in 1960 it changed almost beyond recognition; and it is of the earlier *Bulletin*, that had lived in an unbroken tradition from its foundation in 1880 to the day of the take-over, that I wish to speak.

I find it curiously pleasing that JF Archibald, who was the moving spirit in the *Bulletin*'s development, was of Irish descent. He was born at Kildare, near Geelong in Victoria, in 1856, and his father was a sergeant of police who, like all good Irishmen, is said to have been deeply interested in literature. So JF Archibald is one of that distinguished company of Celts—the Scots and the Irish—who from Adam Lindsay Gordon and AB Paterson to Hugh McCrae and Shaw Neilson, from Christopher Brennan to Robert D Fitz-Gerald, have contributed so much to this country's literature, especially its poetry.

Archibald, however, was unique amongst this company in that he claimed to be not only Irish but French. Having been baptised under the Christian names of John Feltham, early in life he began to call himself, instead, 'Jules François'. With his pointed beard and gold-rimmed glasses, half hidden under his big wide-brimmed hat, as he is portrayed in photographs and in the caricatures by David Low, there was in fact a French look about him; and he himself was to declare that his mother, whose maiden name was Charlotte Jane Madden, and who came from an English family, was of French and

Jewish descent; but the story remains mysterious. Though there is a useful account of his life by Sylvia Lawson in the *Australian Biographical Dictionary*, besides many articles in the *Bulletin*, the full-scale biography that might explain this aspect of his character has yet to be written.

It was clearly his devotion to his adopted nationality that led him to bequeath the Archibald Fountain to Sydney. It was intended to commemorate the association of France and Australia in World War I, and Archibald insisted that a French sculptor should be chosen for the work—that is why we have the statuary of François Sicard.

At any rate, French or Irish, what a great man, how noble a patron of Australian art and letters, Jules François Archibald was. To have founded and edited the *Bulletin* would surely have been enough for any one man. But then in 1907, as a kind of overflow from the *Bulletin* and his own energy, he joined in founding the *Lone Hand*, which, crowded with famous names in stories, verse and black-and-white art, is now much cherished by collectors. Then, in 1919, the last year of his life, five years after he had sold his interests in the *Bulletin*, he became literary editor of the new-born *Smith's Weekly*—a very lusty infant—after it had been founded by Joynton Smith, Claude McKay and Robert Clyde Packer.

And still, after his death, Archibald continued under his will to shower new benefactions on Sydney. In a fine gesture of affection to his profession, he left over half his fortune of £90,000 to the Australian Journalists' Association 'for the relief of distressed journalists'. He gave the city, as we have seen, the Archibald Fountain, duly sculpted by a Frenchman—though for fear that Sicard's original design of Hercules slaying the lion might be thought to be a dastardly Gallic plot to degrade the British lion, Lionel Lindsay, as a member of the committee in charge of the project, persuaded the sculptor to change to the more tactful theme of Theseus slaying the Minotaur. I don't know if we have missed anything by this. A bull is perhaps a more powerful, as well as a more tactful sculptural form than a lion; and Archibald's red granite fountain, with its Minotaur and dolphins and gods and goddesses and turtles lolling about in bronze and spouting among the green trees of Hyde Park is still surely by far the noblest group of public statuary in Sydney; for ever, as Archibald said any rich man could achieve, writing its donor's name across the city.

And finally, as if all that were not enough, this great man also left in his will provision to establish the Archibald Prize for portraits, awarded annually by the trustees of the Art Gallery of Sydney. Longstaff, Lambert, Henry Hanke who later painted Unk White as a fencer, Nora Heysen, Max Meldrum, William Dargie, Arthur Murch, Ivor Hele, the powerful and controversial Dobell, just about every Australian portrait painter of note from WB McInnes to Clifton Pugh has won the Archibald Prize since it was first awarded in 1921, and it still confers more distinction on its winner and arouses far more public interest than any other art award in Australia.

Away back in 1880 when in partnership with a journalist named John Haynes, Archibald founded the *Bulletin*, he was only 24 years of age. However, he had already had considerable experience in journalism.

His career had started when he was 14, as an apprentice to the printery of Fairfax and Laurie who were lessees of the *Warrnambool Examiner*, in Victoria. Later, when the same company founded the *Warrnambool Standard*, he joined the staff of that paper and from its editor, Henry Laurie, afterwards to become Professor of Philosophy at the University of Melbourne, he learnt the art of ruthless sub-editing which, on the *Bulletin*, he was to practise with great gusto. Writers who were afterwards troubled at what Frank Dalby Davison was to call 'the somewhat surprising adventures' of their stories when the *Bulletin* got hold of them should have blamed JF Archibald, or Professor Laurie. It became the custom to cut or polish or on occasion virtually re-write the contributions as the sub-editors thought fit; and during my first years on the paper I used to watch with amazement while John Brennan, then the short-story editor, serenely pruned the stories into shape. Once I submitted to him a 10,000 word short story of my own about a bush shepherd; and he promptly cut 9000 words out of it. I remember, though, that he consulted me about that, and I agreed. Later I used to do the same kind of thing myself to both the short stories and the bush ballads and other 'popular' kinds of verse. Never, or hardly ever, did I lay sacrilegious hands on what I thought was the more serious sort of poetry, though I would often write to the author with suggestions for an alteration. Sometimes our authors, after we had improved them, were delighted to discover how well they seemed to be writing, and sometimes they were furious. One indignant poet even wrote to Robert Graves—why Robert Graves?—to tell on me, and asked him if I had any right to tamper with his masterpiece. Graves, who had inspected the poem, very decently replied that while I really shouldn't have done it, it was just as well I had.

But to return to JF Archibald. After his days with the slashing Henry Laurie, Archibald, at 18, set out to conquer Melbourne. That city, to his grief, paid scant regard to his genius and though he got a job as a stone-hand on the *Herald*, then as a reporter on a weekly called the *Echo*, then as court and parliamentary roundsman for the *Daily Telegraph*, he could never get onto the *Argus*, where he longed to be. He found the management of the *Telegraph* too mean and the staff too alcoholic—a not uncommon state of affairs in journalism— and in a moment of desperation, when he was 20, became a clerk in the Victorian Education Department. Here, predictably, he didn't last very long. In January 1878, he found himself sacked in a general economic blitz known as Black Friday; and, despairing of the civil service as earlier he had despaired of journalism, fled to Maryborough in Queensland, where he got a job as a clerk with an engineering firm with the stimulating name of John Walker and Co. He dreamed of going to Edinburgh to study medicine, but by good chance the Walkers sent him away up north to the Palmer River goldfields, to look after a crushing mill the firm owned at a settle- ment named Maytown. It was a crucial experience for Archibald. Living in a hut with the miners, sharing their perils and privations in that hot and isolated place, he developed an abiding respect for them, and for all such battlers of the outback, that was soon, and permanently, to be reflected in the *Bulletin*.

In 1879 he found himself in Sydney and, with John Haynes, planning the great venture. At the time, both he and Haynes were working for the *Evening News*, a paper which by a happy coincidence was later to be edited by 'Banjo' Paterson. Haynes, who was six years older than Archibald, had got him his job on the *News*. Another Irishman, credited by AG Stephens with a love of poetry, he seems to have been a very amiable fellow, who was to be of great use on the *Bulletin* not only in directing its politics and writing bright copy for it but also in the very necessary art of raking in advertisements. WH East, a compositor who helped put the first issue into type and stayed with the paper for the next 49 years, said in his reminis- cences that Haynes had 'a perennial smile which was calculated to disarm the unwary' and which with his florid complexion and twinkling blue eyes got him the nickname of Happy Jack. Archibald described him as 'half fat priest and half comedian' and said he 'looked to him as a brother, for he was almost ever hopeful'. WH East also said that he wondered how Haynes and Archibald could ever have joined forces, for in contrast to his happy partner, Archibald was 'morose and taciturn'; but surely East was remem- bering him in one of his bad days or bad years and forgetting the livelier side of his character. Archibald was in fact subject to attacks of melancholia, and no doubt at those times was morose enough, yet Norman Lindsay, recalling their first meeting when Archibald had summoned him over from Melbourne at the age of 22 to join the *Bulletin*, and whisked him round from Circular Quay to the Botanic Gardens to see the city, wrote of him as a man 'on wires with vitality and interest in the spectacle of life'. The keynote of Archie's being, he said, remembering and paying tribute to the journalist in him, was 'a passion for copy'.

It is not quite certain which of the two, Haynes or Archibald, suggested starting the new paper. William Macleod, who drew Nosey Bob the hangman for the first issue, and who was to become managing director for 40 years from 1887 to 1927, said in the fiftieth jubilee issue that he didn't know which of them conceived the idea and he didn't think Haynes or Archibald knew either. On the other hand, WE FitzHenry, who was more-or-less the paper's own official historian and had been a member of the staff since 1917, said without reservations in the seventieth jubilee issue that the first suggestion came from Haynes. It seems possible that Haynes had originally had a notion of starting some sort of Catholic paper, and that as the two men talked over the project, it soon evolved into the broader idea of the *Bulletin*.

Nor is it certain which of the two suggested calling the *Bulletin* by that title. Haynes wanted to call it the *Tribune* and to model it on an American paper called the *San Francisco News Letter and Californian Adviser*, which was 'famous', as FitzHenry said, 'for its boldness of expression, pithy paragraphs and devastating cartoons'—it certainly sounds like a suitable model for the *Bulletin*. Archibald, remembering the Palmer River, wanted to call it the *Lone Hand*, a title he kept up his sleeve to use later on. His model, again highly suitable, was in FitzHenry's words, a 'short-lived audacious Sydney weekly called the *Stockwhip and Satirist* which made the ears of the respectable burn during the middle of the 1870s'.

Whoever first suggested it, the *Bulletin* was the title they eventually settled on, taken from another San Francisco paper; and on 31 January 1880 their first issue came out.

The opening numbers, which Archibald years later was unkindly to describe as 'a poor thing', were nevertheless bright enough, and in their witty and irreverent paragraphs, their cartoons and caricatures and poems, their theatre notes and their hard-hitting attacks on authority, clearly indicated the lines on which the paper would develop. The first issue, in words said to have been added by Archibald to Haynes' draft, boldly proclaimed that 'the public eye rejects as uninteresting more than half of what is printed in the publications of the day; it is only the other half which will be found in the *Bulletin*'. The aim of the proprietors, Archibald declared, was 'to establish a journal which cannot be beaten—excellent in the illustrations which embellish its pages and unsurpassed in the vigor, freshness and geniality of its literary contributions'. Later he was to say that one of their chief aims had been to attack the 'mean subservience to a spirit of snobbery and dependency' and the 'apish imitation of London ideas' which they thought was undermining the true spirit of Australia, especially in Sydney.

Despite these high ambitions, and despite a ready enough welcome by the public, the paper had need of Haynes' optimism, for in its first few years it was continually short of money and plagued by debt collectors. On 8 January 1881 WH Traill, a journalist born in the Orkney Isles who had worked on the *Courier* in Brisbane, had been editor of the *Sydney Mail* and was now Reuter's correspondent in Sydney, landed the struggling company with a libel action based on an article he had written on the popular pleasure resort of Clontarf. It was a rather surprising document for the generally broad-minded *Bulletin* to have published, a roaring wowseristic attack on the dances at Clontarf attended by larrikins and their girls. The dancing, said Traill, 'was that of satyrs and bacchantes, but of satyrs and bacchantes in soiled tweed suits and squalid finery or rumpled gowns that had first been stiffly white'. Panting bevies of young girls, he went on, could be seen 'clinging in romping abandon to promiscuous partners . . . Drink and excitement . . . and, above all, example and evil associations, were doing their work and breaking down the last barriers of modesty'.

Heaven knows what was to follow; but since the moralist had rashly said that these naughty goings on were fostered 'by scoundrels who gained a livelihood by ministering to the orgies of the vicious', it is not surprising that a man who ran a picnic-ground at Clontarf, and who received further provocation in a letter from Haynes, took the *Bulletin* to court. In the event, he was awarded only a farthing's damages—so things at Clontarf may really have been pretty hot—but Haynes and Archibald were unable to raise £700 of the £1500 costs awarded against them, and consequently in March 1882 were sent to Darlinghurst Gaol. There they lingered for six weeks until the £700 was raised by public subscription. By this time, coming to the rescue of the paper in its desperate financial position, Traill had bought a controlling interest in it for £2000 and had become proprietor and editor. Haynes could not get along with him, and three years later he resigned and went into politics. But Archibald stayed on. He said afterwards that the term in jail gave him the longest holiday he had ever had; and of Traill he said generously, 'Before his day we were puny little paragraphists—hurlers of squibs merely . . . From his time onwards the Bulletin became a solid political and social power'.

Traill, said Macleod, gave the Bulletin a national character. More-over, not only did he give force and direction to its politics, but he greatly improved the quality of its black-and-white art. No doubt with the enthusiastic support of Archibald, who, as we have seen, had begun the policy of black-and-white illustration in his very first issue, he imported such renowned penmen as Livingston Hopkins, better known as 'Hop', from America, and the inimitable Phil May from London. Hop, incidentally, was to become not only one of the Bulletin's most celebrated cartoonists but also the founder of the art of etching in Australia.

But, valuable though his achievements were, Traill stayed only five years with the Bulletin, then followed Haynes' example and went into politics as member for South Sydney. Then he went into pigs. He wasn't, as it turned out, very happy in either of those profes-sions, and with some nostalgia for his journalistic days, told Macleod that on the whole he preferred poets to pigs. And so, in 1886, the year Traill left, came Archibald's first real chance to show what he could do with the Bulletin: with himself in full control as editor and the paper on a sound financial footing.

By this time, moreover, he had brought James Edmond on to the staff to look after the politics for him. Though he held the most impassioned views about a few great issues of the day— his concern for Australian nationhood and independence; his opposition to capital punishment, and to the Boer War— Archibald cared little for politics in general and indeed, said Macleod, 'knew nothing about them'. James Edmond, an all-rounder from Rockhampton, born in Scotland, who could write an eloquent short story with his left hand and a hard-hitting leader with his right, was just the man to help him. The famous story about him is of the occasion when EW Cole of Cole's Book Arcade offered prizes for the best essays for and against Federation, and Edmond won both. Cole wouldn't give him the money for one of the awards, though, because he said it was contrary to the spirit of the competition to enter for both. Edmond, who afterwards became editor, was to give the Bulletin almost the whole of its political platform and to quote Macleod again, 'was almost entirely responsible for its increasing political flavour even in Archibald's day'.

So Archibald was free to develop the human, the literary and the artistic aspects of the Bulletin which from the start had been his main concern.

Archibald saw himself, as he so modestly said, as essentially a cobbler, 'a soler and heeler of paragraphs'. And so, in part, he was. He wanted the ordinary people of the bush and the street to write the *Bulletin* for him, or for themselves, on any vital subject that interested them; and his job was to see that they expressed themselves pithily and entertainingly. 'Archibald sat, with bright eyes and brighter brains,' said AG Stephens, 'cutting, pointing and vitalising. No writer was safe from his improving pen; and generally he bettered what he touched.'

But his aim to express the spirit of Australia also of necessity involved, as he had foreseen from the start, searching out and publishing the best work of its black-and-white artists, its balladists and poets and story writers, who could express that spirit at its finest or its richest; and that is what he did. In June 1887, for instance, to give just one example of the kind of thing that was happening and about to happen, four lines of a poem by a young man 20 years of age, named Henry Lawson, were published in the *Bulletin* as a token of encouragement and young Lawson was advised to 'try again'. He did. In October that same year his poem 'Song of the Republic' was printed in full. The next year, on 22 December 1888, his first short story, 'His Father's Mate', was published; and so, as a direct result of Archibald's encouragement, Lawson's career began.

In 1893, in one of those inspired touches of editorial acumen that had already led him to choose James Edmond to be his expert on politics, Archibald invited AG Stephens, who had made a name for himself in journalism and criticism in Queensland, to come back from London, where he was then working, and join the *Bulletin* as a sub-editor, which, in 1894, Stephens did. In that year the red-papered front inside cover of the *Bulletin* became a page of book advertisements; and soon Stephens began to comment on books and literary affairs among the advertisements; and so, almost by accident it might seem, but really because both Archibald and Stephens, and the paper itself, were inevitably moving that way, by 1896 the advertisements had been transformed into the Red Page, with AG Stephens as editor of it, and the *Bulletin* began its service as a centre of Australian literary criticism. Stephens by no means confined himself to reviewing Australian books. On the contrary, he was interested in the whole course of literature, from the ancient Greeks to the modern French and Americans, and held himself free to comment on or quote from anything that caught his eye. But, steadily, wittily, fearlessly and usually sympathetically, with judgement nearly always sound and in a style that is always a pleasure to read for its lyrical cadences when he wanted them, or for its salty and amusing use of Australian idiom, rather like Mencken's use of American, he did criticise Australian books and set Australian literature on the proper course for it to follow. Some of his criticism was collected by Vance Palmer in 1941 in a book called *A. G. Stephens: His Life and Works*; but many more essays, and many fascinating biographical notes on the writers of his time, remain uncollected. All in all, leaving aside HM Green's magnificent *A History of Australian Literature*, Stephens' criticism is probably still the finest and most substantial body of such writing that we have. I can think of no other critic who has made so resounding a name. It is time we had a comprehensive view of him.

As well as establishing the Red Page, Stephens was entrusted by Archibald with responsibility for the quite considerable amount of book publishing the *Bulletin* was doing at that time. But I shall be discussing him as a publisher later in this series of talks.

And of course, as a natural conjunction to criticism and publishing, Stephens was fully engaged with Archibald in discovering new writers. Of his own particular discoveries, the two that stand out are Joseph Furphy's novel *Such Is Life*, and the poems of that most delicate of lyricists or visionaries, John Shaw Neilson. It was a grievous loss to the *Bulletin* when in 1906, upon his resignation from the paper, Stephens took the poet off to contribute mainly to his own literary magazine, the *Bookfellow*.

As well as the early Shaw Neilson, there were memorable names enough among the poets, as distinct from the bush balladists, who appeared occasionally or regularly in the *Bulletin* during the 1890s and early 1900s: Christopher Brennan as a rare visitant, Hugh McCrae, Bernard O'Dowd, Mary Gilmore, Victor Daley, Roderic Quinn, the light but always charming Louis Esson, Dowell O'Reilly, John le Gay Brereton . . . But the massive and distinctive contribution to Australian verse which the *Bulletin* made in this period was the bush ballad, that popular and enjoyable form of poetry in which Australian writers, with some help from Bret Harte and Kipling and their own old bush songs, and the model of Adam Lindsay Gordon, found a form of their own and for virtually the first time began to feel at home and at ease in their own country and their own idiom.

The *Bulletin* arrived too late on the scene for Adam Lindsay Gordon, but it published nearly every other leading balladist you can think of. To name just some of the more prominent there were AB Paterson, Henry Lawson, Will Ogilvie who went back to Scotland too soon after writing some of the finest and most musical of our ballads, Harry Morant 'The Breaker', who was shot by firing squad in South Africa, the grim Barcroft Boake who hanged himself with his own stockwhip, EJ Brady of *The Ways of Many Waters*, and WT Goodge who wrote that delightfully rude poem 'The Great Australian Adjective'. Then in 1913 and 1914 came that immensely popular narrative, akin to the ballad, CJ Dennis' *The Songs of a Sentimental Bloke*, which when printed in book form by Angus & Robertson in 1915 sold, in its first 18 months, over 66,000 copies.

So vital was the *Bulletin's* influence in the bush ballad that Frederick T Macartney in *The Australian Encyclopaedia* roundly declared that, though there were other influences on it, the whole movement was essentially set going by JF Archibald. 'Thus,' he says, referring to Archibald's fostering of native talent, 'thus arose the bush ballad'. HM Green, in similar terms, confirms him. 'Finally,' says Green, summing up on the literature that sprang from the Australian soil in the 1890s, 'came the *Bulletin* . . . encouraging, selecting, intensifying local characteristics, and, on the literary side, pruning and shaping them into effective form. The core of the nationalistic achievement of this young literature,' he goes on, 'was the ballad, which represented something essentially new.'

It was the same with the short story. Once again I turn to HM Green for an evaluation; and here he says bluntly that the short story of the 1890s 'may be said to have been a creation of the *Bulletin*'.

This is a challenging statement, but few would doubt that it is correct. I demonstrated to my own satisfaction, and even a little to my surprise, how right Green was when in 1967, after I had left the *Bulletin*, I helped Beatrice Davis of Angus & Robertson to edit a two-volume anthology which we hoped would represent the best short stories that had been written in Australia. The volume I edited, intended to cover the field from the times of Governor Phillip to the 1940s (quite a large stretch of time) was called *The Lawson Tradition*. It might just as well have been called *The Bulletin Tradition*, for that is what it turned out to be.

After reading as widely into the field as I could, from John Lang's *Botany Bay* in 1859, right through the 1890s to round about 1950, I came to the opinion that, as I said in my introduction, 'properly speaking, if we look to quality and influence, the Australian short story did not begin with John Lang but with Henry Lawson and . . . all the other talents which JF Archibald and AG Stephens fostered in the *Bulletin*.' I was glad to find a place for such writers outside the fold as Henry Handel Richardson, in a pretty story about schoolgirls taking a bath, and the poet William Baylebridge who wrote those extraordinary stories about Gallipoli; I left out, for one reason or another, mostly because I felt they were what we call 'magazinish', such highly respected Bulletin writers as HE Riemann, Ernest Favenc, Randolph Bedford, Dowell O'Reilly, Albert Dorrington and Ernest O'Ferall who wrote that popular drunk story 'The Lobster and the Lioness'. Yet even with these inclusions and omissions, of the 21 writers whom I selected as having most firmly in my view withstood the buffeting of time, no fewer than 19 were regular contributors to the Bulletin. They included Lawson, EJ Dyson, James Edmond, Louis Becke and Steele Rudd; the haunting and powerful chronicler of the convict days, Price Warung; dark Barbara Baynton; and that strangely neglected master of both the comic and the macabre, Frank Penn-Smith; and on then to Bulletin writers of the 1930s and '40s.

If I may turn now for a moment to black-and-white art, a vital element in the Bulletin contribution to Australian culture but which I can only briefly touch on here, it is astonishing to realise how many artists, destined to make great names in other fields of Australian art, in etchings and woodcuts, in oil paintings or watercolours, were content in those far-off days to draw the humble joke-block. Perhaps they did it simply because they were young and hard up. Perhaps in the bohemian and democratic spirit of the times they had no false pride to make them disdain such work. Perhaps the Bulletin's prestige was so high that they were delighted to appear in its pages with any kind of drawing whatever. At any rate, draw for the Bulletin they did.

The famous Lindsays were there in all their prodigality: Norman, drawing everything from the thundering main cartoon to that much cherished joke-block of the old spinster looking at the baby and saying 'If my memory does not deceive me, it's a boy'; Percy Lindsay, best known for his beautiful small landscapes in oils; Lionel, who besides illustrating verse and stories, drew the brilliant set of advertisements, called the Chunder-loo series, for Cobra bootpolish; Ruby Lindsay, who was to die so tragically in the influenza epidemic after World War I; and, last of the clan, Daryl Lindsay who illustrated, among other tasks for the Bulletin, a serial by Vance Palmer.

The Lindsays' practical, down-to-earth attitude to their art, and to the pride and necessity of making a living from it, is well known from Norman's and Lionel's autobiographies. But who could have imagined the lordly George Lambert, stalking through life like an Elizabethan prince and known in London to AJ Munnings and his circle as 'George the Genius', drawing mere joke-blocks for the Bulletin? He did. So did Fred Leist, afterwards an oil painter of note. So did that admirable watercolourist BE Minns, celebrated in serious art and the *Bulletin* alike for his portraits of the Aborigines. So, coming towards our own times, did GK Townshend.

Then, still among famous men, but among those whose reputations were chiefly founded on their black-and-white work, there was Percy Leason, who, after many years of contributing to the *Bulletin* and Melbourne *Punch*, went away to America in 1939 and worked as an illustrator and teacher; and John Richard Flanagan, whose flair with the pen seemed almost as if it would rival Norman Lindsay's. He too went to America and became that country's highest-paid magazine illustrator. Hop and Phil May, the great cartoonists, have already been mentioned; and alongside them one must place David Low, whom William Macleod brought to the *Bulletin* from New Zealand in 1911, and who, after having a carnival of delighted satire with Billy Hughes, won world renown as a cartoonist on the London *Evening Standard* and the *Manchester Guardian*.

For a picture of what the *Bulletin* was like in its early days, not only as a paper but as a centre where these legendary figures met and talked to each other, I turn to my old friend Billy FitzHenry again. Fitz was always a little sentimental and some of his swans may have been geese; but a lot of them were genuine swans, too, and I know nobody else who has so warmly and memorably brought the period to life. On the Red Page in the seventieth Jubilee number, in 1950, he described the counter that, when the *Bulletin* was at 24 Pitt Street, down near Circular Quay, was put up in the front office, to stop drunks and deadbeats roaming all over the building, and the bench in front of the counter where contributors waited to get their cheques from Tom McMahon, the accountant.

'On the bench,' he said, 'Louis Becke, home from the South Seas, often had a pleasant snooze, and Ernest Favenc and poet John Farrell swapped many a yarn. From the old bench Harry Morant ("The Breaker") said goodbye to a host of Bohemian friends before his departure to the South African war . . . Phil May, one foot resting on the bench, is said to have modelled the comical caricature of himself which he labelled "That's Me When I'm Old". On the bench Rod Quinn smiled at Hugh McCrae, who roared with wild laughter at Rod's gentle humour. Or Fred Broomfield boomed the literature of the world at all who would listen.

'Names that are forgotten now,' FitzHenry went on, 'sat on the bench awaiting a cheque from Tom McMahon: P. T. Freeman, Steve O'Brien, Perce Abbott, Stefan von Kotze, Archibald Preston and Phillip J. Holdsworth.' Holdsworth, he added, was celebrated for wearing a high hat, frock coat and spats and, in consequence, was regarded with great suspicion by the *Bulletin* bohemians.

Well, that was the tradition set up by Archibald and Stephens; and that was the tradition that, in my own days on the *Bulletin*, from 1938 to 1961, in what I hope was all due humility, we inherited.

Sir Gustav Nossal

Gustav Nossal has been both a scientific researcher in immunology and a scientific policy formulator at national and international levels. He was born in Bad Ischl, Austria, in 1931, and came to Australia with his family in 1939. Educated at St Aloysius College, he studied medicine at the University of Sydney and, after two year's residency at Royal Prince Alfred Hospital, moved to Melbourne to work as a research fellow at the Walter and Eliza Hall Institute of Medical Research, gaining a PhD. Apart from two years as Assistant Professor of Genetics at Stanford University, one year at the Pasteur

Institute in Paris, and a year as a special consultant to the World Health Organisation, all Nossal's research career has been at the Hall Institute, of which he was director from 1965 to 1996. he was also Professor of Medical Biology at the University of Melbourne, now Emeritus.

Nossal's research is in fundamental immunology, and he has written a number of books and articles in this field. He was president from 1986 to 1989 of the International Union of Immunological Societies, president of the Australian Academy of Science (1994–98), and a member of the Prime Minister's Science, Engineering and Innovation Council (1989–98). From 1990 he chaired the committee overseeing WHO's global program for vaccines and immunisation, and he is on the strategic advisory council for the Bill and Melinda Gates children's vaccine program. He is also deputy chairman of the Council for Aboriginal Reconciliation and deputy chair of The Global Foundation.

Gustav Nossal was knighted in 1977 and made a Companion of the Order of Australia in 1989. Among his other honours are the ANZAAS Medal, the Advance Australia Award, the James Cook Medal of the Royal Society of New South Wales, the Robert Koch Gold Medal, the Albert Einstein World Award of Science, the Emil Von Behring Prize, West Germany; the Rabbai Shai Shacknai Prize, Israel; and the Phi Beta Kappa Science Award, USA.

He was Australian of the Year in 2000.

Leaving his work as a science policy maker to one side, Sir Gustav Nossal's Boyer Lectures went to the heart of his research work in immunology and were titled *Nature's Defences—New Frontiers in Vaccine Research*. He sought to bridge the 'wide gulf between scientist and layman. The public wants and needs information about modern science; the scientist is reluctant to give it, and mistrusts the media'. Less now, one would hope. His individual lecture titles were: 'Vaccines and History'; 'Strategies of the Cellular Defence System'; 'Diseases due to Civil Warfare'; 'Immunology and Cancer' and 'Immunology and Genetics'; reproduced here, a subject of particular current interest.

IMMUNOLOGY AND GENETICS

Nature's Defences —
New Frontiers in Vaccine Research

Sir Gustav Nossal

• 1978 •

To one who has spent practically all his working life in the laboratory, the pace of progress often seems frustratingly slow. It is not
wise to focus on the achievements of the past month, or even the
past year, for fear of becoming disheartened. The consoling thing is
the historic dimension of medical research. A real discovery once
made cannot be undiscovered. In its own small way, each discovery
alters the history of the human race. Viewed in this light, and taking
a scientist's creative achievements in five or ten year segments, many
of today's new breed of full-time professional researchers have no
cause to be ashamed. TS Kuhn, a contemporary American philosopher of science, refers to this slow creep forward as 'normal science'.
Sometimes, however, a kind of tidal wave sweeps over a field, a revolutionary surge of insights and possibilities, that is so exciting in its
impact, so destructive of old complacencies, so energising to all the
workers in the subject, so magnetically attractive to others at the
margins of the field, as to turn science upside down in a brief
space of time. Kuhn calls this 'revolutionary science'. Consider
Rutherford's belief in 1932, that nuclear fission by fast neutrons,
discovered in his laboratory, would never be of any practical use. A
scant seven years later, Leo Szilard and others persuaded Albert
Einstein to write the famous letter to President Roosevelt that
launched the Manhattan project. Only six years after that, the atomic
age had descended irrevocably on mankind. The events of modern
genetics belong to this category of tidal wave, and my belief is that
the practical results will be overwhelmingly for the good of mankind. Furthermore, when one considers how much has happened in
genetics between 1974 and 1978, one sees how the pace of things
has accelerated even since Rutherford's day. In this lecture we shall
look at the possibilities that genetic research offers for the production of new and exciting vaccines. To do so, we must first learn a
little about new ways of studying DNA through genetic engineering.

We have known for a quarter of a century that the coded instructions for the synthesis of proteins reside in the nucleus of the cell in long, double-stranded, helical molecules called deoxyribonucleic acid, or DNA. The stretch of DNA which contains the code for a given protein constitutes the gene for that protein. Lederberg and others discovered ways of artificially ferrying these bits of DNA containing the code from one bacterium to another, thereby giving us the chance to perform genetic engineering on these lowly species. A new technology, pioneered by Stanley Cohen at Stanford University, goes a step further and allows genes from higher species, even humans, to be inserted into bacteria.

This new form of genetic engineering is quite simple in concept. Many bacteria carry inside them small particles called plasmids. These plasmids are also constituted from DNA and they are circular as well as helical in shape, rather like a necklace with twirled strands. In genetic engineering a particular gene, say a gene from a rat, is snipped out from the natural helical strand of rat DNA. The circular DNA molecule of the plasmid is then snipped open, the rat gene is spliced into place in the plasmid and the circle is reformed. The plasmid which now carries the rat gene is reinserted into the bacterium where it lives and reproduces itself in the normal way. Because a bacterium, along with the plasmid inside it, can multiply in about 20 minutes, it is easy to see how large quantities of the recombined plasmid DNA can be obtained in a day or two, thus providing ample samples for close chemical study in the laboratory.

It is highly significant that the Nobel Prize for Medicine for 1978 was awarded not to the prominent genetic engineers but rather to three scientists who made the first essential breakthrough, namely the discovery of the special enzymes, the biological tools which make it possible to split the DNA double helix in the correct manner. The Nobel Committee is imaginative, but also necessarily conservative. Its endorsement of genetic engineering certainly means that the work is now thoroughly respectable. Nevertheless, recombinant DNA research (to use the proper technical term) has aroused worldwide controversy. Fears have been expressed that hideously dangerous micro-organisms might be tailormade by scientists and escape from the laboratory, or that genes of a cancer virus might be planted into simple intestinal bacteria. As a result, the research is now permitted only under stringent safeguards in laboratories specially designed to prevent microbes from escaping. I first became involved in the controversy surrounding genetic engineering in 1975, when I joined a special World Health

Organisation Committee on the subject, which I subsequently chaired for two years. We quickly realised that recombinant DNA research could only be put into proper perspective if regarded as a small part of the overall problem of microbiological safety. In fact, we found much more glaring examples of potentially risky procedures requiring correction, such as the shipment of dangerous bacteriological specimens under inadequate packaging. There is now a general consensus that, given proper safeguards, the risks of recombinant DNA research are negligible.

Why have scientists gone to all this trouble just to put a few genes into bacteria? The first reason is that the technique has given us fundamental knowledge of the most unexpected and profound kind. Now for the first time we can read and analyse the make-up of human genes, and some of our most cherished pre-conceptions formed through previous studies confined to bacterial genes have gone out the window. As recently as two years ago, it was thought that the string of coded instructions in the DNA of the gene was copied directly into a single-stranded molecule called RNA. This was seen as a messenger moving from the control centre in the nucleus of the cell to the cytoplasm, or the works department of the cell. Here proteins are assembled from their individual building blocks following the code in the messenger RNA. One gene was supposed to code for one protein, and the messenger RNA was supposed to reflect faithfully the gene sequence. Now, thanks to recombinant DNA technology, we know that this is far from the truth. The genes for most proteins of higher organisms contain lots of bits and pieces that are not translated into the final protein. The genes are far more complex than we imagined, with long stretches that appear to exert some controlling function rather than just a coding function. The RNA copy of a gene is also more complex than was thought, and has to be split and spliced inside the nucleus before it is fit for export into the cytoplasm. There is a whole new world of gene physiology just waiting to be discovered.

This brings us to a consideration of some of the uses of recombinant DNA technology. Suppose we wish to obtain large amounts of a medically useful human protein, such as insulin for the treatment of diabetes. We currently treat diabetics with beef or pig insulin prepared from pancreas glands obtained from the abattoirs. This material gives a significant proportion of side-reactions due to its foreign nature. Would it not be wonderful if pure human insulin could be made in huge vats of growing bacteria at less cost than the present animal products? This dream may not be so far away using genetic engineering. It is being actively pursued by several teams in the United States. A young Australian, Dr John Shine, recently returned to Canberra from San Francisco, was a prominent member of a Californian research group that has actually transplanted the insulin gene of rats into bacteria, and as a result bacteria are now making an insulin-like molecule, although not very efficiently. Dr Walter Gilbert of Harvard University is on record as saying that human insulin for clinical use could be made four years from now. Given the pace of progress over the last two years, this appears quite realistic.

The rules that will be uncovered as we learn how to make insulin through genetic engineering will certainly be applicable to other proteins. For example, clotting factors for the treatment of haemophilia, which must today be made from specially collected, fresh human blood, could be next on the list. But the subject of special interest from the viewpoint of these lectures is the use of genetic engineering in the manufacture of vaccines.

I mentioned in the first lecture that the World Health Organisation was sponsoring a major new research programme aimed at the control of serious third-world diseases such as malaria and schistosomiasis. Let us consider the case of malaria in some detail. Normally, the starting point for manufacture of a vaccine has to be a substantial amount of pure organisms. Malaria is due to an invasion of red blood cells by a single-celled parasite which enters the body following a bite by a mosquito. The insect carries malaria in its salivary glands. A vaccine would have to be prepared from parasites harvested from the salivary glands of infected mosquitoes, or from parasites purified from infected human red cells. In the long term, it should be possible to grow the mosquito forms in tissue cultures of mosquito salivary gland. This technical feat has not yet been accomplished. However, scientists have learnt how to take normal human red blood cells, infect them in the test tube with malaria parasites, and propagate indefinite growth of the parasite in culture. As red blood cells cannot divide, fresh blood has to be added to keep the process going, and the yield of parasites is not yet very high. In other words, if present technology were to be employed, enormous numbers of blood donors would be needed to manufacture enough vaccine for wide deployment.

How could genetic engineering help? By an approach simple in concept but difficult in execution. Take malaria, for example. A malaria parasite is in fact a single cell, quite as complex in its chemical constitution as a human cell. It contains literally thousands of antigens. As a result, the malaria sufferer makes a wide diversity of different antibodies. When a malarial parasite grows and divides inside a red cell, the infected cell finally bursts. Unless the daughter parasites liberated from the burst red cell rapidly enter another red cell, they die within minutes. To enter the next red cell, the parasite must knock on the door in a very special way. There is a specific molecule, a receptor, on the red cell surface acting as a lock, and an equally specific receptor on the malaria parasite surface, acting as a key. The key must fit the lock for the parasite to gain entry. The wrong sort of red cell, with the wrong sort of locks, cannot be infected. In fact, certain individuals are genetically resistant to some forms of malaria because their red cells do not have the right lock. Imagine, now, if the malaria parasite's key were covered up with antibody. It could not fit into the lock. So the antibody we want is an antibody to the key, or to the specific receptor on the malaria parasite that allows it to slip into a red cell. It follows, then, that the antigen we want in a vaccine is the key itself. We want large quantities of the parasite's specific receptor molecules.

Obviously, the first step is the identification of the receptor This is the subject of much current research including a major programme at the Hall Institute. This phase should not take more than two years. The next step is where genetic engineering comes in. The messenger RNA for the receptor will have to be isolated. This will be a tough and demanding task, possibly the hardest part of the operation. If this can be achieved, the steps leading to large-scale manufacture of vaccine resemble in most essentials those for insulin manufacture. For those of you interested in technical aspects, they would be as follows: first, a DNA copy of the messenger RNA would be made. Then it would be inserted into a plasmid, the recombined plasmid would be inserted into bacteria and grown in large-scale culture, the new gene would be activated and the malarial molecules would be isolated and given as an injection. For those who prefer not to struggle with the technology, the 'take-home' message is simply this. Instead of having to collect huge quantities of human blood as the growth medium for the vaccine, the malaria antigens would be made by bacteria growing in vats of a simple nutrient broth, as we call it in the trade. The cultures themselves would be no more difficult than making cheese or brewing beer, but the subsequent chemical purification, would of course, be a substantial technological exercise.

An important point to realise is that the new, genetically recombined bacteria would have to be made only once. If the piece of malarial DNA has been correctly inserted, the property of carrying that gene will belong to all the progeny of the recombined bacteria. The relevant cultures could be shipped from manufacturer to manufacturer, or even from country to country, just like a particularly good strain of brewer's yeast.

If this dream can be realised in the case of malaria, there is no reason why it would not work for a wide variety of other diseases. It would be wrong of me, however, to gloss over the large number of major technical hurdles that stand between enunciation of the ideas and their realisation as an experimental vaccine.

Let me turn briefly to another achievement at the interface of immunology and genetics; this time a major triumph that is actual rather than anticipated. It relates to the prevention of Rh disease in babies. The structure of our red cells is controlled by a number of genes. One important gene set is that which makes us either Rh-positive or Rh-negative. In Australia, about 85 per cent of people are Rh-positive, 15 per cent Rh-negative. An Rh-negative woman will, therefore, marry an Rh-positive man 85 per cent of the time. The risk of Rh-disease is confined to such marriages. The problem is that the Rh-negative woman is not immunologically tolerant of Rh-positive cells. In fact, she can and frequently does make antibodies against them. Suppose an Rh-negative woman becomes pregnant and her baby is Rh-positive, having inherited the Rh genes from the father. A few baby red cells leak through into the mother's circulation during pregnancy. However, during labour, the strong contractions of the uterus squeeze many more baby red cells through the placenta and into the mother's blood stream. The tiny number of Rh-positive cells that leaked during pregnancy are not enough of an antigenic stimulus to the mother's immune system to cause antibody formation, but the substantial leak during delivery frequently is. With the rarest of exceptions, the first baby born to the Rh-negative woman is quite all right. Consider now, a second pregnancy. Of course, if this time the baby is Rh-negative, it will come to no harm. If it is Rh-positive, the tiny numbers of Rh-positive baby red cells that leak into the mother's blood during the new pregnancy will act like a 'booster' shot of vaccine. The mother, already sensitised by the first pregnancy, is far more reactive to the relevant antigens and this time makes large amounts of antibody against the baby's Rh antigens. This passes across the placenta and back into the baby's circulation. The baby, as a result, develops a severe anaemia, which may kill it. Alternatively, it may start a chain of events which ends up with a child that is badly spastic. The situation, tragic enough anyway, becomes particularly agonising for couples whose religious beliefs prevent them from using birth control. In such families, child after child may be stillborn or destined for life in a spastic centre.

Now let us see how a mixture of immunology and genetics has come to the rescue. Simple genetic tests determine the Rh groups of mother and baby. If an Rh-negative woman gives birth to her first-born child, and it is Rh-positive, further tests can quickly show whether significant numbers of Rh-positive cells have entered her blood. In that case, or, in some clinics in every case whether a trans-placental transfer of red cells has been demonstrated or not, the mother is given an injection of anti-Rh antibodies. This 'swamps' the Rh antigen present on the baby cells. It essentially stops the vaccine from taking. The injected antibodies stop the mother from making her own antibodies. The mother does not become immu-nised, and does not give a booster reaction when she falls pregnant again, and so has perfectly healthy second and subsequent children. As a result, the grave problem of Rh disease has all but disappeared in communities where advanced obstetric facilities are widely used. I consider this thoughtful and imaginative use of immunological principles to be one of the real triumphs of modern medicine. An Australian, John Gorman, working in New York, was one of the co-discoverers, and I like to think that his frequent visits to my labora-tory might have pushed the idea along. Our Commonwealth Serum Laboratories were among the first manufacturers of the anti-Rh antibodies, which are purified from blood taken from volunteers.

This happy event in obstetrics reminds me of yet another unex-pected area where a vaccine approach is looking promising, this time not to save babies but to stop them from coming. A birth control vaccine is on the horizon. The world population problem has not been solved by 'the pill', and a wider range of safe and effec-tive measures for family planning is certainly needed. If women could be vaccinated against pregnancy, this would provide an inex-pensive option with long-term efficacy. The line of thinking behind the planned contraceptive vaccine is ingenious, and involves various teams of researchers in Australia, the United States and India, under the coordination of the World Health Organisation. Here is how the vaccine should work. There is a special hormone made in early pregnancy called HCG. In contrast, to the hormones present in the oral contraceptive pill, which resemble those always present in a woman's blood stream though in amounts that vary throughout the monthly cycle, HCG is made only in pregnancy. Interference with HCG could in no way affect the non-pregnant woman or her hormonal balance. If HCG were neutralised by antibodies the instant it was formed, the fertilised ovum could not implant and no pregnancy could occur. So the idea is to make a vaccine containing part of the HCG molecule, causing anti-HCG antibodies to be

produced, and rendering the woman incapable of becoming pregnant while the antibodies persist. An Australian, Dr Frank Morgan,
worked out the chemical structure of HCG. Some sections of the
protein resembled other hormones. There was a special section of it,
consisting of 35 amino acid building blocks, which was unique to
HCG, and not present in any other hormone. Then Drs Hugh Niall
and Geoffrey Tregear, working at the Howard Florey Institute in
Melbourne, synthesised this section of HCG in the test tube. Rabbits
vaccinated with it produced antibodies which specifically
neutralised HCG and had no effect on any other hormones. In
America, the vaccine was injected into baboons. Early results
suggest that it works as a contraceptive. Now human trials are
planned. If present hopes are realised, the vaccine will protect so
long as annual booster shots are given, but will allow the woman to
conceive again, perhaps a couple of years after the last injection.
Once again, the example illustrates how pure research in biochemistry, physiology and immunology preceded a practical application,
potentially of global importance.

Of course, birth control is a controversial subject. My experience
in international health has convinced me that population control
will only work when it is seen as part of a total health care package.
It can only gain community acceptance as standards of nutrition,
education and health care rise. Any campaign that isolates birth
control out of this context, as happened recently in India, is
doomed to failure. The role of the researcher is to come up with a
variety of methods to suit the social, cultural and religious needs of
different communities.

We have reached the end of our exploration of vaccines and of
nature's defences. I hope I have shown you what makes the immune
system so special. So much of medical practice consists of giving
drugs to reverse some established illness, or to alleviate its symptoms. In contrast, the immune system is an extraordinary and
sophisticated mechanism for keeping us healthy using natural
processes. If we can harness it, improve and strengthen it, in order
to prevent disease, this must be a more sensible approach to the
health of mankind than to treat diseases once they have emerged.
Immunology is no longer a subject confined to infectious disease
control. Its emergence into general medicine is really quite recent.
I am convinced that many practical advances, including ones that
have not yet been imagined, remain to be discovered using
immunological principles.

The health of mankind is a deep and important subject. I have
been disappointed by the level at which the public debate on health

in Australia has been pitched in recent years. It seems to me that most of the debate has centred on who pays whom how much for what. There has been great discussion about the quantitative aspects of health care and very little about its quality. The issue of preventive medicine has hardly been raised; nor has the question of how to find better treatments for the chronic diseases that put such a great strain on the health care system. Public health remains a minor issue, swamped by the largely illusory triumphs of crisis medicine. Health education is given little but lip service. Contrast, for example, the massive amounts spent each year on the treatment of lung cancer versus the miniscule sums devoted to anti-smoking education, particularly in schools. Perhaps most regrettably, medical research is rarely the subject of serious political debate. In fact, in Australia we have the almost childish situation where most of the discussion is between medical academics who need more funds, and officials who believe that medical research is too remote and airy-fairy to warrant their serious attention. Contrast the total budget of our National Health and Medical Research Council, 85 cents per Australian per year, with the cost of a single prescription, $3.70; or a single visit to a general practitioner, $9. Will our children and grandchildren thank us for our choice of priorities? Surely the questions we have discussed in this series of lectures merit canvassing on a wide scale.

In the longer term, the only approach to both prevention and cure is through the understanding which comes from research. The process of discovery, which must start from fundamental probings on how things work normally, is capricious, unpredictable, frequently slow-moving. The disciplined application of fundamental discoveries to real-life problems is equally arduous, costly and challenging. The whole future of the health of the world depends on society understanding this nexus between fundamental science and disciplined application. Both limbs must be suitably supported. If these lectures have done no more than to give you a glimpse of this fascinating continuum between creative ideas and disease eradication, then both your effort and mine will have been worthwhile.

RJL Hawke

Bob Hawke was born in 1929 in Bordertown, South Australia. He was educated at the Perth Modern School and at the University of Western Australia from which he graduated with the degrees of Bachelor of Arts (Economics) and Bachelor of Laws.

He went to Oxford University as a 1953 Rhodes Scholar. He returned in 1956 to undertake research at the Australian National University, and then joined Australian Council of Trade Unions in 1958 as a research officer and advocate. He became president of the ACTU in 1970.

Hawke served for five years as president of the Australian Labor Party, beginning in 1973, and was also a member of the governing body of the International Labour Organisation.

His first attempt in 1963 to enter politics was unsuccessful. In 1980, however, he won the seat of Wills and immediately became shadow spokesman for industrial relations and employment. He took over leadership of the party when Bill Hayden resigned on the day that Prime Minister Malcolm Fraser called a Federal election in February 1983.

The Labor Party won in a landslide. In July 1987, Hawke led his party to a fourth term but in December 1991 he was replaced as Prime Minister by Paul Keating after a leadership challenge.

Bob Hawke has been a member of the Board of the Reserve Bank of Australia (1973–80), of the Australian Population and Immigration Council (1976–80) and of the Australian Manufacturing Council (1976–80). He was honorary visiting professor in Industrial Relations at the University of Sydney from 1992 to 1997 and adjunct professor at the Australian National University between 1992 and 1995. He is a business consultant and a director of a number of corporations.

Mr Hawke was awarded the Companion of the Order of Australia in 1979 for services to trade unionism and industrial relations.

His series of Boyer Lectures attracted great attention and won the 1980 United Nations Association Media Peace Prize. The title was *The Resolution of Conflict*. As he remarked in his introduction, the ambitious nature of his theme 'does not imply that there are more than suggested avenues' but he had one certainty and one hope—'that we are in dangerous times and my efforts may provoke thought and public debate on these issues.' They were: 'How We are Governed' parts 1 and 2; 'Australia in Crisis' parts 1 and 2; and 'The International Context', which is reproduced here. All still make interesting and enjoyable reading but Mr Hawke's shift in attention in the fifth lecture to the international scene was particularly interesting, written as it was on the eve of his entry into parliament.

THE INTERNATIONAL
CONTEXT

The Resolution of Conflict

RJL Hawke

• 1979 •

In the first four lectures, I have been talking about aspects of conflict in Australia and their possible resolution. In most of the matters I have traversed there is obviously room for argument and strongly diverging points of view. But on one point there can be no argument. All our endeavours to create a better and more harmonious society in this country will have been a monumental exercise in futility if the world blows itself apart as a result of the failure to resolve conflict between nations or groups of nations. If that awesome bell tolls, it will have tolled for us.

Let me repeat what I said at the beginning of the first lecture—our capacity to influence these global issues is minimal. Our fourteen million people represent about one-third of one per cent of the world's population and will be an even smaller proportion by the end of this century.

This very fact, however, makes it imperative for us to recognise the forces of change and sources of conflict within our world which are operating today and are likely to be with us for the rest of this century. We should attempt to understand these factors so we can appropriately fashion our internal decisions and act in international councils in a way relevant to this changing global environment which will shape the destiny of future generations of Australians.

As with our own country, we can best begin to comprehend the possible dimension and direction of future change in the international arena by appreciating the magnitude of what has occurred from the time of the Second World War, a cataclysm which irreversibly altered the course of world history. A starting point to this understanding is provided by an observation in a recently released OECD publication, *Interfutures: Facing the Future:*

When the invasion of Poland began, 80% of the earth's land areas and 75% of the world's population were controlled by the West as it then was, while 25% of each belonged to the British Empire.[1]

When that war was ending, the delegates of the 50 countries meeting in San Francisco in 1945 knew they were drawing up a United Nations Charter for a different world; none of them, however, would have foreseen just how different that world would become in the next 35 years as a result of the geopolitical forces which had been unleashed by the recent conflict. Under the pressure of these forces the old colonial structure disappeared and the proliferation of new states has trebled the membership of the United Nations. Of the 152 countries now members of that organisation, 119 belong to what is designated the Third World. The report recently submitted to the Australian government by the Harries' committee—'Australia and the Third World'—underlined the significance of this grouping:

> Taken together, Third World countries account for about half the world's land area, about half its total population and around 17 per cent of its total production. They supply approximately 90 per cent of world oil exports and 32 per cent of world exports in non-fuel ores and minerals. They include in their number countries ... which are middle-ranging military powers, possessing substantial and in some cases very sophisticated arsenals. If determined to do so, some Third World countries would be able to deploy nuclear weapons within a few years. Third World countries control access to canals, straits, waterways, bases, ports, airspace and airports which if denied could weaken the defences of the Western powers and affect adversely their economic prosperity. In some instances, such action by one or several Third World countries would produce an unfavourable and direct effect on Australia's strategic environment and economic prosperity ... relatively small groups of Third World countries have the capacity, through changes in their international alignment, to alter profoundly the strategic balance between the West and the Soviet Union and its allies.[2]

This analysis, of course, does not assume that the Third World is some homogeneous entity. Their common achievement of national independence is reflected in a general consensus of Third World countries on such issues as colonialism, racism and concepts of a new international economic order within the various organs of the United Nations. But in demographic and economic terms these countries have quite differentiated experiences and likely growth paths which of themselves will be a possible cause of future conflict.

In the period from 1945 the *increase* in population of all Third World countries more than equalled the developed world's present population of approximately one billion. It is estimated that by the end of this century, of a world population of some six billion people, about 60 per cent will live in Third World countries, or 80 per cent if China is included for these purposes; by that time 70 per cent of the total population of the Third World, so defined, will live in eight countries—China, India, Indonesia, Brazil, Bangladesh, Pakistan, Nigeria and Mexico.

Economic growth rates have ranged from negative to well above the average of 3 per cent for the Third World as a whole and, as the *Interfutures* document points out:

> per capita incomes in the Third World range from $110, at 1974–76 prices, in Bangladesh, through $610 in Ivory Coast, $2,700 in Singapore, $6,300 in Libya to $15,000 in Kuwait.[3]

The evidence suggests that these disparities within the Third World in growth and per capita income will widen into the future with several Third World countries (in addition to the oil exporters) achieving, by the year 2000, income standards similar to those of some developed countries at the present time. It should perhaps be of some interest to us that on current projections Singapore is likely by then to have a higher per capita Gross National Product than Australia.

At the other end of the scale, poverty is currently a prevailing characteristic of the Third World. According to World Bank estimates, 800 million, or 40 per cent of the Third World's two billion people—or in other words a number equivalent to the total population of all OECD countries—exist in conditions of 'absolute poverty'; and that level is only expected to fall significantly by the end of the century, on the basis of the more optimistic economic and demographic projections.

Clearly, there is not sufficient time in this lecture to elaborate adequately on all the significant aspects of the changes which are occurring in what I have referred to as our global environment. I have tried briefly just to give you some conception of the massive nature of these changes. What I hope I have succeeded in doing is to show just how futile it will be for us to imagine that we fourteen million Australians can proceed into the future upon some insular assumptions derived from a distant past.

To give point to this warning, let me dwell for a short time upon some features of these changes which are of immediate relevance to us. Our trading patterns have already changed dramatically in the past generation. As we observed in the Crawford Report, we have moved from a position 25 years ago when the United Kingdom took more than one-third of our exports and provided nearly one-half of our imports, to a point where that country takes only one-twentieth of our exports and provides only one-tenth of our imports. Japan has become our dominant trading partner, taking more than a third of our exports and providing more than a fifth of our imports. The eight market economies of South-East and East Asia, that is the five ASEAN countries: Indonesia, Malaysia, Singapore, Thailand and the Philippines—together with Taiwan, Hong Kong and South Korea—include the fastest-growing economies in the world and will, on present trends, within a matter of less than five years be as significant in world trade as Japan is today.[4]

These countries have married the latest technology to relatively low wage rates and are producing an increasingly wide range of sophisticated manufactured goods; in fact almost half of all the Third World's exports of industrial production comes from four countries in this area—Hong Kong, Taiwan, South Korea and Singapore.

As we seek to export to the countries of this area our minerals and rural products and, hopefully, specialised manufactured products of our own, we will have to provide greater access to this increasing range of their manufactured products. This will be a challenge containing sources of external and internal conflict but it is not one Australia will be able to ignore. I remind you that we have attempted in the Crawford Report to point the way to the possible resolution of these conflicts, by urging the adoption of an industrial adaptation policy which would (a) encourage the emergence of a more competitive manufacturing sector (b) promote flexibility and adaptability in the economy and (c) ease the adverse consequences of adjustment.

Any discussion about the future international context is obviously incomplete without reference to China, a country included in the Third World for some purposes but properly to be considered in a separate category. The inevitable importance of a country of some 900 million people has assumed an increased significance with the radical change of direction adopted by the Chinese leadership in February 1978 in its commitment to the program of economic development referred to as the 'Four Modernisations'—agriculture, industry, science and technology, and defence. There was some suggestion early this year, sparked by references to possible suspensions of certain negotiations with the Japanese, that this commitment was substantially in question.

I believe it is not, for the very simple reason that there will be no significant locus of power within China which will wish to divert the basic thrust of this policy. The armed forces will certainly want to see a strong and expanding economy, as will the potential elites in the educational, technical and professional fields who can perceive a more fulfilling and rewarding role in the massive infrastructure required to give effect to the four modernisations. And there is clearly no shortage of enthusiasm on the part of Japan and the Western powers to be associated with the program. There will, of course, be modifications, but the concept and course are irreversible.

This has important economic implications for Australia, which already has substantial trade with China. But I believe the issue of longer-term significance is the nature of the developing relationship between China and Japan. Japan last year enjoyed one-quarter of China's overseas trade; under the long-term Trade Agreement between the two countries updated in March of this year, two-way trade will increase enormously in the period to 1990, with the possibility that the value of each country's exports to the other could total $US30 billion between now and that time.

I believe that Chinese pressure for the supply of military equipment will be one of a number of influences leading in time to a resurrection of the heavy armaments industry in Japan and a significant growth in the defence forces of that country. This belief does not of itself involve any value judgment about such developments, but I suggest that such a possibility is relevant to any assessment of potential conflict in the rest of this century.

Certainly, the Soviet Union, which professes considerable cynicism about the capacity of China to achieve the targets of the new economic development program, is nevertheless deeply concerned at this intermeshing of the Sino-Japanese economies. Senior spokesmen for the Soviet have specifically expressed the view that this cooperation could last perhaps 20 years but that conflict would arise when Japan decided to become the third thermo-nuclear power. The relevant point for us is not the accuracy or otherwise of these prophecies but rather that we should not allow our thinking about the future to be entirely determined by comfortable assumptions as to what we would expect or like to happen in that time scale.

Although the world has avoided the ultimate disaster of the nuclear holocaust, war has in fact been the constant concomitant of our affairs since 1945. And for most of that period no area has been watched by the world with more consistent apprehension than the Middle East. The Arab-Israeli conflict has erupted into war on four occasions since 1948; and, because of the violent emotions involved and the energy imperatives which increasingly dominate the thinking of nations, it remains a major threat to the peace of the world.

For that reason and because, as you know, I have a particular interest in this area, I would like to talk briefly about this issue, particularly as I do believe there is a possible way through what appears to be a virtual stalemate, and it does seem to be one where it is perfectly appropriate for Australia to take an initiative, given our good standing with the countries directly involved and with the United States. In this discussion I, of course, put to one side, with contempt, those extremists who conceive of only one resolution of this conflict—the obliteration of the state of Israel.

While there are several difficult aspects, the critical question in the current negotiations is the future status of the West Bank. It is quite clear that President Sadat (and probably President Carter) have a quite different view to Prime Minister Begin as to what is meant by the documentation which emerged from and followed the Camp David summit in September 1978. The agreement provided for a one-year negotiating period between Israel and Egypt (and hopefully Jordan). The two relevant and related passages are to be found first in the joint letter of Sadat and Begin to President Carter dated 25 March 1979:

> The two governments agree . . . that the objective of the negotiations is the establishment of the self-governing authority in the West Bank and Gaza in order to provide full autonomy to the inhabitants . . .

and second in paragraph 1(c) of the *Framework for Peace in the Middle East Agreed at Camp David* (17 September 1978) which says:

> When the self-governing authority in the West Bank and Gaza is established and inaugurated, the transitional period of 5 years will begin. As soon as possible, but not later than the 3rd year after the beginning of the transitional period, negotiations will take place to determine the final status of the West Bank and Gaza . . . The solution resulting from the negotiations must also recognise the legitimate rights of the Palestinian people and their just requirements . . .

Sadat argues that these words allow for the emergence of a separate Palestinian State, a proposition resisted by Begin. On this point I find it impossible to disagree with what was said by Aharon Yariv— Israel's military negotiator at Kilometre 101 after the 1973 Yom Kippur war—in an article in the *Jerusalem Post* on 30 March of this year:

> Without a doubt, different and conflicting interpretations of this paragraph can lead to serious difficulties between Israel and Egypt as well as between Israel and the United States. We should be realistic and recognise that autonomy, whether we like it or not, carries the seed of a Palestinian political entity.

But the basic and totally understandable Israeli fear is that the creation of an independent Palestinian entity on their immediate border would provide a strategic launching pad for an attack upon Israel and thereby threaten the very viability of the state. Egypt and the United States (together with a number of remote and comfortably placed armchair strategists) assert that this is a groundless apprehension. And this is the sticking point.

The realities are apparent—the reality of a Palestinian aspiration, the reality of Israel's fear, the reality of the Egyptian and American belief that guarantees can be provided to prevent the realisation of this fear. The question is—how to translate those realities into an acceptable settlement?

I believe this could be done in the following way. As Israel is assured that the new entity will not be used as a base for an attack upon her, a term is inserted into the treaty giving substance to that assurance by providing that should this in fact occur and Israel be forced as a result into war, then any new territorial lines emerging from such a conflict are non-negotiable.

The virtues of such a proposal are: first the aspirations of the Palestinians for their own separate entity are satisfied (as in fact they could have been at any stage for the 19 years between 1948 and 1967 when the territories in question were under Arab and not Israeli control), and *second*, Israel is not left with a mere guarantee that it will not be attacked—which, in the light of their experience since 1948 and the existing PLO Charter calling for the destruction of Israel would, to the Israelis, seem somewhat less than convincing. In sum, if the assurances to Israel are sincere, those giving them should have no difficulty in agreeing to such a provision and would have every incentive to see that the assurances were in fact respected; for its part, Israel, if the assurances were broken, would have to defend itself, as in the past, but would do so in the knowledge that it would not subsequently be subject again to interminable international pressure on the crucial question of the security and recognition of its borders.

Complementary provisions would be necessary to cover any dispute as to whether an attack was in fact pre-emptive in character as was the case with Israel in 1967. This issue, I suggest, could be dealt with by the two sides agreeing in advance upon a panel of countries to be incorporated in the treaty, whose responsibility it would be to make a decision in the event of any such dispute.

Israel may well argue that the risk in these proposals is unconscionably high. I would like to comment upon that possibility by repeating some observations I made in April 1979. These remarks are, I believe, relevant not only to the precise subject of which I have just been speaking, but to other considerations which are at this time in the forefront of our minds; indeed, in some respects they capture very much of what I wish to convey generally of the need for new, bold and imaginative thinking about issues which can, literally, be a matter of life and death for us all:

> The agreements between Egypt and Israel have helped to dispel the illusion of hopelessness which had overwhelmed many men and women of goodwill around the world on this issue of the Middle East. The pattern of recurrent and increasingly devastating war had seemed to them irreversible. And despair is rarely a useful handmaiden to decent policy-makers or opinion-formers. These historic events have shown that there can be 'another way' than conflagration and death—that the crucible of war can be replaced by the councils of peace.
>
> The overwhelmingly important question is what will be the longer-term course of action of the other Arab States and the PLO in response to the treaty, both in relation to Israel and Egypt—and also in relation to the economic stability of the rest of the world. Short of war, as previously experienced, these States (and Iran) have it within their capacity to create continuing turmoil.
>
> The United States, Western Europe, Japan and their major trading partners are increasingly vulnerable in relation to Middle East oil. The United States is now importing 8.8 million barrels of oil per day (forty-six per cent of its needs)—some 2.3 million of these are from Arab producers, with more than one million a day from Saudi Arabia alone. And in strategic terms it should be remembered that the eastern end of Oman commands the Strait of Hormuz, through which passes between sixty-five and seventy per cent of Western

Europe's imported oil, ninety per cent of Japan's and thirty per cent of America's. And the Strait of Hormuz is susceptible to blockade.

In this context the position of Saudi Arabia is of crucial importance, and the evidence in that respect is not reassuring. On March 31, 1979, Saudi Arabia decided to support the Arab boycott of Egypt formulated at the Baghdad conference. How far, in fact, Saudi Arabia will go down that road is not yet certain, but without doubt this is one of the biggest question-marks over the whole future course of events in the Middle East, as indeed is the very question of whether the present regime survives or is moved to one more squarely in line with the Rejectionist Front . . .

In these processes of peace there are, and will be heroes, just as surely as there are in times of war. And just as there are risks in war, so there are risks in these processes of peace. The heroes will be those who see and know the risks and are prepared to face them . . .

The great *achievement* of recent times is that Israel has been recognised by the major Arab State. The great *task* of the immediate future is to ensure that this recognition is explicitly embraced by all other protagonists. The great *challenge* then for Israel will be to accept the reality of that recognition. Justice demands that these things go together—Israel cannot be expected to accept the one without the other.

Those thoughts, expressed in April 1979, seem to me even more valid today.

Apart from the Arab-Israeli question I have not specifically talked about avenues for the resolution of international conflict. My main concern has been to promote an understanding of the fact that we are part of a surging, unparalleled torrent of change in the world's history. To believe that we can isolate ourselves from the waves of that torrent would make Canute look like a calculating realist. Peoples have come to experience that political structures and divisions of power are not immutable. Nor will they perceive the distribution of wealth and resources between nations to be unalterably ordained in heaven and incapable of drastic rearrangement by the less than gentle manipulation of man. It is right and, to put the matter in the lowest possible denominator, it is in our self-interest, that Australia should join with other developed nations to accelerate the flow of appropriate assistance and technology to less privileged communities—and what is appropriate should not be left to the unfettered discretion of transnational corporations whose interests are by no means necessarily identical with those of such communities.

In this matter of our international relations and the diversion of resources it is a sad commentary upon our global community that the *Interfutures* document is able to make this stark comment:

> The overall figures for military expenditure are simply stupefying: the annual military budget of all the nations of the world is in the region of $US350 billion in 1976 terms—an amount equivalent to the annual gross product of the poorest half of the world population.[5]

Through history the factor that has consolidated previously warring tribes or groups has been the appearance of some common external threat—perhaps we do need a signal that the Martians are coming.

But now, if I can, let me in conclusion try to bring together the threads of these last five lectures.

Our country and our world are in this turmoil of change. There are many aspects of that change about which we can do nothing, and many which indeed we should welcome. But much of this change, unless properly understood and sensibly handled, has the capacity to diminish or destroy the environment within which the freedom of the human spirit may flourish. And there are forces which would feed upon these changes to achieve precisely that result.

More and more of our people, especially the young and under-privileged, will be increasingly susceptible to the blandishments of these forces if we do not provide them with employment or security with a sense of fulfilment. If we do not do this we have no right to demand or expect their adherence to the values of a free society.

Countries, and individuals, when threatened with the forces of change and conflict have the option of withdrawing into an isolationist shell, putting up the barriers of their own material achievements and hoping those forces will dissipate or pass by leaving them unscathed. This 'I'm all right, Jack' syndrome is morally bankrupt and strategically barren. There is an alternative.

We have a magnificent country—land, unlimited natural resources, and a fine people enriched by one of the great migration waves of history. We have the capacity to do justice to all those people, and through the sensible utilisation of those human and natural resources to make a significant contribution to the welfare of those beyond our shores who are considerably less fortunate than ourselves.

However, we totally delude ourselves if we imagine these things will happen by a mindless adherence to past assumptions or a blind belief in the adequacy of existing structures and attitudes to meet these volcanic forces of change. The world will not wait for us.

Let me say again, finally, that I make no claim to certainty for the prescriptions I have advanced for some paths to the resolution of the conflicts we face. If I have, in any way, stimulated you to engage in the greatest adventure of all—to think new thoughts—I rest content.

1   *Interfutures: Facing the Future*, Organisation for Economic Co-operation and Development (1979), p66
2   'Australia and the Third World', Report of the Committee on Australia's Relations With the Third World, Chaired by Professor Owen Harries, September 1979, p14
3   *Interfutures*, p72
4   Report, Study Group on Structural Adjustment, Chaired by Sir John Crawford, Chapter 9
5   *Interfutures*, p376

EVENTS 1980 – 1989

1980

JANUARY	Soviet invasion of Afghanistan
	Indira Ghandi won Indian election
MARCH	Robert Runcie became Archbishop of Canterbury
	Robert Mugabe elected Prime Minister of Zimbabwe
APRIL	Jean-Paul Sartre died
MAY	Quebec voted against leaving Federation
	President Tito died
	New High Court opened in Canberra
JUNE	Australia's first test tube baby born in Melbourne
JULY	Moscow Olympics opened
AUGUST	Independent trade union federation Solidarity triumphed in Poland
	Azaria Chamberlain disappeared at Ayers Rock
OCTOBER	Fraser Government returned in general election
	Bob Hawke elected to Parliament
	Queen Elizabeth visited Pope John Paul II at the Vatican (first time by a British monarch)
NOVEMBER	Ronald Reagan won US Presidential election, defeating Jimmy Carter. Republicans controlled Senate for first time in 26 years

1981

JANUARY	Sir Harry Gibbs replaced Sir Garfield Barwick as Chief Justice
	Rupert Murdoch bought *The Times*
FEBRUARY	Margaret Thatcher met Ronald Reagan
MARCH	Florence Bjelke-Petersen nominated to Senate
	President Reagan wounded in assassination attempt
APRIL	Andrew Peacock resigned from Fraser Ministry
MAY	Pope John Paul II wounded in assassination attempt
	François Mitterand became President of France
JUNE	Sir Russell Drysdale died
JULY	First woman appointed to US Supreme Court—Judge Sandra O'Connor
	Prince of Wales married Lady Diana Spencer
SEPTEMBER	London Stock Market suffered second worst fall in history
OCTOBER	Anwar Sadat assassinated

NOVEMBER — Tonkin Government returned 10 per cent of South Australia to Pintjantjatjara Tribe

DECEMBER — Sir Reginald Ansett died

As yet unnamed, HIV-AIDS reported in San Francisco

1982

JANUARY — Lindy and Michael Chamberlain committed for trial

APRIL — Argentina captured the Falkland Islands

Israel returned Sinai to Egypt

MAY — Pope John Paul II made first papal visit to Britain

JUNE — Britain won Falklands war

President Reagan visited Britain

Israel invaded Lebanon

JULY — ABC celebrated 50 years

Sir Ninian Stephen became Governor-General

AUGUST — Israelis drove PLO out of Beirut

SEPTEMBER — Margaret Thatcher visited China

Princess Grace killed in car crash

OCTOBER — National Gallery opened in Canberra

Chamberlains found guilty, Lindy Chamberlain given life sentence

Helmut Kohl elected Chancellor of West Germany

NOVEMBER — Leonid Brezhnev died; succeeded as USSR general secretary by Yuri Andropov

1983

JANUARY — Sutherland–Pavarotti concert at Sydney Opera House

FEBRUARY — Tennessee Williams died

Seventy-two died in Ash Wednesday fires

Malcolm Fraser called a snap election; Labor switched leaders from Bill Hayden to Bob Hawke

MARCH — Labor wins election in landslide, Bob Hawke became Prime Minister

Malcolm Fraser resigned from Parliament; Andrew Peacock became Liberal leader

APRIL — Federal Court dismissed Chamberlain appeals

Gough Whitlam made Ambassador to UNESCO

JUNE — Margaret Thatcher re-elected in landslide

JULY	High Court blocked Franklin River dam
AUGUST	Philippines opposition leader Benigno Aquino assassinated
SEPTEMBER	Australia won America's Cup
OCTOBER	Yitzhak Shamir takes over from Menachem Begin as Israeli Prime Minister
DECEMBER	Polish union activist, leader of Solidarity, Lech Walesa wins Nobel Peace Prize

1 9 8 4

FEBRUARY	Yuri Andropov died; succeeded as USSR general secretary by Konstantin Chernenko
JUNE	Sikh Golden Temple stormed by Indian troops
JULY	David Lange became Prime Minister of New Zealand
	Mick Young resigned from Federal Parliament over Paddington Bear affair
AUGUST	Los Angeles Olympics opened
SEPTEMBER	UK and China agreed on the return of Hong Kong in 1997
OCTOBER	IRA bomb blast at Grand Hotel, Brighton UK—killed four at Conservative Party conference
	Bishop Desmond Tutu won Nobel Peace Prize
	Victorian Arts Centre, Melbourne, opened
	Indira Gandhi assassinated
NOVEMBER	Rajiv Gandhi became Indian Prime Minister
	Writer Xavier Herbert died
	Ronald Reagan won US Presidential election with George Bush as vice president
DECEMBER	Hawke Government re-elected in close poll
	Ted Hughes succeeded John Betjeman as United Kingdom's Poet Laureate
	Grace Cossington Smith died

1 9 8 5

JANUARY	Former Governor-General Sir William McKell died
MARCH	Mikhail Gorbachev became Soviet leader on death of Konstantin Chernenko
APRIL	Rupert Murdoch became Hollywood mogul with 50 per cent purchase of Twentieth Century Fox
MAY	Rupert Murdoch bought six US television stations

JULY	Greenpeace *Rainbow Warrior* sunk in Auckland Harbour
	Lionel Murphy found guilty in conspiracy trial
AUGUST	Sir Macfarlane Burnet died
SEPTEMBER	Lionel Murphy appealed
	Simon Crean became President of ACTU
	French Government admitted that French secret agents sank
	Rainbow Warrior; Defence Minister resigned
OCTOBER	Orson Welles died
	Rock Hudson died
	Yul Brynner died
NOVEMBER	Reagan and Gorbachev meet in Geneva
	Tennis great Harry Hopman died

1986

FEBRUARY	Lindy Chamberlain released following discovery of further evidence—a white matinee jacket
	Margaret Thatcher and François Mitterand signed agreement to build a Channel Tunnel
	Swedish Prime Minister Olof Palme assassinated
	Ferdinand Marcos overthrown; Cory Aquino became Philippines President
MARCH	Queen Elizabeth proclaimed Australia Act in Canberra on 2 March
APRIL	Duchess of Windsor died
	Simone de Beauvoir died
	Lionel Murphy acquitted on appeal
	Fire in Ukraine's Chernobyl nuclear reactor
JUNE	Kurt Waldheim elected president of Austria
JULY	Fringe Benefits Tax (FBT) introduced
	Two Australians—Barlow and Chambers—hanged in Malaysia for drug trafficking
AUGUST	Sculptor Henry Moore died
SEPTEMBER	Desmond Tutu became Archbishop of Cape Town
	Australia and India tied first Test in Madras
	Sir Robert Helpmann died
OCTOBER	Queen Elizabeth visited China—the first visit by a British Monarch
	Lionel Murphy died

NOVEMBER	Cary Grant died
	Pope John Paul II visited Australia
DECEMBER	Rupert Murdoch took over Herald & Weekly Times Group
	Harold Macmillan died
	Crocodile Dundee success

1987

JANUARY	Sir Warwick Fairfax died
	Alan Bond bought Nine Network for $1000 million
FEBRUARY	Sir Anthony Mason succeeded Sir Harry Gibbs as Chief Justice of the High Court
MAY	'Four Corners' screened program on Queensland police corruption
JUNE	Thatcher Government won third term
	Fred Astaire died
	Sir Billy Sneddon died
	Michael and Lindy Chamberlain pardoned
JULY	Christopher Skase bought Seven Network
	Hawke Government won third term
	Pat Cash won Wimbledon final
SEPTEMBER	Fitzgerald Royal Commission opened into allegation of Queensland police corruption first aired on 'Four Corners'
OCTOBER	Stock market 'Black Monday', 19 October
NOVEMBER	Free trade agreement between Australia and New Zealand
	Joh Bjelke-Petersen forced to resign as Premier of Queensland after 20 years
DECEMBER	US President Reagan and Soviet leader Gorbachev signed missile treaty

---

1988

JANUARY	Australian bicentenary celebrations
MAY	Queen Elizabeth opened new Parliament House in Canberra
	Brisbane Expo '88 opened
AUGUST	Church of England voted for ordination of women
	Margaret Thatcher visited Australia
SEPTEMBER	Seoul Olympics opened
	Four referendum questions on four-year parliamentary terms rejected by electorate

NOVEMBER	George Bush elected US President
	Benazir Bhutto became Prime Minister of Pakistan
DECEMBER	Pan American flight crashed in Lockerbie, Scotland

1989

JANUARY	Japanese Emperor Hirohito died
	Salvador Dali died
FEBRUARY	FW de Klerk became leader of South Africa
	Bill Hayden succeeded Sir Ninian Stephen as Governor-General
APRIL	Solidarity declared legal in Poland
MAY	Tiananmen Square demonstrations
	Hungary lifted the Iron Curtain
JUNE	Solidarity beat Communist Party in Polish election
	Troops massacred protestors in Tiananmen Square
	Ayatollah Khomeini died
JULY	Laurence Olivier died
	Fitzgerald Royal Commission report presented
	Herbert von Karajan died
AUGUST	Airline pilots' strike began
SEPTEMBER	Hungary opened its borders to East German refugees
	Irving Berlin died
OCTOBER	San Francisco earthquake
NOVEMBER	Berlin Wall came down
	Czech Communist leadership resigned; Alexander Dubcek welcomed back to Prague
	Christopher Skase's Quintex group applied for receivership
	Bond Corporation burdened by huge debts
DECEMBER	Mikhail Gorbachev meets Pope John Paul II in Rome; first meeting between a Soviet leader and a Pontiff
	Nicolae Ceausescu, President of Romania, overthrown and executed
	Newcastle struck by earthquake

Bernard Smith

Bernard Smith is an art historian, educator and critic. He was born in Sydney in 1916 and educated at the University of Sydney, the Warburg Institute, University of London and the Australian National University.

He began his teaching career in the New South Wales education department in 1935, but then in 1944 became education officer in the Art Gallery of New South Wales. There he compiled the first complete catalogue of Australian oil paintings at the gallery in 1953. His reputation was established with the publication in 1945 of his first book, *Place, Taste and Tradition*, on general art history.

From 1955 to 1966, Professor Smith was a member of the staff of the Department of Fine Arts, University of Melbourne, first as a lecturer, then senior lecturer, and from 1964 to 1966 as Reader. From 1963 to 1966, he was also art critic for the *Age*, Melbourne.

He was the first director of the Power Institute, founding head of the Department of Fine Arts, and first Power Professor of Contemporary Art at the University of Sydney, holding these positions from 1967 to 1976.

Smith painted briefly in the 1940s, but then resumed painting in the 1980s, holding a one-man exhibition under the pseudonym Joseph Tierney in 1985.

He has received honorary degrees from the Universities of Melbourne and Sydney, and in 1976 was made a *Chevalier dans l'Ordre des Arts et des Lettres* by the French Government. He received the Henry Lawson Festival Prize for Poetry in 1964 and the Ernest Scott Prize for Australian History in 1962.

Smith's publications include a number of highly influential works such as *European Vision and the South Pacific*, *Australian Painting 1790–1960*, *The Antipodean Manifesto*, *The Boy Adeodatus*, *The Critic Advocate*, *Imaging the Pacific*, and *Noel Counihan: Artist and Revolutionary*, and a collection of poems.

Professor Smith gave his Boyer Lectures the collective title *The Spectre of Truganini*; the title is the message. Their individual titles were: 'The Ethical Roots of Culture'; 'The Mechanism of Forgetfulness'; 'The Concerned Conscience' reproduced here; 'Black Voices' and 'A Cultural Conveyence?'. These lectures could be regarded as an artist's response to the issues raised by Professor Stanner in 1968. In his opening lecture, Professor Smith notes that: 'Despite the amused scepticism which the mateship ethic arouses among many today, it is to be noted that it was in the years when that ethic flourished that Australia . . . gained a reputation for being not only an advanced democratic society, but a humane and compassionate one. The greatest weakness of the mateship ethic however was that it did not include the Australian Aborigine.'

THE CONCERNED
CONSCIENCE

The Spectre of Truganini

Bernard Smith

• 1980 •

The British Library in London, among its many treasures, possesses a small sketchbook kept by Sydney Parkinson, the artist, during his voyage on the *Endeavour* with Captain Cook. One page contains two drawings of Australian Aborigines, the only original drawings of Aborigines from the voyage to survive. The drawing on the left side of the page is a strange one. The men of the Botany Bay tribe, now extinct, wore a characteristic body-paint design. Triangular in form, it stretched from both shoulders to the centre of the chest, then down the centre of the body to the waist. But Parkinson, in making his drawing, perceived these tribal markings in the form of a crucifixion, for reasons which I feel will never be fully explained. As a botanical draughtsman he was not given to fantasy. In no other drawing that he made, to my knowledge, does his Christian upbringing, for he was a devout young Quaker, impose itself so forcibly upon his perception. Was Parkinson subject, we might well ask, to a visionary experience? Did he perceive that with Cook's coming these 'merry and facetious people', as he himself described them, would be subjected by his own race to a prolonged humiliation and degradation best symbolised by the tortured body of the Man of Sorrows. We do not know. But the drawing is evidence that at the first moment of European contact on our eastern coast one conscience at least was troubled.

In the subjugation of a defeated people, I would suggest, two forms of control emerge, a physical control, which is maintained by the laws of the victors over the laws of the vanquished, and a psychological control by which the victors suppress their own moral doubts concerning the more brutal facts of conquest, such as gave rise, as I mentioned in my previous lecture, to the myth of Ham. But human nature being what it is, control is never, short of genocide, complete. Physical control is eventually modified by reform or by violence; psychological control by a concerned conscience. The history of the concerned Australian conscience in its awareness of the degradation of the Aboriginal people has not been written. Should it ever be written it will not, of course, be victory history, and it will find its evidence mostly in the work of novelists, poets, dramatists, artists, film-makers and some anthropologists and archaeologists. It will not be easy to write. For such a history could readily fall into sentimentality, making oppressive institutions and practices tolerable, even enjoyable, in the very process of exposing them: a contribution as it were to a national masochism.

> 'I weep for you,' the walrus said,
> 'I deeply sympathise,'
> With sobs and tears he sorted out
> Those of the largest size
> Holding his pocket handkerchief
> Before his streaming eyes.

We must keep such a danger in mind; but it must not blind us to the liberating power of sympathy. Cynicism, like laughter, may become an excuse for doing nothing.

A concerned conscience about the Aboriginal people did not originate among the Australian born. It may be first observed in the half-hearted attempts made by the colonial administrators, military men and others, to close the gap which they experienced opening out between the high-minded ideals of Enlightenment jurisprudence and the brutal facts of white settlement. They became aware of that steady deterioration in the quality and administration of law as settlers removed Aborigines from their tribal lands, a deterioration best summed up in Professor Rowley's memorable phrase 'from the principles of humanity to those of animal husbandry'.[1]

The heart of the dilemma lay at the point of physical contact between black and white; the Australian locale of Malinowski's 'third cultural reality', of Professor Stanner's 'weird set of shapes'. When was it that a band of blacks first confronted a gang of convicts working under the eye of their gaolers? There were no rules, no rituals to cope with such a situation. If the tension did not lead to violence it was probably dispensed by laughter; a kind of laughter which teetered upon the edge of violence. Such situations I would suggest were the original source of a kind of humour which is typically Australian; the same kind of humour which that very Australian character Blue exhibits in Patrick White's novel *Riders in the Chariot* when he submits the Jew Himmelfarb to a mock crucifixion, as a kind of Easter joke. The clash between convict and

Aborigine was more often than not a no-hope situation into which pity rarely entered. This is revealed clearly by the one important novel by a convict which has survived, James Tucker's *Ralph Rashleigh*. The hero Rashleigh, during his four years with a black tribe, learnt, he tells us, to love his lubra as he once loved his sister and mother. But even this makes no difference to the prevailing mutual hatred. The novel concludes telling us how Rashleigh is speared to death, 'his remains . . . cruelly maltreated by these bloodthirsty barbarians, whom the mock philanthropy of the age characterises as inoffensive and injured beings'.[2]

That was the convict attitude to blacks and it spearheaded the growth of white racism in Australia. A special role however was found for the Aborigine in his contact with Europeans. He was required to play the clown, as a kind of initiation rite to civilised life. Convict artists first developed the stereotype of the comic Aborigine and its course may be traced through the early nineteenth century to the graphic illustrations of the *Bulletin* and the world of advertising art of our own time. Characterised by a brutal insensitivity to humiliation it also invaded poetry. Let me quote a few lines from James Brunton Stephens' poem 'To a Black Gin' written in the 1870s:

> Daughter of Eve, draw near—I would behold thee.
> Good Heavens! Could ever arm of man enfold thee?
> Did the same Nature that made Phryne mould thee?
>
> Eve's daughter! With that skull! and that complexion?
> What principle of 'Natural Selection'
> Gave thee with Eve the most remote connection?

and he concludes:

> Thy primal parents came a period later—
> The handiwork of some vile imitator;
> I fear they had the devil's *imprimatur*.

I have inflicted these dreadful lines upon you for two reasons. First, because such racist verse was very popular at that time. Second, because Brunton Stephens was regarded for years after his death by many Australians, especially in Queensland, to be Australia's greatest poet. Even as late as 1961 HM Green, in his definitive history of Australian literature, could describe Stephens as 'Australia's first scholar-poet . . . the first to introduce into

Australian poetry an element of broader culture ... the first to introduce wit and humour into Australian poetry'.[3] Yet I must hasten to add that Green did not share Stephens' racist attitudes; his book contains many criticisms of the outrageous treatment which Aborigines have suffered.

The comic stereotype of the Aborigine erected a wall against feeling which was not easily broken through. It was not until some 60 years after settlement that Charles Harpur, poet and son of convicts, expressed some human sympathy for the Aborigine in a work of art. The best of his 'black' poems as we might call them were written in the 1840s at the height of the pastoral confrontation, when the extermination of blacks reached alarming proportions. Harpur was not alone, at this time, in his concern, but he felt that his vocation as a poet required him to speak for others. In his poem, *Ned Connor*, a stockman boasts to his friends how he had killed an Aborigine who had led him to safety through the bush. This apparently, even for them, is taking the new Australian humour a bit far. They do not approve. When later Ned goes to fetch water the spectre of the slain Aborigine rises before him; he becomes ill and dies a few days later. In Harpur's *Creek of the Four Graves*, one of the best short narrative poems in our literature, four white settlers are killed by Aborigines and a fifth manages to escape by hiding in a spot sacred to the tribe. In such poems we may witness how tragic events became a geographic presence endowing the landscape with melancholy.

Harpur published his *Creek of the Four Graves* in 1853. Six years later the tragedy of Aboriginal society first engaged the attention of a painter. In 1859, the year in which Darwin's *Origin of Species* appeared, Robert Dowling painted his *Tasmanian Aborigines*, a version of which is in the Queen Victoria Museum, Launceston. As a youth growing up in Launceston he had been deeply affected by the tragedy of the Tasmanians. His painting is a sad but dignified monument to their passing. Each individual in the doomed group stares into nothing. There is no longer any sense of community. Despair is absolute.

After Harpur and Dowling a white blanket of forgetfulness covers the plight of the Aborigines from the emerging Australian culture for almost 70 years. Hidden from sight in missions and reservations they made little impact upon the Australian consciousness. Henry Kendall's *Last of His Tribe*, with its sentimental pathos, records the general belief encouraged by social Darwinists that the race would gradually vanish away. Yet Kendall could write comic poems about blacks as cruel as those of Brunton Stephens.

Australia as a pastoral Arcadia had no place for them. In Boldrewood's *Robbery Under Arms*, the most successful of the pastoral novels, Warrigal, the part-Aboriginal servant of Starlight, the bushranger, is an embodiment of all evil. The disturbed conscience of Boldrewood, in his treatment of Aborigines in his novels, has been shrewdly observed by Professor JJ Healy. Boldrewood is an interesting test case because he was involved with frontier conflict with blacks as a squatter in western Victoria during the 1840s; but when he came to write his novels 40 years later, his imaginative transformations, as Healy reveals, elided 'the darker shadows of the past' in order to present the colonial period as 'almost Arcadian in peaceful simplicity'.[4]

Rosa Campbell Praed's experiences parallel those of Boldrewood. She grew up in the Burnett District of Queensland with black children as fond playmates. But she also experienced personally the Fraser massacre of 1857. It is clear that she was too close to the horror of it all, too personally involved as a child to be able, when she began to write her novels years later, to resolve her experiences into a coherent imaginative whole. For so long as Australian cultural values were dominated by the ethos of the pastoral life and social Darwinism its ethical support, the tragedy of the Aboriginal society could not make any serious entry into Australian culture. It is remarkable how long the old stereotypes were sustained. Andrew Pike has indicated how in the early Australian film industry from 1912 to the 1940s Aborigines, invariably played by whites with blackened faces, were cast as offsiders to bushrangers. But instead of being villainous, as in the original role of Warrigal in *Robbery Under Arms*, they were now represented as loyal, worthy fellows. The purpose, however, was obviously no more than local colour.

It was not possible for Australian writers to reach out and grasp imaginatively the spiritual values of Aboriginal culture and the modern plight of the Aboriginal people until the moral authority of biblical fundamentalism and social Darwinism were successfully challenged. This only became possible after the end of World War I, when deep cracks began to appear in the certitudes of Victorian beliefs. The work of the great synthesisers of anthropological thought, whom I mentioned in my last lecture, Fraser, Freud, Durkheim and so on, and also the novels of DH Lawrence, began to create a new framework of options within which the imagination might operate more freely in its contact with the so-called primitive cultures.

A forerunner of the new situation was Grant Watson, an Englishman who spent a couple of years (1910–11) in close association with Aborigines in Western Australia, in the company of the anthropologist Radcliffe Brown, and Daisy Bates. In the novels which Watson came to write, in the light of his Australian experiences, the Aborigine is no longer a fringe dweller adding a bit of local colour, he is drawn into the centre again, to question the validity of white civilisation. But the position which Watson tentatively explored is not taken up by Australian writers until some time later, first in Katharine Susannah Prichard's *Coonardoo*, published in 1929, and then in Xavier Herbert's *Capricornia*, published in 1938. Both writers worked from direct contact and knowledge of Aborigines and part-Aborigines, and placed them at the centre of their imaginative vision. Prichard is more lyrical in tone, has a finer ear for language than Herbert, but Herbert works on a grand scale, figuring forth the complexity of the social textures of North-Australian society by means of a fierce and corrosive, but liberating imagination. The literary achievement of these two writers has often been discussed but their significance for the development of Australian culture as a whole has not, it seems to me, been fully appreciated. It is in their work, surely, that our culture first begins to be built upon firm ethical foundations; that it begins to speak for the human condition, rather than for a privileged section of the human race. By contrast the culture that flows from Lawson ends up in a blind alley of white racism; the culture that flows from Norman Lindsay and Christopher Brennan to a displaced Europeanism seeking to avoid the moral imperatives of place with a false doctrine of universals. What Prichard and Herbert grasped was that at the heart of the Australian experience lay a sexual tragedy of enormous historical dimension in which love, mockery and hatred battled for the mastery, and that the tragedy was performed across the bodies of Aboriginal women. Speaking of part-Aboriginal girls, Herbert wrote bitterly: 'They're looked upon from birth as part of the great dirty joke'.[5] Norman, the half-caste hero of *Capricornia*, is the first man of his kind to be presented by an Australian writer with a mature feeling for the elementary human decencies; Prichard's Coonardoo, whose life is a long allegory of suffering, is the first Aboriginal woman in our literature to be realised by a compassionate imagination. With the creation of Coonardoo and Norman, Australian culture begins a process of atonement, the concerned conscience is pointed a way by which it might be quietened, and Truganini laid to rest behind her mountains. Prichard and Herbert had grasped that black and white alike in Australia are involved in a common destiny. Years later Judith Wright gave a classic expression to their pioneering intuition in her poem *Nigger's Leap*:

> Did we not know their blood channelled our rivers,
> And the black dust our crops ate was their dust?
> O all men are one man at last. We should have known
> the night that tided up the cliffs and hid them
> had the same question on its tongue for us
> And there they lie that were ourselves writ strange.

In 1940 came the Jindyworobaks, a group of poets centred in Adelaide. They stressed the connection between poetry and place, invoking Aboriginal culture as a model. Though their influence was transitory they helped to give our poetry more of a local flavour and reduced its European pre-occupations.

In the years between the wars it was not the problems of the Aboriginal people but the formal and colourful beauty of traditional Aboriginal art which began to impress Australian artists. First in the field was Margaret Preston who, both in her art and writing, suggested that it should form the basis of modern Australian art. Though the immediate influence of her work was small—direct perhaps in the decorative work of Byram Mansell, indirect in the paintings and illustrations of Elizabeth Durack—in a more general way her influence has been widely pervasive. Aboriginal art strongly influenced the styles of Ian Fairweather and Anthony Tuckson— who did much to gain a recognition for Aboriginal art as art in our museums and galleries. The influence of Aboriginal art is present also in the personal styles of some of Australia's best known artists such as John Olsen, Fred Williams and Leonard French. This overall influence needs to be studied more carefully than it has been. It may well be one of the significant components by which modern Australian art, at its best, has been able to crystallise itself out from its primary European and North American sources.

For most of our artists the Aborigine has been an aesthetic rather than a moral presence; influencing the sensibility rather than disturbing the conscience. There were some, however, of a more realistic persuasion, for whom the image of the Aborigine in modern Australia remained a compelling concern. In 1933 Arthur Murch visited the Hermannsburg Mission and drew fine portraits of the Aranda which, had they been executed 100 years before, twentieth-century critics might have called portraits of noble savages. During the early 1940s the young refugee Jewish artist, Josl Bergner, perceived a striking parallel between urbanised Aborigines in Melbourne and the degradation and persecution to which his own people were being then subjected in Nazi-occupied Europe; and he painted them so. The comic stereotype was being challenged and the image of the Aborigine becoming a moral presence in Australian art. About the same time Russell Drysdale began his memorable series of station blacks.

'They have to me,' he wrote some time later, 'a peculiar dignity and grace, not the sort of dignity . . . that one thinks of in the Apollo Belvedere, but the way in which a man comports himself in an environment which . . . has been his and his alone.'[6] Australian painters however were not disposed for the most part to follow the leads given by Murch, Bergner or Drysdale. But in 1958 Arthur Boyd, drawing upon memories of a visit he had made to central Australia in 1951, exhibited a series of paintings entitled *Love, Marriage and Death of a Half-Caste*. It is an allegorical narrative in which 'a half-caste man wooing a half-caste bride' finds himself 'haunted by the dream image of a white bride and by his fear of white society'.[7]

Like Prichard's *Coonardoo* and Herbert's *Capricornia*, Boyd was dealing with the problem of Aboriginal identity under pressure from white society. It is the only series of paintings to my knowledge which attempts to enter the world of moral and racial ambiguity which part-Aboriginal people inherit. Shortly after Arthur Boyd completed this series of paintings his brother David exhibited a group which was concerned with the life of Truganini. They included some of the best paintings of his career. But the critical hostility with which they were met has not perhaps been paralleled in the history of Australian art criticism. Although the protests were usually mounted in the terms of aesthetic quality, it seems clear that the subject had touched a raw nerve in the Australian racial consciousness. One critic wrote that 'most Australians neither think nor care about the plight of the Aborigines' and suggested that pictures devoted to the Melbourne Cup and Stiffy and Mo might be more worthy of the artist's concern.[8]

The situation is the reverse in the case of the novel. The years following World War II witnessed increased industrial and political activities among blacks in north-western Australia. In 1946 a group of Aboriginal stockmen maintained a successful strike as a result of the discovery of minerals. The Pindan co-operative established by Don McLeod, who has become a legend in his own lifetime, brought Aboriginal affairs to the forefront of political interest. Professor Rowley has described its unprecedented achievements as follows:

An Aboriginal community was finding itself and maintaining itself economically in the face of real hardship. The members had broken out of legalised and institutionalised dependency, and were living as *political* men and women, using the legal and administrative institutions of the Australian community to advance their own interests and thus finding their own ways into the culture of institutionalised democracy, so long closed to them, and at their own pace, retaining those remnants of their culture which were important to them.[9]

From the heightened political situation in Western Australia, symbolised by the success of Pindan, came an important crop of novels by FB Vickers, Donald Stuart, Gavin Casey, Mary Durack, Randolph Stow and Richard Beilby. These novels brought a new awareness to the Australian community of the legal disabilities suffered by Aborigines, the atrocious standards of health care to which they were subjected, the degraded conditions under which they lived. They also brought a new realisation of the realities of economic and political organisation among blacks. The work of these westerners was complemented in the east by several highly distinguished novelists, notably Thomas Keneally, Peter Mathers, David Ireland, Patrick White, and Xavier Herbert again in his monumental epic *Poor Fellow My Country*.

Not surprisingly these novels vary greatly in literary quality; but as a whole they have performed an invaluable function. They have developed a heightened state of awareness concerning a moral issue central to the nation's existence. Yet oddly enough this heightened awareness has, it seems to me, placed all Australians with any sense of concern for the Aboriginal people in an increasingly embarrassing position. Because there is now a considerable morality gap between our sympathies and our achievements; between the conscious concern now held by the majority of Australians for the well-being of the Aboriginal people and their actual living conditions: their health, legal status, and hopes of leading a normal Australian life or preserving a traditional one. Some maintain that this gap is widening. So I should be inclined to call the years through which we are presently passing, taking a cue from Lewis Carroll, whom I quoted at the beginning of this talk, the Years of the Walrus, the years of a manifest hypocrisy, during which we extend our sympathies increasingly to the Aboriginal people while our institutions, legal and otherwise, continue to permit the cannibalisation of their culture and their aspirations in the name of technological progress.

1   CD Rowley, *The Destruction of Aboriginal Society*, Australian National University Press, Canberra, 1970, p137
2   James Tucker, *Ralph Rashleigh*, Angus & Robertson, Sydney, 1952, pp277, 303
3   HM Green, *A History of Australian Literature*, Angus & Robertson, Sydney, 1961, Vol 1, p166
4   JJ Healy, *Literature and the Aborigine in Australia*, University of Queensland Press, St Lucia, 1978, p51
5   Xavier Herbert, *Capricornia*, Angus & Robertson, Sydney, 1943, p82
6   Quoted in Geoffrey Dutton, *White on Black the Australian Aborigine Portrayed in Art*, MacMillan, Melbourne, 1974, pp62–3
7   Ursula Hoff, *The Paintings of Arthur Boyd*, Meanjin, xvii, No 2, 1958, p146, published University of Melbourne
8   Robert Hughes, *The Art of Australia*, Penguin, Harmondsworth, 1970, pp249, 250
9   CD Rowley, *The Remote Aborigines*, Australian National University Press, Canberra, 1971, p257

John Passmore

John Passmore is a distinguished philosopher and gentleman of letters. He was born in Manly, NSW, in 1914. He was educated at the University of Sydney where he studied under, and was influenced by, Professor John Anderson and took the university medal in philosophy.

He taught philosophy there until he left Sydney in 1950 to become Professor of Philosophy at the University of Otago, returning to Australia in 1955 to join the Australian National University, first as reader, and then as Professor of Philosophy. He held the chair from 1959 to his retirement in 1979, when he

became Emeritus Professor. From 1982 to 1993 he was attached to the History of Ideas Unit at the university as a university fellow and then as a visiting fellow. Since 1994 he has been visiting fellow of Historical Studies.

Professor Passmore first established his reputation as an historian of philosophy, and his best-known work in that field is *A Hundred Years of Philosophy*. Among his books are *The Perfectability of Man, Responsibility for Nature, Science and its Critics, The Philosopy of Teaching, Recent Philosophers*, and in 1997, *The Environment, Education, The Arts: Memoirs of a Semi-detached Australian*.

John Passmore has lectured extensively in Europe, Asia and America, and twice was a visiting fellow at All Souls College, Oxford, and Clare Hall, Cambridge.

He is a former president of the Australian Academy of the Humanities, a Fellow of the Academy of the Social Sciences, a foreign fellow of the British, American and Danish Academies, a member of the Institut de Philosophie, and a trustee of the International Council for the Future of the University.

He has received honorary doctorates from a number of universities in Australia and overseas. He has been a member of the Australian Research Grants Committee, the Australian Science and Technology Council, and a director and a governor of the Australian Elizabethan Theatre Trust, where I, for one, was grateful for his presence and contribution.

Professor Passmore was made a Companion of the Order of Australia in 1992.

The title of Professor Passmore's Boyer Lectures *The Limits of Government* is still an arresting one. Concerned by what he saw as an increasingly doctrinaire intellectual environment, John Passmore's intention was clear: 'Painful, dangerous even, though the exercise may be, we are forced to think.'

The titles of his individual lectures were 'The General Problem'; 'Coercion'; 'Protection'; 'Subsidisation' and 'Conclusions and Reflections', which is reproduced here. All display his special clarity of thought and gentle good sense.

CONCLUSIONS
AND REFLECTIONS

The Limits of Government

John Passmore

• 1981 •

I have talked about three closely related ways in which a government exercises its powers: coercion, protection and subsidisation. Let me now sum up what I have said. Each such power, I suggested, has its limitations. Some of these limitations apply to any government anywhere. Take coercion. No government can coerce its citizens into being imaginative, and imagination lies at the heart of every creative enterprise, whether in industry, art or science. Some limitations will vary with circumstances. Without ceasing to be democratic, a democratic government cannot engage in forms of coercion which an authoritarian government takes for granted. As for protection, there will be ills against which no government can protect its citizens: they arise out of human ignorance or human limitations or the operation of natural laws. Other ills a particular government will not be able to protect against without bringing to ruin the social system on which it depends.

Each of these powers, one can add, has its darker side. By its very nature, coercion is in itself an evil. It is a *necessary* evil in so far as without the help of governmental coercion a community is not able to go about its business or enjoy its pleasures in reasonable security. Yet coercion can also be used in order to destroy our freedom to do so. As for its other powers, by protecting, as by subsidising, government can enlarge the range of activities which are available to individuals. It can help to make possible the emergence or the continuance of voluntary associations. But it can also, deliberately or inadvertently, reduce its citizens to the condition of slaves, destroying their capacity for independent action and the voluntary organisations through which that capacity finds expression. Setting out to protect, a government can create a form of society in which atomised individuals, their organisations destroyed, are at the mercy of a government against which there is no protection.

One could tell a similar story, did time permit, about other government powers: about its power to persuade, about its control over information. But rather than exploring such themes, let us turn our attention to the Australian scene, and ask how what I have been saying bears upon it. Our attitude to government has traditionally been a rather complicated one. On the one hand, we automatically turn to government for help in an emergency, to protect and to subsidise. We do this whoever we are. Academics, farmers, businessmen have this much in common. It seems to us very natural, too, to cope with a social problem by legislation. 'There ought to be a law about it', we say with indignation. The total number of Acts passing through Australian legislative bodies in a single year, so I have credibly been told, approaches the thousand mark. There is not a single citizen of Australia, I feel confident, however law-abiding he may think of himself as being, who has not broken the law, not once but very many times. Our law courts are clogged. Organisations find it necessary to protect themselves by engaging lawyers rather than more directly productive staff—as universities may be forced, in self-protection, to engage lawyers rather than scientists and scholars. Each separate legislative act may have its justification, but the multiplicity of regulations destroys the efficiency of regulation. Yet we go on law-making, as if its social costs simply did not exist. There is a further point to be considered: ask a government to do too much and the really important decisions are not made or are inadequately considered, as Confucius long ago pointed out.

But if, in Australia, we turn readily to governments for protection or assistance by regulation, it is still true that on the other side we display a marked mistrust for government. That is apparent in our political institutions. In some measure, of course, every democracy mistrusts government. That is precisely why democracies have free elections, with opposition parties, open parliamentary debates, independent news media, a relaxed censorship, freedom of information. If these institutions operate in an imperfect fashion, there is still no mistaking their general intent, to limit the powers of government.

Nevertheless, Australia carries mistrust for governments beyond what democracy inevitably demands, further than it is carried in, let us say, Great Britain and New Zealand, if not, in every respect, as far as it is carried in the United States. Our elections, to take one case, are held every three years, where four or five years is the more normal period of office. Furthermore, when we elect a government we by no means say to it: 'There you are now; do as you choose.' A new government is slotted into a set of pre-existing institutions—

judicial, administrative, coercive—over which it has only a limited degree of control. Take the federal government. Its legislation, in the federal sphere, has to be approved not only by a lower house, as in all democracies, but by a Senate with real teeth. Even then it may be ruled unconstitutional by the High Court, to say nothing of the powers of the Governor-General. Only by referenda can a government loosen the bonds imposed upon it by the federal Constitution. Voters in such referenda have been conspicuously unready to agree to proposals which would enlarge the government's powers.

Regular elections, constitutional rules, federalism—these are by no means the only ways in which we limit the powers of our governments. Our suspicion of government also finds expression in our fondness for statutory authorities and public companies. Even when an organisation is largely, or totally, funded by governments, we do not always bring it under the direct control of the public service, we do not subject it to governmental intervention in its day-to-day activities, we do not administer it in the manner which we take to be typical of government-run services, bureaucratically. Our government-funded radio and television stations, to take a case, are governed by a commission; they are not under the direct supervision of a ministry. That, of course, is the government's doing. But in Australia even governments mistrust governments; if they do not mistrust themselves, they mistrust their possible successors. By this indirect method of rule, governments both assuage the qualms of electors and diminish the power of subsequent regimes.

Not only do we traditionally subdue the immediacy of government control in the life of the community by the device of statutory authorities, we also permit, in a great many instances, commercial competition against government-funded enterprises. We display indeed, an exceptional fondness for that type of dual arrangement, which, so far as I know, no political theorist, no political party, has ever explicitly advocated. We have private and government banks, insurance companies, airlines, hospitals, schools, broadcasting and television stations, travel agents, theatrical entrepreneurs, book shops. Encountering so broad a range of governmental activities, American observers often describe our society as 'socialistic', whereas in the eyes of Continental observers, not necessarily from eastern Europe, we are a strange people indeed, in funding a government enterprise and yet not subjecting it to direct government control. We are stranger still in their eyes when, as often happens, the competitor is government-subsidised or, at the very least, assisted with loans and protected against further competition in a manner which can indeed approach the farcical, as in the two airline system.

In yet another respect, not so readily specifiable, we limit the power of our governments by our attitudes as distinct from our constitutional provisions. In many societies, the strength of a government depends, at least partly, on the fact that it possesses a special charisma. It is thought of as being in some sense holy, sacred, so that criticism, let alone rebellion, is sacrilegious. Emperors and kings have often sought to represent themselves as being divine beings, as gods, descended from gods, or at the very least as ruling by divine right. Democracy in England arose out of a rejection of that view; governments were conceived of as secular devices for protecting contracts. But attempts were still made to bestow some charismatic legitimacy on governments by suggesting that they represent the general will, or the people as a whole, or some mysterious metaphysical entity called 'the State', or the proletariat become conscious of its true nature. Or perhaps that by becoming the government, the politicians who make it up have divested themselves of all particular interests and now wholly concern themselves with the national interest—whatever that is supposed to be. In one way or another a government is turned into something not merely powerful but grand, peculiarly deserving of our respect and loyalty, not merely because half the population, many of them with distinct reservations, has voted for it but for some deeper, metaphysical, reason.

In Australia the charismatic power of government, by international and historical standards, stands very low. Much of the charisma attaches to a Royal Family twelve thousand miles away. Its reflection at Yarralumla is feeble indeed. Our Prime Minister does not possess the charismatic authority of the French, or even the American, President. It is characteristic of our way of thinking that we are about to construct a Parliament House which instead of standing grandly on top of a hill burrows into that hill so that one can actually walk over it. Nothing could more accurately depict the Australian spirit. Yet even that Parliament House has been condemned as too grand. Professor Manning Clark laments our lack of a sense of grandeur and does what he can to impose grandeur upon us, whether by elevating our past or by envisaging for us an apocalyptically conceived future. But some of us see our lack of grandeur as a cause for self-congratulation. We would not welcome a republic out of a fear that we might come to attach a reverential authority to a President. It is our historic task to show the world what can be created by a resolute pursuit of mediocrity. I mean mediocrity in the original sense of that word—the full recognition that we are all human beings, with all the limitations of human beings. We are none of us superhuman, we are not gods in the making, our government no more than the rest of us.

It is not necessary to agree with Tom Paine that 'the trade of governing has always been monopolized by the most ignorant and most rascally individuals of mankind'. Some of our politicians are reasonably well-informed and no more dishonest than the rest of us. We do well to think of them in this way, as none of them saints and few of them scoundrels. They are not parasites, just as public servants are not parasites. Their role in our society is a very important one and the best of them work very hard to fulfil it. But it is as dangerous to think too well of them as it is to think too badly of them. Commonsense, astringency, a refusal to take pretensions seriously, these are the qualities for which we are valued in the counsels of the world and I hope it will always be so. No doubt, these virtues can degenerate into cynicism, or into mediocrity in the bad sense of the word, a loss of any ability to distinguish what will just pass muster—'she'll do', as we say—and the genuinely good, a refusal to try to accomplish what lies well within our powers, let alone what will stretch them to the utmost. Understood, however, as I have understood it, our mediocrity is our saving grace.

So far I have been developing my original claim: that in Australia we mistrust governments. Then how are we to account for the proliferation of our government enterprises? In the United States, after all, there is no government broadcasting, there are no government trading banks, no government air lines, to take only the most obvious instances. Well, if we mistrust governments, we also mistrust private enterprise. Many of us read with sympathy Adam Smith's remark that 'people of the same trade seldom meet together but the conversation ends in a conspiracy against the public'. That is the other side of our fondness for an arrangement by which government enterprises compete with private enterprises. It is a way of mistrusting private enterprise and government simultaneously. One must add, as illustrating our mistrust of private enterprise, the sufficiently obvious point that it is in any case restricted by a formidable array of legislative and administrative rules, designed to protect the worker, the consumer, the environment, or some more vaguely conceived 'national interest'. To sum up, the majority of Australians—there are, of course, many individual exceptions—have not been won over by either of the two most sharply delineated political philosophies, by libertarianism on the one hand or by totalitarianism on the other hand, even in the form of state socialism.

Let us consider, nevertheless, how a full-blooded libertarian would respond to the Australian situation as I have described it. He would look favourably on the restrictions we have imposed on government. Indeed, he would wish to strengthen them, as we saw, by introducing constitutional amendments of the same general sort as the American Bill of Rights. He would add to the Constitution amendments which would limit the total expenditure of governments, compelling them to balance their budgets, to restrict their total expenditure—with allowances, of course, for special circumstances. (You can find a set of proposals of this sort in the appendix to Milton Friedman's book *Free to Choose*.) I do not think these proposals should be dismissed out of hand as worthless, difficult though they may be to implement. A despotic government can destroy our rights, a spendthrift government can lead us into an inflation from which it can be difficult, even impossible, to recover. Yet I have reservations, as I have already made plain, about the necessity, and the desirability, of the first of them, the Bill of Rights. The limitation on the spending powers of government, similarly, might greatly diminish its flexibility, its capacity to respond to rapidly changing circumstances. If both proposals nevertheless deserve serious consideration, it is as emphasising the kinds of obligation which, in a democratic society, a government ought to regard as tacitly binding upon it: to leave us as free as possible and to restrain its spending.

What else would a libertarian say as he looked at our society? He would not at all like our habit of running to the government for subsidy. I agree, as I have already made plain, that there are grave dangers in doing so. There are at least three advantages in obtaining our ends by voluntary organisations, supported by private donations, rather than by government hand-outs. The first advantage is that the running of such organisations gives individuals an opportunity to learn the arts of cooperation, to exhibit imagination and initiative, to stand in closer relationships with their fellow human beings. The second advantage is that the activities of such organisations are not then subject to the fickleness of government, which is as ready to withdraw support as to offer it. And a third advantage is to obviate the risk that government, operating on the principle that he who pays the piper calls the tune, will move from subsidising to controlling, subverting the original intention of the organisation.

These grounds are not strong enough, I however argued, to allow the deduction that the government should withdraw from subsidising, that it should never, that is, transfer income from taxpayers in order to subsidise activities. The voluntary activity may simply not be able to survive without subsidy; its loss would have the effect that our society would lose its diversity, that valuable activities would no longer take place in it.

The libertarian would also object to our social services. They, too, were once left to voluntary effort. Anybody who believes that this was the ideal state of affairs had better read George Orwell's *Down and Out in London and Paris*. If he grumbles about the indifference or hostility of bureaucrats he might also recall that the phrase 'cold as charity' pre-dates the welfare state. So far as social services are employed as a way of helping the handicapped, in the broadest sense of that word, in a manner which relieves the suffering of those who are incapable of helping themselves and assists those who can partially help themselves to maintain maximum independence, I am not prepared, as I have already said, to support the libertarian case against them. But it is also true that, as libertarians argue, social service policies have often been notably unsuccessful in obtaining their ends. They have too often been motivated not by a desire to relieve suffering or to turn dependence into independence but by a totally insane attempt to equalise, even between relatively well-off citizens, to equalise, for example, by reducing the need for such relatively well-off citizens to sacrifice part of their income to support children whom other people on the same income do not have to support. Often enough, the effect has been that the low-income tax-payer has had to meet the expenses of the relatively well-off. The libertarian argument should at least provoke us into looking very carefully at our support programs, examining their necessity and their effectiveness. One of the major problems, as I see it, is to distribute such support only to those who really need it, without making use of means tests, which are both undignified and costly to police. Here is a field where there is clear need for practical inventiveness.

One other aspect of our society a libertarian would certainly object to. We have government enterprises, even when we permit competition from private enterprise. Much of the libertarian's criticism is based on the assumption, derived from American experience, that government enterprises are bound to be badly run. This, I have suggested, is simply not true. It is particularly not true when the enterprise is permitted the degree of liberty from civil service regulations which is possessed by statutory authorities and private competition is allowed. But it does not follow that in every case in which we now do so we are right to employ this dual system, let alone that it ought to be made universal. We need to look much more closely than we have so far done at the question under what circumstances such private–public competition is desirable, what good it can achieve and what evil it can prevent.

We have given the libertarian his head. Now let us look at those who would like to see the power of government extended. They will certainly not be content with the Australian scene as it is. The first thing they commonly want to do is to destroy the federal system, by abolishing state governments, so that the federal government will be all-powerful except on questions of purely local concern— which can be left to municipal bodies. They would abolish the present Senate and they would not permit the High Court to declare legislation invalid. That implies a confidence in government which I am quite unable to share. But the government, the reply may come, is elected by the people. So it is, or more accurately, as I have several times insisted, by about half the people approving of some elements in the government's policy. But once it is elected it always, by the nature of the case, does a great many things which it had not announced it would do. It has to respond to changing circumstances, but it may also be corrupted by the experience of power so corrupted indeed that it takes steps to ensure that it will never have to face the electors again. That has happened elsewhere, it could happen here, and has indeed already happened when electorates are gerrymandered. In the past, we were saved both from a government's attempt to ban the Communist Party and from the nationalisation of the banks by the complexities of our constitutional system. Never trust governments absolutely, and always do what you can to prevent them from doing too much harm. That is the very sound principle which our political system has enshrined. Compared not only with what governments have done but with what they are doing here and now, in one part of the world or another, Jack the Ripper was an innocent babe-in-arms.

Of course, we hear a lot nowadays about 'socialism with a human face'. But the Soviet Union is right about this; there can be no such thing. Any state socialist government which tries to humanise itself will find itself moving in bourgeois directions. The face of bourgeois society, like human faces in general, is no doubt often hideous. I yield to nobody in detesting a great number of its expressions, the greed, cruelty, unscrupulousness, complacency, heartlessness, so often visible there. Nevertheless, I still believe that it is the only form of society within which great changes can take place without the apparatus of the concentration camp, murder, the suppression of opposition, the muzzling of the artist, the thinker, the critic, the independently minded worker. State socialism is a paradise for the intellectual who is prepared to conform and for the bureaucrat, but for no one else. To travel out of Hungary, as I recently did, in a train from which the roof-panels were removed at the Austrian border, in case some dissident were concealed there, trying to escape, is to be reconciled to a great deal in Australia. But such a reconciliation should lead one to be more, not less, wary of threats to liberty in one's own society—threats which can come from any of our political parties. Nor should it lead one to be afraid of change. I am not suggesting that, for example, our present distribution of powers between state and federal governments is ideal. Mr Hawke was right when he suggested in his Boyer lectures that we ought to be seriously considering changes in our system of government to make it more genuinely representative. Those changes should not, however, be of such a character as to weaken our protection against the rise of tyranny.

The full-blooded state socialist, of course, would want to abolish the dual system of competition between private and public by nationalising the private. I have to confess that I simply cannot understand why, at this stage of our social experience, anyone should want to nationalise, deliberately to create a monopoly. Who can now possibly believe that nationalised monopolies would be more responsive to the public, more efficient, more profitable, offer a better life to their employees, be less subject to industrial disputes? The sole possible justification of national monopolies is in those rare instances where it is not desirable that the user should pay in direct relationship to his use. As it is not desirable for it to cost more to send a private letter from Perth to Brisbane than from one suburb of Perth to another.

If we believe that governments are so endowed with economic knowledge that they can run the economy more effectively than anybody else, or than the free market, then we might also be prepared to believe that certain key enterprises should be nationalised. But why should we suppose that governments possess this wisdom? As the German sociologist Max Weber pointed out, politics as a profession attracts a very special class of human being. The most innovative, daring, imaginative, enterprising members of the community do not enter politics. So government control means, in practice, control by a very special limited class of human beings. Political animals, working through bureaucrats. Why should we entrust to them or indeed to anybody else, even the most gifted, the power to plan our lives?

My conclusion will be very unsatisfying to those who like to believe that there is some single, sweeping, social change that will solve all our problems, whether it be the withdrawal of government or its total supremacy. Substantially, I am defending our mixed economy, without for a moment suggesting that we have the mixture right or that we are under no necessity to make any kind of political or social change. If I have some degree of sympathy with the libertarians, it is in so far as they have a genuine enthusiasm for liberty, an enthusiasm which, however, their conservative imitators only partially share. Many of the changes we need to make are, I believe, in the libertarian direction. The libertarians accuse me, however, of letting my heart rule my head because I am not prepared to accept their view that nineteenth-century industrial society was a Garden of Eden from which we were expelled for eating the apple of welfare. I grant that when governments do good it is with the slap of command. Nevertheless in my judgment they can sometimes do good, did so in industrial England, have done so in the post-war years, here in Australia. Yet we should never forget the limits of government. Governments cannot create liberty, imagination, affection, the desire to understand, the capacity to co-operate, generosity, tolerance. Indeed, a government has good reason to fear each and everyone of these qualities, if it is intent on extending its power. That is why we have good reason, in our turn, for fearing it. No doubt, it can equalise. But it is no accident that 'equaliser' is American slang for gun. We can be sure that if we abandon liberty in the name of equality it will be equality at the point of a gun, equality in misery.

Sir Bruce Williams

Born in Warragul, Victoria, in 1919, Bruce Williams was educated at Wesley College, the University of Melbourne and the University of Adelaide. He lectured in economics at Adelaide and at Queen's University of Belfast until 1950. Following work on the theories of employment and expectations he became Foundation Professor of Economics at the University College of North Staffordshire, now the University of Keele. He went to the University of Manchester in 1959, as Professor of Economics and subsequently as Professor of Political Economy and Cobden Lecturer. He worked in the fields of technical change and economic growth, and in the application of science to industry.

In 1967 he was appointed vice-chancellor and principal of the University of Sydney, chairing the vice-chancellors' committee from 1972 to 1974. He returned to Britain in 1981 and became the first director of The Technical Change Centre and visiting professor at the Imperial College until 1986. He was a Fellow of the University of Sydney Senate from 1994 to 1998.

He chaired the Australian Government's Committee of Inquiry into Education and Training from 1976 to 1979. From 1969 to 1981 he was on the Board of the Reserve Bank of Australia, a member of the Immigration Planning Council from 1968 to 1973, and on the advisory council of the CSIRO from 1968 to 1974. He chaired the New South Wales Cancer Council from 1967 to 1981, the Westmead Project Committee from 1968 to 1980. He has been chairman of the Sydney International Piano Competition and president of the Sydney Spring Festival of Contemporary Music.

Sir Bruce is a fellow of the Australian Academy of the Social Sciences and has honorary doctorates from the universities of Sydney, Melbourne, Manchester, Queensland, Keele and Aston in Birmingham.

He was knighted in 1980 for services to education and government.

Sir Bruce's Boyer Lectures entitled *Living With Technology* were individually titled 'Dynamic Technology'; 'Technological Employment and Unemployment'; 'Education Skills and the Working Life'; 'Run Over by Technology?', which is reproduced here, and 'Possible Futures' in which he concluded that the greatest problems come from the need to reconcile interests, which is always difficult. His concluding words are: 'No-one can say just how hard the path will be. For this is a case of: Traveller, there is no path, Paths are made by walking.'

RUN OVER BY TECHNOLOGY?

Living with Technology

Sir Bruce Williams

• 1982 •

We have come to treat the creation of new technologies as a normal feature of life. That however is a fairly recent development. At the time when the First Fleet left England to establish a British colony in New South Wales, economic conditions did not differ greatly from those in the Roman Empire nineteen centuries earlier. However the Industrial Revolution that was to become cumulative and spread throughout the world had already started in Britain.

In my first lecture I referred to the costs as well as to the benefits of continuing technical change. New technologies have added greatly to production and to the range of goods and services, have eliminated most very heavy and dangerous work, have made possible improved standards of housing, diet, health, education and the forms and levels of scientific activities that have greatly enriched human culture.

Costs

The main cause for worry about technical change in the last 200 years is the increase in the destructive power of weapons. The technologies of nuclear, chemical and biological weapons have reached such a stage that the future of mankind is threatened.

New technologies have also created serious problems of pollution and generated costly fluctuations in the levels of employment and the locations of employment.

High levels of investment in new technologies create a strong demand for labour, and the demand for labour in new activities absorbs labour made redundant by innovations in older activities. But investment in new technologies has never been stable and when it falls off we are faced with a serious problem of unemployment.

The innovation process has had other disturbing effects. Both within and between countries technical changes have induced shifts in the location of industry and employment, creating temporary shortages of labour, housing, transport, schools and hospitals in some regions, and more lasting surpluses in other places.

Technical changes have often reduced the demand for mental and manual skills that were in good supply at the time and increased the demand for skills that were not—so creating the need for re-training, and for changes in pre-employment and on-the-job training.

The benefits and costs of technical change have been very unevenly spread, though somewhat less so since the increase in the social services, and to those made redundant by technical change the costs will seem much greater than the benefits.

Apart from the effects of fluctuating levels of investment in new technologies on levels of employment, and the uneven distribution of benefits and costs of technical change, there have always been critics of various aspects of industrialisation. There have been many critics of rural depopulation and urbanisation, critics of the cash nexus and the strained pursuit of material riches that competition encourages; critics of the effects of occupational and geographical mobility in undermining the strength of the extended family; critics of the attempts of applied science and engineering to make man 'the conscious lord of nature'.

In recent years the extent of criticism and foreboding has increased. There are strong fears that the costs of further technical change are rising faster than the benefits. Lewis Mumford, for example, wrote in The Myth of the Machine that technological innovation has become so rapid and general in its effects that continuity and security in modern society have been destroyed. Technology, he said, must be tamed if society is to survive; while Heidegger in Discourse on Thinking wrote that technological forces have moved beyond man's will. Other critics have maintained that over-cropping and over-grazing, the depletion of sea food stocks, the exhaustion of non-renewable materials, and the pollution of the land, the sea and the atmosphere will soon bring crisis and collapse if the growth of population and production are allowed to continue.

In a statement to the United Nations in 1969 U Thant issued a sombre warning from a rather different standpoint in that it implied the need for much further growth in developing countries:

> I can only conclude that members of the United Nations have perhaps ten years left in which to subordinate their ancient quarrels and launch a global partnership to curb the arms race, to improve the human environment, to defuse the population explosion, and to supply the required momentum to development efforts. If such a

global partnership is not forged within the next decade, then I very much fear that the problems I have mentioned will have reached such staggering proportions that they will be beyond our capacity to control.

Adapting to Technology

Heidegger's view that technological forces have moved beyond man's will is shared by many writers. Galbraith has written that in thought as in action we are becoming the servants of our machines. The film *Colossus* is built on a dramatic version of man as a slave of his own machines. Colossus, a very powerful computer, has taken control of the economic and defence systems of the United States of America and Russia. The President of the United States and Dr Farbin the inventor attempt to bring Colossus under control, but Colossus decides to keep control and to do so has the President and Dr Farbin, his creator, put in prison.

In this literature on the impact of technology on society there are two conceptually distinct themes—one that by adopting new technologies we commit ourselves to adapting our ways of life to them; the other, more deterministic, that the technologies we use have an inherent dynamic and change independently of us.

Ways of life were certainly changed by industrialisation. The factory brought the separation of the home and the work place, and the greater discipline of the clock and the tempo of machines. Patterns of consumption were changed by increases in incomes, the range of goods and town living. The sharp reduction in the proportion of agricultural workers undermined the belief that man is at the mercy of natural forces, and continuing innovations in technologies in the production of food and raw materials and in manufactures, encouraged belief in man's power to control the forces of nature.

Making the best use of technological possibilities has required progressive changes in the division of labour. Some changes have been de-skilling, as in the case for example of workers on assembly lines in motor car factories. Other changes have required the development of new skills, for example to operate chemical process plants, to program computers and to manufacture chips for computers and micro controls. Other new technologies have brought changes in location; the change from steam power to electric power for example had a major effect on location of industry. But unless the new skills are required and unless workers do move to the new locations, the new technologies will not be used effectively and could fail. The invention of new technologies cannot of itself ensure that society will create the conditions for their effective use.

Changes in the organisation of work may also carry over into social life. Thus the introduction of coal-cutting machinery in British mines, and the introduction of tunnel ovens in the British pottery industry, so changed work roles and relative wages that pecking orders in social life which had carried over from the workplace were undermined.

Management methods and the organisation of industries were also changed by new technologies—or rather, to realise the potentialities of new technologies it was necessary to change methods of management and industrial organisation. In some industries new technologies brought such economies of scale that only a few firms could survive. In other cases new technologies created great opportunities for small and new firms. There was need also to change the law. Industrialisation in Britain and in other countries would not have got far without considerable legal change to remove restrictions on trade and methods of production, and to introduce limited liability and the joint stock company—for the accumulation of capital is a critical factor in industrialisation everywhere. Currently, some of the potentialities of information technology will not be fully used without changes in laws relating to copyright and to the separation of speech and other data in communication networks.

There is no doubt that new technologies have brought great changes in our attitudes and manners of living. To make good use of the latest technologies it will continue to be necessary to make changes in and beyond the work place, and the adoption of new technologies will create pressures to make these changes. But it does not follow that the changes will be made. Britain, for instance, has fallen behind in economic growth precisely because it has not adapted institutions and attitudes to fit in with the new technologies.

Autonomous Technology

Marx once wrote that the hand mill gave us the feudal society and the steam mill the capitalist society. Wilhelm Leibnecht in his autobiography recounts a visit to London to see Marx and Engels. He found them greatly excited by an exhibition in Regent Street of a model train powered by electricity. This, they thought, could be the new source of power that would give us the socialist society. Years later at the outset of the communist revolution Lenin reflected that hope in a qualified form in his slogan 'Soviets plus electrification equals socialism'.

The combination of the views that technologies determine ideas and social systems and that new technologies evolve autonomously produces a very deterministic theory of change. The concept of autonomous technology is reflected in the growing tendency to describe technical change in biological terms—to refer, for example, to *generations* of computers.

Invention is a cumulative process and each extension of knowledge and each new solution to a technological problem creates the potentiality for further inventions. With some new technologies—for example, computers—the potential for further development may be enormous. But the development of that potential does not take place automatically. It requires a considerable human effort and commitment of resources. The planned development of 'the fifth generation computer' in Japan requires such a large commitment of resources that the Japanese government has organised a consortium of government and private agencies to make the invention and is providing substantial financial backing.

In industrialised countries a substantial part of the work force is engaged in research and development activities—almost 13 per cent in the United States of America and between 10 and 12 per cent in Germany, the United Kingdom and Japan. If we take away such activity, about half of which is financed by governments from taxes there would be much less technical change. And if governments ceased to provide substantial finance for education—about 8 per cent of the Commonwealth government expenditure—further technical change would be severely impeded by a shortage of scientists, technologists, technicians and craftsmen.

Technical change does not proceed independently of human decision. In part it may often appear to do so because much technical change is induced by the pressures, or the compulsions, of competition.

To understand the social role of competitive pressures it helps to recall a very influential book which was published in Britain just a few years before Governor Phillip established the colony in Sydney. That book was Adam Smith's *Inquiry into the Nature and Causes of the Wealth of Nations*. When Adam Smith wrote there was an extensive network of government and corporate controls over trade, methods of production and location. Smith's book showed that this network of controls restricted the growth of wealth. By limiting the market, it hindered the growth of the more productive division of labour, and it reduced pressures to invent and install machines to make workers still more productive.

In the circumstances of the time Smith's book was very persuasive. Changes in attitudes and in the laws and their administration then created a competitive system which induced remarkable increases in production.

During the depression of the 1930s there were growing doubts about whether competitive pressures could continue to induce technical change and economic growth. In some areas new technologies had reduced the number of firms to two or three, and business and professional associations and trade unions—often with the help of governments—were able to reduce the rigours of competition.

However, partly as a consequence of a growth in organised research and development during and after the Second World War, competitive pressures played a very important part in inducing technical change during the long post-war boom. Competition did not operate in just the same way as it did when there were many firms in every industry. But in science-based industries, where organised research and development made possible planned invention and innovation, competition among the few proved to be very powerful and productive.

This innovation puts pressures on traditional industries to find more efficient methods and to improve their products. Thus bricks faced competition from plastics and glass in buildings and the cotton and wool textile industries faced competition from nylon and terylene.

Compulsions of Competition

Competition between firms has the effect of reducing prices and profit margins and gives them an incentive to reduce costs or find a more attractive product. When a firm which has a substantial output introduces a new technology which reduces costs or improves quality it gets a competitive advantage and puts pressures on others to improve their products or methods of production. To the extent that this competitive pressure spreads the new technologies throughout the industry, consumers of the products will gain. However the profits from the innovator, before the diffusion of the technology, will disappear and the incentive to innovate is re-created.

Competition is a very rough social control. Even governments that proclaim the virtues of competition sometimes use tariffs and quotas to reduce the strength of international competition. But if firms abroad adopt new technologies, unless the home firms innovate to keep the protection effective, the tariffs and quotas would have to be raised each time the foreign firms innovated. An Australian firm may be forced to introduce new labour-saving technologies to avoid bankruptcy and, when such a compulsion is based on a foreign producer's actions, it is particularly likely to produce the response that we are being rolled on by technology, or that technical change proceeds independently of our willing.

Of course not all competition that induces technical change is beneficial. In military technology there is a fierce competition between the major powers to make their technologies ever more advanced and to make the weapons systems of their opponents obsolete. Such competition is very costly and dangerous.

Competition may also encourage firms to adopt new technologies that have harmful side effects which could have been avoided by adopting more expensive solutions. When the competition is purely internal it should be easy for governments when they have the relevant information to see that the firms carry the full costs of preventing harmful side effects. But where the competition is international, governments will be pressed strongly not to disadvantage the home producers. In this case also it may seem that technology is out of control, though the real problem is an unwillingness to pay the price of a lower rate of economic growth.

Competitive systems are not, as Adam Smith believed, part of a natural order of things. They are products of social engineering designed to increase the wealth of nations. The object is to provide opportunities to introduce new products and more efficient methods of production and to put pressure on others to follow suit. We continue to accept the compulsions of competition—often under protest—because we are keen to have the bigger post-tax incomes and the progressive expansion of the social services that economic growth makes possible.

On occasions innovations produced from competitive pressures have some unpleasant side effects because the side effects were not foreseen. That happened with thalidomide. In some cases it happens because governments did not care about pollution or the degradation of the environment. Even now the response that 'if it grows cut it down, if it moves shoot it' is not entirely out of fashion. But there is a greater public interest in preserving the environment and in reducing pollution, and governments are paying more attention to formulating the appropriate rules for the operation of competition.

The appropriate rules are sometimes outright prohibition on discharging noxious substances and sometimes taxes to give producers an incentive to find new methods with less undesirable side effects and to provide funds to make good damage done. Unfortunately there is not as yet sufficient knowledge of the damage done by various levels of pollution to guide the legislators, or sufficient power to foresee all the side effects of new products, including the ethical drugs.

The real issue is not whether technology is autonomous—it is not—but whether we are setting the right objectives for research and development. We are now much more aware of the dangers of technical change induced by competition under out-of-date rules. There is a passage in Francis Bacon's *Essay on Innovations* that is worth recalling: 'He that will not apply new remedies must expect new evils, for time is the greatest innovator'.

There is a danger that the ratio of benefits to cost from future innovative activities will become less favourable unless we change the rules and insist on a new direction in government-financed research and development. But although by taking thought we should be able to reduce the costs of change, we will not be able to eliminate them. Some hard-won skills will be made redundant, some career expectations will be dashed, some industries and regions will decay, and some seemingly well-tested ethical drugs will prove to be health hazards. Even that most urgent change, universal disarmament, would have costly side effects. For apart from the extensive redundancies and serious problems of re-deployment that would follow a rapid run-down, wars and preparations for wars have been important factors in the invention process and it would take time and a great ingenuity to develop peaceful substitutes.

In my final lecture I will consider some possible futures. Was U Thant's sombre warning justified? Are the problems of the arms race, environmental degradation and population growth now beyond our capacity to control? What if we survive? What will be the trends in output, in material standards of living, in education, in leisure, in employment? Of course I do not know the answers. But it is interesting to speculate, and our speculations might help us to avoid some of the worst of the possible futures.

Michael Kirby

Michael Kirby was born in Sydney in 1939. He was educated at Fort Street High School and the University of Sydney. He practised for a time as a solicitor and, later, as a barrister.

In 1974, he became a member of the New South Wales Bar Council and was appointed deputy president of the Australian Conciliation and Arbitration Commission. There followed numerous appointments to Federal and State statutory authorites and offices. From 1975 to 1984 he was the first chairman of the Australian Law Reform Commission. He has been a member of the Administrative Review

Council of Australia (1976–84), the Australian Institute of Multicultural Affairs (1979–83) and the executive of the CSIRO (1983–86).

He was made a judge of the Federal Court in 1983, which position he relinquished when he was appointed a judge of the Supreme Court, then President of the Court of Appeal of the Supreme Court of New South Wales. In 1996 he was appointed to the High Court of Australia.

Michael Kirby was a Fellow of the Senate of the University of Sydney from 1964 to 1969. He was deputy chancellor of the University of Newcastle from 1978, and chancellor of Macquarie University from 1984 to 1993.

Justice Kirby has also been involved in many international organisations, including UNESCO, WHO and the OECD. He was a member of the International Labour Organisation Commission in South Africa (1991–92) and chair of the International Commission of Jurists in Geneva in 1992.

He has published several books and is connected with a number of scholarly journals. Justice Kirby is also associated with numerous cultural activities.

In 1983 he was named a Companion of the Order of St Michael and St George, and in 1991 he was made a Companion to the Order of Australia.

Michael Kirby gave his Boyer Lectures the title *The Judges*. Individually they were 'Behind the Curtain'; 'Selection, Training, Function'; 'Judicial Method'; 'Human Error and Human Frailty'; 'Judges as Reformers', which is reproduced here, and 'The Future?'. Writing in 1983, in his conclusion he predicted that court dress would fade away by the turn of the century. Well, not quite. More importantly he concludes by referring to the judiciary's great strengths: 'Personal integrity, intellectual ability and diligence are chief amongst them. These strengths deserve to be celebrated. In a changing world they remain a sheet anchor for our civilisation.'

The Judges

Michael Kirby

• 1983 •

Fairy Tales

I want to start with a fairy tale. It is a very popular fairy tale. The public, and especially newspaper editorialists, hate to see it doubted.[1] Once upon a time, the Parliament made the law. The Judges only interpreted and applied it. The Executive enforced it. In this Kingdom of 'strict and complete legalism'[2] it was considered that the Judge certainly never made new law himself.[3] He had no democratic legitimacy to reform the law or to express views of what the law should be.[4] Those were tasks left to Members of Parliament—people elected to reform the law. Indeed, there was a quaint myth, which I thought almost sexual when I first heard it. The common law was to be 'discovered' in the bosom of the Judges. Imagine the image that phrase conjured up in the mind of generations of young law students. The Judge, faced by a difficult problem, was somehow to look downwards and there, lo and behold, in his bosom, would be the pre-existing law just waiting to be discovered by him.

This view of the judicial function was faithfully held for hundreds of years—into our generation. In fact it is still held by many Australian Judges who feel distinctly uncomfortable in the notion that they are making law, new law, reformed law—not simply applying, in a mechanistic way, the preordained rules of the system.

During the last century[5] and with growing insistence in this century, commentators and Judges themselves came to acknowledge frankly the uncomfortable fact that, in our common law system, Judges do make the law. Views differed as to the extent of the legitimate field of judicial creativity. The great American Judge, Benjamin Cardozo, earlier this century suggested that it was in no more than 10 per cent of cases. Even then, only in the higher courts did Judges have the rare choice that called on them to be creative. Only in this small proportion of cases did the Judge have the opportunity to exercise reforming skills in court.[6] Other top Judges became more assertive. In the context of appellate court decisions, Lord Macmillan once said:

> In almost every case, it would be possible to decide the issue either way with reasonable legal justification.[7]

Certainly, it has been hard to take the old theory seriously since the great Scottish Law Lord, Lord Reid, finally denounced it in 1972 as a 'fairy tale'.

> There was a time when it was thought almost indecent to suggest that judges make law—they only declare it. Those with a taste for fairy tales seem to have thought that in some Aladdin's cave there is hidden the Common Law in all its splendour and that on a judge's appointment there descends on him knowledge of the magic words Open Sesame. Bad decisions are given when the judge has muddled the pass word and the wrong door opens. But we do not believe in fairy tales any more.[8]

The inclination to be bold, creative and reformist varies in society. The same variations are to be found in the judiciary. Some Judges in Australia and Britain remain terribly cautious. Others, whilst acknowledging a creative function, are keen to underline, like Cardozo, the limited opportunities and the care and caution that must be exercised when they stumble upon them. Lord Wright described the way in which the common law had been developed:

> From case to case, like the ancient Mediterranean mariner, hugging the coast from point to point and avoiding the danger of the open sea of system and science.[9]

But other Judges are plagued with fewer doubts. They see more openings. They perceive the urgent need for modernisation and reform in the law. They harken back to the great common law Judges of the past who, with determination and assurance, developed the common law from precedent to precedent. In Australia our exemplar in this respect is Justice Murphy of the High Court. In Britain, Lord Denning was the boldest exponent of the reforming function of the Judge on the Bench. But might not this conception of the judicial functions lead to uncertainty in the law?

> I would agree it does, because in a sense I concentrate on the rights and wrongs of the individual before me, and if it does lead

to uncertainty—so it does, but there's no certainty in the law. It's a complete will o' the wisp . . . It really depends on the department of law in which you're dealing. With commercial cases and conveyancing cases, these kind, people must know what the law is, and so forth. But when it comes to injuries to individuals, for instance. They aren't concerned with any particular strict rules of law. They want justice in the particular case—their compensation, it may be. Or it may be the husband and wife cases, or unfairness in inquiries. All these are not capable of being guided by strict rules, and therefore in all these cases I strive to do justice, knowing that the law is necessarily uncertain in these areas.[10]

Now, not all Judges agree with Lord Denning. But whether in the lowest courts or the highest courts, and whether it is in 10 per cent of cases, more or less, there are few observers of the judiciary today who would deny that Judges have a function in *making* the law. If they have a function in making the law, they have a function in its *reform*. The debate today, in Australia at least, is rather about the extent, the preconditions and the principles by which these un-elected lawmakers will perform their creative duties.

Circumstances of Law Making

Some circumstances of judicial law-making are absolutely clear. For example, when Judges make rules of court, they can sometimes affect very significantly substantive or procedural rights. The High Court of Australia, for example, adopted a Rule of Court requiring that any application for leave or special leave to appeal should be made to a Full Court by counsel. In 1975 the court refused an application for a prisoner to appear personally in his appeal.[11] Clearly that Rule made by the Judges, not by Parliament, affected the prisoner's legal rights.

For centuries the Judges have been making the rules of practice and procedure by which trials are conducted. Yet these rules too, by controlling which persons have standing, which can be called, what evidence they can give and how, all of these rules profoundly affect the outcome of cases. By and large, few would question this function of the judiciary in laying down the rules of the game.[12] Then there are the rules of common law itself: precedents developed by Judges over 800 years. In a sense, the common law is the embodiment of the common sense of the English-speaking people, as perceived and expressed by Judges. In previous times, many value judgments could be avoided by the Judges simply passing such questions over to the jury. But three features of our century have accentuated the policy making role of Judges:

- The first is the declining use of juries in civil and even criminal cases
- The second is the growth of judicial discretion by which binding cases or even Acts of Parliament leave it to the Judge to do justice according to his assessment of the particular case, and
- The third is the growth of legislation itself, so often couched in words of uncertain meaning, such a requirement that the Judge shall act 'in the public interest'[13] or that the Judge shall determine the matter according to the 'fairness of the case'.

Just as Judges have differing inclinations after certainty and flexibility, rules and discretions, so too do Parliaments. Different generations reflect differing inclinations to search for

- *strict rules* (with the advantage of certainty but the possible disadvantage of injustice) or
- *discretion* (with the advantage that justice may be done but with the disadvantage of uncertainty).[14]

Judges also differ in their willingness to offer up litigants before them as victims 'at the altar of regularity'.[15] Some can do it without blinking an eyelid. Most, remembering their oath to do *justice according to law*, look hard amongst the precedents to see if there is not something that can be done. Lord Denning would search them high and low until he had found a satisfactory principle to justify the just and fair conclusion, as he saw it.[16] Most Judges are more cautious. One probably summed it up for the majority. If the facts lead inevitably to only one just conclusion but the law points you to the opposite result, the consequence is a remarkable concentration of the mind upon that law. Is it authoritative? Is it binding? Has it been distinguished or varied? Has it been doubted? Is it capable of another interpretation? If the answer to all of these questions is 'No', the duty of the Judge, unless he is at the very apex of the judicial system, will be plain. He must do justice *according to the law*. The law must win the day. But according to one's inclinations, skills, ingenuity and courage, the answer 'No' will come with more or less frequency.

Stretching, moulding and adapting the old precedents of the common law has been the way of our legal system for centuries.[17] Until lately it has been done under the guise of 'discovering' rules that theoretically pre-existed the search. Now, a new realm of creativity looms on the horizon. The democratic Parliament has been most prolific in law-making. Every year more than one thousand Acts of Parliament are made throughout Australia. In addition, there are countless by-laws, regulations and ordinances. The function of the judiciary is changing. From an expositor and developer of the common law, the Judge is increasingly becoming the interpreter of legislation. Whether it is a Magistrate applying a liquor statute, a trial Judge interpreting a criminal code, the Federal Court struggling over the meaning of the Conciliation & Arbitration Act or the High Court seeking to divine the intention of taxation legislation, judicial officers today are devoting increasing proportions of their time to the construction of legislation.

Legislation is cast in words. The pride of the English language is its literature. Our tongue is rich in words which enjoy many meanings. But if this is an advantage in literature, it is a decided disadvantage in the law where precision, clarity and certainty are at a premium. But it is a disadvantage we have to live with.

It has long been a principle accepted by the Judges that they should endeavour to uphold, where the words permitted it, the intention of Parliament.[18] But until now the Judges have limited themselves in the background material they would read, for the purpose of determining the policy to be found strictly within the words of Parliament. In Europe, Judges never hesitate to look to a whole range of associated documents. In the United States, although a common law country, there is a similar willingness to go behind the language of Congress where this is unclear. Until very recently, Judges of our tradition stuck rigidly to the text of the statute. Initially they took this view as defensive of the freedoms of citizens. Those freedoms could not be diminished unless Parliament spelt out the diminution in words of great clarity. But the result of this judicial approach has been legislation of great detail and complexity. Parliament and the Executive Government are determined to ensure that Judges will not frustrate their intention. Accordingly, they spell out that intention at inordinate length. One has only to contrast the general language of legislation in Europe with the highly technical and often unreadable language of our legislation, to realise what an impact Judges have had upon the way in which our laws are drafted.

Lately, there has been a softening. The demand for simpler legislation, more simply expressed, is now universal. Judges themselves are beginning not only to look at the Hansard debates on legislation but to acknowledge that they do so. Justice Mason of the High Court of Australia admitted this at a recent symposium on statutory interpretation held in Canberra:

> Like Mr Justice Murphy, I often look at Second Reading Speeches. Unlike him, I do not confine my attention to those made by Senator Murphy. Of course, Judges are infinitely curious. It is better that their curiosity should be satisfied publicly rather than privately. Despite this, I can see that there is some problem of accessibility— important for the client in obtaining accurate advice and important for the practitioner who is conscious of his potential liability for negligence. But I am not inclined to think it is a serious problem.[19]

Many Judges, and still more legal practitioners, remain dubious about Judges looking beyond the text of legislation. Some Judges will never do it. Other are now clearly doing it.[20] Governments are proposing new techniques to enhance the capacity of Judges to flesh out the bare bones of legislation in accordance with its intent.[21] Though editorialists remain dubious about this enlargement of the judicial function[22] many of their reservations are based upon the myth that the Judge's function is exclusively mechanical with no room for creativity. It took hundreds of years for Judges themselves to acknowledge, with candour, the creative work they were doing. Acceptance of this role in the general community and editorialists cannot be expected overnight. The price of simpler legislation, which ordinary people can readily understand, is a new confidence that Judges will wholeheartedly implement the policy behind legislation compatible with the use of brief and general language. That confidence will only be earned if Judges assume a more active role in discovering that policy and enlarge the range of materials they will examine in aid of construction. It constantly amazes non-lawyers to find that most Judges will not look at a Second Reading Speech. They will not look at Parliamentary Debates. They will not examine reports on which legislation may be based. They will not even look at what legal text writers say unless the text writer be dead. The reasoning behind this rule (now substantially relaxed of late) is that the text writer might change his mind so long as he is alive. With the law changing so rapidly today, not many texts of deceased authors are worth quoting. The caravan almost surely has moved on.

Words of Caution

For every reformer on the Bench—whether a Murphy or a Denning—there are many more who have their doubts. Some, like Sir Garfield Barwick, deny that even the highest court may legitimately 'change' the law.[23] Others, whilst acknowledging that Judges may be good 'contributors and formulators'[24] do not believe that they are the stuff of which reform is made.[25] On this view enthusiasm is not and cannot be a judicial virtue.[26] Even if not mere ciphers, mechanically discovering, declaring and applying the law, they see the judicial role as very severely circumscribed by its lack of democratic legitimacy. Judges are not elected.[27] Parliaments, in our generation at least, are. On this view, whatever may have been permissible to the Judges of ancient times, it is impermissible today. Moreover, it flies in the face of the community's simplistic notion of democracy. If too candidly disclosed, it may undermine the appearance of judicial impartiality and neutrality.[28]

Judges are urged by people who hold this view not to confuse their role with the frank law-making function of a legislature.[29] They do not have its warrant from the people. They are generally members of the older generation. They are not reflective of the whole variety of the population.[30] If the law is not satisfactory, the people can blame Parliament. If the shoe pinches, the brake on reform is a brake applied by Parliament not by the Judges.[31] Where Parliament fears to tread, the courts should be specially careful.[32]

The establishment of permanent law reform commissions, to help Parliament with the reform of the law, provides the Judges who held to these views with further ammunition against their reformist brethren. Law reform bodies have developed techniques of widespread community consultation which are not available to Judges. At best, Judges merely have only the parties before them. They might not be representative of the whole community. Almost surely they would not provide the Judge with the economic, scientific and other expertise available to professional law reformers. The first Chairman of the English Law Commission, now a Judge of England's highest court, Lord Scarman, referred to these matters in distinguishing his approach to law reform, as a Judge, from Lord Denning's:

> I disagree with Lord Denning. I believe in law reform by statute, and preferably by statutes introduced after full consideration of the problem by the Law Commission, or other body charged with considering law reform, or the implications of law reform. Lord Denning thinks that one can take a short cut by judicial decision, avoiding all the parliamentary delays, and indeed the delays associated with a thorough-going and patient examination of the problem by a body like the Law Commission. I profoundly disagree with Lord Denning on this. And I think if I had any criticism of Lord Denning

as a developer of the law, it is that he develops it at a cost of uncertainty. The question is where the line is to be drawn. I go along with Lord Denning to this extent, that I think there is room for a certain degree of development of the law by judicial decision. But I do think that the development has to be in the minor key. One cannot change a Rule of Law which is clear and well established merely because it produces a hard case, that is to say, works injustice.[33]

In response, Denning puts the judicial reformers' point of view. Judges have been developing the law for centuries. Parliament has neither the time nor the inclination to attend to all the necessities of law reform.[34] If it does attend to some of them, the delay is crippling.[35] It will not help the litigants in the particular case before the Judge:

> Well, I am afraid the present trend is that the Judges shouldn't do anything new. They shouldn't alter the law. There should be no law making by the Judges. Everything should be left to Parliament or to the Law Commission. I take a completely different view. I think the Judges alone can deal with the instant case, to remedy the wrong in the case which is before them. If you wait for legislation you may wait for years and years and that can't affect the instant case—only the future cases. So I hope the Judges, if they're strong enough, will continue to develop our law as by history they've done in the past . . . If you've got Judges of the best kind, who are ready to take a broad view, you can get it done as well or better by Judges than from all these long inquiries by Law Commissioners and the like. But of course, it depends on the Judges.[36]

Standing halfway between Denning and Scarman, Lord Justice Kerr, also a former Chairman of the English Law Commission, could not disguise his admiration for Denning's approach. Perhaps it takes a professional law reformer to know the limitations of institutional law reform. Will a reference be given? How quickly can the report be made? Will it get through the bureaucracy? Will Parliament have the time to consider the report? Will Parliament change the recommendations?:

> I do feel very strongly that when you've got a supremely able person, as Lord Denning is, it's a good thing to have what you might call a pacemaker—somebody who, if you like, goes a little bit too far and then others can put him right under our ordinary process of the courts and appeals and so forth. But it's a good idea to have some-

body there who's a bit more visionary than the rest. And he is the ideal person.[37]

Finding the Balance

That seems to be the conclusion—as true for Australia as for Britain. Judicial creativity and law-making must be cautious. It must normally be done 'in the minor key'. It should be done with sufficient care that it avoids, where possible, interference in the party political debates.[38] Yet even this will not be possible in Australia where the Federal Constitution is about power and a bench of Judges must determine, from language that is old and general, where that power lies.

If we have thrown away the fairy tale, there is still a natural disinclination for Judges to embrace too stridently the assertion of their law-making functions. The passive and mechanical view is deeply embedded in the community's consciousness.[39] The suspicion of too much candour or too much activism in judicial law-making arises from a fear of idiosyncratic personal judgments not grounded in a coherent framework of legal rules. This, for example, was Lord Hailsham's criticism of Lord Denning:

> I think there is a want of coherence in his approach to things. He has a very highly subjective view of the world, I think. Speaking simply now as one who has appeared before him, as well as read his judgments in the reports, one's never quite sure with Tom whether one's going to meet with the lion under the throne or the tribune of the people.[40]

Lord Denning once said that Judges divide neatly into 'bold spirits' and 'timorous souls'.[41] But this is to oversimplify things. There is a spectrum here and Judges may be found at different points of the spectrum in different cases and at different times of their judicial development. You can call the tension that between 'activism' and 'constraint' or between 'certainty' and 'justice'.[42] You can ascribe it to differing views about the desirability of candour in what the Judge is actually doing and the desirability of avoiding damage to public confidence by too frank an assertion of the Judges' right to choose. There is a need for a mixture of reformers and traditionalists in our courts. This, at least, is Lord Hailsham's own view. And it is my own. In America, reformers have long had a voice in the highest courts. In England, at least since the 1960s, there have been notable and outspoken reforming Judges. We have had fewer in Australia. The reasons for this are many and complex. They include,

I think, a certain provincialism and lack of self-confidence in our capacity to develop a law appropriate for Australian conditions. The final total release from the apron strings of the Privy Council, promised for the end of 1983, may, symbolically, help in the intellectual liberation of Australia's Judges.

Extra-curial Reform

I have not dwelt on the role of Judges as reformers, outside their function of deciding particular cases. Some Judges, as you have heard, serve in law reform commissions. All of the States and Territories of Australia have such bodies. Most are headed by Judges, often working part-time.[43]

But even in court, where the law constrains a Judge to reach a conclusion which he regards as unsatisfactory or unjust, he can play a role in law reform. He can draw the needs of reform to the attention of Parliament. Many Judges do this. In the past their words were often lost in the casebooks. Nowadays, the Law Reform Commission extracts judicial suggestions for law reform and includes them as an appendix in its annual report to Parliament. If the shoe pinches, Parliament now has even less excuse for inactivity.

Some Judges will not even refer to the need for reform. They think this is no part of their proper task. But this is nowadays a minority view. Indeed calls are now being urged by Judges themselves to take their law-reforming function further. In France, the highest court reports annually to Parliament and to the President, collecting the aggregation of judicial experience in the law over the year and recommending necessary improvements, identified by the cases heard. Such reports are known in other common law countries.[44] But, in Australia, if courts make an annual report (and most do not) they are generally confined to statistical and financial matters of housekeeping.

It is wrong to think that the need for law reform will be self-evident. It is foolish to believe that Parliament or law reform commissions can tackle the myriad of problems necessary for the reform and modernisation of our legal system. Keeping within proper bounds, I believe the judiciary should aggregate its experience and report collectively each year to the Parliament and to the public on the improvements that are shown to be needed. Parliament should establish committees to process and act upon at least those recommendations that are agreed. Too often we accept injustice with a shrug of resignation. The Judges do more than most to right wrongs. But they could still do more.

This series now approaches its close. In the final program I will endeavour to look forward and to offer suggestions about the future of the judiciary. In the age of computers and intelligent machines, some even ask, do the Judges have a future? For the answer to that question, I must keep you in suspense.

1 See e.g. 'Judges' Laws', *Sydney Morning Herald*, 10 February 1983, 6. See also G Robertson, 'Trial and Error', *New Statesman*, 23 May 1980, 782, 'The Denning Method', (1980) 130 *New LJ* 126; 'The Judge as Lawmaker' (1980) 130 *New LJ* 150; J Jowell, 'Lord Denning, The Courts and the Administration', *The Listener*, 22 May 1980, 644; A Pidgeon, 'The Agatha Christie of the Law', The *Age*, 22 April 1983

2 Chief Justice Dixon, 'Speech on Swearing in as Chief Justice', (1951-2) 85 CLR xiv

3 SF Milsom, 'The Past and Future of Judge-Made Law', 10th Wilfred Fullagar Memorial Lecture, (1981) 8 *Monash Uni L Rev*, 1

4 GE Barwick, 'Judiciary Law: Some Observations Thereon', (1980) 33 *Curr Leg Prob*, 239. See also Sexton & Maher, 63

5 J Bentham, 'Judiciary Law', cited in Barwick, n4

6 B Cardozo, *The Growth of the Law*, 1924, 60

7 Lord Macmillan, *Law and Other Things*, 48. Others have suggested the figure is twenty or fifty per cent of cases. See Paterson, 173

8 Lord Reid, 'The Judge as Lawmaker', (1972) 12 *Journal of Public Teachers of Law*, 22

9 Lord Wright, 'The Study of Law', (1938), 54 LQR 185, 186

10 Lord Denning, interviewed by H Young, *Talking Law*, BBC, 16 September 1979

11 *Collins v The Queen*, (1975) 133 CLR 120

12 It has been otherwise in the United States. Justice Douglas, for example, dissented from the view that the Supreme Court of the United States could promulgate the Federal Evidence Rules. In the result, an Act of Congress was passed in 1975.

13 Griffith, 196

14 Paterson, 124, 130

15 BN Cardozo, *The Growth of the Law*, 1924, 66

16 Lord Denning, 'The Way of an Iconoclast', (1959) 5 JSPTL 77, 89

17 BN Cardozo, *The Paradoxes of Legal Science*, 116. Cf Lord Denning, quoted Paterson, 180

18 *Heydon's Case*, (1584) 3 Co Rep, 7a; 76 ER 637, 638

19 Justice Mason, summing up, Australia, Attorney-General's Department, *Symposium on Statutory Interpretation*, 81, 83. See also (1983) 57 *Australian Law Journal*, 191

20 See eg *South Australian Commissioner for Prices and Consumer Affairs v Charles Moore (Aust) Limited*, (1977) 139 CLR 449, 479–81; *Wacando v The Commonwealth*, (1981) 37 ALR 317, 335–6; *Commissioner of Taxation v Whitfords Beach Pty Limited*, (1982) 39 ALR 521, 533; *TCN Channel 9 Pty Limited v AMP Society*, (1982) 42 ALR 496

21 See eg proposals for an explanatory memorandum and comments in *Symposium*, n19, 5ff. The Law Reform Commission has produced one such explanatory memorandum. See *Insurance Contracts* (ALRC 20), 1982, 279ff (Appendix A). See also Acts Interpretation Act 1901, s15AA

22 See eg 'Judges' Laws', *Sydney Morning Herald*, 10 February 1983, 6; 'In Judgment', *Melbourne Herald*, 7 February 1983, 6
23 Balwick, *Judiciaq Law*, 247
24 Devlin, 12
25 Griffith, 208
26 Devlin, 5
27 Devlin, 10; Abel-Smith & Stevens, 121
28 Lord Reid, quoted in Griffith, 179
29 Lord Jowitt, in Abel-Smith & Stevens, 287
30 Devlin, 53
31 Lord Parker, *Hansard*, 5th Session (HL), Vol CCLVIII, 9 June 1964, Col 1071–2
32 Lord Reid, in Griffiths, 183
33 Lord Scarman, interviewed by Hugo Young, BBC, n. 10, 11–12
34 Lord Denning, in Paterson, 181
35 Lord Reid, in Paterson, 182
36 Lord Denning, interviewed by Hugo Young, n.10, 14
37 M Kerr, interviewed by Hugo Young, 12
38 *Duport Steels Ltd v Sirs*, [1980] 1 All ER 529 (HL)
39 Lord Radcliffe, quoted in Cappelletti, 65
40 Lord Hailsham, interviewed by Hugo Young, n.10, 10
41 Lord Denning, in *Candler v Crane Christmas & Co*, [1951] 2 KB 164, 178
42 Griffiths, 300
43 For example, Justice Zelling (SALRC); Justice Kearney (NTLRC); and Justice McPherson (QLRC)
44 See, for example, the report of the National Court of Papua New Guinea, noted *Canberra Times*, 15 February 1983, 5

Shirley Hazzard

Expatriate novelist, essayist and biographer Shirley Hazzard was born in Sydney in 1931. She grew up at Mosman, NSW, receiving all her formal education at Queenwood School. From 1947 to 1951, in consequence of her father's employment in the Australian government service, she lived in Hong Kong and New Zealand, and travelled to England and the United States.

In 1952, Shirley Hazzard joined the United Nations secretariat in New York. During a decade on the UN headquarters staff, she travelled in Europe, and worked during 1957 in Naples.

In 1961, she resigned from the United Nations to give full time to writing. She has contributed to the *New Yorker* magazine since 1960. Indeed, her first book, a collection of short stories, *Cliffs of Fall*, contain some stories that were first published there. The book was published in 1963.

Shirley Hazzard has published a number of novels, including *The Evening of the Holiday*, *People in Glass Houses* and *The Bay of Noon*, together with numerous articles on literature and international affairs, and also non-fiction, among which was her analysis of the UN: *Defeat of an Ideal: A Study of the Self-destruction of the United Nations*. Another, published in 1990, was *Countenance of Truth: The United Nations and the Waldheim Case*. Her most recent work, a memoir called *Greene on Capri*, was published in 2000.

Her 1980 novel, *The Transit of Venus*, won the National Critics Book Award in the United States in 1980. She was a Guggenheim Fellow in 1974, and in 1982 she was elected to the American Academy and Institute of Arts and Letters.

The title of her Boyer Lectures was *Coming of Age in Australia*. They made a significant impact at the time and are still widely read. They are characterised by an intellectual and linguistic elegance. Individually they are: 'An Air of Disbelief'; 'Into the Mainstream'; 'Australia and the Menace of Eternal Youth' and 'To Live Without an Enemy' which is reproduced here.

Her special tone of voice, as well as her themes, are to be discerned in her introductory note in which she said these lectures 'are an appeal to Australia to consider and value the entire context of civilised human endeavour, so that their own rich patrimony may take its place there, and ripen, and fulfil its destiny.

'It seems to me that Australia has long since come of age. Experience is there, and humanity, character and conscience. Only the realisation is awaited, and the inspired acceptance.'

TO LIVE WITHOUT
AN ENEMY

Coming of Age in Australia

Shirley Hazzard

• 1 9 8 4 •

In the course of these talks I have given the view that the great mutation confronting Australia is not so much one of identity as of maturity: reciprocal maturity of the individual and the nation. Perhaps that holds true for all the world. We might define maturity as wholeness, as equilibrium. For most of us it can never be an established, undeviating condition. It is more like a sustained effort to know ourselves and the world around us. What does stop men and women and nations from developing their best selves? What makes it possible for some to realise their full stature? We have all seen, in the young and not-so-young, how impetus can falter or diverge. What comes between all the truths we know within ourselves, and the lives we actually live, the words we find ourselves uttering? Much of thought and art has been concerned with illuminating that dichotomy—that form of the self-destruction, the fatal flaw, to which the Greeks gave the name *hamartia*.

Poets and philosophers throughout the centuries have urged us to mistrust whatever too eagerly gratifies our sense of our own righteousness. To question the sources of our promptest emotions, lest they should derive from self-flattery. In these days we are deluged with incitement to vicarious heroics by reports and depictions of terrible wrongs which wring our sentiments but cost us no sacrifice. We surface from these immersions as if from a play or a film that has moved us, imagining that by our indignation and emotion we have actually performed some moral action. But if our moral outrage is to have meaning, to amount to something more than self-dramatisation, then the conduct of our daily lives will reflect it. If we are in earnest about all of this, will we not hesitate before adding our own private particle to the mockery and hatred in the world? After all, it is fairly easy to look at the past with insight and virtue: we all know what should have been done. The difficulty is to bring that large, clear-eyed view, that generous humanity and that humility to bear on the present moment and the future, where it might truly serve us.

In these talks, I have tried to take as my theme the cumulative value of the conscious human experience, as a civilising continuity. Our human past and present, overwhelmingly in error, have nevertheless preserved and developed a filament of self-recognition and recorded wisdom, and a body of humane gesture. Rejection of that knowledge is the ever recurrent human tragedy. How many of those, throughout the world, who maintain that the great evidence—the best of the human experience—no longer speaks to us, how many have truly listened to those voices? If we tend rather to turn up the telly, or flip through the ads, if we limit ourselves to the approved and current intellectual fare, it is not usually because we are satiated with the masterworks of all the ages. Isn't it more generally because we doubt our own powers of comprehension; or because the sustained private exercise of thought is growing alien to our leisure hours; or because our capacity for inward effort is enervated by the passivity implicit in much technology and by the circus of spectatorism?

The great works don't lose power merely because they lose the power to influence. Embodied human knowledge resides in them, just as truth abides in events, unaffected by ignorance or falsehood or the craving for cachet. At various stages of our history we have been allowed to recover—even dramatically—the power of past knowledge, like patients recovering from a long bout of amnesia. If we are now to cast memory wilfully aside, why should we expect another chance?

I do not underrate the difficulties for a society wishing to assimilate the best qualities of the past while evolving the character of a distinct and growing nation—particularly when this is occurring simultaneously with swift migrational change, and in the contemporary mood of acceleration which seems to insist that any human enterprise, however complex, can instantaneously come right. What I doubt is that the difficulties facing Australia are now predominantly those of a cultural and psychological overshadowing by older civilisations, or the imposition from abroad of unwanted and irrelevant intellectual concepts.

Throughout history, as new nations have come to birth, their citizens have commented on the struggle to create afresh in the light and shadow of history. Some have commented wryly and wittily, some with indignation, some with keen application to their own failings. There is Horace two thousand years ago reminding us that when Greece was enslaved by Rome she made in turn a slave of her rough conqueror by teaching him the arts.[1] We have Juvenal, inveighing against the patronising airs assumed by Greeks in Rome.[2] There is Horace Walpole, assuring us with a smile that eighteenth-century Englishmen catch cold because they have acquired, through reading classical poets, the open air habits of the Mediterranean.[3] There is the Japanese mediaeval court earnestly speaking Chinese—and leaving it to their womenfolk, unworthy of that ceremonial honour, to create the richest works of literature in the Japanese tongue.[4] There is cultivated Russia speaking French, and fashioning a resplendent city in the Italian image. There is— most poignant for Australia—the United States, looking to Europe and to Asia, and looking also to herself. Much of what we praise or deplore, in art or life, as deeply Roman or Japanese, American or British, would in fact be unthinkable without those formative influences. It is impossible to divide them simplistically from the style and character of the emerging nation: at their best they have provided much of the stimulus through which self-recognition can eventually occur.

Writer after writer in this country, and many who are not writers, have spoken of the Australian identity as a new appreciation of this land by its citizens—with the implication that Australians had been prevented, until now, from enjoying the interest and beauty around them, and that this pall had been cast by the infectious indifference of other peoples towards Australia. Perhaps this belief needs some examination before it is received into Australian mythology.

The discovery and settlement of this continent was not exclusively a story of violent inhumanity. The great explorations and navigations carried out from the fifteenth to the nineteenth centuries were, in addition to all else, an immense exercise of curiosity. Great empires are established in pride, cruelty and greed; but in the process they carry with them some at least who wish to learn and know. As the ancient world had, for erudition and advantage, studied and adopted many discoveries and practices of Egypt, Persia and China, and transformed domestic life by importations of plants and animals, so the newer empires bore forward those who were eager for new sights and sensations, scholars who risked their lives for knowledge, and many who wished to bring the revelations of other lands to the attention of the known world. The Dutch sailors who, in 1697, carried off black swans from the mouth of the Swan River—finding them, incidentally, proof negative of the contrariness of the Antipodes—these were early envoys, on the Australian scene, of an intense and sustained interest taken in this continent by its European discoverers.

The history of Australia's settlement—the story, in Robert Frost's words about early America, of a 'land vaguely realising westward, but still unstoried, artless, unenhanced'[5]—that Australian narrative is, of course, dense with the courage of discovery and also with the attention that discoveries here aroused elsewhere. Yet it was when I left these shores that I first was made aware of the body of interest and scholarship directed to Australia's indigenous life and its Pacific setting. It was in Asia and in Britain in the post-war years that I first heard such things knowledgeably discussed, was made aware of the study of Asian and Pacific languages and peoples, and saw their works of art displayed and appreciated. Some of this interest did exist then in Australia itself; but it was subdued, it was exceptional; it wasn't free. In the museums of Rome and Florence I was to discover Australian and Polynesian artifacts—many of them bought in the 1780s by Sir William Hamilton from Captain Cook, and presented to the kings of Naples. I was to learn how one of those Bourbon kings exchanged a set of precious papyrii from the Herculaneum excavation for a group of live kangaroos. I was to find in the notebooks of Leonardo da Vinci a reference to a weapon, mentioned by classical writers, that was used by German tribes in antiquity: a weapon that could be artfully thrown a certain distance, and recalled at will;[6] and I saw that one of Virgil's modern English translators had rendered its Latin name as 'boomerang'.

From the outset, a close interest was taken in the natural phenomena of Australia. Joseph Banks was one of a succession of naturalists who observed Australia—Brown and Flinders, Ferdinand Bauer, John and Elizabeth Gould. There was the Frenchman François Peron, to whom Darwin paid tribute; and there was Darwin himself. There was Ferdinand von Mueller, the German from Rostock, a hero of Australian botany, who caused the eucalyptus to be known and grown throughout the world; and there was the Duke of Newcastle's expedition, with which he served. It is impossible here to do more than suggest that multitude of spirited and devoted people, soon joined by Australians born, who thought and wrote about, and depicted, the natural attributes of these regions. In this century, they continue to arrive: the painter Emil Nolde, as commissioned artist with the German expedition to New Guinea on the eve of the First World War; and the immigrant from Lithuania, Olegas Truchanas, reaching Hobart in 1948, and subsequently revealing rivers, lakes, mountains, forests and plants to Tasmanians themselves.[7]

It is not entirely mysterious that Australians themselves, although given that early stimulus, did not at once take a wider pleasure in the natural gifts of their country. The settlers of this land had over-whelming cause to find their new home formidable and unlovely, and to associate beauty with the countryside of their native north. That reason was rooted, almost literally, in the matter of fertility; in the need for arable soil, for crops and edible plants. It was rooted in survival. Even the most appreciative Australian of the 1980s does not cultivate a taste for the food of the Aboriginal peoples; nor does the importation of most of his diet from the northern hemisphere cause him nationalistic qualms. Fertility is survival. No wonder it is celebrated.

For the first settlers, fertility did not exist. It is almost impossible for us to imagine the task that faced those who landed here—to a sandy soil, a sparse and precarious supply of water, and a virtually complete absence of recognisable edible vegetation. None of this was to be quickly transformed. The plants, trees, crops—the animals and fowl—for subsistence and survival had to be procured from across the world. They had to be slowly and painfully cultivated in new conditions and with experimental methods. If the early settlers felt aversion to the inedible produce of an arid soil, it was not simply from myopic northern insularity. They had to create fertility. And then, too, in their desperate situation, was it not natural that they yearned for the familiar?

So far the story is comprehensible. But why, as conditions of Australian life grew more hospitable, why was the Australian eye and mind so little engaged with the natural character of this country? It is said with truth that Australia assumed the stodgy aspects of nineteenth-century British life. But why only the stodgy aspects? It was also a time when a number of Britons were acquaint-ing themselves with the habits and tongues of peoples throughout the world; it was a time of prodigious inventiveness and creativity in Britain itself; it was a period of genius. It is not enough to dismiss that stimulus as the work of a small minority. Ideas begin with minorities, they begin with individuals; and any prolonged indif-ference to them deserves pondering.

In early Australia—in the Australia of the mid-nineteenth century—there was a wish to cultivate intellectual curiosity on these shores; and for a time this seemed to flourish. There were movements towards tolerance, and towards equality of the sexes. I have seen that Australian writers—Manning Clark, Geoffrey Blainey,

Bernard Smith, Richard White—I've seen that these and other writers are exploring the conditions in which that openness, that curiosity, became somehow clouded and took so long to re-awaken. Earlier in these talks, speaking of the narrower outlook of Australia in my own childhood, I said that Australians then felt safe with what they were accustomed to. But why had they accustomed themselves to an existence so little varied by knowledge? Many many Australians were readers in that era; and many read stories and poetry, histories and lives, by the best writers. Latin was taught in the schools, and some French. But that had failed, even into the early 1950s, to generate wider eagerness for information and for exigent intellectual standards. It had failed to influence the eye with which Australia looked at her own earth and her indigenous peoples; at her neighbours in Asia, and her fellow-beings around the world.

I have come to doubt whether these matters can be attributed to oppressive British influence. Our own choice was involved in it, and a pride—as it sometimes seems—a pride in immaturity.

A few moments ago I quoted Robert Frost's lines on the evolving United States—the land, as he describes it:

> the land vaguely realising westward,
> But still unstoried, artless, unenhanced'.[8]

In the same poem, Frost wrote this also:

> Something we were withholding made us weak
> Until we found out that it was ourselves.

Politicians to the contrary, I believe that men and women, and nations can be weakened by quite other things than a paucity of lethal weapons or a shortage of foreign exchange. They can be weakened by anger, by dwelling on past grievance, by a need to boast or blame. They can be weakened by hostility or envy, disguised by the name of self-assertion; and self-assertion can sweep them, too, into conspiracies and wars. They can be weakened by the suppression of sensibility, and the elevation of material gain. In any lasting sense, they can only be given strength by knowledge and self-knowledge, and by a sense of common humanity.

It is the boast of our era that we deal in what are called 'realities'. This is put to us, in the intellectual or aesthetic context, as a rigorous advance over the deluded sentiment of less enlightened times.

Yet we must remind ourselves that many people on earth are enduring drastic realities, and need no instruction in defining them. And that these veterans themselves occasionally testify, from their irrefutable experience, that our concept of 'reality' has limits, and that they are often narrow ones. We might reflect for a moment, for example, on the conviction which moved Alexander Solzhenitsyn, in his Nobel acceptance speech, to quote Dostoievsky's words: 'Beauty will save the world'.

I cannot tell you what reality is, or what portion it forms of all the truth. I know that each person's reality is a different one; and that any compulsion to narrow, to unify and classify, to exclude meaning, is at root a wish for ignominious safety. In thought and art, the use of the term 'reality' can be self-serving. It can come from a wish to silence enquiry, and is therefore to be feared.

In preparing these talks I have found myself thinking time and again of two writers—one a poet, the other a philosopher—two masters of different temperaments and nations, who lived through approximately the same segment of our century and were concerned that new definitions of 'reality' might carry with them a form of intellectual tyranny. I have thought of the Italian philosopher Benedetto Croce, a figure heroic in the quality of his thought as in the conduct of his life, for whom the profound unity of all the arts and of spiritual and ethical values gave universality to life across the ages. Croce believed in the power we possess, through thought and perception, to influence and even to form our realities and give them a lasting and favourable meaning in human affairs. He not only saw that inestimable power decline, with the degeneration of humanist principles; he saw it deliberately abandoned. As the poet Eugenio Montale has said, in a tribute to Croce, 'The very notion of an art destined to last disturbs a humanity that no longer wants to reflect, suspended as it is between anxiety and the obscure need to put an end to every individual difficulty'.[9] Yet Croce never lost faith in the endurance and regenerative powers of our civilised life.

On the other hand—but not by contrast—William Butler Yeats is the poet who has come often to my mind as I prepared these talks. Yeats, who died in 1939, was one of the last masters in an almost unbroken succession of the great poets in our language. At the time of Yeats' death, the darkness in which the world was soon to be re-submerged was thickly gathering; and a stark new climate of reality had been rife for 25 years—since August 1914. In Britain and throughout Europe—in the countries which had most to lose, which had lost most heavily to this new ethos, and were now to lose yet more—a diversity of gifted persons was endeavouring to express loss, change, and apprehension: not to define these things in the factual terms of Dickens' Mr Gradgrind,[10] but in the common human tongue of poetry and philosophy. These people, with their diverse genius, these people gave hope, even in articulating despair. They gave hope, because articulation itself is civilisation. It is the means by which our human nature has managed to retain consciousness.

If Yeats confronted the new reality with despair, it was a despair to which he brought as powerful and personal a lyrical passion, and as great a beauty, as he had brought to his lifelong celebration of a hopeless love. In his daily conduct, he appeared maddened by his sense of human folly—by what he called 'the growing murderousness of the world'[11]—and he indulged in discreditable actions and statements. Yet, as sometimes happens in such cases, his gift remained free. His anguish was roused not only by the disappearance from the world of civilised works and concepts nurtured with genius and tenacity, but by what he saw as a veritable complicity in their extinction on the part of the intelligentsia itself, in the name of 'reality'. This danger had been signalled through the preceding century and a half by other great poets. Yeats knew—as did Croce—Yeats knew that what we call civilisation exists only as faith; as a tenuous agreement. And has no other 'reality' than that with which we endow it. Yeats felt antipathy to an era which seemed to mock at that civilised agreement: an era which preferred, as he put it, to 'traffic in mockery'.[12] Some of the words of Yeats, from this vision of his later life, are universally known—the often quoted lines, for example, from his poem 'The Second Coming', that 'things fall apart; the centre cannot hold'.[13] I would like to remember here a less quoted poem by Yeats—a brief late poem, which opens with the following lines:

> Civilisation is trooped together, brought
> Under a rule, under the semblance of peace
> By manifold illusion; but man's life is thought,
> And he, despite his terror, cannot cease
> Ravening through century after century,
> Ravening, raging, and uprooting that he may come
> Into the desolation of reality.[14]

At the beginning of these talks I spoke about a feeling of helplessness that characterised life in the Australia of my own childhood, in the 1930s and early 1940s. Looking back, I don't believe we were as helpless as we felt. For many Australians, as for people throughout the world then, energies and sensations were consumed in toil and in the struggles of a lean peace and a cruel war. But our resources were also *wasted*. They were consumed in needless antagonism towards those who had not harmed us, and in resistance to, and fear of, what would have helped us to endure and enjoy life.

History suggests to us the terrible possibility that humankind cannot live without an enemy: that, deprived of one antagonist, we will soon settle on another; and that our individual lives set the scene for this tragedy with the little private wars we are forever declaring among ourselves. If we are not to accept that fated view of our past and our future we must learn to develop our faculties— to open our eyes and ears and minds. We need to listen and to enquire. To have thoughts in which we have no enemies. To equip ourselves for living to the full, in Australia and the world.

1   Horace, *Epistulae*, 11, i, 156
2   Juvenal, *Satire III*, 58–146
3   Horace Walpole, Letter of June 15, 1768, to George Montagu
4   See, *inter alia*, Ivan Morris, *The World of the Shining Prince*, Ch 1 ('The Heian Period'), Oxford University Press, London, 1964, p13.
5   Robert Frost, 'The Gift Outright'
6   Leonardo da Vinci, *Notebooks: Warfare*. See 'cathegia'. See also Virgil, *The Aeneid*, Book VII, line 741, translated C Day Lewis
7   See Max Angus, *The World of Olegas Truchanas*, Olegas Truchanas Publication Committee, Hobart 1975
8   Robert Frost, 'The Gift Outright'
9   Eugenio Montale, 'L'estetica e la critica'. Address in commemoration of Benedetto Croce, delivered at the Teatro Eliseo, Rome, December 1962. Subsequently published in *Il Mondo*, December 11, 1962, and collected in diverse editions. In translation, see *The Second Life of Art: Selected Essays of Eugenio Montale*, edited and translated by Jonathan Galassi, Ecco Press, New York, 1982. (Chapter entitled 'Aesthetics and Criticism')
10 Charles Dickens, *Hard Times*
11 WB Yeats, *The Trembling of the Veil* (years 1887–1891)
12 WB Yeats, 'Nineteen Hundred and Nineteen', Part V, *The Tower*, 1928
13 WB Yeats, 'The Second Coming', *Michael Robartes and the Dancer*, 1921
14 WB Yeats: 'Meru', *Supernatural Songs*, XII, *A Full Moon in March*, 1935

Robert Frost 'The Gift Outright', reprinted by permission of the Estate of Robert Frost and the *Poetry of Robert Frost* ed Edward Connery Lathem, published by Jonathan Cape Ltd.

Helen Hughes

Helen Hughes was born in Prague in 1928. When Germany invaded Czechoslovakia in 1939, her parents immigrated to Melbourne. She was educated at Melbourne University, from which she graduated with Bachelor of Arts and Master of Arts degrees in history and economics. She studied at the London School of Economics for a PhD.

Professor Hughes worked in market research and business economics on her return to Australia, and then taught economics at the universities of New South Wales and Queensland. In 1963, she began to work on development issues at the Research School of Pacific Studies of the Australian National University, with particular emphasis on development in the Pacific and Southeast Asia.

She joined the International Bank for Reconstruction and Development (World Bank) in 1968. She added to her southeast Asian experience of development by working in Latin American, South Asian, Middle Eastern and African countries, becoming chief of the Industry Division, deputy director of the Development Economics Department, and finally director of the Economic Analysis Department, which provides the central intelligence for the World Bank's annual borrowing and lending operations.

Professor Hughes returned to the Australian National University in 1983 to take up a chair in economics in the Research School of Pacific Studies, and to head the National Centre for Development Studies. She retired in 1993. In 1994 she became director of the University of Melbourne's Full Employment Project.

She was the deputy chairperson of the Committee to Review the Australian Overseas Aid Program in 1984, deputy chairperson of the Fitzgerald enquiry into immigration in 1988 and adviser on the export credit scheme in 1989. As well she has been a member of the board of AUSSAT, and of the Australian Manufacturing Council. She has been on several academic boards and the boards of several major Australian corporations.

In 1985, Professor Hughes was made an Officer of the Order of Australia, and has been elected to membership of the Australian Academy of the Social Sciences. She has published widely on the economics of industrialisation and development, and on international economies.

Professor Hughes gave her Boyer Lectures the overarching title of *Australia in a Developing World* and in them she ranges over the global economic environment; her concerns include employment, protectionism and population policy. The individual titles of the lectures are 'The Global Background'; 'The Right to Work'; 'The Role of Government'; 'A People and an Environment' and 'Policies for Progress'. Her third lecture, 'The Role of Government', which is reproduced here, is clear and challenging, providing an interesting companion piece to John Passmore's 1981 series on the limits of government.

THE ROLE OF GOVERNMENT

Australia in a Developing World

Helen Hughes

• 1985 •

Autralia's convict origins and the extensive pastoral and mining frontiers of its early development are reflected in the pervasive role of government in the economy. When things go wrong, often because of changes in the international sphere, Australian entrepreneurs turn to government. High protection and extensive regulation encourage this approach. The proper functions of government in the economy are often lost as a result.

Running the economy is one of the key functions of a national government. Whether explicitly or implicitly, through economic policies or their absence, governments play a dominant role in the economy. They establish the climate of growth or stagnation which shapes the attitudes of producers and consumers; they determine the policies which influence economic decisions by affecting relative prices; and they play a direct role in the economy by ensuring law and order, by providing such social infrastructure as education and health services and by investing in such physical infrastructure as roads and airports. In addition, Australian governments over the years have directly intervened in the economy taking over marketing functions, regulating industries and owning enterprises such as banks and airlines. Together, these strands of public intervention make up the 'rules of the game' which determine Australia's economic performance.

The interface between government policies and people's actions is, of course, complex. The world, and hence the Australian economy, is constantly changing, analysis always lags behind events, and the future is unpredictable. This leads to differences of opinion among economic analysts. But economic analysis is strengthening its grasp and depth. Rapid improvement in economic policies played a key role in the worldwide prosperity of the 1950s and 1960s. In the early 1980s it prevented a repetition of the depressions of earlier times. Current economic difficulties largely result from an unwillingness to take the political steps necessary to adjust to changing conditions. In contrast, a will to implement appropriate economic policies has been crucial to the high growth and poverty alleviation policies of such 'catching up' developing countries as Singapore, Malaysia and Thailand. Industrial countries such as Sweden and Denmark have been able to turn troubled economies around.

Education is a prime government responsibility. A country's education policy permeates all aspects of economic productivity. It influences social and cultural life and it has an important influence on political maturity. Expenditures on education are key national investments.

In the second half of the nineteenth century, Australia's emerging school system led in providing basic education for the majority of the population. Universities were founded. Apprenticeship provided training in craft skills. Later, public high schools gave access to academic education to those who could not afford or did not want to patronise private schools. Australia also led in the provision of education for children in the outback.

But during the 1920s and 1930s Australian education fell behind other industrial countries, and by the 1950s it was starved of funds. Reviews of education policy led to a considerable expansion in education expenditures in the 1960s, so that education now has roughly the same share of public expenditures in Australia as in other countries. Physical conditions in schools, including recreational facilities, have improved enormously. Class sizes have been reduced so that they compare well with other industrial countries. The hours worked by teachers have fallen. Teachers' remuneration is high by international standards. Nonetheless, primary and secondary education is neither appropriate nor of adequate quality.[1] Almost half of the students leave the education system before they are properly equipped to participate in a modern, flexible and upwardly mobile workforce.

The growth of private school attendance, and the keen competition to secure private school places, confirm that state schools do not carry out their task satisfactorily. Increasing numbers of parents are opting out of the state systems despite the considerable cost of doing so, but more than 75 per cent of children must make do with the state system. Australian education has thus not only declined in quality, but it has also become less, not more, equitable than in the past.

Australia is falling behind other countries, including East Asian industrialising countries, in technical education. Apprenticeship training no longer provides the skills necessary for a modern work-force. Workers in the Republic of Korea receive better technical training than Australian workers. And low labour costs often reflect higher productivity rather than sweated labour. In the past, whenever shortages of skilled labour have occurred, skilled immigrants were brought to Australia. This is again beginning to happen. Yet the high unemployment of young people is building up an army of untrained workers, and at the same time many training facilities are under-utilised. Some industrial training facilities are used as little as four hours a day. Recent government measures have been designed to stimulate young people's interest in training, but even more could be done. Unemployment benefits for young people could be tied to participation in technical, accounting and academic training with bonuses for successful performance to stimulate interest. Facilities for retraining workers to keep up with changing technology are inadequate.

Participation in tertiary education is low by international standards. The abolition of university fees and the introduction of centralised funding that is divorced from university administration has broken the connection between the demand for tertiary places and their supply. As is often the case with services provided free of charge, relatively low standards of teaching have come to be accepted in some courses. A division of labour between universities and other tertiary institutions is lacking.

The absence of a national system of matriculation and national objective performance tests largely confines students to tertiary education in their own states. Together with the immobility of university staff, even among closely allied subjects, this has led to a very costly duplication of facilities for disciplines in low demand at the expense of those in high demand. For example, at the beginning of 1985 there were not enough computing or commerce places to satisfy demand, but there were ample places in classics and Slavonic languages. There is no reason why tertiary teachers who are among the best educated people in the community should be exempt from the restructuring pressures exerted on the rest of the population. They would find alternative employment easily if they sought it realistically.

Despite the great increase in knowledge and techniques which makes undergraduate training inadequate for a wide range of professional jobs, graduate education, the rapidly expanding sector of education in other industrial countries, is still largely in a monastic mould in Australia. Graduate teaching on lines developed in the

United States and countries such as the Netherlands has to be undertaken by subterfuge. Research and development in the economy depend on graduate training and they suffer accordingly.

Poor education policies are closely linked to unemployment. Young people who cannot find a point of entry into the workforce usually lack basic and vocational skills. And because they lack the skills necessary for upward mobility, many workers cannot leave activities in economic decline. Instead, they appeal for protection particularly in low skill industries such as clothing and footwear. Australian workers are generally fearful of technological change because their basic education is not sufficient to enable them to train for the new jobs that are opening up. New technologies do not displace workers. They create higher incomes by increasing productivity and international competitiveness. This means new jobs to satisfy the new incomes at home, and possibilities of new export-oriented employment.

The training of women is dominated by outdated attitudes. They are not entering highly paid trades such as plumbing or electronics in significant numbers. It is rare to see a female crane driver or commercial pilot. The airforce has difficulty in recruiting women for its electronic maintenance needs.

In tertiary education women still enter predominantly 'women's' occupations such as nursing and teaching, and they are not well represented in engineering, economics or graduate studies. A large part of the Australian education system still encourages girls to opt for second class citizenship. They do not take their career prospects seriously. Many are still afraid of appearing to be 'too clever'. Schools are not doing enough to prepare girls and boys for a society of equals. Most Australian girls now in school are going to spend 40 years or more in the paid workforce. They need training for the same occupations as boys. If they miss out on education while at school their work will be largely in 'women's' occupations, earning less than men of equal ability.

A vast expansion of the educational bureaucracy has unfortunately not led to the efficient management of education. But while dissatisfaction is widespread, there is almost no information about the costs of educating students to various levels of competence. Huge sums of taxpayers' money are poured into education every year without any knowledge about the relative efficiency with which it is utilised. The benefits that result to individuals and society from education are not calculated. Cost comparisons among educational institutions in Australia, and with other countries, are not available. The lack of objective nationwide examinations makes it impossible to compare educational achievements among the states and over time. The education establishment has either not been aware of the importance of such comparisons or, worse, it has sought to obfuscate issues of cost effectiveness and efficiency. Education is not properly costed or valued. Students and their parents are not encouraged to make career investments.

When mass access to primary and secondary education was being established, the emphasis on a basic, uniform and public education was clearly desirable. However, in a world in which growth depends on productivity, and productivity depends on the application of new technologies, it is essential to move to a more diversified, higher quality educational system that is responsive to the need for rising productivity in the economy. Increasing cost effectiveness and efficiency will need a shift in emphasis from tenure and seniority to performance by teachers and students. Syllabuses and teaching methods need to be improved, the range of subjects available requires enlargement and Asian languages need to be emphasised. Australians should be as fluent in Thai, Bahasa Indonesian, Chinese and Japanese as Europeans are in the languages of their neighbours. Children and adolescents, partic-ularly girls, need to become more interested in formal learning than they now are.

At the tertiary level a dramatic change of policy is needed to increase the number of student places, particularly at graduate levels. The present system is highly inequitable. The most important determinant of access to tertiary education is the educational status of a student's parents.[2] The children of university graduates go to university. Combined with traditional Australian hostility to 'tall poppies', the effect of present tertiary education policies is to deny education for the professions and the accompanying career oppor-tunities to children of working class families. The abolition of university fees has enabled a wealthy elite to perpetuate itself at the cost of lower income groups. The reintroduction of a fee system, with merit and 'needs' scholarships, is essential if discrimination against low income groups is to end and if the number of student places is to be expanded. Such expansion would not need vast new expenditures. Inter-state consolidation of courses to utilise economies of scale would lower the cost of tertiary education. Australian tertiary institutions could sharply reduce the capital costs of adding student places by adopting the year-round teaching system which many American universities use instead of the present three terms or two semesters that leave classrooms, residential colleges and other buildings idle for more than three months of the year. Each lecturer would still only teach for nine months of the year, leaving three months for research.

Tenure cannot continue to be an excuse for failure to evaluate performance in tertiary teaching and research. At present young graduates are being denied teaching places by policies that protect incompetent staff against change. Australia cannot become a technologically advanced and highly productive society while there are insufficient places for students wishing to learn computing skills! Some centralised funding would continue to be necessary for research, scholarships and subsidies for other socially desirable ends even if fees were reintroduced. Such funding should be used to establish national mobility in education for both students and teachers.

Industrial countries are now looking critically at the high cost and low productivity of their public sectors. And by any standards Australia stands out as a heavily governed country. A population of fifteen and a half million people supports the Commonwealth government, six state governments, the Northern Territory and the Capital Territory administrations and a large number of local governments. Inevitably their functions overlap. In addition, Australian governments have taken on many functions often left to private business even in welfare-oriented countries such as Sweden and Denmark. Australian governments have also been extraordinarily industrious in creating marketing boards, regulating productive activities, inventing zoning regulations, engaging in industrial promotion, and in many other economically related activities. To do this they have often neglected investment in infrastructure and other essential tasks of government. Regulatory activities have been steadily increased with the very best of intentions. They seek to protect one group or encourage another. But the total effect is to reduce Australia's competitiveness and thereby create unemployment.

The operations of public enterprises are also coming under greater scrutiny. This is occurring because of the growing dissatisfaction of industry and household consumers. Profitability is not necessarily a sign of efficiency. Public enterprises such as power companies, state railways or Telecom are natural or mandated monopolies. Not having any competition they can be grossly ineffectual, provide very poor services and still be profitable. Hiding behind the slogan of financial responsibility they can charge high rates to users. Their relative efficiency is not known. More open dealings with the public would persuade the consumers that rising utility and other charges are not the result of managerial incompetence. Greater business acumen and more advanced professional skills at management and board levels would enhance efficiency. Improvements are also needed in overview functions. At present neither state nor Commonwealth administrations have socio-economic auditing capacities that can assess public enterprises in public interest terms.

State involvement in the marketing of products such as eggs, milk and wheat has reached ludicrous levels in Australia. Farmers enjoy the protection of public marketing and price fixing thereby subsidising inefficient producers at the consumers' expense. Such government intervention often impairs marketing efficiency, reducing prices received by the farmer and increasing those paid by the consumer for poor management of such 'middlemen' functions as storage. Interstate egg and milk 'wars' highlight the costs of public marketing. Like industrial protection, public marketing measures were generally introduced in response to well organised political lobbies, and these insist on their maintenance through skilful use of the media. The measures are supported by the employees and managers of other industries that enjoy similar protection. Marginal operators who should be encouraged to find alternative, profitable production or employment are helped to keep inefficient farms and other enterprises in operation.

State health, labelling, transportation and building, retailing and a myriad other regulations increase tendencies toward the fragmentation of production and low capital utilisation. For example, each state's individual food labelling and container requirements raise the cost of producing goods such as margarine. The original aim was to protect producers in one state or industry at the cost of others. But from a national viewpoint such regulations are counterproductive. Where one or two plants would suffice for efficient national production, several firms produce for each state market. And there are usually enough close substitutes to keep the market competitive without any regulation. For example, margarine products compete with butter and vegetable oils.

Australian zoning and building regulations are examples of intervention run riot. Local regulations differ for trivial reasons, necessitating a larger range of builder's hardware than that available in the huge United States market. Many regulations are technologically outdated and others arise from ignorance, poor taste or extremes of paternalism. However, the results, such as the high social and economic costs of Canberra's vast sprawl, are not subjected to either professional or democratic review.

Some local governments insist that a house must have a bath; in the bureaucrats' view a shower will not suffice to keep the occupants clean. In other jurisdictions a washing machine must be in a separate room from a kitchen. The efficient bureaucrat must presumably protect the absent-minded housewife from the dangers of putting the dirty clothes in the oven and the roast in the dryer! Petty bureaucrats lacking appropriate professional training and experience thus interfere with the 'quality of life' in Australia, making intolerable intrusions into privacy as well as undermining economic efficiency.

The strict control of the hours of opening of retail and service establishments no longer protects workers as it was properly designed to do in the nineteenth century. Employees' rights have improved dramatically, and it is working people, particularly working wives, who would most benefit from longer shopping hours. But limitations on hours of opening reinforce the power of arbitration and trade union prohibitions on part-time work, reducing part-time employment opportunities. They also reduce capital productivity to intolerably low levels. Consumer choice is narrowed.

As the arbitration system has eliminated regional differences in wages, state governments have tried to substitute for the absence of such differences by 'industrial promotion'. 'Decentralisation' policies lead to 'beggar-my-neighbour' policies. States raid firms in other states to capture employment by providing subsidised public land and power. Promotion and research activities are duplicated.

State government purchasing preferences have also contributed markedly to the fragmentation of Australian industrial production, with resulting losses of productivity and competitiveness. Negotiations to eliminate these practices are moving very slowly.

The scope for effective state government promotion is limited. It should be focused on natural resources, transportation and labour cost differentials. Unfortunately the real effect of state government promotional activities is to increase greatly the cost of government and reduce Australia's industrial potential.

In the present climate of opinion, the public service is also being more carefully examined. An improvement in its efficiency and cost effectiveness is urgently needed. Low entry standards, lack of subsequent formal training and weak management are all part of the problem. Public service technology is often out of date and new equipment functions badly because of inadequate professional support. Public service regulations are designed to discourage young people from investing in their careers through education. Competition is discouraged. The Reserve Bank, for example, only accepts new staff aged more than 26 years in exceptional circumstances! The present largely clerical public service has to be transformed into a corps of professionals in the near future if Australia is to be able to increase productivity and reduce employment in the public service. Entry standards and promotion qualifications need to be raised and accountability increased. Formal qualifications cannot substitute for experience, but either one or the other is necessary where often neither exists at present. The elimination of redundant and counterproductive regulations would free up thousands of administrative workers for more productive purposes. Australia has to face up to the implications of having more than a quarter of its workforce in the public sector. Half as many would still represent almost twice the public share of the workforce in Japan!

In the absence of a medium to long term perspective for the Australian economy, the burden of economic management largely falls on the Treasury's annual budget, and the Reserve Bank's (short term) management of the money supply; that is, demand management through fiscal and monetary policies. The annual budget exercise is dominated by the need to hold at bay distortions created by protection, manpower and other policies albeit by focusing on narrow and short term issues. Often the distortions created by one set of regulations are offset with yet another set of distortions and regulations. In addition Australian fiscal policy clearly has acute problems on both the revenue and expenditure sides. A succession of major tax enquiries and a considerable technical literature have concluded that our tax system is neither efficient nor equitable.[3] In the absence of political rectitude we have used inflation to increase tax revenues to meet increasing demands on government expenditures, particularly as welfare costs have risen with unemployment. The consequent high marginal tax rates discourage work effort. Nevertheless government revenue has still not been adequate, and budget deficits have risen. Tax avoidance and evasion are rampant. The absence of capital gains taxes has diverted efforts from production and exports to company merger and real estate speculation.

The financial sector is also critical to the health of an economy. If monetary and financial policies are managed well, they are invisible. If they are inappropriate, either in themselves or as a result of fiscal profligacy, they can lead to an economy's collapse. Australian monetary policy has traditionally had a stabilising effect offsetting budget deficits and the inflationary pressures created by other policies. But the positive effects were, until recently, negated by protective controls in the financial sector. The regulation of financial markets (together with protection and other appropriate policies) leads to distortions in savings and investment. Despite the valiant attempts of merchant bankers to provide venture capital in the interstices of the financial system, entrepreneurs found it difficult to respond to business opportunities. This contributed to excessive borrowing abroad.

Government is not well suited to conducting business in the private sector. Private enterprises have to be risk takers; public servants have to be risk averters. But much of the current debate about privatisation is beside the point. Natural monopolies such as railways or mandated ones like airlines either have to be run by public companies or have to be regulated if the community is not to be exploited.

It is time that Australia began to abandon its convict origins. Government has a key role to play in the economy. However, in Australia this role has become as fragmented as the rest of the economy, and much government intervention is ineffectual. Less intervention in a more efficiency and growth oriented framework would be far more effective.

1 See Lauchlan Chipman, *Education—An Agenda for Reform*, The 1985 Alfred Deakin Lecture, 27 June, 1985, The Alfred Deakin Lecture Club, Melbourne, 1985
2 Sue Richardson, 'Who benefits from higher education?', MG Hogbin (ed), *'Withering Heights':The state of higher education in Australia*, Allen & Unwin, Sydney, 1988 (but forthcoming when this lecture published).
3 Notably Taxation Review Committee, *Full Report* (Asprey Report), Canberra 1975, and *Inflation and Taxation*, Report of the Committee of Inquiry Into Inflation and Taxation (Matthews Report), Canberra 1975

Eric Willmot

Eric Willmot was born in southern Queensland in 1936. His parents moved around during his childhood, and he attended primary school in various places in Queensland and the Northern Territory. He did not go to secondary school and spent his youth as a drover and horse breaker. At the age of 18, after a rodeo accident, he decided to continue his schooling. He graduated from Newcastle University with a science degree, gained a diploma of education, and spent the next decade teaching mathematics at schools in New South Wales, Victoria and Papua New Guinea.

Returning to Australia, he completed a masters degree in education and planning, and in 1972 joined the Commonwealth Department of Education.

His academic career began in 1978 as a lecturer in the school of education at Canberra College of Advanced Education. Then he moved to the Australian National University as director of research of a project on indigenous teacher training. He was instrumental in the development of Aboriginal Enclave programs across Australia to assist people who did not complete secondary school to go through university.

In 1981, Professor Willmot was appointed principal of the Australian Institute of Aboriginal Studies in Canberra. He left the Institute in 1984 to become deputy secretary of the Commonwealth Department of Aboriginal affairs, a position he held for one year before being appointed Professor of Education at James Cook University in Townsville.

In 1987 he joined the ACT School Authority, and from 1991 to 1992 he was secretary of the ACT Department of Education and the Arts. In 1992 he was appointed director general of the Education Department of South Australia and from 1992 to 1994 he was CEO of the Department of Arts and Cultural Heritage in that state.

Eric Willmot is also an award-winning inventor, most notably of a variable-ratio gearing system. He has written a number of books including the acclaimed *Pemulwuy: The Rainbow Warrior*. He has received honorary doctor-ates, and in 1984 was made a Member of the Order of Australia.

The title of his Boyer Lectures, *Australia—The Last Experiment*, derives from his argument that Australia's polygeneric society, like the US and South Africa, may be the last such deliberate experiment. His lectures' individual titles are 'A Different Genesis'; 'The Embedded Dolls', which is reproduced here; 'The Dragon of the New Eden'; 'Lushy Country Dreaming'; 'A Rational Differential' and 'A Choice of Destinies'. As Professor Willmot concludes in his last lecture: 'We are our own judges—we will know before anyone else whether we've succeeded or failed as the last experi-ment.'

THE EMBEDDED DOLLS

Australia: The Last Experiment

Eric Willmot

• 1 9 8 6 •

Australia is not alone in the way its modern population was formed. Australia is part of a family that I have called polygeneric nations.[1] The world can be divided broadly into two kinds of human societies, indigenous and polygeneric. Indigenous societies are those whose populations are made up substantially of indigenous people; that is, people who have no other race memories except from the place where they live. Such nations include Nigeria, Britain, France, and perhaps Japan.[2] The polygeneric nations are made up of human groups from different origins and with different race memories. Quite often one of the groups may be described as aboriginal or indigenous. Canada, the United States of America, the Central and South American states, New Zealand, Australia, Fiji and South Africa all belong to this group. There were others where the experiment in polygenesis failed. One relatively recent failure is that of Rhodesia, which has now become an essentially indigenous nation again, today known as Zimbabwe.

This process of polygenesis is certainly not a new phenomenon, because human beings have always moved about the globe, and every nation on earth has undergone such a process at some time in its past. It is very difficult to know what these past processes might have been, except that they resulted in the formation of largely indigenous societies. I have come to the conclusion, however, that modern polygenesis is somewhat different from that of the past.

Polygenesis is very much a dynamic process, it describes a society in a state of change, and there is a notion of eventual resolution. This ending of the process is not all positive. It involves a cost. For instance, for many modern Australians, an indigenous resolution of our social experiment would mean the loss of a very real European heritage in exchange for something both new and ancient, a very uncertain place in the sun. In any case, how could such a thing happen?

There are a number of easily understandable ways in which history

343

and prehistory indicate that past polygeneric societies have resolved themselves towards an indigenous form. The first is genocide—where one group manages to completely eliminate another. The tendency to do this is still alive in modern times. Adolf Hitler was determined to apply such a solution to the Jewish population of Europe. Some elements of Israeli society seem now to be occupying themselves with a similar proposal in relation to the Palestinians.[3] Even in Australia, the new British arrivals in the nineteenth century, quite officially,[4] decided to practise genocide on the Aboriginal population of Tasmania. It is worth observing at this point that genocide is a very difficult process to carry out perfectly. And if one fails to achieve it, then genocide becomes a two-edged sword, as most historic perpetrators of genocide have discovered. As a result, genocide is not a popular public policy these days.

The next simple and direct resolution of polygenesis is miscegenation, the mating between races. This process obliterates races by creating new ones. Genocide and miscegenation, together, were probably the predominant processes of the past. Genocide is much more rare in modern times, and, while miscegenation is common, it only appears as a major process in central and southern America. But even then there still remains the need to remove old race memories.

Obliteration of the memory of their origins, if accomplished by all groups, provides a feasible resolution to polygenesis. This was certainly true and practical in ancient times. Five thousand years ago, twelve generations of people born in a strange land was probably enough for them to lose the critical memory of their origins. They could become, at least culturally, indigenous to the place where they dwelled. The method seems to have been to enshrine the memory of their origins in mythology. Even if this mythology contained migration legends, it would not detract from their new indigenous status. This was most probably the case in many relatively recent indigenous nations, such as the Maoris of New Zealand.[5]

The sharp difference, however, between ancient polygenesis and its modern form is that the old process of forgetting or replacing memory with mythology is no longer possible. By the time societies become literate and this literacy becomes popularly based, the forgetting of origin memories is not possible. This is even more the case with the introduction of photographic and electromagnetic recording.

Neville Bonner has described migrants as people who have a race memory from somewhere else. This would mean that every element of a modern polygeneric society, except the original aboriginal group, is doomed to remain forever migrants. Indeed a strange situation, which seems to suggest that the status of people in modern polygeneric societies will remain forever unresolved. If this were true, then modern polygeneric societies are a totally new social phenomenon. This is all the more fascinating when one realises that the world's most powerful society, the United States, is such a nation. The world's most troubled society, South Africa, is one. And so is Australia.

On the earth today polygeneric societies can be found in all the stages of evolution. Modern polygeneric societies have not ignored their special situation. Indeed they have applied a number of official and informal social and cultural policies in an attempt to resolve their status.

The first of these strategies is partition—the process of socially separating the various cultural groups into sub-societies that communicate with each other at their boundaries. This was certainly attempted in the United States and Canada in relation to their aboriginal populations and was part of the essence of the Waitangi Treaty in New Zealand. Its worst and most unsuccessful form is South Africa's apartheid.

Notwithstanding the problems that arise in this approach, it has demonstrated its usefulness, at least as a developmental measure. It has certainly been used with some success in relation to Canadian and United States aboriginal groups. It has also been used in Australia in relation to the same groups. It seems to be useful in the short term, providing the partition is created on an agreed basis and that basis is associated with land. On the other hand, experiments with partition in New Zealand have not been so successful. And both Fiji and Hawaii are presently undergoing considerable social stress in their attempts to apply similar policies, to say nothing of Australia's land rights impasse.

The failure of partition generally seems to be associated with miscegenation and acculturation. Intermarriage of people of different races and acculturation, or at least the rate at which they take place, vary from society to society. The rate of miscegenation seems to be directly connected with changes of views of cultural solutions in polygeneric societies. Since most approaches to census do not allow accurate data to be gathered in regard to the mixing of races, it is useful to use indicator groups in examining this phenomenon.

I have found that Japanese groups are good indicators. It seems that they react quickly, in terms of intermarriage, to the movement of polygeneric societies towards cultural solutions. For instance, the average rate of intermarriage among Japanese in contact with other societies tends to be between 4 and 6 per cent. In Hawaii at present the rate of miscegenation is over 30 per cent.[6] This indicates to me that the islands of Hawaii are moving into a cultural solution phase.

Before going any further let me define what I mean by a cultural solution. This form of resolution involves a change in the culture of one or more of the groups involved. Cultural solutions vary greatly and are quite often difficult to understand. Whenever they're observed in action, cultural solutions are usually in a state of fairly rapid change, and cross-sectional views do not give a lot of information. Notwithstanding this, there is one interesting case of the application of a cultural solution where an end point can be observed: this is in the Pacific island state of Western Samoa.

In relatively recent times, Western Samoa has gone through two situations that would normally give rise to some sort of polygenesis. The first appears to have occurred about 300 years ago, when the island was invaded and occupied by people from Tonga.[7] It is difficult to say what happened during this period, but about a hundred years later, the Tongans left. Culturally, Western Samoa seemed largely unaffected. Later, during the German occupation of Western Samoa, Chinese labourers were brought in to work on copra plantations on the island. These labourers were all male, and after some time the Germans pressed the Samoans for their cooperation in allowing the importation of Chinese women, but the Samoans steadfastly refused to allow it.

At that stage a simple solution of partition had been applied. The partitioned groups were the Samoans, the Chinese men, and the Germans. Following their refusal to allow the importation of Chinese women, the Samoans removed the partition between themselves and the Chinese. It soon became apparent that the Samoan tradition prescribed that not only were the offspring of a Samoan mixed marriage Samoan, but the alien partner in the marriage also became Samoan. Today it is possible to find the extraordinary situation of a *matai* (leading person) in a Samoan village who is of predominantly Chinese descent.[8] Such a person is regarded as Samoan.

If we sweep across the Pacific to Canada, we find not only the application of partition between the French, the British and the aboriginal population, but also another partition of mixed race people, known as *matis*. In a sense, this was a cultural policy, as any mixed race offspring between the Europeans and the aboriginal population were regarded as being part of a new race, *matis*. This policy has continued into the present century among Canada's aboriginal people. Here even more complex partitioning rules were applied. Certain forms of miscegenation were regarded as moving in one direction and another form in another. For instance, an aboriginal woman marrying a non-aboriginal man became herself non-aboriginal, or rather a non-status Indian, and her children were similarly classified. A non-aboriginal woman marrying an aboriginal man, however, became herself a status aborigine and her children were also aborigines.

Although partitioning was applied initially in the United States of America in relation to aborigines and to Africans, America was the first place to construct a more revolutionary cultural ideology for the resolution of their polygenesis. This was the well known idea of multilateral assimilation: the melting pot. It was assumed that the various groups that formed the modern United States would eventually become a single cultural entity to be known as American.

By the late 1950s and early 1960s, the melting pot strategy had failed and America drifted again into a complex system of voluntary partition. These partitions gathered up within them black Americans, aboriginal Americans and South Americans, and even formed partitions within the European population, such as the Italians and the Irish.

I don't wish to suggest that partition cannot offer a long-term solution—both China and Russia, for instance, seem to have resolved an ancient polygenesis this way. I have not examined either country closely, but I assume that some special sort of cultural interface (to use computer terminology) must have developed between the partitions. Modern polygeneric partitions, on the other hand, tend to be unstable at their cultural boundary areas.

Central and South America continued on the path of miscegenation solutions. Countries like Mexico managed to form large central populations with up to 60 per cent of their people being of new mixed-race origin. These people began to dominate both the physical and cultural nature of those societies. In more recent times, partition has again become apparent, possibly as a result of experience with polygeneric neighbours. In fact this kind of voluntary partition has become characteristic of the Americas. One possible cause for the existence of these relatively stable partitions is the appearance of higher order identity, most noticeable in the United States.

Identity in its simplest form is a subjective notion that humans hold as to what they are. It is clearly related to culture and is perhaps the most important expression of culture. Somewhere in the massive information store within each of our heads is one part of the recipe for our identities. That is the part which we, as individuals, generate. It is what we see ourselves to be. The other part of our identity is produced by the shared perception of us by others.

Let us consider that this recipe is written on an imaginary slate. As adults, we encode the information about who we are and what we are. Our children read it and assemble the recipe of their identities. The information each generation encodes upon the slate may change from time to time, but the slate is always there to be seen, provided that children are in contact with their parents, or at least with other members of their racial or cultural group.

This is how identity would arise in an indigenous society. But for members of a polygeneric society, identity is no simple matter. I would like to illustrate something of this complexity by recounting an interesting experiment, carried out by Geoffrey Coyne in South Australia.[9] The study made use of Rokeach value inventories.[10] The inventories were placed before a group of Aboriginal students and a group of non-Aboriginal students. When their responses were analysed, no significant difference in values was found to exist between the groups, and yet it was clear to the researcher that these groups were not only different, but they also saw themselves to be different and so did others. The next part of the experiment involved a projective operation in which each group was asked to project the values of the other group, that is to use the inventories to describe what each group thought were the values of the other. Very significant differences were found between the two projections. The conclusion is obvious: the values of the two groups, ascertained in this way, were very little different. But the way in which the groups perceived each other's values was quite different.

This is an extraordinary phenomenon: two ethnically different groups, with very similar values exhibit strongly different primary identities. The question is, how does such a thing come about? I believe some understanding of this can be gained by examining a traditional Russian doll. This artefact consists of many hollow dolls each carved identically but in different sizes, so that each fits precisely inside another. If one begins to take the dolls apart, there is an expectation that the end of the process—that is the innermost doll—will provide the reason or meaning for the dolls. The innermost doll, however, is no different from the first and contains no more information. It is quite a different matter to put the dolls back together. The secret of the dolls becomes rapidly apparent. It lies in the way in which the dolls fit together, the way they are embedded one into the other. It is this characteristic of embeddedness that makes the individuals in a polygeneric society distinctive and different from the inhabitants of an indigenous society. When one ethnic group in such a society writes upon the slate of their primary identity, they also write upon the slate of others. These others reciprocate the process. The children of these societies read not simply the identity of their ethnic ancestor, but also the projected identity of their ancestors' co-adventurers in polygenesis.

The significance of this is that in polygeneric societies there is no such thing as a pure ethnic identity. The primary identity of an Italian Australian will be quite different to the primary identity of a native Italian who lives in Italy. We have become embeddlings. Like the Russian dolls, we have all become intrinsic parts of each other.

Not only is the primary identity of people in modern poly-generic societies different from those in indigenous societies— secondary or higher-order identities that are even more complex also exist. By higher order identity, I mean that identity which an individual has ascribed to him or herself in relation to a nation. For instance, when an American is described as a 'Yank', the description could apply equally to an American of indigenous descent, a black American, or one of the wide variety of European Americans. This is a very real identity for Americans. It is able to exist alone and beyond primary identities yet be consistent with them. This coexistence of primary and secondary identities seems to be the most advanced end point of modern polygenesis that I have yet been able to observe. Australia has not yet developed a substantial higher order identity. Some of the Australian partitions try to project their primary identity as the national identity. This leads to social power struggles, arguments over flags and anthems, and indeed arguments about what we are.

Primary identities are the swaddling clothes of our children. It is most unlikely that we shall give them up until indigenisation is complete, if indeed that is any longer possible. Higher order, or national, identity, on the other hand, is an evolutionary process, and would be expected to be more advanced in older polygeneric societies such as the United States. Nevertheless it does sometimes appear in younger societies. New Zealand exhibits a relatively stable higher order identity. New Zealand, like Australia, is a young member of the polygeneric family. This leaves us with somewhat of a puzzle as to why Australian higher order identity is so poorly developed; I shall address this question in a later lecture.

The age of a polygeneric society is not the only factor in the evolution of higher order identity. Social modelling, the way a society thinks of itself, or is promoted to think of itself, has a fairly profound effect. Unfortunately such constructed models are often faulty and lead to blind alleys.

The Americans see their society as a great cultural mosaic. When the many different parts are drawn together into a single whole, the image of America is created. This particular conceptualisation has influenced social policy thinking in almost all of the polygeneric nations, including Australia. Unfortunately, it has an underlying fallacy. It is easy to observe that the parts of these societies within their partitions are not as they arrived in the new worlds. They also change, and nowhere is this change noticed so much as in the Central and South American states. But even within North America it is clear that the people of various descents have changed remarkably from the communities of their origins. In fact, I would argue that the mosaic is an unfortunate and incorrect construction for describing polygeneric societies, because it assumes that, while the total image can change, the elements making it up remain unchanged. A better model, I believe, is that of the matrix. The matrix is certainly constructed of a wholeness of different parts, but its changing form is the product of changes within the cells that form it as well as the location of the cell in an array. It is this changing dynamic that makes the polygeneric societies so distinctly different from the older indigenous forms. These new societies are the centres of rapid cultural change. But, more importantly, the Earth's polygeneric societies are the source of new culture. New human culture is the generator of intellectual evolution. The new frenetic power of the polygeneric world has become internationally active, invading the old world and infecting it with our visions. With our visions, for we are the children of the future.

1   EP Willmot, *New Models for Populations in Polygeneric Societies*, ANZAAS, Australian National University, Canberra, 1983.
2   The existence of the remnants of an earlier population, the Ainu, indicate polygenesis in the not too distant past.
3   Kahane, a rabi and member of the Israeli Parliament presents a stance of determination to rid Israel of the Palestinians.
4   VR Ellis, *Trucanini, Queen or Traitor?*, Australian Institute of Aboriginal Studies, Canberra, 1981.
5   Maori occupation of New Zealand appears to have taken place within the last 3000 years.
6   Author's research.
7   Author's research.
8   Author's research.
9   G Coyne, *Value Conflict and Change Among Aboriginal Students*, Report to SA Dept of Education, 1975.
10 M Rokeach, *The Nature of Human Values*, Free Press, New York, 1973.

Davis McCaughey

A distinguished theologian and former Governor of Victoria, Davis McCaughey was born in Ireland in 1914 and emigrated to Australia in 1953. He was educated at Campbell College, Belfast, at Pembroke College, Cambridge, at New College, Edinburgh, and at the Presbyterian College, Belfast. He was ordained a minister of the Presbyteerian Church of Ireland.

After moving to Melbourne to become Professor of New Testament Studies from 1953–64, he was Master of Ormond College at the University of Melbourne from 1959 to 1979. He served on the University's council for three-year periods in three decades from the

1960s, and served as deputy chancellor in 1978–79 and 1982–85. He also served as a member of the interim council, and then on the council of La Trobe University from 1965 to 1974.

Dr McCaughey was the president of the first Assembly of the Uniting Church in Australia. He had also served in the Faith and Order Commission of the World Council of Churches from 1961 to 1975.

Davis McCaughey was appointed Governor of Victoria in 1986, serving with distinction until 1992. He has been a professional associate in the history department of the University of Melbourne since that year.

He has received honorary degrees from the universities of Melbourne, Queens Belfast and Monash, and is an honorary fellow of Pembroke College, Cambridge. Among his publications are The Christian in the World Struggle (jointly), Victoria's Colonial Governors 1839–1900 (jointly) and Tradition and Dissent.

He was made a Companion of the Order of Australia in 1987.

Piecing Together a Shared Vision, written while he was Governor of Victoria, is Dr McCaughey's title for his Boyer Lectures in which he asks whether we are able to share a sense of direction that gives coherence to our lives. What one might describe as a Presbyterian clarity and firmness underlies these gentle lectures. 'Who Are We?' was his first lecture, followed by

'Something Beyond Ourselves'; 'Professions and Conventions: A Matter of Trust' then 'Ourselves Writ Strange' and 'Some Larger Love or Loyalty', which is reproduced here. Throughout them all he encourages a curiosity about the beliefs of our neighbours and a respect for them and, ultimately, a hope that we might love them.

SOME LARGER LOVE
OR LOYALTY

Piecing Together a Shared Vision

Davis McCaughey

• 1987 •

In a previous chapter I spoke about some of the ways in which our patterns of behaviour are controlled by conventions. I introduced this by references to the behaviour of members of professions. But conventions influence other relations of life. Gilbert Harman writes:

> Moralities are social. They are defined by the conventions of groups. But you belong to more than one group, and different groups have different conventions. Which conventions determine your moral obligations? They all do. Since you belong to a number of different groups, you are subject to a number of different moralities—the morality of your family, perhaps your school, a professional morality (your 'business ethics'), the morality of your neighborhood, the various moralities of various groups of friends, the morality of your country, and finally, perhaps, a limited morality you share with most of humanity. These moralities will sometimes be in conflict, and give rise to a tragic situation in which you are faced with a conflict of loyalties. In that case, there is no clear moral solution to your problem. You must choose the group which is most important to you and act on its conventions.

I do not suppose that Professor Harman would offer that as an exhaustive list. We in Australia would certainly want to draw attention to the conventions that determine moral obligations as we have inherited them in different ethnic groups: our cultural conventions, our conventional moralities deriving from different religious positions, or political convictions. The question that we have set ourselves is this: Are there any perceptions that we have in common that transcend these differences? There are some, we said; or there should be some. A healthy, and to some extent cohesive, society depends upon a reasonable proportion of its citizens having a common respect for certain things (what we called an awareness of the sacred); it equally depends on groups of people working out the ethical implications of being members of a particular profession, or of pursuing a particular occupation; and all the time we need to be having our outlook enriched and transformed by the quickening of our imagination's.

Is there anything more to be said about our shared vision, matters that we could look at through common eyes in such a way as ultimately to determine public policy? I have no doubt that there are several, but I want to select three: a common awareness of the importance of the family as the basic unit of society; a common determination that every member of the community should be provided with an opportunity to work; and a commitment to improve the quality of life for all citizens but especially for those whose lives have been rendered poor or mean.

The many cultures to which we in Australia belong bring with them a great variety of patterns of family life, from the tribal loyalties of Aborigines to the small unit of the nuclear family with its 2.4 children. Few institutions in our society have been subjected to closer analysis. The family has been dissected and defended from as many points of view as there are articulate social scientists or imaginative writers. We are all experts on families, for we have all been— all are—members of families, whether they are happy and contented or places of tension and disruption.

After all the battering that the family has received from supporters and critics, two things seem to have emerged, which must belong to our shared vision. The first is that the family, nuclear and where possible extended, continues to be the primary unit in which we care for one another, not only at the beginning of life (infancy and childhood) or at the end of life (old age, declining powers, decrepitude), but also in the middle of life when apparently we are strong. The second is that the family is the primary place of experience of moral realities: the place where we learn to talk, and to speak the truth, to love and be loved.

Because the family is the primary unit of care, its protection has almost always been the subject of legislation. For long that seemed to be confined to laws relating to marriage, but when social legislation gained in prominence and the state took responsibility to support families, at least families in need, the focus shifted from concern with marriage to concern with the protection of women and children. The state today has to recognise a greater variety of patterns of family life than in the past—for instance, with the growing incidence of one-parent families—but a responsibility towards the family in some shape or form is one from which no government can be allowed to walk away.

At the other end, from matters on which we depend on legislation, the family is shaped by conventions that we observe. These conventions include family Christmas parties or the observance of Mother's Day or of birthdays. For centuries Jews have known the value of the observance of Sabbath Eve in the home. There are, however, other kinds of conventions that need to be observed. It is difficult to state them without sounding banal or naive, but a fundamental convention is a respect for truth. By this I do not mean that members of a family should always, painfully, be telling each other what they think. I mean rather what some Hebrew and Greek writers meant when they equated truth with reliability. Members of a family should be able to depend upon one another.

This is most vividly expressed in the commitment made by a man and a woman each to the other in marriage. Today there may be more de facto relationships than heretofore: many would claim that they have as deep a commitment to each other as married couples. Nevertheless, most children are born within a formalised marriage relationship, and there is much to be learnt from that relationship. Both by common law and by the law of the church, men and women married each other in the exchange of vows. A vow is something different from an aspiration or a good intention. An exchange of vows is something more than a legal contract (though it may involve that), more than a socially convenient way of announcing to friends and relatives that a couple now intend to live together (if they have indeed not already been doing so), more than a dramatic way of expressing a romantic attachment; it is a determination to live together for better for worse, for richer for poorer, and so on—till death do us part. Life is no longer to be lived by inclination but to be controlled by commitment.

We can say that and still be sympathetic when things go wrong. Few experiences are more painful than disruptions within a family. But the point is that we can and should use the phrase 'things go wrong'. WH Auden wrote a poem entitled *Their Lonely Betters*. He describes how he 'listened . . . in the shade/To all the noises that my garden made'—the robins singing and the flowers rustling.

> No one of them was capable of lying,
> There was not one which knew that it was dying . . .
> Let them leave language to their lonely betters
> Who count some days and long for certain letters;
> We, too, make noises when we laugh or weep:
> Words are for those with promises to keep.

It is in the family that we learn to speak, it is there that we should learn to speak the truth, it is there that we have to learn to abide by promises. It is in the family that we learn that there are other people in the world who are more important than we are; and that moving out in concentric circles we should enter into relationships of confidence and trust, in which constancy and loyalty are regarded as virtues.

After the family I suppose that one of the next areas in which most men and women find themselves in contact with other people is the workplace; and I have suggested as part of our shared vision a common determination that every member of our community should be provided with an opportunity to work. There are some resemblances and some differences between life in the family and life at work; and they may both—the resemblances and the differences—be instructive.

First we might note in passing that, as with the family, we all tend to have opinions about work: we have worked, or we hope to work, or we have been denied work, or we have had work to do that was satisfying or not satisfying. Some have had experience of working with their hands, some predominantly working with their brains, some know a lot about working at a desk—on paper or with a computer—some spend most of their time working with people, seeing them face to face, cooperating with others obtaining their cooperation, in competition with others, outwitting them perhaps. And the relation between effort and financial reward varies enormously. Some know what they will earn this week, this month, this and next year; and the sum is not going to vary according to the amount of effort put into their work. Others find their income affected directly by the number of hours given to their work, and the quality of their performance. Some again find that their earnings depend on factors largely beyond their own control, the weather, the price of basic commodities in overseas markets, or what the public (which is fickle in this regard) is prepared to pay for works of art or regards as entertainment.

These distinctions do not exhaust accounts of the different ways in which we experience work, or the different points at which we are denied it; but they suggest that when we talk about the importance of providing men and women with opportunities to work we are talking about a lot of different situations in life. Just as the family provides men and women and children with the primary unit in which they are cared for (or at least that is as it should be), so work and the workplace provide or should provide men and women with the security of having a purposeful existence. Different cultures will give different reasons for this phenomenon. That is to say, there will be a variety of explanations at the ultimate level, arising from fundamental convictions about man's nature. For our purpose we may observe that we deny men and women something that belongs to their human nature when we deprive them of the opportunity to work. Work can be part of their joy in sharing in creative activity, whether it expresses the human race's relation to nature, industrial development, commercial expansion, economic growth, or social organisation: in all these ways, men and women fulfil a part of their nature through work. One strand in our cultural tradition—that which goes back to the Hebrews—while stressing that work should be enjoyable notes also that work is an economic necessity, and that it sometimes involves drudgery. These are important reminders that the criterion by which we judge work is not simply whether it is invariably enjoyable; we judge it rather by whether it is genuinely creative and productive. In passing we might note that it is always safer to apply this reminder about the drudgery that is part of work to ourselves than it is to apply it to others. It would be a distortion in our understanding of what work does for a man or woman— giving them a joyful part in creative activity—to chain some to a ceaseless drudgery.

Again just as surely as the family is the place where we first meet the moral reality of other people with whom we must live, so the workplace in its way is also an arena where moral considerations enter into our relations one with another. The way in which we describe the moral considerations that enter in differs in the two cases. The family operates on ethical considerations expressed in terms of love and trust and forgiveness. The workplace operates with a more impersonal morality of loyalty, reliability and above all fairness or justice. Archbishop William Temple once described justice as love operating at a distance. I cannot express my concern for my fellow human being in Africa through the exercise of personal virtues which I must practise inside my family. If I really care for him or her, if I really want to love those distant neighbours as myself, I will seek justice for them—a fair deal, access to the courts to right their wrongs, an impartial hearing of cases, a just reward for labour. Such matters may require political and legislative action: only thus can justice be done, or attempted, and love become effective at a distance.

Similarly with the provision of work for every man or woman who wishes to take advantage of it. There is an abiding imperative, to provide work for others because to deny it is to destroy part of what it is to be human—just as surely as the destruction of a man's language reduces his humanity. Not any work on any conditions, but work that is rewarded on a scale consistent with a man or woman's dignity as a citizen of this country in the closing decades of the twentieth century. If that is too general and vague, then let us discover what it means; but we have set the problem for economists and politicians and social workers and theorists to solve. We do not accept as inevitable that a considerable residue of man and woman power in this country is condemned to be without purposeful work.

If Hugh Stretton is right in saying that a return to full or fuller employment can not be achieved by the traditional macro-economic means alone, then, in his words:

> We need also some old and some new micro-economic policies. They might include more education, training and retraining; more work-sharing by a range of means from part-timing through shorter working hours to wider uses of sabbatical long-service and retraining leave; some increase of taxation and collective spending on public goods and services; some public or subsidized-private 'employer of last resort'.

It is no part of the purpose of these lectures to discuss the economic or political actions necessary for the restoration to the vast majority of citizens of this country the opportunity to work, to work productively and to be given a fair reward. It is appropriate to say that these must be part of the shared vision of our society, and that we look to those in authority to tell us not what will not work but of those things to which we may put our hand that may be effective.

Let me repeat: the demand for work for all is rooted in a conviction that a man or woman's humanity is to a high degree bound up with his or her having meaningful work to do. And the provision of work must be within terms that are just and seen to be just. Augustine said:

> Set justice aside and what are kingdoms but large robber bands, and what are robber bands but little kingdoms . . . Excellent and elegant was the pirate's answer to the great Macedonian Alexander, who had taken him. The king asking him how he durst molest the seas so, he replied with a free spirit, 'How darest thou molest the whole world? But because I do it with a little ship only I am called a thief, thou doing it with a great navy art called a conqueror.'

Justice demands a certain degree of equity, of fairness.

This leads to the third of our considerations: a shared vision will include a commitment to improve the quality of life for all citizens. In the second chapter I spoke of some of the things that point beyond ourselves, indicators of the sacred. I suppose it might have been entitled 'Man does not live by bread alone'. Throughout I have tried to say that there are considerations that make life worth living that go beyond what can be required by law, that there are people and values that triumph over brute force, and that our own concern that our fellow man or woman should have meaningful work is rooted not simply in the economic self-interest of the community—namely, that we cannot afford to have so much labour power idle, although that is true—it is rooted rather in what is their due as human beings. We now note that part of our shared vision is of a community that cares for the quality of life of its members.

In 1940, when Britain was desperately fighting for survival, the historian EH Carr (himself certainly a realist) wrote in an editorial for The Times:

> If we speak of democracy, we do not mean a democracy which maintains the right to vote and forgets the right to work and the right to live. If we speak of freedom, we do not mean a rugged individualism which excluded social organization and economic planning. If we speak of equality, we do not mean a political equality nullified by social and economic privilege. If we speak of economic reconstructions, we think less of maximum production, though this too will be required, than of equitable distribution.

A year later William Temple, then Archbishop of Canterbury, first used the term, 'welfare state': this in contrast to what Carr had called the 'night watchman state' of the nineteenth century. The state was there, it was argued, not simply to guard you against night marauders but to promote the health, education and welfare of all its members.

The notion of the welfare state is now less popular than it was. Indeed, some in public life compete if not in denigrating it then in distancing themselves from the term and the reality that it represents. Nevertheless, it is worth taking it out and examining it again. Is it true, for instance, that we cannot afford to have a universal welfare system? We are told that it is too costly and that taxes must come down not go up. But it has been pointed out that the tax revolt of recent years did not occur in the countries with the highest level of taxation (Scandinavia and the Germanic countries) but in Anglo-Saxon countries with relatively low levels of tax by OECD standards.

It may be significant that the higher taxed countries also had a universal welfare system from which both rich and poor benefited. Everybody could see how their taxes might help them. In countries like ours, where it is thought that benefits should be directed to the needs of the poor alone, there is a demand for tax cuts: the rich and the middle class feel that they are being asked to provide for the poor, and there are even some who say that they are being asked to provide for the improvident. The situation might be quite different if we were more actively concerned about the quality of life of the whole community.

Another example: never before in the history of Australia have works of art been purchased for such inflated prices as has happened in the art auctions of recent months and years. Private individuals are spending a lot of money on what we might term aggrandisement. Yet we have museums and galleries and libraries quite inadequately supported by private or public funds. We're back at the bad old contrast: private affluence, public, if not squalor, then need. There is a terrible nemesis ahead for a country that allows expenditure on higher education to decline over a 12-year period from 1.73 per cent to 0.9 per cent of gross domestic product.

I cite these instances not in order to offer solutions but to raise questions for debate and to ask how serious we are about the improvement of the quality of life for all citizens. Such a quality of life, of course, has to be paid for. In the process, some of the rich will be a little less rich and some of the poor a little less poor. It is by no means clear, however, that this country would be less secure financially and economically if we were to pay as much attention to the quality of life as to the quantity of goods which we possess or process. Nor is it by any means clear, despite some current ortho-doxies, that public expenditure is rarely as beneficial as private expenditure or that public borrowing is more improvident than private borrowing. There would seem to be a case for looking at instances on their merits.

Because the examples given are worrying, I could leave a nega-tive, not to say depressing impression. If we look at the three areas about which I have been speaking in this chapter—family, work, quality of life—there is much to hearten us. Many of the cultures now present in this country have brought with them a strong family life and loyalty: where they are available, within reach, members support each other to an impressive degree. Many of the educa-tional initiatives, some of them taken quite locally, say in TAFE colleges, have prepared young people for specific occupations in the areas in which they live, and have re-trained older people (not least middle-aged women) to enable them to undertake satisfying, useful and productive work. No one can travel through the country districts of Victoria, or (I imagine) of other states, without coming across heartening instances of local government, in the words of one municipal officer, discovering afresh that their responsibility is not only to the preservation and enhancement of property, but also to serve people: quality of life is on the agenda, but it is also on the ground, with initiatives being taken by local business sometimes quite small but contributing to employment, to the enrichment of life and to the country's export earnings; also quality of life, in the growth and development of crafts, in the provision of sporting facilities and the encouragement of physical fitness.

So we could multiply examples of what is heartening. This needs to be said to offset the widespread preoccupation with self and self-fulfilment: too many marriages break up because I, the first person singular, am not satisfied or fulfilled, or because I the first person singular, have become tired of making a daily effort to live with and to love this partner or take daily responsibility for these children. We are surrounded by public exhortations to gain satisfaction by a therapy that will look after me, the first person singular now in the accusative case, to make purchases, even to borrow from the banks to do so in such a way as to make me ride higher, look more beautiful or successful among my contemporaries. There is nothing wrong with beauty or success, but plenty that is questionable about the way in which it is to be achieved. What Hugh Stretton has called the cult of selfishness has to be resisted. Self-respect is one thing; self-obsession is another.

If we are to withstand the massive self-centredness that characterises personal and organised or institutional life at the end of the twentieth century, many people will have to live in ways that cost them something: the only way to overcome selfishness is by unselfishness. Is there, in a phrase of Reinhold Niebuhr, 'some larger love or loyalty which qualifies the self-interest of various groups'— something that we have or could have in common, at what I have called the penultimate level? I think there is.

Many men and women came to this country, many men and women have grown up in this country, with a hope in their hearts that they and their children might see and know a fairer, more just and compassionate society than has been known in previous generations in this country or in the countries they came from. We should be careful not to allow that hope to grow dim. Many men and women have believed that there is an order of truth and beauty and goodness that transcends their immediate desires and judges their earthbound self-regarding natures. We should be careful not to denigrate the intellectual curiosity, sensitive imagination, or religious conviction on which such a belief depends. Many men and women have perceived—in another phrase of Niebuhr—that 'nothing we do, however virtuous, can be accomplished alone; therefore we must be saved by love'. We should be careful not to quench that fire: it is altogether too easy to stop loving your fellow man or woman, and to stop them loving each other.

Hope, faith, love: they are the conditions of civilised life in a secular society just as surely as they have their roots for some in a religious context. And did not somebody say that the greatest of these is love?—the eye that is constantly looking out on the world in all its wonder, and on the neighbour in his or her need.

The poem by WH Auden 'Their Lonely Betters' may be found in *Collected Shorter Poems 1927-57* (Faber, London, 1966). The quotation from Hugh Stretton is taken from his *Political Essays* (Georgian House, Melbourne, 1987), a book demonstrating an unusual blend of social and economic analysis and moral indignation, which if taken seriously could have a salutary effect on public attitudes. The reference to EH Carr's editorial in *The Times* I owe to Asa Briggs, *A Social History of England* (Weidenfeld and Nicholson, London, 1983). Had space permitted I would like to have referred to Stuart Macintyre, *Winners and Losers: The pursuit of social justice in Australian history* (Allen & Unwin, Sydney, 1985), a reminder of how difficult it is to realise the vision of a more just society. Archbishop Temple's use of the term 'welfare state' appears in *Citizen and Churchman*: see Ronald Preston's article, 'Welfare State' in *A New Dictionary of Christian Ethics*. The quotations from Reinhold Niebuhr are taken from *Christian Realism and Political Problems* (Faber, London, 1954) and *The Irony of American History* (Scribner, New York, 1962).

Max Charlesworth

Philosopher and ethicist Max Charlesworth was born in 1925. He studied at the University of Melbourne and at Louvain University in Belgium.

He lectured in philosophy at the University of Melbourne from 1959, progressing to senior lecturer in 1962, reader in 1968 and chairman of the department of philosophy in 1975. In 1976 Professor Charlesworth took the chair in philosophy at Deakin University in Victoria and also became Foundation Dean of the School of Humanities, a post he held until 1983. Professor Charlesworth retired in 1990 and became Professor Emeritus the following year.

His interests span a number of areas: education, Aboriginal culture and religion, as well as bioethics—the study of the moral and social implications of biotechnology. During his career he sat on a number of committees: from 1983 he was at the Monash Centre for Human Bioethics; The Victorian Standing Review and Advisory Committee on Infertility (1983–93); the National Bioethics Consultative Committee (1988–91); the Australian Health Ethics Committee (1991–93); and the NHMR Council (1991–93). He was director of the National Institute for Law, Ethics and Public Affairs in 1993–94.

Professor Charlesworth has been a visiting professor at a number of universities—in the United States, Canada, and Belgium, and has held a fellowship at London University. He has published many books on the subjects of philosophy, ethics and religion.

Life, Death, Genes and Ethics was the great sweeping title chosen by Professor Charlesworth for his Boyer Lectures on his richly interesting subject matter. As he says in his introduction: 'The new forms of biotechnology-genetic engineering, genome analysis and genetic therapy, in vitro fertilisation and other modes of artificial reproduction—all promise great human benefits. At the same time, they also raise formidable ethical and social problems for which there is no precedent'. These technologies have brought about new situations which are difficult to relate to our ordinary ethical and legal principles and to the religious beliefs of many.

All of the lectures from 'New Ways of Birth', written just nine years after the birth of the first Australian test tube baby, to 'New Ways of Dying' to 'The Ethics of the Genes', and 'Bioethics: Committees, Experts and the Community' are immensely important, but his concluding lecture 'Controlling the Biotechnological Genie', which is reproduced here, is particularly useful to lay readers. He deals with difficult issues with insight and delicacy.

CONTROLLING THE BIOTECHNOLOGICAL GENIE

Life, Death, Genes and Ethics

Max Charlesworth

• 1989 •

The object of this Essay is to assert one very simple principle, as entitled to govern absolutely the dealings of society with the individual in the way of compulsion and control, whether the means used be physical force in the form of legal penalties, or the moral coercion of public opinion. The principle is, that the sole end for which mankind are warranted, individually or collectively, in interfering with the liberty of action of any of their number, is self-protection. That the only purpose for which power can be rightfully exercised over any member of a civilised community, against his will, is to prevent harm to others. His own good, either physical or moral, is not a sufficient warrant. He cannot rightfully be compelled to do or forbear because it will be better for him to do so, because it will make him happier, because, in the opinion of others, to do so would be wise, or even right. These are good reasons for remonstrating with him, or reasoning with him, or persuading him, or entreating him, but not for compelling him, or visiting him with any evil in case he do otherwise ... Over himself, over his own body and mind, the individual is sovereign.

John Stuart Mill, *On Liberty*[1]

Legal Versus Voluntary Regulation

I have said several times that Australia has been a leader not only in scientific research in the new reproductive technology but also in bioethical reflection on the thorny issues raised by that technology. One can go further and say that Australia has also been in the forefront as far as the legal control of artificial birth technology is concerned. The first legislation in the world regulating in vitro fertilisation and other forms of reproductive technology was enacted in 1984 by the Victorian Parliament in the shape of the Infertility

(Medical Procedures) Act and in 1988 the Reproductive Technology Act was passed by the South Australian Parliament. Other Australian states are presently considering similar legislation. I believe that the Australian experience, particularly in Victoria, of this kind of legislative regulation of artificial conception technology has a good deal of relevance for other countries. In fact, the Victorian legislation has already aroused considerable interest overseas. Two French experts have, for example, concluded that the Victorian Infertility (Medical Procedures) Act offers the best model for the protection of the interests of all concerned in in vitro fertilisation and other forms of artificial reproduction.[2]

This kind of control of in vitro fertilisation and other procedures by legislation has been strongly opposed by many of the medical scientists involved and also by the Australian National Health and Medical Research Council. They argue that the control and regulation of the new biotechnology is best done by the scientific community itself through its own Ethics Committees operating within the guidelines laid down by the National Health and Medical Research Council. Legislation, it is said, is of its very nature inflexible and cannot possibly cope with the incessant change and development in the volatile reproductive technology field. Again, legislation restricts and inhibits the freedom of scientific enquiry and places Australian scientists at a disadvantage as against scientists in other countries where there are no legal restrictions on research. More fundamentally, legislation such as the Victorian Infertility (Medical Procedures) Act involves the law interfering in an area which is not the law's business. People should be free to make their own reproductive choices without the state putting its oar in. Just as couples are free to procreate children in the normal way without interference by the law, so couples should be free to have children by in vitro fertilisation or other means without interference by the law.

I personally have a good deal of sympathy with this latter argument since in a liberal democratic society, such as our society is supposed to be, people should, as far as possible, be left alone to make their own autonomous decisions. The law should be called in only where obvious harm is being done to others or where there is a clear and unambiguous justification for paternalism. As it was put by John Stuart Mill, one of the founding fathers of liberal democracy: ... 'The only purpose for which power can be rightfully exercised over any member of a civilised community, against his will, is to prevent harm to others ... Over himself, over his own body and mind, the individual is sovereign'.[3] Many people tend to think that if some line of behaviour is morally wrong or questionable there ought to be a law prohibiting it. Some time ago I was watching my favourite football team playing and, after a number of clearly dubious decisions against us by one of the umpires, a large and vocal fellow-supporter near me shouted to the umpire: 'There ought to be a law against you'. That, I think, is a fairly common view: if something is wrong there ought to be a law against it.

The Law and Morality

But, of course, there are many kinds of behaviour that we may consider immoral or objectionable or undesirable, but which are not the business of the law. In a liberal democratic and pluralist society such as ours the law is not really concerned with the enforcement of morality but rather with providing a framework of peace and order within which people may exercise their personal liberty to the greatest possible extent and make their own personal moral choices and engage in what John Stuart Mill calls their own 'experiments in living'. In a liberal democratic society I may believe as I like and do as I like provided that I do not by the expression of my beliefs or by my actions cause 'harm' to others and prevent them from exercising their liberty to do as they please. We cannot then expect the law to seek to enforce virtue in general and prohibit vice in general; rather the law restricts itself to a very small area of immorality—those activities that harm others and prevent them from exercising their own free choice in matters of morality. An important part of this function of the law is the protection of the rights of those who are unable to protect their own rights.

We must, then, not expect the law to be the agency by which a common morality should be enforced in the community. Equally, we must resist the idea that if the law is silent on a particular issue, then it is condoning a line of action in conniving in it. As an American thinker has put it:

> We are a pragmatic and litigious people for whom the law is the answer to all problems, the only answer and a fully adequate answer. Thus many people confuse morality and public policy. If something is removed from the penal code, it is viewed as morally right and permissible. And if an act is seen as morally wrong, many want it made illegal. Behold the 'there ought to be a law' syndrome. This is not only conceptually wrong, it is also conversationally mischievous. It gets people with strong moral convictions locked into debates about public policy, as if only one public policy were possible given a certain moral position.[4]

It may then very well be the case that some of the practices and procedures in the area of biotechnology are held to be *immoral* or *unethical* by many people, but that nevertheless they are not made *illegal* or subject to legal control. To be made illegal it has to be shown not just that they are unethical or raise social problems but in addition that they are likely to have harmful implications for others, that is, violate people's rights in some clear and obvious way. It needs also to be shown that the prohibitions of the law are likely to be obeyed by the generality of people and that enforcement of the law will not bring about more harm than good in a society where there is a plurality of widely differing moral views and convictions. For many people this is why prostitution and abortion should be decriminalised. While they are in themselves morally objectionable, the attempt to legislate against them would, so it is argued, bring about more harm than good. As Governor Mario Cuomo of New York (himself a devout Catholic) replied to the US Catholic bishops' demand that abortion be legally prohibited:

> . . . Legal interdicting of abortion by either the federal government or the individual states is not a plausible possibility and even if it could be obtained, it wouldn't work. Given present attitudes, it would be Prohibition revisited, legislating what couldn't be enforced and in the process creating a disrespect for law in general.[5]

Similarly, one may be uneasy about the *moral* implications of certain aspects of biotechnology, while nevertheless accepting the fact that formal *legal* control would be inappropriate or counter-productive.

This disjunction between the sphere of law and the sphere of morality cuts both ways. For if to settle the *moral* question about IVF is not thereby to settle the *legal* question as to whether and how IVF should be controlled and regulated, so also to settle the legal question is not thereby to settle the *moral* question. In other words, we must resist the idea that if the law is silent about a given area then 'anything goes' in that area. Some bioscientists say things such as: 'I'll press ahead with my research until the law tells me to stop', as though the silence of the law enables them to escape making any ethical judgements of their own on the work they are doing. None of us can lead our normal lives simply by acting within the law; so also bioscientists cannot really fulfil their responsibilities as scientists and as human beings simply by acting 'within the law' and pressing ahead with their experiments until the law calls a halt.

What then in general terms is the proper province of specifically *legal* control and regulation with regard to the new biotechnology in a liberal democratic society such as ours?

The Public Interest

As I said before, couples should as far as possible be able to make their own procreative choices and to form their families by various means—through ordinary sexual intercourse, adoption, artificial insemination, in *vitro* fertilisation, gamete inter-fallopian transfer, even through surrogacy—without the state stepping in. However, in *vitro* fertilisation and related research clearly raise such important issues of moral, social and legal concern that some kind of regulation is needed. One obvious concern is the status of the children born from artificial birth technologies, especially where donors are involved. Whose daughter or son is the child born from artificial insemination, or in *vitro* fertilisation using donor sperm or ova or even a donor embryo? Similar questions arise about frozen embryos when the parents die or separate. Again, in adoption procedures the best interests of the child have to be taken into account and so the state steps in to safeguard, by regulation, the interests of the child. In the same way the interests of the children must be considered in artificial insemination, in vitro fertilisation and surrogacy— although the analogy with adoption cannot be pressed too closely since with artificial insemination, in *vitro* fertilisation and surrogacy a child is not already in existence. The 1985 report of the Australian Family Law Council, *Creating Children*, placed great stress on 'the paramountcy of the welfare and interests of the child born of reproductive technology', and argued that in *vitro* fertilisation should be seen primarily as a way of creating children and, if one may so put it, only incidentally a means of alleviating infertility in couples or an area of biomedical research.[6] However, others have argued that if we take this position too far we will end up saying that in *vitro* fertilisation couples should have to pass the same stringent tests as adoptive parents have to do before they are allowed to have children. We should therefore, so it is said, see in *vitro* fertilisation and other forms of artificial procreation as being closer to ordinary procreation than to adoption.

In this view then, although parents should be free to make their own reproductive choices, there is a justification for some kind of legal control and regulation by the state since the status and interests of the children brought into being need to be defined and defended, and also of course because some limit needs to be set on experimentation in this field.

In the case of surrogacy other public policy interests apply since it is important that the surrogate mother be able to give completely free and informed consent to the surrogacy arrangements and that there be no kind of 'baby selling' involved. For this reason the state has a right to step in to regulate surrogacy arrangements so that the kind of private entrepreneurship practised in some parts of the US, and which involves the commercialisation of surrogacy arrangements, is banned.

Again, particularly with regard to issues which are completely novel or about which there is division in the ccommunity, the intervention of the law often has a symbolic function in that it signifies to the community that these issues are under surveillance, so to speak.

In a recent article Professor Bernard Dickens of the University of Toronto had this to say about legislation in the area of artificial reproduction:

> Not all of the issues . . . need to be determined by legislation. Common law evolution through case-by-case judgments may be adequate to deal with many issues, such as whether a child born in consequence of negligent genetic screening of a sperm or ovum donor can succeed in a claim for wrongful life. Nevertheless, many issues arising in the practice of artificial reproduction are not amenable to systematic or consistent accommodation by a legal system dependent only upon declaratory or *ex post facto* judgment of the courts. The issues are of such social significance, and potentially of such major impact upon children to be born, that a responsible society must address them through specific, informed and perceptive legislation. We cannot evade the challenge of legislating for the Brave New Children.[7]

I have so far been concentrating on matters related to reproductive technology, but much the same goes for the issues related to the prolongation of human life by biomedical means. In one sense, as I have argued before, one ought to be able to make up one's own mind as to when and how one dies. But because of possible abuses, and also because of powerful symbolic reasons, the state has a right to step in to control when patients may legitimately request medical help in bringing about their death. This is, in effect, what the medical treatment legislation of Victoria, South Australia and the Northern Territory tries to do.

Even though the state may intervene, through legislative control, in the areas we have been discussing, on grounds of public policy, we must not conclude from this that that legislation has a directly moral end and purpose. In a liberal democratic society matters of morality and religion ought as far as possible be left to personal decision and the law should not be used to enforce a common morality or a common religious belief and practice. This is, after all, the crucial difference between democratic societies and traditional or 'confessional' or ideological societies, where the state enforces on all its citizens a particular moral or religious or ideological view. One gets the impression that some of those who want to use the law to prohibit in vitro fertilisation or other forms of reproductive technology want to return to some kind of confessional or ideological society.

Despite what I have said about the right of the state to control reproductive technology by legislation, it is worthwhile noting that there have not been any moves in Australia to use legislation to control genetic engineering or recombinant DNA technology. Genetic engineers are able to introduce new organisms into the environment to produce better plants or better animals and fears have been raised that these new organisms may have unexpected effects and bring about what has been called a 'biological melt-down' or a 'biologic Chernobyl'.[8] In Australia, however, control over genetic engineering is at present ensured through guidelines of the Genetic Manipulation Advisory Committee, a federal committee reporting to the Minister for Industry, Technology and Commerce. The National Health and Medical Research Council has also formulated guidelines on genetic engineering with respect to human beings.[9] Compliance with these guidelines is voluntary and there is no legal way to compel compliance.

In a recent report the Law Reform Commission of Victoria concluded that the present system of voluntary guidelines and self-monitoring should remain, although it conceded that legislation may be necessary in particular areas.[10] It must be said, however, that this view is not shared by many people in the US, the UK, and Europe. Whatever individual scientists may do, it is argued, large and powerful international biotechnology companies are not likely to observe any voluntary guidelines they may deem to be inconvenient.

The Victorian Experience
I have already mentioned the Victorian Infertility (Medical Procedures) Act of 1984. Under that Act a Standing Review and Advisory Committee was established to interpret the legislation and decide whether applications for research in the in vitro fertilisation area should be approved or not. It also has the task of advising the

Minister of Health on matters to do with infertility. The Committee had its first meeting in October 1985 and has since had more than 50 meetings.[11] It is worthwhile considering the experience of this Committee since it is directly relevant to the question we are concerned with here.

In my view the work of the Committee over the last four years has shown how unfounded were the fears originally expressed by the medical scientists engaged in infertility research, as well as by the National Health and Medical Research Council and other parties, that legislation in this field must necessarily be rigid and inflexible and unable to respond to the rapid and radical developments in reproductive technology.

In 1987, for instance, the Committee was confronted with a request to allow experimentation, under strictly controlled conditions, on embryos before the developmental stage known as 'syngamy' when the embryo is about 20 hours old. The Committee decided that the Act would have to be amended to permit this kind of experimentation which it considered would help to alleviate some kinds of infertility. The amendment specified that the ova used must come from a married woman; that the woman and her husband must consent in writing to the procedure; that the couple must be participants in an IVF program; that the experimentation must be likely to produce information which would enable a woman in an IVF program to become pregnant; that donor semen must not be used unless the donor and any spouse had been counselled and had consented to such use. In other words, the medical scientists could not form embryos for experimental purposes of an open-ended kind by using gametes from anywhere, so to speak, and without reference to the wishes of the providers of the gametes. This amendment was accepted by the Victorian government, and after being debated in the Parliament and the community, it became law at the end of 1987, some nine months after it was first proposed by the Committee. This shows convincingly that legislation is not necessarily inflexible or hard to change.

Again, during the operation of the legislation so far it has become evident that the Act does not merely restrict or inhibit scientific research into infertility but also provides a framework of protection for such research. So long as medical scientists work within the provisions of the legislation they are safe. There is some opposition in the Australian community to biotechnological research—particularly among fundamentalist groups where it is seen as an attempt to 'play God'—and the legislation serves both to safeguard legitimate scientific activity in this field and also, as I remarked before, to symbolise that it is under community surveillance and control.

Further, it has become evident that the choice is not just between heavy-handed and inflexible legislation on the one hand and voluntary professional self-regulation on the other hand. Willy-nilly the law must be involved in the biotechnological domain, for example in determining the status of IVF children. The question is not whether the law should be involved at all, but to what degree it should be involved. To use an analogy: it would be fatuous to argue that adoption procedures should not be regulated by law but should be left to voluntary self-regulation by adoptive parents. The 'best interests of the child' require that legal control be established in this area. Similarly, with medical procedures whose aim is to alleviate infertility and create children, the law cannot be indifferent to the interests of the children that are likely to result from such procedures. In particular, provision needs to be made for the maintenance of records so that IVF children may eventually enjoy the same rights of access to information about their biological parentage as adopted children. Again, there needs to be provision for the proper regulation of IVF clinics and for appropriate counselling of IVF couples. Even if the sections on embryo experimentation were deleted from the Victorian Infertility Act, some kind of legal control would still be needed for these purposes.

The institution of the Standing Review and Advisory Committee under the Victorian Infertility Act is the clue to the success of the Victorian legislation. The Committee has a broadly based membership (the Act specifies the categories of membership of the Committee—a philosopher, a legal practitioner, a social worker, a person with an interest in community affairs, two representatives of religious bodies and two medical practitioners) and it acts as a kind of mediating agency between community opinion and the scientific world. The majority of members of the Committee are not scientists and they have to inform themselves of the scientific import of the proposals put before the Committee. This has involved frequent meetings with the various groups of medical scientists and practitioners working in the field of infertility and a developing appreciation by the members of the Committee of the attitudes and views of the medical scientists involved. (I must say that I have moved from being mildly suspicious and apprehensive about medical scientists working in this field to being very impressed by their seriousness and sensitivity. There are, of course, some 'cowboys', but they are not typical.) On the other hand the Committee has been able to convey to the medical scientists and practitioners a sense of community attitudes towards their research and has forced them to explain themselves better and in general to improve their 'public relations'. Scientists, alas, usually do not take this aspect of their work seriously enough. As has recently been remarked, apropos embryo experimentation:

> the problem lies with the failure of the scientists to come to grips with the essentially political nature of science, the extent to which political and ethical choices are an integral part of the whole human embryo experimentation debate, not some kind of tacked-on, tiresome, time-wasting issue dredged up by troublemakers keen to strangle progress.[12]

A number of points may be made about the Victorian Committee. First, it is not merely an advisory body but has the power to approve applications to conduct experimental procedures. Although this means that neither the Minister of Health, nor the government, nor Parliament as a whole, can veto the decisions of the Committee, I believe that the Committee's power to approve experiments is necessary, given the difficulty and complexity of the problems in the reproductive field. Whether or not experiments involving, for example, the microinjection of sperm into ova should be allowed or not is hardly the kind of issue that can be usefully debated in a party-political way on the floor of Parliament. Given the difficulties of similar committees in the US, I believe that it is of the greatest importance to avoid politicising the discussion of these issues, although of course they must be subjected to community appraisal and discussion.

Second, the Victorian Committee is not a representative body: in other words, its members do not formally represent groups with interests in the IVF area. There has been a great deal of pressure from certain groups to gain representation on the Committee, but in my view much of its strength comes from the fact that its members do not formally represent the interests of various groups such as IVF couples, feminists, pro-life groups and so on. Once again, the fate of similar committees overseas shows how divisive so-called representativity can be. Those who call for representation usually want their own groups to be represented, but they see no reason why opposing groups should have equal representation.

Third, the main task of the Committee is to interpret a piece of legislation, the Infertility (Medical Procedures) Act 1984. The Committee is not a miniature government enquiry nor a Royal Commission free to range over all the implications of reproductive

technology. Some people have criticised the Committee for allowing experimentation on so-called spare or untransferred embryos
and also on pre-syngamous embryos. But the possibility of embryo
experimentation is clearly allowed by the legislation and the
Committee has simply declared that it is. If some are unhappy with
this then they should seek to amend the legislation. (It is at this level
that political debate is perfectly appropriate.) One would hope,
however, that, before they did this, they would re-read the reports
of the Victorian Waller Committee which investigated all these
matters in 1982–4 and made recommendations accordingly. Those
recommendations were endorsed by the Victorian Parliament, and
presumably by the community at the time, and the present legislation enacted.

Conclusion

Let me sum up, very briefly, some of the main themes that have
been running through these lectures. First, I have been insisting that
the new biotechnology in all its forms presents us with novel and
unprecedented problems for which there are no clear answers. In
my view we must get away from the idea that for every such
problem there is, if only we search long and hard enough, a clearcut solution: all that we have to do is to wheel out the appropriate
ethical principle, 'apply' it to the case in question and read off the
answer. QED! Very often we find ourselves in situations where there
is a genuine moral dilemma, or where we simply don't know what
to say, or where the best we can do is to opt for the lesser of two
evils. The artist Georges Braque once said that in art you do not do
what you want to do but what you *can* do, and the same is true in
the ethical sphere.

In this sphere also we need to have a great deal of moral imagination so that we are willing to contemplate situations which a few
years ago would have seemed utterly bizarre: I am thinking here, for
instance, of the possibilities that have come about through in vitro
fertilisation where the process of conception takes place outside the
mother's body. By this simple fact all kinds of quite novel situations
arise which we find it difficult to face up to or get our minds
around. At the same time we also need to have a healthy sense of
realism and commonsense and not be too impressed by some of the
wilder science fiction scenarios projected by some people—
mechanical wombs, genetically designed 'parahumans', 'neomorts'
or brain-dead people being kept alive artificially and used as incu-
bators. What is really possible and feasible and what is merely
theoretically possible are two very different things. Theoretically we

could, within certain limits, genetically redesign human beings, but that is not a real and feasible possibility and we should not base our bioethical thinking on such extreme scenarios.

Again, we should refuse to be bullied by the so-called 'slippery slope' argument: if you allow X then you take the first step on a slope that will land you in absurdity or in some monstrous conclusion. Thus, it has been argued that if we allow *in vitro* fertilisation then we will end up by completely technologising human procreation and eventually with something like the mechanical womb. However, the answer to this is that if you are on a slippery slope you must take care to secure your footing and not to slip. There is no reason why you cannot welcome *in vitro* fertilisation as a means of alleviating infertility and allowing couples to have children and yet reject the technologising of human procreation. Equally you can welcome gene therapy as a way of avoiding genetic disease and yet reject the eugenic reshaping of human nature. John Stuart Mill once remarked that 'there is no difficulty in proving any ethical standard whatever to work ill if we suppose universal idiocy to be conjoined with it'.[13]

What is remarkable in the field of reproductive technology is the gradual acceptance by the community of developments which were at first thought to be beyond the ethical pale. Artificial insemination by donor was, only a few years ago, thought to be quite unacceptable—a threat to marriage and to parenthood—but it no longer excites any opposition. It is well-known that some lesbian couples have had children through artificial insemination but there have been no calls to ban artificial insemination by donor, as there have been vociferous calls to ban surrogate motherhood. (Here, as elsewhere, we strain at gnats and swallow camels.) Two American observers made the following remarks about artificial insemination over 20 years ago:

> Any change in custom or practice in this emotionally charged area has always elicited a response from established custom and law of horrified negation at first: then negation, without horror; then slow and gradual curiosity, study, evaluation, and finally a very slow but steady acceptance.[14]

I think that one can discern this change from horrified negation to slow and gradual curiosity, study, evaluation and then finally acceptance in many other areas of artificial reproduction.

A second theme that has run through these lectures is a questioning of the curious kind of pessimism about technology in general and biotechnology in particular that comes from groups as diverse as fundamentalist Christians, radical feminists and 'Green' movement activists. I do not believe that technology and biotechnology have their own autonomous momentum that we cannot resist, as though once having got on the technological train we cannot get off. Equally I do not believe that we ought to do everything that technology allows us to do or that there is some kind of 'technological imperative'. But I also do not think that there is some kind of *prima facie* presumption that developments in biotechnology are likely to be dangerous and that we must know and assess all the implications and possible risks of a piece of biotechnology before we go ahead. Again, we are all too well aware of the mixed blessings of the technology that came out of the Industrial Revolution, but I cannot imagine anyone really wishing that industrial technology, with all its immense plusses and all its immense minusses, hadn't happened. The same is true of the new biotechnology: it can be used to help human beings to become more really human, and it can also be used to technologise and dehumanise central areas of human life such as birth and death. But surely no one can really wish that the biotechnological revolution hadn't occurred. As we know, human sexuality is deeply ambivalent in that it has enormous possibilities both for human creativity and human destructiveness. As Freud put it, human sexuality is caught between love (*eros*) and death (*thanatos*). But that is, I hope, no argument against sexuality.

My third theme connects with the second: that we are not powerless before the possibilities opened up by the new biotechnology and that we can control it and, as best we can, make it serve human purposes. Legislation is certainly needed: however, in a liberal democratic and pluralist society the role of state control through legislation is severely limited, and the part of other agencies and community groups is correspondingly important. The present debate in Australia and other countries between fundamentalist and other Christians, feminists, bioethicists, bioscientists, Green activists, law reform commissions, pro-life groups, is not something to be regretted; on the contrary, it is to be welcomed. We need as many groups in the community as possible keeping watch on developments in biotechnology, raising questions, initiating discussion, issuing reports. The community as a whole needs to educate itself so that it can deal in a positive way with the possibilities disclosed by the new biotechnology. In a very real sense, as I said before, we must all become bioethicists! In particular the media has a central function here, avoiding sensationalism and what I call the science fiction approach and trying to promote a genuine and responsible public debate on what are really matters of life and death. In my opinion that debate is of the greatest importance and my hope is that these six lectures may have contributed to it.

1 On Liberty and Considerations on Representative Government, ed. RB McCallum, Blackwell, Oxford, 1946, pp8–9
2 See Genevieve Delaisi de Parseval and Anne Fagot, 'The Status of Artificially Procreated Children: International Disparities', Bioethics, Vol. 2, no. 2, 1988, pp136–50
3 JS Mill, On Liberty, pp8–9
4 Richard A McCormick, How Brave a New World? Dilemmas in Bioethics, Doubleday, New York, 1981, p185
5 Mario Cuomo, 'Religious Belief and Public Morality: A Catholic Governor's Perspective', in Patricia B Jung and Thomas A Shannon (eds), Abortion and Catholicism, Crossroad, New York, 1988, p212
6 Creating Children: A Uniform Approach to the Law and Practice of Reproductive Technologies in Australia, Family Law Council, AGPS, Canberra, 1985
7 Bernard M Dickens, 'Legislating for The Brave New Children', in Barbara Landau (ed.), Children's Rights in the Practice of Family Law, Carswell, Toronto, 1986, pp364–5
8 W John Moore, 'Genes for sale', National Journal, 21 June 1986, pp1538–32
9 National Health and Medical Research Council, Ethical Aspects of Research on Human Gene Therapy, 1987
10 Genetic Manipulation, Law Reform Commission of Victoria, 1988, para 85
11 On the work of the Committee see Louis Waller, The Law and Infertility, CJ La Trobe Memorial Lecture, La Trobe University, 1988
12 Rosaleen Love, 'Promises, promises', Australian Society, July 1989, p15
13 John Stuart Mill, Utilitarianism, ed. M Warnock, 1962, p221
14 SJ Kleigman and SA Kaufman, Infertility in Women, FA Davis Co, Philadelphia, 1966, p178. See also Bernard M Dickens, 'Legislating for the Brave New Children', in Barbara Landau (ed.), Children's Rights in the Practice of Family Law, Carswell, Toronto, 1986, pp345–65

EVENTS 1990 – 2000

1990

MAY   South African President PW de Klerk and Nelson Mandela
           held amicable talks about the country's future
JULY   Kerry Packer regained control of the Nine Network from
           Bond Corporation
OCTOBER   East and West Germany reunited on 3 October
NOVEMBER   Mary Robinson became first woman President of Ireland
           Margaret Thatcher replaced as Prime Minister by John Major
DECEMBER   Fairfax publishing group collapsed with debts of $1.5 billion
           Patrick White died
           Dame Joan Sutherland retired

1991

FEBRUARY   Gulf War liberated Kuwait from Iraqi occupation
MAY   Indian Prime Minister Rajiv Gandhi assassinated
AUGUST   Revolutionary week in Russia saw the final downfall of Mikhail
           Gorbachev with Boris Yeltsin in full command, and the end of
           control by the official Communist Party
DECEMBER   Bob Hawke replaced as Prime Minister by Paul Keating
           Soviet Union officially ended
           Manning Clark died

1992

MARCH   Sarajevo bombarded after majority voted for independence of
           Bosnia and Herzegovina as the Yugoslav Federation continued
           to fall apart
MAY   Alan Bond sentenced to 4 years' jail
JUNE   Brett Whitely died
AUGUST   Barcelona Olympic Games opened
OCTOBER   Canadians voted overwhelmingly against granting autonomy to
           Quebec
NOVEMBER   Bill Clinton elected US President
DECEMBER   Sir Sidney Nolan died

1993

JANUARY   Audrey Hepburn died

MARCH	Labor Government returned at general election with Paul Keating as Prime Minister
SEPTEMBER	Sydney won right to present Olympic Games in 2000
DECEMBER	Native Title Act passed in Federal Parliament
	South African Parliament voted itself out of existence, clearing the way for an all-race election

1994

APRIL	Nelson Mandela elected President of South Africa
	Anarchy and genocide in Rwanda
	Richard Nixon died
	Jacqueline Kennedy Onassis died
MAY	Channel Tunnel opened
DECEMBER	Russia attacked Chechnya

1995

APRIL	Russia captured Groznyy, capital of Chechnya
SEPTEMBER	French nuclear tests at Mururoa
NOVEMBER	Israeli Prime Minister Yitzhak Rabin assassinated
	Bosnian war over

1996

FEBRUARY	Prince and Princess of Wales' divorce announced
MARCH	Liberal–National Party Coalition Government elected with John Howard as Prime Minister
MAY	Port Arthur massacre
	Likud Alliance elected to government in Israel with Benjamin Netanyahu as Prime Minister
JULY	Atlanta Olympic Games opened
OCTOBER	Nobel Peace Prize shared by East Timorese Bishop Carlos Belo and Jose Ramos-Horta
NOVEMBER	Bill Clinton elected for second term as President of the USA

1997

FEBRUARY	Deng Xiaoping, paramount leader of the Chinese people died
MARCH	Geoffrey Rush wins Best Actor Oscar for *Shine*
MAY	British Labour Party won general election, Tony Blair becoming Prime Minister

JUNE	Britain leaves Hong Kong
JULY	Landslide at Thredbo village
AUGUST	Diana, Princess of Wales died
SEPTEMBER	Mother Teresa died
	Asian financial crisis
OCTOBER	Cheryl Kernot defected to Labor Party
NOVEMBER	Michael Hutchence died
DECEMBER	Kofi Annan succeeded Boutros Boutros-Ghali as Secretary-General of the United Nations

1998

FEBRUARY	Constitution Convention recommended that a referendum question be put to the people for the establishment of a republic and the appointment of a president
MAY	Indonesian President Suharto resigned to be succeeded by Dr J Habibie
	Frank Sinatra died
JULY	Wik Native Title Bill passed
OCTOBER	Liberal–National Coalition Government returned at general election
	Australian Stock Exchange demutualised and became a company listed on its own sharemarket
	Australia Women's Hockey Team won their second World Cup

1999

FEBRUARY	Blair Government in Britain reformed House of Lords by removing automatic right of hereditary peers to sit
	Impeachment trial of US President Clinton, who was acquitted of perjury and obstruction of justice
	King Hussein of Jordan died
MARCH	Yehudi Menuhin died
	Six members of IOC expelled over their involvement in Salt Lake City corruption
	All 20 members of the European Commission resigned amid charges of incompetence
APRIL	NATO began bombing campaign in Kosovo
	Arthur Boyd died
MAY	First members of the Scottish Parliament sworn in

	Mahendra Chaudhry became first Indian leader of Fiji
JUNE	Israeli Prime Minister Netanyahu quit following a landslide win by Labor's Ehud Barak
JULY	Legislation for Goods and Services Tax passed to become effective on 1 July 2000
	Bill Skate resigned as Prime Minister of Papua New Guinea after corruption accusation
	King Hassan of Morocco died
AUGUST	Federal Parliament passed a motion declaring 'deep and sincere regret' for past injustices to Aborigines
SEPTEMBER	Australian troops entered East Timor as the major part of a UN peace-keeping force, led by Australia
OCTOBER	People's Republic of China celebrated 50th anniversary
	World population reached 6 billion
	Australia's population reached 19 million
	Abdurrahman Wahid became first democratically elected President of Indonesia with Megawati Sukarnoputri as Vice President
	Morris West died
	Albert Tucker died
NOVEMBER	Referendum to establish the Commonwealth of Australia as a republic defeated in all states
DECEMBER	Malaysian Prime Minister Mahathir re-elected
	Helen Clark became Prime Minister of New Zealand, defeating incumbent Jenny Shipley

2000

MAY	Vladimir Putin elected President of Russia
	Mahendra Chaudhry overthrown as Prime Minister of India
	High world oil prices led to protests from motorists and truckers around the world
JULY	Goods and Services Tax and income tax cuts introduced
SEPTEMBER	Sydney Olympic Games opened
OCTOBER	Sydney Paralympics opened
	South Korean President Kim Dei-jung awarded Nobel Peace Prize
NOVEMBER	US Presidential election hung in the balance for over a month resulting in the election of George W Bush

Notable deaths in 2000 were:

Charles Perkins

Pierre Trudeau, former Canadian Prime Minister

Sirimavo Bandaranaike, former Sri Lankan Prime Minister and world's first female prime minister

Judith Wright

A D Hope

John Perceval

Tom Fitzgerald

Tom Fitzgerald was born in 1918 and educated in economics at the University of Sydney.

He began his career in the Federal Treasury and served in the RAAF during World War II. He became a journalist after the war, first editing *Wild Cat Monthly* and then moving to the *Sydney Morning Herald* where he was the paper's finance editor from 1952 to 1970.

In 1958, with George Munster, he founded *Nation*, 'an independent journal of opinion', published each fortnight and examining emerging social and cultural issues. *Nation* merged with *Sunday Review* in 1972 to become *Nation Review*.

Fitzgerald moved to Canberra to the secretariat of the Senate Committee on Securities and Exchange. In 1974 he released his provocative report into the mining industry concluding that there was massive tax avoidance on the part of major mining companies despite government subsidies. He also served as a member of the Royal Commission into Australian Government Administration. He next became an economic adviser to the Wran Labor Government in New South Wales.

In retirement Tom Fitzgerald was a book reviewer for leading newspapers.

He died in 1993.

Fitzgerald gave his Boyer Lectures the title *Between Life and Economics* because he was concerned that economics has profound but barely understood effects on everybody's life. He believed 'the public has a right to expect and demand nimbleness and adaptability from its policy makers.' Writing in the midst of recession and some extraordinary media corporation collapses and restructures which must have amazed him, Fitzgerald produced six lively essays: 'Early Perspectives on Life'; 'Economics, Broad and Narrow'; 'Japan in Fact and in Theory' (how surprised he would have been by that country's current circumstances); 'Capital Disaster';

'Canberra's Manufacturing Capacity' and 'No Dialectic', which is his summary and is reproduced here. Through them all runs his passionate dissent from the whole prevailing climate of economic opinion.

NO DIALECTIC

Between Life and Economics

Tom Fitzgerald

• 1990 •

Members of the first generation of the Canberra Press Gallery still have no doubt—for some of them remain hale and hearty—as to what was the most impressive moment in the history of the House of Representatives. They say it was on a May afternoon in 1942 when the Prime Minister, John Curtin, told the House that a big naval battle had begun in the Coral Sea. A Japanese fleet proceeding towards Port Moresby was being engaged by American and Australian vessels and aircraft. When the message from General Douglas MacArthur was handed to him in the House, John Curtin stood up and spoke spontaneously. To a reader of Hansard now, the brief and simple words, expressing everyone's indebtedness to the Allied sailors and airmen and hopes for their well-being, are not remarkable, nor meant to be remarkable. It was Curtin's presence, the aura about him, a vibrancy conveyed with calmness, that moved even the least friendly of the journalists to write in the *Sydney Morning Herald* that this was Curtin's greatest speech, a 'dynamic and imperishable moment'.

On the other side of the coin, the passage in Hansard that sticks most in my mind from leafing through old volumes is one that neither the journalists nor the members of the House found worthy of report or comment. This also was an impromptu affair, late in an October night in 1927, soon after the Parliament had been moved to the former sheep station in Canberra. There were lots of workmen around the place engaged in road laying and landscaping and general jobs that went by the name of earthworks. A member from South Australia told the House how he had been scandalised from watching the labourers. Some of them were going too slow. Not all; some of them only speeded up when the overseers came by. Having watched many gangs in South Australia, he said, 'I have been amazed and astounded at the sort of thing I have seen going on here'. Shortly afterwards Frank Anstey, the Labor member for an inner Melbourne seat, was allowed five minutes before the House rose. He touched on several matters that had been raised that evening. On the subject of the labourers, he did not pick up the line of comedy that was offering. He conceded that some of the labourers seemed to be slow, and said he didn't think he would go any faster if he were out there with them. Then he added:

> If I had the chance of doing their work for the remuneration I secure as a member of Parliament, or of fulfilling the exacting and tiring job of a member of Parliament for the little remuneration that these men receive, I should say 'Give me the workman's wages and my present position, and give them the one thousand pounds a year.'

This strange, subversive moment of reality in the House evidently sprang from long-held feelings. Anstey contrasted the hard physical work he had been required to do for many years with what he called the 'indolent life' of a member of Parliament, and he showed total recall of a passage he had read somewhere in Mark Twain:

> Looking back after the lapse of years, Mark Twain remarked, 'I have done all sorts of intellectual work, but I am prepared to do the most arduous intellectual work for a small reward, because I know that when I am tired of it, I can always take up the pick and shovel for recreation.'

Radical though he was, Anstey had no program of change to offer. A lifelong enemy of cant was just clearing the air. He thanked Providence that he had moved from the one kind of work to the other, and suggested that other members of Parliament might do something similar.

Long before Frank Anstey spoke those words, his young friend and protégé John Curtin had acknowledged that even his taking a position as a trade union official as the first step in a personal career was a separation from the working class. From that moment, the young man said, you begin 'receiving more than you justly earn'. He, too, could only express a sense of inner conflict without being able to propose a resolution of it. The important thing is that neither Curtin nor Anstey suppressed or denied the responsibility that their privileges entailed.

It seems to me that the human awareness of these men is an aspect of the same intelligence that made them outstanding representatives of a Labor tradition of hard, independent thinking on economic subjects and most particularly a tradition of distinguishing the interests and demands of the financial sector from considerations of the welfare of the whole economy. They were always alive to the potentiality for conflict between the two. From about the age of 30, John Curtin pursued his own line of study in economics, independently of Anstey. He attended university courses in the subject and kept abreast of some advanced professional writing. But he never wavered from the older man's first precept that money must be made the servant, instead of master, of the people and industrial life. Anstey had known the consequences of the bank crashes of 1893; both men saw bankers overrule the elected Labor government in the 1930 Depression in a manner that was to be condemned by a subsequent Royal Commission.

On his appointment in 1917 as editor of a Labor newspaper in Perth, John Curtin accepted a responsibility to be aware of current economic thinking. He read, or at least examined, each of the books that Keynes wrote in 1919, 1921, 1923 and 1930, as well as numerous articles. He read some writings of another Cambridge economist, AC Pigou, among others. He made comments on or references to all of these. He had discussions with several Australian professors of economics: Edward Shann, Douglas Copland and Lyndhurst Giblin. He engaged Giblin in debate in print. At the beginning of a pamphlet he wrote in the Depression of 1930, when Australia had a large public-sector debt, Curtin indicated an under-standing of the inherent difficulties in economic analysis. A passage such as the following has a topical air, and one might wish that the intelligence it expresses was available now:

> The cross currents in the reactions emerging from what has happened make it almost impossible to present the case in the proper sequence of cause and effect. Far back in the hills there is little difference observable between what ultimately becomes a great river and what merely serves as a minor tributary to it. But for the number of lesser streams feeding it, however, the river itself might not have become of any great historic or national importance. So it is with the study of Australia's economic problem. What appear to be minor elements are so mixed with those that are admittedly major in significance, that the only safe thing to do is to consider them whenever and wherever they present themselves.
>
> We are a debtor country . . .

When Curtin came to office, therefore, he had wrestled with the economic complexities to arrive at his own position, founded on principles that would not be quickly engulfed or swept away by advisers in Treasury or anywhere else. Professor Giblin later acknowledged that this was the case, from his experience as a senior economic adviser to the Curtin government. He recalled a remark that the Prime Minister made to him one day: 'I have attended the funeral of so many economic theories . . .' Giblin had the grace to add the comment: 'It must be admitted that the advice of economists has always been apt to neglect John Locke's warning against believing anything more strongly than the evidence warrants.'

Curtin, along with Anstey and EG Theodore, had, since the time of World War I, called for the establishment of a real central bank with control over the money supply. The absence of such a body left the economy exposed to a mixture of forces and decisions which they summed up, with differing connotations, as the 'money power'. On Curtin's first meeting and conversation with the governor of the Commonwealth Bank in 1941, while he was Leader of the Opposition, he formed a judgement that the governor's attitude to national economic issues was, even in wartime, dominated by the interests of the banks, and he spoke out sharply to that effect. His government's banking bills of 1945 were intended as a lasting protection against the dangers. Control over the money supply was entrusted to a central bank that would be subject to the elected government.

If anyone today chooses to dismiss a suggestion that a considerable part of our economic sovereignty has passed to a new, farcical version of the money power, let such a person explain how the government would be able tomorrow morning to reduce the exchange rate and interest rates for the purpose of correcting the fundamental structural imbalance between the traceable and non-traceable sectors of the economy. It is a nice question as to how much the Treasury's disinclination to address that imbalance in public, and its retreat into aggregate savings and investment figures, is due to a perception that a necessary correction cannot be executed, and how much to an inability, based on unwillingness, to recognise the existence of the imbalance.

Drawing together some of the main threads of the analysis of the two previous talks: the dash for financial deregulation got off on the wrong foot from the start because deliberate Treasury policy had already, at the beginning of the 1980s, put Australia into a condition of heavy deficit in the current balance of payments along with the unprecedented habit of resorting to high interest rates to induce short-term foreign money into the system to cover the deficits. The abandonment of such controls over the domestic money supply that had existed, leaving the conduct of monetary policy solely to interest rates, not as a check on the supply but an attempted restraint on the demand for money, was compounded when the deregulation was extended to the foreign exchange markets late in 1983, not only by floating the Australian dollar but also by removing all controls on capital flows in and out. The new reciprocating mechanism of very high interest rates (compounding rapidly to swell the overseas debt) and corresponding high exchange rates has worked consistently to put the trading sector of the economy in fundamentally disadvantaged imbalance. High interest rates have not been the only factor making for the high and volatile exchange rate; it appears that the very short term commitment of most of the foreign-owned deposits encourages speculative play with our dollar in disregard of the underlying payments problem. But the high interest rates have been the essential underpinning for the overvalued dollar. The cumulative damage has by now become severe in the usually resilient rural industries. The more precarious manufacturing sector, already weakened by previous misfortunes and now suffering from the general structural imbalance, somehow remains a target for special hostility in Canberra, and the flame of enterprise in manufacturing appears to be at its lowest in 50 years.

Financial deregulation has been considered only in its macro-economic effects in these talks, leaving aside its other consequences in the financial and property markets. Those macro-economic effects, given the initial starting circumstances, have been disastrous.

One of the most fortunately endowed nations on earth for its natural resources has recently been pronounced by its federal Treasurer as 'a poor country'. After all his years of declaring the sovereignty of market forces, the Treasurer has felt obliged to appeal to industrialists to commit money for capital expenditures in disregard of the hostile realities of the foreign exchange market for them. As citizens of the world, we have reduced the proportion of our national product going to overseas aid by about 40 per cent in the last five years, while the net income deficit in our balance of payments, mostly interest payments at exorbitant rates, has risen in that period from $6.5 billion to $15.8 billion a year. There is more than a whiff of mental bankruptcy in the air.

In the necessary dialectic over issues of policy in changing economic circumstances, it had been the Labor Party's traditional function to maintain a vigilant eye in the interests of preserving the nation's financial independence. By suddenly lunging in the direction of the opposite camp, and capping this with the elimination of dissent even within the public service, this government has abolished the normal avenues for a dialectic in a period when a long succession of its predictions have been unfulfilled.

So it is that these Boyer talks have been mostly devoted to expressing dissent from a whole climate of economic opinion: from what I suspect is a consensus view only among members of an extremely vocal and therefore influential, but essentially narrow, group. The new orthodoxy is of very recent and sudden origin, and waves of new orthodoxy in economics sometimes prove to be short-lived. Public opinion could blow this one out like a candle.

The purpose of the talks has been descriptive: to explain what I believe is the case. That must always precede any proposals for action, however urgent may be the need for change. It is doubly necessary now to seek as wide a recognition of the present state of affairs as possible, because the required changes will be of a technical nature in their implementation, and these affairs remain predominantly in the hands of a relatively small band of technicians who, however well intentioned they were, have heavily miscalculated. This is the kind of situation in which, on some past occasions, the Labor Party played the indispensable role of challenging the pretensions of financiers to possess arcane knowledge that transcended ordinary public perceptions. We have been compelled to recognise something that earlier Labor leaders might have regarded as inconceivable: given the quirks of personality, it is possible for a Labor Party in office to be far less effective in preserving common-sense economic principles than it would have been if it had remained as a challenging Opposition.

The practical task facing us is plain enough. We must regain a decent measure of control over our exchange rate and our money supply; and, on a parallel path, we need to bring to our industrial policy a true understanding of circumstances in the manufacturing sector, recognising its peculiar character among the trading industries. The undertaking on the financial front is much more intricate than the industrial one. They should complement each other in working towards a re-establishment of economic sovereignty, after years when misguided approaches on both fronts have colluded in the heavy diminution of sovereignty.

On the details of implementation, the greatest complication to be addressed is the enormous build-up of flighty, short-term foreign money in our financial system that the present government has permitted under highly paid advice. So it has to be addressed, not dismissed in a single word, *irreversible*, that the new Reserve Bank governor drops from time to time, or with the tale about the genie that could not be put back in the bottle, which his successor as head of Treasury favours; each of them appears to draw personal satisfaction from these oracular pronouncements. What the country needs is that some people who recognise the necessity for change should be given entrée inside the portals. There is no single messiah inside or outside to provide pat solutions; the various possible options have to be submitted to cooperative discussion and development. The options range from moves to restore an equivalent of the former regulatory system, perhaps with a revival of techniques such as the old variable deposit ratios to be applied to overseas funds in some circumstances, and on to questions of a possible linking of our dollar to another currency or currencies. My inquiries do not indicate that the present position is irreversible. In fact, defeatism is no more of an available alternative than the procrastination in facing realities has been a solution in the past seven years. From the present condition of bankruptcy, a well considered change of policies cannot fail to produce some improvement.

Since manufacturing generally calls for higher organisational skills and a stronger spirit of sustained enterprise and adaptation than other business activity, it needs to attract some of our best brains and to have the close understanding of persons of comparable quality in government, as has long been the case in Japan. After the first requirement of a corrected structural balance, especially in the exchange rate, for the traded-goods sector, it is likely that incentives on a phased and conditional basis, as in depreciation allowances, will sometimes prove to be of net public benefit. Above all, this is an area requiring a change of mind and tone in government. And, subject to your judgment, I think it would be splendid if the force of public opinion helped bring about changes of that kind in both the financial and the industrial fields.

Economics drove out the wider universe from most of these talks, as it usually does when it gets a foot in. Until a quite late stage of the preparation, I had hoped that some word indicating a reconsideration of official policy would allow a contraction of the economic argument and a return to more exciting things in life. It was not to be. Even so, we have been able to recall the qualities of some great human beings in our past, and perhaps to draw encouragement from that. Meanwhile, the embryos of the barnacles have been pressing on as efficiently as ever, and our daunting descendants of one or two billion years hence remain where we tried to pay our respects at the beginning. Anything more that might have been said would have made no difference at all.

John Curtin's announcement of the Coral Sea naval engagement, timed by the Hansard reporters as taking one minute, is in the Commonwealth Parliamentary Debates, volume 170, pages 1060-61. Ross Gollan reported in the *Sydney Morning Herald*, 11 May 1942, that no more than a third of members were present in the House of Representatives when the Prime Minister spoke. 'The words . . . were redoubled by that indefinable projection of personal sincerity which, on subjects that stir him greatly, gives Mr Curtin a grip over actual audiences that can never quite be conveyed to those who hear only his broadcasts or read reports of what he has said. No one who participated in the few minutes in which Mr Curtin was addressing the House failed to come out of them a better Australian.' Curtin had not magnified the importance of the naval engagement. He said, 'This battle will not decide the war; it will determine the immediate tactics which will be pursued by the Allied forces and by the common enemy.

Frank Anstey's remarks about the slow labourers in Canberra are in CPD volume 116 (26 October 1927), pages 768–69. Among Frank Anstey's early appeals to the Fisher Labor Government to establish a full central bank was an article, 'Today, Today's the Time', published in several Labor papers, including *The Timber Worker*, Melbourne, edited by John Curtin, in its issue of 12 December 1914.

The quotation of John Curtin in 1930 is taken from page 5 of his pamphlet, *Australia's Economic Crisis and the £55,000,000 Interest Bill*, published in October of that year.

Professor LF Giblin's recollection of Curtin as Prime Minister is from his book, *The Growth of a Central Bank*, Melbourne University Press, 1951, page 298.

Fay Gale

An outstanding educator and tertiary education administrator, Fay Gale was born in 1932 and was educated at the University of Adelaide.

Initially a geography mistress at Walford Church of England Girls' School, she undertook postgraduate studies and held a postdoctorate fellowship at the University of Adelaide in 1965. She was lecturer in geography there from 1966 to 1971, senior lecturer from 1972 to 1974, and reader from 1975 to 1977, before taking the chair in 1978, the first woman to become a professor of geography in Australia. She became Emeritus Professor in 1989 and in 1988–89 she was pro-vice chancellor of the university.

From 1990 until her retirement in 1997, Professor Gale was vice-chancellor of the University of Western Australia, only the second female vice-chancellor in Australia. She was president of the Australian vice-chancellors' committee in 1996–97.

Professor Gale has held a number of visiting professorships and lectureships at universities and colleges in England and America. She has also been the president of the Academy of the Social Sciences in Australia and vice president of the Association of Asian Social Science Research Councils. As well she has been a member of the National Committee of UNESCO and of the council of the Australian Research Council. She has been a member of the Prime Minister's Science and Engineering Council, chair of the Social Justice Advisory Council, commissioner of the Australian Heritage Commission from 1989 to 1995, president of the Institute of Australian Geographers 1989–90, and a member of the Australian Institute for Aboriginal and Torres Strait Islander Studies since 1964.

Professor Gale has published widely. She was made an Officer of the Order of Australia in 1989.

Changing Australia was the 1991 Boyer Lecture title shared by Fay Gale and Ian Lowe. Professor Gale's titles were 'Change in Universities—

396 • THE BOYER COLLECTION

Evolution or Revolution'; 'Equity—It is a Cover for Uniformity', which is reproduced here, and 'Technology-driven Education'. At the conclusion of her first lecture to illustrate the tension and dilemma she discerns, Fay Gale quotes from *The Rocks* by TS Eliot:

Where is the Wisdom we have lost in Knowledge?

Where is the Knowledge we have lost in Information

Ian Lowe

Ian Lowe's career has been devoted to science and technology policy, and to environmental and population issues. He was born in 1942 and educated at Bowral High School, the University of New South Wales and the University of York. His teaching career began in 1971 with the Open University in the United Kingdom; he was ultimately sub dean of the Faculty of Technology from 1978 to 1980.

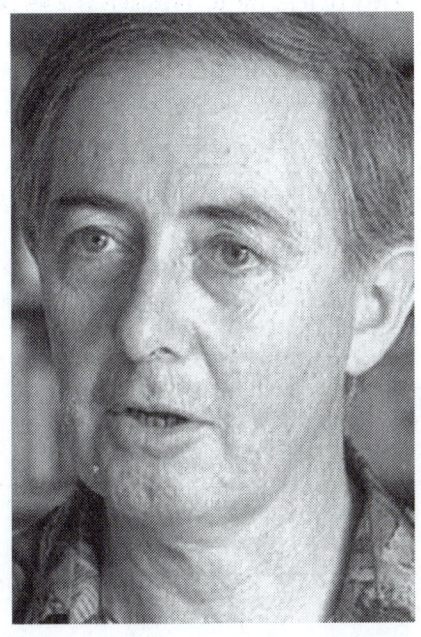

Professor Lowe returned to Australia to take up the appointment of director of the Science Policy Research Centre at Griffith University in 1980. He was Associate Professor of Science, Technology and Society from 1985 to 1994 and head of the School of Science in 1994–95. He has been honorary Professor of Science, Technology and Society since 1994.

From 1983 to 1989 Professor Lowe was a member of Australia's National Energy Research, Development and Demonstration Council and chaired the Council's standing committee on social, economic and environmental issues. He chaired the Commonwealth State of the Environment Advisory Council, which produced the first independent national report on the environment in 1996, and, from 1994 to 1996, he chaired the Queensland Health Promotion Council. From 1994 to 1998 he was on the National Greenhouse Advisory Panel and a member of the Bureau of Immigration and Population Advisory Committee 1994–95. He was a member of the Administrative Review Council from 1995 to 1998.

Since 1997 Professor Lowe has been a member of the board of the National Science and Technology Council.

As well as his extensive academic publications, he writes regularly for the *New Scientist*.

Changing Australia was the 1991 Boyer Lecture title which Ian Lowe shared with Fay Gale. Ian Lowe's three lectures were titled 'The Search for the Engine of Change'; 'Who's Paying the Driver?', which is reproduced here, and 'Change and our Future'. He pugnaciously poses a series of questions in his first lecture: 'So who is to blame for the stunning mediocrity of television, its image as a sort of chewing gum for the mind: John Logie Baird? The media barons? The government? Advertising agencies? I could ask the same sort of questions about the car, who is to blame for its negative effects on our society?' He is interested in the forces driving technological change, and the problems in the wake of its benefits.

EQUITY—IS IT A COVER FOR UNIFORMITY?

Changing Australia

Fay Gale and Ian Lowe

• 1991 •

Fay Gale

Equity has become a major platform in the reorganisation of higher education in Australia. Every university is now expected to have an equity program which forms part of its annual profile submission to the Department of Employment, Education and Training (DEET), and indeed one which appears to assume equal importance with its research program. Since the allocation of student places and ultimately of federal funds is based on this profile submission, equity management, and with it research management, is seen as the centre stage on which both the reform of the older universities and the transformation of the former colleges into universities are being engineered.

I would like to question the position of equity in this program. It is not that I am opposed to equity nor to the focus of it as a central feature of a university. On the contrary I have been a very active supporter of equal opportunity in a number of areas. It is not that I oppose the opportunity for Aboriginal people to come to university, or for women to be given an equal chance to enter higher education and gain university positions, or for people from rural areas to be encouraged to see a university education as something worthwhile and accessible to them.

Education may have the effect of enhancing people's social and economic opportunities, but a university education is really about broadening minds, extending knowledge, to enable participants to see and experience new horizons. It is fundamentally about providing people with equal chances to participate, but based on intellectual quality. A university is not about equal access for all—it is about equal access for all who are intellectually qualified—irrespective of gender, ethnicity or age. Thus my objection is not to the concept of 'equal opportunity' or its significant role in universities but rather to the political use being made of the concept of equity. Equity is a misnomer for what is currently being proposed and promoted in higher education. Equity does not seem to be, in this present form, about equal opportunity; rather it seems to be another lever for managing what takes place in universities. It is this apparent misuse of equity principles that concerns me.

In my first lecture I talked about the need for freedom: the importance of the freedom of the mind in developing new ideas, in going to the edges of knowledge. That knowledge is not something which can be controlled, managed, ordered into straight lines, and determined by so-called national priorities. Knowledge comes from the freedom of the creative person; from the breaking of the bonds of control and management; from experimentation, albeit sometimes ending in failure. Similarly, equity will not come from managed programs—from controls, and from centrally determined numerical targets.

I said in the first lecture that my opposition to many of the changes in higher education was not because I was completely satisfied with the status quo and saw no need for change. There are in fact several areas in which both traditional universities and the former colleges had become stultified and which needed to be changed. It is the 'revolutionary' and highly controlled manner of the change and therefore its destructive down side that I protest about. Similarly, it is not the concept of equity itself but the way it is being managed that concerns me. If we do not ask the right questions, we cannot possibly get the right answers and in the equity issue certainly it is the wrong questions that have been asked. The question put is not 'Why are there so few women in education?', or 'Why are there relatively so few Aboriginal people there?'. These in my view should be the questions, but those asked are questions like 'Why are people kept out?', 'Why are the entry requirements not comparable from one institution to another?'!

One result of this inability to frame the right questions is that under the guise of equity, the binary divide has been removed and all higher education institutions are now called universities. I have no complaint about that. The name is of little significance. The complaint I have is that in the pretence of equity, all are now treated as if they *are* the same. The so-called unified national system has been a great push to uniformity and equity has been misinterpreted in this process. Equity is not uniformity. Equity is about equal opportunity. But in this new guise—really uniformity—all universities (and all institutions of higher education *are* now universities) must have the same equity program—must take in a proportion of 'this group' or 'that group' and must follow the same kinds of strategies to do so. This is uniformity. This is not equal opportunity.

The process therefore has led not to an 'equalling up' but to a 'levelling down'. Australia as a nation has protested against apartheid, against the processes of separate opportunities, but the move to uniformity has given only a second-rate opportunity to many people who deserve a first-rate opportunity. It is not equity to run down and impoverish the traditional universities. We hear a great deal about 'levelling the playing field' in the name of equity, but that is the very process of levelling down. Australia cannot afford to do this. Australia is a very diverse country socially, culturally and physically. To cater for those differences we need diversity not uniformity. I see a real danger that the current equity programs are being misdirected to achieve uniformity. The policy of levelling the playing field or, as one public servant in education recently said, 'spreading the manure evenly' is not tackling the heart of the problem.

For women the earlier barriers to entry have now been pushed on to other levels. Equity which is allowed to operate if only intellectual qualities are counted is evident now at university entry level. But for women this newly won equality quickly vanishes at the senior levels.

The problem in essence is that white Anglo-Saxon males predominate in senior education positions on the whole in Australia more than any other group of people. This is not because they are brighter, but because of the differential opportunities given as they proceed in establishing their careers. Equity should be about equal opportunity to ensure that educational opportunity in academic teaching, research and administrative positions reflects intellectual ability not Anglo-Saxon masculinity.

Student intakes have changed over the years and where social barriers have been removed those admissions reflect actual ability more so now than at any previous time in our history. For example, where there are tight entry requirements such as experienced in the older universities, women achieve entry as frequently as men. Therefore in medical schools and law faculties for which entry requirements are often very rigorous, there is now a student body made up of roughly 50 per cent males and 50 per cent females.

A recent British study (1988) by Dr Isobel Allen, *Any Room at the Top*, showed the disparity between the numbers of women entering medical courses and the number in prestigious posts available to them as graduates in medicine. In Britain (and the study would apply elsewhere) women make up some 50 per cent of students graduating from medical school but only 1 per cent of consultant general surgeons. Why the fall-off? What are the blockages? What are the missed opportunities? This disparity is seen in almost every field of academia. Whilst women make up close to 50 per cent of those entering all of the competitive areas in university education, they make up only 5 per cent of professors, for example, in traditional Australian universities. These great proportional differences scarcely point to equal opportunity. In 1977 I made a study of academic women in Australian universities. At that time women accounted for 2.4 per cent of all academic staff at the level of professor, associate professor and reader. By 1987 when I repeated the study of the same universities I found that the proportion of women in the senior academic positions had doubled. That sounds good but doubling meant only rising to just over 5 per cent of senior positions and that over a decade of great political activity in affirmative action.

We need therefore to ask what the real questions are. 'Spreading the manure evenly' may present a graphic illustration of the government's commitment to equity in higher education but it will not address the discrimination which women face for a large number of social reasons. The disadvantages which women face in reaching senior positions in academia are largely structural and reflect the underpinning attitudes of Australian society. The problems belong to a much broader field than those which can be simply answered by equity management within universities. Thus the pressure being put on universities to develop equity management plans is wrongly based on the assumption that management and special planning can answer the problems of society. We do not need to have an affirmative action policy to allow women to enter university. Where ability is the sole criterion women are not disadvantaged. But we do need to have an anti-discrimination policy to enable women to go on beyond the student stage. The discrimination which women face is not conscious—in most cases it is accidental, part of the structure of our culture. It is about 'old boys' networks: 'it is not what you know, it is who you know'.

Our society is finding it very difficult to make the kind of major adjustments that are really necessary for change in the status of women. One of the reasons advanced by Dr Allen, in the study referred to, for women dropping out or being poorly represented in senior levels of the medical profession is that by the time women have completed their training and their hospital registration years they are about 27 or 28 years of age. This is the time of life when women realise that they cannot delay much longer their family role if they wish to take part in the reproduction of the human race. Thus, it is not a time at which most women can afford, in social or biological terms, to go into a job with long hours of hard work, said to be anything up to 90 hours a week for trainee surgeons, or to be prepared to take jobs anywhere in the country—in other words, to undergo the kind of training that is required to become a surgeon, since these are the very years of their lives when family responsibilities begin to take over. Quite different attitudes to their dilemma would be necessary to enable them to succeed in such careers.

Work published by Sylvia Kirov of the University of Tasmania (Kirov 1991) echoes the British study of Isobel Allen I referred to earlier. To explain the question 'Why are so few women reaching the higher levels in medical academia and research?' she finds the same child-bearing, long training, long hours at work and lack of flexibility in the workplace were all factors in holding women back. When searching for solutions—in career structures, in societal and institutional changes—it is really to attitude change that the author points.

This same kind of structural discrimination holds women back in almost every area of Australian society. The time out they must take from the career market if they wish to have children is simply not recognised in most professional or promotional areas.

In the academic world, for example, promotion comes largely by research publication and there are various ways in which this is defined. One is publication in refereed international journals, but quite often access to those journals is a result of being part of a network. That social network comes from the ability to travel frequently, attend conferences, take positions overseas—in other words from great mobility. Whilst men assume that wives will follow them around the world in pursuit of their careers, women do not make the same assumptions of their husbands, and very few husbands are prepared to take on such mobility and sacrifice of career for the sake of their wives. There is a clear discrimination against women's career developments.

In academia, promotion also results for people who have had a variety of experiences in many different areas. Again, the limited mobility facing most women is a disadvantage to them. The time out needed by women to care for young children works only to their disadvantage. I doubt if I have ever been on an appointment or promotion committee where I have heard the fact mentioned that a woman has taken leave from her academic career to raise children, let alone be taken as a positive advantage in developing social skills, or tolerance and understanding, or even responsiveness to community needs, yet these valuable skills learnt during the family phase in a woman's life are often quite evident in the female application and are often lacking in the male applicants. Why is such experience totally ignored? The ground rules have been set by males and are not readily changed. Thus, if a woman of 35 is judged alongside a man of 25 and her publication list seems to be much the same, the conclusion is that she is not as bright. The conclusion is never the obvious one, that the time out was for raising a family which has brought its own rewards in terms of experience and personal development and the management of human resources. And thus women will return fresh to academia and go on to be very productive and will not face the burnout symptom quite common in men who started earlier on their career paths.

The equity programs now dominating universities in a uniform style across Australia are rarely able to face the real issues of why so few women go on to senior positions. It is not that we have a problem about getting highly capable women into universities, the problem is the way in which we discriminate against them on graduation because society cannot yet take on board the dual role that most women play. For this reason the DEET-required profiles insisting on equity programs to broaden entry simply miss the real issues.

In my experience in universities, women are not discriminated against on the basis of their sex, at least not overtly these days, but they are discriminated against on the basis of age. They are also discriminated against on the basis of a wrongly perceived lack of experience. Because women, due to greater family responsibilities, are less mobile than men, this is viewed as lack of broad experience.

I am frequently tempted to ask in such discussions when men are comparing the relative merits of a male and a female candidate whether the favoured man has actually had more experience than the woman or just the same experience ten times over albeit over a longer period of time and in different places. But does that really add up to greater experience?

This same lack of acknowledgment of the value of the different experiences of women, of appreciation of different needs at different times in one's life, travels right across Australian culture. It is to be found in the difficulties Australians have in appreciating the rich cultural variety amongst various groups in the enlarged twentieth century Australian community. And, in particular, the cultural complexity amongst Aboriginal people is not understood. Environmentally Australia is a very diverse continent. From alpine climates to desert to tropical coast or from rolling plains to high mountains or eroded plateaux the differences are enormous. Across this highly varied country lived a great diversity of people in pre-European times. These were the original Australians, the Aboriginal people, who in each place developed a special, intimate relationship with the land in which they lived. That relationship was vastly different from one part of the country to another, just as the country was different from one place to another.

The complexity of the Australian landscape and its people was a concept well understood by Aboriginal people before Europeans arrived. Many dreaming stories reflect this understanding.

For example the Adnyamathanha people of the Flinders Ranges explain the differences between themselves, the people of the hill country, and those of the plains through a story about a kangaroo and a euro. Euros inhabit only the ranges but kangaroos live out on the plains. I retell it here in the words of an Aboriginal narrator as published in Dorothy Tunbridge's book, *Flinders Ranges Dreaming*.

Once upon a time the whole country was flat. There were no hills at all. There was a buck kangaroo called Urdlu and a buck euro called Mandya who both lived at Puthadamathanha. These two used to travel around together in the same country. One of their favourite foods was the wild pear root.

Urdlu the kangaroo and Mandya the euro dug for tucker in separate holes. Urdlu found a lot of tucker, but Mandya found only a little. Urdlu, however, wouldn't tell Mandya where his hole was. Poor Mandya was getting thinner and thinner and Urdlu was getting fatter and fatter. In the end Mandya came to Urdlu and asked: 'Give me some of your mai (food). I'm hungry. Come on Vurlka, give me some mai.' Urdlu said to Mandya: 'There's some mai in that bag there. You can take that.' As he ate it, Mandya said: 'This is really good tucker! Where did you get it?' Urdlu said with a wave of his arm: 'Oh, I found it over there.'

The pair of them went to sleep. In the morning Urdlu got up and went to look for water. While he went around looking here and there for water to drink, Mandya got up and went to find the hole where Urdlu got his tucker. He picked up Urdlu's tracks and followed them. He went along steadily down the track made by the kangaroo, until he came to his hole. He dug out a big heap of tucker from it. He was so pleased he stayed there digging and eating without even looking up.

Urdlu came back from having a drink. 'Now where on earth has the old fellow got to? I know, he's gone to my hole!' He took off after Mandya. He tracked him. His fresh tracks were there, all the way down to the hole. He could see where Mandya had dug up the dirt as he went along. He sure had dug up the dirt!

When Urdlu arrived at the hole Mandya was so busy digging he didn't even see Urdlu coming. Mandya was digging like mad. Urdlu called out: 'Why did you come to my hole?' Mandya said he was starving and Urdlu was mean not to tell him where there was tucker. He just went on eating. Now this made Urdlu really angry, so the pair of them were soon having a big fight over the tucker. Mandya pulled at Urdlu's arms and all. He stretched his arms, he stretched his fingers, he stretched his legs. They got very long. Then Urdlu pressed Mandya's fingers and his legs; he pressed his back, his chest; he thrashed him. Then they separated.

The wounded Mandya went off to Vadaardlanha to camp. While he was lying there trying to go to sleep, his hip started to hurt. In fact, he had a sore. He reached down and took out a little stone from the sore. He blew on it and in a flash hills came up from the plain. Indeed, several ranges of hills came up. The more Mandya blew, the more the hills kept coming up.

Meanwhile Urdlu headed down towards Varaata. He moved that big flat along as he went. He was lying out there on the flat when he looked back and saw the hills coming down the plain. He said: 'Hey! What's the old fellow up to? Over that way there's a big range of hills coming up! If he keeps that up I won't have anywhere to live!' So, with a big sweep of his tail Urdlu pushed the ranges back to where they are now.

The Adnyamathanha, who are proud of their hill country and its mythical origins, are now reviving their cultural roots and publishing these secular stories of their ancestors. This one explaining the difference between the euro or small rock wallaby and the large kangaroo of the plains also describes why they now live in different country. There are many such stories that reflect the historical differences in groups of people and their understanding of the differences in the landscape.

I am trying to say that 'equal opportunity' is not the same as equality. There is a real danger that the present thrusts on equity lead ultimately to a common approach without necessarily redressing the real structural discrimination faced by so many different groups in Australian society. Australian universities do not require the kind of uniformity that underpins many of the centrally driven equity programs. Because of the enormous diversity in the Australian people, it is differences in educational opportunities we need, not similarity. The medical example I gave illustrates how women need different kinds of opportunity from men if their education is to lead to equal chances in employment. Similarly, equal opportunity for Aboriginal people will only come when we all recognise the differences. Their Aboriginality does not make them all the same and their needs and interests are not all the same. Not only are there big differences in Aboriginal culture from one part of Australia to another but also there are vast differences between those who have grown up as urban people and those in traditionally oriented areas. In pre-European times there was enormous diversity based on geographic variation. That has increased, rather than diminished since the arrival of Europeans in this country. Thus to place too much emphasis on programs especially identified for Aborigines can suggest that all Aborigines are the same and that all Aborigines need special treatment. Whilst such programs will greatly advantage some Aboriginal people, they will not necessarily advantage all. In fact there is a real danger that too great an emphasis on Aboriginal special entry or separate quotas will ensure that all people of any Aboriginal origin at all identify first and foremost as Aboriginal people before they are identified as male or female or urban or rural or wanting to do medicine or arts. This is not to decry such enclave programs They are essential to give Aboriginal people equal opportunity to benefit from university education. I am merely warning against too much planning and uniform direction that can limit rather than expand options.

Similarly my research on Aboriginal juvenile justice has shown Aboriginal youths to be seriously discriminated against by our so-called justice system.

This research my colleagues and I published in a book entitled *Aboriginal Youth and the Criminal Justice System; the Injustice of Justice?* The subtitle underlines the basic findings. The book demonstrates that Aboriginal youths are not treated differently primarily because they are Aboriginal. This is not the major reason; the study revealed that in South Australia where Aboriginal youth account for just over 1 per cent of all young people, they represent just on 8 per cent of all those apprehended by police, 14 per cent of youth who go to court and 28 per cent of young people who are placed in detention. The extremely disproportionate number who are incarcerated compared with non-Aboriginal youth was not found to be primarily due to their being Aboriginal nor was it due to the crimes they commit. Rather we found that Aboriginal youth are penalised because they are unemployed, poorly educated, do not live primarily in nuclear families and live in lower socioeconomic areas of our cities or in the fringe areas of country towns or more isolated settlements. It is thus their low socioeconomic status and their residential location which determine their different treatment before the law.

Affirmative action entry quotas to universities will not give equity to women in their career paths in the universities any more than the law courts can be expected to solve Aboriginal crime rates which are related to social conditions. The real issues belong in the community attitudes and opportunities in career structures. Thus if we do not ask the real reasons for the disproportionate numbers of white males occupying all of the senior positions in academia, the professions and management, we will not be able to provide the right answers. If we do not seek and find the real causes we will not find the right solutions.

There is no doubt that Australia desperately needs equal opportunity in education. It is well known that intelligence, skill, initiative and creativity are not gender or ethnically determined and that if we are to obtain the best brains in the country taking the leading education or management roles, then we must have mixes proportionate to the general population. This would mean that the male–female mix would be approximately 50:50 of those making up senior university staff or in senior management in industry, or in other such posts—as many women as men. Similarly, one would expect that there would be a proportional number of Aboriginal people in senior management positions, related to population numbers.

The reality, however, is that this is not achieved by central planning from Canberra making decisions about equity intake. These are major social changes that are not achieved by dominance or direction, which is in fact counterproductive. The experience in eastern Europe is surely evidence that central planning, uniformity and central decision-making stifle rather than encourage intellectual thought, creativity, originality; the very things that will lead to enlightened senior management and to educational change in Australia.

Allen, Isobel, *Any Room at the Top? A Study of Doctors and Their Careers*, Policy Studies Institute, London, 1988

Gale, Fay, Bailey-Harris, Rebecca & Wundersie, Joy, *Aboriginal Youth in the Criminal Justice System: The Injustice of Justice?* Cambridge University Press, Cambridge, 1990

Gale, Fay & Lindemann, Sandra, 'Women in the Academic Search for Excellence', *The Australian Universities Review*, Vol. 32, No. 2, 1989, pp2–6

Kirov, Sylvia M, 'Women in Medical Research and Academia: What Future?', *The Australian Universities Review*, Vol. 34, No. 1, 1991, pp38–43
Tunbridge, Dorothy, *Flinders Ranges Dreaming*, Aboriginal Studies Press, Canberra, 1988

WHO'S PAYING THE DRIVER?

Ian Lowe

The broad issue of equity in modern Australian society is a most important factor to consider in a time of rapid change, for it is easy for such change to be socially divisive. We should think about what happens when new technology causes a fundamental change to the way a task is done. When I was hacking away on a typewriter producing news reports for a student paper in the 1960s, a whole string of skilled trades was necessary to turn my fractured prose into the printed word. Linotype operators set the story in hot-metal type, it was placed in galleys and galley proofs were pulled and carefully read, sub-editors laid out the pages and designed headings, compositors made up the page, page proofs were scrutinised before the paper was printed and so on. Until a recent change in senior management, I was writing a regular column for a national newspaper. I wrote my column on a laptop computer and used a modem to send it down a telephone line, directly to the newspaper's computer. The sub-editors did their thing on another screen and the electronic mess went down the wire to a typesetting machine. The words didn't appear on paper until the newspaper was printed.

Now think about how the changes have affected different people. For the writer or the sub-editor, there has been little fundamental change. The job may have become a little more satisfying; it is certainly easier to revise a story and get it right if you can play around with it on the screen, rather than screwing up the first piece of copy paper and trying again. Now think what has happened to the jobs of the linotype operator or the compositor, those skilled artisans who used to produce the metal form of the words from which the paper was printed.

Those jobs no longer exist. In terms of the workforce of a newspaper, those people are not employed any more. There are other examples; those who used to work in service stations pumping petrol usually lost their jobs when the self-service pumps were installed, for example. If you think that this problem only affects the unskilled or blue-collar workers, reflect on the revolution which has hit banks in recent years. Like I do, you probably often forget to go to the bank on Friday, but the day is saved by the automatic teller which will give you folding money at 11 pm, or early Saturday on your way to do the shopping. You, as a consumer, have benefited from the introduction of the automatic teller machines. Look around your bank branch some time, and compare the number of people behind the counters with the workforce of five or ten years ago. The banks no longer employ large numbers of bright young school leavers to begin work on the counter dealing with customers and gradually work their way up through the system. Computer experts are employed, but the banks are no longer recruiting large numbers of school leavers, so a steady stream of traditional white-collar jobs has dried up.

Earlier, I talked about the variety of forces which motivate the introduction of new technology. Social equity was not one of them. Indeed, the most common motivations for new technology, such as technical advancement or economic gain, make no pretence to incorporate the equity dimension. Whether or not a new tech-nology is accepted is usually determined by the market, by the decisions of individual consumers and corporate groups.

Economists tend to believe in markets because they think that they are the most efficient means of allocating resources between competing interests. Whether that is true or not, even the most besotted admirer of markets would probably not claim that they contain any feature or mechanism which could promote equity, even in principle. Indeed, there is a fundamental sense in which markets will always promote inequity. If a market is used to all-ocate a scarce resource, whether it is beach-front land or accom-plished professional footballers, those with large bank accounts will always be able to outbid those with lighter wallets. Thus allocation through a market means that those who are rich will get what they want and those who are poor will miss out. Those of us who are not rich are limited to competing for those things which the rich do not want sufficiently to bid the price up out of our reach.

This is a compelling argument for government intervention in the marketplace. At the economic feeding trough, the strong and aggressive piglets will always push aside those which are scrawny or meek if government abdicates its responsibility to produce some form of order. Leaving things to the market constitutes acquiescence by government in concentrations of power which we know will be abused. It has been wisely said that in any struggle between the powerful and the powerless, to do nothing is not to be neutral but to side with the powerful.

Leaving our economy to the forces of the market is simply an abdication of the historic responsibility of government to restrain the power of those who could otherwise use their economic clout against the interest of the community as a whole. As the divisions between the powerful and the powerless are widened by technological change, there is a greater responsibility on our political and legal system to ensure that power is moderated in the public interest.

It's helpful in reaching an understanding of the economic dimension of technology to go back 200 years to the founder of serious economics, Adam Smith. He has been much maligned because of the simplistic views of some of his modern disciples, but Adam Smith actually had quite a sophisticated understanding of the way the world works. As Tom Fitzgerald pointed out in the 1990 Boyer Lectures, we would probably be much better governed if those countless economic advisers who assist government had actually read all of Adam Smith's key work, The Wealth of Nations. This first analysis of technological change was based on the view that there were three key factors needed to produce anything useful enough for people to want to buy it. The three factors were land, labour and capital. In that fundamental sense, his analysis was more complete than the picture used by many modern neoclassical economists, who ignore the vital input from land or natural resources to reach the absurd conclusion that perpetual growth is possible in our closed system.

In the case of technological change, Smith saw the crucial trade-off as being between capital and labour. He thought that entrepreneurs who behaved rationally would work out the balance between two competing ways of carrying out a job: paying wages for human labour or investing capital in a machine. A factory owner will buy a machine if the cost of production is reduced: in other words, if paying interest on the money borrowed to buy the machine costs less than wages for workers to do the same job.

Of course, real life is more complicated than that simple trade-off. The first factories were built to control the workforce rather than to cut costs. Once the workers were in the factories, it was often possible to force them to accept lower wages by the threat of mechanisation, thus complicating the trade-off between equipment and labour. In modern Australia, the comparison is weighted toward mechanisation by the reprehensible payroll taxes imposed by state governments, since these form an economic penalty for employing people rather than machines.

A further complication is the issue of what happens to the extra productivity when machines are used. Smith saw the increase in output as being universally beneficial. New technology would only be introduced if it made the business more profitable. The extra profits can only be distributed as either higher wages to the workers or larger dividends to those owning the company. In either case, Smith argued, the extra cash would be spent in the community, thus providing extra work for the butcher, the baker and the candlestick maker, so the whole community would benefit. A modern version of this argument was put forward in the Myers Report on techno-logical change in Australia, concluding that the community as a whole would benefit from new technology. The fallacy of applying this argument to our modern economy was pointed out by Professor Ron Johnston, who noted that a significant number of our productive enterprises are owned by overseas interests. That means, in turn, that a significant fraction of the extra wealth produced by technological change does not flow into the com-munity, but instead flows off to the United States or Britain or Japan or wherever the stakeholders happen to be based, benefiting their local economies rather than ours.

The question of the economic role of technology in the modern industrial state has been analysed by the American economist JK Galbraith. He points out that many of the characteristics of modern organisations stem from what he calls the imperatives of technology. He argues that the harnessing of technology to the production of goods and services has irreversibly changed the nature of the firms engaged in those tasks, leading inexorably to an increasing time span for completion of production tasks, an increase in the capital investment required, more specialised labour, an increasingly important role for organisation as a feature of production, a greater need for long-term planning and an increas-ing tendency to want the state to bear major risks.

Galbraith argues that these trends have ended forever the era of large corporations run by one entrepreneur, such as Henry Ford. In the modern era, corporations are controlled by technical experts, who hold between them 'the diverse technical knowledge, experi-ence or other talent which modern industrial technology and planning require'.

The massive investment of capital, equipment and labour in the productive process leads to fundamental changes to the theoret-ical interactions between producers and consumers in a market.

Producers can no longer afford to allow the demand for their goods and services to be determined by the whim of the consumer, and so set out to create and manage demand. It could be claimed that the main purpose of the advertising industry is to ensure that consumers do not make economically rational decisions. Many large corporations, especially in countries such as the USA, rely mainly on military contracts: the ultimate form of insulation from the pressures of market forces and consumer demand. To quantify this effect, US military contracts in 1989 added up to US$129 billion, equal to more than half of the total economic output of Australia.

Large modern corporations typically don't attempt to maximise their profits, but aim instead at corporate survival and growth. The scale of investment and the time scale of planning lead corporations to be risk-averse and seek the support of the state for their activities. As Galbraith put it, 'The decisive power in modern industrial society is exercised not by capital but by organisation, not by the capitalist but by the industrial bureaucrat'. He argued that complex organisation, and therefore bureaucracy, is inescapable in advanced industrial society.

This analysis was a brave attempt by a leading economist to explain the real world of today; by comparison, simple market economics is of little assistance in understanding the modern technological state. Galbraith's insights are vitally important. We can only see what future options we have if we understand the limitations imposed by the general properties of technology.

First, modern technology requires a highly developed system of division of labour; modern work is increasingly specialised. The general mechanic gave way to specialists like the motor mechanic, who today is likely to concentrate on one area, such as brakes, or one brand of car. Complex tasks are subdivided into jobs suitable for the various specialists.

Second, we have a highly centralised production and distribution system; when I go to the shop I am unlikely to be offered local produce or even Australian produce if the shop has been able to buy cheaper goods from further away. The extreme example of this effect is the spreading network of so-called fast-food outlets, taking pride in producing the same bland taste in Melbourne as in Miami, Milan and even Moscow.

A third characteristic is that the economic system is oriented towards wants, rather than needs; think about the fraction of your income spent on basic needs compared with indulgences such as fashion, entertainment, travel, sport and hobbies.

We now have a regulated market system for goods and services; not only does government control such basics as hygiene and food quality, it also regulates trade practices, consumer rights and even shopping hours. Overall, the state has a greatly increased role. Even in Australia which has, despite the constant claims that we are over-governed, a smaller government sector than most industrialised countries, it is still true that the state is a major supplier of goods and services and the major purchaser of high-technology products.

One of the most interesting developments in recent years has been the massive growth in world trade, especially in value-added goods and services. Simple commodities account for a relatively small fraction of economic activity. There is a very good reason for this development. Modern technology is more sophisticated and so uses smaller quantities of raw materials to do the same job. Today's computers are much smaller than those of a decade ago, and use smaller amounts of minerals. The same is true of TV sets, cars and a range of other devices in common use. Minerals and other raw materials are of decreasing importance in world trade. Australia is very unusual in having a trade pattern dominated by minerals and agricultural produce, when world trade is dominated by information and highly transformed manufactured goods.

We should also recognise that politics in the complex modern industrial state is mainly concerned with economic management; think about the extent to which the political agenda in Australia is dominated by interest rates, trade figures, wage settlements and the public sector borrowing requirement. Keeping a complex modern economy operating is almost a circus act, so many different factors need to be kept in balance.

Finally, there is widespread use of elaborate structures for management of the process of production and distribution; even such areas as marketing now boast sufficient complexity to merit academic appointments in many of our universities, and graduate schools of management are devoted to the arcane skills of keeping the modern company functioning.

The general point is that modern industrial society is complex and relies on a high level of interconnection, regulation and government intervention. Additionally, most big corporations take great trouble to insulate themselves from the sort of random fluctuations which occur in a market economy. Those who argue for a simple approach of leaving the modern state to market forces are being at least as unrealistic as those who seek a return to a pre-industrial state of Arcadian bliss. Just as we could not hope to feed the current population from an agrarian economy, we could not support our industrial system on the basis of an eighteenth century free market.

Galbraith's analysis is an updated version of a theory put forward 50 years ago by James Burnham in his book *The Managerial Revolution*. Burnham saw the world of his time undergoing what he regarded as a social revolution to a new 'managerial society'. He saw the control of corporations being taken away from the owners by the managers, a process which has continued to this day. The nominal owners of large companies—the shareholders—have very little control over what is done. By controlling the flow of information to the nominal owners, the managers retain control of the key investment decisions affecting the future of the corporation.

Burnham foresaw the erosion of national sovereignty which has recently occurred. He argued that a traditional sovereign nation made its own laws, set its own tariffs and other controls on imports and exports, regulated its own currency and set its own foreign policy. He saw all these activities as incompatible with the needs of modern technology such as 'the complex division of labour, the flow of trade and raw materials'. As I have mentioned, world trade and commerce are now dominated by intangibles rather than physical objects. As a consequence, increasing integration of the world economy is a fact of life. National governments can and do regulate the flow of physical commodities into and out of their countries; they erect customs barriers at their borders and tax flows of commodities. But governments have difficulty even detecting the flows of information, let alone regulating these areas of economic activity. It has been said that the political union of Europe in 1992 is merely giving political recognition to what has become a financial reality, which is that the borders between the separate nations of western Europe have very little significance in today's world.

I want to make one more general point before putting these ideas into a local context and exploring their implications for Australia. The recent dramatic rise in the importance of information technology has changed the world in some fundamental ways.

Where energy technology has been the key to most of the past industrial development, information technology will play a similar role in the future modern society because it has a great capacity to influence other technological developments. Modern information technology has facilitated the implementation of change in a wide range of areas, as well as accelerating the pace of transfer of ideas and developments from one place to another. Not only does this result in more rapid diffusion of new ideas, but it also removes the need for innovations to occur in particular geographical areas. The smokestack industries of the original Industrial Revolution developed where the appropriate resources were located; for example, steel-making was carried out where coal, iron ore and water for transport were close to each other. Newcastle and Wollongong are Australian examples. The industries of today and tomorrow are much less likely to be tethered to physical resources, and much more likely to be located near markets or sources of skilled labour.

Information technology has also fundamentally changed the power relations in society. Large corporations are now equipped with global communications networks, but so are governments and various non-government organisations, such as conservation groups, indigenous people and political oppositions. The very success of contemporary technology has placed powerful communications capacity within the reach of a mass market. This has led to some unexpected consequences. Let me give you four examples.

Where once only large corporations could afford computers and high-quality printing, those technologies are now within the reach of small companies, community groups or individuals. Second, conservation groups are playing an increasingly important role in the negotiation of global treaties, because their sophisticated use of information systems often means that they are better informed than the diplomats negotiating on behalf of governments. As a third example, indigenous peoples in the Amazon have begun using video to record negotiations with city entrepreneurs to ensure that agreements are honoured. Finally, opposition to the regime of the Shah of Iran was built up despite total control of the mass media, by smuggling tape cassettes of speeches by the Ayatollah Khomeini from mosque to mosque. Thus information technology has become a powerful levelling tool. Where George Orwell foresaw our leaders using video to spy on us, through the media we are now using video to spy on our leaders!

This whole analysis of the characteristics of technological society has implications for Australia at three levels: our internal structure of states and territories, our overall national economy and our relationships with other countries. There are important ways in which our federal system is a handicap in the modern world. I mentioned that the barriers between the separate nation-states of Europe are becoming less important. By contrast, we still behave largely as if we were a series of warring tribes. Our states have separate legal systems, different tax structures, individual approaches to education, even different road rules. The changes necessary in moving between our various states are often greater than those in moving between the separate nations of Europe. It was recently observed that we are the most competitive nation on earth, as we spend most of our time and energy competing with each other.

We certainly do not present a united or even coordinated approach to the rest of the world. As far as the structures of our national economy goes, we are also out of step with the rest of the industrialised world. In overall terms, we are already what has been called a post-industrial society. About three-quarters of our wealth is produced by the broad area of services, with only about a quarter coming from physical commodities: agricultural produce, minerals and manufactured goods. However, our trade pattern is still heavily oriented toward the export of minerals and farm produce, with a massive trade imbalance in manufactures. As the value of commodities has been falling in relative terms for at least 40 years, and arguably for most of this century, our terms of trade have inevitably declined.

Conventional economic wisdom has encouraged us down this path by its belief that we should pursue activities in which we have a comparative advantage over other nations. Some people even believe that the solution to our current economic problem consists of exporting more minerals, even though this approach would entrench more firmly a trading pattern characteristic of a Third World country. With our national waggon hitched firmly to the fading star of commodity exports, we would experience continuing economic decline to the only status even worse than the banana republic threatened by Paul Keating: becoming a banana monarchy.

I have mentioned that the world economy is increasingly an international organism. This has a clear effect on economic management. Our government now frames its Budget and waits with almost pathetic eagerness to see what the New York money market thinks about it. We think it is a good budget if the verdict is that the Americans want to buy still more of our productive assets. We have little room for manoeuvre as a result of our trade structure and the level of foreign investment that has been encouraged in the past by our short-sighted leaders.

We need to outgrow the short-term economic approach which allows the future to be determined by simple considerations of profit, whatever the long-term consequences for our living standards or even our political independence. We should be making a concerted effort to plan rationally for the future. I can't see that the current pattern of economic activity in Australia makes sense even in economic terms. It has very serious potential social and political consequences. Additionally, it does not appear to be ecologically sustainable.

I will be looking in my last lecture at our options for avoiding further economic decline. They hinge crucially on the current enthusiasm for becoming what has been called a clever country. Like former Science Minister Barry Jones, I would much prefer that we become an intelligent society, but that is another story.

I want to turn, finally, to the issue of our economic relationships with other countries. Technology being now a powerful economic force, the nations which are doing well economically are those which have successfully harnessed technology to their needs: countries such as Sweden, West Germany and Japan.

Take the case of Japan, a dramatic example of the saying that past trends are not future destiny. Forty years ago, Japan was a middle-rank economic power with a reputation for shoddy goods. Today it is the dominant economic power of the world, with all ten of the world's largest banks and over a third of all the deposits in all the banks of the world. This is precisely because of the way the Japanese economy has specialised in the sort of value-added products which are the key to economic success in the modern world.

During the same period the United States has failed to maintain its technological competitiveness. In fact, the United States has declined in two decades from the richest nation on Earth to the largest debtor in human history. The indebtedness of the USA is two to three times the amount per head of the next worst case, Brazil. Its debt position is much worse than ours. Furthermore, the USA is increasingly moving toward the trading pattern of a Third World country, exporting raw materials and buying its elaborately transformed manufactured goods from Japan and other countries of east Asia. The USA has been described, like Australia, as a very rich Third World country.

The changing economic relationship between Japan and the United States should command our attention, as should the growth in the economic influence of other countries of east Asia. As a nation, we are still alarmingly ignorant of the history, the politics, the culture and above all else the diversity of the nations to our north. It is difficult to see a long-term benefit in this strategy.

In the absence of any alternative plan we are likely to see Australia moving more comprehensively into the role of an economic colony of Japan, doing the things which colonies traditionally do: supplying raw materials, acting as a market for manufactures and providing a suitable site for holidays. If we want to shape our own future rather than have it shaped by others, we need to adopt a different approach; the future is bleak if we continue to pursue our traditional emphasis on the export of primary produce.

While there is a strong argument for trying to become at least more self-sufficient in value-added goods and services, we might not want to emulate Japanese society for a variety of reasons. Not only is there a dedication to the work ethic and a degree of pressure to conform that we would probably find uncomfortable, but the Japanese approach suffers from a fundamental problem of ecological illiteracy. When he visited Australia in 1988, the Canadian scientist Dr David Suzuki urged us not to follow the path of Japan, the country of his ancestors. He pointed out that we are self-sufficient in most important ways, whereas Japanese society can only survive with massive imports of food, minerals and energy. In terms of political and economic independence, there are obviously great advantages in having a lifestyle which is both sustainable and self-sufficient.

Let me summarise what I have said in this lecture. I have discussed the complex economic role of technology in modern industrial society. The future is likely to see technology playing an increasingly important role, not just in economic terms but also as a social and political force. The world of today is one in which the economic and political roles of nations are increasingly determined by the way they manage technological change. This poses a clear challenge for Australia. The recently retired professor of science and society at Bradford University, Tom Stonier, has said that technological change represents opportunity to those who are well educated and aware, but is a threat to others. That observation applies to nations as well as to individuals. Our education system is the key to ensuring that we are equipped, as individuals and as a nation, to shape our own destiny in a rapidly changing world. Rapid change is assured; what prospects are there for managing the changes in ways we would want?

One of the keys to our chances of becoming more self-reliant in the crucial area of value-added goods and services will be the research and teaching efforts of our universities. In her third lecture, Fay Gale examined the pressures on universities to act as the wellspring of ideas for a new and transformed Australia, and I will return briefly to this question in my final lecture.

Geoffrey Bolton

One of Australia's most highly regarded historians, Geoffrey Bolton was born in 1931 in Perth. He was educated at Wesley College, Perth, the University of Western Australia and at Balliol College, Oxford.

He was Beit Senior Research Scholar at Oxford in 1956 and returned to Australia to take up a research fellowship at the Australian National University in 1957. He was senior lecturer in history at Monash University in 1962 returning to Perth to become Professor of Modern History at the University of Western Australia from 1966 to 1973. He was dean of the Faculty of Arts from 1967 to 1968. He was appointed Professor of History at Murdoch University in 1973 and held the chair there until 1989. As well, he had terms as dean of the School of Social Inquiry (1973–75 and 1988) and pro vice chancellor (1973–75).

Professor Bolton was visiting Commonwealth fellow to St John's, Cambridge in 1978–79, and in 1982 he became the first head of the Australian Studies Centre at the University of London, where he remained until 1985.

He returned to Australia and in 1989 became Professor of Australian History at the University of Queensland. Returning once more to Perth, he took up the chair of history at Edith Cowan University in Western Australia, which he held until his retirement in 1996. He has been Professor Emeritus there since 1997 and is senior scholar in residence at Murdoch University.

Professor Bolton was visiting fellow at All Souls, Oxford in 1995. In 1999 he joined the Senate at Murdoch University. He was on the council of the Australian National Maritime Museum from 1985–90.

He has written extensively on Australian social and political history. Not only was he general editor and author of volume five of the *Oxford History of Australia*, but among his books are *A Fine Country to Starve In*, *A Thousand Miles Away*, *Spoils and Spoilers* and *Dick Boyer: an Australian Humanist*, his biography of Sir Richard Boyer, and, most recently, in 2000, his splendid biography *Edmund Barton—The One Man for the Job*.

He was made an Officer of the Order of Australia in 1984.

Geoffrey Bolton gave his Boyer Lectures the title *A View from the Edge: An Australian Stocktaking*. The 'edge' for Geoffrey Bolton is Western Australia where he has lived and worked for most of his life and, to a lesser extent, Queensland. His is a different perspective from 'the usual orthodoxy' of the Canberra–Melbourne–Sydney triangle. His individual lectures are titled 'Human Resources', used in the proper sense of the words; 'Resourceful Humans', which is reproduced here; 'The Belly and the Limbs'; 'Australoedipus'; 'International Debits and Credits' and 'Taking Stock: The Choices Before Us' which he concludes by quoting Edmund Barton's reminder to Australians that 'we are a free people of keen insight and active reason.' As Bolton concludes: 'We have the capacity to learn from experience and to cherish our achievements, so that although the immediate future may not be easy, we shall encounter it resolutely.'

A View from the Edge: An Australian Stocktaking

Geoffrey Bolton

• 1992 •

It is hard to persuade the Australian people to think well of themselves when we are in the middle of a major depression. We live in a culture where the value of a citizen is often judged by his or her work. Without a job it is easy to lose self-respect. Despair is particularly widespread among many young Australians, because youth unemployment is not simply a phenomenon of the last few years. It has been around since the early 1970s, and since 1982 the rate of youth unemployment has never dropped below 20 per cent. There is a nasty irony in the words of our national anthem, 'Australians all, let us rejoice/ For we are young and free;/ We've golden soil and wealth for toil', before lapsing into the safer, if rather obvious comment, 'Our home is girt by sea'. Almost since the day Australia adopted that national anthem its words have been a lie. Nobody under 25, and that means nearly one-half of our population, can have any clear recollection of a time of economic security based on virtually full employment.

It is probably cold comfort for a historian to point out that this is not the first time in Australia's modern history that we've undergone a major economic depression. It is in fact the fourth; depressions occur about every half century. The first was in the early 1840s, following over-speculation in the pastoral industry; the second was in the early 1890s, arising from a number of causes, but most spectacularly from the excesses of a property boom based on 'marvellous Melbourne'; the third, still lingering in the memories of the elderly, was the depression of the 1930s; and the fourth, which we try to disguise under the name of a recession, is with us today. Each of the first three depressions, of course, eventually came to an end. The hard times of the 1840s were followed by the prosperity resulting from the goldrushes in New South Wales and Victoria in the 1850s. In the 1890s also, gold in Western Australia helped recovery in Victoria and South Australia, and the coming of federation in 1901 gave a stimulus by unifying Australia into a common market; but because of the great drought culminating in 1902, recovery was slower. In the 1930s gold played a lesser role, and it was not until the coming of the Second World War that it could safely be asserted that the depression was over. In each of these three depressions many young, unemployed men took to the roads and went bush, looking for work in the pastoral, farming or mining industries. This outlet is largely denied to the young unemployed of the 1990s. Primary production has ceased to be labour-intensive, and there is no incentive to leave the cities. A few have chosen to join the alternative-lifestyle communities established in rural districts since the early 1970s, but, so far as the majority are concerned, it is simply unrealistic to imagine that a goldrush or mineral boom will somehow transform their prospects.

However, it would be a mistake to imagine that the Australians of earlier generations, confronted by economic depression, simply sat tight waiting for a goldrush. The more one digs into the past, the more one is struck by the ingenuity and resourcefulness of Australians in the face of crisis. In the 1840s, for instance, some entrepreneurs responded to the downturn by developing exports to South and East Asia. Contrary to popular belief, it is not true that Australia has discovered Asia only in the last few years. As Professor AS Yarwood has shown in his book, *Walers: Australian Horses Abroad*,[1] Australian pastoralists developed a trade in horses for the cavalry in India, and this trade lasted for 100 years until the coming of motor transport in the 1930s. Australian exporters established themselves in the face of competition from South Africa and from local breeders in India because their product was better. Translated into terms that we might understand today, it is as if an Australian equivalent of Volvo or Range Rover captured and kept a distinctive share of the world market against all competitors for the best part of a century. Meanwhile, also in the 1840s, Western Australians began to take a share in exporting sandalwood to China. These were imaginative responses.

Nor was it surprising that such examples of resilience in adversity should be found in the Australia of the 1840s. Although it was barely half a century since the first convicts had arrived in Sydney colonial self-confidence was already strong. This may seem surprising, considering those convict origins. British commentators in the early nineteenth century were on the whole dubious about the future of a community whose initial genetic stock was largely drawn from the criminal classes. Even so liberal-minded a commentator as Sydney Smith thought it would take some generations for

Australians to cast off the ancestral taint. But others were more hopeful, and it is curious that one source of hope came from the Greek and Roman classics then taught at the best British and colonial schools. More than one writer remarked that ancient Rome had risen to great heights after its foundation by a gang of bandits led by Romulus and Remus. Why shouldn't it be the same for Australia? John West, the scholarly historian of Tasmania, pointed out that Rome was built on seven hills, and as Hobart was also built on seven hills the hopeful parallel was irresistible. More modern-minded Australians drew challenging comparisons with the United States. The full title of WC Wentworth's *History of Australia* published in 1819 reads: 'A Statistical, Historical, and Political Description of the Colony of New South Wales and its dependent settlements in Van Diemens Land: with a particular enumeration of the advantages which these colonies offer for emigration and their superiority in many respects over those possessed by the United States of America. By William Charles Wentworth, a native of the colony'.[2] In short there is very little to suggest that the shame of convict origins produced a sense of inferiority in the first generation of white Australians, and much to suggest a greater self-confidence than is always evident in our own day.

In such an environment it isn't surprising to find a high degree of initiative and inventiveness, much of it naturally enough directed to the improvement of Australia's staple industries. Agriculture benefited in successive generations from John Ridley's invention of a reaping machine fit for Australian conditions, HV McKay's harvester, and William Farrer's development of strains of wheat capable of surviving low rainfall. Shearing machines were invented by Frederick York Wolseley and improved by Arthur Howard. Behind these relatively well-known names there were hundreds more tradespeople in Australian country towns, blacksmiths, millers, leatherworkers, with enough technological skills to devise some improvement which would fit local conditions. Consider, for instance, the speed with which electricity was introduced into Australia and note the places where it was first put into use. Electric lighting was demonstrated at the Melbourne Exhibition of 1880, but because of competition from the gas companies the cities were slow to adopt the new medium. Instead the first street-lighting by electricity anywhere in Australia was installed by the Tamworth Municipal Council in 1888, followed within two years by Young, Penrith, Moss Vale and Broken Hill. Rural ingenuity was further demonstrated at Thargomindah, 1200 kilometres west of Brisbane, where in 1893 the township's electricity was powered by an artesian bore which continued in operation for over 50 years. In 1895 Launceston was lit by hydro-electricity powered from the South Esk River. Such episodes must be pondered by those who see culture and technology as diffusing largely from the metropolis. Instead it suggests a resourceful and intelligently adaptable people, able even in times of commercial depression such as the 1890s to modernise their technology.

But of course there were limitations. For some forms of research, such as aviation, there was neither the capital nor the engineering infrastructure to support innovation, so that pioneers such as Lawrence Hargrave or Alfred Alcock, inventor of the hovercraft, remained frustrated and unrecognised. Social circumstances also restricted others, such as the Aboriginal David Unaipon who certainly invented an improved handpiece for shearing and was throughout his long life obsessed with the problem of perpetual motion. Of greater importance was the difficulty for Australia, with its small population and its restricted home markets, to compete with overseas manufacturers who could benefit from the economies of large-scale production. Thus in the early decades of the twentieth century the horse-drawn sulkies and ploughs which could be provided locally were gradually superseded by motor transport and motorised tractors, mostly of American origin and offering the advantages of standardised parts and servicing. The Australian virtues of making do, of rural ingenuity, could not match the advantages of American mass production. By the time the Americans came to Australia during the Second World War, there was, as the historians Kay Saunders and Lyn Finch have shown, a yawning gap between American technology and Australian under-development.[3] Australians marvelled at American four-wheel drive vehicles, post-hole diggers, and semi-trailers; Americans shook their heads at a country which they saw as like their own at the turn of the century. Australian improvisation was still sometimes useful: when it became necessary hurriedly to build an airstrip at Mareeba the Australians produced a tarmac laid on an undercovering of molasses. But in military technology, household technology and a number of other respects, Australians now saw themselves as lagging behind.

Australian entrepreneurship also drew in its horns during those early decades of this century. In the 1880s and the 1890s, despite a heavy dependence on wool and gold, the Australians could be seen as enterprising traders. In 1888, only three years after the first cattlemen arrived in the Kimberleys, they were sending trial ship-ments of beef cattle to Singapore. During the next 20 years cattle were shipped from Australia's northern ports to destinations as far afield as Manila, Vladivostok and Durban. New South Wales exported coal to Chile—our major overseas customer—and to the Philippines. But the Americans who governed the Philippines imposed barriers on Australia's beef and coal trade, and elsewhere in the northern Pacific economic nationalism was on the rise. For the Australians of the early twentieth century it seemed logical and safer to impose protective tariffs behind which local manufacturers could be encouraged and to rely for export markets on the security offered by the British connection—especially after the First World War disrupted commerce with Germany and Russia. Those who spoke of increasing trade links with China and Japan were countered by champions of the White Australia policy who feared that Asian nations might use trade as a lever for demanding the easing of immigration restrictions. Consequently the initiative which had been so marked a feature of Australians in the nineteenth century became somewhat subdued in the 1920s and 1930s. Some creative spirits could still be found in the business world: Walter Hume's use of a centrifugal process for the manufacture of cement pipes provides a solitary example of an Australian firm pioneering a new technology and exporting it throughout the world. The Holden family of South Australia became the biggest manufacturers of motor-car bodies in the British Empire during the 1920s, but were forced by the depression into a takeover by General Motors. But there were not many more like them.

No completely satisfactory explanation has been advanced for the loss of confidence which seems to have overtaken Australians in the early years of this century. Two generations of historians have dated the change from the slump of the early 1890s, the most recent of them Beverley Kingston in *The Oxford History of Australia*: 'What took place was like the ending of a childhood: the curtain's fall on wide-eyed expectation, the entrance instead of uncertainty, doubt and mistrust: "never glad confident morning again"'.[4] But there was optimism enough among the makers of the Australian federation of 1901; and in the early years of the Commonwealth there seems still to have been a widely shared sense of Australia, together with New Zealand, as a social laboratory which was in some ways leading the world. Australia and New Zealand were among the earliest nations to admit women to the vote, to establish a comprehensive arbitration system and a minimum wage, to grant on contributory old-age pensions. Consider the language of the first prime minister, Sir Edmund Barton, defending the federal constitution: 'I have no fear whatever as to its strength against attack or as to its fitness to do its appointed work in the interests of a free people of keen insight and active reason'.[5] 'A free people of keen insight and active reason'; when was the last time one of our nation's leaders referred to his or her fellow-Australians in terms of such confidence? This may have been politician's rhetoric, but it was a rhetoric which took it for granted that the audience would share a resolutely hopeful view about Australian capacity.

I am one of those who believe that the First World War was the undoing of Australian confidence. It wasn't simply the damage inflicted when, out of a total population of five million, of whom no more than one million may have been adult males of military age, sixty thousand were killed in action and another three hundred thousand exposed to the hazards of modern war. This culling of a generation must have deprived Australia of too much good human material, as well as traumatising the survivors and their families. But the war was also divisive in stirring up powerful ethnic rancours: first through the harassment of citizens of German background, later through the conscription crisis which placed so many Irish-Australians at odds with the governing classes. The war also strengthened the belief that Australia was incapable of self-defence except as the auxiliary of great and powerful allies—a lesson later reinforced by the Second World War. But none of these factors entirely explains the lack of original initiative among so many of the Australian business community for so much of the twentieth century. There were honourable exceptions. BHP owed much of its progress to Guilliame Delprat's adaptation of the flotation process for treating sulphide ores, and later to Essington Lewis's grasp of new technology. Consolidated Zinc and Mount Lyell also showed an awareness of research. But even in these cases progress was due to the initiative of individual managers rather than forming part of the corporate culture. In general, research and development was left to the government.

The first major initiative was taken in 1926 by that underrated prime minister, Stanley Bruce, who set up the Council for Scientific and Industrial Research which later became CSIRO. CSIRO has an impressive record; it is a substantial national achievement. Think of the millions that have been added to Australia's export income over the last 50 years by the discovery of the role of trace elements in farming. We owe that to CSIRO. Consider the benefits to our pastoral industry through the eradication of pleuro-pneumonia in cattle and the development of pasture plants such as Townsville lucerne. We owe that to CSIRO. Remember how the timely intro-duction of myxamatosis at last enabled graziers to control the rabbit population, thus reaping the maximum benefit from the wool boom of the 1950s. We owe that to CSIRO. Even at the regional level, let us look at the boost given to a remote part of northern Australia by the surveys which led to the establishment of the prawning industry in the Gulf of Carpentaria. We owe that to CSIRO. On the industrial side there have been valuable contributions to our textile industry. But in general, although primary industry has contributed significantly to the funding of CSIRO, secondary industry has been less forthcoming. When attempts were made around 1960 to foster chemical engineering the petro-chemical companies gave minimal support, preferring to import their technology. Unfortunately this attitude has been all too widespread. We have very few, if any, equivalents of firms such as Siemens in Germany, Philips in Holland, or ICI employing well-funded research teams. In two decades after the Second World War fewer than one-seventh of Australia's more than six hundred chemistry postgraduates were employed by industry. The philanthropists who have endowed Australian scientific and medical research have been mostly of continental European origin. But for every Adolph Basser promoting scientific research, or George Henry Bosch endowing a medical school, one can name 20 more businessmen who showed no sense of social responsibility to the country in which they enriched themselves. The Walter and Eliza Hall Institute of Medical Research at Melbourne, under Sir Macfarlane Burnet and Sir Gustav Nossal, is a great example of what good can come from a posthumous benefaction. But even in death Australia's rich have often been selfish.

This points to a flaw in our corporate culture. In 1963 a CSIRO survey of 75 manufacturing firms found only one which could claim to be a world leader in innovation, and only about seven more sympathetic to innovation. Management, said the report, was dominated by older men who thought 'in terms of what they remember of their own understanding of technology twenty or thirty years ago'.[6] Although the Vernon committee in 1965 urged the Commonwealth government to encourage industrial research and development in the private sector, it was 12 years and six governments later before anything was done. Attitudes have not improved more recently. During the 1980s Australia's entrepreneurs seemed able to lay their hands on vast amounts of capital for the purpose of buying breweries and television stations at inflated prices, thus helping to swell the country's overseas debt. Some, like Lang Hancock, were prepared to spend up to $30 million on providing themselves and their families with a roof over their heads. If these amounts had been applied to research and development it is likely that Australia's economic position today would be noticeably stronger than it is. Many virtues are claimed for a marketplace freed of government regulation, but it hasn't done much towards making us a 'clever country'.

It is unlikely that the seventeen and a half million Australians of 1992 are less talented and less innovative than the three and a half million of a hundred years ago. With five times the population there should be five times the creativity. Instead too few Australian firms maintain a substantial research effort, while government support for CSIRO and university research has increased only in parsimony. Yet at a time when the old mechanisms which produced full employment no longer work, there was never a greater need for sustained research; not only in the technological and physical sciences, but also in the social sciences and humanities from which we might learn how to adjust our society's expectations to a future in which there will not be work for all. It is a time, not to restrict education to school-leavers, but to expand the facilities available to the mature-aged in search of a second chance. We probably need fewer 21-year-old graduates in commerce and management who know nothing else, and more middle-aged men and women retrained to update their skills. We might even update the thinking of our professional and business executives. In shaping our national policies on research and education, we should hear less of the miserable skinflint catchcry of 'user pays', and more of developing the skills and confidence latent among the Australian people. Our political and business leaders need to recover the sense that our first prime minister, Sir Edmund Barton, expressed: that Australians are a free people of keen insight and active reason. In the past this vision may have been obscured. Two of the factors sometimes blamed for this are our division into six competitive states and our prolonged links with Britain and the British Commonwealth. I'm not sure that either of these factors has been crucial as a limitation on Australia's progress, but both need to be looked at in the next instalments of this series before we return to our central theme: the fostering of a collective Australian self-confidence.

1   AS Yarwood, *Walers: Australian Horses Abroad*, Miegunyah Press, Melbourne, 1989
2   London 1819
3   K Saunders and L Finch '"In imitation of our progress": American perceptions of Australian underdevelopment during the Second World War', *Australian Studies*
4   B Kingston, *Glad Confident Morning: The Oxford History of Australia Volume 3*

1860–1900, OUP Melbourne, 1988 p314; quoting B. Fitzpatrick, *The Australian People 1788–1945*, Melbourne, 1946 p217

5   *Sydney Morning Herald*, 8 January 1920
6   SH Bastow 'Research in the manufacturing industry of Australia', *Journal of the Institute of Engineers, Australia* 36, 1964, ppN37–N40

Ian Anderson

Associate Professor Anderson is currently the director of the Centre for the Study of Health and Society in the School of Population Health at the University of Melbourne. Over the past three years, he has been focused on the development of the VicHealth Koori Health Research and Community Development Unit within the Centre.

He has worked in Aboriginal (Koori) Health for about 15 years, which has involved a number of different roles, such as Aboriginal health worker, health educator and general practitioner. More recently he was chief executive officer for the Victorian Aboriginal Health Service, prior to becoming the medical adviser to the Office for Aboriginal and Torres Strait Islander Health in the Commonwealth Department of Health and Aged Care.

Over the years, Ian Anderson has developed a national profile for his work on Aboriginal health policy and strategy. He has been involved in a number of policy development processes, including chairing the working party that developed the National Indigenous Sexual Health Strategy.

Professor Anderson is Koori and has a professional background in medicine and social sciences. He has written widely on issues related to Aboriginal health, identity and culture, and has a broad interest in the sociology of health and illness, related policy analysis, and theory development in the social sciences. His Boyer Lecture, *Towards a Koori Healing Practice*, provided evidence of his ability to draw these disciplines together in a useful and coherent form.

In 1993, to mark the International Year of the World's Indigenous Peoples, the Boyer Lectures were presented by seven Aboriginal and Torres Strait Islander people. This anthology includes two of the lectures, those given by Professor Ian Anderson and Noel Pearson. The other 1993 Boyer Lectures and their titles were: Mandaway Yunupingu, 'Yothu Yindi–Finding Balance'; Dot West, 'Indigenous Media'; Jeannie Bell, 'Australia's Indigenous Languages'; Getano Lui Jnr 'A Torres Strait Perspective'; and Helen Corbett, 'International Efforts'.

Noel Pearson

Born in 1965, Noel Pearson is
from the Hopevale community
on Cape York Peninsula. He was
educated at Hopevale School and
St Peter's Lutheran College,
Brisbane. He has an honours
degree in history from the
University of Sydney, and
completed a law degree in 1993.

Mr Pearson was an adviser to
the Hopevale Aboriginal Council,
and helped establish the Cape
York Land Council in 1990. He
was part of the Queensland
Government's working group to
establish the 1991 Aboriginal
Land Act, but resigned in protest
over deficiencies in the proposed
legislation. Noel Pearson was

executive director of the Cape York Land Council and subsequently chairman. He was one of the team who dealt with the Federal government on
its response to the Mabo Native Title decision.

Noel Pearson now manages the Cape York Partnership Plan working to
bring together business, government and the community. He is active in
the Cape York Charitable Trust, a body established to facilitate income in
the communities of Cape York.

In 2000, he published *Our Right to Take Responsibility* and delivered the
2000 *Light on the Hill* Ben Chifley Lectures at Bathurst.

Noel Pearson's 1993 Boyer Lecture, delivered when he was only 28 years
of age, and titled 'Mabo: Towards Respecting Equality and Difference'
opens with an elegant link to Professor William Stanner's 1968 Boyer
Lectures *After the Dreaming*. While his current focus may be on practical work
for the betterment of the Cape York community, he continues to be a
significant contributor to the public discourse on Aboriginal matters. His
1993 Boyer Lecture remains an important element in the public understanding of indigenous land rights.

TOWARDS A KOORI HEALING PRACTICE

Voices from the Land

Ian Anderson and Noel Pearson

• 1993 •

Ian Anderson

On 11 June 1987 Arthur Moffat, a 51-year-old Aboriginal man, was found dead in a cell in the Warragul Police Station. He had been taken to the police station from the platform of the railway station, having been removed thereto from a train on which he had been travelling. Everything done to Arthur Moffat—the removal from the train, the placing on the railway platform, the removal to the police station and the detention in the cells—was based on the assumption that he was simply intoxicated. The only basis for this assumption was that he smelt of alcohol, was only partly conscious, and was an Aboriginal. The police called ambulance officers to the police station who confirmed this assumption.

The assumption was unsound. Arthur Moffat was most probably suffering a hypoglycaemic reaction due to the combination of diabetes, heavy drinking and not eating. Very simple attention could have saved his life.

(Wootten, 1990: 1)[1]

The police and ambulance officers who were a part of this series of errors should have known that the assumptions under which they were operating were unsound. In the case of the police their actions were directly contrary to the spirit of their standing orders. This is not a matter of a single incorrect diagnosis. It was a series of social interactions in which police and ambulance officers made dubious assumptions. On every occasion they confirmed each other's judgement. I doubt those involved would have been so certain about their judgement if Arthur Moffat was not an Aboriginal man left semi-comatose on a country railway station. If Arthur Moffat had been dressed in a business suit and found on the steps of the stock exchange he would very likely be alive today.

Arthur Moffat, just like 10 per cent of the adult Aboriginal community, was diabetic. Knowing this problem is very common in the Aboriginal community may have saved this man's life. Yet all involved presumed a semi-conscious Aboriginal man was a mere drunk. So that it is unlikely that technical knowledge alone about Aboriginal diabetes would have altered the behaviour of the police and ambulance officers. Their behaviour only makes sense by reference to particular racist stereotypes of Aboriginality.

These stereotypes have their own logic, having grown out of the social relations between Aboriginal people and non-Aboriginal people on the colonial frontier. This coloured lens of white colonial heritage represents Aborigines as naive primitives unable to handle the dangerous moral products of civilisation such as the grog.

In the south-east, where I live, most interactions between Koories and non-Aboriginal people are fleeting. So when encounters do occur people often resort to those colonial images, and act accordingly. I see this encounter between an Aboriginal man and the health and custodial systems as entrenched in the broader context of relations between Aboriginal and non-Aboriginal Australia. Experienced, skilled workers do make mistakes of this order when dealing with Koori people—not only because they lack technical knowledge, but because their actions continue to be driven by a colonial view of Aboriginal Australia.

The case of Arthur Moffat raises a series of problems about medical practice and Koori people.[2] Firstly, how do the submerged assumptions and biases of medical practitioners colour the perception of Aboriginal people and consequently shape their diagnosis and treatment of Koori ill-health? Following on from this, how do the experiences of Koori people shape their encounters with medicine? I am deeply concerned about the persistence of tragedies such as Arthur Moffat's death. Yet I also feel we need to aim for more than disaster prevention. We must take heed of these experiences, and prevent them being repeated. But we also need to move beyond them, to realise the powerful potential of a healing practice based on Koori values—a truly Aboriginal approach to health care.

Just as our existing Aboriginal health services helped to open new ground in community health, I believe we can lead the way again, with a healing practice based on Koori ideas of well-being. But we can only do this if we accept that Aboriginal people's experience of medicine is part of a history which includes invasion and on-going colonisation. This colonial process has dis-empowered people, controlling their intellectual life, taking from them their right to organise their collective life. An anti-colonial project like this must empower Koori people by acknowledging their experience of medicine, and their understanding of health issues.

I don't consider my knowledge of Koori health issues to be an 'expertise'. The academic tradition creates so-called truths about health and healing which are accessible to only the specialist few. I consider my knowledge to be a product of my own particular experiences, certainly in professional training, but equally in being a part of and working within the Koori community.

In an education system which deifies textual knowledge, other ways of knowing or learning get poor recognition. It sometimes seems as if intellectual activity develops in a social or experiential vacuum—a kind of divine inspiration. That's not the case. So I want to acknowledge, and pay respect to, those individuals who have been (and continue to be) my teachers within my own community. Their experiences and knowledge have been influential in shaping my understanding of the issues in Aboriginal health.

This approach has two implications. First, it means I am speaking from the experience of being Koori. I am not speaking for indigenous Australian communities in general. I can't speak for Murris, Nungas, Noongars, Yolngu, Anangu or any other Aboriginal or Islander mob. Second, in speaking from a Koori experience, I am well aware of the common prejudice that we Aboriginal people in the south-east have lost our culture as well as our land. I don't accept this. I am quite passionately committed to working within what I see as being a Koori tradition.

Working as a doctor within my sense of the values or practices of Koori tradition, I need a framework for thinking critically about medical work in Koori communities. I need to consider the extent to which the practice of Western-derived medicine is counter to the empowerment of Aboriginal people, and the Aboriginalisation of health care. For me, this understanding is the outcome of a commitment to working with Koori communities who seek to redefine medical work in order to better service their own mob.

An alternative healing practice may remain centred on the needs of the Koori body, but it has to comprehend the body holistically. I see the Koori body as much more than an interconnected system of muscles, bone or fat. The bodies which we inhabit also have cultural and social dimensions. In fact the cultured nature of our experience of bodies is such that even the so-called objective body of clinical science is in itself a culturally shaped perception of the body.

Medicine doesn't operate only in the realm of organic disease. Healing practices also impact on the development of a sense of self, and on how you value your body. Illnesses such as diabetes, even though they may eventually threaten life or result in debilitating complications, often have minimal symptoms in the short term. For many Koories, looking after their diabetes is embedded within other needs and experiences, like finding work, finding suitable housing and getting a useful education.

I want to see a form of healing practice which constructively engages with all those processes which contribute to the development of Koori well-being, rather than one which is only concerned with bugs and tumours and suchlike. This is obviously an ambitious project. In a moment I want to lay out some of the ground-work, by outlining the important issues which underlie such a transformation. We can realise the visionary potential of Koori health by thinking with our hearts, but with one eye on the past and one towards the future.

The Aboriginal Health Services

Before I talk about a future Koori health care practice, let's consider the history that makes these questions possible. The community-controlled Aboriginal Health Services emerged at a key moment in the history of the Aboriginal political movement. Until the 1960s, Aboriginal political activity was essentially a civil rights movement, concerned with issues like citizenship and equal pay. When the 1967 referendum removed the constitutional barriers to Aboriginal citizenship, Aboriginal politics was transformed. Ideas of autonomy, self-determination and sovereignty became central to the new political terrain. The new attitude was crystallised by the words of Kevin Gilbert: *Because a White Man'll Never Do It*.[3] Koories, frustrated with continuing poor access to health services, were convinced the Aboriginal community had to take into its own hands the responsibility for delivering its health services. In this new era the key issue became how Koories would exercise their rights to health care.

Koories have had good reason for anger with the inadequacies of the mainstream health system. Prior to the development of the Aboriginal health services, access to any form of health care service could not be guaranteed. The most significant barrier to health care was poverty, and the indifference, even frank hostility, of some health care providers. Stories like Arthur Moffat's were all too common in those days.

Aboriginal people were only able to interact at the margins of the system—and then often with difficulty. The Koori experience was to be treated on the hospital verandah, or having to 'trouble' a resentful private practitioner. In the 1960s, the Victorian Aborigines Welfare Board[4] wrote to medical practitioners in Victoria requesting information on the health of Victorian Aborigines. One doctor replied in 1966 that:

> I do think of them as 'pests' by and large because the 5% of [A]boriginal patients would account for perhaps 50% of late night calls and week-end work . . . In my earlier days here, I would sometimes try to collect a fee, particularly if a group arrived in a taxi from 40 miles away, but now do not—it upsets me—not them . . .
>
> I resent them for this double imposition—this is a busy practice and sleep can be precious and I get very little time to spend with my family of five . . .[5]

This doctor thought of his patients as pests, so it is likely that they were treated as such. Koories were resented for intruding into his private time. We may sympathise with someone whose family life suffers because of his work. But his patronising attitude is inexcusable and it betrays a complete lack of understanding of how the conditions of Koori life shaped their encounters with medicine.

It's attitudes like this that promoted the very problem he's complaining about. Knowing they would be unwelcome pests, Koories were hardly likely to make an appointment for a routine check-up. They were far more likely to wait until they needed urgent care, possibly late at night and certainly far sicker than they needed to be. In the design and delivery of health services Koories were perceived and treated as if they were outside of the health system. They were seen as an unnecessary burden, rather than people who were the entitled recipients of health care.

Coinciding with the growth of a vigorous Aboriginal health movement there was also a shift in the relationship between the Australian state and Aboriginal people. After decades of imagining itself as a dominion of the British empire, the Australian nation awoke from its post-World War Two slumber to find such an attitude was no longer possible. In this context the policies and practices of Aboriginal assimilation became increasingly untenable. They merged into the more pluralistic policy model of welfare colonialism.

Unlike the older idea of nationhood, it was now possible to be Aboriginal and be considered a part of the Australian community. In place of the old Protection Boards and their mission managers we now have a large bureaucracy which administers Aboriginal programs. The political activities of the Aboriginal health movement managed to drive a wedge into the space opened by this shift in colonial relations. One outcome of this wedge of conflict was the Aboriginal health services.

These health services were created by the community to be controlled by the community. They operate under an elected community board of management. This organisational structure gives Koories the opportunity to design and deliver health programs for their own people, and to develop health policy and strategies. Aboriginal health workers collaborate with largely non-Aboriginal practitioners such as doctors, nurses and dentists. Koori people are able to choose staff who they judge will work as their advocates, and demonstrate respect for their culture.

By creating these centres the Aboriginal health movement has created Aboriginal places where health care services can be delivered. Koori communities have defined through collaboration and dispute how the health services should be administered, how accountability should be ensured, and how work roles should be defined. The services have worked hard to ensure that individuals working in Aboriginal communities operate within the parameters set down by the community.

I don't wish to naively idealise these services. But they have created primary health centres where Koories can comfortably go, see a Koori health worker, and be treated with respect by people who know something of their lives and culture. But the doctor they see will most likely be non-Aboriginal and working with an often inappropriate biomedical model of health. This is about more than whether or not individual practitioners are sensitive to individual and community experience. We need to develop a new form of practice which we can use to better realise the visions of Koori people.

Koories and Medicine
To tackle the problems of the relationship between Koories and the institution of medicine, we need to examine the social context of medical practice. One of the key factors which enabled the profession of medicine to develop its dominant position within the health system was an alliance, albeit an often troubled one, between the state and medicine. Medicine has, for example, the power to certify absence from work, and regulate access to a vast number of pharmaceutical and other therapeutic substances.

More fundamentally medical practice is premised on people consenting to change their life practices to take medication as directed, present for surgery or perhaps change their diet. In this form of practice, relief from suffering depends on the patient submitting to medical authority. By intervening in people's life practices at the moment of actual or potential harm medicine transforms our bodies. It does this by imposing particular values on how we should be or behave.

The medical knowledge of the body conveys a claim to 'truth', that the doctor knows your body better than you ever will. This scientific knowledge of the body has its cultural origins in the late eighteenth century development of the clinic. Within the clinic it became possible to investigate and examine bodies and locate diseases in particular sites within the emerging cultural construct of the scientific body.

In the twentieth century, with the development of sophisticated mechanisms of population surveillance and new research methodologies, this terrain has extended to include not only actual disease, but also potential disease. The emphasis within contemporary medicine on prevention is founded on the notion that risk, like actual illness, can be managed by changing lifestyle.

So according to this perception, diabetes is an abnormality in the regulation of blood glucose which has particular effects on organs such as the heart, kidney and eyes. Medicine can intervene once the disease occurs in order to alleviate sickness. Alternatively, diabetes may be prevented by adopting particular dietary or exercise practices. Both in its broader social context, but also in the day-to-day relationships between doctors and patients, medicine has the power to very literally regulate or shape people's lives. This power depends on the medical perception of the body.

Good outcomes are of course possible. But it does depend on whether patients and doctors agree on strategies of care. For the patients such interventions must be economically and socially possible and desirable. This can be difficult enough when patients and doctors share a class and cultural background. You can imagine how much more difficult it is if the advice is being given by a member of a colonising culture to a member of a colonised one.

When doctors talk about how patients respond to intervention and instruction, they talk about compliance. And it's not unusual to hear doctors voice concern of 'poor compliance' among Koori patients. This is important because the extent to which a patient is seen to comply sometimes decides their access to health care. For Koories, well-being as a value has as much to do with family relationships as it has to do with their experience of their physical body.

A Koori person with kidney failure who is treated with dialysis may find their commitments to their kidneys conflicting with the needs of their family. It's sometimes difficult to respond to the demands of an extended family with limited resources, and balance this with a strict regime of dialysis. In cutting dialysis time, the Koori patients aren't necessarily neglecting their own well-being. They are operating within the framework of Koori notions of well-being. Doctors may view such patients as poorly motivated or insufficiently compliant.[6] A patient deemed to be poorly motivated risks being judged as undeserving of costly resources such as transplant services. In this regard medical practitioners are brokers—they regulate access to particular resources. The so-called better patients may indeed have better access to more specialised and costly resources.

My point is, medical interventions are not value free, and doctors are powerfully positioned to transform the lives of their patients. These transformations are not limited to the organic realm. Medicine is as an agent of cultural change. It seeks to relieve suffering by modifying how people act and how they think. This process has profound implications for who Koories are and how Koories imagine themselves to be. In a moral sense this is neither necessarily good nor bad. Healing practices of any kind have such implications. However, Koories are entitled to a healing practice which bears out our vision of ourselves, and not one which reinforces the coercion and the helplessness of colonial stereotypes. This problem is integral to the operation of clinical medicine, regardless of where it's practised.

In thinking about the practice of medicine this way I'm not saying anything particularly new. Neither am I debunking the need for this type of healing. However, I am committed to the idea of a Koori healing practice which maintains the benefits of a biomedical practice, but takes the implication of these criticisms seriously.

Koori Healing Practices

This is not just a clinical or intellectual problem, it is also a matter of imagination. The doctor in the clinic needs to consider that their interpretation of patient experience is as subjective as it is objective. A Koori healing practice would require a more disciplined form of imagination in order to better understand how someone comes to call on health service resources. People seek health resources because of the experience of their body. This experience has a number of inextricably linked aspects—there's the interpretation of body senses, interaction with other people through time, and a history of prior encounters with the health system. The body which enters the clinic is a product of organic and social processes which are so intertwined it's impossible to engage with, or intervene in, either realm without impacting on the other.

The Koori body develops and transforms in a particular set of personal historical and social circumstances. For Koories, important aspects of this growth are the experience of an extending kinship system and an experience of non-Aboriginal institutions and society. Through the process of development certain values become embodied. For example, our concept of well-being is not only an idea which we use to assess body experience, it also drives our body in particular ways. This transforming experience of who I am and how I experience my body, as a Koori, is a key dynamic. It shapes how people come to the health system and, following each encounter, it continues to give form to their behaviour.

So Aunty's experience of a diabetic leg ulcer isn't just an experience of pain or discomfort. It also incorporates the difficulties she has in meeting family needs, getting the transport or money to see a doctor, and the humiliation she feels when the doctor berates her for not looking after herself.

The impact this might have on the clinical interaction can be realised if practitioners look beyond the body parts made available to them by the coloured lens of clinical science. They need to engage with the other abstract forms bodies can take. Healing is not only an empirical science. It is not just a question of choosing the appropriate treatment. By giving a name and conferring meaning to the patient's problem, the doctor takes the first step in narrowing the range of solutions available to the patient. To do this constructively in a Koori healing practice we need a new form of medical imagination. This is possible if we take into account how the overlaying dynamics of the doctor/patient and the Koori/non-Aboriginal relationship shape the perception of the Koori body. Certainly this would have helped Arthur Moffat. Likewise, it may cause some doctors to question their ability to judge a Koori patient as poorly motivated.

Some aspects of the embodied experience of Koories in the clinical encounter are simply beyond, or incommensurate with, standard medical practice. The Koori Aunt with diabetes who lives in an overcrowded inadequate house and has considerable difficulty in achieving good diabetic control, has a body which bears the experience of poor housing. In cramped and inadequate living conditions, the need to negotiate a diabetic diet is likely to be one of many unnecessary stresses. Even though Aunty may say she wants to maintain good diabetic control, her will may not be sufficient when a feed of fast food is both the one and only treat for the day and keeps a mob of kids' bellies quiet.

Now it's a difficult argument to sustain, using the logic of a rational clinical science, that Aunty's poor housing causes her diabetes to be unmanageable. However, if we take into account all the possible dimensions of her embodied experience we might be able to develop strategies which would not be made apparent by scientific reasoning alone. Finding better housing for Aunty might achieve better control of her diabetes. With a few less mouths to feed in the one household it would be easier for her to negotiate her diet.

Koori life experience and medical practice are not diametrically opposed. There is basis for interaction. They have much in common, such as a concern for control of pain or the alleviation of suffering. However, the skills required in getting consensus on such concerns are not intuitive. Nor are they necessarily facilitated by traditional modes of clinical interaction.

Understanding the relationship between Koories and medical practice has certain profound implications. Firstly, the set of conditions which shape these encounters such as the experience of poverty, poor housing conditions or conflicting values of well-being, can't be viewed simply as constraints on medical practice. It's not good enough for doctors to maintain the attitude, 'given an ideal world what we would do is . . . .'

Rather, these so-called constraints on medical intervention must be understood as integral to the practice of healing. So for the diabetic Koori living in an inadequate house, getting reasonable housing is as integral to the problem of diabetes as is the choice of medication. Doctors must see that the extent to which people incorporate medical advice is not the responsibility of the patient alone. It's a problem of the doctor–patient relationship.

A new Koori healing practice would recognise that historically medicine has been poorly attuned to Koori values of well-being and the conditions which have shaped this. We would need to move beyond the traditional encounter between one doctor and one patient. We have to find new forms of interaction between doctors and patients and other staff such as Aboriginal health workers. This would shift our focus from the diagnosis and treatment of disease. It would enable patients to actively engage in negotiating their problems and their healing strategies. This reorientation takes the health care provider out of the individual client–practitioner consultation into the social realm in which the patient's well-being develops.

The dynamics of families and communities are fundamental to a

Koori vision of well-being. So only focussing on Aunty's blood sugar readings will miss some of the most important influences on Aunty's well-being. Is Aunty's dietary change only to be achieved by persistently telling her how to eat better? How might our strategies change if we focussed on the family and not the individual? We could even go beyond that and develop strategies for community healing.

Until recently few people in the broader community cared if medical practitioners considered Aboriginal patients pests. Over the last two decades some sections of the health bureaucracy have demonstrated some interest, often after considerable political debate, in improving their performance on Koori health issues. But in the politics of Aboriginal health, the institution of medicine has been somewhat more peripherally involved. Academic centres and professional bodies have taken up issues of Aboriginal health, but to date they have had a secondary role in the development of Aboriginal health services.

The death of Arthur Moffat was a tragedy. Yet on a daily basis this tragedy is re-enacted, albeit in a more mundane way. Changing the relationship between medicine and Koori communities is more than removing the veneer of bigoted language. It requires us to question the very values inherent in medical practice. This requires an ongoing cultural activism, questioning the cultural basis of medical practice. Such activism takes the struggle for better health services into the academy where medical knowledge and medical practitioners are made.

1   Wootten, JH (Commissioner), Report of the Inquiry into the Death of Arthur Moffatt Royal Commission Into Aboriginal Deaths in Custody, Canberra, Australian Government Publishing Service, 1990
2   My intention is to focus my remarks on the aspect of health care work which I am primarily, but not exclusively involved in. Medicine has a particular position within a larger occupational field of health services which adds another dimension to the issues which I will discuss.
3   Gilbert, Kevin J, Because a White Man'll Never Do It, Angus & Robertson, Sydney, 1973
4   The Aborigines Welfare Board was created under the Aborigines Act with the function to 'promote the moral, intellectual and physical welfare of [A]borigines . . . with a view to their assimilation into the general community' (Lyons, G, 'Official Policy Toward Victorian Aborigines 1957–1974', Aboriginal History, 7, 1983, pp61–81).
5   From documents in the author's possession.
6   Anderson, Ian, 'Access, equity and the ethics of resource allocation for minority groups: A Koori perspective' in Choice or Chance? The Ethics of Resource Allocation for Minority Groups: Ethics of Resource Allocation in Health Discussion Paper 3, Australian Health Ethics Committee, 1992

MABO: TOWARDS RESPECTING EQUALITY AND DIFFERENCE

Noel Pearson

The Boyer Lectures of the eminent Australian anthropologist Professor William Stanner entitled *After The Dreaming* hold their own amongst this country's finest writings on matters black and white.

Today, more than ever, the series which Professor Stanner delivered for the ABC in 1968 makes compelling reading. His lectures articulate, illuminate and provide some guidance, with questions that will consume the people of this continent for as long as we need to consider them. Such questions as: the future of nationhood and the equivocal citizenship of those with whom a settlement of great grievance remains outstanding; indigenous rights and notions of new partnerships; constitutional and institutional renovation; the never-decreasing need for social reconstruction and renewal; and the great imperative for an equitable distribution of the hitherto not so common weal.

Stanner wrote one year after the 1967 Referendum which, amongst other things, finally incorporated into the Commonwealth the indigenous people of the country. In this lecture I propose to reflect on some aspects of Stanner's lectures, whilst tracing some of the developments of the past two decades, leading to the watershed decision of the High Court of Australia on 3 June 1993 on the question of native title to the Murray Islands in the case brought by the late Eddie Mabo and others.

I stood but a child of tender years when Professor Stanner spoke hopefully about our entry with a vengeance into the country's history. To tell the story of that time and the changes which have happened and the changes which, like Stanner, we still await, it is appropriate first to tell of the man who commandeered Aboriginal policy in the state of Queensland for more than two decades.

In 1989, on a bright Sunday morning, Joh Bjelke-Petersen stood at the front of the old church at Hope Vale, surveying the long wide street, framed by mango trees and frangipannis with barking dogs idly chasing horses.

Earlier the former state Premier, whose once authoritarian aspect had by now waned considerably, had regaled the congregation of black faces in the weather-board church with stories. Stories of how they had transformed dense woodland into paddocks and rows of tin shacks with wide streets, named after German missionaries now long departed. How they had built this glorious church from the timber that had stood on the paddocks where cattle now grazed. He had returned to the mission to commemorate a community milestone: it was 40 years since the Guugu Yimithirr people had returned, largely through his agency as a young Country Party backbencher, from seven years' exile in central Queensland. The mission which had been established in 1886 was closed down in the war, and the people removed when the resident German missionary was interned in 1942.

After the church service, a journalist asked the former Premier about land tenure for the people of the community. With perhaps accidental candour he replied that the land had always belonged to the Guugu Yimithirr. It was just that the government had been looking after it for them. And now they had handed the land back to the rightful owners.

It was a startling admission—*that the land had always belonged to them*—from one who had made an international reputation of denying Aboriginal human rights in the state of Queensland and had steadfastly opposed the notion that indigenous people had certain inherent, traditional rights to their homelands. His government could scarcely bring itself to mention the word 'traditional' without suffering acute political nausea.

In the early years of government policy, Aborigines were different and, because of their alleged backwardness, could be treated unequally. Discriminatory treatment of the mission and reserve inmates during those years, when it was said *we lived under the Act*, arose out of their constitutional perceived lack of quality: black people were innately unequal, therefore special laws where the state governed aspects of people's lives which were beyond the reach of law makers for other citizens were justified.

This policy of innate difference and inequality was underpinned by a policy of assimilation for, by a process of training, civilising and indeed *breeding out* their backwardness, the blacks could lose their difference and become like everyone else. They could come out into the mainstream society as people exempted from the Act and finally equal. The Churches would assist in this endeavour and to that end no church body broke more sweat than the Hope Vale Lutheran Mission Board under Bjelke-Petersen's ten-year chairmanship.

My parents watched their contemporaries pack up their young families, leave the mission and go south to live near Lutheran congregations: to milk cows, pick peanuts, cut cane and work on highways. Just like poor whites did.

I don't recall wishing that my family had also gone south. But I do recall the strange tolerance that my father and the older people showed those who administered the paternalistic regime which was our life in the mission: the missionaries and the managers. This was explicable by their over-riding devotion to the Church, a fierce sense of the mission's history and the community's tribulations and survival through times of extreme hardship, loss and dislocation. Like those born before us and indeed those who would follow, the collective psyche of myself and my schoolmates was dominated by the Moses-like figure of George Heinrich Schwarz of Neuendettelsau, who had died six years before I was born.

Old missionary Schwarz had first landed at Cape Bedford in 1887, by which time Guugu Yimithirr people had been reduced to a demoralised fringe-dwelling existence following the establishment of Cooktown. Many of their number now exterminated, their bones lined the blood-stained tracks to the Palmer River Goldfields. There was gratitude for Schwarz's lifelong effort to provide a shelter from a colonial storm whose waves had almost completely swamped the Gungu Yimithirr, drowning many of the descendants of those who first met James Cook at the Endeavour River in 1770.

Who of those who saw the sails disappear north after the crew of the *Endeavour* had effected repairs on the vessel, would have thought that four generations later the Captain's descendants would return with such vengeance, with a fever for gold and for land, leaving demoralised strugglers, begging, sneaking and apologising for an existence in their own country?

Given the Church's role in the secular administration of the mission, and the fact that the government was now headed by a *church friend*, indeed a *mission friend* during the years of my early youth, the older people forgave and suffered government paternalism in much the same way that they had suffered the paternalism of old Missionary Schwarz.

But as with the old missionaries who had gone, there was increasing disquiet among the younger people about the government and Church-sanctioned policy of inequality justified by difference. Why were people prohibited from buying motor-vehicles, why should they have to seek permission from the manager to leave the reserve, why did the money that they earnt have to be kept and managed by the mission, why could not the community have title to their land in their own hands?

The increasing awareness that Queensland legislation and policies concerning Aboriginal people breached fundamental human rights, and that our mission friend was a leading and vehement opponent of Aboriginal rights, brought on a significant identity crisis for the community. It was a crisis which led to a realisation that paternalism whilst in a fraternal context might be a natural relationship of affection, but when it concerned adults of different races it was undeniably racist, and arose from a fundamental assumption of inferiority and superiority. The government and indeed the Church had assumed our innate inferiority and their own superiority. Like many paternal relationships put asunder, the bitterness of this realisation was painful.

As with the memory of the old missionary, the pain was most acutely felt by those who had watched their parents and grandparents endure a system which treated them as state wards, as incapable and undeserving of equality and dignity. It was within the young hearts of those who contemplated this history that indignation burned, and it found resonance in the memories and secret, long-suppressed feelings of those who had endured it.

There arose a movement for change and a demand for equality.

The Brisbane Commonwealth Games in 1982 and Aboriginal protests focused international attention on Queensland's record on human rights and land rights in particular, and signalled a change in the direction of the National Party government's policies on Aboriginal Affairs. The infamous *Aborigines Act* was repealed and new and less draconian legislation governing communities was introduced. Together with legislation granting a form of land title to Aboriginal Reserves under an instrument called a Deed of Grant in Trust, this heralded a new era where the government strove to address the long-standing and widespread criticisms of its discriminatory laws.

Rather than sanctioning difference and inequality, the new policy urged equality and sameness. Aboriginal people were no longer to be distinct from the rest of the Queensland community, they were equal and this meant that they could not be allowed to be different. Aborigines were to be considered merely dark-skinned Queenslanders.

Communities which had endured terrible histories of repression and stranglehold government management, in which social problems were rife, lacking basic health, housing, educational and other services, were by semantic fiat to have been transformed into wholesome country towns with black yokels sitting on verandahs contemplating cows and the sorghum harvests.

Formal equality was now largely a fact. The government's policies were therefore difficult to reproach. The response was always that it now treated Aborigines as equal *like any other Queenslanders*.

Of course, the respect in which Aborigines were most similar to their fellow Queenslanders was that they had no special claim or right to their traditional homelands. Non-Aboriginal Queenslanders had no such inherent rights, and it would be discriminatory to accord *special rights* to compensation or land ownership to Aborigines. All rights to land in the state were granted by the Crown and there was neither any legal nor moral claim on behalf of indigenous people to what they claimed were their lands. How can you have an equal society when one group sets itself apart with claims to separate rights?

Therefore, whilst a substantial change occurred in policies in the 1980s from inequality and difference to equality and sameness, both policies were discriminatory and were premised on a vehement denial of the notion of traditional rights to land.

Thus whilst Professor Stanner confronted the myth of waste and desert lands and said that if Crown title were paraded by, every Aboriginal child would say, like the child in the fairy tale, 'But the Emperor is naked . . .', in Queensland the government continued to insist that the Emperor was decently attired in its Crown titles. It was on this insistence that the Bjelke-Petersen government moved at a night sitting of the Parliament to pass the *Queensland Coast Islands Declaratory Act 1985*. This Act purported to retrospectively extinguish any native title that might have existed in the Murray Islands. If valid, the legislation would bring to an end the court action brought by Eddie Mabo and others three years before, challenging the Crown's power to grant title to people who claimed they already held a pre-existing title to their homelands.

Before dealing further with the question of pre-existing title and the outcome in what is the most important and controversial decision of the High Court of Australia, I would like to survey briefly the developments which unfolded at the national level following the 1967 Referendum and Stanner's hopes for a final breaking of the Great Australian Silence and his hopes for Aboriginal land rights recognition.

Prior to his Boyer lecture, Professor Stanner had been to Yirrkala on the Gove Peninsula, consulting the Aboriginal people in relation to bauxite mining leases granted to Nabalco. He spoke in his lecture about the people's anxiety about the proposed development, and the strong feelings the people expressed about their homelands and what lay ahead with the mining development.

The Yirrkala people launched an action in the Supreme Court of the Northern Territory against the mining company, claiming that they held a communal native title, recognised by Australian common law, to their traditional lands. Professor Stanner gave expert evidence for the plaintiffs.

In a 1971 decision now known as the *Gove Land Rights Case*, Justice Blackburn of the Northern Territory Supreme Court found that there was a traditional system pertaining to the claimed lands which he described as 'a government of laws and not of men'. Nevertheless his judgement denied that native title was part of Australian common law, and he confirmed the assumed doctrine of *terra nullius*: an empty land without owners.

However, the negative finding in the *Gove Case* combined with increasing political agitation by Aboriginal people in the early 1970s gave rise to a political imperative to address land rights. If Aboriginal people possessed no inherent rights to land at law, then a moral onus fell upon Parliament to create rights to land. The Woodward Commission, established by the Whitlam Labor government, eventually led to the enactment of the *Northern Territory Land Rights Act 1976*. This followed moves in South Australia to address land rights.

Similar if increasingly inadequate legislative measures on land title were taken in New South Wales, Victoria and eventually Queensland. As each state eventually dealt with the imperative to address the question of land rights within their jurisdiction, it is true to say that each subsequent measure was less inspired than the last.

What has resulted is a patchwork of legislative regimes which have made provision for some areas of the country and no provision in respect of others. Moves in the mid 1980s at the federal level to introduce a national land rights model failed to fulfil the need for a national provision. The well-spring of goodwill, which erupted after *Gove*, had petered out to a trickle by the time Michael Mansell made his assessment in 1989 that no more would we see land rights legislation in this country. The question, so far as the material Australians of the 1980s were concerned, had been more or less addressed and, if not addressed, then at least attempted. In confirmation of Mansell's assessment, in 1991 the Queensland Labor Party adjusted its land rights policy platform downwards to match its recently introduced legislation. The outcome determined the policy.

It therefore appeared that there would be no more political or social impetus for any national movement on land rights. At this point, Mansell quite correctly asked whether our better prospects lay outside of the nation rather than within it.

The constitutional mandate over Aboriginal Affairs which the 1967 Referendum gave the Commonwealth has been infrequently exercised. Aboriginal Affairs and matters concerning our entitlements have too often been left to the states to repeat the long history of neglect and denial which had given rise to the need for constitutional change in the first place. One of the few assumptions of constitutional responsibility for peoples of the Aboriginal and Torres Strait Islander races was the Whitlam Labor government's enactment of legislation outlawing Queensland's discriminatory laws. And, of course, the most significant exercise of the race power came in the last days of that government with the enactment of the *Racial Discrimination Act* in October 1975.

The Act has proved to be pivotal in respect of the protection of native title as established in the *Mabo* cases. The High Court's finding in the 1992 decision, that whilst under Australian common law the British Crown acquired sovereignty over the country, it did not thereby extinguish the beneficial title of the indigenous inhabitants which they held under their own laws and customs, has revolutionised the nation's understanding of its land laws and indeed its history.

There are historical truths which are difficult for some to accept given that history is so important to contemporary political ideology. There are prescriptions which taste like too many bitter pills to many Australians who have alternately lamented, grieved and felt betrayed by the Court's decision.

There may now be some remnant rights which must be accounted for and will no longer suffer denial. This is being met by the complaint of politicians and interest groups that many in the desert areas of Western Australia and elsewhere in remote Australia, where there may be such remnant rights, have not been as comprehensively dispossessed and, better still, obliterated like so many have been in settled Australia. If only their ancestors had achieved in the Pilbara what they achieved in Van Dieman's Land!

There are black Australians too who will also feel betrayed by the Court's decision on native title, who will feel short-changed by history and white law.

But for many Australians, both black and white, *Mabo* represents an opportunity for the achievement of a greater national resolution of the question of Aboriginal land rights, and an improvement in relations between the new and old of this land, a first step in a new direction which might yield the changes necessary for indigenous people to be genuinely repossessed of their inheritance.

Given the hope and doubt which Aboriginal people feel about the court's decision and the responses of various governments and the non-Aboriginal public to native title, how can we proceed with feet laden by such trepidation?

Mabo is an attempt by the colonialist legal system to accommodate Aboriginal land rights. It is by no means the most perfect accommodation between rights under Aboriginal law and the white legal system. But, from all assessments, it is close to the best accommodation achievable within the Australian legal system. It stands creditably against similar accommodations in Canada, the United States and New Zealand.

The significance of the decision is that it recognises Aboriginal law and custom as a source of law for the first time in 204 years of colonial settlement. For the great part, however, Aboriginal law remains unrecognised. Nevertheless, the breadth of the context of this recognition sets the stage for an interaction which has never before been possible.

Colonial law has been a reality in Australia since 1788. Aboriginal law has always been a reality and we are unanimous in our resolve that it continue to be so. Colonial law is part of our indigenous reality here in Australia; it determines and controls our ability to exercise our law, enjoy our rights, maintain our identities.

With *Mabo*, the colonial system is saying: Yes, we do recognise Aboriginal law in certain circumstances relating to land but our law also says that there has been extinguishment which is legal in many circumstances. As to the balance of Aboriginal law, well, the colonial law is saying: It has no reality, in so far as we are concerned and in so far as we are prepared to act.

No matter the illegitimacy of the imposition of colonial law; no matter how revisionist and how artificial and pragmatic the High Court's recognition of indigenous law in the Murray Island case might be said to be—it is nevertheless the prevailing reality.

They are saying to us: This is the position, this is the reality, what can you do about it?

If this is the situation—that Aboriginal law has restricted recognition and there is little prospect for an extension of recognition through agitation of the common law—what strategies do we pursue to make Aboriginal law have a reality, have consequence for our colonial condition?

For the most part, the Aboriginal political system occupies a sphere which is quite distinct from the white political system. Indigenous political activity and philosophy are largely spinning in an orbit that does not have much relevance to, or impact upon, the dominant sphere in which many of the critical developments are taking place. We need a new political ideology for indigenous political strategy.

Uncle Tom and Malcolm X represent the two extreme characterisations of racial-ethnic politics in the United States, where the pan-Afro-American struggle has provided an image of the way black politics ought to be understood. At one end of the spectrum is the sell-out, at the other the radical activist. These characterisations are largely white constructs. The colonists have defined the way in which our struggle is to be understood—they, the media, the wider colonial society, define our struggles as moderate or radical, conservative or activist, to suit themselves, and we have internalised these characterisations and made them our own.

Early black leaders in Australia seized upon the politics of liberating victims which defined the black struggle against segregation in America. The emergence of radical activism changed the way in which Australians were forced to take account of the victims, but it did not always change the stance and the position from which the victims spoke—as the powerless and oppressed minority.

The language of victim politics positioned the rest of Australia as guilty perpetrators. It is an uncomfortable position and not one which will sustain a political cause. The Australian body politic will salve its conscience so far and then react in an indignant backlash, the 'we can't be blamed for what happened' response.

To that constituency, a reminder that such conscience-salving is to be particularly observed in the ready agreement of those most vehemently opposed forces who nevertheless concede the need to address the shameful health, sanitation, educational, employment and housing conditions of black Australians.

Rather than land rights this view urges conscience-salving through the pursuit of what Stanner called the 'hobby horses'. But as in 1968, with many of the statistics deteriorating rather than improving, Stanner's questioning of this approach is relevant to 1993: He said:

> They are all in part right and therefore dangerous. If all these particular measures, with perhaps fifty or a hundred other, were carried out everywhere, simultaneously, and on a sufficient scale, possibly there would be a general advance . . . But who shall mobilise and command this regiment of one-eyed hobby horses? And keep them in column?

For the indigenous quarter, the fact of our changing political circumstances calls for us to re-evaluate our political strategies. People aren't moderates or conservatives on the one hand, and radicals and extremists on the other. Rather, it is actions and strategies which should be seen as moderate or radical. There is a world of difference between black radical cheek and black radical chic. The test of credibility of a strategy is not whether the approach is radical or conservative, but whether it is smart or dumb, and whether it enhances or jeopardises the rights and interests of one's people.

The politics of victims asserts that unless the dominating state accepts us on our own terms, any complicity, any dealing constitutes an unacceptable relinquishment of our power. For a long time, the only political currency which Aboriginal people could use was their refusal to be involved. Now that the non-Aboriginal legal system has offered something in the way of rights, however narrow, to refuse to engage in the game and to fail to appreciate the rules and its limitations—even if our purpose be to disrupt the game— no longer seems smart. The challenge is to negotiate the expansion of those rights without losing ground and without surrendering the chances of future advances in a struggle which has incrementally advanced and whose destination is still long in arriving.

Kerry Stokes

A major media proprietor, Kerry Stokes was born in Melbourne in 1940, and educated at St George's Christian Brothers College and the Western Australian Technical College. He has lived in Perth since 1959. His company, Australian Capital Equity Pty Ltd, has held a variety of media and other business interests, including at one time the newspaper the *Canberra Times* and currently, the Seven television network of which he was chairman from 1995 and executive chairman since 1999. He has also had interests in the pastoral industry, real estate and manufacturing.

He has had a strong influence in the arts and was chairman of the National Gallery of Australia from 1996 to 2000, and chairman of the Art Gallery Foundation of the Art Gallery of Western Australia and a director from 1989–91. He was a director of the Canberra Theatre Trust and in 1980 a director of the Sydney Dance Company. He is a life member of the Variety Club of Australia.

In 1994 he received the West Australian Citizen of the Year Award in Industry and Commerce. In 1995 he was made an Officer of the Order of Australia.

Kerry Stokes gave his six 1994 Boyer Lectures the overall title of *Advance Australia Where?*. It is also the title of his concluding lecture. His passionate concern was the communications media. The engaging titles of the lectures are: 'Don't Shoot the Pigeons Just Yet'; 'Evil Communications Corrupt Good Manners'; 'Culture—It's Yoghurt for American'; 'The Hand that Rocks the Cradle . . .'; and 'Double Jeopardy: Double Expense', which is reproduced here.

Kerry Stokes articulates clearly his concern about official and commercial obsession with new communications technology, together with massive investment relatively unprompted by consumer demand or social need. He is also concerned about the risk of cultural imperialism facilitated by the new technology so that 'the unique Australian cultural identity is in danger of being overwhelmed by foreign produced material.'

DOUBLE JEOPARDY:
DOUBLE EXPENSE

Advance Australia Where?

Kerry Stokes

• 1994 •

Dazzling as the new technology is, it is no good having extra channels and fancy information delivery systems if the flow of information is impeded by law, and the quality of information is corrupted
by the people who handle it. No matter how solid the policy
foundations, or how good the technological framework, it all
comes down to people in the end: we need good craftspeople
working in a creative environment to put the media house in order.

I want to turn away from the owners and the federal government
and look at the responsibilities of the people who work in the
media, particularly journalists, and the rights of consumers, particularly their right to be informed.

As the technology develops, it becomes more important to
ensure that the legal and self-regulatory framework which governs
the conduct of people in the media is working well. At present, I
think there are some major impediments to the proper working of
our media in a democratic society. The defamation law is far too
draconian. It inhibits free speech because it is too heavy-handed. Yet
those whose complaints fall outside the defamation law or those
who cannot afford the risk of running a defamation action have no
redress. In short, the present regulatory system gives little or no
protection to the average person who suffers abuse from the media,
but gives too much protection for the rich and powerful.

Unfortunately, these twin defects feed off each other. The more
ordinary people see they have no effective redress from media
misconduct, the more they applaud the restrictive defamation laws
which serve the rich, the powerful, the politicians and the big name
sports and entertainment stars. All of which does nothing to
encourage the formation of an informed society. Unless there is
some reform, as technology develops this is likely to get worse
rather than better.

Many people in Australia today believe our media do not serve us well. A lot of their dissatisfaction is directed at the journalists them-selves. That is evidenced by fairly regular opinion polls which rank journalists at the level of car sellers and real estate agents and a long way below even politicians. That hurts!

Given this low public rating of journalists, the public would perhaps be reluctant to grant them any further leeway than they already have. So when any proposals to liberalise the defamation laws come up, people are at best apathetic and at worst openly hostile. They perhaps see the defamation law as one of the few weapons to keep journalists under control.

This is unfortunate. Whereas the strict defamation law might be one of the few restraints on journalists, it has a worse side effect in that it sometimes enables the rich and powerful to silence critics. It permits people in the professions to escape scrutiny, and it prevents full and frank discussion of some matters of public importance.

Reform is needed, but it will not come while we see so many instances of journalistic misconduct. Those who have called for reform may have put the cart before the horse. Until the profession of journalism puts its own house in order, there will be little public sympathy and no political sympathy for reforming defamation law.

At present there are very few constraints against journalists' misconduct. Unlike nearly every other profession, there is no statu-tory or professional body that oversees the profession of journalism. There is the Media, Entertainment and Arts Alliance, but this is an industrial union, not a professional body. It embraces most practis-ing journalists, but not all. More significantly, it does not have open and independent procedures to scrutinise journalists' conduct and to discipline errant journalists.

Perhaps the journalistic sin most condemned by the public is invasion of privacy. Invasive television cameras intruding into people's grief, foot-in-the-door journalism and publication of irrelevant details of people's private lives are, I suggest, the things that cause journalists to be held in such low esteem. Yet there is no legal protection against this sort of journalism. This is because there is no general legal right to privacy in Australia. Further, the pro-fession itself provides no redress against it and no disciplinary measures against it. This is because the journalists' code of ethics puts the public 'right to know' ahead of all else.

The tragedy, I think, is that there is a misguided belief that the defamation law is the only restraint against even further excesses, when it is no such thing at all.

One of the difficulties is that defamation is directed at the publishing company, not the individual journalist. The journalist's conduct is rarely brought under scrutiny. And the case usually comes to court years after the event.

We should look at a three-way reform: a recognition of a general right of privacy; an open and independent system of making individual journalists accountable for misconduct; and a fundamental change to the defamation law. They should go hand-in-hand.

Let us look at privacy first. At present there is no general redress against invasions of privacy. Some regulatory bodies deal with particular areas, such as abuse of the telephone system or in relation to provision of credit. But intrusions by the media go largely unredressed.

Technology, of course, has made invasion of privacy easier. We saw just recently the example of a miniature camera being used to get pictures of the Princess of Wales in a gymnasium. We have seen the publication of politicians' private car-telephone conversations. Hidden cameras, infrared devices and smaller and more sophisticated bugs are becoming cheaper and more available to privacy invaders, who might include the media.

It would be helpful if the industry could agree on a form of privacy guidelines and impose them by self-regulation. The present guidelines in the journalists' code of ethics of the Media Alliance are unsatisfactory. They call on journalists to respect privacy, but that is cancelled out by the overriding requirement of the public's right to know. Moreover, the code of ethics privacy clause is expressed in very general terms.

If self-regulation fails, then a change in the law might be needed. This would be unfortunate as the law is often an inflexible and expensive way of achieving social goals, and it rarely keeps abreast of technical developments.

What about general misconduct, beyond invasions of privacy? What restraint is there against misconduct by individual journalists for things such as breaches of confidence, bias, racism, unfairness, misleading conduct and so on? A member of the public can complain to the editor, who is also a journalist, and hope to extract a correction or the publication of a letter to the editor. However, any hope of discipline against the errant journalist is a faint one because editors are subject to a virtual union closed shop and face the threat of strikes if anyone is fired. Besides, termination of employment may often be too drastic, though industrial law doesn't allow for lesser penalties of fines or suspension.

Television and radio, of course, do not have a daily equivalent of the Letters column and only broadcast corrections and apologies under grave legal threat. The Australian Press Council is supposed to be the self-regulatory industry association to deal with complaints against the press. Alas, it does not embrace the electronic media. Nor do all newspaper publishers accept its jurisdiction. Moreover, even those that do, do not publish many of its rulings other than those about themselves. Without the sanction of publicity, the Press Council does not have a bark, let alone a bite.

A further weakness with the Press Council is that complaints are addressed to the publisher, not the individual journalist. Obviously, publishers must carry the lion's share of the blame when things go wrong, because they have the overall control. However, journalism is a profession, even if nearly all its participants are employees rather than private practitioners. Individual journalists must be held responsible and accountable for misconduct, not just to their employer in terms of continued employment or promotion chances, but to the public at large. They have that responsibility, just like an employed doctor, engineer or solicitor.

In all, the present system makes things very difficult for the ordinary member of the public who has been mistreated by the media.

The introduction of pay television and the potential of converging technologies make the situation even more acute. What we actually need now is a uniform complaints system that covers all media. It must be an Australia-wide system that is accessible to the public and run openly and independently.

The important point is that once the media and the people who work in it become more accountable to the general public, it is likely that the media will be trusted with a more liberal defamation and contempt law and protection of sources than we have at present.

Take the protection of sources as one example. Lawyers and doctors have the confidences with their clients generally respected by the courts. They also have reasonably strong professional ethical monitoring. Journalists, however, can be forced to divulge their confidential sources on pain of a fine or even imprisonment. This is unsatisfactory because if the confidentiality of journalists' sources is not respected, a lot of sources will dry up. Those sources will not risk their jobs and in some cases their lives or limbs, if there is a chance their identities will be disclosed. And then important information which should be made public would remain secret. It is iniquitous for journalists and not in the public interest that the present law does not give even limited protection for journalists' sources.

Let us now turn to the defamation law. In all states and territories, publishers are required to prove the truth of what they write.

The High Court has recently modified this in relation to the discussion of government and political matters, where publication can be protected from defamation action providing the publisher can prove it was acting honestly, not recklessly, and reasonably. However, this modification applies to a relatively narrow area. For the broad brush of everyday reportage you still have to prove truth, and this is more difficult than it sounds.

It is in fact an extremely expensive, hit-and-miss affair. By the time the lawyers representing both sides have gone to town on all the witnesses, no-one can tell where the truth lies. And in those circumstances, the law and practice is to say the defence has not been made out and the defendant publisher must pay (usually large damages out of all proportion to the real injury). The end result is that speech and writing are inhibited.

If you can only publish and say what you can prove to be true, you say little. This was eloquently put by Justice William Brennan in the US Supreme Court in 1964:

> Erroneous statement is inevitable in free debate. It must be protected if the freedoms of expression are to have the breathing space that they need in order to survive . . . A rule compelling the critic of official conduct to guarantee the truth of all his factual assertions— and to do so on the pain of libel judgments virtually unlimited in amount—leads to a comparable self-censorship . . . Under such a rule, would-be critics of official conduct may be deterred from voicing their criticism, even though it is believed to be true, and even though it is in fact true, because of doubt whether it can be proved or fear of the expense of having to do so.

Instead of putting the onus on the publisher, as in Australia, the US puts the onus on the person suing, just as in every other area of the law (medical malpractice, breach of contract and so on). The person suing has to show 'malice', 'negligence' or no public interest. These principles mean that the publisher would be safe if he or she made reasonable inquiries, gave the other side an opportunity to respond, honestly believed the truth of what was being published on at least some grounds (even if they could not be proved) and published in the public interest.

What effect would that have on Australian journalism if applied broadly? At present, the truth requirement effectively results in self-censorship. The public, of course, cannot see that because the material subjected to self-censorship of its nature is not public. The main evidence of it, though, is there in the news pages of Australian newspapers with the high percentage that is reportage of protected courts, parliamentary reporting, government reports, human interest stories and the odd science bit. With the truth test hanging over them, journalists either give up altogether or self-censor because it is too hard.

A reasonable-grounds test would have a different outcome. Broadly applied, it would put journalists and journalism to the test. It wouldn't be a case of lawyers going off in an expensive search for an elusive objective truth. Journalistic conduct itself would actually be called into account. Journalists would have to answer the tough questions such as: Did you behave reasonably? Did you give the other side a reasonable opportunity to respond? Did you make reasonable inquiries? Were you malicious? Did you honestly believe your story? Where are your notes and records of conversations to back this up?

Furthermore, editors would have to insist on journalism being conducted in such a way as to answer those questions so their defamation defences are secure.

Also under these sorts of principles, people confronted with allegations wouldn't be able just to say: publish and I'll sue, or you try and prove it. They would have to respond or the defence of absence of malice would be made out. These changes can only improve public discourse.

There are other facets of the defamation law which do little to help the general conduct of the media in Australia. It is expensive, the delays are legendary, success for both sides is very hit and miss, and the remedy of paying money years after the event is not related to the nature of the injury, which is damage to reputation now.

Swift corrections and a climate of negotiation and give and take, away from the fear of huge damage pay-outs on one side or the lure of the pot of gold on the other, would make the parties address the main issues: the reasonableness of the publisher's conduct and the restoration of wrongly damaged reputation.

The cry for reform in defamation has been agonisingly long. The recent High Court ruling on free speech has certainly put the issue on the political agenda—Attorney General Michael Lavarch sees it as the first step on the road to the creation of a national uniform defamation code. However, it is still up to the politicians to act, and the momentum will not be sustained without public pressure. That sort of public involvement won't come about until something is done about invasions of privacy and other media excesses. Reform of both, as I say, will have to go hand in hand.

As newspapers start electronic delivery, the need will be greater for a regulatory system that focuses on the reasonableness of the conduct of the journalist, rather than on proving the elusive truth of what was said. This is because electronic publication is more instant and the temptation to get the story on the database without checking is higher.

So far we have looked at the conduct of the people in the media, and how the law and practice have not been very satisfactory in improving standards. Before leaving discussion of the legal-regulatory regime of the media and communications industry, I want to give a couple more examples of how technology is getting ahead of the game in terms of both legal and self-regulatory mechanisms.

The first example is new graphics technology and the second relates to copyright. Many newspapers have already introduced or are about to introduce new computer methods of producing pictures, replacing the darkroom and its enlargers and developing tanks. However these computer methods give the photographer or picture editor great scope to manipulate the image to give a false impression, well beyond the normal darkroom techniques. The computer allows seamless erasure, transplanting or moving of people or things. On one hand the technology provides great creative potential and great economies, but on the other it also gives rise to a potential for great harm and embarrassment.

Some newspapers have worked out rough guidelines. Some state if a picture is a concoction or has been tampered with. But there is no enforcement and the public has no way of knowing whether or not the camera or the computer are telling a lie. This is not a call for regulation by government, far from it. Rather it is a call for better self-regulation and more public involvement in self-regulation.

The other example I wish to cite concerns copyright law, where technology has left the framers of the law trailing hopelessly behind. For 30 years or more technology has outstripped the law, with virtually every major change in technology leaving the law floundering in its wake. This timelag has allowed widespread theft of intellectual property, with relative impunity or with remedies so cumbersome as to be virtually useless. Audio tapes, photocopies and VCRs are major examples. People have copied without paying copyright and for years there was no sensible administrative means whereby they could pay copyright even if they wanted to. When the law eventually caught up, it imposed tape levies and permitted sampling of educational and government photocopying.

Now another major technological change looms and poses another challenge for the lawmakers. As with previous technological changes, they are aware of the problem, but whether that awareness will be translated into law in the next half decade is another matter. The technological change is convergence. Present copyright law still talks about literary, musical, artistic, photographic, and film works as if they are separate things, and as if the way they are reproduced or copied is different. Nowadays, of course, they are all the same thing and can be copied and reproduced the same way: digitally. Beethoven's Ninth, the photo on page one of today's newspaper, the words of the text next to it and the sound of my voice talking to you can all be reduced to computer files, to strings of ones and zeros, then copied and reproduced exactly.

Digital technology and convergence means some of the natural restraints against unauthorised copying are removed. Why go to a music store when you can get your music CDs free down the phone line from a bulletin board? This is not fanciful. The Recording Industry Association of America is alarmed. It said it was very troubled about how easy it was to upload sound recordings and other information and put them on a bulletin board on the 20 million-member Internet for anyone to download.

The law as it now stands could leave the owners of this intellectual property unprotected. A recent copyright convergence seminar in Canberra revealed the slowness of some of the thinking. At present, copyright law deals with literary, musical, artistic and film works separately. But as we have seen, they can all now be similarly reproduced in computer code which leads to a blurring of the distinction between different media.

Further, the existing law does not cater for the new technology of multi-media which can creatively combine, say, a clip of Madonna music, the words of a Keneally novel, some moving pictures from *Mad Max*, an Aboriginal motif and so on. The Federal Justice Department's Copyright Convergence Group in deliberating on this issue has kept the distinctions between the various artistic works and suggested that the law be amended separately with respect to each. This seems to fly in the face of the way the technology is changing, and offers cold comfort for the many local artists who seek protection for their intellectual property.

My point here is that a purely legalistic approach may not work in the face of rapidly moving technology. A technological solution as well as a legal one is needed. Piracy by audio tape, for example, was addressed not by catching and fining or suing the pirates, but by levying the tape they bought and later by delivering music on CDs, which until very recently were not easily copied.

If protecting Australian culture is the aim, we may have to take a

broader view rather than adopting the piecemeal approach governments have adopted up to now.

To conclude this lecture, much of what Australian journalists,
artists, writers and musicians do is world class. My concern is that
we should create an environment that encourages and enforces high
standards and protects Australian culture in an age where changes in
technology point to ever-increasing internationalisation and mass
marketing. This will require greater public and industry participation and a broader governmental vision. Without it, the technology
will drive our media and communications industry in a haphazard
way. That may not result in the best outcome for Australia.

Over the course of the past five lectures, I have examined various
aspects of what I have termed the communications evolution. It is a
complex subject, but that is the nature of communication itself. And
we have seen that many issues are inter-related (culture and foreign
ownership, for example), which makes it even more difficult to find
appropriate solutions.

It is this complexity which poses the central dilemma, as far as I
am concerned: there is a danger that in dealing with the welter of
technological options our response is fragmented. We may be
tempted to tackle problems piecemeal instead of formulating a
coherent strategy. And by focusing on the fragments we may miss
important cross-connections. The trees may lead us to lose sight of
the wood.

In my last lecture, I intend to confront this dilemma head on,
examining the avenues for action that may offer the best result for
Australia.

Eva Cox

Eva Cox was born in Vienna in 1938 and immigrated to Australia in 1948. She was educated at Sydney Girls' High School, the University of New South Wales and the University of Sydney.

From 1977 to 1981 she was the director of the New South Wales Council of Social Services. In 1981–82 she was a senior adviser to the Federal shadow minister for social security. She then became senior assistant director of the NSW Department of Youth and Community Services. From 1990 to 1994 she was the managing director of Distaff Associates before becoming a lecturer in the department of

humanities and social science at Sydney's University of Technology in 1994.

She has held numerous consultancies and has been an active member of the boards of many organisations. These include the Australian Council of Social Service, the NSW Council of Social Services, Community Child Care, Women's Economic Think Tank, which she helped to found, and the Women's Electoral Lobby, of which she was also a founding member. She was also active in the Media Women's Action Group, and in 1983 was involved in the Alternative Economic Summit. She has been a regular commentator on the ABC and she is the author of *Leading Women*.

Eva Cox was made an Officer of the Order of Australia in 1995.

A Truly Civil Society was the title given by Eva Cox to her six 1995 Boyer Lectures. Their individual titles were 'Broadening the Viewing Points'; 'Raising Social Capital', which is reproduced here; 'The Dark Side of the Warm Inner Glow: Family and Communitarians'; 'The Companionable State'; 'Change, Diversity and Dissent' and 'A Utopian Road Movie'. In describing these lectures, Eva Cox said: 'They look at our collective responsibilities; at ways in which we can move back from the possible undermining of society; how we move on towards a humanly comfortable future which values our connections and validates debates and dissent.' Her respect for debate and dissent is never far from the surface of these lectures.

RAISING SOCIAL CAPITAL

A Truly Civil Society

Eva Cox

• 1 9 9 5 •

We invented money and, from coins of precious metal, we created the convenient fiction of finance. This fiction has unfortunately become the ultimate public record of human connections—what we now call transactions.

Journalists, treasurers and business lobbies use financial data as pressure points to influence political decisions. We worry constantly about whether our ill-defined Gross Domestic Product is growing too fast or not fast enough, even though it measures only part of our production and wealth. Finance capital movements determine exchange and interest rates and usurp the roles of the sovereign state. Electronic pulses are invested with so much meaning that they have the power to destroy governments and increase the private affluence of a privileged few.

What is meant by wealth? Wealth has become a very disputed term, particularly with the recent World Bank claims that Australia is the wealthiest country in the world.

Marilyn Waring described the faults in measures of national production in her ground-breaking book *Counting for Nothing*. Crime is counted, traffic accidents because of potholes are not but car repairs are. Plantation trees are counted, self-sown saplings are not. If we sell sex, cooking and child care they are counted, but unpaid housework is not. Growth in GDP may come from oil spills, bush-fires, wars, epidemics or the destruction of wilderness. GDP is reduced by a lower road accident rate and fewer heart attacks.

The public finance system does not debit financial capital with the destruction of physical capital such as the uncounted wealth of clean air, water resources, trees and the rest of the natural world. So aspects of daily living, such as unpaid production and gifts of time, are not counted as part of the wealth of nations.

There are four major capital measures, one of which takes up far too much policy time and space at present. This is financial capital.

Physical capital makes it onto the agenda because of the environmental movement. So there are fierce debates on trees, water, coal and what constitutes sustainable development. Some types of physical capital and financial capital deplete with overuse, or become scarce and too expensive. We occasionally mention human capital—the total of our skills and knowledge—but rarely count its loss in unemployment.

There has been too little attention paid to social capital—the last of the four horseriders of another apocalypse. Social capital refers to the processes between people which establish networks, norms and social trust and facilitate coordination and cooperation for mutual benefit. These processes are also known as social fabric or glue, but I am deliberately using the term 'capital' because it invests the concept with reflected status from other forms of capital. Social capital is also appropriate because it can be measured and quantified so we can distribute its benefits and avoid its losses.

We increase social capital by working together voluntarily in egalitarian organisations. Learning some of the rough and tumble of group process also has the advantage of connecting us with others. We gossip, relate and create the warmth that comes from trusting. Accumulated social trust allows groups and organisations, and even nations, to develop the tolerance sometimes needed to deal with conflicts and different interests.

We must put a high priority, therefore, on growing social capital by offering opportunities for trust and cooperation. The social institutions which govern and influence us must operate in ways which value diversity and belonging. They must also be able to withstand debate and questioning. If the social system isolates people, discourages informal and formal contact, or just fails to offer the time and space needed for social contact, then social capital is under threat.

Lack of time is an increasing problem as time becomes commodified through ever longer hours of paid work, isolation in cars and as increasing options for individual working and leisure intrude on our once informal meeting times. We rarely have time to walk, often avoid public transport, shop hurriedly and use technology to provide home-based entertainment and work. We need to make time for social interactions and the development of trust relationships. What once happened by accident needs to be recognised and encouraged. We need to examine how we can use technology to enhance social capital, and we must look at lifestyles and life cycles to make sure there is space and time.

Social capital should be the pre-eminent and most valued form of capital as it provides the basis on which we build a truly civil society. Without our social bases we cannot be fully human. Social capital is as vital as language for human society. We become vulnerable to social bankruptcy when our social connections fail. If most of our experiences enhance our sense of trust and mutuality, allowing us to feel valued and to value others, then social capital increases. This is why I want to use the concept of social capital as a major thread in these lectures.

In a recent article called 'Bowling Alone: America's Declining Social Capital', American political scientist Robert Putnam describes the need for a strong active civil society to make democracy work. He quotes many studies that show a correlation between high levels of civic culture, comfortable lifestyles and positive economic outcomes.

Putnam claims that the interactions which create social capital are most likely to occur in egalitarian communities where people voluntarily contribute time and effort and receive positive reinforcement. Experiences which engender trust and recognition of common ground allow people to move comfortably from the defensive 'I' to the mutual 'we'. A sense of reciprocity, he claims, is more than just a utilitarian trading relationship. It creates complex social relationships.

Spending time together, working cooperatively and enjoying each other's company create social capital. This seems to be heresy indeed. In an age when competition is the only solution on offer, social capital theory suggests another option: that humans achieve more by cooperating. Indeed much of what we, as a society, have achieved has been by cooperation. If cooperation works so well, we should be wary of accepting competition policies.

Putnam's work in regional Italy offers statistical evidence that cooperation pays off socially, bureaucratically and economically. High levels of social capital bring cooperation and norms which may be called civic virtues. These virtues in turn are the basis of truly civil societies where the law rests lightly. If we trust others as we trust ourselves, prosperity and economic growth follow.

Social capital is the social glue, the weft and warp of the social fabric which comprises the myriad of interactions that make up our public and private lives—our *vita activa*. Distrust, loss of social cohesion and short-term self-interest breed conflict and social isolation, demands for law and order and a contempt for power and authority.

So how do we create social capital? Putnam suggests it is the trust we develop through active relationships with each other. Accumulated trust is based, at least in part, on working together in 'civic' groups. These are the familiar community groups: non-profit organisations such as P&Cs, local environment groups, Rotary, craft groups, neighbourhood centres, local sporting groups, some ethnic and religious groups, reading groups, fundraising organisations, playgroups and others which have an egalitarian voluntary structure. Such groups are generally run democratically: people participate because they want to and their processes involve members working together on tasks, developing trust and mutually rewarding relationships.

Trust should be defined as inexhaustible because it is increased, rather than depleted by positive use. The more we work together with others in environments which encourage cooperation the more likely we are to trust others, and the occasional failures of trust will be less damaging. Social capital is therefore increased by use. It can be depleted by widespread lack of trust or by our failure to trust others. Without trust we avoid contact with others because we fear betrayal. This is the core component of social connections.

When people meet to clean up a city, a suburb or a local park, they are amassing social capital. Indeed we amass social capital when we work on the school fete, talk to our neighbours about the street plants, drop some soup into a sick friend, meet a regular group at tennis or bowls, join a local choir, commit ourselves to making uniforms for the junior sports group, arrange theatre parties, or whatever we do with friends and sometimes strangers.

Even in paid work we may often want to give more than the minimum. There is pleasure in providing a better service. It is a small gift to help, to smile and to satisfy another. We do this not just for commercial reasons but because as the shop assistant, nurse or car detailer we like the customer and want to give them something extra.

Competing against each other leaves little space for reciprocity and the growth of social capital. Running against another in a race may benefit our speed, but jointly organising the sports day produces cooperation and trust. There are many situations where cooperation and reciprocity are more effective than competition. Civic virtues come from building on what we have in common rather than by using our differences to create in-groups, outgroups and fear-driven competition.

The value of belonging to voluntary organisations is often misinterpreted by those on the political right who use Putnam's work to claim that we should replace governments with any voluntary organisation. This ignores Putnam's point that it is not the auspice of the organisation that counts, but the way it operates. Many of these groups on the Right are authoritarian in structure and want to impose their norms on others.

As Putnam says:

> On the demand side, citizens in civic communities expect and get better government . . . they are prepared to act collectively to achieve shared goals. . . . Most fundamental to the civic community is the social ability to collaborate for shared interests. Generalised reciprocity . . . generates high social capital. . . . A conception of one's role and obligations as a citizen, coupled with a commitment to political equality, is the cultural cement of the civil community.
>
> Without norms of social reciprocity and networks of social engagement, the Hobbesian outcome of the Mezzogiorno—amoral familism, clientelism, lawlessness, ineffective Government and economic stagnation—seems likelier than successful democratisation and economic development. Palermo may represent the future of Moscow.

Putnam's work shows that community groups, workplaces or other organisations which are authoritarian and paternalistic do not create trust and civic virtues. They distribute favours to the chosen and compliant, or demand blind loyalty. The consequences are competitive and suspicious interactions. Unity is created by identifying an outside enemy and closing ranks. Mafia-style patronage breeds competition—not cohesion.

What Putnam's data suggests is that the removal of government—destroying the legitimacy of its laws—may create gangs and militias as is occurring in the USA. We need to remember that there is nothing naturally virtuous in communal organisations, nor anything inherently wrong with government.

I was excited when I found Putnam's work because it offered a framework for pulling together many of my diverse concerns. The idea of social capital as a measure of the social health or otherwise of communities, societies or nations has a certain unifying elegance.

However, I think his viewpoints are still too narrow. He focuses on definable organisations which work formally in the public arena but he does not include the many informal groups. His limited view reflects the usual masculinist assumptions about the separation of the public and private spheres.

I want to extend the social capital concept to include the household and informal sectors which can also create social trust relationships and forms of civic wellbeing. I would include certain extended household operations, neighbourliness and community support, all of which informally link people. These informal help and support measures are functional as well as creating recognition and identity.

Social capital accumulators work best as open systems which allow entry for newcomers who may be different. Informal networks may cluster around a formal institution such as a school or community centre, or less visible locations like the house where people gather, a local shopping centre, coffee shop, or parks.

These informal networks fit Putnam's models of democratic, egalitarian web-like structures which offer shared positive experiences through collaboration. The experiences provide a comfort zone for recognising our communalities and choosing to look for collective rather individual benefits.

There is another related area of possible accumulation of social capital that struck me on reading Putnam. What he describes as civic culture is very similar to what is increasingly being recognised as workplace culture. Again, the rules and formal structures of workplaces may be similar, but the actual cultures of staff relationships within workplaces may affect the way the organisation works as well as how productive it is.

Some workplace cultures model open and relatively egalitarian relationships. Others are closed and authoritarian, immune to change or to the entry of outsiders. A level of collegiality and trust between workers creates workplaces where authority is worn lightly but responsibly and productivity are high. Where the workplace is redolent with distrust and suspicion, the rule books grow in size because everything has to be documented. Disputes are always bubbling, and there are likely to be complaints of harassment and discrimination.

It is interesting to note that at the same time as there is a government policy of imposing competition between firms, there is a recognition that the best working teams are based on cooperation. Indeed competition would seem to militate against the levels of trust and cooperation that are emerging in studies of best practice. We need to consider whether the loss of social capital through workplace competition may also prove in the not-so-long run to reduce productivity and profits.

What are the elements of social systems which increase social capital? They are mainly based on interactions. They involve space, time, opportunities, precedent and the valuing of processes.

We need the opportunities to interact with a reasonably broad spread of people, and to build up a level of trust through positive rather than negative experiences. We need the time to engage in satisfactory processes of discussion, to acknowledge the input of others, and to develop outcomes which reflect inputs.

Public life and activities take time, and time is an ever decreasing 'commodity' for many people. Full time work often extends well past the eight hour day, yet time is available in excess to those who have no paid work. This is one of the diseases of our present community. There is a constant trade-off between time and money.

If we decide to value all aspects of the *vita activa*, we should be able to spend time in paid work earning money, using our skills and contributing to the workplace community. We should also be able to spend time on interpersonal relationships and the daily tasks of care for self and others, including the rearing of children. And we should also be able to spend time in the public sphere producing ideas, running small communal groups or large institutions and involving ourselves in making decisions that affect the way we live.

We must validate the social and remember that humans were never disconnected individuals. We have always been social. Our human ability to reason has never removed us from our interdependence. In fact, it is through our ability to cooperate, as well as compete, that we have developed what passes for civilisation. I want to reclaim the concept of civic virtue as a collective rather than an individual manifestation of a truly civil society. The types of civic structures which develop social capital are not created by removing the underpinnings of the state, but by giving people time, skills, encouragement and resources.

What happens when we run down our social capital? This raises the issue of whether we live in communities or nations which offer sufficient possibility for experiencing social trust. Are there societies with an adequate level of social capital? Is there a social plimsoll line, a marker which, once passed, reduces the levels of civic virtue to the point of no return?

If our communities are already low in social capital, or even in deficit, their reconstruction will be slow. Putnam talks of the problems of countries where communism wiped out much of the civic culture. There are others where centuries of top down feudalism was never replaced by any democratic structure.

The process of replenishing or developing social capital takes a long time. The Italian examples Putnam quotes are the results of centuries of civic cultures. Losing social capital should therefore be identified as a serious problem. The question Putnam asks of the USA, and I am raising the same question here, is: Are we running our social capital down and even out?

We have a different political culture from the United States of America. The American colonies had a much stronger emphasis on free enterprise and individualism than on government. Our colonies were started by government fiat and we continue to have a closer relationship to the public sector than our American peers. Trust in government I suspect, is one of our social capital indicators.

In Australia, opinion polls over time suggest there is increasing cynicism about government and politicians. There are diminished levels of trust in public utilities, particularly when they corporatise and treat us as customers not citizens. These days, our utilities delivering phones, gas, water and electricity behave like any other big business. Yet when they are sold, the public feels a loss of common property.

I have a strong sense that we are unravelling and tearing the social fabric, replacing it with a safety net that catches some of the poor and leaves the rest to flounder. We are losing some of the sense of belonging and of the common wealth that is part of our public selves. We are left to retreat into the presumed safety of the private world.

We need to recognise that a loss of social capital may cost us financial capital. For instance, an increased fear of crime, when the crime rate is not rising, is a more significant measure of social distrust than an actual increase in crime. The unreasoned fear of other people's criminal intent signals a decline in social capital.

It is this unwarranted fear that leads to a demand for more government spending on crime prevention measures, gaols and other forms of social control. The last New South Wales state election was a case in point, when the then government and Opposition tried to outdo each other in their promises to punish criminals. Yet there was no real evidence that crime was on the increase, nor that the proposed measures would curb it.

Expenditure in this area was seen as politically necessary but was unlikely to be effective because it failed to address the real problem. In fact more law and order measures would probably exacerbate the problem because they would lift the levels of anxiety and do nothing to reduce the level of crime.

It is an interesting contradiction that increased rates of imprisonment and policing under conservative governments leads to the higher spending they claim to be against. And expenditure on social control often exceeds the cost of those government services which increase social capital—for instance more jobs in the community services sector.

We are left with the contradiction that a government's failure to spend on enhancing social capital will actually reduce the level of financial capital. Indeed, high social capital may well be the prerequisite for economic growth.

Pierre Ryckmans

An elusive philosopher, Pierre Ryckmans was born in 1935 in Brussels and was educated at the University of Louvain. He settled in Australia in 1970 after living and teaching in Hong Kong for a number of years. In Hong Kong he taught history of art at the Chinese University. In Australia he has taught Chinese literature at the Australian National University. From 1987 to 1993 he was Professor of Chinese Studies at the University of Sydney.

Professor Ryckmans is the author of a number of books, several critical of the Chinese regime, particularly under Mao. Many were written under the pseudonym Simon Leys. His *Chinese Shadows* and *The Chairman's New Clothes: Mao and the Cultural Revolution*, both published in translation in 1977, stirred considerable controversy in certain literary and scholarly journals. He is also the author of *The Burning Forest*, *The Death of Napoleon*, an acclaimed translation of *The Analects of Confucius*, *Essais sur la chine*, and *The Angel and the Octopus*. Professor Ryckmans also contributes to a number of international journals.

He is a fellow of the Australian Academy of the Humanities, a member of the Academie Royale de Literature Francaise (Belgium). Among his awards are *The Independent* (UK) Foreign Fiction Award, the Christina Stead Prize for Fiction (NSW Premier's Literary Awards), and the Victorian Premier's Prize for Literary Translation.

Geoffrey Bolton's 'view' was from the 'edge' for his geographical reasons; Pierre Ryckmans' 'view' is from a 'bridge' that may be between cultures, or lives, or experiences. Bridges can carry us forward, they can also allow us to return.

The View from the Bridge—Aspects of Culture consists of four lectures: 'Learning'; 'Reading', which is reproduced here; 'Writing' and 'Going Abroad and Staying Home', published with two appendices— 'Perplexities of an Electronically Illiterate Old Man' and 'Barcelona by Robert Hughes'. They are elegant, absorbing and stimulating.

Pierre Ryckmans' introduction begins with gardening and philosophers. He goes on to say: 'John Henry Newman's magnificent statement on spiritual development— "πGrowth is the only evidence of life"—might as well have been issued by an old farmer. Since the dawn of cilivization— actually, since Neolithic times when prehistoric man first began to settle down, to sow, to plant and to harvest— "culture" has sustained and defined us, and it is not by chance that we use the same word when we speak both of "cultivating" our gardens, and of "cultivating" our minds.' Dr Ryckmans is quite a gardener.

READING

The View from the Bridge: Aspects of Culture

Pierre Ryckmans

• 1996 •

In the memoirs of a contemporary Chinese writer, I found an intriguing anecdote. During the war, the author had fled the Japanese invasion and taken refuge in the countryside. For a man who only knew modern city life, the sudden discovery of a traditional peasant world that had hardly changed in two thousand years proved full of surprises. One day, as he had to write an article for a magazine, he went out in the fields, in search of inspiration. He sat under a tree, scribbled a couple of pages, but, feeling dissatisfied with his work, threw the draft away and pursued his walk. An old peasant who had been watching him for some time, ran after him with the discarded manuscript, and, invoking all the authority of age, gave the young man a stern dressing down: 'Shame on you! You are an educated man, you ought to know better! One does not treat writing like garbage!' Taken aback at first, the writer finally understood—and was moved: in this remote corner, the illiterate villagers still respected writing as something sacred—for it was a rule in traditional China that no writing of any sort should ever be randomly discarded; manuscripts and papers bearing inscriptions, if no longer needed, had to be carefully stored while waiting to be incinerated on a certain day of every year, all at once, in the local temple of Confucius.

The script is at the root of Chinese civilisation in a way that has no real equivalent anywhere else in the world. Western literary culture, on the contrary, developed at first from the oral tradition of the Homeric poems; and later on, in the classical period, it was still the spoken word that continued to dominate the intellectual and literary life, through the major disciplines of theatre and eloquence. In China, by contrast, the written word has played the commanding role from the very beginning. The script was vested at first with magical power; eventually it became the exclusive key to political power—hence the prestigious aura that always surrounded it.

Of course, this is not the place to examine how and why, in China, the written word came to occupy a position of such exalted importance, but since this chapter is devoted to books and their function in our lives, it seems to me that passing reference to the Chinese experience might be of some relevance. After all, the Chinese have enjoyed a particularly long and rich acquaintance with books (in fact, by the end of the eighteenth century, more books had been published in China than in all the rest of the world). Sometimes, one wonders if their particular reverence for books might not be missing in our modern world?

Some years ago, Peter Weir directed a film in the United States, *Dead Poets Society*, which was shown here to considerable acclaim. I generally admire the works of this director, and I accept that this particular film has genuine merits—yet it provoked in me a genuine *revulsion*, which, I think, bears examination.

The film describes the experiences of an original and inspiring young teacher in a very conservative and elitist boarding school. Against the heavy conformity generated by the school discipline, the teacher—who is also a poet—displays a refreshing iconoclasm. Importantly, he succeeds in communicating to his students his enthusiasm, his love of literature, and his respect for individual expression. At the end of the year, a tragedy occurs; the teacher is victim of a slanderous accusation, and is dismissed from the school; yet, as he leaves, we can see that a majority of his students will remain faithful to the spirit of his teachings.

Obviously, the general theme of the film is morally uplifting and unimpeachable. An early incident in the plot, however—of considerable symbolic importance—not only alienated my sympathy, but placed me completely at loggerheads with the director's intentions. The textbook prescribed by the school authorities for the literature course was an anthology of English poetry compiled and introduced by a pompous moron. The brilliant young teacher explains to his students why this introduction is philistine and stupid; in conclusion, he advises them to discard it—not metaphorically, but literally and physically. In front of them, he tears the offending pages from his own copy of the anthology, and he instructs them to submit theirs to the same treatment. Initially, the students are shocked and perplexed, then hesitantly at first, one of them begins tearing pages from his textbook, and is soon followed by others, and in no time nearly the entire class explodes in a joyous iconoclastic frenzy. Only two or three dour conformists (who, in the end, will prove to be traitors) resist the movement—and we are meant to despise them. All along, the film director was tugging at our emotions with rather thick strings—but at this early point, he lost me for good. I rebelled and broke free. My heart went to the villains—after all, alone among their peers, they became the brave minority that dared to swim against the new tide—and, in the end, I even felt that the school principal, for all his despotic, ugly and obtuse ways, basically did the right thing when he sacked a teacher who, however idealistic and talented, would instruct his students to tear pages out of a book.

I am still at a loss to understand how an intelligent and sensitive film director could have hit such a jarring note. It was as if, in a noble and lofty romance, one were suddenly exposed to a passage of gross pornography. Could it be because Weir, being an Australian working in America, belongs in fact to two young cultures equally blessed with the same innocence? I mean, both Australia and the United States, in their short histories, have been spared the direct experience of totalitarian terror—this rape of the collective consciousness, which finds its most basic expression in the destruction of books. Conversely, for anyone who has cultural roots in Europe for instance—or in China—the sight of books being ripped apart by a mob of enthusiastic young people presents necessarily a connotation of unspeakable brutality and horror: it is the quintessential Fascistico-Nazi, Stalino-Maoist gesture; in no context could it ever conceivably be turned into a metaphor for liberation; it is a plain and arrogant display of barbarity, immediately conjuring up Orwell's memorable image of a jackboot crushing a human face—forever.

It is within civilisations where books were most revered that their periodic destruction has been pursued with the greatest ferocity. This fury is a measure of the prestige and authority that are usually vested in them. Without a sense of the sacred, no sacrilege is possible. Illiterates can have no real quarrel with books.

The first emperor of China, a fearsome tyrant who achieved the unification of the country 2200 years ago, remained notorious through the ages for two crimes against the spirit: he buried scholars alive, and he burned all the books. These two deeds have been viewed with equal horror by later generations. The point is not that a book can be considered to have as much value as human life, but that, simply, when a man is bent on destroying books, you know that he is capable of anything, since his aim is not merely to kill people, but to kill their souls.

Yet the destruction of books was perpetrated at different times for a variety of reasons. In a later period, a highly cultivated emperor who had gathered an immense and priceless library, was eventually overthrown by a rebellion. As the victorious rebels reached the gates of his palace, the ruler set his library on fire: he had read all these books, yet found himself incapable of saving his throne. All this accumulated wisdom had proved pointless in the end, so he felt that these books deserved to be turned into ashes.

Thus, one despot destroyed books out of fear: they contained a power that could challenge his rule; and another destroyed them out of resentment: they had failed him at the moment of greatest need. In both instances, however, books were equally supposed to exert decisive action, to deliver effective solutions.

Such a view, in fact, is far more universal than one might imagine. Some time ago, a popular literary program on French television conducted an interesting inquiry. The same question was put to various writers, artists and intellectuals: Is there any book that has actually affected your life? Try to play this game for yourself; if you strive to answer the question with absolute sincerity, without any attempt at impressing the public, you might find your own answer disconcertingly anticlimactic. Shall I confess what I came up with?

In George Orwell's essays, there is a whimsical little piece on the subject of tea drinking. Orwell explains that you cannot really enjoy tea unless you drink it without sugar or milk and he challenges any dissenting reader to an experiment: for three days, force yourself to drink your tea without putting anything in it. It will taste bitter and unpleasant at first, but you will progressively get used to it; in the end, you will prefer the new taste to such an extent, that you will never revert to your former habit. Of course, as regards tea, having lived for some years in East Asia, I knew long ago the advantage of drinking it straight; but I wondered if Orwell's experiment could not be extended to coffee. And indeed, his forecast proved absolutely accurate; in fact, it took me much less than three days to effect a complete and definitive conversion in my coffee-drinking habits. I had enjoyed sweetened coffee for the first 25 years of my life; but since the Orwellian experiment, the taste of coffee with sugar has become genuinely and utterly revolting to me.

Now, returning to the original question: I have been an avid reader for more than half a century; yet, in the end, if I have to make an honest, conscientious assessment of the most real and concrete impact that any of these thousands of books ever directly exerted upon my life, I am afraid I can only point to this single item— ridiculous, absurd and irrelevant: I do not put sugar in my coffee anymore.

Before you dismiss this testimony of mine as frivolous, contrived or flippant, please carefully examine your own experience, and see if you can produce something more significant and impressive.

Should we then conclude that books are essentially *useless*? I would indeed suggest that we subscribe to this conclusion, so long as we remain aware that uselessness is also the hallmark of what is truly priceless. Zhuang Zi (from whose wisdom I have already drawn in the first chapter, and who will guide me again later on) summed it up well: 'People all know the usefulness of what is useful, but they do not know the usefulness of what is useless'.[1] On this theme, he developed a number of parables such as this:

> A carpenter on a journey came to a village where he saw an enormous tree—so huge that the villagers worshipped it as their local Spirit. It was broad enough to give shade to several thousand oxen, and its trunk measured a hundred spans round. It was taller than the surrounding hills, and its lowest branches were seventy feet up. It had dozens of boughs out of which you could have carved entire boats. The crowd of people gazing at it was like the throng in a market; but our carpenter did not give it a glance, he passed straight on, without even stopping. But his apprentice stood staring at the tree for a long time, and then ran after the carpenter and said: 'Master, since I first took up the axe to serve you, I never saw timber as splendid as this. But you did not even bother to look, and went straight on your way, without stopping. Why is that?' 'Forget it, say no more,' replied the carpenter. 'This tree is useless: make boats from its timber and they will sink; make coffins and they will rot; make vessels and they will break at once; use it for making doors, and it will sweat its sap; turn it into posts and pillars, and the worms will set in. This tree is wretched timber—of no use whatsoever. And that is why it was able to remain undisturbed for so long, and to grow to such proportions.' The same night, as the carpenter was asleep, the tree appeared to him in a dream and said: 'What would you compare me with? Would you compare me with *useful* trees? The cherry-apple, the pear, the orange, the persimmon—as soon as their fruit is ripe, they are torn apart, ripped of their fruit, and their limbs are subjected to abuse. Their usefulness makes life miserable for them; they die in mid-journey without lasting out the full span of years which Heaven had allocated them. Such is the fate of all creatures who fall prey to worldly vulgarity. As for me, I have always endeavoured to remain of *no* use at all; it was not always easy, but I finally made it. I am absolutely *useless*, which proved to be of the greatest use to me, since it is thanks to my uselessness that I was allowed to grow undisturbed to my present size.'[2]

The other day I was reading the manuscript of a forthcoming book by a young journalist—a series of profiles of women living in the Outback—farmer wives battling solitude and natural disasters on remote stations in the bush. One woman expressed concern for the education and future of her son, and commented on the boy's choice of exclusively practical subjects for his courses at boarding school. She remarked: 'I can't say I blame his choice, as I too would prefer to be out in the bush driving a tractor or building cattleyards rather than sitting in a classroom *learning about Shakespeare, which is something he'll never need*. But it worried me to think that if in a few years time he decides to do something else, but cannot qualify because he lacks the required school subjects, then it will be my fault, because I didn't supply him with the education he needed . . .'

In this passing remark there is something which I find simply heartbreaking. For a woman who single-handedly raises and cares for a large family—while sharing in many of the men's tasks—worrying about mortgage repayments, fighting loneliness and depression, bolstering her husband's crumbling self-respect in front of looming bankruptcy, fending off the menaces of alcoholism and social disintegration, and who meanwhile drives tractors and handles cattle, and faces a thousand emergencies—it would appear indeed that 'Shakespeare is something one will never need'. And on what ground would we dare to challenge her view?

Oddly enough, this disarming remark on the uselessness of literature unwittingly reduplicates, in one sense, a provocative statement by Nabokov: in fact the brave woman from the Outback here seems to echo a sardonic paradox of the supreme literary aesthete of our age! Nabokov wrote this (which I shall never tire of quoting—perhaps because I myself taught literature for some time): 'Let us not kid ourselves; let us remember that *literature is of no use whatever, except in the very special case of somebody's wishing to become, of all things, a Professor of Literature*.'[3]

And yet even Professors of Literature, when they are originally made of the right mettle, but find themselves in extreme situations—divested of their titles, deprived of their books, reduced to their barest humanity, equipped only with their tears and their memory—can reach the heart of the matter and experience in their flesh what literature is really about: our very survival as human beings. I know of one Professor of Literature at least, who would be qualified to teach the brave woman from the Outback how, even for people in her situation—*particularly* for people in her situation—there may be a very real need for reading Shakespeare.

The name of that Professor is Wu Ningkun. He is an elderly

Chinese scholar; nearly 50 years ago, moved by patriotism, he gave up a promising (and cosy) academic career in the United States, where he was teaching English literature, and returned to China, knowing that his talents and expertise were sorely needed there. But, under Maoism, there was no place in China for refined, cultivated and cosmopolitan minds. He was immediately suspected, ostracised, persecuted, and for the next 30 years, became a victim of the totalitarian paranoia that sees humanist culture as a treason, intelligence as an ideological crime, and presumes that whoever reads TS Eliot in the original must be a dangerous international spy.

He has written a book about his experiences, *A Single Tear*, which is, to my mind, the best written and most essential reading on a subject on which so much has already been published, and yet so little is understood.

The darkest depth of his ordeal was reached when he was sent to a labour camp in the barren wilderness of north-eastern China, close to the Siberian border. Around him, many inmates were crushed to death by the horrors of the camp—they were dying of starvation, brutal treatment, exhaustion and despair. Under such conditions, physical resilience alone was not enough to stay alive— one needed spiritual strength. Wu Ningkun sustained his spirit with poetry. He had succeeded in smuggling with him two small books: a copy of *Hamlet* and a collection of the Tang dynasty poet, Du Fu. Formerly he had only *studied* Shakespeare; now, for the first time, he was truly *reading* it. Occasionally, when a blinding blizzard blew from Siberia, and the prisoners had to spend the day cooped up in a cell, he could come back to *Hamlet*:

> *Hamlet* was my favourite Shakespearean play. Read in a Chinese labour camp, however, the tragedy of the Danish prince took on unexpected dimensions. All the academic analyses and critiques that had engrossed me over the years now seemed remote and irrelevant. The outcry 'Denmark is a prison' echoed with a poignant immediacy and Elsinore loomed like a haunting metaphor of a treacherous repressive state. The Ghost thundered with a terrible chorus of a million victims of proletarian dictatorship. Rosencrantz and Guildenstern would have felt like fish in the water, had they found their way into a modern nation of hypocrites and informers . . . [As to Hamlet himself], his great capacity for suffering gave the noble Dane his unique stature as a tragic hero preeminently worthy of his suffering. I would say to myself 'I am not Prince Hamlet, nor was meant to be . . .' echoing Eliot's Prufrock. Rather I often felt like one of those fellows 'crawling between earth and heaven' scorned by Hamlet

> himself. But the real question, I came to see, was neither 'to be or not to be' nor whether 'in the mind to suffer the slings and arrows of outrageous fortune', but how to be worthy of one's suffering.[4]

That a man may survive for quite a while without food, but cannot live one day without poetry, is a notion which we tend to dismiss too lightly, as a sort of nineteenth century romantic hyperbole. But our gruesome century has provided enough evidence: it is true, in a very literal sense. Wu Ningkun's testimony which I just invoked confirms from the other end of the world an earlier voice from another 'House of the Dead': Primo Levi who, having survived Auschwitz, wrote the classic account of the death camps, *If this is a Man*, devoted one entire chapter to an experience very similar to the one described by the Chinese scholar. One day, as Levi and another inmate were on duty to fetch soup for the entire barrack, on their way to the kitchen, with the heavy soup bucket hanging from a pole which they carried on their shoulders, they enjoyed the brief respite of a summer day, and started chatting. The other prisoner was a clever young Frenchman, with a gift for languages. Levi who had been teaching him some Italian, suddenly was moved by a crazy and irresistible impulse to introduce him to Dante. He began to recite a passage from the *Divine Comedy*, the Canto of Ulysses, clumsily translating it for the other man, verse by verse: 'Here, listen, open your ears and your mind, *you have to understand, for my sake.*' The effect of this recitation of a few stanzas was 'As if I also was hearing it for the first time: like the blast of a trumpet, like the voice of God. For a moment I forget who I am and where I am . . . [The companion] begs me to repeat it. How good he is, he is aware that it is doing me good. Or perhaps it is something more . . . perhaps he has received the message, he has felt that it has to do with him, that it has to do with all men who suffer, and with us in particular; and that it has to do with us two, who dare to reason of these things with the poles for the soup on our shoulders.' Then, sudden catastrophe memory fails at the end of one stanza—to reach the end of the Canto, a crucial connection is missing. 'I have forgotten at least twelve lines . . . I would give today's soup to know how to connect the last fragment to the end of the Canto. I try to reconstruct it through the rhymes, I close my eyes, I bite my fingers—but it is no use, the rest is silence.'[5]

The depth and truth of this particular moment were such that, 30 years later—the year before he died—Levi returned to it in the last book he wrote, *The Drowned and the Saved*. Summing up his experience of the death camp, he concluded: 'Culture was important to me, and perhaps it saved me . . . When I wrote "I would give today's soup to know how to retrieve the forgotten passage", I had neither lied nor exaggerated. I really would have given bread and soup—that is, blood—to save from nothingness those memories which today, with the sure support of printed paper I can refresh gratis whenever I wish, and which therefore seem of little value.'[6]

In Auschwitz, the forgotten poem became literally priceless in that place, at that instant, the very survival of Primo Levi's humanity was dependent on it.

Earlier on, I made the point that no book in particular can actually affect your life, except in a ludicrously limited sense. Having said that, I must now hasten to add if individual books have no such power, what can most certainly transform your life is the very experience of *reading* itself. In fact, reading not only transforms your life, sometimes it competes with it—even eclipses it—a situation which was memorably evoked by Logan Pearsall Smith: 'People say that life is the thing, but I prefer reading'.

Jorge Luis Borges (whose real importance as a *writer* is perhaps still debatable, whereas his supreme excellence as a *reader* is definitively established) was once asked by an interviewer if he did not regret having spent more time reading than actually living. He replied: 'There are many ways of living, and reading is one of them . . . When you are reading, you are living, and when you are dreaming, you are living also.'

Anyone with a passion for reading has measured the truth of this observation. Looking back into your own past, among the landmarks of your life, you will find that great readings occupy a place no less significant than actual happenings—for instance, a long and adventurous journey through strange lands, which you undertook in a certain year, may in retrospect appear no less memorable than your first exploration of *À la recherche du temps perdu*; or again, you might realise that your encounter with Anna Karenina, or with Julien Sorel proved more momentous than meeting most of your past acquaintances. Who is to assess the relative significance, the specific weight that should be ascribed to these diverse experiences in the shaping of your personality?

Our minds are an incredibly complex cluster of thoughts and emotions, of beliefs and passions, of facts and feelings, of images, impressions, memories and dreams, of reality and myth. Our actions are the outcome of this rich chemistry. Who is to determine in what proportion this creative mixture was made fecund by the actual happenings of our life, or by our readings? As Borges pointed out, our readings too were real events, and without them our life would have been different— and certainly the poorer.

The classic statement on the experience of reading was made by CS Lewis, at the end of the last book he wrote. It is worth quoting at length, and pondering at leisure:

> Literature enlarges our being by admitting us to experiences not our own. They may be beautiful, terrible, awe-inspiring, exhilarating, pathetic, comic, or merely piquant. Literature gives the entrée to them all. Those of us who have been true readers all our life, seldom fully realize the enormous extension of our being which we owe to authors. We realize it best when we talk with an unliterary friend. He may be full of goodness and good sense, but he inhabits a tiny world. In it, we should be suffocated. My own eyes are not enough for me. The man who is contented to be only himself, and therefore less a self, is in prison. My own eyes are not enough for me . . . Even the eyes of all humanity are not enough. I regret that the brutes cannot write books. Very gladly would I learn what face things present to a mouse or a bee; more gladly still would I perceive the olfactory world charged with all the information and emotion it carries for a dog . . . In reading good literature, I become a thousand men, and yet remain myself. Like the night sky in a Greek poem, I see with a myriad eyes, but it is still I who see. Here, as in worship, in love, in moral action, and in knowing, I transcend myself; and am never more myself than when I do.[7]

It is said that the ancient Greek philosopher Antisthenes advised his disciples *not* to learn how to read. A modern commentator observed cynically: Antisthenes was right, for reading is not something that can be learned.[8]

True readers are very rare indeed. This affirmation seems at first to be given a spectacular refutation by the industrial development recently achieved by the great publishing houses, and by the impressive stacks of best-selling books piled up in bookshops, just like tins of sardines in supermarkets. But are these best-sellers *real* books? Or, when they are, are they read by the people who buy them? The fact is, we are now witnessing a proliferation of *non-books* (a subject which I have already dealt with elsewhere): they present the physical appearance of books, but an essential book-component is missing: time. Hastily conceived and produced, their life expectancy is as ephemeral as that of yesterday's newspaper. Like the secret instructions of *Mission Impossible*, the non-book self-destructs after you have read it—sometimes even *before*.

Still, there are best-sellers which also happen to have genuine, or even outstanding merit. By accident, or by the prowess of a publisher's salesmanship, copies suddenly sell in the hundreds of thousands, but they are not necessarily read; or, if they are read, they are largely misunderstood. A law of diminishing returns has been defined by perceptive experts: a good writer who is read only by a thousand readers can expect to be understood by 90 per cent of them; if he is read by ten thousand readers, he will probably be understood by a mere 10 per cent; and if he is read by a hundred thousand readers, it is most likely that no more than 1 per cent will get his point. In other words, although the figures of sales may greatly vary (for reasons that have little to do with the book itself), the size of the genuine readership remains roughly constant. For an author, the price of popular success is widespread misunderstanding. This sort of misunderstanding, however, has a sweet financial compensation, but then, the least a good writer should expect from his bad readers is that they should make him rich—even though this is not his original motivation. On being asked why he wrote, EM Forster replied, that he did it merely to win the approval of two or three individuals whom he respected. This defines nicely the responsibility of a true reader. Conversely, to an obviously incompetent reader who had sent him some very nasty critical comments, Lamartine replied finally and immortally: 'Sir, it is not for you that I write.'

To analyse the absurd mechanism that can turn an excellent book into a best-seller *for the wrong reason*, a good case may be provided by a study of the recent success of Robert Hughes: *Barcelona*. This work is remarkable for its intelligence, scholarly information and wit, but its topic is highly specialised. Without a strong curiosity about Catalan cultural history, and about the phenomenon of provincial culture, I doubt if many readers would have the time and patience to read it from cover to cover (it took me nearly a month). Yet copies of the book sold in industrial quantity: the publisher had had the preposterous *and* brilliant idea of putting it on the market at the time of the Barcelona Olympic Games. Now, here is an intriguing problem of Logic:

1 Only a person interested in Catalan culture would enjoy reading *Barcelona*.
2 Any person interested in Catalan culture would naturally curse the Olympic Games and avoid visiting Barcelona on such a moronic occasion.
3 Only a moron would wish to attend the Olympic Games.
4 Evidently, no moron will ever read *Barcelona*.

These are all the elements of the riddle posed by the extraordinary popular success of Hughes's book. Try and solve it if you can.

All the people who have been taught how to read, think they can read. In this sense, one could say on the subject of reading what La Rochefoucauld noted about love: 'Most people would never love, had they not firstly been told about it'.[9] (And indeed, the fact is: we would never have the ambition to direct a symphonic orchestra, or to compose a great epic poem, without first possessing a very particular talent and training—whereas we all naturally presume that we should be able to love someone else for a lifetime—an undertaking that requires a much more rare genius.* But this is another story.)

Love and reading provide good metaphors for one another. There can be no meaningful reading without loving what you read. Nabokov was right to say that a book is either for the bedside table or for the waste-paper basket: either you enjoy passionately its company—so much so, that you cannot bear to part from it; or it does not mean much to you, and you should not be wasting your time with it.[10] And this is precisely the reason why literature and scholarship are so often at loggerheads. A 'literary scholar' appears to be a contradiction in terms: a scholar must read all the books that are relevant to his research—however mediocre, dreary and boring. A true lover of literature only reads the books he loves. The conflict between the two can sometimes become acute, and though there are a few instances of good writers who are also literary scholars, on the whole, there is little sympathy wasted between the two camps. Novelists love to lampoon academic critics; thus for instance, with an unerring ear for fashionable cant, Vikram Seth caught this snippet of dialogue between literary pundits: 'What utter nonsense! . . . Don't pay any attention to him: *he's just a writer, he knows nothing about literature!*'[11] And the academics retaliate with their own weapons: for example Nabokov was denied a Chair of Comparative Literature at Harvard—his appointment having been rejected by the faculty committee after a senior scholar had argued that 'One does not appoint an elephant as Professor of Zoology'.[12]

An entire anthology could be compiled from the various gibes which creative writers never tire of addressing to scholars and

* It is, in fact, in a very literal sense, a *supernatural* feat. But, as Chesterton said, if you take the supernatural away, you are left with the unnatural.

critics. The artist's impatience towards the parasitic and artificial sophistication of literary theoreticians was best expressed by Chekhov, who, with his characteristic contempt for empty rhetoric, stated that all books were simply divided into two categories: those which he did like, and those which he did not.[13]

But it is probably Jules Renard who identified the true reason at the heart of the writer's hostility towards the critic: 'I refuse to know how people who have got talent are being judged by people who have got none.'[14]

Sometimes a creative writer may be forced by circumstances into the position of literary academic. Such a predicament can be experienced as sheer torture. Indeed, it was movingly described by the Polish writer Kazimierz Brandys, who, having had to flee the Communist regime of his country, became a political refugee, and had to teach in France and in America for a living:

> I am now teaching Polish literature at Columbia University. I have some twenty students. My objective is to make then understand that they are in front of a man who is in *total despair*—a man who, since he was a child, always *hated* all analyses of literary works, but who now needs to analyse literary works in order to earn a living . . . What an absurd task it is to teach people how to understand a work of literature! I have never read any book with the purpose of understanding it. To read and simultaneously to explain is as inconceivable for me as it would be to complete the act of love with a medical examination. I was not devouring books—books were swallowing me. *They* spoke to me about life and death, *they* spoke to me about myself, whereas I myself never had anything to say about them . . . I knew a student from Yale; one day, as he saw Faulkner in front of a bookshop on a corner in Fifth Avenue, he had the impulse to go down on his knees and to kiss his hand. To my mind, such a gesture is exemplary: it is the only suitable attitude towards literature.[15]

Brandys then issued a cautionary warning, which seems very important to me, and is too often overlooked:

> It may sound strange, but there are people for whom an acquaintance with works of art can be harmful: it puts on them obligations that are beyond their means; it forces them to abandon their own original simplicity; they suppress their own qualities, fearing that, in being natural, they might appear common. When in contact with art, these people fall under an evil charm, they become deeply

disturbed and anxious. Uncertain of their own taste, not daring to trust their own eyes and their own ears, they seek salvation in artificiality; they worship and they condemn in pure conformity with conventions. They turn into monsters of insecurity, their mouths are permanently twisted into a grimace of contrived admiration or contempt. I know many people of that sort—specially women—who are being damaged by art.[16]

Brandys here reminds us of a profound truth the handling of all things spiritual is always fraught with dreadful perils: *if you wish to use them for your own purposes, they will turn against you with a vengeance.* Naturally, it is in religious matters that this phenomenon can be observed with the greatest clarity. Thomas Merton noted in one of his diaries: 'Religion is not understood. Those who wish themselves pious in order to admire themselves in that state *are made stupid by religion.* What is needed is to lose ourselves completely in God; what is needed is perfect silence. Pious talk has something revolting about it.' In this passage, if you transpose the religious terms into literary concepts, the statement retains its full relevance: 'Literature is not understood. Those who wish themselves cultured in order to admire themselves in this state are made stupid by literary studies. What is needed is to lose ourselves completely in literature; what is needed is perfect silence. Literary theory has something revolting about it.'

1   Zhuang Zi, chapter 4 'In the world of men'. For English translations, see Burton Watson, *The Complete Works of Chuang Tzu*, Columbia University Press, New York, 1986; see also AC Graham, *Chuang Tzu: The Inner Chapters*, Unwin Paperbacks, London, 1986.

2   In AC Graham's translation, see op. cit., pp72–3; in Burton Watson's, pp634

3   V Nabokov, *Lectures on Literature*, Weidenfeld and Nicolson, London, 1980, p125

4   Wu Ningkun, *A Single Tear*, Hodder & Stoughton, London & Sydney, 1993, pp100–1

5   Primo Levi, *If this is a Man*, Abacus, London, 1987, chapter 11, 'The Canto of Ulysses', pp115–21

6   Primo Levi, *The Drowned and the Saved*, Abacus, London, 1988, p112

7   CS Lewis, *An Experiment in Criticism* (1961), Cambridge University Press, Canto, Cambridge, 1992, pp137, 139, 140–1

8   JF Revel, introduction to *Sade: 120 Journées de Sodome*, Pauvert, Paris.

9   La Rochefoucauld, *Maxims*, CXXXVI: 'Il y a des gens qui n'aurient jamais été amoureaux s'ils n'avaient jamais entendu parler de l'amour.'

10   On this point, see Anthony Burgess, *Homage to Qwertyuiop*, Abacus, London, 1968, 'The Nabokov—Wilson Letters', p456

11   Vikram Seth, *A Suitable Boy*, Phoenix House, London, 1993

12   Andrew Field, VN: *The Life and Art of Vladimir Nabokov*, Crown, New York, 1986, p263; also Brian Boyd, *Vladimir Nabokov:The American Years*, Chatto and Windus, London, 1992, p303

13   The very idea of literary criticism filled Chekhov with horror. He wrote: 'When I am told of what is artistic and inartistic, of what is stage-worthy and unstageworthy, of commitment, realism and all that, I am baffled, I tentatively nod agreement, and I answer with banal half-truths, not worth a brass farthing. I divide all works into two kinds: those I like, and those I don't like. I have no other yardstick, and if you ask me why I like Shakespeare and don't like Zlatovratsky, I shall have no answer. Perhaps I shall grow wiser in time and acquire a criterion, but meanwhile all aesthetic discussions just exhaust me and seem like continuations of scholarly disputes with which people wearied themselves in the Middle Ages', (Letter of 22 March 1890, quoted in Ronald Hingley, *A Life of Anton Chekhov*, Oxford University Press, Oxford, 1989, p126.)

14   Jules Renard, *Journal* (entry of 22 April 1899): 'Je refuse de savoir ce que peut penser des hommes de talent un homme qui n'en a pas.'

15   Kazimierz Brandys, *Carnets: Paris–New York–Paris 1982–1984*, Gallimard, Paris, 1987, pp115–7

16   Ibid., p119.

Martin Krygier

A lawyer who is also a philosopher and is wary of classification, Martin Krygier was born in Sydney in 1949, the son of Polish immigrants. Educated at Sydney Grammar School and the University of Sydney, he obtained a PhD at the Australian National University. He has, since 1996, been Professor of Law at the University of New South Wales.

Professor Krygier's work spans a number of fields, particularly legal, political and social philosophy, legal sociology, communist and post-communist studies, and the history of ideas. He has been invited to lecture in universities in North America, Great Britain, and Europe—west, central and east. He is the chairman of the editorial board of *East Central Europe—L'Europe du Centre Est*, a journal published in Budapest. He has been president of the Australian Institute of Polish Affairs since 1997. His publications include *Bureaucracy: The Career of a Concept* (co-ed), 1979; *Marxism and Communism; Posthumous Reflections on Politics; Society and Law* (co-ed), 1994; and *The Rule of Law After Communism* (co-ed), 1999.

Between Fear and Hope: Hybrid Thoughts on Public Values was the densely elegant title given by Martin Krygier to his 1997 Boyer Lectures. His six lectures were 'Hybrids and Comparisons', which is reproduced here; 'Between Fear and Hope'; 'The Uses of Civility'; 'Pride, Shame and Decency'; 'The Good that Governments Do' and 'In Praise of Hybrid Thoughts.'

Professor Krygier, like many Australians, is both insider and outsider, a 'cultural hybrid': Australian-born but carrying the historical and cultural residues of his refugee parents' backgrounds. From this vantage point, and the taste for comparison that it encourages, he analyses differences among societies, evaluates the role of government and law within a good society, and defines the values that help shape one that is civil and decent. He is intrigued by false dichotomies and believes we are too often pressed to make choices between alternatives that are both attractive and possibly compatible: 'realism and idealism, fear and hope, survival and flourishing, individual and community, ethnics and Australians, symbols and practices, pride and shame. There is room for them all, and an important place for each.

HYBRIDS AND COMPARISONS

Between Fear and Hope: Hybrid Thoughts on Public Values

Martin Krygier

• 1 9 9 7 •

This has been a remarkable year, for it has seen the return to Australian public life of truly political conflict. By politics, I have in mind here not what Leon Trotsky used to call 'corridor skills'— about which we are all too well informed—but something larger: public conflicts over public values. Recent controversies have raised questions of tolerance, civility, decency, responsibility, nationality, pride and shame, among others. More broadly, of course, values are in play whenever we wonder about the sort of society we are and would like to be. There are times when it can be useful to raise one's head from the particulars of current disputes to focus on some of the values at stake. This seems to me one of those times.

It was always false, and it can no longer be pretended, that government is just a matter of selecting the best means to achieve agreed-upon ends. For, manifestly, we differ about ends. Nor are these mere technical differences, or differences between the schooled and the ignorant, as recent technocratic mythologies have implied. They are differences about what matters and what should matter to us. And there are no experts in that. Political institutions have to deal with conflicts over values. If they are good institutions they will ensure that these conflicts are peaceful and solutions stay within civilised limits. But they will not ensure that conflicts will go away. They will never go away. Or as some do, others will arise.

And this suggests a problem. Many of us disagree over matters of value, but few of us are used to arguing about these sorts of things in any sustained way. Our newspapers are full of facts and details, and often vehemently expressed opinions about them, but the values informing those opinions are rarely closely examined. Much of the time we take our values off the shelf where they have been put by our parents, our friends, our cultural inheritances, our time and place. Though our values may well change over time, we rarely examine or rearrange the shelf deliberately or thoughtfully. And often we feel confused. We are confused about what is going on in the world and we are confused about what we think should go on. At least many of us are, and that causes us unease.[1] We often feel passionately about what happens or should happen, but we find it hard to articulate our values or defend them. We act on our values, or feel that something is right or wrong, more than we discuss or know how to discuss them.

In these lectures I will try to discuss some of them. I will suggest some of the values that I think appropriate to thinking about several of our current controversies, some of the implications of these values, and some ways of thinking through such values.

I do not argue for specific solutions to vexed problems, for to do so requires much more than values. Local knowledge and close familiarity with particular circumstances, and often particular expertise, are necessary to resolve practical problems. Yet they are not all that is involved. For it is a mistake to think that our views of things are simply the results of the things themselves or what we know of them. We filter anything we care about through our deeper commitments and approaches to the world, even when we are not sure what these are. That is why people so often continue to disagree over the things that matter to them. These are rarely disagreements which one unnoticed fact, or even a bunch, could dissolve. And yet we are bombarded with facts, or sound-bite judgments about them, rather than with reflection on what we bring to bear, or should bring to bear to the viewing of the facts. I want to encourage that sort of reflection.

As a way of putting in question what is familiar and seems natural, I begin in this lecture by advocating *comparisons* with circumstances which are neither. In this light, I seek in what follows to explore the worth and conditions of several inter-related but distinct practical ideals[2] for our society. These ideals are practical because they can be attained; if never completely, then still with varying degrees of success. They are ideals because they are worth attaining, and then sustaining, against any threats to them. They also demand to be made good locally, wherever they have not been.

In the next lecture, I introduce one sort of comparison which I consider crucial though it is often ignored: that is, comparison with the worst that people do to each other. I argue that we should always begin by considering how to avoid evil, even if our deepest ambition is just to do good. Ideally we will be able to do both. If we can successfully stem some of the worst sources of fear, we might clear some space for hope. I then commend a particular kind of society which avoids certain evils, and allows some important goods. Like many writers, I prefer a 'civil society' to an uncivil one, and will seek to show why. I also think a society should be decent. In the fourth of these lectures, I reflect on one of the major issues of our time—the variety of differences among members of our society. I ask about the place for pride and shame, and about the bearing of civility and decency in response to it. In the fifth lecture, I ask what roles government and law might usefully play and what sorts of government and law might usefully play these roles. Finally, in a deliberately untidy way, I try to knit together some of the underlying themes of these particular discussions. I have no systematic doctrine to sell, but I do have some values to commend, and some ways to think about values, whatever we end up believing. My hope is that both those who value what I value, and those sad few who don't, might find something useful to take away, to be used in other places on other days.

There is no way ultimately to resolve conflicts over values, but that doesn't mean that anything goes. There are ways of arguing about values, and some ways and some values are more defensible than others. Some, indeed, are indefensible, as I will seek to show. Others, mine as it happens, are solid as rocks. Or so I want to believe. If I were a philosopher, I would simply rely on the power of my argument to convince you to share my values. But I am not, so I will say something about their sources and character to try to convey why I find them attractive and why they matter so to me. Of course, I would not be disappointed if you found them attractive as well.

I am an Australian. I was born, brought up and educated here. I have spent the bulk of my life here. I watch cricket for days without being bored. I expect Christmas to be hot. These facts are central to my makeup. Were they otherwise, so would I be. And yet they are not the only pieces that make me up. For, like so many Australians, I am the lucky beneficiary of other people's tragedies, most immediately those of my parents. That, too, is relevant to who I am and what I think about.

My parents arrived here during the Second World War, Polish-Jewish refugees from Nazism. Their lives, families, friendships and country were ripped apart by the war. Both my mother's parents and her brother were murdered by the Nazis; other relatives spent years fighting or being imprisoned by them, and what was left of the family was dispersed around the world. My parents left Poland from necessity, arrived in Australia by accident, and stayed because, after the Communist take-over of Poland, they couldn't go home.

They came to love this country and to participate actively in its affairs, but that was later.

I mention these far from exceptional facts not to claim some exotic authority for my views, nor—in accordance with a budding Australian tradition—to launch a prize-winning novel but because they inform the way I think about things, what I think about and—above all—what I think matters. Combined with my birthplace, they have made me what I am: a congenital cultural hybrid, a hybrid from birth. If you prefer, a mongrel.

My parents were already hybrids in Poland, since they were culturally both Polish and Jewish. Each ish had significance for them, and so their lives were already complicated. They became Australian hybrids differently, however, over time. What they came to learn and expect, and grew to be, in Australia interacted with their already formed personalities and cultural identities. Their hybrid condition was acquired, as is that of most, if not all adult migrants: they become culturally something different from what they once were while remaining something different from those among whom they now are. Since over 20 per cent of Australians were born overseas, and 40 per cent were either so born or their parents were, there are a lot of us about.

There is also a third sort of hybrid, and I am one of them too. I study and write about the societies of post-communist Europe, and their fate matters a lot to me. So I am also a vocational hybrid: coming from one world, and preoccupied with another. There are, of course, fewer vocational hybrids than congenital and acquired ones, and many of them are hybrids of the other kinds as well, a connection which is psychologically not difficult to explain. Perhaps it is just a way of mixing business with pleasure, but it has consequences. When I am there I think of here; when here, of there. That makes comparisons ever-present and unavoidable.

All hybrids are affected, some afflicted, by overlapping cultural residues within them. Pure vocational hybrids might slough such residues off as simply parts of their jobs, but congenital and acquired hybrids often find that difficult to do. They often discover to their surprise, rather than as a matter of deliberate choice, aspects of their personality—their sense of identity, belonging, sometimes longing—which define them and have moulded them, whether they like it or not.

There is no reason to romanticise hybrids. Sometimes their cultural condition is just a source of confusion, sometimes of defensive fundamentalism, sometimes of unattractive social climbing, sometimes of raw pain. Some hybrids find the combinations within unbearable, and some try to suppress some of their cultural elements, usually the foreign ones, for their own sakes or those of their children. That is often an excruciating experience, particularly for those who find that cultural integration comes more slowly than the wish for it. Worse still must be the discovery that it can all be for nothing: the host and dominant culture, which you imagined you were joining or had long joined, spits you out and then tramples on you. At its most tragic, that was the discovery made by German Jews in the 1930s.

Even when the threat is incomparably less, it must always be a source of immediate shock and continuing distress when people who have adopted a country and with it aspects of a culture, discover that they are nevertheless still, or again, treated as aliens. Were the Pauline Hanson phenomenon to be generalised and sustained, I imagine that many Asian-Australians, even those who have lived here for generations, must feel something of that shock and distress. To say nothing of Aborigines, who have lived here forever and whose cultural adaptation was, to put it gently, not of their choosing.

Other times, or for other people, there is nothing problematic about being a hybrid. Some rejoice in the variety of their inheritance and find it, or make out of it, a rich and coherent whole. Some just do, and others just don't, feel that particular aspects of their cultural inheritance matter to them, are significant parts of what they are. Many children of migrants naturally or deliberately leave their parental culture behind and think little of it, in both senses of that phrase.

All these responses can change over a person's life, and over generations. Resolutely Aussie kids of hybrid parents—I was one— can gradually find themselves resonating to cultural melodies which had earlier left them cold. And whatever they do, they might, to their surprise, find their own children re-establishing links with the culture of their grandparents, links which the generation in-between rejected, ignored or simply forgot.

Even contented congenital hybrids, like myself, at times find themselves envying people whose sense of who they are and where they belong seems uncomplicated: grounded in local geography, family and tradition; supported and interwoven with others by generations of overlapping public and private narratives; apparently settled, and settled here, for longer than life. For many hybrids, however happy in the condition or unconscious of it, there are moments of awkwardness when we don't quite know where we belong, or when it occurs to us that there is no group which we feel completely inside, though there are several where we don't feel completely outside, either. Of course not only hybrids have this experience and it's by no means all bad. Indeed, I've come to think that such complication has compensations. Hybrids share a particular condition which might yield some insights.

Hybrids have a specific resource available to them: a range of values, experiences, traditions, which are different from others that circulate in their heads and in the heads of those with whom they mix. That can be enriching both to them and those who meet them. Moreover, where these components are psychologically salient— where they have meaning and significance for the hybrids themselves—they are not merely options from which to choose, like goods in a shop, or a background of exotic food, strong coffee or stronger spirits. They enter into people's lives and souls. They shape values, ambitions, horizons, expectations, ways of talking, of drinking, of laughing and of loving. And they shape the values (and all the rest) which people from these traditions pass on to their children. Whether these are good values, and whether they mesh easily or well with local ones, are particular and variable matters. Some are good and do mesh, some are good and don't, some aren't and do, some aren't and don't. All that has to be worked through and worked out.

There is something else hybridity can generate, however, which I think is a totally good thing. Comparisons. Part of a hybrid's make-up grows out of experience, cultural traditions, a sense of other histories and possibilities, modes of thought, speech and behaviour, which are different from local ones. On the one hand, this can open windows for them into other, often very different and complex, cultures which complete outsiders find harder to penetrate. On the other hand, it offers to hybrids a vantage point, a perspective, and a quite peculiar place to stand. That metaphorical space is simultaneously inside and outside the cultures in which they were raised, in which they live, of which they are parts and which are parts of them. That can make them critical of some things. It can also allow them, however, to appreciate distinctive accomplishments that non-hybrids, who have not known their absence, might regard as natural and unremarkable. More generally, it can offer a powerful antidote to parochialism, which has, perhaps, cosy charms as a way of life, but is not much help in understanding or evaluating a way of life.

Parochialism is common enough everywhere, though its sources and character differ widely. There is a lot of it in America, for example, because it's often hard for Americans to imagine that anything important happens anywhere else. In Australia, by contrast, so much that is important happens somewhere else, and everywhere else is a long way away. A common response is to overrate the importance of that far-away stuff and then court the risk of cultural cringe, which is a wonderful Australian phrase but a far from exclusively Australian disease. It is found in all provincial settings. Since there are many ways of being provincial, one can find it among east Europeans when they listen to westerners, particularly rich ones, and among Americans, and some Australians, when they listen to Alistair Cooke. The opposite extreme is to puff up whatever is near at hand and insist that Australians have nothing to learn from the experience of anyone else. That also is not a specially Australian condition, and everywhere it is a silly one. It allows one to be not only provincial but a little ridiculous, and narcissistic as well.

For narcissism is not just an individual phenomenon. The morbid self-obsession characteristic of narcissistic individuals can be observed among groups too. What I have elsewhere called 'national narcissism'[3] thrives in many countries, in both positive and negative varieties. Positive narcissism is more familiar. The positive narcissist is confident that his country is the centre of the world. What matters happens there, and it can't be bettered. This is a viewpoint well captured in Saul Steinberg's marvellous *New Yorker* cover, 'View of the world from 9th Avenue'. The foreground, which occupies half the canvas, is occupied by one New York block, between 9th and 10th Avenues. Beyond the Hudson River, there are a few major American states and cities and then, across the ocean, small in the far distance, China, Japan and Siberia. Australia doesn't appear.

Positive narcissism is easy to mock, and it is rightly mocked. We have seen quite a bit of it in Australia in the last couple of years, and it is not a pretty sight. It contrives to combine boastfulness, ignorance, insecurity, and hostility in ample and self-reinforcing measures.

Not that its melancholy twin, negative narcissism, is more attractive or less parochial. It differs from the celebratory kind, but only by inversion of value, not of subject. The subject is again one's own country and it's also superlative, in a way. However, what occurs there is not the best but the worst.

America has always had plenty of positive narcissists. From the 1960s, for a decade or two, it gained many negative narcissists as well. (Australia had some too, though ours have often been happier to damn the Americans, and us only secondarily as their satraps or cultural colonies. This is another provincial privilege.) In a century which boasts Stalin's Russia and Mao's China, Hitler's Germany and Pol Pot's Kampuchea, this position was always absurd, though it was popular enough, particularly among intellectuals. More gener-ally, unless one has really thought about the many goods and evils the world has to offer, narcissism—both positive and negative—is a frivolous way to think about anything that matters.

One antidote to such narcissistic tendencies, whether positively or negatively charged, is to look around. Anyone can do it. Hybrids merely have a strong temptation and good access. They have the option close at hand, indeed under the skin. That option, more specifically, consists in reflecting upon a deceptively simple ques-tion which I consider one of the most important of all for social understanding and evaluation. That question, in all its glory and complexity, is: *Compared to what?*

I have observed or participated in many discussions of the justice, decency, adequacy, and so on of our society, and its legal and polit-ical arrangements. Again and again I have been left wondering what other participants, so often firm in their (frequently contradictory) judgments, had in mind as standards of comparison. After all, compared to the Kingdom of God, we all do rather poorly, and compared to the other place, we do pretty well. What counts, and for what purposes? If these are not the standards, or not the only ones, against which one should compare everyday life, what are? These are not small questions, even less—God forbid!—'academic', and these lectures will often return to them.

I have started with hybrids because being one drove me in the particular direction I am describing. Also I quite like the breed. But of course the hybrid route to comparison is not the only one. There are other ways to get there. The greatest observer of the United States was a Frenchman, Alexis de Tocqueville. A lesser but acute observer of Tsarist Russia was another Frenchman, the Marquis de Custine. Neither was a hybrid though it is significant that both viewed what they analysed from a cultural platform outside it.

Hybrids and foreigners are fortunate, in this one respect at least. Hybrids have access to sources of comparison, which are unearned but built in. Foreigners do too, if they interest themselves in another culture closely enough. They may be alive to these comparisons and make use of them, or they may not.

What hybrids and foreigners have built in, others can gain. And there are other relevant endowments, available and useful to anyone. A strong historical sense is indispensable to any compara-tive consideration of human possibilities. Not all hybrids have it, nor all foreigners. And conversely, as many historians have shown, it can be obtained without moving from a well-stocked library.

Also crucial is a political imagination that is open equally to catastrophes that must be avoided and hopes that might be realised, whether or not they have been matters of local or immediate experience. Though George Orwell encountered aspects and consequences of totalitarianism as a fighter in the Spanish Civil War, he never experienced the societies he characterised so extraordinarily in 1984 and *Animal Farm*. These were works of imaginative genius, all the more because some totalitarian societies came to mimic them. We can't all be Orwells, but as Pierre Ryckmans eloquently reminded us in last year's Boyer lectures, books can—and travel needn't—help expand our imaginations too.

However we get there, I want to advocate thinking *comparatively* about whatever matters to us. If local non-hybrids want to take comparison seriously, that is open to them and they can do it as well as anyone, though they will have occasionally to leave home, in fact or in thought. In particular, they must work at wondering about, as seeing as problematic, what we commonly take for granted. This will not guarantee them answers to complex social problems, but it might expand their horizons and imaginations, and might refine the questions they think it important to ask.

I have not seen this point made better than by the late Robert Haupt, who went from being a good Australian journalist to a great one, when he moved from Australia to become the Moscow correspondent for my local, and often parochial, newspaper, the *Sydney Morning Herald*. I found the passage I will quote so arresting, that I have appropriated it in several places. It bears repetition.

In October 1993, shocked by the way in which Boris Yeltsin had managed, bloodily and for the time being, to re-establish control in Moscow, by storming the Russian house of parliament—the so-called 'White House'—Haupt was moved to reflections of a sort rarely evident among Australian political journalists, or among Australians generally, but which are nevertheless distinctively Australian in character. He wrote:

> Acres of scholarship have been devoted to the question of how Russia—rich, cultured, the bridge between East and West—got to this constitutionless point. Square-inches are given in the Australian syllabus to how we arrived at Federation. Is it time, one wonders, for a comparative study between [sic] the thought of Sir Henry Parkes and of Bakunin, the relative achievements of Lenin and Deakin? When one sees Russians killing Russians in a country 88 per cent Russian while Serbs and Croats apparently live in peace in Australia, an explanation must be sought beyond the effects of SBS and surf.
>
> Here [in Moscow], all the boring things of life are missing. There

are no Premiers' Conferences, no shire councils, no chambers of commerce, no solicitors, accountants, real estate agents, no double-entry bookkeeping. There are soldiers everywhere, but very few police, and none you could rely on for help in a sticky situation. There is no head of State, no Scout movement, no civic progress associations and few charitable groups.

All of this, the texture of civic order, strikes an Australian as so natural and ordinary that to investigate its origins seems super-fluous, while to speculate on how evanescent it might become is an exercise in sheer wonder, or perverseness. Yet the worth of something can generally be better seen from its absence than its presence.[4]

Like Haupt, I believe that one can better appreciate what seems 'natural and ordinary' by comparing it with circumstances where it is neither. One can always ask, and it is commonly worth asking: Why here and not there, or there and not here? This naive question can help us to see more distinctly—rather than merely see through—much that frequently goes unobserved, because it so often goes without saying.

Compared to what, then? Anyone is in a position to compare—for better or worse—what they have with what they had, the present with the past. This is often useful and it is often done, whether it is useful or not. It is common both for reactionaries within a dominant culture, and for unhappy immigrants, to compare the present unfavourably with the past, but the pasts they have in mind often have little to do with each other, and often not much to do with what actually happened either. We can also compare what we have and do with what others like us have and do. This can be an important stimulus to reform or, if we're lucky, satis-faction. Thirdly, we can compare what we have with what we would like to have, or believe we should have. Hopes and ideals drive us to these comparisons.

All of these are legitimate comparisons to make and to draw upon, so long as we are conscious of what in particular we are comparing and why. Critics often fail to make clear whether they think things are worse than before, worse than elsewhere, worse than they should be, or all of the above. Those happy with the way things are are often equally undiscriminating. They are all important sorts of judgments to make, but they are not the same judgment. There is not even much reason to assume that they will point in the same direction.

The first and the third of these comparisons—with the past and with an idealised future—can largely be accomplished without leaving home, actually or even imaginatively. The second—with societies similar to one's own—requires some physical or mental travel, but if you choose your comparisons right it can be quite comfortable. It is useful to know what happens in societies with which one shares many features but not all, and it is not too hard—particularly if everyone speaks English there.

But there are some comparisons which are culturally more taxing, and which take up most of my time. One is with societies and cultures which seem utterly or drastically to lack what seems normal at home. Another, really the converse of the first, is with societies which seem to regard as normal what is inconceivable here. Each of these comparisons raises questions about the naturalness of what otherwise goes without saying (here or there), and each encourages thought about the causes and worth of whatever matters to us, when we find it is not universally shared.

Sometimes these sorts of comparisons can be made through deliberately fanciful but finely constructed thought experiments, as in the novel *Lord of the Flies*, where William Golding transports his fictional young characters to an uninhabited island, and has us observe their behaviour—*our* behaviour—in these culturally and institutionally unconstrained circumstances. The great eighteenth century French analyst of political institutions, Montesquieu, populated his fictional *Persian Letters* with stories of Persian despotism and its consequences, about which he knew nothing much, but which were intended to warn of dangers of French despotism and despotism in general, about which he knew a great deal. Or we can reflect on the *Utopia* of Sir Thomas More and its many successors, or the unsettling dystopias—Zamyatin's We, Huxley's *Brave New World*, Orwell's 1984—in which our century is so unusually rich.

More deeply and powerfully, Thomas Hobbes, the greatest of English political philosophers, asked us to consider the uses of political authority by inviting us to consider what life would be like without an established state, law, and the related institutions of which many people complained in the war-torn century and country— seventeenth century England—in which he lived. His argument is relentless and his conclusion quite fearfully grim: life in what he called a 'state of nature' would be a predicament so terrible that people would lay down everything save their lives to escape it. So the existence of a state is a powerful good, as long as it can protect our lives. If it does that indispensable job, Hobbes notoriously insisted, little else can be demanded of it. For without institutions powerful enough to keep the lid on, life would necessarily be plagued by constant, unremitting insecurity, the consequences of which he portrayed in one of the most famous and most eloquent passages in political philosophy:

> Whatsoever therefore is consequent to a time of war, where every man is enemy to every man; the same is consequent to the time, wherein men live without other security, than what their own strength, and their own invention shall furnish them withal. In such condition, there is no place for industry; because the fruit thereof is uncertain: and consequently no culture of the earth; no navigation, nor use of the commodities that may be imported by sea; no commodious building; no instruments of moving, and removing, such things as require much force; no knowledge of the face of the earth; no account of time; no arts; no letters; no society; and which is worst of all, continual fear, and danger of violent death; and the life of man, solitary, poor, nasty, brutish, and short.[5]

Though such hypothetical comparisons might not be provable, they need not be empty. Many thinkers have disagreed with Hobbes about what a society of people something like us might be like without a political order something like ours. But only frivolous or privileged people can ignore the depth and fearfulness of the comparisons he made and the dangers of which he wrote.

This sort of comparison does not have to rely merely on intuition and speculation. International relations have often amounted to a state of nature. Countries riven by civil war too. Think of Bosnia or Somalia or Zaire or Cambodia or whatever other country is being ripped apart by the time this lecture goes to air. And really to think about such possibilities is especially important in a society like ours, just because they are so alien from everyday experience (though not everyone's experience) here. It is one thing to know that the world is full of strange and tragic places and events. Another harder and more important thing, to try to learn about and from them.

Of course, few lessons can simply be transferred from one society to another, still less from fantasy to reality, and it is not for recipes that one makes comparisons. It is to help consideration of one's own circumstances from a vantage point not limited by one's own horizons.

We belong to a privileged group of countries—relatively rich, peaceful, democratic, and law-governed—whose apparent successes some people are trying to emulate. This is especially true of the post-communist world which interests me, where many would like to witness similar successes without having to travel. It is worth examining what our luck might rest upon, both for their sakes and our own. That must involve self-examination, but not self-absorption. We should be in a position to say why here and not there or there and not here. That we are not yet in that position is clear from the fate of some of our prescriptions, for other societies' ills and for our own. Thinking about our values, in the light of apt comparisons, might enable us better to help others; but it also might allow us to help ourselves, and to discover how much or little we know about ourselves. It might reveal how well or ill our rights are secured, and it might reveal, too, how well or ill we have discharged our responsibilities. It might also reveal to us costs, failures and inadequacies in the social accomplishment we represent. For we will not do well out of every comparison, and we should pay equal heed to those where we don't as to those where we do.

And if we are encouraged to try some new initiative—ignorant, belligerent and racist populism, to take a random example—we should certainly think about the fate and consequences of similar initiatives wherever else they have been tried. Conceivably we might find the comparisons encouraging. More likely, we will not. Either way we will be less ignorant for having made them. In any event, that is what I believe. In these lectures I will try to lead you to think about it, and perhaps believe it as well.

1   For a sensitive exploration of the extent of our confusion and unease, see *The Mackay Report: Mind and Mood*, Mackay Research, Sydney, July 1997.
2   I borrow the idea of practical ideals from Philip Selznick, 'Legal Cultures and the Rule of Law', in Adam Czarnota and Martin Krygier, eds, *The Rule of Law after Communism*, Dartmouth, Aldershot 1998.
3   Martin Krygier, 'Marxism, Communism, and Narcissism' (1990), 15, 4, *Law and Social Inquiry*, 70–30.
4   Robert Haupt, 'It's no way to run a country', *Sydney Morning Herald*, 9 October 1993, p27.
5   Thomas Hobbes, *Leviathan*, edited with an introduction, by Michael Oakeshott, Basil Blackwell, Oxford, 1946, p82.

David Malouf

David Malouf was born in Brisbane in 1934 and educated at Brisbane Grammar School and the University of Queensland.

Initially a lecturer in the English Department at the University of Queensland until 1957, he spent almost ten years abroad teaching and writing in England and Italy. He returned to Australia in 1968 to become a senior tutor and lecturer at the University of Sydney, a post he held until 1977.

He is the author of a number of works of fiction, including *Johnno*, *An Imaginary Life*, *Fly Away Peter*, *The Great World*, *Remembering Babylon*, *Conversations at Curlew Creek*

and *Dream Stuff*. He is also a playwright, poet and a librettist. His work has been translated into most European languages, and into Arabic and Chinese.

David Malouf is a multi-award winner. Among those awards he has won are the NSW Premier's Literary Award in 1979 for *An Imaginary Life*; the *Age* Book of the Year Award for 1982 for *Fly Away Peter*; and the Australian Literature Society's Gold Medal in 1983 for *Child's Play* and *Fly Away Peter*. *The Great World* won the Adelaide Festival Prize for Fiction, the 1991 Miles Franklin Award, the Commonwealth Prize for Fiction, and the Prix Femina Etranger in France. *Antipodes*, a collection of stories, won the Vance Palmer Prize for fiction in the 1985 Victorian Premier's Literary Awards. In 1988 Mr Malouf was awarded the inaugural Pascall Prize for excellence in creative writing. *Remembering Babylon* was shortlisted for the Booker Prize, and won the NSW Premier's Prize for Fiction in 1993, the *Los Angeles Times* Prize for Fiction, and the inaugural International IMPAC Dublin Literary Award. He was named the 2000 Laureate of the Neustadt International Prize for Literature by the Oklahoma University.

David Malouf was made an Officer of the Order of Australia in 1997.

A Spirit of Play was the overall title David Malouf gave to his Boyer Lectures, with a secondary title of 'The Making of Australian Consciousness'. The six lectures were 'The Island', which is reproduced here; 'A Complex Fate'; 'Landscapes'; 'Monuments to Time'; 'The Orphan in the Pacific' and, finally, 'A Spirit of Play'. Throughout the lectures, David Malouf observes an interplay of inventiveness and openness—a spirit of play—against the fears of our isolation and difficult beginnings. He remarks in his final lecture on the pressures of the globalised world, the risks of fragmentation: 'But we have faced changes before. What saved us on those earlier occasions was neighbourliness, the saving grace of lightness and good humour, the choice of moderation over the temptation to any form of extreme.'

THE ISLAND

A Spirit of Play: The Making of Australian Consciousness

David Malouf

• 1 9 9 8 •

Looking down the long line of coast this morning as I begin these lectures, I see the first rays of the sun strike Mount Warning and am aware, as the light floods west, what a distance it is to the far side of our country—two time zones and more than three thousand kilometres away, yet how easily the whole landmass sits in my head—as an island or, as I sometimes think of it, a raft we have all scrambled aboard, a new float of lives in busy interaction, of assembly lines and highways, of ideals given body as executives and courts, of routine housekeeping arrangements and objects in passage from hand to hand. To comprehend the thing in all its action and variety and contradiction is a task for the imagination, yet this morning, as always, it is simply there, substantial and ordinary.

When Europeans first came to these shores one of the things they brought with them, as a kind of gift to the land itself, was something that could never have existed before: a vision of the continent in its true form as an island that was not just a way of seeing it, and seeing it whole, but of seeing how it fitted into the rest of the world. And this seems to have happened even before circumnavigation established that it actually was an island. No group of Aboriginal Australians, however ancient and deep their understanding of the land, can ever have seen the place in just this way. It has made a difference. If Aborigines are a land-dreaming people, what we latecomers share is a sea-dreaming, to which the image of Australia as an island has from the beginning been central.

This is hardly surprising. Sydney, in its early days, was first and foremost a seaport, all its dealings were with the sea. Our earliest productive industries were not wheat-growing or sheep-raising but whaling and sealing. It took us nearly 30 years to cross the first land barrier. Right up to the end of the nineteenth century our settlements were linked by coastal steamer, not by road or rail. In his sonnet 'Australia', Bernard O'Dowd speaks of Australia's 'virgin helpmate, Ocean', as if the island continent were mystically married to its surrounding ocean as Venice was to the Adriatic.

As the off-shoot of a great naval power we felt at home with the sea. It was an element over which we had control; more, certainly, than we had at the beginning over the land. It was what we looked to for all our comings and goings, for all that was new—for news. And this sense of being at home with the sea made distances that might otherwise have been unimaginable seem shorter. It brought Britain and Europe closer than 10,000 miles on the globe might have suggested, and kept us tethered, for longer than we might otherwise have been, by sea-routes whose ports of call in the days before air travel constituted a litany of connection that every child of my generation knew by heart. Distance is not always a matter of miles. Measured in feelings it can redefine itself as closeness.

And this notion of an island continent, contained and containable, had other consequences.

Most nations establish themselves through a long series of border conflicts with neighbours. This is often the major thrust of their history. Think of the various wars between Germany and France, or Russia and Poland, or of British history before the Union of the Crowns.

Australia's borders were a gift of nature. We did not have to fight for them. In our case, history and geography coincided, and we soon hit upon the idea that the single continent must one day be a single nation. What this means is that all our wars of conquest, all our sources of conflict, have been internal. Conquest of space to begin with, in a series of daring explorations of the land, which were also acts of possession different from the one that made it ours merely in law. This was possession in the form of knowledge by naming and mapping, by taking its spaces into our heads, and at last into our imagination and consciousness. Conquest of every form of internal division and difference: conquest of the original possessors, for example, in a war more extensive than we have wanted to recognise. Later, there was the attempted resolution, through an act of Federation, of the fraternal division between the states; and, longer lasting and less amenable of solution, of the conflict, once Federation had been achieved, between the states and the federal government. Also, more darkly, suppression, in acts of law-making and social pressure and through subtle forms of exclusion, of all those whom we have, at one time or another, declared to be outsiders among us, and in their various ways alien, even when they were Australians like the rest. That early vision of wholeness produced a corresponding anxiety, the fear of fragmentation, and for too long the only answer we had to it was the imposition of a deadening conformity.

In time, the vision of the continent as whole and unique in its separation from the rest of the world produced the idea that it should be kept separate, that only in isolation could its uniqueness—and ours—be preserved.

Many of the ideas that have shaped our life here, and many of the themes on which our history has been argued, settle around these notions of isolation and containment, of wholeness and the fear of fragmentation. But isolation can lead to stagnation as well as concentrated richness, and wholeness does not necessarily mean uniformity, though that is how we have generally taken it. Nor does diversity always lead to fragmentation.

As for the gift of those natural, indisputable borders, that too had a cost. It burdened us with the duty of defending them, and the fear, almost from the beginning, that they may not, in fact, be defendable.

Our first settlements outside Sydney, at Hobart in 1804 and Perth in the 1820s, were made to forestall the possibility of French occupation (and it seems Napoleon did plan a diversionary invasion for 1804). Then, at the time of the Crimean War, it was the Russians we had to keep an eye on. The Russian fleet was just seven days sailing away at Vladivostok. And then, from the beginning of this century, the Japanese. This fear of *actual* invaders, of being unable to defend our borders, led to a fear of other and less tangible forms of invasion. By people, 'lesser breeds without the Law',[1] who might sully the purity of our stock; by alien forms of culture that might prejudice our attempt to be uniquely ourselves; by ideas, and all those other forms of influence, out there in the world beyond our coast, that might undermine our morals or in various other ways divide and unsettle us. All this has made little-islanders of us; has made us decide, from time to time, to close ourselves off from influence and change, and by settling in behind our ocean wall, freeze and stop what has been from the beginning, and continues to be, a unique and exciting experiment.

Australia began as an experiment in human engineering. We should not allow the brutalities of the age in which it took place to obscure the fact that among the many mixed motives for the founding of the colony there were some that were progressive and idealistic. The eighteenth century was as troubled as we are by the nature of criminality and, in dealing with it, the need to balance deterrence, or as they would have called it, terror, with the opportunity to reform. Botany Bay was not just a dumping ground for unwanted criminals. It was also an experiment in reformation, in using the rejects of one society to create another.

What seems astonishing when we look about at the world we live in here, this clean and orderly place with its high level of affluence and ease, its concern for rights and every sort of freedom, these cities in which a high level of civility is simply taken for granted and barely remarked upon, is that it should have emerged from a world that was at the beginning so un-free, so brutal and disorderly. It did so because these rejects of society, of whom so little might have been expected, *made* it happen. Out of their insistence that they were not to be so easily written off.

Charles Darwin, who was not always a sympathetic observer of the Australian scene, has two things to tell us of the colony as he first saw it in 1836, not quite 50 years from the beginning. 'Here', he writes in his *Journal of the Voyage of the HMS Beagle*, 'in less promising country, scores of years have affected many times more than the same number of centuries has done in South America'. That is a tribute to the pace of development in Australia, and also, no doubt, to British efficiency and moral fibre as opposed to Spanish and Portuguese fecklessness. But he has something else to say as well. 'As a means', he tells us, 'of making men honest—of converting vagabonds the most useless in one hemisphere into active citizens in another, and giving birth to a new and splendid country—and a grand centre of civilisation—it has succeeded to a degree perhaps unparalleled in history'.

When we think of our beginning, we are inclined to emphasise what is sensational in it, the many horrors, and this is understandable.[2] They were real, and indignation at injustice does credit to us—so does a passionate sympathy for its victims. Fellow-feeling for the weak and for those who fail, out of bad luck or bad judgment or ordinary human hopelessness, is one of our strongest national characteristics and has its beginning here. Our attitude to welfare, for instance, and to those who need it, is very different from the way these things are seen in some other places.

But victims, and sensational brutality and misery, are easy to imagine and identify with. What is harder to think our way into is ordinariness, the day-to-day routine of lives that, however brutal they may have been by our standards, were unremarkable except in the astonishing capacity of those who lived them (and we need to think hard about what this must have meant to individual men and women) to endure, but even more, to change; to take hold of their lives and remake themselves in terms of the opportunities offered by a second chance in a new place.

Eighteenth-century playwrights and novelists often made a criminal—a highwayman or confidence trickster or thief—their hero. Gay's *Beggars Opera*, Defoe's *Colonel Jack* and *Captain Singleton*, Fielding's *Mr Jonathan Wild*, all play with the interesting and subversive notion that the qualities that go to the making of a successful criminal—entrepreneurial egotism, an eye for the main chance and for the weakness of others—may be the same qualities that in other circumstances make a politician or businessman. Botany Bay in some ways put this cheeky proposition to the proof.

John Locke claimed that men join a civil society or commonwealth 'for mutual protection of their lives, liberty and estates, which I call', he says, 'by the general name of property'.[3] Now, if it is the need to protect property that makes men join together and become citizens, mightn't it be possible to make citizens out of vagabonds, as Darwin calls them, by giving them property, that is, land, but in a place so far off that they would not be tempted to return; a place where possession of property would lead them to *settle*, even when their term of exile was up? Land, that real yet mystical commodity of measured dirt that can raise a man, or a woman, from a mere nothing to an individual of status and power, and eventually, since this is what land usually ensured in the days before universal suffrage, the right to vote and have a voice in the making of the laws.

It was the promise of land, 50 acres for a man, 30 more for his wife, and 30 for each child, that was the new element in this experiment and a defining one in our history, not least because of the conflict it involved with the original owners. That is another story, another and darker history interwoven with our more triumphal one, and the conflict over land that is at the centre of it is not just about occupation and ownership; it is also about what land means. For Aboriginal people land is the foundation of spiritual being. For Europeans it represents security and status, or it is a source of wealth. The desire of ordinary men and women to become property owners was the making of this country. To own a piece of Australia, even if it was only a quarter-acre block became the Australian dream. The desperation that lay behind it, the determination of poor men and women to grasp what was offered and raise themselves out of a landless poverty into a new class, was the source of a materialism that is still one of our most obvious characteristics. It has taken us 200 years to see that there might be another and more inward way of possessing a place, and that in this, as in so much else, the people we dispossessed had been there before us. But the fact is that for those convicts who did succeed, all this was a fairy tale come true. Samuel Terry, for instance, was transported in 1801 for stealing 400 pairs of stockings; he seems always to have done things on a large scale. He served his seven years, and when he died in 1838 owned 19,000 acres, more than the greatest lord in England.

Of course, opportunity, however great, was also limited. Not everyone ended up as a merchant prince. But when all the savageries have been taken into account, and the disruption and pain of leaving loved ones, and a life, however unsettled, that in their mind, in their hearts too, was home, transportation worked for most of these men and women. To suggest otherwise is to deny the extent to which so many of them *did* change and become the active citizens who made our world. And there must have been some among them, like Simeon Lord and Mary Reibey or Esther Abrahams, for whom Botany Bay was not just the underside of the world but the realisation of that dream of radical English thinkers in the seventeenth century, the world turned upside down.[4] Esther Abrahams, who was transported in the First Fleet for theft, set up with, and later married, Major George Johnston, and was, for a time, the First Lady of the colony. It is Mary Gilmore who has given us our most memorable statement of all this. The old convict in her poem 'Old Botany Bay' gives a voice to many thousands who have no other voice in our history.

> I'm old
> Botany Bay;
> Stiff in the joints,
> Little to say.
>
> I am he
> Who paved the way
> That you might walk
> At your ease today.
>
> I was the conscript
> Sent to hell
> To make in the desert
> The living well
>
> I bore the heat,
> I blazed the track—

Furrowed and bloody
Upon my back.

I split the rock;
I felled the tree;
The nation was—
Because of me!

Old Botany Bay
Taking the sun
From day to day . . .
Shame on the mouth

That would deny
The knotted hands
That set us high!

I would want to add that it wasn't just muscle and dumb endurance that these people brought, and which we enjoy the fruits of, but also native wit, inventiveness, imagination and, most of all, the amazing human capacity to re-imagine and remake themselves.

One surprising detail leaps out of the various accounts we have of the First Fleet voyage. It is this: on the night of 2 January 1788, some of the convicts on one of the ships, the *Scarborough*, as their contribution to the possibilities of diversion and simple enjoyment in the place they were coming to—and in defiance it seems, of the misery of cramped conditions and whatever terror they may have felt at their imminent arrival on a fatal shore—got up a dramatic entertainment, some sort of play.

So, smuggled in on one of those eleven little ships, along with their cargo of criminal rejects and all the necessary objects for settling a new place the handsaws and framesaws, and the steel spade and iron shovel and three hoes and an axe and tomahawk for each man, and the woollen drawers and worsted stockings for the men, and linsey-woolsey petticoats and caps for the women, and Lieutenant George Worgan's piano,[5] and the rights and obligations that, in being argued back and forth between authority and its many subjects, would make the new place they were coming to so different from the one they left—was this spirit of make-believe, of theatre, of play. And along with it, an audience's delight, and practiced skill no doubt, in watching and listening.

The fact is that the whole of a culture is present, in all its complexity, in small things as well as large. What arrived here with those eleven ships was the European and specifically English culture of the late Enlightenment in all its richness and contradiction, however simple the original settlement may have seemed. From the moment of first landing a dense, little new world began to grow up here. Out of the interaction of Europeans with a new form of nature that put to the test all their traditional assumptions about farming methods and how to deal with weather and soil. Out of the interaction of authority with the mass of convicts, around questions of right and obligation, force and consent—these were open questions in some ways because the status of convicts was different here from that of convicts At Home. Out of the interaction between men and women in a place where women were freer than men (they did not have to perform government labour for their food), and freer than women were at home—a good many of these women became independent traders and land holders. Out of the interaction between all these newcomers and those, the original possessors, who were already on the ground. Before long, and well within the first two decades, all the amenities of an advanced society had been conjured up.

Craftsmen of every sort—furniture- and cabinet-makers and long-case clock-makers—had got to work, using Home designs but local woods. Only some of them are known to us by name. John Oatley is one. He made the turret clock that can still be seen in the tympanum of Francis Greenway's Hyde Park Barracks. Then there were brass-founders and tinsmiths, pottery-makers like Samuel Skinner, whose wife Mary took over the business when he died; and quality silversmiths, many of them Irish and most of them transported for forgery, a common crime in that profession. John Austin and Ferdinand Meurant, for example, were both transported from Dublin in 1798 and pardoned four years later, Meurant for knocking £50 off the price of a necklace he made for Governor King's wife. Austin, in a nice colonial irony, went on to become an engraver for the newly established Bank of New South Wales. All these many artisans and makers of fine goods were convicts. They got conditional pardons quickly because the colony needed their skills.

There is something very moving, something we can feel close to, in all this. It speaks of inventiveness and industry beyond the level of mere making do; of a determination to create a world here that would be the old world in all its diversity, but in a new form—new because in these new conditions the old world would not fit. But what is newest of all is the opportunity that was offered to those who might have believed that, in being transported, all future opportunity had been closed to them. In the more relaxed conditions of this new world even convicts had a kind of power they could never have exercised at home. The System had holes—air holes through which a man could catch a second breath and through which a new form of society could be breathed into existence, a society that was rough perhaps, but full as well of the raw energy that comes with opportunity. If I settle on this occasion on just one of this little new world's many re-creations, it is because it seems to me to look forward more evocatively than most to the future, and in a particular way.

In January 1796, just eight years from the beginning, a playhouse was established, a local habitation for that spirit of theatre smuggled in on the *Scarborough*. It was a real theatre, Georgian in design, with a pit, a gallery and boxes. Entrance to the boxes cost five shillings, to the pit two and six, to the gallery a shilling, and those who had no ready cash could pay in kind, that is, in meat, flour or spirits. It was a convict enterprise of the colony's baker, Robert Sidaway, and seems to have established itself (this too might tell us something about the kind of society we were to become) rather more easily than the first church. The Reverend Johnson had to build that for himself, and his first Christmas service, in 1793, drew only 35 worshippers. Sidaway's theatre, presumably, did better than that.

An audience is a mysterious phenomenon and subject to mysterious and unpredictable forces. Made up of individuals who shift their attention and their sympathies from moment to moment under the influence of strong emotion or an appeal to their imagination or their sense of humour, but also of a sharpened critical sense in the matter of watching and listening, it is a little society of its own, reconstituted at each performance inside the larger one, and mostly outside its control. Not a mob, but a cohesive unity, with its own interests and loyalties, but unpredictable and therefore dangerous. And this must have been especially true of this audience, composed as it was of convicts and their guards but in convict hands. Fascinating to wonder how far such an audience might constitute the beginnings here of an integrated community, one in which, given the differences—of status, as between convicts and guards, bound and free; of origin, English and Irish; of education, religion, fortune—a various crowd could nonetheless become one.

On 8 April 1800, Shakespeare's *Henry IV Part One* was played. It must have had a special appeal, a special relevance for this audience; one wonders how the authorities allowed it. Political rebellion presented as a falling out between thieves; a tavern underworld of sublime exuberance, where a light-hearted attitude is taken to highway robbery and the picking of pockets; a Lord Chief Justice openly insulted; every sort of high principle roundly mocked. Old hands might have recognised, in the improvised play in which Falstaff and Prince Hal alternately plead for mercy to the King, a version of the mock trials that were one of their chief entertainments in Newgate, a learning-place for first offenders in how to defend themselves in front of the beak. (And Shakespeare's scene may have just such occasions as its reference.) The play's language must have been a particular delight, with its thieves' cant so like the convicts' own 'kiddy' language.[6] And how comically liberating to see lordly authority taken out of the realm of the distantly sacred and brought up close, as they must have seen it every day in the streets of Sydney, in the form of Lieutenant-Governor King for example, blustering wrangling, breaking out in the same bad language as themselves.

An extraordinary achievement, and so early in the piece, this alternative stage for action, this exercise in audience-making, society-shaping in the spirit of play. But risky. Dangerous.

Governor King must have thought so anyway. In one of those about-turns that are so common a feature of our history, when all that seems given is taken back again, in September 1800, when his Governorship was confirmed, he closed the playhouse and had it razed to the ground.

1   Rudyard Kipling, 'Recessional', 1897.
2   Sydney, who as Secretary for the Home Department was responsible for the establishment of the colony, seems to have intended that transported convicts, once they arrived at Botany Bay, should be 'free on the ground'; that is, their sentences, 7 or 14 years or life, were terms of exile, not of bondage. One of the arguments in favour of Botany Bay as the site for the colony was that there were no people there who might put the men and women who were sent there under bond, as they had been, for example, in Virginia. As for labour, the convicts might work for their keep until the colony was established but forced labour had been declared unconstitutional in 1783, on the grounds that it reduced a man to slavery and no free-born Briton, even a convicted felon, should be put in the same condition as a slave.
      Governor Phillip chose to ignore all this. He put his convicts in bond to the Crown and, unless they were pardoned, until the last day of their sentence. There is the pathetic case of William Bradbury who had, it was thought, served his 7 years, partly on The Hulks (those old prison ships anchored in the Thames and off Portsmouth), partly on the voyage out, and who was granted land at Parramatta. But when the Second Fleet arrived with the records, his sentence was found to be for life. Phillip took him back into bondage, and when he protested had him flogged. In despair, Bradbury ran off into the scrub and was never heard of again.

In this business of flogging, too, Phillip's decision was to be fateful. Civil floggings were largely symbolic, their aim to humiliate the victim in front of his peers, not to break him physically. What Phillip did was impose on the civilian convicts the naval practice of flogging by numbers and to the last lash.

These decisions had their severest consequences long after Phillip had left the colony when, at the end of the Napoleonic wars, large numbers of convicts began to arrive at Botany Bay, and the demand for labour in the colony, both for public works and for work on private farms, made bonded labour both useful and profitable. But it is worth noting that one of the privileges allowed to convicts in New South Wales was the retention of their property. A man who could support himself and did not draw food from the Stores could exempt himself from government labour, as James Grant did, for example, in 1804. And once a man had completed his government labour he was free to hire himself out for private work. When the price of labour in the colony rose to 4 and 5 shillings a day, a skilled workman, such as a bricklayer or carpenter, could work for himself and pay another man to do his government work for him. Women from the beginning did no government work at all. As Alan Atkinson puts it in The Europeans in Australia, 'In these first years of European settlement (after Phillip's time and up to Macquarie's) even convict men and women who came with no money entered a market as much as they did a penal system.'

3   John Locke, Second Treatise on Civil Government, 1690. One of the cornerstones of English political thinking.

4   At the debates held at Putney in 1649, at the end of the English Civil War, the Diggers and Levellers and other pre-communist groups who made up a large part of Parliament's New Model Army argued for the establishment of an egalitarian commonwealth and for universal male suffrage independent of the ownership of land. They were defeated by Cromwell and the other Grandees, and when some of them, the Diggers, being landless, occupied and began to dig common land, they were driven off in a series of bloody skirmishes. These sects were the organised and articulate nucleus of what Christopher Hill, in his The World Turned Upside Down, calls 'masterless men', who in the breakup of the old feudal system constituted a new class, of vagabonds, beggars, itinerant labourers, and the urban poor. As early as 1594 we hear of them being rounded up and transported to Ireland as a way of relieving the kingdom of its 'superfluous people'—Ireland, in this way, preceding Virginia and, later, New South Wales as repositories of the unwanted and refractory.

We see something of the ideas common among utopian radicals in the early seventeenth century from Gonzalo's speech in The Tempest:

> I' the commonwealth I would by contraries
> Execute all things; for no kind of traffic
> Would I admit; no name of magistrate;
> Letters should be unknown; riches, poverty,
> And use of service, none; contract, succession,
> Bourn, bound of land, tilth, vineyard, none;
> No use of metal, corn, or wine, or oil,
> No occupation; all men idle, all;
> And all women too, but innocent and pure;
> No sovereignty...

This was a religious as well as a political vision, in which the ownership of property, the use, through monopoly, of common goods, the rule of one man over another as king or bishop or magistrate, the use of one man's service in another's interest, was a result of the Fall, and Abel's murder at the hands of Cain the origin of one 'brother's' ascendancy over another in a fallen world.

5   When Worgan left the colony, his piano passed into the hands of Elizabeth Macarthur. It still exists. See *The Oxford Companion to Australian Music*.

6   One of the privileges of convicted felons in New South Wales was that all charges by or against them had to be heard by a magistrate. By a legal fiction they appeared not as felons but under their old designation, as labourer or hedger or haberdasher, and had the right as well to use their own slang, their thieves cant or 'kiddy' language, which the court, if necessary, translated.

Inga Clendinnen

Now a Queensland island dweller, Inga Clendinnen was born in
Geelong in 1934, educated at
Morongo Presbyterian Girls'
College, Geelong, studied history
and literature at the University of
Melbourne, and took a D. Litt. at
La Trobe University. She taught in
the history department of Melbourne University for a number of
years from 1956, before moving
to the newly established La Trobe
University in 1969, where she
taught until 1991, being made
emeritus scholar in 1992.

Her books, *Ambivalent Conquests:
Maya and Spaniards in Yucaton
1515–1570* and *Aztecs: An Interpretation*, and scholarly articles on
the Aztecs and Maya of Mexico and their encounter with invading
Spaniards in the sixteenth century have won a number of international
awards. Over recent years, she has also published literary essays and short
fiction. Her immensely impressive *Reading the Holocaust* won the NSW
Premier's General History Award 1999 and the United States Jewish
National Book Award for Holocaust Studies. She has also written a memoir
entitled *Tiger's Eye*.

Inga Clendinnen has been a Visiting Fellow at the Shelby Cullom Davis
Center for Historical Research at Princeton University, and at the Institute
for Advanced Study at Princeton. She is a member of the Australian
Academy of the Humanities.

Dr Clendinnen gave the title *True Stories* to her 1999 Boyer Lectures. They
were 'Incident on a Beach', which is reproduced here; 'Pilgrims, Stains and
Sacred Places'; 'Back to the Past: Victoria 1841'; 'Arnhem Land 1931–7';
'Inside the Contact Zone: one and two'; 'What Now?' Moving on from her
background as a formal historian, Dr Clendinnen works with retrieved
fragments to construct a highly personal and challenging review of race
relations in this country since first contact, so we may better understand
how our nation has come to be what it is today. In the conclusion of her

final lecture she asserts: 'We need history; not Black Armband history and not triumphalist white-out history either, but good history, true stories of the making of this present land, none of them simple, some of them painful, all of them part of our own individual histories.'

INCIDENT ON A BEACH

True Stories

Inga Clendinnen

• 1999 •

I begin with the story of an incident on a beach. The place is the southwest coast of what we now call Western Australia. The year is 1801. A French scientific expedition is coasting those shores, with the official blessing of their First Consul, Napoleon Bonaparte. Their main job is to collect samples of flora and fauna which might be useful back home in France, but they are committed scientists, and they are curious about the human population too: indeed, one of the naturalists aboard has a special interest in the infant discipline of Anthropology. But while they have seen the smoke of many fires they have not sighted a single native until they surprise a solitary man, fishing in waist-deep water. The encounter is not encouraging as the Frenchmen advance, waving glass necklaces at him, he shouts, who knows what, shakes his fish spear at them and disappears into the scrub.

Then they come upon a man and woman digging for shellfish. The man runs, but the woman, 'seized with fright', we are told, flings herself down and flattens her face and body into the sand, arms and legs bent 'like a frog on the edge of a pond'. The Frenchmen surround her. One lays presents beside her—a mirror, a little knife—while another quickly checks to see whether she still has her front teeth. (Dampier had reported that the people he encountered had lost theirs.) He finds that she does.

Then, hoping she might stop crying, the men withdraw twenty feet or so. But she remains pressed into the sand, save that she once lifts her head and looks at them. So they come back and pick her up and hold her suspended so they can examine her. Then, 'as she still would not stand, they laid her on her back on the sand.'

The leader of the expedition continues the account:

> I saw then that she was pregnant—that is probably what prevented her from fleeing . . . This woman had a small round face with pronounced features . . . She was of small stature, but well-made . . .

I judged from her breasts that she had had many children, although she appeared not to be more than twenty or twenty-two years old. Her only clothing was an old skin . . . a piece of the same skin forming a kind of pocket, which contained several small onions, similar to the roots of orchids . . . At last, as this woman showed no sign of life, we left her. We were hardly more than thirty paces from her when we saw her stealing away on hands and knees into the bushes, leaving behind our presents and her stick.

This is the story as Nicolas Baudin recorded it in his report to his superiors.[1] The story was told honestly: Baudin was confident that he and his men had conducted themselves correctly, and that they had done no harm. Clearly they intended none. In one sense the woman was lucky: these strangers didn't rape her, they didn't abduct her, they didn't kill her. Three centuries earlier Spaniards might well have done any or all of those things. The Frenchmen had treated her gently. Of course they would not have treated a Frenchwoman met on a beach like that, but these heirs to the French Revolution certainly recognised her as a fellow human, black and near naked though she was—they gave her both time to stop crying, and her little gifts, and they molested her only in so far as their scientific purposes required. They were only doing their job—and they did her no harm.

Or so they thought. Now, consider the matter from her perspective. She had been surrounded; she had been paralysed with terror. One of the strangers had forced his fingers into her mouth. At that point she had been lying face down, so he must have turned her head to the side before he could thrust them in. Then they had lifted her and stared at her and tugged at her garment as she hung in their hands like a frozen frog. Then they laid her down and stared some more. And then they went away. So what had happened to her?

What is terrifying is that we do not know, even as we watch her press herself into the sand, as we watch her crawling away. We see her body, but we do not see her mind. What did she think was happening as she felt the hands of these very material apparitions? What did she think was happening to the child in her belly, the child she was desperately trying to protect from their sight and touch? And later, when she crept back to her people, how was she received? Was she received at all? Was she shunned? Was she killed? They would have been watching what happened. They would have seen her hanging in those strange bleached hands. What did they think had happened to the child in her belly? Did they decide to kill it, too? And the man who fled in terror, abandoning his pregnant woman to the strangers. Where would he find his manhood now?

We don't know the answers to any of these questions. All we do know is that no harm was intended, and that harm was almost certainly done. We also know the Frenchmen's story, a story told honestly from their perspective, despite all the things it leaves out, of what happened on the beach. We don't know the woman's story at all. We can only infer what it might have been by exercising our imaginations.

It is also worth thinking about the gifts the Europeans brought to bestow upon these as yet unknown locals: glass beads, knives, mirrors. This is the standard inventory of the smiling face of imperialism. Columbus took beads, knives and mirrors with him to America. Why knives? Because knives are seriously useful in any economy? Why beads? Because savages are vain? Because all men are vain? Why mirrors? A usefully portable fragment of white man's magic? A joke on the savage? The woman had just been subjected to the novel experience of the sustained European scientific gaze. Is she now being invited to scrutinise herself? She leaves the European things anyway— along with her digging stick, which is her essential equipment for life. What I most notice about this aborted transaction is that the Europeans bring no mirrors for themselves.

There is little point in apportioning blame close to two hundred years after the event. What interest me are two things. First is the intellectual and imaginative exercise we have just been through in doing this little bit of history: retrieving just what happened, thinking about its possible consequences, deciding from their words and actions just what the Frenchmen were up to and the kind of men they were, and doing our best to imagine the thoughts and feelings of the silent players in the scene. Second, there is the separate matter of clarifying and examining our own responses to what happened.

What I feel, to my surprise, is anger. In part this is because she is a woman, young, pregnant and alone, she is being manhandled, and as a woman I resent that. But I have to admit to a deeper response which is an anachronistic absurdity. What I want to say is: 'Take your hands off her, you Frenchmen.' I see them as foreign intruders molesting my countrywoman, someone from my territory—a territory my forebears will not even enter for several decades, forebears who could well perform actions much worse than these earnest Frenchmen. Nonetheless, that is what I feel. And I do not feel in the least implicated in what was done to her: I am on her side. What, I wonder, do you feel?

As to why this small long-ago event should matter to any of us— well, I will make a large claim for it: I believe its examination is conducive to civic virtue, and therefore to the coherence of a democratic liberal state. The philosopher Martha Nussbaum identifies three qualities as necessary for responsible citizenship in a complex world: an ability to critically examine oneself and one's traditions; an ability to see beyond immediate group loyalties and to extend to strangers the moral concern we 'naturally' extend to friends and kin; the development of what she calls the 'narrative imagination': the ability to see unobvious connections between sequences of human actions, and to recognise their likely consequences, intended and unintended.[2]

Nussbaum believes that these three things sustain the political health of a democratic nation, and so do I. I also believe that these things can be achieved, indeed are possibly best achieved, by the close analysis of past situations like the one we have just been looking at. Reflection on such situations liberates our imaginations to taste experiences other than our own—what it was like to be that woman on the beach, what it was like to be one of those rather embarrassed French scientists. That imagining expands our moral comprehension. We are also led to reflect on unobvious connections and the range of possible outcomes—what Nussbaum would call the narrative imagination at work.

Such analyses also help us to know ourselves more exactly, and more critically. For example: What is this territory I discover I feel so powerfully about? Why did I feel invaded, too? Some years back one of those books appeared which precipitate ideas lurking in the corners of the mind into clear view. Benedict Anderson asked what holds nations together. Think about it. What set of experiences signifies 'Australia' to you? What do you directly know of it? You know your family, your friends, the people at the school, your workmates if you still have a job, the lady in the corner shop if there is still a corner shop, the people at the fruit stall, a cloud of relations, your football team, some people on radio and television. You will have travelled over bits of it, some bits often if your social or economic work takes you there. But it is still a very patchy mental map. There will be suburbs even in your home city as unvisited as Marco Polo's China.

So where is 'Australia'? As Anderson makes clear in his *Imagined Communities*—it's in your mind.[3] Nations are imaginary communities, and none the less real for that. And nations, especially democratic nations, especially democratic ethnically and religiously diverse nations like our own, cannot hold together unless they share a common vision as to how the world works, what constitutes the good life, what behaviour is worthy of respect, what behaviour is shameful. Present input clearly matters—the journalists of the ABC and SBS influence my image of Australia and the world every day—but our understanding of our nation is also profoundly shaped by our view of its past, of its history—however vague that view might be.

That the study of history can encourage civic virtue is not a fashionable view in 1999. This has been the bloodiest century in human history, which makes it a bad time for the notion that good will and mutual respect can come out of reflection on the past. Most people would say that Yugoslavia has been destroyed by its history: by unassuaged passions and unforgiven wrongs. Michael Ignatieff has written a fine book arguing that it is not the past dictating to the present which has devastated Yugoslavia, but present politicians ruthlessly manipulating the past: that it is bad history, not true history, which has reduced the place to ruins. He may be right.[4] I think he is right. But what is clear is that it is too late for good history to help Yugoslavia now. Once civil order breaks down, vengeance becomes a dangerously attractive existential choice, giving purpose to every action, significance to every thought. It cripples the moral imagination, freeing people to act towards their neighbours, now become their 'enemies', in any way they like—'look what you've made me do!' To consolidate good history made out of true stories we need time, and peace, and we need the will. We also need to keep in mind that truth is a direction and an aspiration, not a condition.

Other people would say I am too ambitious in wanting true stories to make up the history of a nation rather than one simple and therefore necessarily false one: a story about how fine and great we are, how fine and great we have always been. They would say that people need simple stories which will make them proud of their country; that too many stories, especially if they are as lumpy as true stories tend to be, will only confuse them.

We have a prime example of the dangers of a simple story powerfully and repeatedly told close to hand in the United States of America, where American History is on the syllabus at most years in primary and secondary school, where the American flag is worshipped daily, and where 'America' officially can do no wrong. Teach grown men and women a nursery version of their history and you will make babies of them when it comes to grasping the actual workings of their own society, and of their nation in the wider world. The hypocrisy of much American foreign policy is only possible because so many of its people believe that the USA simply could not engage in dishonourable actions. They believe in their nursery version. So, even more alarmingly, do many people within the United States government.

One example only: in the course of snatching their one-time friend, later arch-enemy, President Noriega from Panama, in an operation they code-named 'Just Cause', the invading US troops and air force killed somewhere between 3000 and 7000 people, nearly all of them civilians going about their ordinary business—not drug dealing, not engaging in subversive political activity, just shopping, working, going to school. And all to lay hands on a single villain. Those thousands of dead Panamanians simply do not exist in American consciousness, much less burden their conscience. They have been comprehensively 'disappeared'. The internal problems of the United States polity—angry black men and women in the cities, armed white men in the hills—have a lot to do with that insistent but spurious national story.

By contrast, there are, increasingly, at the end of this terrible century, examples of divided nations who are making the choice for good history. Let me offer you two. First, South Africa. Under the old régime, racial division and gross inequality were sustained by state violence, and caused incalculable social misery. That régime was ended by negotiation, so there could not be a criminal tribunal, a Truth and Justice Commission. Instead, a Truth and Reconciliation Commission was set up.

The commission's aim was to open the circumstances of secret killings to the light. What all the people attending the commission, victims and perpetrators alike, were doing was a painful kind of public history: establishing precisely what had happened, in scrupulous detail, then recording it. Even the triumphant African National Congress, to the continuing rage of some of its members, found its wrongdoings exposed, and soberly set down.

The man who headed the Truth and Reconciliation Commission, Archbishop Desmond Tutu, wanted the new state to begin not with no history, not with false history, but with a true history forged out of its divided but shared past. And it worked. Vengeance, reparation, even justice, turned out to be less important than knowledge. From now on, no one in South Africa can deny the past or falsify it. South Africans, black and white, have their true stories. Some will still cry for justice, but the worst of the agony has been assuaged and rendered unavailable for disreputable use by that extraordinary collective enterprise in good history.[5]

My second and still problematic example is Ireland, where over the last few years we have watched not so much the forging of a new history, but a halting, difficult movement away from bad history. We have watched a people extricating themselves from the tyranny of legends, from corrupted histories which have been used to promote murderous division. The burning in their beds of three young brothers, the bomb at Omagh, made manifest what can happen when grossly simplified and distorted myths are declared to be the one and only true history. The growing accord depends on many things, not least Ireland's new prosperity, but I think they can do what they were beginning to do politically only because some good history had already been done, for example and in particular on the history of the Irish famine.

It had been a central tenet of Irish republican mythology that the Great Famine of 1847 occurred because wicked men organised the export of corn to foreign Protestant landlords in England while Catholic Irish men, women and children were left to starve. As Colm Tóibín puts it, 'the Famine had to be blamed on the Great Other the enemy across the water, and the victims of the famine had to be this entire Irish nation rather than a vulnerable section of the population'.[6]

Over those few years a million people out of eight million people starved to death or died from disease. Two million more emigrated, with thousands of them dying en route to the United States or Canada or Australia. The famine was certainly made worse by bungling, by adventurism, by coldheartedness. It was made the occasion for a cynical land-clearing exercise, with evictions and forced expropriations. And the Irish were despised by the British ruling caste: The Times of March 1847 declared them to be 'a people born and bred from time immemorial in inveterate indolence, improvidence, disorder, and consequent destitution'—not an encouraging evaluation on the eve of the third year of the failure of the potato crop.

Nonetheless, recent research—research too detailed and thorough to be denied—has established that Ireland remained a net food importer during the hungry 1840s, that many members of the Catholic Irish middle class profited from the anguish of their compatriots, and that some of the most mean-minded of the Poor Law administrators were not Protestant landlords, but Irish Catholics.[7]

End of legend. During the presidency of Mary Robinson, the Famine was brought back into Irish history as the tragic shared legacy it is, with the parts analysed, responsibilities allocated, and the victims memorialised and mourned. Good history at last, with each side having to acknowledge the truth of stories different from their own preferred versions.

So what kind of history do we need here, in this fortunate slice of the world called Australia? We have already had a tussle over that question. Geoffrey Blainey began it. Blainey has always had a knack for titles: *The Tyranny of Distance*, *The Triumph of the Nomads*, *The Rush that Never Ended*. He is also moved by the stories of small men who dream large dreams, like the immigrant lad who began by boiling up sugar and water in his parents' bathroom and peddling toffees from a tray at weekends, and turned into Mr Macpherson Robertson the lollies baron, bringing joy and tooth decay to generations of Australians.[8] Blainey sees the romance in mercantile and industrial endeavour, and he makes us see it too. He tells us true stories which other historians neglect to tell.

I was therefore taken aback when Blainey deployed that deft wit to abduct the phrase 'Black Armband History' from the Aboriginal protest movement of the 1970s, because the phrase was altogether too dismissive of those other stories which were part of the stories of his favourite Aussie battlers, and certainly part of the one big story of how we have come to be as we are. I was shocked by John Howard's adoption of the Black Armband History tag. The Prime Minister's leap to appropriate it seemed to me an act of partisan opportunism. What Howard wanted, transparently, was white-out history, a simple tale of the triumph of the Anglo-Celts over deserts and empty places, ignoring the mosaic of different peoples we have always been, ignoring our first people. He wanted bad history, and, as I have tried to show you, bad history has a very bad record.

Which brings me to the matter of these talks. It was easy to decide on the theme: the practical usefulness of good history both morally and politically. Initially I wanted to avoid Aboriginal issues, as being at once too complicated, and too politicised. I thought and I still think that the most urgent issue before us today is the demor-alisation, the social disaffection, the sheer human misery attached to chronic unemployment and chronic job insecurity. I also thought that the term 'Aborigine' obscures almost as much as it illuminates, bundling together people living in quite unlike circumstances—in remote communities, on the fringes of country towns, in the deep interior of cities.

However, there is a 'we' and a 'they' in this country, a divide between Aborigines and the rest of us. Wherever they live, they are the product of their distinctive history, as we are of ours. Their expe-rience of their unique past crucially matters to their present situa-tion, and to their view of their possible future. Our ignorance of their history, or our denial of it, is a threat to us all, because it is the major impediment in the way of general agreement as to what constitutes justice and decency, which are core issues in any democracy.

To put my one card on the table: while I am a historian and an Australian, I am not an Australian historian. I have no specialist knowledge of the affairs of this country. Until about a year ago, my attitude on Aboriginal issues was the usual confused liberal one: I knew they had been dispossessed, often murderously, and I also suspected that today too many of their wounds—the malnourished babies, the suicidal young people, the diseases, the drunkenness—were self-inflicted. I did not know what had happened in between. What I have been doing over these last months is curing my ignorance.

To Aboriginal listeners I say: you have lived your history, while I have only retrieved what I can from books. I must ask your tolerance for the liberty I am taking—a necessary liberty, because it is through reading that most of us come to understand our fellow humans better.

Twenty years ago, in his Boyer Lectures, Bernard Smith described what whites have done to Aborigines in the times of violence and what came after as 'the locked cupboard of Australian History'.[9] That was nearly 20 years ago, and the cupboard is locked no more. The ghosts swarm like angry bees: Henry Reynolds' work on the early wars, the Stolen Children report, the devastating health statistics, the extravagant incidence of self-destructive acts among Aboriginal adolescents, too high among teenagers everywhere, highest among them. There has also been a deal of talk about 'guilt' and 'shame', and what precise mixture of each non-Aboriginal Australians should be feeling.

Back in 1980, Smith's concerns were different. He claimed that the 'new awareness of what actually occurred', that is, of true history, constituted a 'central problem for the integrity and authenticity of Australian culture today'. 'Authenticity'. 'Integrity'. These are interesting words. They are not to do with economics. They are not to do with political stability. They are not to do with Australia's international reputation. They are not to do with interests at all. They are to do with national morality, and the inner coherence of that morality—a thing at once more obscure and more real than any of the others. Can a culture be inauthentic? Yes, if, for example, systematic injustice to a particular group is accompanied by a general conviction of a commitment to 'a fair go', to egalitarianism, which I believe to be an authentic and distinctive element in Australian culture.

Over these next weeks, I want us to do some history together to look at a handful of the stories I uncovered, like the story about the woman on the beach, so that we as individuals can decide first, what we make of them, then what we feel about them, then what we think we should do about them. That, after all, is the ambition of civic nationalism: for citizens to be sufficiently informed factually and exercised morally to be competent to make decisions for themselves.

First I need to identify what I see as the peculiar characteristics and the strengths of the European 'Australia' which has evolved over these past two hundred years, and that is how I will begin next week.

1   Frank Horner, The French Reconnaissance: Baudin in Australia 1801–1803, Melbourne University Press, 1987, p152. Horner is quoting from Baudin's letter to the Minister of Marine, written from Timor.
2   Martha Nussbaum, Cultivating Humanity: A Classical Defence of Reform in Liberal Education, Harvard University Press, Cambridge Mass., 1997.
3   Benedict Anderson, Imagined Communities: Reflections on the Origin and Spread of Nationalism, Verso, London, 1983.
4   Michael Ignatieff, Blood and Belonging: Journeys into the New Nationalism, Vintage Books, London, 1994. For an examination of historical fabrications and falsifications, see Noel Malcolm, Kosovo: A Short History, Macmillan, London, 1998.
5   See also the report titled Memory of Silence brought down by the UN-sponsored Commission for Historical Clarification and presented to the Government of Guatemala in February 1999, which established that the military were overwhelmingly responsible for the atrocities which marked Guatemala's thirty-six-year-long civil war, and that the Cuban and United States governments had both lent active support to its illegal operations. President Clinton has now formally apologised for his government's role. Recovering victims' true stories is a dangerous business: two days after the release of the report of an earlier human rights inquiry, the Recuperación de la Memória Histórica, in April 1998, the Catholic bishop who had been its chief patron was found bludgeoned to death.
6   Colm Tóibín, 'The History of the History of the Irish Famine', London Review of Books, 30 July 1998, pp17–23; p18.
7   See e.g. Joel Mokyr, Why Ireland Starved: A Quantitative and Analytical History of the Irish Economy 1800–1850, Allen & Unwin, London, Boston, 1983.
8   Geoffrey Blainey, Our Side of the Country: the Story of Victoria, Methuen Haynes, North Ryde, 1984, p70.
9   Bernard Smith, The Spectre of Truganini: 1980 Boyer Lectures, Australian Broadcasting Commission, Sydney, 1980, p10.

Murray Gleeson

The Honourable Murray Gleeson, AC, is the Chief Justice of the High Court of Australia.

Born in Wingham, New South Wales in 1938, Murray Gleeson was educated at St Joseph's College and the University of Sydney, where he studied law. Initially practising as a solicitor, he was admitted to the Bar in 1963. He took silk in 1974 and, after being a member of the Council of the New South Wales Bar Association, served as president in 1984 and 1985. In 1988, he was appointed Chief Justice of the Supreme Court of New South Wales, a position he resigned in 1998, when he took up his

appointment at the High Court. From 1989 to 1998 he was Lieutenant-Governor of New South Wales.

He was made an Officer of the Order of Australia for services to the law in 1986, and a Companion of the Order of Australia in 1992.

The Rule of Law and the Constitution is the overall title given by Chief Justice Gleeson to the important and admirably clear 2000 Boyer Lectures, which he delivered on the eve of the Centenary of Federation. The individual lectures were: 'A Country Planted Thick with Laws'; 'Becoming One People'; 'Aspects of the Commonwealth Constitution'; 'Constitutional Rights', which is reproduced here; 'The Keystone of the Federal Arch' and 'The Judiciary'.

Our ancestors did a great thing one hundred years ago: they made a nation. Driven by a passionate belief that they had within their grasp a continent which could become a nation, against all the odds, they made a nation for a continent.

Federation wasn't easy and it wasn't inevitable; when it finally occurred on 1 January 1901, it was the result of a long process of negotiation and compromise between the often competing desires of the uniting colonies.

Much of that careful negotiation involved the creation of the Australian Constitution, the legal instrument that brought the new nation into being.

It lays out the terms under which the colonies agreed to join the newly created federal union. It is the basic law of our country.

The constitution directed the creation of a Federal Supreme Court, to be called the High Court of Australia. The High Court has two main functions; one is as the final court of appeal in all civil and criminal matters. But it is also the keeper of the Constitution, interpreting its meaning in a changing society and enforcing its observance.

Of his lecture series, Chief Justice Gleeson said: 'The Centenary of Federation provides Australians with an opportunity to re-examine a fundamental aspect of our national identity. We are members of a society committed to the rule of law. Our basic law is the Australian Constitution. Maintaining the vitality and relevance of our legal and constitutional arrangements is a subject which affects all citizens.'

CONSTITUTIONAL RIGHTS

The Rule of Law and the Constitution

Murray Gleeson

• 2000 •

When we hear Americans refer to their 'constitutional rights', they are usually speaking about a series of amendments to their original Constitution. Those amendments make up what is referred to as a Bill of Rights. They are constitutionally entrenched guarantees of certain rights, which are enforceable in the courts. They limit the law-making power of legislatures, and control the executive.

The Australian Constitution, as a plan of government for a federal union, is largely concerned with pragmatism rather than ideology. It does not take the form of a Bill of Rights. Yet it would be a mistake to think that it does not contain guarantees of rights, freedoms and immunities.

The establishment of representative parliamentary democracy as the method of government for our Federation has been held to carry implications for freedom of political debate and comment.[1] The exact nature and extent of these implications is a matter of debate amongst constitutional lawyers.

The structure of the Constitution reflects the principle of the separation of legislative, executive and judicial powers. That principle was embedded in the Constitution of the United States, which so attracted the founders. It has major consequences because it denies complete power to any one arm of government. One of the most effective restraints upon power is a division of authority, so a constitution is important not only for the power it gives, but also for the power it does not. A constitution that vests legislative, executive and judicial power in different organs of government, and makes them institutionally separate, builds into the system a constraint on power. Yet the separation is not in all respects strict. For example, responsible government requires that the executive be responsible to Parliament. Even so, the principle of separation is to a substantial extent institutionalised.

Some members of the High Court have discerned in the

Constitution implications of equality and, in particular, equality before the law.[2] As Justice Gaudron has pointed out[3] equality 'is an infuriatingly elusive concept'. If the statement in the American Declaration of Independence that all men are created equal were treated as a proposition of fact, then it would be manifestly untrue. There is nothing more obvious than that people are, in most respects, unequal. That is the evidence of our senses. The problem of inequality may be alleviated by seeking, at least, equality of opportunity. However, that is not a complete answer because people have different capacities to take advantage of opportunities. Thus, in many circumstances, equality of opportunity results in inequality of outcome. (Ask any parent or teacher what the result will be of giving a group of children an equal opportunity to read books.) Yet most Australians share a belief that all people are equal—and they are right. This is because the proposition that people are equal is not a statement about a fact; it is an expression of an ethical principle. It reflects a value, not an observation. The source of that ethical principle, however, may be a matter of disagreement. For some people, it is based upon religious conviction. For some, it is derived from an ethical system that is independent of any religious notion. For others, it is purely intuitive.

Whatever the source, the value of equality before the law is deeply ingrained in our legal system, and in the Constitution. As with other such values, it is imperfectly realised, and its practical implications may lead to legitimate disagreement. Consider, for example, the subject of the right to legal representation, and legal aid. No one suggests that every person charged with a traffic offence should be entitled to be represented in court, at public expense, by a senior counsel of his or her choice. Questions of degree are involved. Issues of competing priorities in relation to the expenditure of scarce resources arise, as do questions of efficiency and accountability in the use of public funds. In a democracy, issues of that kind are usually resolved through the political process. But constitutional guarantees of equality before the law, or due process in the administration of justice, where they exist, draw a line beyond which political choice cannot reach. Ultimately, deciding where that line is to be drawn may require judicial decision. When that occurs, we are at the interface between political and judicial power—this problem underlies a good deal of human rights debate.

A constitutional guarantee follows from the provision in s 71 that the judicial power of the Commonwealth is to be vested in the High Court of Australia, and in such other federal courts as the Parliament creates, together with State courts invested with federal juris-diction.[4] This means that a citizen cannot be subjected to the exer-cise of Commonwealth judicial power except by a court. This, coupled with the principle of separation of powers, and the inde-pendence of the judiciary, denies to Parliament and the executive government the capacity to administer civil or criminal justice. It is an assurance of due process. It means, for example, that a citizen cannot be tried and punished for an offence by an officer of a government department. It means that disputes about civil rights and obligations, including disputes between citizen and govern-ment, can be conclusively determined only by an independent judi-ciary. These are fundamental principles affecting the basic structure of our society. Most people take them for granted. But they were built into the Constitution by the founders, and they cannot be altered by Parliament.

There are important guarantees in express provisions in the Constitution. There are prohibitions against certain forms of discrimination.[5] There is a prohibition against making a law to establish a religion, or imposing a religious test as a qualification for public office.[6]

To some people, that last guarantee may seem of little modern relevance, but it was significant in 1901. The religious tolerance and diversity that we now accept did not exist then. An example of the spirit of the time can be seen in a problem encountered by Australia's first Prime Minister. In 1902, Edmund Barton took a trip to England. On his journey he passed through Rome where he paid a courtesy call on Pope Leo XIII. The result was that a petition, said to have been signed by 30,000 Australians, was addressed to the Federal Parliament, praying that it would 'strenuously oppose the conferment [sic] upon [Mr Barton] of any position of honour or dignity in the Commonwealth until his actions have received the endorsement of an electorate of the Commonwealth'.[7] At the time, an observer wrote:

> Knowing the fierce hatred which secretarian strife engenders, the incident by itself was of no great moment; but it was not without significance—if the alleged number of signatories to the petition was correct—that 30,000 people could be found in Australia to put such a ban on the political future of a man, whom two years before they had tumultuously acclaimed as 'Australia's noblest son', and who had just been the recipient of titular and academic honours in England.[8]

The power of the Federal Parliament to make laws with respect to the acquisition of property is subject to the qualification that such an acquisition must be upon just terms.[9] This restraint on legislative power protects citizens from having their property acquired by a Federal government without compensation. In that respect it recognises and guarantees a right of private property. It means that, if Parliament decides that it is in the public interest to acquire a citizen's property and use it for public purposes, the individual citizen does not have to bear the cost. This protection of private rights of property against public interference was largely modelled on one of the amendments to the United States Constitution.

Section 92 of our Constitution contains a famous guarantee. It says that trade, commerce and intercourse between the States shall be absolutely free. To some people, this might seem a commendable use of plain English, but the meaning of the guarantee was found to be obscure. It gave rise to almost a century of litigation. Everybody could agree upon some of the things that it included, but what were its outer boundaries? Obviously, it prevented the states from setting up customs barriers at their borders. That was one of the primary objectives of federation. But what, if anything, did it have to say about the power of the states to tax interstate road carriers who used their road systems? What did it say about the power of the states, or the Commonwealth, to establish schemes for marketing primary products involving the compulsory acquisition of goods intended for interstate trade? These and other questions occupied the courts many times throughout the twentieth century. The problem is that there is a mismatch between the simplicity of the language and the complexity of the problems to which it might apply. Simple language is not always plain if the issues it addresses are not simple.

It was a combination of the guarantee of freedom of interstate trade, and the requirement of just terms for an acquisition of property, that was held in the late 1940s to invalidate the Federal Parliament's attempt to nationalise the banking system.[10] That legislation provides an example of the way in which over time a Constitution must accommodate changing circumstances and political theories. We now live in an age of economic deregulation, with bipartisan support for free markets and competition policy. Yet, only fifty years ago, the Federal Parliament enacted a law to give a monopoly upon banking business to a government instrumentality. The very bank that has recently been privatised was intended not only to remain public but to take over the business of all the private banks. Who is to say that, fifty years from now, in the economic and social conditions of the time, the idea might not again have political attraction? If it does, it may have to be measured once again against the Constitution, and the interpretation that is then given to its language.

There is, in the Constitution, in a provision expressed in terms that are both legalistic and archaic, a basic guarantee of the rule of law. The High Court is given jurisdiction in matters in which a writ of mandamus or prohibition or an injunction is sought against an officer of the Commonwealth.[11] This jurisdiction cannot be altered or taken away by Parliament. It confers on the High Court the power, by making certain forms of order that historically followed judicial review of executive action, to compel officers of the Commonwealth to act according to law. The expression 'officer of the Commonwealth' includes the Prime Minister and Ministers, and all public servants. The effect of the provision is that no one is above the law. Thus government officials must exercise their powers according to law. If they do not, then, in the last resort, the High Court may order them to do so. The Constitution, which is the basic law, itself declares that the government must obey the law, and gives the High Court the jurisdiction to compel such obedience. That jurisdiction cannot be removed or modified except by constitutional amendment. Parliament, if acting within the limits of the powers assigned to it by the Constitution, may change the law. But the executive government must obey the law. That is what the rule of law means.

As explained earlier, we do not have, either in our Constitution, or in legislation, a comprehensive statement of human rights and freedoms along the lines of a Bill of Rights. This is a controversial issue in current political debate. It is not my purpose to advocate a point of view, but it is worth identifying some of the issues involved.

Although the most extreme violations of human rights are usually associated with repressive and undemocratic governments, there is an aspect of democracy itself which requires vigilance in order to protect individual rights and freedoms. A democratic government seeks to represent the will of the majority. It is the support of the majority that gives legitimacy to the laws made by, and the powers exercised by, such a government. That is what makes them acceptable—or at least tolerable—even to those who disagree with them. The electoral process is designed to ensure that governments are responsive to the wishes of the majority; but majorities cannot always be relied upon to be sensitive to the interests and the legitimate concerns of minorities. The problem is compounded because society is not neatly divided into one majority and a number of minorities. The attribute that makes a person a member of some minority group does not define that person for all purposes. In reality, most of us belong to some kind of minority. How then does a democracy, which functions on the basis of majority rule, institutionalise protection of legitimate minority interests? This is the essential problem underlying debate about human rights.

One way, which has been adopted to a limited extent in Australia, and to a greater degree in the United States, India and South Africa, is to entrench guarantees of rights and freedoms in a written constitution. The power of judicial review of legislative action then makes the courts the ultimate protectors of these rights, giving judges, who are unelected, and who do not seek—or need—electoral popularity, the power to declare laws to be unconstitutional and invalid. Clearly, rights and freedoms entrenched in that way must represent values that are fundamental and enduring. If they did not, the democratic system itself would be subjected to unbearable stress.

To establish a right in a constitution is to deny to a democratically elected Parliament the power to make a law inconsistent with that right. The whole point of having a constitutional right is to put it beyond the reach of Parliament. It gives judges the power to declare that the will of Parliament shall not prevail. If the Constitution is silent on a subject, then it is up to Parliament, from time to time, to deal with that subject—or not to deal with it—as it thinks fit. When the Constitution speaks, it limits the power of the Parliament, and if the courts find that legislation is inconsistent with the Constitution, it is therefore invalid.

Not all formal declarations of rights and freedoms are of that kind. For example, *The Canadian Charter of Rights and Freedoms*, enacted in 1982, contains legally enforceable guarantees, but they are not absolute. They are instead subject to such reasonable limits prescribed by law as can be demonstrably justified in a free and democratic society. Certain of the guarantees can be overridden by Parliament. The political implications of overriding a guarantee may be serious; but it can be done. The *New Zealand Bill of Rights Act 1900* does not empower courts to invalidate legislation inconsistent with the rights it declares, but the courts are required to interpret legislation consistently with the Bill of Rights, and there are mechanisms for parliamentary scrutiny of compliance with the Bill. The *Human Rights Act 1998* of the United Kingdom incorporates the European

Convention on Human Rights into the law of the United Kingdom. Its main provisions took effect in England in October 2000. English courts will have to decide whether breaches of the provisions of the European Convention have occurred. Austria, Belgium, Denmark, France and Germany have all incorporated the European Convention into domestic legislation.

Some commentators have expressed concern about what they describe as a process of judicialisation of public policy. Some fear that judges are being given too much power; others see judges as the natural protectors of minority or individual rights. The fact that judges are unelected is regarded by some as undemocratic. Others consider that the very fact that judges do not need electoral popularity makes them the most effective guardians of the rights of unpopular people. Rights are often important precisely because of the unpopularity of the people they are meant to protect. People who only say things that are ppular and that are greeted with general applause do not need a right of free speech. Freedom of speech only matters when a person wants to say something that will displease somebody else. It may matter a great deal when a person wants to say something that will displease a lot of people.

The Lord Chancellor of England said, concerning the *Human Rights Act* 1998:

> [T]he new legislation has been carefully framed to preserve the traditional constitutional restraints on judicial interpretation of the law, particularly the sovereignty of Parliament. The Human Rights Act, for example, will lead the Courts to exercise a more intensive form of scrutiny over Government and public authorities. The judges will have to deploy such concepts as proportionality and necessity, permitting the Government to cut down human rights only if it does so in response to a pressing social need. The courts will be drawn into a greater number of politically controversial issues. But they will not as a result be enabled to strike down Parliamentary legislation, although they will be able to declare it incompatible with the European Human Rights Convention.[12]

The Lord Chancellor's reference to 'the sovereignty of Parliament' has to be understood in the context of the United Kingdom, which does not have a written constitution. In a federal system, such as Australia's, there is no sovereign Parliament. The law-making power of Australian parliaments, Federal and state, is limited by the Constitution. If there is a dispute about those limits, it is determined by the courts, in particular by the High Court.

Whether they are expressed as constitutional guarantees or take the more restricted form just described, the content of declared rights, freedoms or immunities may itself be a subject of contention. Freedoms and immunities are usually easier to agree, because they do not involve the expenditure of public funds. But rights can be of a different order. What are sometimes advanced as rights are in truth political claims or aspirations that can never be fully satisfied, and which may involve demands upon limited government resources. They may also conflict with other rights and freedoms. Consider, for example, the matter of access to health care. Although it may come as a surprise to some members of my profession, many people regard access to medical services as even more beneficial than access to legal services. Governments of all political persuasions accept an obligation to assist people to obtain medical and hospital services, but they inevitably have to face issues of cost. More significantly for present purposes, they may also have to face issues as to the individual rights of the providers of medical services. This is a matter addressed in the Constitution. It also provides a good example of the manner in which rights can conflict.

One of the express guarantees contained in the Constitution is that laws with respect to the provision of medical services must not authorise any form of civil conscription.[13] The reason for this is obvious. One way for a government to provide wide and affordable access to health care would be to prohibit private medical practice and to force all doctors and nurses to work for the government. But if that occurred the individual rights and liberties of the doctors and nurses would be overridden. The Constitution prevents that. As with the provision concerning acquisition of property, the rights, interests and liberties of individual citizens are protected against government encroachment, even though the government may be motivated by considerations of public welfare. What may be thought surprising, however, is that the prohibition only applies to civil conscription in relation to the provision of medical services.

Legal rights are sometimes confused with economic claims. Such claims may constitute legitimate political objectives, but they are of a different order from enforceable rights. Their practical attainment might also involve measures that are inconsistent with the rights or liberties of other people. Reconciling conflicting rights, or resolving inconsistencies between the claims of some and the liberties of others, is a common political problem. When it becomes a matter of legal disputation, however, the issue takes on a new dimension. In the arena of political debate, a dispute is resolved through the ordinary democratic process. But when it comes before the courts, it is resolved by judges whose duty is to act without regard to popular opinion.

Human rights discourse is entering a new phase in this country. The issues are complex, and they have major implications for the role of the courts and for relations between the judiciary and the other branches of government.

The protection of the rights and freedoms of individuals and minority groups has always been an essential part of the role of the courts. The law, in its nature, is a constraint upon power. Whether the power is that of individuals or corporations or governments, the restriction on that power that comes from the law is a powerful civilising influence. Working out the principles according to which the will of an elected Parliament that is responsive to popular opinion must bend to the law, as enforced by unelected and independent judges, is one of the most important and difficult issues of current debate.

1   Theophanous v Herald & Weekly Times Ltd (1994) 182 CLR 104; Lange v Australian Broadcasting Corporation (1997) 189 CLR 520.
2   Leeth v Commonwealth (1992) 177 CLR 455, p487
3   Justice Mary Gaudron, 'In the Eye of the Law: The Jurisprudence of Equality', 1990 Mitchell Oration, Adelaide.
4   Street v Queensland Bar Association (1989) 168 CLR 461, p521 per Deane J.
5   Constitution, s 86, 88, 90, 99.
6   Constitution, s 116.
7   Henry Gyles Turner, The First Decade of the Australian Commonwealth, 1911 and 1995, p55.
8   Ibid., p55.
9   Constitution, s 51 (xxxi).
10 Bank of New South Wales v Commonwealth (1949) 76 CLR 1.
11 Constitution, s 75 (v).
12 Third Worldwide Common Law Judiciary Conference, Edinburgh, 5 July 1999 [12].
13 Constitution, s 51 (xxiiiA).

For permission to quote copyright material, the publishers thank:

Australian Consolidated Press and the *Bulletin*; Curtis Brown for poetry by AD Hope; ETT Imprint for 'Nigger's Leap' from *A Human Pattern: Selected Poems* by Judith Wright (ETT Imprint, Sydney, 1996) and 'Old Botany Bay' from *Selected Poems* by Mary Gilmore (ETT Imprint, Sydney, 1998); John Fairfax Holdings Ltd and the *Sydney Morning Herald* for material by the late Robert Haupt; and Dorothy Tunbridge for material from *Flinders Ranges Dreaming*.